Lecture Notes in Computer Science   556

Edited by G. Goos and J. Hartmanis

Advisory Board: W. Brauer   D. Gries   J. Stoer

J.-M. Jacquet

Conclog: A Methodological Approach to Concurrent Logic Programming

Springer-Verlag
Berlin Heidelberg New York
London Paris Tokyo
Hong Kong Barcelona
Budapest

Series Editors

Gerhard Goos
Universität Karlsruhe
Postfach 69 80
Vincenz-Priessnitz-Straße 1
W-7500 Karlsruhe, FRG

Juris Hartmanis
Department of Computer Science
Cornell University
Upson Hall
Ithaca, NY 14853, USA

Author

Jean-Marie Jacquet
Centre for Mathematics and Computer Science
Kruislaan 413, 1098 SJ Amsterdam, The Netherlands
and
Department of Computer Science, University of Namur
Rue Grandgagnage 21, 5000 Namur, Belgium

CR Subject Classification (1991): D.1.3, D.2.10, D.3.1, I.2.3, I.2.5

ISBN 3-540-54938-2 Springer-Verlag Berlin Heidelberg New York
ISBN 0-387-54938-2 Springer-Verlag New York Berlin Heidelberg

This work is subject to copyright. All rights are reserved, whether the whole or part of the material is concerned, specifically the rights of translation, reprinting, re-use of illustrations, recitation, broadcasting, reproduction on microfilms or in any other way, and storage in data banks. Duplication of this publication or parts thereof is permitted only under the provisions of the German Copyright Law of September 9, 1965, in its current version, and permission for use must always be obtained from Springer-Verlag. Violations are liable for prosecution under the German Copyright Law.

© Springer-Verlag Berlin Heidelberg 1991
Printed in Germany

Typesetting: Camera ready by author
Printing and binding: Druckhaus Beltz, Hemsbach/Bergstr.
45/3140-543210 - Printed on acid-free paper

To my parents
who began this whole work

Preface

Content

As suggested by the intensive activity in logic programming both in the research and the application areas, the use of logic as a programming language is now widely accepted. Besides, the recent development of parallel architectures of computers has strengthened the interest for concurrent computations. Concurrent logic programming has emerged from these two fields of activities. It seems particularly promising because of its declarative and symbolic appeals and because of its inherent non-deterministic feature, which makes it very well suited for parallel executions. This book is a step in the study of concurrent logic programming. It discusses the design of a concurrent logic programming language, named Conclog, and a methodology for constructing programs in this language.

(i) The language

The main features of Conclog originate from the approach adopted in its design. Instead of directly dealing with operational tricks to ensure efficiency, the ideal logic programming paradigm has been taken as a reference. A sound and complete parallel execution model of Horn clauses is described first. It uses or-parallelism and full and-parallelism. Subgoals of conjunctions are reduced independently, regardless of shared variables. Subsequent conflicting bindings are reconciled intermittently by equation manipulations. This basic scheme is then extended to incorporate negation. To that effect, substitutions are generalized and inequations are introduced in the reconciliation process. The extended scheme turns out to be sound and as complete as possible when the negation-as failure-rule and the resolution principle are used. Finally, extra-logical features are defined for optimization and practicability purposes.

We claim that the resulting language allows an easy declarative programming. As a consequence of our concern of computing general Horn clauses in a sound and as complete as possible way, problems can be solved in a declarative manner. In particular, annotation handling is not required to obtain soundness and completeness. Furthermore, multi-directional and multi-solution procedures are supported quite naturally. Nevertheless, efficiency has also been taken into account. Assuming suitable hypotheses on their use, procedures can be transformed into very efficient ones through the introduction of appropriate control information.

Since our main concern is the ease of programming, extra-logical features are kept minimal and have a simple semantics. These properties are not obtained at the expense of generality. Examples ranging from pure logical to classical concurrent applications are developed to support our claim.

(ii) The methodology

The proposed methodology is aimed at guiding the construction of a program in Conclog in a rigorous way. Although Conclog has been taken as target language, we believe that it can be easily adapted to other concurrent logic languages.

The methodology covers the entire programming process, from informal specifications to efficient Conclog programs. It is based on three phases. The first phase is dedicated to writing specifications. A specification consists essentially of a structured description of the computed relation in natural language. Necessary types, environment conditions and operational properties may be specified as well. The second phase consists in constructing a description in (pure) first order logic. Such a description is composed of two parts: a definition of predicates and a set of properties relating them. The last phase consists in deriving Conclog programs from the logic description. It proceeds in two steps. A first correct program is derived from the logic description. It is then transformed into more efficient versions by means of correctness-preserving transformations.

Structure

The book is structured in twelve chapters organised in four parts: an introductory part, a concluding part and two main parts discussing the design of Conclog and programming in it.

(i) The introduction part

The introductory part is composed of two chapters. Chapter 1 presents the goals of the book and places it in the concurrent logic programming context. Chapter 2 provides the background material necessary to understand it.

(ii) The design part

The design of the language is described in six chapters. Chapter 3 presents the auxiliary reconciliation calculus. Chapter 4 discusses the design of the parallel execution model of Horn clauses. Chapter 5 extends it to tackle negation. Chapter 6 describes the Conclog extra-logical features. Chapter 7 examines a possible extension of the resulting model. Chapter 8 compares Conclog with other parallel schemes and concurrent logic languages.

(iii) The programming part

Three chapters are devoted to programming in Conclog. Chapter 9 presents the methodology. Chapter 10 and Chapter 11 apply it to concrete examples ranging from applications free from behavioral requirements (Chapter 10) to the simulation of dynamic systems (Chapter 11).

(iv) The conclusion part

Finally, the conclusion part, composed only of Chapter 12, sums up our work and suggests subjects for future research.

Guide to the reader

Conclog has been designed in full details. Theoretical properties have been proved too. It follows that some parts are necessarily specific and/or theoretical. They may discourage the reader interested in using Conclog or interested in having just an overview of it. To this end, the chapters of the book have been conceived in order to allow some parts to be skipped without any trouble. In a first reading, we suggest that the reader consult the introductory Sections 3.1.1, 3.2.1, 4.1, 5.1, 6.1 and Section 6.2. He should get enough information to understand the language and to use it.

Similarly, Chapters 10 and 11 have been written in such a way that a minimal knowledge of the methodology is necessary to understand them. The reader just interested in the direct coding of programs can thus just read the introductory Section 9.1.

Our methodology does not intend to be a universal panacea. Nevertheless, it aims at easing the construction of the programs. We thus warmly recommend Chapter 9 explaining it.

Finally, this book has been conceived to be as self-contained as possible. The reader unfamiliar with logic programming can read it without first consulting other books. Nevertheless, we have been quite concise in recalling the basic foundations of logic programming. References are given where the reader can find complementary information, if necessary.

Acknowledgments

This book is a revised version of my Ph.D. thesis ([Jacquet, 1989]), accepted by the University of Namur (Facultés Universitaires Notre-Dame de la Paix de Namur), Belgium, in November 1989. Most of the work presented here was carried out when I was there as a Research Assistant supported by the Belgian National Fund for Scientific Research. The final version was written when I was participating in the ESPRIT Project Integration at the Centre for Mathematics and Computer Science (CWI) in Amsterdam, The Netherlands. I would like to thank all these institutions for having supported my work and for having provided me with optimal facilities to achieve it. It also gives me great pleasure to thank the people who so ably helped me in writing this book.

I am indebted to Axel van Lamsweerde, my supervisor. He introduced me to logic programming several years ago and initiated my research in concurrent logic programming. His careful reading of earlier versions has substantially improved the quality of this work.

I wish to acknowledge Yves Deville, my office mate at the University of Namur, as well. Much of the material presented subsequently has been influenced by our numerous discussions. I am also pleased to acknowledge Baudouin Le Charlier for his pertinent remarks.

I am grateful to Ugo Montanari for his interest in my work. His comments and advice on my Ph.D. thesis have been very useful for its publication. I am also grateful to Maurice Bruynooghe and Jean Fichefet for having served on my Ph.D. thesis committee. Their comments on the draft version of the thesis have also been of great aid.

I wish to thank the members of the ESPRIT Project Integration and especially Krzysztof Apt, Jaco de Bakker, Keith Clark, Frank Mac Cabe, Luis Monteiro, Catuscia Palamidessi, Antonio Porto, Jan Rutten, for their interest in my work and helpful discussions.

Several members of the Institut d'Informatique of the University of Namur, of the Ecole de Langues Vivantes of the University of Namur and of the Centre for Mathematics and Computer Science in Amsterdam were so kind to read parts or previous versions of this book: Jorge Barreto, Mete Celiktin, Pierre De Boek, Guy Deville, Pierre Flener, Naji Habra, Rosane Pagano, Daniele Turi, Fer-Jan de Vries, Jeroen Warmerdam. I take this opportunity to thank them. I am also particularly indebted to Dominique Adams and Anne Collard who carefully checked each word of this book. All remaining faults are, of course, mine.

I am also grateful to Springer-Verlag, in particular to Alfred Hofmann and Hans Wössner, for their help in getting the manuscript published.

Last but not least, special thanks are due to my family. Their permanent support throughout these years substantially contributed to the completion of this book. The interest of friends and colleagues has also been much appreciated. May they all find my gratitude here.

September 1991 *J.-M. Jacquet*

Table of contents

PART I : INTRODUCTION   1

Chapter 1 : Introduction   3
1.1 Requirements from an idealized view of logic programming 4
1.2 Real logic programming 5
1.3 Conclog : a concurrent logic programming language 7
1.4 Towards a methodology of concurrent logic programming 11
1.5 Overview of the book 12
1.6 Contribution 16

Chapter 2 : Logic programming   21
2.1 Syntax 21
2.2 Declarative semantics 23
2.3 Operational semantics 27
2.4 Relating the declarative and operational semantics 43

PART II : DESIGNING CONCLOG   47

Introduction   49

Chapter 3 : A reconciliation calculus   51
3.1 Reconciling substitutions 51
3.2 Reconciling n-substitutions 86
3.3 Application : parallel unification through reconciliation 110
3.4 Comparison with related work 117
3.5 Conclusion 121

Chapter 4 : A basic scheme for concurrent logic programming   123

4.1 Introduction 123
4.2 Basic concepts 144
4.3 The Conclog model 150
4.4 Variants of the model 194
4.5 Theoretical properties 205
4.6 Comparison with related work 225
4.7 Conclusion 236

Chapter 5 : Incorporating negation   239

5.1 Introduction 239
5.2 Basic concepts 261
5.3 The Conclog model 290
5.4 Variants of the model 324
5.5 Theoretical properties 334
5.6 Comparison with related work 345
5.7 Conclusion 370

Chapter 6 : Adding extra-logical features   373

6.1 Sources of inefficiencies 374
6.2 The extra-logical features 378
6.3 The Conclog model 422
6.4 Theoretical properties 428
6.5 Comparison with related work 428
6.6 Conclusion 436

Chapter 7 : Event-driven reconciliation   437

7.1 Description 437
7.2 Analysis 439
7.3 Conclusion 447

Chapter 8 : Comparison with related work   449

8.1 Parallel Prologs 449
8.2 Parallel execution models of Horn clause programs 456

8.3 Guarded Horn clause languages 456
8.4 Distributed logic languages 467
8.5 Constraint concurrent logic programming languages 469
8.6 Parallel implementations of logic languages 471

Conclusion 473

PART III : PROGRAMMING IN CONCLOG 477

Introduction 479

Chapter 9 : Towards a methodology of concurrent logic programming 481

9.1 Introduction 481
9.2 Writing a specification 484
9.3 Constructing a logic description 497
9.4 Deriving a concurrent logic program 512
9.5 Comparison with related work 550
9.6 Conclusion 552

Chapter 10 : Programming non-behavioral applications 555

10.1 Introduction 555
10.2 Relational database programming 555
10.3 Simple multi-directional list processing 558
10.4 Single-solution directed list processing 568
10.5 Handling trees 606
10.6 Generate and test programming 616
10.7 Conclusion 621

Chapter 11 : Programming behavioral applications 623

11.1 Introduction 623
11.2 Programming infinite processes 623

11.3 Programming abstract data types 627
11.4 Programming systems of processes 634
11.5 Classical concurrent programming 699
11.6 The producer-consumer paradigm 707
11.7 Conclusion 716

Conclusion 719

PART IV : CONCLUSION 721

Chapter 12 : Conclusion 723

12.1 The Conclog language 723
12.2 The methodology 726
12.3 Future work 728

APPENDICES 731

Appendix 1 : The perm and element procedures 733
Appendix 2 : An airline reservation system 735
Appendix 3 : An operating system 737
Appendix 4 : A lift system 747

REFERENCES 753

INDEX 775

Part I

Introduction

Chapter 1

Introduction

Since the very old days, human reasoning is a matter of interest. Aristote already formulated inferences in his syllogisms four centuries A.C.. Since then, thought has progressively been studied and formalized. This has given rise to a discipline in its own right, named logic.

In the last decades research in logic has investigated the mechanical character of proofs of theorems. This has progressively resulted in a new way of computing, called logic programming. Milestones in this direction are Herbrand's work on automatic theorem proving ([Herbrand, 1930]), Robinson's work on a machine-oriented resolution inference rule for first order logic ([Robinson, 1965]) and Green's result that a resolution theorem prover can simulate a computation ([Green, 1969]). Shortly after, Kowalski ([Kowalski, 1974]) and Hayes ([Hayes, 1973]) gave an explicit procedural interpretation to resolution inference - the former for the Horn clause subset of predicate logic, the latter essentially for logic programs made of first order equality statements. Concurrently, Colmerauer developed a new language, called Prolog (for PROgramming in LOGic). It has revealed to be successful for programming a wide variety of applications ranging from the more elementary programs to the more sophisticated ones such as symbolic integration, plan formation, computer aided design, compiler construction, data base description, drug analysis and natural language parsing. Prolog has provided the final credibility of using logic as a means of computing.

Since its creation, logic programming has raised much interest in the Computer Science community. Although some of them have addressed other kinds of logic, most works belong to first order logic and even to a subset called general Horn clauses. The recent development of computers with parallel architectures has motivated a new area of research : concurrent logic programming. It seems particularly promising because of the inherent non-deterministic feature of first order logic. This book belongs to this trend. It is twofold. On the one hand, a new concurrent logic programming is proposed. It aims at tackling concurrent executions in logic programming while conserving the declarative appeal of first order logic. On the other hand, a methodology is associated for further easing the programming using it.

The remainder of this chapter intends to sketch the main features of our work. To that effect, some theoretical limitations of any logic programming language are first recalled. They are contrasted with what could be an (unachievable) ideal of logic programming. Then, objectives underlying the design of our language are explained and the need for a methodology of concurrent logic programming is motivated. This already points out some original features of the work. Our contribution is further precised in a third part.

1.1 Requirements from an idealized view of logic programming

Most of the interest taken in logic programming comes from the possibility to ascribe two different complementary semantics to logic programs. The *declarative semantics* refers to the semantics of first order logic. Roughly stated, a program is seen as a set of implications and a computation consists in giving values to variables in order to make a submitted formula a logical consequence of the program. At the opposite, the *procedural semantics* is machine-oriented and refers to a model of execution. A program is then seen as a set of multiple entry point procedures. The execution of a procedure call results in the successive symbolic reductions of formulae and in the production of values for the variables.

In an ideal world, one would like these two semantics to be equivalent. This would exhibit a very attractive feature of logic programming : the programmer would ideally pay no attention to program execution and would concentrate his efforts on the logic description of the problem to be solved. This ideal view would contrast with imperative programming where one has rapidly to compose loops, destructive assignments, procedure calls, etc.

This idealized view is however not feasible. Church (1936) has indeed proved that first order logic is undecidable. In fact, first order logic is just semi-decidable : it is possible to automatically prove all formulae that are consequences of a set of formulae but not always to automatically disprove any non-consequences.

Nevertheless, this idealized view suggests two important properties that should be afforded by any logic programming language : completeness and soundness. Additional desired properties include fairness, multi-solution and multi-directionality.

1.1.1 Completeness and soundness

Completeness and soundness properties formulate together the equivalence between the declarative and procedural semantics. We state them informally in this introductory chapter. They will be refined in Chapters 2 and 5.

The completeness property requires that every formula that is a logical consequence of the program under consideration (declarative reasoning) is indeed provable by the procedural execution (procedural reasoning). The soundness property states the converse property, namely every formula that is provable from a procedural execution (procedural reasoning) is indeed a logical consequence (declarative reasoning).

It is worth noting that the undecidability property of first order logic prevents these properties from being extended to disprovable formulae and non logical consequences. In practice, this means that the termination of the execution of a formula under a program cannot be required in any case. Any model of execution has a program and a formula for which it does not halt. One significant situation where termination can be required is however that where all instances of the treated formula F that are logical consequences of the considered program are instances of a finite number of instances of F. This situation is subsequently referred to as *LP-situation*.

1.1.2   Multi-directionality

Another desired property is that of multi-directionality. As logic programs manipulate relations, one would like them to be used with different patterns of instantiation of their arguments. Procedures programmed so as to achieve this property are called *multi-directional*.

1.1.3   Multi-solution procedures

A fourth hoped property also arises from the handling of relations. In general, several sets of values may be computed for the variables of a submitted formula. One would then like the execution model to compute all of them. Procedures programmed so as to achieve this property are called *multi-solution*.

1.1.4   Fairness

Finally, fairness would also be suitable. Sometimes, the number of such value sets is not finite. In such a case, one would like the execution model to compute eventually any of them. Such execution models are called *fair*.

1.2   Real logic programming

Care for practicability must furthermore be added to the theoretical constraints stated in the previous section. Obviously, any language must act somewhat efficiently. A compromize must thus be made between a fully declarative, expressive and non-executable view and a fully procedural efficient view.

A first concession for efficiency is generally to restrict to Horn clause programs (instead of using full order logic programs) because an efficient complete and sound interpretation of them is known ([Colmerauer et al., 1973], [Kowalski, 1974]). Basically such clauses take the form of universally quantified implications involving at most one positive literal as consequent and a possibly empty conjunction of positive literals as antecedent :

$$\forall \, (p_1(...) \Leftarrow p_2(...) \wedge ... \wedge p_m(...))\ ^1$$

Questions that can be asked as candidate theorems take the form

$$\exists \, (\, q_1(...) \wedge ... \wedge q_n(...) \,)$$

where the q_i's represent positive literals. They are answered by successively replacing each q_i by the body of a clause in which it appears as consequent part. The reduction ends when there remains no such q_i to reduce.[2]

The resulting loss of expressiveness appears quite clearly. For instance, expressions of the form

$$A \Rightarrow B \vee C$$

cannot be expressed directly. In fact, what is really lacking is the possibility of having negative literals in the antecedent part of the implications. In practice, this is circumvented by allowing such negative literals to indeed occur. The extended clauses are called *general Horn clauses*.

To conserve the efficiency of the resolution, the common way of handling negative literals consists of first reducing the associated positive literals and then of inverting the success/failure of their reduction, thus making the reduction of the negative literals succeeds or fails according as the reduction of the associated positive literals fails or succeeds, respectively. Hence, the negative literal not(p(...)) is interpreted as

$$\neg \, \exists(p(...))$$

that is as

$$\forall \, (\neg p(...)).$$

In view of the form of the query, the expected meaning would however be

$$\exists \, (\neg p(...))$$

Some problem of soundness are thus to be feared. Problems of completeness may then result when negation is involved twice.

Nevertheless, even if negative literals were interpreted as $\exists \, (\neg p(...))$, problems of completeness may arise from the non-termination problem. Consider, for instance, the following fragment of program where p is defined as

---

[1] We use $\forall(A)$ and $\exists(A)$ to represent the universal and existential closures of the formula A, respectively.
[2] This rough description will be made more precise in subsequent chapters. It is however sufficient for understanding this introduction.

$\forall$ X : p(X) $\Leftarrow$ q(a);

$\forall$ X : p(X) $\Leftarrow$ not(q(a)).

Assume the reduction of q(a) never terminates. Then, so is that of p(X) although one trivially has

$\forall$X: p(X).

It is worth noting that negative literals are theoretically not necessary. All computable functions have indeed been proved to be computable in Horn clause logic ([Tarnlund, 1977]). However, they are useful and even sometimes practically essential.

A second compromize towards efficiency is the introduction of control information in Horn clause programs although this again is not theoretically necessary. The most well-known example is the Prolog cut. Other examples include goal annotations (IC-Prolog [Clark et al., 1982], Concurrent Prolog [Shapiro, 1983]), mode declarations (Parlog [Gregory, 1985]), wait declarations (Mu-Prolog [Naish, 1985b]) or clause annotations (UNSW-Prolog [Vasak, 1986]). Furthermore, antecedent conjunctions are also often judiciously ordered in order to ensure termination and/or more efficient computations.

Finally, built-in primitives have to be introduced. To be usable, a language must at least incorporate input and output primitives. Moreover, other primitives such as meta-call, assert, bagof, setof, ... are useful for some kinds of applications. All such primitives are outside the scope of first order logic though essential from a practical point of view.

Summing up, practicability further enlarges the gap between the declarative and procedural semantics. The price to pay for efficiency is restriction to general Horn clauses. This involves some problems of loss of expressiveness, soundness and completeness. Moreover, some extra-logical built-in primitives and control information should be introduced. All these impurities cannot be blamed to the logic programming language but should be addressed by the programming process at a coding level. Restated in other terms, the non-equivalence of the declarative and procedural semantics does not mean that logic cannot be used as a basis for programming. Simply, some non-logical issues will have to be tackled too. We will extend this view to the context of concurrent programming by supporting a design phase, where the declarative semantics is of primary concern, and a coding transformational phase, where impure features can be introduced in a controlled fashion to improve efficiency.

1.3 Conclog : a concurrent logic programming language

As hardware technology evolves, highly parallel computers become realizable. This implies a radical departure from conventional sequential programming since new problems like interference, deadlock, starvation, ... are introduced. It is furthermore believed that the success of parallel computers will depend on the software technology being used ([Takeuchi and

Furukawa, 1986]). In particular, the design of parallel languages is of importance. Even more important is the availability of methodologies for building correct parallel programs.

Research in parallel logic programming can be classified in three levels ([Ueda, 1986a]).

1) *Parallelism at the implementation level.* The objective at this level is to implement logic languages on parallel architecture computers. Work here is mainly concerned with the design of abstract machines ([Kimura and Chikayama, 1987], [Hermenegildo, 1986], [Levy, 1987], [Warren, 1987a], ...) and compilers ([Codish, 1985], [Hermenegildo and Nasr, 1986], ...).

2) *Parallelism at the language level.* The design of languages that are parallel by nature or incorporate parallel features is addressed at this level. It should be noted here that logic programming is particularly well suited for parallel executions. Indeed, disjunctions and conjunctions of general Horn clauses involve no a priori ordering. They thus inherently embody a great source of non-determinism.

3) *Parallelism at the application level.* Finally, parallelism can also be thought at the application level. It consists in the construction of algorithms including as many parts executable in parallel as possible.

It should be noted that these three levels are not necessarily dependent on each other. For instance, parallel algorithms need not be physically executed on parallel machines. Moreover, sequential languages can be implemented on parallel architectures. A convincing example is the use of vector processors to compute Fortran programs. However, parallel algorithms only make sense if parallel languages can be used to write them. As far as parallel languages are concerned, one trend is to design such languages in order to take profit of the computational power supplied by parallel architectures; parallel languages then only make sense if parallel architectures are available. Another trend is to exploit the possibilities of a "developed form of co-routining"; in this case, the availability of parallel machines is not so significant.

A word should be added on the difference between concurrency and parallelism. The word concurrency refers to parallel executions with possible interference due to their competition for shared resources and/or their cooperation. It is opposed to pure parallelism where parallel executions are totally independent and never cooperate. Our language involves interdependent computations and is thus qualified of concurrent. We will generally speak of concurrency rather than parallelism to stress this point. Nevertheless, some well-established concepts, such as and-parallelism, or-parallelism, stream-parallelism refer to parallelism rather than concurrency. In these cases, for consistency, we will use the usual terminology and thus will employ the term parallelism.

Given this context, our objective is to conceive a language expressing concurrent executions in the classical logic programming framework and standing as close as possible to the ideal of logic programming. Consequently, we aim at designing a concurrent logic programming language meeting the following requirements.

1) *Language based on the conventional logic programming framework.* Our first requirement is to restrict the language to the manipulation of general Horn clauses and to base it on the resolution principle ([Robinson, 1965]) and its procedural interpretation ([Kowalski, 1974]). We might have considered other kinds of logic programs such as those based on Temporal Logic ([Abadi and Manna, 1987]) or other resolution strategies. However, our choice should guarantee a certain level of performance without sacrificing too much to expressiveness. Moreover, we can take advantage of a 15-year experience and of many theoretical results.

2) *General-purpose language.* Second, we aim at a concurrent general-purpose language that allows to support all problems according to the schemes of reasoning usually employed in logic programming. In particular, no simplifying assumption on the number of computable solutions or on the form of the computed relations may be accepted. Hence, multi-directional and multi-solution procedures must be supported. A total independence of target machine must be ensured too.

3) *Concurrency expressing language.* The language should not be a sequential logic language augmented with primitives for concurrency. It should express concurrent executions in an implicit way and use by default and-parallelism and or-parallelism.

We could have taken an opposite approach and try to parallelize Prolog. However, this would have been somewhat conflictory at the basis. Indeed, the logic programming framework inherently parallel would have been first sequentialized to produce Prolog and then parallelized. Furthermore, most of the Prolog problems of completeness and soundness would have certainly been conserved too.

4) *Simple though powerful language.* The two previous sections have demonstrated that a complete abstraction from any execution model cannot be achieved. Nevertheless, our aim is to construct a language as declarative, as expressive and as simple as possible. In particular, the completeness, soundness and fairness properties are desired. Multi-directional and multi-solution procedures should also be supported when wanted. Furthermore, extra-logical features and control information should be kept minimal and should have a simple procedural semantics. This objective should make the language easy to program with.

Some schemes of parallel computations have been proved useful : back communication, eager evaluation, lazy evaluation, ... ([Clark et al., 1982], [Gregory, 1985]). We would like to support their coding too.

Such declarative and expressive aims certainly run against efficiency. One further goal is to allow multi-solution multi-directional procedures to be optimized when their use is in practice restricted. This should be achieved so as to reach performances similar to those obtained in other concurrent logic programming languages.

5) *Implementable language*. Although the language is not dedicated to a particular machine, it should also be implementable on parallel machines. In particular, no control information or primitive should be difficult to implement.

As it will be argued in detail in Chapter 8, such objectives depart from existing concurrent programming languages such as Concurrent Prolog ([Shapiro, 1983]), Parlog ([Gregory, 1985]), Guarded Horn Clauses ([Ueda, 1986a]), Strand ([Foster and Taylor, 1989b]), Delta-Prolog ([Pereira et al., 1986]), P-Prolog ([Yang, 1986]), Pandora ([Bahgat and Gregory, 1989]) and the cc family of languages ([Saraswat, 1989]).

Although we do not want to fight against them, it is worth noting that the first four languages essentially support single-solution directed procedures. The single-solution character results from the fact that, due to the commitment mechanism they embody, only one clause can be selected at each reduction step. At most one solution can thus be produced. The directed charateristic of the procedures results from the fact that for efficiency purposes but also for correctness ones, annotations have to be introduced in the programs. They imply a reasoning in terms of a strict data flow. Those languages are thus not complete. When negation is involved, they also turn out to be unsound. One of their interest is that they can be implemented very efficiently. However, we believe that this is obtained by sacrificing too much the expressiveness. We take an opposite course. We aim at building a language supporting fully multi-directional and multi-solution procedures. We mainly concern for completeness and soundness. Nevertheless, we also aim at supporting the coding of single-solution and directed procedures with similar performance as the committed-choice languages do. This will be achieved by using annotations forcing similar dataflows. How to introduce them safely will furthermore be addressed at the methodological level.

P-Prolog attempts to introduce multi-directionality in the committed-choice framework. It is based on the nice concepts of clauses mutually exclusive and non mutually exclusive. The first clauses are devoted to the coding of single-solution directed procedures and involve commitment. The last clauses are related to the coding of multi-solution multi-directional procedures; they exclude commitment. However, the mutual exclusive declaration of the clauses involves some patterns of use. The same procedure cannot be used, on the one hand, in one pattern of instantiation of the parameters to produce just one solution by taking profit of commitment and, on the other hand, in another pattern of instantiation to produce all solutions. This will be made possible in Conclog. This feature essentially results from the above objectives. Procedures are first coded in very declarative way and thus are multi-solution and multi-directional. At this point, because of our concern for completeness and soundness, the concurrent execution model can almost be discarded. The procedures are then optimized by the introduction of suitable annotations. The set of annotations will turn out to be richer than that of P-Prolog. It is also more flexible than that introduced in the CP family of languages ([Saraswat, 1987]).

Pandora - which can be viewed as a successor of P-Prolog - also suffers from the impossibility of using a procedure in one pattern to produce several solutions and in another pattern to produce just one solution by involving commitment.

Delta-Prolog addresses another issue than ours: the distributed programming in logic programming. Roughly speaking, the execution of a Delta-Prolog program consists of the parallel executions of Prolog programs that communicate by means of message passing. Its foundation rests on a new logic, called distributed logic ([Monteiro, 1984]). This language thus contrasts with our first objective of using the conventional framework of first order logic.

Our third requirement makes our research different from those trying to parallelize Prolog (e.g. [Clark and Mac Cabe, 1979], [Wise, 1984], [Overbeek et al., 1985], [Butler et al., 1986], [Shen, 1986], [Hausmann et al., 1987], [Whesphal et al., 1987], [Warren, 1987a], [Ali, 1988], [Calderwood and Szeredi, 1989], [Szeredi, 1989]).

Finally, our first requirement limits the investigation of our work to classical logic programming. We believe that the ideas presented in [Saraswat, 1989] for constraint concurrent logic programming, a generalization of concurrent logic programming, are orthogonal to our work and could be used to extend the cc family of languages to new (quite interesting) constraint logic programming languages.

1.4 Towards a methodology of concurrent logic programming

Sections 1.1 and 1.2 have discussed the gap existing between the declarative and procedural semantics of any logic programming language. Despite our concern of building Conclog as close as possible to the ideal of logic programming by ensuring soundness and completeness, by supporting multi-directional and multi-solution procedures, Conclog is not an exception to the rule. Hence, some programming reasoning should also be applied when using Conclog. It is thus important to combine its design with methodological guidelines for narrowing this gap in a safe way.

To be useful, we believe, following [Deville, 1990], that such guidelines should cover the entire construction process. Furthermore, logical aspects should be separated as much as possible from the operational ones. The proposed methodology is composed of three phases. The first phase addresses the specification of the procedure to be coded. The second consists in building a logical characterization in first order logic of the relation computed by the procedure. Finally, the third one is concerned with the derivation of Conclog programs. In particular, it provides correctness preserving transformations for inserting (safe) annotations.

One feature of Conclog is that our concern for completeness, soundness, multi-directionality, multi-solution certainly eases the program construction task. In particular, the logical and the procedural aspects can be separated quite clearly. In contrast, if committed-choice languages were used as target languages, some characterization of the procedures and the functionality of the predicate should already be addressed at the second logical characterization phase in order to derive (more or less easily) programs reflecting their logical characterization. This is not required when Conclog is used. Nevertheless, we believe that some parts of the methodology could be used to construct a methodology for these languages.

1.5 Overview of the book

The book is composed of two main parts : the design of Conclog and the related programming aspect. They are encapsulated between this introductory part and the conclusion part.

A. The introduction part

The introductory part is composed of two chapters. This chapter introduces the book. Chapter 2 aims at introducing some background information from the logic programming framework. It is suggested that logic programming is parallel by nature. The various sources of parallelism are discussed, namely or-parallelism, and-parallelism and parallel unification. The declarative semantics is recalled in a model theoretic framework. Finally, classical concepts from the procedural semantics are also recalled : substitutions, unification, resolution, and/or search trees. In particular, a special class of substitutions, namely the idempotent substitutions, is highlighted. Their interest arises from their close connection with equations. This feature will turn out to be particularly well-suited for reconciliation purposes.

B. The design part

The design part constructs the Conclog language in three steps. A parallel execution model of Horn clauses is first constructed. It is then extended to incorporate negation. Finally, extra-logical features are introduced. The language is of course designed with respect to the objectives of Section 1.3. In particular, it uses and-parallelism. Full and-parallelism is in fact used. That is subgoals of conjunctions are reduced in a fully parallel and independent way. Conflicting bindings for shared variables may then result. How to combine them is tackled by means of an auxiliary reconciliation calculus.

Precisely, the design part is organized in the following six chapters.

B.1 CHAPTER 3 : THE RECONCILIATION CALCULUS

Chapter 3 addresses the reconciliation calculus. It is composed of three parts.

1) First, the reconciliation calculus of substitutions is introduced. It rests on an equational interpretation of substitutions. Reconciliating substitutions then amounts to solving systems of equations. Some theory of the reconciliation of substitutions is elaborated. In particular, the relationship between the unification of substitutions and their reconciliation is established in the context of idempotent substitutions. Algorithmic issues are also addressed. It is shown how the

algorithm of [Martelli and Montanari, 1982], initially developed for the unificiation of terms can be exploited for reconciliation purposes.

2) This theory is extended in a second part to a generalization of substitutions, called n-substitutions. This generalization issues from a natural introduction of negation : equations are negated. Introduction of inequations results. Negative information must then be introduced in the substitutions in order to provide a finite representation of the solutions of systems of equations and inequations. This leads to the concept of n-substitutions. Their interpretation is also equational. Their reconciliation thus consists of the resolution of systems of equations and inequations. Classical concepts on substitutions (such as their composition, their idempotence character) are also extended to the n-substitutions. This extension allows us to extend the properties developed for the reconciliation of substitutions. Finally, an algorithm for the extended reconciliation is also proposed.

3) The third part of the chapter deals with parallel unification algorithms based on reconciliation.

B.2 CHAPTER 4 : THE BASIC EXECUTION MODEL

Chapter 4 introduces the basic execution model. It uses or-parallelism and full and-parallelism. The reconciliation calculus of Chapter 3 is used to combine the substitutions computed from subgoals of a conjunction.

The model is described according to two complementary views.

1) A tree view characterizes any execution in a global way in terms of and/or search trees. According to this view, any computation appears as the progressive construction of an and/or search tree slice by slice. This is achieved by means of cycles, each one composed of a generation phase and a reconciliation phase. The role of the generation phase is to expand the constructed part of the tree of one slice. The role of the reconciliation phase is to restore consistency in the part resulting from the previous generation phase, pruning it from the branches that are detected to participate to any solution, communicating bindings and delivering newly computed answer substitutions as results of the computation.

2) A process view refines the tree perception of the computation in the more dynamic real behavior. Any computation is then described in terms of the behavior of processes. Many sources of parallelism are pointed out as a result. In particular, the apparent strict interleaving of the generation and reconciliation phases is relaxed. Furthermore, substitutions may be produced whereas others are still under computation.

The depth of the slices generated is a parameter of the model. A class of execution models is thus in fact defined. All of them are proved to be sound and complete.

B.3 CHAPTER 5 : INCORPORATING NEGATION

Chapter 5 incorporates negation in the basic model. Negation is introduced as a new form of the negation as failure rule. It takes profit of the equational interpretation of substitutions. Consequently, systems of equations involved in the basic model are generalized in systems of equations and inequations. The generalization of substitutions to n-substitutions results. As negative information can be communicated by n-substitutions, goals are generalized to incorporate this negative information. Generalizations of the instantiation concept, of the unification concept and of the reconciliation calculus follow.

This given, the basic computing scheme is preserved. The newly introduced negative subgoals are manipulated in order to behave as the negator of the set of n-substitutions computed for their associated positive literal. Some care is furthermore taken to the implicit way in which variables are quantified at each reduction step. A form of negation very close to the real negation results. It is proved to be sound with respect to the completion understanding of the programs. It is also argued to be as complete as possible when the negation as failure rule and the resolution principle are used. Furthermore, as negative literals behave actively, the floundering problem is shown to be of no concern.

B.4 CHAPTER 6 : ADDING EXTRA-LOGICAL FEATURES

Chapter 6 incorporates extra-logical features as a final design step. Their design has been guided by optimization and practicability purposes. On the one hand, annotations are provided to optimize logic programs. In contrast with many languages such as the committed-choice ones, their insertion is optional; in no way they are required to ensure soundness and completeness. On the other hand, built-in primitives have been introduced to make Conclog practical. The whole set of extra-logical features is argued to be minimal and "reasonably complete" in the sense that

- for any extra-logical feature, it is practically not convenient to simulate it by a combination of other ones (minimality);
- most desirable forms of synchronization, communication or, more generally, computations can indeed be programmed by using the Conclog extra-logical features ("reasonable completion").

B.5 CHAPTER 7 : EVENT-DRIVEN RECONCILIATION

Chapter 7 discusses one possible extension of Conclog. It consists in forcing processes to perform reconciliation when some events occur. The feasibility of this extension is analyzed. It is argued why it is not incorporated in Conclog.

B.6 CHAPTER 8 : COMPARISON WITH RELATED WORK

Finally, Conclog is compared with other parallel logic schemes and parallel logic languages. More specific comparison are also included in Chapters 4, 5 and 6. In particular, the Conclog basic model is compared with other parallel execution models of Horn clauses in Chapter 4. The Conclog negation is compared with other forms of negation in Chapter 5. The Conclog extra-logical features are compared with existing annotations in Chapter 6.

C. The programming part

Programming in Conclog is addressed in the third part of the book. It is organized in three chapters.

C.1 CHAPTER 9 : TOWARDS A METHODOLOGY OF CONCURRENT LOGIC PROGRAMMING

Chapter 9 presents our methodology for programming in Conclog. It extends the methodology proposed in [Deville, 1987] and [Deville, 1990] to the concurrent programming context. As announced in Section 1.3, it covers the entire cycle of the construction : from the specifications to the concurrent logic programs. It is composed of three phases.

The first phase concerns the specifications. Our specifications basically consist of a structural natural language description of the relation. Type information, environment conditions and operational properties may be stated as well.

The second phase consists in constructing a description of the relation in first order logic. This description is split up into two parts. On the one hand, the relation is defined by means of a well formed formula of first order logic. It is called logic definition. On the other hand, the relations appearing in this formula are characterized by properties. They express, at the logical level, data dependency properties, test dependency properties and mutual exclusiveness properties.

The final phase consists in deriving a concurrent logic program from the logic description. It is itself composed of two steps. In a first step, a set of general Horn clauses is derived from the logic definition. It is then made correct. In a second step, this first correct version is transformed to more efficient versions by means of correctness preserving transformations. Some of these transformations take profit of the logic properties.

It is worth noting that, although Conclog has been chosen as target language, parts of the methodology can also be applied to other concurrent logic programming language such as the committed-choice ones.

C.2 CHAPTERS 10 AND 11 : PROGRAMMING APPLICATIONS

Applications are finally coded in Chapters 10 and 11. We distinguish two kinds of applications : the behavioral and the non-behavioral ones.

The behavioral applications consists of the simulation of dynamic systems. Their specification essentially state behavior requirements. They are tackled in Chapter 11. Several examples of such applications have been coded. They include an airline reservation system, a unix shell and a lift system. It is also shown how to simulate semaphores and how to code the seminal dining philosopher problem.

The non-behavioral applications are free from behavior simulation requirements. They can be regarded as the applications to which logic programming is widely acknowledged to be dedicated. In view of this property, they are firstly presented in Chapter 10. It is there shown how to program relational database, multi-solution multi-directional procedures and single-solution directed procedures. Parallelism inherent to trees is also shown to be expressible in Conclog. Finally, the generate and test paradigm is tackled.

The methodology has been used to support the applications. It has been extensively employed for the non-behavioral applications. In particular, it has revealed to be successful for constructing procedures that are widely acknowledged to be of advanced programming. It has been used in a lesser extend to program the behavioral applications. This results from the fact that by nature such applications do not fit in the first order logic framework.

These examples also give the opportunity to test the practicablility of Conclog, its expressiveness and the ease of programming with it. Comparison with other languages is also performed on practical examples thanks to them.

D. The conclusion part

Finally, the fourth part concludes our work and sketches work for future research.

1.6 Contribution

The results of the book are a concurrent logic programming and a methodology for programming in it. We describe hereafter the main original contributions.

A. The language

Originalities of the language may be perceived at four levels : by considering the language as a whole and by analyzing each of the three incremental steps of its construction. To ease the discussion we will further analyze the auxiliary reconciliation calculus in a separate point.

A.1 CONCLOG AS A WHOLE

Considered as a whole, the originalities of Conclog come from the rather original approach adopted in its design. We do not directly deal with operational tricks to ensure efficiency but rather make reference to an idealized view of logic programming. A parallel execution model of Horn clauses which is both sound and complete has then first been designed. Negation is introduced thereafter so that the extended model is sound and as complete as possible while using resolution and the negation as failure rule. Finally, extra-logical features are introduced.

As a result, multi-directional and multi-solution procedures are supported quite naturally. Furthermore, thanks to our concern for soundness and completeness properties, programs containing no annotations can be written in a declarative way. They are already sound and, in most cases, complete. This should be contrasted with committed choice languages where thorough operational behavior of the computations involving annotations handling is required. Finally, annotations may then be optionally introduced to make the programs more efficient. One significant feature of Conclog is that it allows a clear separation of the logical level of reasoning from the operational one.

A.2 THE RECONCILIATION CALCULUS

The theory of reconciliation developed in Chapter 3 is original to our work. Its central idea is to interpret substitutions in equational terms. This interpretation has revealed to be quite suited to reconcile substitutions. Furthermore, it has suggested our way of handling negation. Equations were simply negated, this producing inequations. Systems of equations were then generalized naturally in systems of equations and inequations. This leads us to introduce the new concept of n-substitution. It generalizes the substitutions by introducing negative information. Composition of substitutions has been extended to those n-substitutions. This allows to extend the theory of the reconciliation of substitutions to them. In particular, a new concept, called n-mgu is pointed out.

A.3 THE CONCLOG BASIC MODEL

To date, the idea of using a reconciliation approach as a basis for a parallel execution model is present only in [Pollard, 1981]. Comparison with this work is made in detail in Chapter 4. As a snapshot, our model differs from it in the following three points :
- by the employed reconciliation calculus,
- by the communication of bindings after each reconciliation phase,
- by the way in which pruning of the tree is performed.

A.4 THE CONCLOG NEGATION

The Conclog negation is a new form of the negation as failure rule. It takes benefit from the equational paradigm used in the basic model and from the all-solutions discovery due to the or-parallelism and and-parallelism employed in it. Referring to the completion understanding of the programs, it is proved to be sound and as complete as possible when the negation as failure rule and classical resolution are used. Furthermore, negative literals behave actively so that the floundering problem is avoided.

It is here worth noting that only a few concurrent logic programming languages or parallel execution models tackle negation. To our best knowledge, the parallel Prolog Pepsys is the only one to do so ([Whesphal et al., 1987]).

A.5 THE CONCLOG EXTRA-LOGICAL FEATURES

The Conclog extra-logical features are composed of annotations and built-in primitives. The built-in primitives are not so much original. They include the usual input/output primitives, the arithmetic ones, ... Primitives for testing the variable or ground nature of a term have been adapted to the Conclog context. Some of them further suspend until their parameter becomes non variable or ground. Another primitive adapts the Parlog three-argument meta-call primitive to our context.

The Conclog annotations are more original. Read-only annotations, suspension declarations, activator commit operators, the del and sol operators and the reduction operators are also peculiar to our work.

The read-only annotations review those of Concurrent Prolog. Two kinds of read-only annotations have been provided. The first ones act in a global way. They are used to state once that the reduction cannot instantiate the annotated variable. The last ones are weaker. They act locally and allow back communication to take place.

Such a distinction between local and global annotations is peculiar to our work. The Concurrent Prolog read-only annotations act in a more ambigous way. They furthermore suffer from problems (see [Saraswat, 1986]) that are avoided by the Conclog ones.

We furthermore allow them to be completed in order to force suspension until the annotated variable becomes non-variable or ground.

The suspension declarations are also original to our work. They have some similarities with the Parlog mode declaration and the Mu-Prolog wait and when declarations. Differences are explained in details in Chapter 6. Their four main features are :
- their non mandatory use;
- the possibility to use several of them for a same procedure;
- the possibility to state local and global constraints corresponding to the global and local read-only annnotations;
- the possibility to include a Cond part that can be used to express many suspension and conditions by using auxiliary reductions.

Two kinds of commit operators are introduced in Conclog. The first ones correspond to the commit operator separating the guard and the body of the clauses used by committed-choice languages. Such operators do not necessarily force the commitment mechanism to be applied in Conclog. To this end, activator commit operators must be involved in the computations. Such operators annotate both calls and procedures. For the procedures, the operators can be used to annotate the whole procedure directly or in association with a suspension declaration. This provides a very powerful combination. It allows procedures to be used in some modes by employing commitment and in others by discarding it. Local and global activator operators can furthermore be stated.

The del and sol operator also limit the computations of a call to the production of some answer n-substitutions. They act in the dual way of the commit operators. The computation is not limited by selecting only one clause to reduce a literal at each reduction step, as the commitment mechanism does. Rather, the computation is halted when the required number of answer n-substitutions have been computed. Such operators have no counterpart in other concurrent languages or execution models.

The reduction operators act on the depth of the generated slices and on the way in which processes of the process model behave. They are thus particular to our work too.

Besides these specific originalities, another significant contribution of our work at this level is to determine a minimal and reasonably complete set of extra-logical features.

B. The methodology

Our methodology is an adaptation of a methodology proposed in [Deville, 1990] for Prolog as target language. It rests on the same three phases. Nevertheless, some significant extensions have been proposed.

B.1 SPECIFICATION

Our contribution at the specification level has been to introduce information specific to concurrent executions. The main originalities are the introduction of invariant properties, event properties and suspension conditions.

B.2 LOGIC DESCRIPTION

Our contribution at the logic description level is to complete the logic definition stated in [Deville, 1990] by so-called logic properties. They are used for concurrency purposes in our methodology but could be employed in sequential languages, for instance to guide the ordering of literals of clause bodies or to introduce cuts.

B.3 CONCURRENT LOGIC PROGRAM

Our contribution at the logic program level is twofold. First, the notion of correctness of logic procedures has been adapted to the concurrent context. We introduce the notions of safety, weak-termination and strong termination. Second, a set of correctness preserving transformations dedicated to the concurrent logic programs has been conceived. Some of them, namely the transformations based on equality substitutions and on generation of equivalent tree, take inspiration from the corresponding ones in the sequential framework. The others are peculiar to our work. Among them are the transformations based on logic properties.

Chapter 2

Logic programming

This chapter reviews the logic programming framework. It does not however intend to be a tutorial to logic programming. Its purpose is rather to make this book as self-contained as possible. The reader is referred to [Lloyd, 1987] for a more extensive introduction.

Logic programming is issued mainly from [Robinson, 1965], [Kowalski, 1974], [Kowalski and van Emden, 1976], [Apt and van Emden, 1982], [Clark, 1979] as well as earlier work on automated theorem proving. It is here sketched according to its usual components : syntax, declarative semantics and operational semantics components. These three components compose the first three sections of this chapter, respectively. Potential sources of concurrency are moreover described in Section 2.3. Finally, Section 2.4 concludes the chapter by presenting properties connecting the declarative and operational semantics.

2.1 Syntax

Let us first precise the form of the programs and well-formed formulas (wff) considered in the book. As usual in first order theories, our first task is to define the syntax of the classes of variables, functions, predicates, connectives, quantifiers and punctuation symbols.

The Edinburgh syntax ([Clocksin and Mellish, 1981]) is subsequently employed in order to represent the first three classes of symbols.
- Variable symbols are strings of letters and digits beginning with an upper case letter. The special "_" symbol is used as a shorthand to reference variables whose names are useless.
- Function and predicate symbols are strings of letters and digits beginning with a lower case letter.

Functions and predicates are also denoted by coupling their name with their arity, as in sort/2, element/3. The sets of variables, functions and predicates are subsequently denoted by *Vars*, *Funcs*, *Preds*.

The logical connectives are denoted by $\neg$ (for negation), $\wedge$ (for conjunction), $\vee$ (for disjunction), $\Rightarrow$ (for implication), $\Leftrightarrow$ (for equivalence). It will furthermore be convenient to write $F \Leftarrow G$ instead of $G \Rightarrow F$.

Finally, the usual existential quantifiers, universal quantifiers and punctuation symbols are employed. Formulae cluttered with brackets are avoided by adopting the usual left association rule and the following precedence hierarchy of operators with the highest precedence at the top

$\neg, \forall, \exists$
$\wedge$
$\vee$
$\Leftarrow, \Rightarrow, \Leftrightarrow$.

This given, the usual notions of constants, terms, atoms, ... are defined as follows.

Definition 2.1
1) *Constants* are functions of arity 0.
2) *Terms* are the expressions inductively defined by the following rules
   (i) variables and constants are terms,
   (ii) if f is an n-ary function and $t_1, ..., t_n$ are terms, then $f(t_1, ..., t_n)$ is a term (n>0).
   The symbol f is called the *functor* of the term $f(t_1, ..., t_n)$. Terms of type (ii) are called *compound terms*.
3) An *atomic formula* or *atom* is an expression of the form $p(t_1, ..., t_n)$ (n>0) where p is an n-ary predicate symbol and $t_1, ..., t_n$ are terms. The p symbol is called the *functor* of the atom.
4) A *literal* is an atom or the negation of an atom. The former is called *positive literal* and the latter *negative literal*.
5) An *expression* is a term, a literal, a disjunction of literals or a conjunction of literals.
6) *Well-formed formulas(wff)* are inductively defined as follows
   (1) atomic formulas are wff's;
   (2) if F and G are wff's, then $\neg F$, (F), $F \wedge G$, $F \vee G$, $F \Rightarrow G$, $F \Leftrightarrow G$ are wff's;
   (3) if X is a variable and F a wff, then $(\forall X) F$ and $(\exists X) F$ are wff's.
   The *scope* of $\forall X$ and $\exists X$ in the above formula is the wff F. An occurrence of X is said to be *bound* if it is under the scope of a quantifier, otherwise, it is *free*.
7) The wff's define the first order language used in this thesis. It is subsequently referred to by $\mathcal{L}$.
8) A *closed wff* is a wff with no free occurrences of any variable. For notational convenience, we will use $\forall(F)$ and $\exists(F)$ to denote the universal closure of F and the

existential closure of F, respectively, that is the wff obtained by respectively adding a universal or existential quantifier for every variable having a free occurrence in F.

9) A *clause* is a wff of the form

$\forall X_1 ... \forall X_n (L_1 \vee ... \vee L_m)$

where each L_i is a literal and $X_1,..., X_n$ are all the variables occurring in $L_1, ..., L_m$. A *Horn clause* is a clause where at most one literal is positive. Horn clauses containing exactly one positive literal are called *definite Horn clauses*. They are subsequently denoted by

$H \leftarrow B_1, ..., B_m$.

or

H.

if m=0. The atom H is the positive literal of the clause. It is subsequently referred to as the *head* of the clause. The sequence $B_1, ..., B_m$ represents the conjunction of the positive literals associated with the negative literals of the clause. It is subsequently referred to as the *body* of the clause.

10) A *procedure* is a finite set of definite Horn clauses with same head functor and same head arity.
11) A *Horn clause program* consists of a finite set of procedures.

Notation 2.2 In view of the clause notation, lists of literals, considered as conjunctions, are subsequently denoted as in

$\leftarrow L_1, ..., L_m$.

The empty conjunction is furthermore denoted by the □ symbol.

2.2 Declarative semantics

The declarative semantics of a logic program is given by the model-theoretic semantics of first-order logic. The notions of interpretation and model are subsequently reviewed. Two particular classes, called Herbrand interpretations and Herbrand models, are pointed out. They will play an important role in subsequent developments. It should be noticed that a version slightly different from the usual one is presented here. It refers to the first order language $\mathcal{L}$ rather than, in each specific case, to the language composed on the considered program. More universal notions follow.

Generality is not pursued here. The results required for understanding the book are thus just given in this section. They are not proved. The interested reader is referred to [Lloyd, 1987] for further details.

Definition 2.3 An *interpretation* of $\mathcal{L}$ consists of four parts :
(i)   a non empty set D, called the *domain* of the interpretation,
(ii) for each constant, the assignment of an element in D,
(iii) for each n-ary function, the assignment of a mapping from D^n to D,
(iv) for each n-ary predicate, the assignment of a mapping from D^n to {true,false}.

Definition 2.4 Let I be an interpretation of $\mathcal{L}$. A *variable assignment with respect to (wrt) I* is an assignment to each variable of an element in the domain of I.

Definition 2.5 Let I be an interpretation of $\mathcal{L}$ and let V be a variable assignment. The *term assignment wrt I and V* of the terms in $\mathcal{L}$ is defined as follows :
(i)   each variable is given its assignment according to V,
(ii) each constant is given its assignment according to I,
(iii) if $t'_1, ..., t'_n$ are the term assignments of $t_1, ..., t_n$ wrt I and V and f' is the assignment of f, then $f'(t'_1,...,t'_n)$ is the term assignment of $f(t_1,...,t_n)$ wrt I and V.

Definition 2.6 Let I be an interpretation with domain D of $\mathcal{L}$ and let V be a variable assignment. Then a wff is given a *truth value* (true or false) wrt I and V as follows :
(i)   If the wff is an atom $p(t_1, ..., t_n)$, then the truth value is obtained by calculating the value $p'(t'_1, ...,t'_n)$ where p' is the mapping assigned to p by I and $t'_1, ..., t'_n$ are the term assignments of $t_1, ..., t_n$ wrt I and V.
(ii) If the wff has the form $\neg F, F \wedge G, F \vee G, F \Rightarrow G$ or $F \Leftrightarrow G$, then the truth value of the wff is given by the usual truth tables for the logical connectives.
(iii) If the wff has the form $(\exists X) F$, then the truth value of the wff is true if there is some d in D such that F has true as truth value wrt I and V[X/d], where V[X/d] is V except that X is assigned to d; otherwise, its truth value is false.
(iv) If the wff has the form $(\forall X) F$, then the truth value of the wff is true if, for all d in D, the truth value of F with respect to I and V[X/d] is true; otherwise the truth value is false.

Clearly the truth value of a closed wff does not depend on the variable assignment. Consequently, we can speak unambiguously of the truth value of a closed wff with respect to an interpretation.

Definition 2.7 Let I be an interpretation of $\mathcal{L}$ and let F be a closed wff. Then I is a *model* for F if the truth value of F wrt I is true.

Definition 2.8 Let S be a set of closed wff. An interpretation of $\mathcal{L}$ is a *model* for S if it is a model for each wff of S.

Definition 2.9 Let S be a set of closed wff. A closed wff F is a *logical consequence* of S iff every model for S is a model for F too. This situation is denoted by

$S \models F$.

By abuse of notation, we will also write S |= G, for any unclosed wff G, to really mean S |= $\forall$(G).

Proposition 2.10 Let S be a set of wff and F be a closed wff of a first order language L. Then F is a logical consequence of S iff S $\cup\{\neg F\}$ has no model.

The basic problem in logic programming is, given a set of Horn clauses P and an atom A, to determine whether P |= A holds. Thanks to the above proposition, this amounts to proving that every interpretation of P$\cup\{\neg A\}$ is not a model. Although this appears simple, it is, in reality, a formidable problem. Fortunately, it turns out that only a smaller class of interpretations, called the Herbrand interpretations, needs to be investigated. They are now defined.

Definition 2.11
1) A *ground term* is a term containing no variables.
2) A *ground atom* is an atom containing no variables.
3) A *ground instance* of a clause C is a clause obtained from C by removing the universal quantifiers and by replacing each variable of C by a ground term.

Definition 2.12
1) The *Herbrand universe* U_H is the set of all ground terms.
2) The *Herbrand base* B_H for $\mathcal{L}$ is the set of all ground atoms.

Definition 2.13 An interpretation for $\mathcal{L}$ is a *Herbrand interpretation* if the following conditions are satisfied :
(i) the domain of the interpretation is the Herbrand universe U_H,
(ii) constants in $\mathcal{L}$ are assigned to themselves in U_H,
(iii) if f is an n-ary function in $\mathcal{L}$, then f is assigned to the mapping from $(U_H)^n$ into U_H defined by $(t_1, ..., t_n) \rightarrow f(t_1, ..., t_n)$.

No restriction is made on the assignment of the predicates in $\mathcal{L}$ so that different Herbrand interpretations arise by taking different assignments. Moreover, since for Herbrand interpretations, the assignment of constants and functions is fixed, *it is possible to identify a Herbrand interpretation by the set of all ground atoms which are true with respect to the interpretation.*

Definition 2.14 Let S be a set of closed wff's of $\mathcal{L}$. A *Herbrand model* for S is a Herbrand interpretation for $\mathcal{L}$ which is a model for S.

Our claim that Herbrand interpretations need only to be considered is now substantiated.

Theorem 2.15 Let S be a set of clauses. Then S has no model iff S has no Herbrand models.

A particular model called the least Herbrand model plays a central role in logic programming. It is usually regarded as the canonical interpretation of a program because it just says what the ground logical consequences of a program are.

Proposition 2.16 Let P be a program and $\{M_i\}_{i \in I}$ be a non empty set of Herbrand models for P. Then $\cap_{i \in I} M_i$ is a Herbrand model for P.

Definition 2.17 Let P be a program. Suppose P has a Herbrand model and note $\{M_i\}_{i \in I}$ the set of Herbrand models. Then the *least Herbrand model* for P, denoted by M_P, is the intersection $\cap_{i \in I} M_i$.

Theorem 2.18 The least Herbrand model M_P of a Horn clause program P verifies $M_P = \{A \in B_H : A \text{ is a logical consequence of } P\}$.

The following proposition gives a further characterization of the least Herbrand model. It is based on a mapping T_P which provides the link between the declarative and the operational semantics. The proof of the theorem is out of the scope of this section and can be found in [Kowalski and van Emden, 1976].

Definition 2.19 Let P be a Horn clause program. The mapping $T_P : 2^{B_H} \to 2^{B_H}$ is defined as follows. For every Herbrand interpretation I,

$T_P(I) = \{A \in B_H : A \leftarrow A_1, \ldots, A_m \text{ is a ground instance of a clause of P}$
and $I \supset \{A_1, \ldots, A_m\}\}$

Definition 2.20 Let L be a complete lattice and $T : L \to L$ be a function from L to L. We define

$T \uparrow 0 = \bot$
$T \uparrow \alpha = T(T \uparrow (\alpha - 1))$, if α is a successor ordinal
$T \uparrow \alpha = \text{lub}\{T \uparrow \beta : \beta < \alpha\}$ if α is a limit ordinal
$T \downarrow 0 = \top$
$T \downarrow \alpha = T(T \downarrow (\alpha - 1))$, if α is a successor ordinal
$T \uparrow \alpha = \text{glb}\{T \downarrow \beta : \beta < \alpha\}$ if α is a limit ordinal

The symbols $\bot$ and $\top$ denote the bottom and top elements of L, respectively. Furthermore, the notations *lub* and *glb* refer to the least upper bound and greatest lower bound, respectively.

Theorem 2.21 Fixed point characterization of the least Herbrand model. Let P be a Horn clause program. Then,

$M_P = \text{lfp}(T_P) = T_P \uparrow \omega$,

where $\text{lfp}(T_P)$ is the least fixed point of T_P.

2.3 Operational semantics

The operational semantics provides a means of transforming a set of Horn clauses into a computational program. There are, in fact, many methods to do this; each of them characterizes a logic programming language. A common framework can nevertheless be pointed out. It issues from Robinson's resolution principle ([Robinson, 1965]), applicable in the more general context of first order logic, and rests on Kowalski's procedural interpretation of Horn clauses ([Kowalski, 1974]). Before recalling this interpretation, the fundamental concepts of substitution and unification are first introduced. Stress is given to idempotent substitutions, of particular interest for subsequent developments.

2.3.1 Substitutions and unification

A. Substitutions

Substitutions may be presented in three ways : as sets of bindings, as functions or as solutions of equations. The first approach is the usual one in the logic programming community. It is also adopted here, for purposes of uniformity. Nevertheless, the two other approaches are not completely abandoned. On the one hand, many concepts and properties reflect their functional counterparts. The reader should thus not be astonished of their presence. On the other hand, the relationship with the equational framework is exploited in the design of Conclog. It is already suggested through the following brief review of idempotent substitutions.

Definition 2.22 A *substitution* is a finite set of the form

$$\{X_1/t_1,...,X_m/t_m\}$$

where each term t_i is distinct from its corresponding variable X_i and where the variables $X_1,..., X_m$ are distinct. Each element X_i/t_i is called a *binding* or an *instantiation* for X_i. The empty set represents the *identity substitution*. It is denoted by $\{\}$.

A *grounding substitution for a set of variables* Svars is a substitution $\{X_1/t_1,...,X_m/t_m\}$ verifying the following properties :

(i) $\{X_1,...,X_m\}$ = Svars
(ii) for any $i \in \{1,...,m\}$, t_i is a ground term.

A *grounding substitution* is a substitution that just verifies the above property (ii). It is thus a grounding substitution for some (unspecified) set of variables.

Definition 2.23 The restriction of the substitution $\theta = \{X_1/t_1,... X_m/t_m\}$ to the set of variables Svars, denoted by $\theta_{|Svars}$, is the substitution obtained from θ by deleting all bindings X_i/t_i for which $X_i \notin$ Svars.

Notation 2.24 In the following, the set of variables appearing in a term, a literal, a wff or more generally any construct S will be denoted by *var(S)*. Moreover, the set of variables $\{X_1,...,X_m\}$ of a substitution $\theta = \{X_1/t_1,...,X_m/t_m\}$ is referred to by *dom(θ)* whereas the set $\{t_1,...,t_m\}$ is denoted by *cod(θ)*. They are named the *domain* of θ and the *codomain* of θ. The set of variables appearing in $t_1,...,t_m$ is designated by *varcod(θ)*.

Substitutions take their meaning through their application to expressions.

Definition 2.25 Let $\theta=\{X_1/t_1,...,X_m/t_m\}$ be a substitution and E be an expression. The construct $E\theta$ denotes the expression obtained from E by simultaneously replacing in E each occurrence of the variable X_i by the corresponding term t_i ($1 \le i \le n$). It is called an *instance* of E. This situation is also referred to as *θ being applied to E*. After such an operation, X_i is said to be *bound* or *instantiated* to t_i. It is said to be *constructed* to t_i if t_i is not a variable, and, to be *grounded* to t_i if t_i is a ground term.

The following proposition characterizes substitutions in view of their application to expressions.

Proposition 2.26 Let σ and τ be two substitutions. The following propositions are equivalent:
  (i)   the substitutions σ and τ are identical
  (ii) for every expression E, the expressions $E\sigma$ and $E\tau$ are identical
  (iii) for every variable X of $dom(\sigma) \cup dom(\tau)$, the terms $X\sigma$ and $X\tau$ are identical.

Substitutions are composed in the following manner.

Definition 2.27 The *composition* of the substitutions $\sigma = \{X_1/t_1,...,X_m/t_m\}$ and $\tau = \{Y_1/u_1,...,Y_n/u_n\}$, denoted by $\sigma \circ \tau$ or $\sigma\tau$, for short, is the substitution obtained from the set $\{X_1/t_1\tau,...,X_m/t_m\tau, Y_1/u_1,...,Y_n/u_n\}$ by deleting any binding $X_i/t_i\tau$ for which $X_i = t_i\tau$ ($1 \le i \le m$) as well as any binding Y_j/u_j for which $Y_j \in \{X_1,...,X_m\}$ ($1 \le j \le n$).

Elementary properties of substitution composition are contained in the following proposition.

Proposition 2.28 Let θ, σ and τ be substitutions. Then
1) $\theta\{\} = \{\}\theta = \theta$
2) For every expression E, $(E\theta)\sigma = E(\theta\sigma)$
3) $(\theta\sigma)\tau = \theta(\sigma\tau)$.

B. Ordering substitutions and expressions

The composition of substitutions introduces a partial pre-order on substitutions. An equivalence may then be induced from it.

Definition 2.29 Let σ and τ be two substitutions.
1) The substitution σ is *more general* than the substitution τ (or the substitution τ is *less general* than the substitution σ) iff there is a substitution γ such that $\tau=\sigma\gamma$. This is subsequently denoted by $\sigma\leq\tau$ (or $\tau\geq\sigma$). [1]
2) The substitutions σ and τ are variants iff the inequalities $\sigma\leq\tau$ and $\tau\leq\sigma$ hold. This is subsequently denoted by $\sigma\equiv\tau$.

Proposition 2.30
1) The $\leq$ relation determines a partial pre-order on substitutions.
2) The $\equiv$ relation determines an equivalence on substitutions.

An analogous partial pre-order and equivalence can be defined on expressions. The same symbols are used to denote them in order to strengthen this similarity.

Definition 2.31 Let E and F be two expressions.
1) The expression E is *more general* than the expression F (or the expression F is *less general* than the expression E) iff there is a substitution γ such that $F=E\gamma$. This is subsequently denoted by $E\leq F$ (or $F\geq E$).
2) The expressions E and F are variants iff the inequalities $E\leq F$ and $F\leq E$ hold. This is subsequently denoted by $E\equiv F$.

Proposition 2.32
1) The $\leq$ relation determines a partial pre-order on expressions.
2) The $\equiv$ relation determines an equivalence on expressions.

The notion of renaming substitutions characterizes the variant substitutions and expressions.

Definition 2.33 A *renaming substitution* is a substitution of the form $\{X_1/Y_1,...,X_m/Y_m\}$ where the Y_i's are variables distinct from one another.

Proposition 2.34
1) Two substitutions σ and τ are variants iff there exist two renaming substitutions ζ and ξ such that $\sigma\zeta=\tau$ and $\tau\xi=\sigma$.
2) Two expressions E and F are variant iff there exist two renaming substitutions ζ and ξ such that $E\zeta=F$ and $F\xi=E$.

---

[1] The qualification "more general than" and the notation "$\leq$" might appear to be conflictory. They are however usually employed in the logic programming community. We also adopt them for purposes of uniformity. Note that the direction of the inequality may be justified by the fact that if σ is more general than τ then σ is also less specific than τ (or contain less information than τ).

The quotient set, say Exprs$_\equiv$, of the set of expressions Exprs by the equivalence $\equiv$ has been carefully studied in [Huet, 1976]. Among others, the following property has been established. It consists, in fact, of an anti-unification result.

Proposition 2.35 For every pair of classes c, d of Exprs$_\equiv$, there is a class of Exprs$_\equiv$, denoted by *inf(c,d)* such that

(i)   inf(c,d) ≤ c and inf(c,d) ≤ d
(ii) for every e of Exprs$_\equiv$, if e≤c and e≤d, then e≤inf(c,d).

The class inf(c,d) is also called the *inf* of c and d.

C. Unification

The central notion of unification is now reviewed. It is presented in the context of the unification of two expressions for the sake of clarity. Extension to set of expressions can however be made in a straightforward way.

Definition 2.36 A substitution θ *unifies* two expressions E and F iff the instances Eθ and Fθ are identical. If so, θ is called a *unifier* of E and F and E and F are qualified of unifiable. The unifier θ is called a *most general unifier (mgu)* of E and F if it is more general than all unifiers of E and F.

Proposition 2.37
1) Each unifiable pair of expressions has an mgu.
2) Mgu's are unique modulo renaming that is, any pair of mgu's (of the same expressions) σ and τ verifies σ$\equiv$τ.

Unification will essentially be used to reduce an atom owing to a definite Horn clause. The following definition extends the preceeding terminology to this context.

Definition 2.38 An atom A and a definite Horn clause C unify with most general unifier θ iff θ is a most general unifier of A and of the head of C. It is assumed that, if necessary, variables of C have been renamed so that no variable of A appears in C. Because of this property, θ can be partitioned into two substitutions : the subset θ$_{atom}$ of bindings of θ including variables of A as left argument and the subset θ$_{clause}$ of bindings of θ including variables of C as left argument. The subsets θ$_{atom}$ and θ$_{clause}$ are called the *atom subset* of θ and the *clause subset* of θ, respectively. They will be referred to by these notations θ$_{atom}$ and θ$_{clause}$, respectively. Finally, given some mgu, the abbreviation *mas* refers to its atom subset.

D. Idempotent substitutions

A particular class of substitutions, called idempotent substitutions, will subsequently play an important role. The interest placed in them essentially arises from their close relationship with equations. These substitutions are briefly reviewed hereafter. Properties are given without proof, except for one highlighting the above relationship. The reader is referred to [Lassez et al., 1988] for further details.

Definition 2.39 A substitution θ is *idempotent* iff $\theta = \theta \circ \theta$.

The following proposition suggests the interest of idempotent substitutions.

Proposition 2.40
1) A substitution θ is idempotent iff $dom(\theta) \cap varcod(\theta) = \emptyset$.
2) Let σ and τ be substitutions. Suppose τ is idempotent. Then $\sigma \geq \tau$ iff $\sigma = \tau\sigma$.
3) Let σ and τ be idempotent substitutions. If $\tau \supset \sigma$ then $\tau \geq \sigma$.

Unfortunately, the composition of two idempotent substitutions is not, in general, idempotent. As an example, consider the two following idempotent substitutions: $\sigma = \{X/f(Y,Z)\}$, $\tau = \{Y/b\}$. The composition $\tau\sigma = \{Y/b, X/f(Y,Z)\}$ is not idempotent since $(\tau\sigma)(\tau\sigma) = \{Y/b, X/f(b,Z)\}$. Nevertheless, the following sufficient condition is usually fulfilled.

Proposition 2.41 Let σ, τ be idempotent substitutions. If $dom(\tau) \cap varcod(\sigma) = \emptyset$ then $\tau\sigma$ is idempotent.

The restriction to idempotent substitutions is not significant in practice. The following theorem provides an important result in this respect. An exception is made to the rule of not proving results mentioned in this chapter. The demonstration is indeed a good opportunity to highlight the close relationship between idempotent substitutions and systems of equations.

Theorem 2.42 Two expressions are unifiable iff they have an idempotent mgu.
Proof The sufficient condition is obvious. The necessary one is established as follows. Let E and F be two unifiable expressions. Let us construct an idempotent mgu for E and F. A simplified version of the first unification algorithm due to Herbrand ([Herbrand, 1930]) is used for this purpose. At each step, our algorithm has a set of equations that it transforms by non-deterministically choosing an equation and by applying an action according to the form of the equation :
  (1) if the equation is $f(t_1,...,t_m)=f(u_1,...,u_m)$, then it is replaced by the equations $t_1=u_1, ..., t_m=u_m$,
  (2) if the equation is X=X, then it is deleted,
  (3) if the equation is t=X with t a non-variable term, then it is replaced by X=t,
  (4) if the equation is X=t and X has another occurrence in the set of equations, then X is replaced by t in all other equations.
The process is repeated until no action can be applied. It starts with the equation E=F.

Obviously, each action transforms the set of equations into an equivalent set of equations. By equivalent, it is understood that all assignations of values to the variables of the former that makes, for each of its equation, its members identical, makes also, for each equation of the latter, its members identical and vice versa. Therefore, as E and F are unifiable, at no point an equation of the form f(...)=g(...) can be created. Furthermore, for each equation X=t, t contains no occurrence of X.

Transformations (1), (2) and (4) strictly decrease the total number of occurrences of variables and function symbols in the left-hand side of the equations. Furthermore, transformation (3) can only be applied a finite number of times. Hence, the algorithm certainly terminates. The delivered system has the form

$$\begin{cases} X_1 = t_1 \\ \ldots \\ X_m = t_m \end{cases}$$

with $\{X_1,...,X_m\} \cap (var(t_1) \cup ... \cup var(t_m)) = \emptyset$. Thanks to the equivalence of the systems of equations, the substitution $\{X_1/t_1,...,X_m/t_m\}$ is a unifier of E and F. It is furthermore an mgu of E and F. Indeed, any unifier σ of E and F verifies the equality $E\sigma = F\sigma$ and, thanks to the equivalence of the systems of equations, the equalities $X_i\sigma = t_i\sigma$ for all $i \in \{1,...,m\}$. It thus also verifies the equality $\sigma = \{X_1/t_1,...,X_m/t_m\}\sigma$. ◊

It is worth noting that the idempotent mgu has been found as the solution of a system of equations. This relationship will be further strengthened by subsequent developments. Note also that the algorithm of the previous proof is very intuitive. This suggests that idempotent mgu's are the intuitive ones. Besides, it is worth noting that efficient unification algorithms delivering such mgu's are known. Martelli and Montanari's one is an example ([Martelli and Montanari, 1982]). Finally, the following proposition further adds to the interest of idempotent mgu's.

Proposition 2.43
1) Let θ be an idempotent mgu of the expressions E and F. Then a substitution σ is a unifier of E and F iff $\sigma = \theta\sigma$.
2) Every idempotent mgu θ of expressions E and F verifies the inclusion
    $[var(E) \cup var(F)] \supset [dom(\theta) \cup varcod(\theta)]$.

2.3.2 Resolution

All logic programming languages (either parallel or sequential) use, with some variant, the following computation mechanism. It issues from Robinson's refutation proof procedure ([Robinson, 1965]), developed in the more general context of first order logic, and Kowalski's procedural interpretation for Horn clauses ([Kowalski, 1974]). Just the latter is presented here.

To be activated, a Horn clause program must be supplied with a conjunction $\leftarrow A_1, ..., A_m$ of atoms. The computation then considers the program clauses as axioms of a certain theory and tries to prove, in this theory, the following sentence

$$\exists X_1, \ldots, X_n : A_1 \wedge \ldots \wedge A_m$$

where $X_1, \ldots, X_n$ denote all the variables appearing in $A_1, \ldots, A_m$. Restated in procedural terms ([Kowalski, 1974]), the conjunction $\leftarrow A_1, \ldots, A_m$ is interpreted as a request to find instantiations for the variables $X_1, \ldots, X_n$ that conjointly solve $A_1, \ldots, A_m$. This can lead to two opposite results : success or failure. In the former case, the values assigned to the variables constitute the output of the computation. In the latter case, no output is performed. Note that several successful computations may exist, each resulting in a different output.

The computation proceeds through non-deterministic steps. Each step transforms a conjunction of atoms

$$\leftarrow G_1, \ldots, G_n \ (n \geq 1)$$

into a new one as follows. One G_i is first arbitrarily selected and next a clause, say

$$H \leftarrow B_1, \ldots, B_k \ (k \geq 0),$$

unifying with G_i is chosen. When need be, the variables of the clause are previously renamed so that none of them appears earlier in the computation and, in particular, in G_i. Let θ be the most general unifier of G_i and H. The conjunction

$$\leftarrow G_1, \ldots, G_n$$

is then transformed in the following new one

$$\leftarrow (G_1, \ldots, G_{i-1}, B_1, \ldots, B_k, G_{i+1}, \ldots, G_n)\theta \ .$$

Such a transformation step is called a *reduction step*. The reduction process ends when the current conjunction is empty or when no reduction step can take place.

The computation successfully terminates if the conjunction $\leftarrow A_1, \ldots, A_m$ can be reduced to the empty conjunction. It fails if whatever goal and clause are selected at each step, the reduction process ends with a non-empty conjunction of goals.

The logic programming languages essentially differ by the strategy they employ to explore all possible reductions. Such strategies are subsequently called *reduction strategies*. It is here worth noting that the choice of a reduction strategy greatly affects the efficiency of the discovering of successful reductions. In particular, non termination of the computation may be induced because infinite sequences of reductions are performed.

Definition 2.44 In view of the procedural interpretation, the following terminology is often employed.
1) The initial conjunction $\leftarrow A_1, \ldots, A_m$ is called the *query* of the computation.
2) Any conjunction of atoms is called a *goal*.
3) Any atom is called a *simple goal* or *s-goal*, for short. In order to strengthen its membership of a goal, it is also called a *subgoal* of this goal.

Definition 2.45 Let $\theta_1, \ldots, \theta_n$ be the successive mgu's involved in a successful derivation for the query $\leftarrow A_1, \ldots, A_m$. The substitution $\theta_1 \circ \ldots \circ \theta_n$ is called a *solution* for $\leftarrow A_1, \ldots, A_m$.

2.3.3 And/or search trees

And/or search trees provide a useful tool for visualizing all alternative reductions in a same picture. They will be intensively used as supports of our developments. They are conceived with respect to a goal and a Horn clause program. The latter is however often kept implicit since there is generally no doubt about it.

Definition 2.46 Let $\leftarrow A_1, \ldots, A_m$ be a goal and P be a Horn clause program. The and/or search tree T for $\leftarrow A_1, \ldots, A_m$ and P is the tree of nodes defined by the following rules.

(i) Its root is the node labelled by the query $\leftarrow A_1, \ldots, A_m$.
(ii) Any node labelled by a goal has as many child nodes as the subgoals contained in the goal. They are associated with these subgoals in a one-to-one fashion. Each child node is labelled by the corresponding subgoal.
(iii) Any node labelled by a s-goal, say G, has as many child nodes as clauses of P unifiable with G. They are associated with these unifiable clauses in a one-to-one fashion. Any child node is labelled by the goal
$\leftarrow Ca\theta$
where
- $H \leftarrow Ca$ is the unifiable clause corresponding to the node
- θ is the mgu of H and G.

Note that, as particular cases of (ii) and (iii), the following nodes have no child :
- nodes labelled by the empty goal
- nodes labelled by s-goals that unify with no clause of P.

The following property gives a recursive characterization of and/or search trees. It is worth noting that it cannot be employed as a definition since and/or search trees are characterized in terms of themselves without decrease of the value of some well-founded function.

Proposition 2.47 Let $\leftarrow A_1, \ldots, A_m$ be a goal and P be a Horn clause program. The and/or search tree T for $\leftarrow A_1, \ldots, A_m$ and P verifies the following properties.
(i) If m=0 (i.e. the conjunction is empty), then T is formed of one node labelled by $\square$.
(ii) If m>0, then T is composed of
- the node labelled by $\leftarrow A_1, \ldots, A_m$, as root node,

- m subtrees $ST_1, ..., ST_m$, attached to the m s-goals $A_1, ..., A_m$, respectively. Each ST_i is defined as follows ($1 \leq i \leq m$). Fix some i in $\{1,...,m\}$. Assume

$H_1 \leftarrow Ca_1.$

...

$H_n \leftarrow Ca_n.$

are all the clauses of P that unify with A_i, say with mgu's $\theta_1, ..., \theta_n$, respectively.

ii.1) If there are none (i.e. n=0) then ST_i reduces to the only node labelled by A_i.

ii.2) Otherwise (n>0), ST_i is composed of
- the node labelled by A_i, as root node
- the n and/or search trees for the goals $\leftarrow Ca_j\theta_j$ and the program P ($1 \leq j \leq n$).

Any and/or search tree is thus composed of two kinds of nodes, labelled by goals and s-goals, respectively. They are usually called and-nodes and or-nodes, respectively. The qualification and/or search tree results from these appellations. We will subsequently adopt this qualification, too. However, we will qualify the nodes by the more suggestive appellation of goal-nodes and s-goal-nodes.

Definition 2.48
1) Nodes labelled by a s-goal are called *s-goal-nodes*.
2) Nodes labelled by a goal are called *goal-nodes*. The goal-node corresponding to the root of the and/or search tree is furthermore particularized. It is called the *query-node*. Finally, goal-nodes associated with an empty conjunction of atoms are called *☐-nodes*.

Convention 2.49 The following conventions will be used for drawing and/or search trees.
1) The label of any goal-node associated with a non-empty conjunction of atoms may be deduced from the label of its children s-goal-nodes. Such goal-nodes are consequently not labelled in and/or search tree pictures but just depicted by a point.
2) Goal-nodes are labelled by the following additional information :
   - the set of variables introduced by the corresponding clause through unification; it is signalled by the Vc abbreviation;
   - the atom subset of the involved mgu; it is signalled by the Mas abbreviation.

The second part is, in fact, related to the reduction from which the goal-node is issued. It should thus be associated with the arc linking the father s-goal-node with this goal-node. The above convention is however taken to ease the presentation.

The clause subset of the mgu is not explicitly represented. It is, in fact, already represented (in an implicit way) through its application to the clause body.

3) To preserve their name as much as possible, variables of clauses are renamed by subscripting their name with integers. For instance, X_2 refers to a renaming of the variable X.

4) S-goals that unify with no clause are stressed by annotating their corresponding s-goal-node by a special pending mark $\otimes$. As a consequence, these nodes are also called $\otimes$-*nodes*.

5) The and/or search trees are depicted so as
   - the left-to-right reading of sibling s-goal-nodes reflects the left-to-right reading of the conjunction associated with their father node;
   - the left-to-right reading of sibling goal-nodes reflects the top to bottom reading in P of the corresponding clauses in P.

6) Usual simple and double arcs are employed for representing subtrees attached to goal-nodes and s-goal-nodes, respectively.

Example 2.1 Figure 2.1 pictures the and/or search tree for the query

$\leftarrow$ p(X,Y), q(Y,Z)

and the program

p(a,a).
p(X,Y) $\leftarrow$ r(X),s(Y).
q(c,d).
q(X,e) $\leftarrow$ t(X,T).
s(b).
t(_,f).

The number between brackets will be subsequently used to refer to the nodes.

Convention 2.50 For ease of the presentation, we will subsequently confuse nodes with their label and thus speak of the node $\leftarrow A_1, ..., A_m$ instead of the node labelled by the goal $\leftarrow A_1, ..., A_m$.

The main default of the and/or search tree representation is that it provides no facility to transmit bindings made in one subtree to others. Restated in other terms, by allowing subtrees generated by a goal-node to be separately computed, we take the risk of binding a same variable to incompatible terms. An example is given by nodes (4) and (6). This will induce later special treatments. This also motivates the following distinction of candidate-solution and solution subtrees.

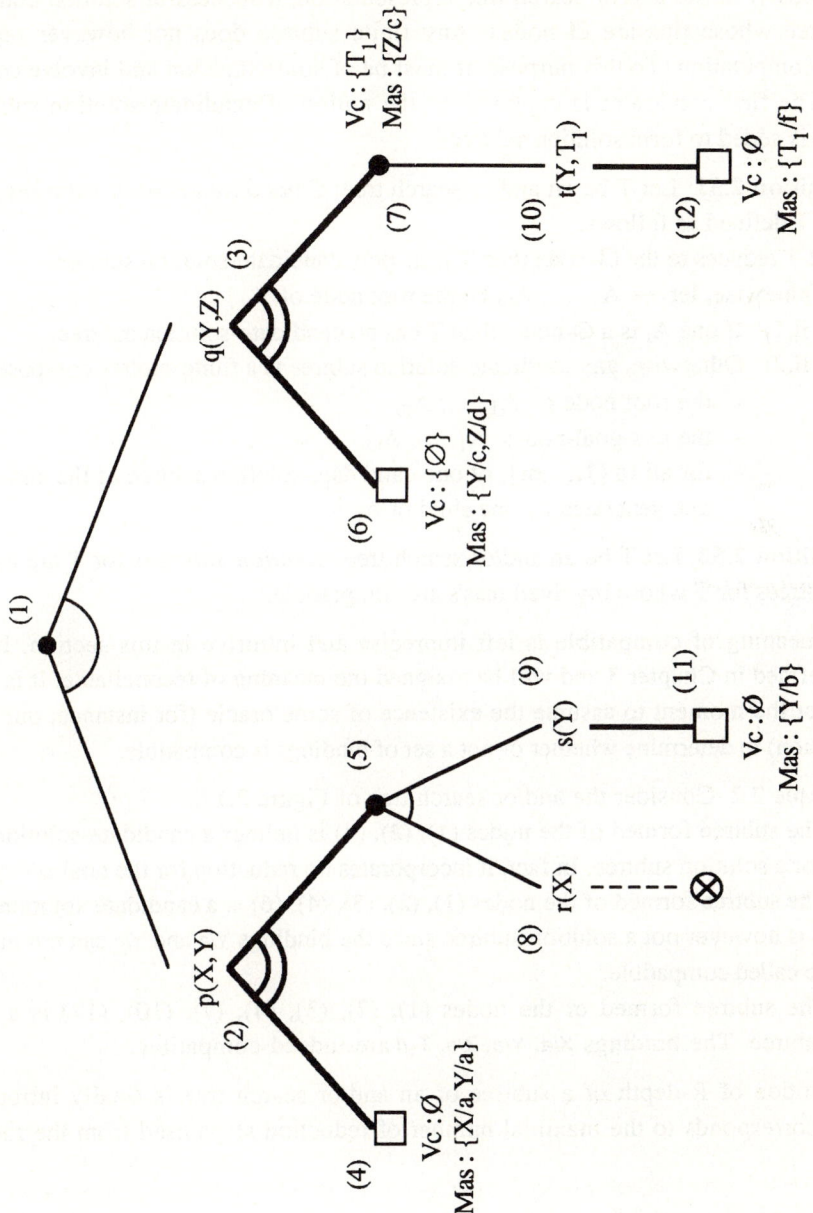

Figure 2.1

Obviously, in the and/or search tree representation, a successful solution consists of a finite subtree whose tips are □-nodes. Any finite subtree does not however represent a successful computation. To this purpose, it must be of some skeleton and involve compatible bindings. The first constraint is captured by the notion of candidate-solution subtree. The second one is added to form solution subtrees.

Definition 2.51 Let T be an and/or search tree. *Candidate-solution subtrees* are finite subtrees of T defined as follows.
  i)   If T reduces to the □-node then T is its only candidate-solution subtree.
  ii) Otherwise, let ← $A_1, ..., A_m$ be the root node of T.
     ii.1) If one A_i is a ⊗-node, then T has no candidate-solution subtree.
     ii.2) Otherwise, any candidate-solution subtree is a finite subtree composed of
       - the root node ← $A_1, ..., A_m$
       - the m s-goal-nodes $A_1, ..., A_m$
       - for all i∈ {1,...,m}, of one candidate-solution subtree of the and/or search tree generated by one child of A_i. [2]

Definition 2.52 Let T be an and/or search tree. *Solution subtrees* for T are candidate-solution subtrees for T whose involved mas's are comptatible.

The meaning of compatible is left imprecise and intuitive in this section. It will be precisely defined in Chapter 3 and will be assigned the meaning of reconcilable. It is however sufficient for the moment to assume the existence of some oracle (for instance, our intuitive comprehension) to determine whether or not a set of bindings is compatible.

Example 2.2 Consider the and/or search tree of Figure 2.1
  1) The subtree formed of the nodes (1), (2), (4) is neither a candidate-solution subtree nor a solution subtree. In fact, it incorporates no reduction for the goal q(Y,Z).
  2) The subtree formed of the nodes (1), (2), (3), (4), (6) is a candidate-solution subtree. It is however not a solution subtree since the bindings Y/a and Y/c can not manifestly be called compatible.
  3) The subtree formed of the nodes (1), (2), (3), (4), (7), (10), (12) is a solution subtree. The bindings X/a, Y/a, Z/e, T_1/f are indeed compatible.

The notion of R-depth of a subtree of an and/or search tree is finally introduced. It intuitively corresponds to the maximal number of reduction steps used from the root of the

---

[2] Note that, in contrast with Proposition 2.47, finiteness of candidate solution subtrees allow to employ this recursive definition. The definition is not circular since the numbers of nodes of the candidate solution subtrees of the and/or search tree engendered by the A_i's are strictly less than that of the candidate solution subtrees under definition.

subtree to one of its tips. It is defined by using the more general concepts of part and well-formed part.

Definition 2.53 Let T be an and/or search tree. Consider the arcs of T as directed from father nodes to their children.
1) A *part* of T is a subset of the set of nodes of T. Connections between nodes of any part are inherented from those of T.
2) A *well-formed part* of T is a part of T that verifies the following properties :
    - every root node is a goal-node
    - every tip node is either a $\otimes$-node or a goal-node.

Note that the notion of part of an and/or search tree includes that of subtree and of slice.

Definition 2.54 Let T be an and/or search tree. Consider the arcs of T as directed from father nodes to their children. Then the *R-depth* of a part P of T is the number of goal-nodes that are not query-nodes on a longest path of P.

Example 2.3 Referring to the and/or search tree of Figure 2.1, the R-depth of the solution subtree $\{(1),(2),(3),(4),(7),(10),(12)\}$ is 2. It corresponds to the path formed of the nodes (1), (3), (7), (10), (12).

Convention 2.55 In contrast with the depth notion, the notion of R-depth is not generally sufficient to characterize some part of an and/or search tree completely. For instance, the concept of slice of R-depth D is ambiguous since paths can be extended from one s-goal-node without modification of their R-depth. This problem is solved by taking the following convention :

- only well-formed parts are considered;
- a $\otimes$-node is a tip node only if, assuming that the pending mark is a child goal-node, this goal-node would be an element of the well-formed part.

As a consequence, the first slice of R-depth D of an and/or search tree denotes the (only) well-formed slice of R-depth D of this tree. For instance, referring to the and/or search tree of Figure 2.1, the first slice of R-depth 1 of the tree is composed of the nodes $\{(1),(2),(3),(4),(5),(6),(7)\}$. The node (8) is a $\otimes$-node that does not participate to this slice. Indeed, if its pending mark were considered as a goal-node, it would not be of an element of the slice.

2.3.4 Sources of concurrency

The previous sections should have suggested the adequacy of the logic programming framework for concurrency. The declarative semantics points out many sources of non-determinism. The truth value of disjunctions, conjunctions, implications can indeed be obtained by, first, evaluating the truth value of their components separately and, then, by combining the results. These sources of parallelism are present at the operational level, too. They are now reviewed from this point of view. By the way, the various forms they can take are detailed. Another form of parallelism arising from unification is described thereafter.

A. Or-parallelism

A first form of parallelism consists of using alternative clauses in parallel to reduce a s-goal. This is called *or-parallelism*. It corresponds, in and/or search tree terms, to the concurrent search of goal-nodes which are children of s-goal-nodes.

The usefulness of or-parallelism has been advocated in [Pollard, 1981]. A first argument concerns database applications. Often, interpreters deliver only one solution. However, in the database context, it is natural to compute the relation associated with the user's goal - and not a single member of it - and, consequently, to compute all the solutions of the query, not just the first one discovered.

However, or-parallelism makes sense even in case only one solution is requested. Indeed, several solutions can be required for intermediate subgoals. Convincing examples are generate and test programs. The naive sort procedure is particularly suggestive. Stated in functional terms, it consists in sorting an input list by generating the permutations of the list and by testing each of them for orderness. Obviously, although only one list is the sorted version of a given list, several permutations need generally to be generated before the ordered one is produced.

Finally, or-parallelism is also desirable when negative literals are involved. As already argued, it is in practice necessary to negate atomic formulae in Horn clause bodies. The way in which these negative literals are handled is usually to solve the associated positive literals and to deduce results for the negated ones. This negation as failure inference rule implies that an exhaustive search for the positive literal should be made. Once again, a parallel search seems natural.

To sum up, in all these situations, or-parallelism is of interest. By adopting it, one can hope to gain efficiency while being sure to execute useful deductions.

B. And-parallelism

The second way of exploiting concurrency in Horn clause programs arises from the evaluation of subgoals of conjunctions. Provided resulting bindings are suitably handled, those subgoals could be evaluated in a parallel way, too. This form of parallelism is called *and-parallelism*. It corresponds, in and/or search tree terms, to the concurrent generation of subtrees issued from s-goal-nodes that are children of a goal-node.

And-parallelism can take various forms depending on the situations where it is applied. The pure form given above is subsequently called *full and-parallelism*. It makes no assumption on the goals or on their eventual synchronization. Other qualifications are based on such assumptions.

A first one concerns the concurrent evaluation of independent subgoals i.e. goals that share no variable. This is called *restricted and-parallelism*. In this case, it is certainly more appropriate to use concurrent executions than to use sequential ones.
- Firstly, as the subgoals are independent, concurrent executions could do no less than speeding up the overall computation.
- Secondly - and more importantly - the application of depth-first interpreters with backtracking like Prolog have, in such a context, a poor behavior. Consider the independent subgoals p(X), q(Y). Let m and n be the number of solutions of p(X) and q(Y), respectively. A Prolog-like interpreter finds the solutions to the query ←p(X), q(Y) by first finding a solution for p(X) and then all the solutions for q(Y). It thereafter finds other solutions by backtracking to p(X) and rediscovering the same solutions for q(Y). An algorithm of complexity m*n results. In contrast, the parallel execution of p(X) and q(Y) leads to an algorithm of complexity m+n.

Stream-parallelism is a form of and-parallelism in which subgoals are evaluated concurrently and communicate incrementally with one another through bindings of a shared variable. This variable is often a list constructed step by step by the successive reductions of a subgoal, called the *producer* of the list, and consumed by another (or other) conjoined subgoal(s), called the *consumer(s)* of the list. As an example, let us consider the append3 procedure. It consists of appending three lists L1, L2, L3, this resulting in a list L. It is computed by appending the lists L1 and L2, forming a list L12 and then by appending L12 and L3. Appending of two lists, say M1 and M2, is performed as follows. The elements of M1 are taken one after the others and are placed in this order to form the prefix of the resulting list, say M. When all the elements of M1 have been taken, the whole list M2 is placed as the remainder suffix of M. This is translated in the following Horn clauses :

append3(L1,L2,L3,L) ← append(L1,L2,L12), append(L12,L3,L).
append([],L,L).
append([H|T],L,[H|L_rem]) ← append(T,L,L_rem).

Figure 2.2 gives a procedural representation of the execution of append3 with [a,b,c], [d,e] and [f,g] as lists L1, L2 and L3, respectively. The elements a, b, c, d, e are produced in this order by the s-goal append(L1,L2,L12). They are also consumed in this order by the s-goal append(L12,L3,L). Stream-parallelism is achieved by the incremental consumption and production described above. To this end, the two append subgoals are executed concurrently but the list L12 is made incrementally produced by append(L1,L2,L12) and incrementally consumed by append(L12,L3,L).

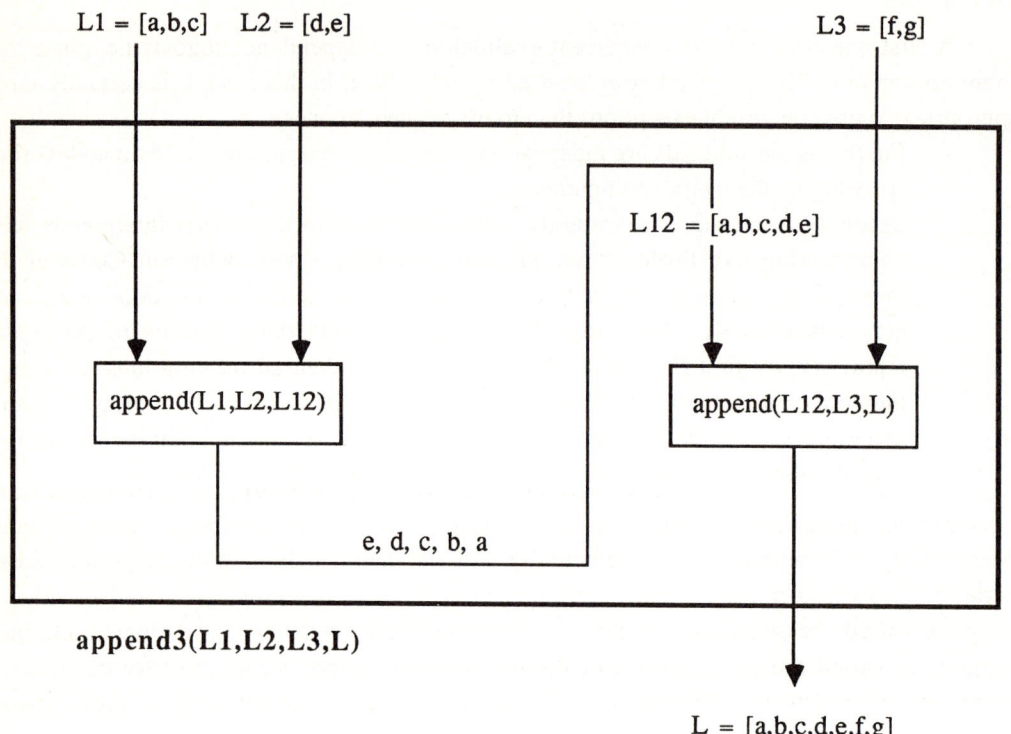

Figure 2.2

Stream-parallelism is used in essentially two modes.
i) The producer is allowed to produce at its rate without care of the rate of consumption. It is then said to be *eager*.
ii) The producer is producing at the request of consumers. It is then said to be *lazy*.

Controlled and-parallelism ([Ueda, 1986a]) is a form of and-parallelism where the reduction of some goals is controlled by the reduction of others. Suppose p(...X...) and q(...X...) are two atoms sharing a variable X. Assume furthermore that p(...X...) delivers many alternative bindings for X whereas q(...X...) generates only a few ones. Then it is useless to solve the query ←p(...X...), q(...X...) by independently solving p(...X...) and q(...X...). A better solution is to force p(...X...) to wait for q(...X...) to bind X. This is called controlled and-parallelism since the concurrent subgoals are executed in parallel except that p(...X...) must freeze until q(...X...) binds X and, consequently, is controlled by q(...X...). As suggested above, stream-parallelism is often achieved as a form of controlled and-parallelism.

It is not always possible to avoid useless computations by such restrictions. In some cases, benefit can be taken from a particular use of and-parallelism, called *earlier detection of failure*. When several conjoined subgoals are solved concurrently, it often happens that a binding for a shared variable generated by the reduction of a subgoal cannot participate in a solution. In this case, the corresponding subtree should stop growing since it is useless. In particular, in a producer-consumer scheme involving a list as shared variable, the list can be rejected in view of one prefix. In this situation, the rest of the list should not be constructed since it is of no help. The naive sort procedure we examined above provides a good illustration: most of the permutations of the list can be rejected in view of a prefix.

C. Concurrent unification

A third area in which concurrent computation might occur is in the unification algorithm. Obviously, it is a form of parallelism at a lower level. It can be closely related to and-parallelism as the concurrent unification of the composed terms $f(t_1,...,t_m)$ and $f(u_1,...,u_m)$ amounts to the concurrent resolution of the conjunction $t_1=u_1, ... , t_m=u_m$.

2.4 Relating the declarative and operational semantics

The declarative and operational semantics are related by the completeness and soundness properties. They have been informally stated in Chapter 1. They are now precisely defined. To this end, the concept of interpreter is first introduced.

Definition 2.56 An *interpreter* is an algorithm that, given as input a Horn clause program and a conjunction of atoms, delivers as output either substitutions for the variables of the conjunction or the answer no. In the latter case, the interpreter is said to fail. An interpreter is allowed not to terminate but must end up immediately after having failed.

The following notations will be helpful to describe the properties of interpreters.

Notation 2.57 Let Int be an interpreter, P be a Horn clause program, $\leftarrow A_1, ..., A_m$ be a conjunction of atoms and θ be a substitution. The notation

$P \mid\text{-}_{Int} (A_1, ..., A_m)$ with θ

means that the interpreter Int, given P and $\leftarrow A_1, ..., A_m$ as input, delivers the substitution θ. The notation

$P \mid\text{-} (A_1, ..., A_m)$ with θ

will be used as a shorthand when there is no doubt about the interpreter Int.

Definition 2.58 An interpreter Int is
1) *sound* iff for any Horn clause program P, any conjunction of atoms $\leftarrow A_1, ..., A_m$, if the property
$$P \vdash_{Int} (A_1, ..., A_m) \text{ with } \theta$$
holds, then so does the property
$$P \models (A_1 \wedge ... \wedge A_m)\theta .$$
2) *complete* iff for any Horn clause program P, any conjunction of atoms $\leftarrow A_1, ..., A_m$, if
$$P \models (A_1 \wedge ... \wedge A_m)\theta$$
holds for some substitution θ, then there is a substitution μ so that the following properties hold
1) $P \vdash_{Int} (A_1, ..., A_m)$ with μ;
2) $(A_1, ..., A_m)\mu \leq (A_1, ..., A_m)\theta$.

Remark 2.59 The last property
$$(A_1, ..., A_m)\mu \leq (A_1, ..., A_m)\theta$$
is sometimes replaced by the following stronger requirement:
$$\mu \leq \theta .$$
However, for technical reasons of composition of substitutions, some interpreters that are intuitively complete would then be no more complete. Consider the one clause program
$$p(f(X)).$$
and the conjunction of atoms reduced to the only atom
$$p(Y).$$
Take $\theta = \{Y/f(1)\}$. Obviously, the property
$$P \models (p(Y))\{Y/f(1)\} \quad \text{(that is } P \models p(f(1))\text{)}$$
holds. Moreover, a very natural (most general) answer for this query is
$$\mu = \{Y/f(X)\}.$$
However, interpreters delivering such answers are not complete. Indeed, the inequality
$$\mu \leq \theta$$
does not hold. To obtain it, one should be able to exhibit a substitution γ such that $\theta = \mu\gamma$ i.e. such that
$$\{Y/f(1)\} = \{Y/f(X)\} \circ \gamma.$$

Any such γ must at least contain the binding X/1 and thus so does the composition {Y/f(X)}∘γ. Hence, for any substitution γ, the composition {Y/f(X)}∘γ always differs from the substitution {Y/f(1)}.

The technical problem is precisely that the binding X/1 is always present in any composition μ∘γ. However, this X is not a variable of the initial query, for which values are expected. It simply denotes some auxiliary variable. It is here worth noting that if the conventional rule of designing two semantically different variables by distinct names is abandoned and, more precisely if X is renamed by Y in Y/f(X), then the above problem is circumvented:

$$\theta = \{Y/f(1)\} = \{Y/f(Y)\} \circ \{Y/1\} = \mu \circ \gamma.$$

However such a practice is very intricate and dangerous. In fact, the requirement that the substitutions μ and θ verify the inequality

$$\mu \leq \theta$$

i.e. that

there is a substitution γ such that tθ = tμγ for every term t

is too strong. The intuition we placed in completeness is that, for all values given to the variables of a query that make it a logical consequence of the program, the interpreter computes a more general set of values for these variables. Restated in more general terms, if Q denotes the considered query and if θ sums up the first set of values and μ the second one, then there must be a substitution γ such that

$$\forall X \in var(Q) : X\theta = X\mu\gamma$$

that is such that

$$Q\theta = Q\mu\gamma.$$

This condition can furthermore be restated as

$$Q\mu \leq Q\theta.$$

The difference with the inequality μ≤θ is that it is no more required that this inequality holds for (uninteresting) variables that are not in Q.

Convention 2.60 All logic programming languages determine a class of interpreters through their operational semantics. By language misuse, we will subsequently say that a language is sound and complete whenever these properties hold for all interpreters induced by the language.

Part II

Designing Conclog

Introduction

This part is devoted to the design of Conclog. The objectives stated in Chapter 1 have, of course, been taken, as references for this purpose. A major one forces the language to employ or-parallelism and and-parallelism. The first source of parallelism is, from a theoretical point of view, easy to handle : multiple environments have simply to be managed. At the opposite, and-parallelism is not so easy to handle : conflicting bindings for shared variables may result from the independent resolution of subgoals. This problem can be tackled in two ways.

(i) The designation approach
A producer subgoal is designated for each shared variable so that no conflicting bindings occur ([Conery and Kibler, 1981], [Conery, 1983], [Woo and Choe, 1986], [Lin et al., 1986], [Li and Martin, 1986],[Conery, 1987b], [Kalé, 1987]).

(ii) The reconciliation approach
Subgoals in conjunctions are allowed to be reduced independently even if they do share variables. A reconciliation process is then provided to extract coherent solutions for the whole conjunction from solutions produced by their subgoals ([Pollard, 1981]).

A major drawback of the designation approach is that it is quite difficult to systematically designate the appropriate producer subgoal in all cases. By appropriate subgoal, we mean one yielding a most efficient and complete computation. This is made clear from the last statement of the ordering algorithm in [Conery, 1983]: it prescribes choosing the leftmost subgoal in the conjunctions in case previous specific rules produce several potential candidates. Furthermore, it is worth noting that determining such an appropriate producer subgoal is computationally not feasible. Indeed, one obvious property of this subgoal is that it must terminate but the automatic proof of termination of calls is known as undecidable. Moreover, we strongly believe that it is impossible to find a sufficiently general class of programs for which the automatic determination of the appropriate producer subgoal for a shared variable would be possible.

We thus turn to the reconciliation approach. Our precise use is progressively revealed in this part. It is organized as follows.

The problem of making substitutions compatible (what we call reconciling substitutions) is addressed in Chapter 3. Generalization to a generalized form of substitutions, called n-substitutions, is furthermore treated. It will be of particular interest to introduce negation.

The Conclog execution model is then designed in three steps. A parallel execution model of (pure) Horn clauses is presented in Chapter 4. It is extended to incorporate negation in Chapter 5. Extra-logical features are introduced in Chapter 6.

A possible extension of Conclog is thereafter discussed in Chapter 7. Comparison with related work is finally made in Chapter 8.

Chapter 3

A reconciliation calculus

3.1 Reconciling substitutions

3.1.1 Introduction

The meaning of the reconciliation of substitutions as well as the way to perform it can be intuitively suggested by applying the reconciliation-based approach on the following simple example of unification. Consider two unifiable compound terms $t=f(t_1,...,t_m)$ and $u=f(u_1,...,u_m)$. Let us solve the goal $\leftarrow t=u$. Manifestly, in the reconciliation-based approach, we would like to make the m unifications $t_i=u_i$ separately and to extract a mgu for $t=u$ from them. Let us apply this decomposition process recursively. Since the terms are finite and unifiable, we eventually obtain unreducable equations of one of the forms

(1) $X=t$,
(2) $t=X$,
(3) $c=c$,

where X is a variable, c is a constant and t is a term. Such equalities can be solved directly. The identity substitution {} is a mgu for unifications of type (3). As far as the first two forms are concerned, {} or {X/t} is a mgu of X and t according as t is X or not.

Two facts are worth pointing out from this example :

- the initial goal t=u has been reduced to a system of equalities;
- solutions to the non trivial equalities of the form X=t, with X syntactically different from t, have been recorded in the substitution {X/t}.

Conversely, it is interesting to make the substitutions reflect equalities, thus interpreting $\{X_1/t_1,...,X_m/t_m\}$ as the equalities $X_1=t_1$, ..., $X_m=t_m$. Indeed, several bindings for a same variable will generally be produced by the independent reductions of conjoined subgoals. In the equality interpretation, all we have to do is to search a common value for the associated right-hand sides. Stated in more general terms, reconciling substitutions amounts to solving a system of equations. As usual, this means that we have to find values for the variables appearing in the equations such that replacing the variables by their corresponding values makes both sides of the equations identical.

This interpretation however induces one restriction. It is due to the transitive nature of equalities. Consider for instance t=h(X,Y) and u=h(1,Z). The substitution {X/1,Y/X,Z/X} can be proved to be an mgu of t and u. It is however not a good mgu for t and u with regards to our interpretation. Indeed it implicitly implies that Y and Z must be equal to 1 whereas the real meaning of the mgu is that Y and Z must be equal. To avoid these undesired implicit consequences, we must make sure that the domain and codomain of the substitutions do not interfere. That is they cannot share variables. We must thus *restrict to substitutions whose domain is disjoint from the set of variables of their codomain*. Such substitutions have been identified as idempotent substitutions in Chapter 2 (see Theorem 2.40).

Nevertheless, the theory of reconciliation developed hereafter may be presented in the more general context of unrestricted substitutions. Just some properties will require the idempotence property, as, for instance, the link with the above intuition. We will thus not restrict to idempotent substitutions at this point but rather require idempotence explicitly when need be.

3.1.2 Basic concepts

Before defining our central concept of reconciliation, let us first introduce some auxiliary concepts related to equations.

Definition 3.1 An *equation* is a construct of the form

$t = u$

where t and u are terms. It is called an *elementary equation* or *e-equation* for short when t is a variable.

Notation 3.2 In order to avoid ambiguity in using the = symbol, we will subsequently denote by

$=_s$

the syntactic equality between terms. The = symbol will be reserved to denote equalities and equations.

Definition 3.3 Equations will, in general, not be manipulated alone but in *systems of equations*. Such systems simply consist of sets of equations. They are called *elementary systems* or *e-systems* when they are only composed of e-equations.

Notions relative to sets may thus be applied to systems of equations. We will subsequently use them and denote, for instance, by

$S \cup T$ and $S \setminus \{E\}$

the system of equations formed of the equations of S and T and the system of equations obtained from S by removing the equation E in it.

Notions relative to unification are extended to systems of equations as follows.

Definition 3.4 A *unifier* of a system of equations S is a substitution θ such that any equation t=u of S verifies $t\theta =_s u\theta$. It is a *most general unifier (mgu)* of S iff every unifier υ of S verifies $\theta \leq \upsilon$. Finally, S is *unifiable* iff it has an mgu.

Properties of the unifiers and mgu's of systems of equations result from those of terms, thanks to the following proposition. In particular,

(1) mgu's of systems of equations are equal modulo renaming,
(2) unifiable systems of equations have an idempotent mgu.

Proposition 3.5 For every system of equations S, there are two terms t and u formed of the variables of S only and such that
   (i) S is unifiable iff t and u are unifiable,
   (ii) every substitution θ is an unifier (resp. mgu) of S iff it is a unifier (resp. mgu) of t and u,

Proof Assume S is composed of n equations

$t_1 = u_1$
...
$t_n = u_n$.

Let h be a n-ary functor. Then, define t and u as $h(t_1,...,t_n)$ and $h(u_1,...,u_n)$, respectively. Obviously, a substitution is a unifier for S iff it is a unifier for t and u. Hence, S is unifiable iff t and u are unifiable. Furthermore, a substitution is an mgu for S iff it is an mgu for t and u. ◊

The following definition further relates substitutions and systems of equations.

Definition 3.6
1) Let $\theta = \{X_1/t_1,...,X_m/t_m\}$ be a substitution. The *system associated with* θ, denoted by *syst(θ)*, is the system of equations obtained by associating the e-equation $X_i = t_i$ to each binding X_i/t_i ($1 \leq i \leq m$).
2) The *system associated with a set of substitutions* $\theta_1, ..., \theta_m$, denoted by *syst($\theta_1,...,\theta_m$)*, is the system of the equations of syst(θ_1), ..., syst(θ_m).

Example 3.1 Let

$\theta_1 = \{X/Y, Z/g(h(3))\}$,
$\theta_2 = \{X/h(T), Y/h(3)\}$,
$\theta_3 = \{X/U, Z/g(U)\}$.

The system syst($\theta_1,\theta_2,\theta_3$) is composed of the equations

X = Y	(from θ_1)
Z = g(h(3)).	(from θ_1)
X = h(T)	(from θ_2)
Y = h(3)	(from θ_2)
X = U	(from θ_3)
Z = g(U)	(from θ_3).

The notion of system of equations leads naturally to the concept of solution of such systems. It is defined as follows.

Definition 3.7
1) A *solution* of a system of equations S is a substitution that is both a grounding substitution for the variables of S and a unifier of S. The notation *Sol(S)* is used to denote the set of solutions of S.
2) A system of equations is *solvable* if it has at least one solution.

The following proposition relates the unifiable and solvable character of systems of equations. One important consequence is that all solutions of any solvable systems are proved to be summed up by one substitution.

Proposition 3.8
1) A system of equation is solvable iff it is unifiable.
2) Any idempotent mgu θ of any solvable system of equation S verifies the following equalities
$$\text{Sol}(\text{syst}(\theta)) = \{\ \sigma_{|(\text{dom}(\theta)\cup\text{varcod}(\theta))} : \sigma \in \text{Sol}(S)\ \}$$
$$\text{Sol}(S) = \{\ \theta\gamma : \gamma \text{ ground substitution for the variables of } S\ \}.$$

Proof 1) By Definition 3.7, any solvable system of equations has a solution. It is a unifier (see Definition 3.7). Any solvable system of equations is thus unifiable. Conversely, any unifiable system of equations is solvable. To prove this assertion, let S denote some arbitrary unifiable system of equations and let us construct some solution of S. Since it is unifiable, S has an idempotent mgu. Let θ be one of them. Let furthermore γ be some grounding substitution for the variables of S. Let us prove that $\theta\gamma$ is a solution of S. On the one hand, since θ is an mgu of S, $\theta\gamma$ is an unifier of S. On the other hand, it is a grounding substitution for the variables of S. Indeed, thanks to Propositions 2.43 and 3.5, θ is formed only of the variables of S. It follows that $\theta\gamma$ is a grounding substitution whose domain dom($\theta\gamma$) consists of the set of variables of S.

2) Suppose that the idempotent mgu θ under consideration is the substitution $\{V_1/w_1,\ldots,V_n/w_n\}$. To prove assertion 2), let us first note that, thanks to Propositions 2.43 and 3.5, for any solution σ of S and for any grounding substitution γ for the variables of S, the substitutions

$\sigma_{|(\text{dom}(\theta)\cup\text{varcod}(\theta))}$

θγ

are grounding substitutions for the variables of syst(θ) and S, respectively. Proving the assertion 2) then amounts to proving the following four inclusions, regardless to the domain constraint and to the grounding character of solutions :

    (i) $Sol(syst(\theta)) \supset \{ \sigma_{|(dom(\theta) \cup varcod(\theta))} : \sigma \in Sol(S) \}$
    (ii) $\{ \sigma_{|(dom(\theta) \cup varcod(\theta))} : \sigma \in Sol(S) \} \supset Sol(syst(\theta))$
    (iii) $Sol(S) \supset \{ \theta\gamma : \gamma \text{ ground substitution for the variables of } S \}$
    (iv) $\{ \theta\gamma : \gamma \text{ ground substitution for the variables of } S \} \supset Sol(S)$

(i) $Sol(syst(\theta)) \supset \{ \sigma_{|(dom(\theta) \cup varcod(\theta))} : \sigma \in Sol(S) \}$

Let us establish that, for any $\sigma \in Sol(S)$, the substitution σ^*

$$\sigma^* = \sigma_{|(dom(\theta) \cup varcod(\theta))}$$

verifies the equalities

$$V_i \sigma^* =_s w_i \sigma^*,$$

for any $i \in \{1,...,n\}$. As θ is an idempotent mgu of S, one has $\sigma = \theta\delta$ for some substitution δ. The idempotence character of θ then establishes the following equalities, for any $i \in \{1,...,n\}$:

$$V_i \sigma = V_i \theta\delta = V_i \theta\theta\delta = (V_i \theta)\theta\delta = w_i \theta\delta = w_i \sigma.$$

Hence, one has

$$V_i \sigma = w_i \sigma$$

for any $i \in \{1,...,n\}$.

(ii) $\{ \sigma_{|(dom(\theta) \cup varcod(\theta))} : \sigma \in Sol(S) \} \supset Sol(syst(\theta))$

Let us establish that for any solution $\tau \in Sol(syst(\theta))$, there is one solution $\sigma \in Sol(S)$ such that

$$\tau = \sigma_{|(dom(\theta) \cup varcod(\theta))}.$$

Let α be some grounding substitution for the variables of the set

$$var(S) \setminus [dom(\theta) \cup varcod(\theta)] .$$

Then the substitution $\theta \circ (\tau \cup \alpha)$ can play the role of σ. Thanks to Propositions 2.43 and 3.5, it is a grounding substitution for the variables of S. It is also a unifier of S since θ is so. It is thus a solution of S. Finally, since, by the definition of τ,

$$dom(\tau) = dom(\theta) \cup varcod(\theta),$$

one has

$$\theta \circ (\tau \cup \alpha)_{|(dom(\theta) \cup varcod(\theta))} = \theta\tau,$$

and, therefore, as $\theta\tau=\tau$ thanks to Propositions 2.43 and 3.5,

$$\theta \circ (\tau \cup \alpha)_{|(\text{dom}(\theta) \cup \text{varcod}(\theta))} = \tau.$$

(iii) Sol(S) ⊃ { θγ : γ ground substitution for the variables of S }

As θ is a unifier of S, the substitution $\theta\gamma$ is also a unifier of S for any subsitution γ.

(iv) { θγ : γ ground substitution for the variables of S } ⊃ Sol(S)

Let us establish that for any solution $\sigma \in$ Sol(S), there is one grounding substitution γ for the variables of S such that

$$\sigma = \theta\gamma.$$

Indeed, let us take as substitution γ the substitution σ itself. It is indeed a grounding substitution for the variables of S. Furthermore, thanks to Propositions 2.43 and 3.6, one has $\sigma=\theta\sigma$. ◊

From an intuitive point of view, two systems of equations sharing the same unifiers also share the same solutions and vive-versa. However, this is not exactly the case. The systems may contain different variables and their solutions may consequently have different domains. Referring to Definitions 2.2 and 3.7, the two systems cannot share their solutions. Consider, for instance, the systems

$$S = \begin{cases} X=1 \\ V=V \end{cases}$$

and

$$T = \begin{cases} X=1 \\ U=U \end{cases}$$

They share the same unifiers but solutions of S and T have {X,V} and {X,U} as domain, respectively. Solutions of S cannot then be solutions of T and conversely. Nevertheless, any solution of S modified

- by extending it by giving arbitrary ground values for the variables of var(T)\var(S)
- by restricting the result to the variables of T

is a solution of T. Conversely, the property holds when S and T are interchanged. Therefore, modulo the syntactic problem of domain, the intuitive idea that both systems share the same solutions holds. This is stated more precisely by means of the concept of solution-weaker system.

Definition 3.9 The sytem of equations S is *solution-weaker* than the system of equations T if for any solution σ of S, for any grounding substitution γ for the variables of var(T)\var(S), the substitution

$$(\sigma\gamma)_{|\text{var}(T)}$$

is a solution of T.

The intuitive property that two systems of equations share the same solutions is captured by the property that any of them is solution-weaker than the other. The equivalence of the sharing of unifiers and solutions is then reformulated as follows.

Proposition 3.10 Two systems of equations share the same unifiers iff any one is solution-weaker than the other.
Proof Thanks to Proposition 3.8, it is sufficient to prove that two systems of equations share the same unifiers iff they share the same mgu's. Manifestly, two systems of equations share the same mgu's when they share the same unifiers. Let us turn to the converse. Two cases must be considered. If the system have no mgu then they are not unifiable and have no unifiers. They then share the same unifiers. Otherwise, they share an idempotent mgu, say θ. Then, thanks to Propositions 2.43 and 3.5, a substitution τ is a unifier of any system iff it verifies the equality $\tau=\theta\tau$. It follows that the two systems share the same unifiers. ◊

The equivalence of systems can now be defined as follows.

Definition 3.11 Two systems of equations S and T are *equivalent* iff they share the same unifiers that is iff any one is weaker-solution than the other. This is denoted by S≈T.

3.1.3 Definition

We are now in position to define what the expression "reconcilable substitution" means.

Definition 3.12 The substitutions θ_1, ..., θ_m are *reconcilable* iff the associated system syst(θ_1,...,θ_m) is unifiable. Any mgu of syst(θ_1,...,θ_m) is called a *reconciliation* of θ_1, ..., θ_m.

Notation 3.13 The fact that mgu's of system of equations are equal modulo renaming allows us to make some abuse of language and speak of <u>the</u> reconciliation of substitutions. It is subsequently denoted by

$\rho(\theta_1,...,\theta_m)$

where θ_1, ..., θ_m are the reconciled substitutions. The notation

$\rho(\text{Ssubsts})$,

where Ssubsts is a set of substitutions, will also be used in order to avoid listing all the elements of the Ssubsts.

Example 3.2 The substitutions θ_1, θ_2, θ_3 of Example 3.1 are reconcilable since the associated system syst(θ_1,θ_2,θ_3) is solvable. One reconciliation is given by the substitution

{X/h(3),Y/h(3),Z/g(h(3)),T/3,U/h(3)}.

3.1.4 Properties

The reconciliation of substitutions enjoys attractive properties. Basic ones are first proved. The relationship between the reconciliation and the unification of substitutions is then established. One of its interests is to link the above definition of reconciliation with one intuitive perception of finding a "most common instance" of the substitutions.

3.1.4.1 Basic properties

Idempotent substitutions are proved unchanged by application of the reconciliation operation.

Proposition 3.14 Every idempotent substitution θ verifies $\rho(\theta) \equiv \theta$.
Proof As θ is idempotent, it is a mgu of the system $syst(\theta)$. Hence, it is equal to $\rho(\theta)$ modulo some renaming substitution. ◊

Reconciliation of substitutions increases with the number of substitutions that are reconciled. In other terms, it becomes more and more specific as more and more substitutions are reconciled. In particular, Proposition 3.14 implies that every idempotent substitution is more general than any reconciliation in which it participates.

Proposition 3.15 Let $\tau_1,\ldots,\tau_m$ be substitutions. For every subset $\{\sigma_1,\ldots,\sigma_k\}$ of $\{\tau_1,\ldots,\tau_m\}$, one has

$$\rho(\sigma_1,\ldots,\sigma_k) \leq \rho(\tau_1,\ldots,\tau_m).$$

In particular, for any idempotent substitution τ_i, one has

$$\tau_i \leq \rho(\tau_1,\ldots,\tau_m).$$

Proof The inequality

$$\rho(\sigma_1,\ldots,\sigma_k) \leq \rho(\tau_1,\ldots,\tau_m)$$

results from the fact that the system $syst(\sigma_1,\ldots,\sigma_k)$ is included in the system $syst(\tau_1,\ldots,\tau_m)$. Thus any unifier of $syst(\tau_1,\ldots,\tau_m)$ is a unifier of the system $syst(\sigma_1,\ldots,\sigma_k)$. Consequently, any mgu of $syst(\tau_1,\ldots,\tau_m)$ - in particular, $\rho(\tau_1,\ldots,\tau_m)$ - is less general than any mgu of $syst(\sigma_1,\ldots,\sigma_k)$ - in particular, $\rho(\sigma_1,\ldots,\sigma_k)$.

Taking $\{\tau_i\}$ as subset of $\{\tau_1,\ldots,\tau_m\}$, we obtain

$$\rho(\tau_i) \leq \rho(\tau_1,\ldots,\tau_m)$$

and thus, thanks to Proposition 3.14,

$$\tau_i \leq \rho(\tau_1,\ldots,\tau_m). \diamond$$

Reconciling the composition $\sigma\tau$ of two substitutions σ and τ with other substitutions amounts to directly reconciling the whole set of substitutions provided the domain of σ and τ are disjoint.

Proposition 3.16 Let $\{\theta_1, ..., \theta_m\}$ be a possibly empty set of substitutions. Let σ and τ be two substitutions such as dom(σ)$\cap$dom(τ)=$\emptyset$. Then
1) The substitutions $\sigma\tau, \theta_1, ..., \theta_m$ are reconcilable iff the substitutions $\sigma, \tau, \theta_1, ..., \theta_m$ are reconcilable.
2) In this case, one has
$$\rho(\sigma\tau,\theta_1,...,\theta_m) = \rho(\sigma,\tau,\theta_1,...,\theta_m).$$
Proof The theorem directly results from the fact that the systems syst($\sigma\tau,\theta_1,...,\theta_m$) and the systems syst($\sigma,\tau,\theta_1, ..., \theta_m$) are equivalent. ◊

Reconciliation is monotonic in some situations.

Proposition 3.17 Let $\pi_1, ..., \pi_m, \sigma_1, ..., \sigma_n$ be substitutions and $\theta_1, ..., \theta_m$ be idempotent substitutions. Assume the substitutions $\sigma_1, ..., \sigma_n, \theta_1\pi_1, ..., \theta_m\pi_m$ are reconcilable. Then the substitutions $\sigma_1, ..., \sigma_n, \theta_1, ..., \theta_m$ are reconcilable as well. Furthermore, one has

$$\rho(\sigma_1,...,\sigma_n,\theta_1,...,\theta_m) \leq \rho(\sigma_1,...,\sigma_n,\theta_1\pi_1,...,\theta_m\pi_m).$$

In particular, for any idempotent substitution λ and any substitution $\mu\geq\lambda$, one has $\rho(\mu)\geq\rho(\lambda)$.

Proof The theorem results from the fact that any unifier of the system syst($\sigma_1,...,\sigma_n,\theta_1\pi_1,...,\theta_m\pi_m$) is a unifier of the system syst($\sigma_1,...,\sigma_n,\theta_1, ..., \theta_m$). Thus, the substitutions $\sigma_1, ..., \sigma_n, \theta_1, ..., \theta_m$ are reconcilable when the substitutions $\sigma_1, ..., \sigma_n, \theta_1\pi_1,...,\theta_m\pi_m$ are reconcilable. Furthermore, any mgu of syst($\sigma_1,...,\sigma_n,\theta_1\pi_1,...,\theta_m\pi_m$) is also a unifier of syst($\sigma_1,...,\sigma_n,\theta_1, ..., \theta_m$). Hence, one has

$$\rho(\sigma_1,...,\sigma_n,\theta_1,...,\theta_m) \leq \rho(\sigma_1,...,\sigma_n,\theta_1\pi_1,...,\theta_m\pi_m).$$

The particular case results. Assume the substitutions λ and μ are such that $\lambda\leq\mu$ and λ is idempotent. Then, there is a substitution γ such that $\mu=\lambda\gamma$. The previous inequality becomes

$$\rho(\lambda)\leq\rho(\lambda\gamma)$$

that is

$$\rho(\lambda)\leq\rho(\mu). ◊$$

Reconciliation is also idempotent.

Proposition 3.18 Let $\{\alpha_1,...,\alpha_m\}, ..., \{\gamma_1,...,\gamma_n\}$ be sets of substitutions.
1) The substitutions $\alpha_1,...,\alpha_m, ..., \gamma_1,...,\gamma_n$ are reconcilable iff
   - the substitutions of each set are reconcilable,
   - the substitutions $\rho(\alpha_1,...,\alpha_m), ..., \rho(\gamma_1,...,\gamma_n)$ are reconcilable.

2) In this case, one has

$$\rho(\alpha_1,...,\alpha_m, ...,\gamma_1,...,\gamma_n) = \rho(\rho(\alpha_1,...,\alpha_m), ...,\rho(\gamma_1,...,\gamma_n)).$$

Proof The theorem results from the following facts
- the systems
$$\text{syst}(\alpha_1,...,\alpha_m), ..., \text{syst}(\gamma_1,...,\gamma_n)$$
are parts of the system $\text{syst}(\alpha_1,...,\alpha_m, ...,\gamma_1,...,\gamma_n)$;
- the systems
$$\text{syst}(\rho(\alpha_1,...,\alpha_m), ...,\rho(\gamma_1,...,\gamma_n))$$
and
$$\text{syst}(\alpha_1,...,\alpha_m, ...,\gamma_1,...,\gamma_n)$$
are equivalent when the substitutions $\{\alpha_1,...,\alpha_m\}, ..., \{\gamma_1,...,\gamma_n\}$ are separately reconcilable. ◊

Reconciliation of substitutions can, in some cases, be related to their composition.

Proposition 3.19 Let σ and τ be two idempotent substitutions such that

$$\text{dom}(\sigma) \cap [\,\text{dom}(\tau) \cup \text{varcod}(\tau)\,] = \emptyset$$

The substitutions are reconcilable and $\sigma\circ\tau$ is a reconciliation.

Proof Let σ and τ be $\{X_1/t_1,...,X_m/t_m\}$ and $\{Y_1/u_1,...,Y_n/u_n\}$, respectively. The system $\text{syst}(\sigma,\tau)$ is

$$\begin{cases} X_1 = t_1 \\ ... \\ X_m = t_m \\ Y_1 = u_1 \\ ... \\ Y_n = u_n \end{cases}$$

It is equivalent to the system

$$\begin{cases} X_1 = t_1\tau \\ ... \\ X_m = t_m\tau \\ Y_1 = u_1 \\ ... \\ Y_n = u_n \end{cases}$$

The thesis results from the fact that one of its mgu's is the substitution

$$\{X_1/t_1\tau, ... , X_m/t_m\tau, Y_1/u_1, ..., Y_n/u_n\},$$

namely $\sigma\circ\tau$, thanks to the hypothesis on σ and τ. ◊

Finally, the mgu of two terms t and u and the mgu of one instance tσ and u can be related by the reconciliation operator.

Proposition 3.20 Let

- t and u be two unifiable terms sharing no variables
- θ be an idempotent mgu of t and u
- σ be an idempotent substitution such that
    - σ and θ are reconcilable
    - tσ and u are unifiable
- μ be an idempotent mgu of tσ and u.

The substitutions θ, σ and μ are reconcilable and verify

$$\rho(\sigma,\theta) = \rho(\sigma,\theta,\mu) = \rho(\sigma,\mu) .$$

Proof Establishing the proposition amounts to proving that the systems syst(σ,θ), syst(σ,θ,μ) and syst(σ,μ) are equivalent. This results from the following equivalences of systems.

1° By elementary system manipulation, the following systems are equivalent :

{t=u} ∪ syst(σ)
{t=u} ∪ {tσ=u} ∪ syst(σ)
{tσ=u} ∪ syst(σ).

2° Thanks to the hypothesis made on θ, the system formed of the equation t=u is equivalent to the system syst(θ). It follows that the systems

{t=u} ∪ syst(σ)
{t=u} ∪ {tσ=u} ∪ syst(σ)

are equivalent to the systems

syst(θ,σ),
{tσ=u} ∪ syst(θ,σ),

respectively.

3° Similarly, the system formed of the equation tσ=u is equivalent to the system syst(μ). The systems

{tσ=u} ∪ syst(σ)
{tσ=u} ∪ syst(θ,σ)

are thus equivalent to the systems

syst(μ,σ),
syst(μ,θ,σ),

respectively.

Summing up, one has

1° syst(σ,θ)
   $\approx \{t=u\} \cup$ syst(σ)
   $\approx \{t=u\} \cup \{t\sigma=u\} \cup$ syst(σ)
   $\approx \{t\sigma=u\} \cup$ syst(θ,σ)
   $\approx$ syst(σ,θ,μ)

2° syst(σ,μ)
   $\approx \{t\sigma=u\} \cup$ syst(σ)
   $\approx \{t=u\} \cup \{t\sigma=u\} \cup$ syst(σ)
   $\approx \{t\sigma=u\} \cup$ syst(θ,σ)
   $\approx$ syst(σ,θ,μ) .

Hence, the following equivalences hold :

syst(σ,θ) $\approx$ syst(σ,θ,μ) $\approx$ syst(σ,μ). ◊

3.1.4.2 Relationship with substitution unification

The unification of two terms points out a common instance for the terms. Mgu's moreover provide most general common instances for those terms. Similar concepts can be defined for substitutions. In particular, mgu's of substitutions provide a most general common instance for the substitutions. This also intuitively corresponds to the result of reconciliation. The relationship between unification and reconciliation of substitutions is clarified in this subsection.

Definition 3.21 Let σ, τ be two substitutions. They are called *unifiable* iff there exists a substitution θ such that $\sigma\theta = \tau\theta$. Such a substitution θ is called a unifier of σ and τ. It is a *most general unifier* or *mgu* of σ and τ iff for every unifier λ of σ and τ, $\theta \leq \lambda$.

These notions can, of course, be extended in a straightforward way to sets of substitutions. However, for the sake of clarity, we will limit our discussion to pairs of substitutions.

Theorem 3.22 Two idempotent substitutions σ and τ unify iff they can be reconciled. In this case, let $\rho^*(\sigma,\tau)$ be an idempotent reconciliation $\rho(\sigma,\tau)$ where bindings corresponding to variables of dom(σ)$\cap$dom(τ) have been removed. The substitution $\rho^*(\sigma,\tau)$ is an mgu of σ and τ. Furthermore, one has

$$\rho(\sigma,\tau) = \sigma \circ \rho^*(\sigma,\tau) = \tau \circ \rho^*(\sigma,\tau) .$$

Proof Let us first introduce some auxiliary systems and terms. Let, on the one hand, the substitutions σ and τ be numbered such that

$$\sigma = \{X_1/t_1, \ldots, X_p/t_p, X_{p+1}/t_{p+1}, \ldots, X_m/t_m\}$$

$$\tau = \{Y_1/u_1, \ldots, Y_q/u_q, X_{p+1}/v_{p+1}, \ldots, X_m/v_m\}$$
$$\text{dom}(\sigma) \cap \text{dom}(\tau) = \{X_{p+1}, \ldots, X_m\}.$$

The system syst(σ,τ) is equivalent to

$$\begin{cases} X_1 = t_1 \\ \ldots \\ X_p = t_p \\ Y_1 = u_1 \\ \ldots \\ Y_q = u_q \\ X_{p+1} = t_{p+1} \\ X_{p+1} = v_{p+1} \\ \ldots \\ X_m = t_m \\ X_m = v_m \end{cases} \quad (S_1).$$

Consider, on the other hand, the terms

$$w_1 = h(X_1,\ldots,X_p,Y_1,\ldots,Y_q,X_{p+1},\ldots,X_m).\sigma = h(t_1,\ldots,t_p,Y_1,\ldots,Y_q,t_{p+1},\ldots,t_m)$$
$$w_2 = h(X_1,\ldots,X_p,Y_1,\ldots,Y_q,X_{p+1},\ldots,X_m).\tau = h(X_1,\ldots,X_p,u_1,\ldots,u_q,v_{p+1},\ldots,v_m)$$

where h is some (m+q)-ary functor.

The following properties will be useful.

1) Obviously, unifying the terms w_1 and w_2 amounts to solving the system

$$\begin{cases} X_1 = t_1 \\ \ldots \\ X_p = t_p \\ Y_1 = u_1 \\ \ldots \\ Y_q = u_q \\ V_{p+1} = t_{p+1} \\ V_{p+1} = v_{p+1} \\ \ldots \\ V_m = t_m \\ V_m = v_m \end{cases} \quad (S_2)$$

where the variables $V_{p+1}, \ldots, V_m$ do not appear in w_1 and w_2.

2) The variables $X_{p+1}, \ldots, X_m$ do not appear in w_1 and w_2 since σ and τ are idempotent. They can thus play the role of the variables $V_{p+1}, \ldots, V_m$. Consequently, the systems S_1 and S_2 are equivalent.

3) Every mgu of σ and τ is obviously an mgu of w_1 and w_2 and conversely.

These properties given, the first part of the theorem is quite easy to prove. It results from the following equivalences

the substitutions σ and τ are reconcilable iff
the system S_1 is unifiable iff
the system S_2 is unifiable iff
the terms w_1 and w_2 are unifiable iff
the substitutions σ and τ are unifiable.

Hence, two idempotent substitutions σ and τ are reconcilable iff they are unifiable. The substitution $\rho^*(\sigma,\tau)$ is furthermore an mgu of σ and τ. Indeed, the reconciliation $\rho(\sigma,\tau)$ is an mgu of S_1, by definition. The substitution derived from it by renaming the variables $X_{p+1},\ldots,X_m$ to $V_{p+1},\ldots,V_m$, respectively, is thus an mgu of S_2. The substitution obtained from it by removing all bindings for the variables $V_{p+1},\ldots,V_m$, namely $\rho^*(\sigma,\tau)$, is therefore an mgu of w_1 and w_2 and, consequently, of σ and τ.

The last part of the theorem is proved by establishing that, for any variable V,

(1) $V\rho(\sigma,\tau) = V(\sigma \circ \rho^*(\sigma,\tau)) = V(\tau \circ \rho^*(\sigma,\tau))$,

thanks to Proposition 2.26.

For this purpose, let us first characterize the substitutions $\rho(\sigma,\tau)$ and $\rho^*(\sigma,\tau)$. The reconciliation $\rho(\sigma,\tau)$ is only made from the variables of σ and τ. It is thus completely defined by giving the bindings corresponding to the variables $X_1, \ldots, X_p, X_{p+1}, \ldots, X_m, Y_1, \ldots, Y_q$ as well as the variables appearing in the codomain of σ and τ. Bindings corresponding to the variables $X_1, \ldots, X_p, Y_1, \ldots, Y_q$ are instances of $t_1, \ldots, t_p, u_1, \ldots, u_q$, respectively. Those corresponding to the variables $X_{p+1}, \ldots, X_m$ are instances of t_{p+1} and $v_{p+1}, \ldots, t_m$ and v_m, respectively. Let us denote by $Z_1, \ldots, Z_r$ the variables of the codomain of σ and τ that differ from their associated bindings.

The reconciliation $\rho(\sigma,\tau)$ thus verifies the equalities

(2) $X_i\rho(\sigma,\tau) = t_i\rho(\sigma,\tau)$ for $i=1, \ldots, p$

(3) $Y_j\rho(\sigma,\tau) = u_j\rho(\sigma,\tau)$ for $j=1, \ldots, q$

(4) $X_k\rho(\sigma,\tau) = t_k\rho(\sigma,\tau) = v_k\rho(\sigma,\tau)$ for $k=p+1, \ldots, m$

(5) $V\rho(\sigma,\tau) = V$ for any variable $V \notin \{X_1,\ldots,X_p,Y_1,\ldots,Y_q,X_{p+1},\ldots,X_m,Z_1,\ldots,Z_r\}$.

As $\rho^*(\sigma,\tau)$ is $\rho(\sigma,\tau)$ where the bindings for $X_{p+1}, \ldots, X_m$ have been removed and since σ and τ are idempotent, we also have

(6) $t_i\rho(\sigma,\tau) = t_i\rho^*(\sigma,\tau)$ for $i=1, \ldots, p$

(7) $u_j\rho(\sigma,\tau) = u_j\rho^*(\sigma,\tau)$ for $j=1, \ldots, q$

(8) $t_k\rho(\sigma,\tau) = t_k\rho^*(\sigma,\tau)$ for $k=p+1, \ldots, m$

(9) $v_k\rho(\sigma,\tau) = v_k\rho^*(\sigma,\tau)$ for $k=p+1, \ldots, m$

(10) $Z_\ell\rho(\sigma,\tau) = Z_\ell\rho^*(\sigma,\tau)$ for $\ell=1, \ldots, r$

(11) $V\rho^*(\sigma,\tau) = V$ for any variable $V \notin \{X_1,\ldots,X_p,Y_1,\ldots,Y_q,X_{p+1},\ldots,X_m,Z_1,\ldots,Z_r\}$.

We are now in a position to verify the equalities (1). Let V be a variable. Five cases must be examined according to the nature of V.

(i) Variable V is a variable X_i with $i \in \{1,\ldots,p\}$

In this case, the thesis results from the following equalities

$$\begin{aligned}
V(\sigma\circ\rho^*(\sigma,\tau)) &= X_i(\sigma\circ\rho^*(\sigma,\tau)) \\
&= (X_i\sigma)\rho^*(\sigma,\tau) \text{ thanks to Proposition 2.28} \\
&= t_i\rho^*(\sigma,\tau) \text{ by definition of } \sigma \\
&= t_i\rho(\sigma,\tau) \text{ thanks to equalities (6)} \\
&= X_i\rho(\sigma,\tau) \text{ thanks to equalities (2)} \\
&= V\rho(\sigma,\tau).
\end{aligned}$$

$$\begin{aligned}
V(\tau\circ\rho^*(\sigma,\tau)) &= X_i(\tau\circ\rho^*(\sigma,\tau)) \\
&= (X_i\tau)\rho^*(\sigma,\tau) \text{ thanks to Proposition 2.28} \\
&= X_i\rho^*(\sigma,\tau) \text{ by definition of } \sigma \text{ and } \tau \\
&= X_i\rho(\sigma,\tau) \text{ by definition of } \rho^*(\sigma,\tau) \\
&= V\rho(\sigma,\tau).
\end{aligned}$$

(ii) Variable V is a variable Y_j with $j \in \{1,\ldots,q\}$

In this case, the thesis results from the following equalities

$$\begin{aligned}
V(\sigma\circ\rho^*(\sigma,\tau)) &= Y_j(\sigma\circ\rho^*(\sigma,\tau)) \\
&= (Y_j\sigma)\rho^*(\sigma,\tau) \text{ thanks to Proposition 2.28} \\
&= Y_j\rho^*(\sigma,\tau) \text{ by definition of } \sigma \text{ and } \tau \\
&= Y_j\rho(\sigma,\tau) \text{ by definition of } \rho^*(\sigma,\tau) \\
&= V\rho(\sigma,\tau).
\end{aligned}$$

$$\begin{aligned}
V(\tau\circ\rho^*(\sigma,\tau)) &= Y_j(\tau\circ\rho^*(\sigma,\tau)) \\
&= (Y_j\tau)\rho^*(\sigma,\tau) \text{ thanks to Proposition 2.28} \\
&= u_j\rho^*(\sigma,\tau) \text{ by definition of } \tau
\end{aligned}$$

$$\begin{aligned}
&= u_j\rho(\sigma,\tau) \text{ thanks to equalities (7)}\\
&= Y_j\rho(\sigma,\tau) \text{ thanks to equalities (3)}\\
&= V\rho(\sigma,\tau).
\end{aligned}$$

(iii) Variable V is a variable X_k with $k \in \{p+1,\ldots,m\}$

In this case, the thesis results from the following equalities

$$\begin{aligned}
V(\sigma \circ \rho^*(\sigma,\tau)) &= X_k(\sigma \circ \rho^*(\sigma,\tau))\\
&= (X_k\sigma)\rho^*(\sigma,\tau) \text{ thanks to Proposition 2.28}\\
&= t_k\rho^*(\sigma,\tau) \text{ by definition of } \sigma\\
&= t_k\rho(\sigma,\tau) \text{ thanks to equalities (8)}\\
&= X_k\rho(\sigma,\tau) \text{ thanks to equalities (4)}\\
&= V\rho(\sigma,\tau).
\end{aligned}$$

$$\begin{aligned}
V(\tau \circ \rho^*(\sigma,\tau)) &= X_k(\tau \circ \rho^*(\sigma,\tau))\\
&= (X_k\tau)\rho^*(\sigma,\tau) \text{ thanks to Proposition 2.28}\\
&= v_k\rho^*(\sigma,\tau) \text{ by definition of } \tau\\
&= v_k\rho(\sigma,\tau) \text{ thanks to equalities (9)}\\
&= X_k\rho(\sigma,\tau) \text{ thanks to equalities (4)}\\
&= V\rho(\sigma,\tau).
\end{aligned}$$

(iv) Variable V is a variable Z_ℓ with $\ell \in \{1,\ldots,r\}$

In this case, the thesis results from the following equalities

$$\begin{aligned}
V(\sigma \circ \rho^*(\sigma,\tau)) &= Z_\ell(\sigma \circ \rho^*(\sigma,\tau))\\
&= (Z_\ell\sigma)\rho^*(\sigma,\tau) \text{ thanks to Proposition 2.28}\\
&= Z_\ell\rho^*(\sigma,\tau) \text{ by idempotence of } \sigma\\
&= Z_\ell\rho(\sigma,\tau) \text{ by equalities (10)}\\
&= V\rho(\sigma,\tau).
\end{aligned}$$

$$\begin{aligned}
V(\tau \circ \rho^*(\sigma,\tau)) &= Z_\ell(\tau \circ \rho^*(\sigma,\tau))\\
&= (Z_\ell\tau)\rho^*(\sigma,\tau) \text{ thanks to Proposition 2.28}\\
&= Z_\ell\rho^*(\sigma,\tau) \text{ by idempotence of } \tau\\
&= Z_\ell\rho(\sigma,\tau) \text{ by equalities (10)}\\
&= V\rho(\sigma,\tau).
\end{aligned}$$

(v) Variable V is not a variable of $\{X_1,\ldots,X_p,Y_1,\ldots,Y_q,X_{p+1},\ldots,X_m,Z_1,\ldots,Z_r\}$

In this case, the thesis results from the following equalities

$$\begin{aligned}
V(\sigma \circ \rho^*(\sigma,\tau)) &= V(\sigma \circ \rho^*(\sigma,\tau))\\
&= (V\sigma)\rho^*(\sigma,\tau) \text{ thanks to Proposition 2.28}\\
&= V\rho^*(\sigma,\tau) \text{ by definition of } \sigma
\end{aligned}$$

$$\begin{aligned}
& = \ V \text{ by equalities (11)} \\
& = \ V\rho(\sigma,\tau) \text{ by equalities (5).} \\
V(\tau_0\rho^*(\sigma,\tau)) &= \ V(\tau_0\rho^*(\sigma,\tau)) \\
&= \ (V\tau)\rho^*(\sigma,\tau) \text{ thanks to Proposition 2.28} \\
&= \ V\rho^*(\sigma,\tau) \text{ by definition of } \sigma \\
&= \ V \text{ by equalities (11)} \\
&= \ V\rho(\sigma,\tau) \text{ by equalities (5). } \Diamond
\end{aligned}$$

This theorem is interesting in two points.

1) One the one hand, it provides a theoretical contribution to the theory of substitutions.

2) On the other hand, it links our definition of reconciliation (Definition 3.12) with the following intuitive perception : the substitution $\theta_1, ..., \theta_m$ are reconcilable iff some common instance, say θ, can be pointed out. With regards to this interpretation, reconciling substitutions amounts to proving the existence of such a θ as well as to produce the most general one. This precisely corresponds to the concept of unification of substitutions so that the above theorem can be rephrased as

- two idempotent substitutions are reconcilable in the above intuitive sense iff they are reconcilable according to Definition 3.12;
- in case the substitutions are reconcilable, what we called the reconciliation of these substitutions (i.e. $\rho(\sigma,\tau)$) is the most general common instance of the substitution (i.e. $\sigma_0\rho^*(\sigma,\tau) = \tau_0\rho^*(\sigma,\tau)$ - recall that $\rho^*(\sigma,\tau)$ is one mgu of σ and τ).

3.1.5 Algorithm

Let us now present an algorithm for reconciling substitutions. In view of Definition 3.12, this amounts to constructing an algorithm solving systems of equations. It turns out that Martelli and Montanari's algorithm ([Martelli and Montanari, 1982]), originally designed for unifying terms, essentially solves such systems. We will basically use this algorithm here and presents a parallel version. Parts of this section are thus based on [Martelli and Montanari, 1982]. The particularity of our approach is to apply their algorithm here to reconcile substitutions rather than to unify terms.

3.1.5.1 Basic concepts

Notation 3.23 Parallel executions are introduced in the algorithms by means of the two following parallel statements :

(1) <u>Parbegin</u> $S_1 \| ... \| S_m$ <u>parend</u>.
(2) <u>Parfor</u> i=1 <u>to</u> m <u>do</u> S <u>od</u>

where the S, S_1, ..., S_m symbols represent sequences of statements composed of the usual imperative statements and the above parallel statements. The executions of these parallel statements is as follows.

- The execution of parallel statement (1) consists of the parallel execution of the sequence of statements S_1, ..., S_m. It ends when all the executions of the S_i's have terminated. It is thus a fork in S_1, ..., S_m followed by a join of them.
- The execution of parallel statement (2) consists of concurrently executing the m executions of S corresponding to the m values of i. It ends when all of them have ended.

Most of the algorithms developed subsequently behave as functions. It will be subsequently convenient to generalize them so that failure is reported as a result. In other terms, the computed functions will be extended and the algorithms will have two issues :
- reporting failure;
- returning the values really expected from the function (e.g. mgu's, ...).

They will be said to *fail* and to *succeed*, respectively.

Failure will be caused by executing the instruction

report failure.

This forces the termination of the sequence in which it appears. The effect on parallel statements may be defined in two opposite ways :

1° Failure of one parallel subexecution implies that of the whole parallel statement. In this case, the execution of concurrent parallel subcomputations should be halted. Such parallel statements are subsequently denoted by

Fparbegin S_1 || ... || S_m fparend,
Fparfor i=1 to m do S od .

2° Failure of one parallel subexecution does not imply that of the whole parallel statement. Instead, it is only when all parallel subexecutions fail that the whole parallel statement fails. This is the meaning we assigned to the parallel statements

Parbegin S_1 || ... || S_m parend,
Parfor i=1 to m do S od .

It turns out that it is worth generalizing equations so that the equality of more than two terms can be expressed. This leads to the concept of multi-equations. It is itself defined by appealing the concept of multi-set.

Definition 3.24 A *multi-set* is a family of elements in which no ordering exists but in which many identical elements may occur.

Classical notions on sets extend to multi-sets in a straightforward manner. For instance, the union of the multi-sets A and B simply consists of all elements of A and B with eventual repetition of the elements. Similarly, the instance $A\theta$ of the multi-set A by the substitution θ is formed of the instantiations by θ of its elements.

Definition 3.25 A *multi-equation* is a construction of the form

$$V = T$$

where V is a non-empty set of variables and T is a (possibly empty) multi-set of non-variable terms.

Notation 3.26 Given a multi-equation E, we subsequently denote by

E_{left} and E_{right}

the left-hand side (LHS) and right-hand side (RHS) of E, respectively.

Multi-equations will, in general, not be manipulated alone but in systems of multi-equations. The notions developed for systems of equations can be extended to such systems of multi-equations in a straightforward way. For instance,

- A *unifier* of a system of multi-equations S is a substitution θ such that for any equation $E \in S$, the set $E_{left}\theta$ reduces to a singleton, say $\{t\}$, and every element of $E_{right}\theta$ is t. It is a *most general unifier (mgu)* of S iff every unifier υ of S verifies $\theta \leq \upsilon$.
- A system of multi-equation is *unifiable* iff it has a mgu.
- Two systems of multi-equations S and T are *equivalent*, what is also denoted by $S \approx T$, iff they share the same unifiers.

Proposition 3.5 can be extended to systems of multi-equations so that properties of unifiers of systems of multi-equations can be deduced from those of unifiers of terms. In particular,

(1) mgu's of systems of multi-equations are equal modulo renaming,
(2) unifiable systems of multi-equations have an idempotent mgu.

Proposition 3.27 For every system of multi-equations S, there are two terms t and u such that
(i) S is unifiable iff t and u are unifiable,
(ii) every substitution θ is a unifier (resp. mgu) of S iff it is a unifier (resp. mgu) of t and u.

Proof Assume S is composed of n multi-equations $E_1, ..., E_n$ (n>0). Let h be a n-ary functor. We define t and u as $h(t_1,...,t_n)$ and $h(u_1,...,u_n)$, respectively, and construct each pair (t_i, u_i) from each E_i as follows. Let E_i be

$$\{V_1,...,V_p\} = \{s_1,...,s_q\}$$

with p>0 and q≥0. We define t_i as $f_i(V_1,...,V_p,s_1,...,s_q)$ and u_i as $f_i(V_1,...,V_1,V_1,...,V_1)$ with f_i a (p+q)-ary functor.

Obviously, a substitution is a unifier for S iff it is a unifier for t and u. Hence, S is unifiable iff t and u are unifiable. Furthermore, a substitution is a mgu for S iff it is a mgu for t and u. ◊

The following definition will be used to relate multi-sets of terms and multi-equations.

Definition 3.28 Let T be a set of terms with at least one variable as term. The multi-equation associated with T, denoted by *eq(T)*, is the multi-equation whose LHS and RHS partition T in its terms that are variables and its terms that are not variables, respectively.

Note that systems of equations can be transformed into (equivalent [1]) systems of multi-equations by rewriting any equation X = t as eq({X,t}).

Example 3.3 The system associated with the substitutions θ_1, θ_2 and θ_3 of Example 3.1 can be transformed into the system

$$\begin{cases} \{X,Y\} = \emptyset \\ \{Z\} = \{g(h(3))\} \\ \{X\} = \{h(T)\} \\ \{Y\} = \{h(3)\} \\ \{X,U\} = \emptyset \\ \{Z\} = \{g(U)\} \end{cases}$$

It turns out that systems of multi-equations must be presented under a special form to justify further treatments. Such systems are called compact.

Definition 3.29 A system of multi-equations S is *compact* iff every pair (E,F) of distinct multi-equations of S verifies $E_{left} \cap F_{left} = \emptyset$.

Compactification algorithm It is easy to construct an equivalent compact system of multi-equations from a non compact one. Let S be a non compact system of multi-equations. Let ~ denote the relation on multi-equations defined by

$E \sim F$ iff $E_{left} \cap F_{left} \neq \emptyset$.

Consider the transitive closure of ~. It partitions the multi-equations of S into equivalence classes. Let us associate with each such class C the multi-equation E_c whose LHS and RHS are the union of the LHS and RHS of the multi-equations of C. It is equivalent to the multi-equations of C. Indeed, for every pair of multi-equations E, F such that E ~ F, the elements of E_{left}, E_{right}, F_{left} and F_{right} must be made identical. Therefore, the multi-equation E_c contains the same information as the class C. The set S_c obtained by merging in this manner the multi-

---

[1] that is sharing the same unifiers.

equations of each class is thus equivalent to S. It is also compact by construction. The set E_c is subsequently referred to as the *compactification* of S.

Example 3.4 The compactification of the system of Example 3.3 is
$$\begin{cases} \{X,Y,U\} = \{h(T),h(3)\} \\ \{Z\} = \{g(h(3)),g(U)\} \end{cases}$$

The benefit of compact systems comes from the following theorem.

Theorem 3.30 Let S be a unifiable compact system of multi-equations. Then, S has a multi-equation E such that the variables of E_{left} do not appear elsewhere in S.
Proof To formalize the thesis, let $\langle$ denote the relation on multi-equations of S defined by

$E \langle F$ iff a variable of E_{left} appears in F.

As S is compact, the thesis amounts to proving that there is at least one equation E in S such that for any other equation F in S : $\neg (E \langle F)$. Let us proceed by contradiction. If this were not the case, it would be possible to construct a finite sequence $E_1, \ldots, E_n$ of multi-equations from S such that

$E_1 \langle E_2 \langle \ldots \langle E_n \langle E_1$.

However, if $E \langle F$ then in all unifiers of S, the term substituted for every variable in E_{left} must be a strict subterm of the term substituted for every variable in F_{left}. This implies that $E_1 \langle E_2 \langle \ldots \langle E_n \langle E_1$ cannot hold. ◊

3.1.5.2 Solving systems of multi-equations

A. Solvable form

Martelli and Montanari's algorithm consists of transforming a system of multi-equations into an equivalent compact one such that

- P_1. the RHS of the multi-equations contains no more than one term,
- P_2. the multi-equations can be ordered such that all the variables belonging to the LHS of some multi-equation can only occur in the RHS of any preceding multi-equation.

The algorithm fails if the transformation is not possible.

Such a system is obviously unifiable. It is furthermore easy to extract one mgu. Indeed, one simply has to substitute the variables backward. That is one simply has to proceed as follows :

(1) thanks to Property P_1, a mgu for the last equation is directly obtained by binding the variables of the LHS to the RHS term if any and to one of them otherwise;

(2) then, in case the rest of the system is not empty,

- the mgu is injected in it;
- the process is recursively applied to it;

(3) thanks to Property P_2, the mgu obtained in (1) associated with that obtained in (2) is a mgu for the whole system.

The following algorithms make this informal process more precise.

Algorithm Mgu_eq(E)

Specification

Let E be a multi-equation such that E_{right} contains no more than one term. The algorithm Mgu_eq(E) determines an idempotent mgu for E only made from the variables of E.

Code

Case E of
    E is $\{X\} = \emptyset$: do Mgu_eq(E) = {} od;
    E is $\{X_1,...,X_m\} = \emptyset$ with m>1 : do Mgu_eq(E) = $\{X_1/X_m,...,X_{m-1}/X_m\}$ od;
    E is $\{X_1,...,X_m\} = \{t\}$ with m≥1 : do return $\{X_1/t,...,X_m/t\}$ od
endcase .

Algorithm Mgu_syst(S)

Specification

Let S be a non-empty compact system of multi-equations verifying Property P_1 and ordered to make P_2 hold. The algorithm Mgu_syst(S) delivers an mgu for S only made from the variables of S.

Code

If S has only one multi-equation, say E,
  then
    return Mgu_eq(Eq)
  else
    { let E be the last equation of S and S_pref be S\E }
    σ := Mgu_eq(E)
    { let S_pref_inst be S_pref where any variable X of dom(σ) has been bound to Xσ }
    τ := Mgu_syst(S_pref_inst)
    return $\sigma \cup \tau$
fi.

Proposition 3.31 The algorithms Mgu_eq and Mgu_syst meet their specification.
Proof The demonstration consists of a straightforward verification. ◊

B. General situation

The triangularized system is obtained by repeatedly transforming the initial system. For convenience, systems of multi-equations are represented as pairs of systems, denoted by (Solved,Unsolved). The names are meaningful. Informally stated, the Solved system has a triangularized form and consists of the solved part of the whole system. The Unsolved system contains the remaining equations. Each step of the algorithm consists in transferring a multi-equation from the Unsolved part to the Solved one.

Precisely, the following properties are maintained invariant before and after application of each transformation step. Let S be the system to be solved.

- P_3. The system Solved $\cup$ Unsolved is compact.
- P_4. The system Solved $\cup$ Unsolved is equivalent to S.
- P_5. The right-hand sides of all multi-equations in Solved contain no more than one term.
- P_6. The system Solved is ordered such that all variables belonging to the LHS of some multi-equation in Solved can only occur in the RHS of any preceding multi-equation in Solved.

Remark According to Property P_6, some order is thus imposed on the system Solved. Strictly speaking, it is thus no more a system - no order can indeed be captured in sets. It is in fact a list of multi-equations ordered in some way. Nevertheless, it will be convenient to abuse language here and still qualify Solved as a system. The notation

Solved | {E}

uses once more this language misuse. It is used to denote the system obtained by appending (as last multi-equation) the multi-equation E to the multi-equation of Solved.

C. Initial and final situations

The initial and final situations particularize this general description. The core of the algorithm is started with the pair $(\emptyset, S_c)$ where S_c is the compactification of S. If S is unifiable, it ends with the pair (Solved,$\emptyset$). Remember that, in case S is not unifiable, failure occurs and no final situation is reached.

D. The transformation step

D.1 Basic ideas

In view of Theorem 3.30, the transformation step is quite easy to find. It only occurs when Unsolved is not empty. In this case, a multi-equation of the system Unsolved such that

P_7. none of its LHS variables appears elsewhere in Unsolved is searched. If there are none, the system (Solved,Unsolved) is not unifiable (see Theorem 3.30) and so is S. In this case, the algorithm fails. Otherwise, let E be such a multi-equation.

(i) If E_{right} is empty, the multi-equation is transferred to Solved i.e. the following statements are operated
Solved := Solved | {E},
Unsolved := Unsolved \ {E}.
Obviously, thereafter, Properties P_3 to P_6 hold. Note that, in this case, the number of variables in Unsolved strictly decreases.

(ii) If E_{right} is not empty, its terms are unified in order to make E verify Property P_5. If the unification is not possible, then the system (Solved,Unsolved) is not unifiable and failure must be reported. Otherwise, let θ be an idempotent mgu; it is made only from the variables of E_{right} (see Proposition 2.43). The multi-equation $E_{left} = E_{right}$ θ can be considered as solved. Bindings from θ are added as multi-equations in Unsolved in order to obtain an equivalent system of multi-equations. The whole system must then be "compacted" in order to make Property P_2 hold. The following statements must thus be operated :

Unify the terms of E_{right}
If the unification fails
   then
      report failure
   else
      { Let θ be an idempotent mgu of E_{right} made from the variables of E_{right}
      Let t be one element of E_{right}.θ }
      Solved := Solved | { E_{left}= {t} }
      Unsolved := compactification of (Unsolved \ {E}) ∪ syst(θ)
fi

Properties P_3 to P_6 are manifestly kept invariant. Note that, in this case too, the number of variables of Unsolved strictly decreases.

D.2 Example

Example 3.5 We illustrate the algorithm by solving the system issued from the substitutions $θ_1$, $θ_2$ and $θ_3$ of Example 3.1 (i.e. by reconciling them). The system syst($θ_1,θ_2,θ_3$) is

$$\begin{cases} \{X,Y\} = \varnothing \\ \{Z\} = \{g(h(3))\} \\ \{X\} = \{h(T)\} \\ \{Y\} = \{h(3)\} \\ \{X,U\} = \varnothing \\ \{Z\} = \{g(U)\} \end{cases}$$

The algorithm is started on the pair ($\varnothing$,Unsolved) where Unsolved is the compactification of syst($\theta_1,\theta_2,\theta_3$). The pair is here

($\varnothing$,
$\begin{cases} \{X,Y,U\} = \{h(T),h(3)\} \\ \{Z\} = \{g(h(3)),g(U)\} \end{cases}$)

As Unsolved is not empty, a transformation step is applied. An equation of the second system such that Property P_7 holds is searched. In the current system, just the last multi-equation verifies it. An idempotent mgu for $\{g(h(3)),g(U)\}$ is then searched. The substitution $\{U/h(3)\}$ obviously constitutes one. Next, the pair (Solved,Unsolved) is modified

- by moving the multi-equation
  $\{Z\} = \{g(h(3))\}$
  in the Solved part
- by adding the multi-equation associated with the mgu $\{U/h(3)\}$ to the Unsolved part
- by compacting the new Unsolved part, namely
  $\begin{cases} \{X,Y,U\} = \{h(T),h(3)\} \\ \{U\} = \{h(3)\} \end{cases}$

The following pair (Solved,Unsolved) results :

($\{Z\} = \{g(h(3))\}$,
$\{X,Y,U\} = \{h(T),h(3),h(3)\}$)

Applying the same process, this pair is transformed into the new one

($\begin{cases} \{Z\} = \{g(h(3))\} \\ \{X,Y,U\} = \{h(3)\} \end{cases}$,
$\{T\} = \{3\}$)

Applying it once more, the solved pair

($\begin{cases} \{Z\} = \{g(h(3))\} \\ \{X,Y,U\} = \{h(3)\} \\ \{T\} = \{3\} \end{cases}$,
$\varnothing$)

is obtained. Note that this delivers the reconciliation presented in Example 3.2.

D.3 Refining the algorithm

Some problems remain unsolved. For instance, how is the above idempotent mgu θ computed? How is the multi-equation E efficiently selected? Is it necessary to apply the complete compactification process to make the system (Unsolved\E)∪syst(θ) compact? We now turn to these problems and furthermore optimize the algorithm for non-unifying data.

D.3.1 Computing the mgu θ

The mgu θ of the multi-set E_{right} is not computed as such but by means of the common part and frontier of E_{right}. Such concepts can intuitively be suggested by considering terms as trees. In this representation, the common part of a multi-set of terms T is the term obtained by superimposing all terms of T and by taking the part which is common to all of them, starting from the root. The frontier of T is a set of multi-equations where every multi-equation is associated with a leaf of the common part of T and consists of all subterms corresponding to that leaf. For instance, the common part of the multi-set

$\{f(g(X),Y,a), f(g(b),h(Z),a), f(g(T),h(c),a)\}$

is

$f(g(X),Y,a).$

Its frontier is

$$\begin{cases} \{X,T\}=\{b\} \\ \{Y\}=\{h(Z),h(c)\} \end{cases}$$

The common part and the frontier of a multi-set of terms are defined as follows.

Definition 3.32 Let T be a non-empty multi-set of terms. The *common part* of T, denoted by $cp(T)$, and its *frontier*, denoted by $front(T)$, are defined iff one of the following conditions holds :

(i) one element of T is a variable,
(ii) all elements of T are not variable, have the same functor, say f, with same arity, say n, and for all $i \in \{1,...,n\}$, the multi-set T_i formed by taking the ith component of each term of T has a common part and frontier.

When one of these two conditions holds, the frontier and common part of T are defined modulo to a renaming substitution as follows:

(1) when condition (i) holds, then
$cp(T) = X$
$front(T) = eq(T),$
where X is some variable of T

(2) when condition (ii) holds, then
$$cp(T) = f(cp(T_1),\ldots,cp(T_n)),$$
$$front(T) = front(T_1) \cup \ldots \cup front(T_n)$$
where the T_i's are defined as above.

The common part and frontier of a non-empty system can be computed according to this recursive definition. This is achieved by the following algorithm.

Algorithm 3.33

Specification

Let T be a non-empty multi-set of terms. The algorithm cp_f(T) succeeds iff T has a common part and frontier. In this case, it returns the pair composed of them.

Code

If there is a variable in T, say X,
    then return (X,eq(T))
    else
        If all terms of T have the same functor f and same arity n,
            then
                If n=0
                      then return (f,∅)
                      else
                          { Let T_i be the multi-set formed by taking the ith component of each term of T }
                        Fparfor i=1 to n do
                            cp_f(T_i)
                        od
                        If one of the computation cp_f(T_i) fails
                            then report failure
                            else
                                Let (cp_i,$Front_i$) be cp_f(T_i)
                                return (f(cp_1,...,cp_n), $Front_1$ ∪ ... ∪ $Front_n$)
                        fi
                fi
        else report failure
        fi
fi

Proposition 3.34 Algorithm 3.33 meets its specification.
Proof The demonstration consists of a simple verification. ◊

The following theorem relates the discovery of a mgu for a multi-set of terms to the computation of its common part and frontier.

Theorem 3.35
1) Every unifiable multi-set of terms has a common part and a frontier.
2) Let E be a multi-equation. If E_{right} has no common part nor frontier, then E has no unifier. If E_{right} has a common part and a frontier, then the system composed of front(E_{right}) and the multi-equation eq($E_{left} \cup \{cp(E_{right})\}$) is equivalent to E.

Proof Property 1) results from the fact that a multi-set of terms only has no common part nor frontier when at least two terms have no common functor or no common arity. This is never the case when the terms of T are assumed unifiable. Property 2) results from an inductive reasoning on the depth of the terms in E_{right} understood as trees. ◊

Hence, the operations of elementary transformations corresponding to case (ii) of Subsection D.1 can be replaced by the following ones

Compute cp_f(E_{right}),
<u>If</u> failure occurs
   <u>then</u> report failure
   <u>else</u>
     { Let (cp,Front) be the results of cp_f(E_{right}) }
     Solved := Solved | E_{left} = {cp};
     Unsolved := compactification((Unsolved \ E) $\cup$ Front).
<u>fi</u>

Note that because E_{right} is composed of non-variable terms, its common part is always a non-variable term.

D.3.2 Improving the algorithm for non-unifying data

The computation of the algorithm cp_f may however succeed when the terms of E_{right} are not unifiable. For instance, cp_f applied to the terms

f(X), f(g(Y)), f(h(Z))

succeeds although the terms are not unifiable. This is because Algorithm 3.33 returns the pair <X,eq(T)>, without examination of T, each time a variable is found in T. This lack of examination does not imply that the algorithm is incorrect; the multi-equation eq(T) will be found not to be unifiable in a subsequent step of the algorithm. It is possible to anticipate this kind of failure by imposing a constraint on the multi-equation. The constraint to be verified is that the terms of any RHS must be consistent.

Definition 3.36 The terms $t_1, ..., t_n$ are *consistent* iff one of the two following conditions holds

(i) One of the terms t_i is a variable.
(ii) All the terms t_i are not variable, have the same functor with same arity n and for all $j \in \{1,...,n\}$, the jth argument of the t_i's are consistent.

Proposition 3.37 All unifiable terms are consistent.

Proof The theorem is obvious if one of the terms is a variable. Assume all terms are non variable terms. Then, to be unifiable, the terms must have the same functor, the same arity and the corresponding arguments must be unifiable. A recursive reasoning on the depth of the terms proves that condition (ii) holds in this case. ◊

Note that all consistent terms are not unifiable. This is because consistency only considers the corresponding terms separately and not together. Consider for instance, the terms f(X,X) and f(a,b). They are consistent since they have the same functor f, the same arity 2 and, on one hand, the terms X, a are consistent and, on the other hand, the terms X, b are consistent. However, the terms f(X,X) and f(a,b) are not unifiable because there is no common value for X such that X and a, on the one hand, and X and b, on the other hand, are unifiable.

Consistency checking remains however interesting. Some kinds of non-unifiable data can be detected with essentially the same effort as previously. To this end, a suitable representation of the RHS of multi-equations is needed. This is achieved by means of multi-terms.

Definition 3.38 A *multi-term* is either $\emptyset$ or of the form $f(T_1,...,T_n)$ where
(i) f is an n-ary functor
(ii) each T_i (i=1,...,n) is a pair $<V_i,M_i>$ where V_i is a set of variables and M_i is a multi-term, not simultaneously empty.

It is worth noting that unifiable multi-sets may be represented by multi-terms. Empty multi-sets are obviously represented by empty multi-terms. Similarly, non empty unifiable sets of terms may be represented by non empty multi-terms. For instance, the multi-set of terms

{f(g(X),Y,a), f(g(b),h(Z),a), f(g(T),h(c),a)}

is represented by the multi-term

f($<\emptyset$, g($<\{X,T\}$,b$>$) $>$, $<\{Y\}$,h($<\{Z\}$,c$>$) $>$, $<\emptyset$, a $>$).

More generally, the multi-term corresponding to a non-empty set of unifiable terms, say t_1, ..., t_n, is defined as follows :
- its functor and arity are those of the terms t_i,
- its jth component T_j is composed of
    - the set V_j of variables occurring as j^{th} component the terms t_i,
    - the multi-term M_j recursively defined by applying the process on the non-variable terms appearing as j^{th} component of one term t_j.

Obviously, such associated multi-terms provide an equivalent representation to the multi-sets of terms. No information is lost by representing the RHS's of the multi-equations in this way. Furthermore, operations that have to be performed on RHS can be achieved very easily and efficiently with the multi-term representation. In fact, two operations must be done : merging RHS's of multi-equations, computing the common part and frontier of RHS's. They can be achieved by the following algorithm. Adequation to the specification directly results from previous results of this section.

Algorithm Merge(T',T")

Specification

Let M' and M" be two multi-sets of terms and T' and T" be the corresponding multi-terms. The algorithm merge has two issues : failure or success with a multi-term. When the algorithm fails, the terms of M' and M" cannot be unified. When the algorithm succeeds, the produced multi-term is the multi-term associated with the multi-set $M' \cup M"$.

Code

```
If T' is ∅
   then return T"
   else
      If T" is ∅
         then return T'
         else
            { Let  T' be f'(<V'₁,M'₁>, … ,<V'ₘ,M'ₘ>) and
                   T" be f"(<V"₁,M"₁>, … ,<V"ₙ,M"ₙ>) }
            If f' is f" and m is n
               then
                  Fparfor i=1 to m do
                     merge(M'ᵢ,M"ᵢ)
                  od
                  If one merge(M'ᵢ,M"ᵢ) fails
                     then report failure
                     else
                        { Let Mᵢ* be the result of merge(M'ᵢ,M"ᵢ) }
                        return f'(<V'₁∪V"₁,M₁*>,…,<V'ₘ∪V"ₘ,Mₘ*>)
                  fi
               else report failure
            fi
      fi
fi
```

Algorithm Common_part(M)

Specification

Let M be a non-empty multi-term associated with a multi-set of terms T. The algorithm computes the common part of T.

Code

If T is a constant, say c
   then return c
   else
      { T is a compound multi-term, say $f(<V_1,M_1>,...,<V_m,M_m>)$ }
      Parfor i=1 to m do
         If V_i is empty
            then Cp_i := common_part(M_i)
            else Cp_i := one variable of V_i
         fi
      od
      Return $f(Cp_1,...,Cp_m)$
fi

Algorithm Frontier(M)

Specification

Let M be a non-empty multi-term associated with a multi-set of terms T. The algorithm computes the frontier of T.

Code

If T is a constant, say c
   then return $\emptyset$
   else
      { T is a compound multi-term, say $f(<V_1,M_1>,...,<V_m,M_m>)$ }
      Parfor i=1 to m do
         If V_i is empty
            then $Front_i$:= Front(M_i)
            else $Front_i$:= Front(M_i) $\cup$ { V_i = {Common_part(Mi)} }
         fi ;
      Return $Front_1 \cup ... \cup Front_m$
      od
fi

D.3.3 Compactifying (Unsolved\E)∪Front

The compactification of the system (Unsolved\E)∪Front does not need to involve the whole application of the compactification process exposed in Subsection A . Profit can be taken from the fact that Unsolved and, consequently, Unsolved\E is already compact.

Assume the systems S_1 and S_2 are compact. The compactification of the system $S_1 \cup S_2$ can be obtained as follows. If S_2 is empty then the compactification is simply S_1. Otherwise, it can be obtained by applying the following operations :

(1) select a multi-equation E of S_2,
(2) create a new system, say Syst_aux, by merging E with all multi-equations of S_1 whose LHS's share variables with E_{left},
(3) recursively apply the process to Syst_aux and $S_2 \setminus \{E\}$.

This process is justified by the fact that S_1, S_2 and Syst_aux are compact. Note that, in a parallel context, the recursive call (3) can incrementally consume the system Syst_aux produced in (2).

Hence, the compactification of (Unsolved\E)∪Front can be obtained by compacting Front and then applying the above process to (Unsolved\E) and the compactification of Front. It is worth noting that the compactification process is only applied on Front rather than on the whole system (Unsolved\E)∪Front.

D.3.4 Selecting the multi-equation E efficiently

The multi-equation E can be efficiently selected by associating a counter with each multi-equation of Unsolved. Its value is the number of occurrences of variables of the multi-equation LHS in the RHS's of Unsolved. Multi-equations to select are then those whose counter is null.

Counters may be quite easily handled. Their initialization is achieved by completely scanning the system Unsolved. Note that this must occur, in all cases, to select the first equation at the first time. For ease of subsequent manipulation, the initial system is furthermore extended, when need be, so that all its variables appear in the LHS of at least one multi-equation. This is achieved by adding, for each variable X that does not verify this condition, the multi-equation

$\{X\} = \emptyset$

to Unsolved.

This given, counters can be efficiently updated. Updating must only be achieved during compactification. The following operations are performed :

(1) counters of multi-equations of Unsolved\E are decremented by one whenever an occurrence of the corresponding variable appears in the LHS of a multi-equation in the computed frontier;

(2) when two or more multi-equations are merged in the compactification process, the counter associated with the new multi-equation is set to a value which is the sum of the contents of the old counters.

D.3.5 Introducing parallelism

As a final optimization to the algorithm, we introduce parallel executions in the transformations by noting that multi-equations like E can be treated simultaneously, thanks to Properties P_3 and P_7. Atomicity of the assignment instruction is assumed for this purpose.

E. The algorithm

Summing up, our parallel version of Martelli and Montanari's algorithm is as follows.

Algorithm Triangularisation(S)

Specification

Let S be a system of multi-equations. The algorithm succeeds iff S is unifiable. In this case, it delivers an equivalent compact system whose multi-equations are ordered so as to verify Properties P_1 and P_2.

Code

{ initialization }
Unsolved := compactification of S
Solved := []

While Unsolved ≠ [] and not failure do
    { invariant : (Solved,Unsolved) verifies Properties P_3 to P_6 }
    Select the multi-equations of Unsolved whose counter is 0 {i.e. such that none of the
        variables of their left side member appears elsewhere in Unsolved}
    If there are none
        then report failure
        else
            { Let $E_1, ..., E_m$ be these multi-equations }
            Unsolved := Unsolved \ $\{E_1,...,E_m\}$
            Fparfor i=1 to m do
                If $E_{i,right} = \emptyset$
                    then
                        Solved := Solved | $\{E_i\}$
                    else
                        Compute cp_f($E_{i,right}$)
                        If failure occurs
                            then report failure
                            else

                    { Let (cp,Front) be the result of cp_f($E_{i,right}$) }
                    Solved := Solved | $E_{i,left}$ = {cp}
                    Unsolved := recompactification(Unsolved ∪ Front)
                 fi
              fi
           od
        fi
     od
If not failure then return Solved fi .

Note that some of the operations described in Subsections D.3.2 to D.3.4 (such as counter manipulation, multi-term representation of multi-equations) are hidden in (re)compactification calls and in operations on Solved and Unsolved.

Proposition 3.39 Let S be a non empty system of multi-equations. The algorithm triangularisation(S) meets its specification.

Proof The theorem results from our construction of the algorithm. The algorithm has been designed so that
  (i)   the initialization operations make Properties P_3 to P_6 hold,
  (ii) any iteration in the while loop maintains Properties P_3 to P_6 invariant,
  (iii) the number of variables in the system Unsolved decreases at each iteration in the while loop.

Property (iii) ensures that the algorithm terminates. There are two issues : fail or success with a system of multi-equations.
- On the one hand, when failure occurs, the system S has no unifier. Indeed, failure occurs only in two places. In the first one, Theorem 3.30 establishes that S has no unifier. In the last one, if one right-hand side member $E_{i,right}$ cannot be reduced to a singleton then obviously S is not unifiable.
- On the other hand, when the algorithm terminates with success, Properties P_3 to P_6 coupled with the fact that Unsolved is ∅ imply that the returned system Solved verifies Properties P_1 to P_2. In this case, S is furthermore proved to be unifiable. ◊

The algorithm triangularisation was initially developed to unify terms. Given the terms t_1, ..., t_n, the call

triangularisation(eq({V,t_1, ..., t_n}))

where V is a variable not appearing in t_1, ..., t_n indeed determines whether the terms are reconcilable and, in this case, delivers a mgu for t_1, ..., t_n. Martelli and Montanri have given an efficient Pascal-like implementation of the algorithm and satisfactorily compared it with other well-known unification algorithms ([Huet, 1976], [Paterson and Wegman, 1978]).

The algorithm for solving systems of multi-equations can now be stated. It is as follows.

Algorithm Solve_syst_meq(S)

Specification

Let S be a system of multi-equations. The algorithm Solve_syst_meq(S) succeeds iff S is solvable. In this case, it delivers an mgu of S.

Code

Triangularisation(S)
If failure occurs
   then report failure
   else
      { Let S_tri be the returned system of multi-equations }
      return the result of Mgu_syst(S_tri).

Proposition 3.40 The algorithm Solve_syst_meq(S) meets its specification.
Proof This results from Proposition 3.31 and 3.39. ◊

3.1.5.3 The reconciliation algorithm

Our use of the algorithm is not to unify terms but to reconcile substitutions. The reconciliation algorithm is now quite straightforward.

Algorithm Reconciliation($\theta_1,\ldots,\theta_m$)

Code

Let $\theta_1,\ldots,\theta_m$ be idempotent substitutions. The algorithm succeeds iff $\theta_1,\ldots,\theta_m$ are reconcilable. In this case, it determines an idempotent mgu for $syst(\theta_1,\ldots,\theta_m)$ that only refers to the variables of $\theta_1,\ldots,\theta_m$.

Specification

Triangularisation($syst(\theta_1,\ldots,\theta_m)$))
If failure
   then report failure
   else
      { Let S_tri be the resulting system }
      Return Mgu_syst(S_tri).
fi .

Theorem 3.41 The algorithm reconciliation meets its specification.
Proof This results from Propositions 3.31 and 3.39. ◊

3.2 Reconciling n-substitutions

3.2.1 Introduction

In view of the equational framework used in Section 3.1, it seems natural to introduce negation by extending systems of equations to systems of equations and inequations. One attractive property of systems of equations is however lost : substitutions are not sufficient to characterize solutions of systems of equations and inequations, as they were to characterize solutions of systems of equations (see Proposition 3.8). Even the weaker property of covering solutions by a finite number of substitutions does not hold in general. Hence, negative information must be introduce in substitutions in some way. This leads us to generalize substitutions in what we call n-substitutions. Reconciliation of substitutions can be extended to reconciliation of n-substitutions. To show how this can be achieved is the purpose of this section.

3.2.2 Basic concepts

The concept of inequation and related ones are first precised.

Definition 3.42 An *inequation* is a construction of the form

$t \neq u$

where t and u are two terms. It is called an *elementary inequation* or *e-inequation*, for short, when t is a variable and u is distinct from it. Inequations will, in general, not be manipulated alone but in systems of equations and inequations. Such systems are called *hybrid systems* or *h-systems*, for short. They are called *elementary hybrid systems* or *eh-systems* if they are composed of e-equations and e-inequations, only.

The following notation will be useful to distinguish positive and negative information of an h-system.

Notation 3.43 Let S be an h-system. We denote by

S^+ and S^-

the system of equations and the system of inequations of S, respectively.

Solvability of an h-system is defined as follows.

Definition 3.44 A *solution* of an h-system S is a grounding substitution for the variables of S that unifies S^+ and that verifies each inequation of S^-. The set of solutions of S is denoted by *Sol(S)*. The system S is said to be *solvable* iff Sol(S)$\neq \emptyset$.

Proposition 3.45
(i) Systems composed of e-inequations are always solvable.
(ii) Let S be a system of equations and $S_1, ..., S_m$ be systems of inequations. If, for any $i \in \{1,...,m\}$, the h-system $S \cup S_i$ is solvable, then so is the system $S \cup S_1 \cup ... \cup S_m$.

Proof The proposition results from the two following facts :
1) the set of terms is infinite
2) for any variable, the terms excluded by the e-inequations can be summed up in a finite number of terms. ◊

The equivalence ≈ of systems of equations is extended to h-systems by means of solutions. As for systems of equations, domain contraints require to define the notion of solution-weaker system.

Definition 3.46 The h-system S is *solution-weaker* than the h-system T iff for any solution σ of S, for any grounding substitution γ for the variables of var(T)\var(S), the substitution $(\sigma\gamma)_{|var(T)}$ is a solution of T. This denoted by $T \supset_{sol} S$.

Definition 3.47 The systems of equations and inequations S and T are *equivalent* iff any of them is solution-weaker than the other. This is denoted by $S \approx T$.

Notation 3.48 It will be convenient to extend the operand of the $\supset_{sol}$ and ≈ to involve "disjunctions" of h-systems. We will write

$(T_1 \vee ... \vee T_n) \supset_{sol} (S_1 \vee ... \vee S_m)$

to denote the following property : for any $i \in \{1,...,m\}$, for any solution σ of S_i, there is a $j \in \{1,...,n\}$ such that for any grounding substitution γ for the variables of var(T_j)\var(S_j), the substitution $(\sigma\gamma)_{|var(T_j)}$ is a solution of T_j. The notation

$(T_1 \vee ... \vee T_n) \approx (S_1 \vee ... \vee S_m)$

is then employed to sum up the two inclusions

$(T_1 \vee ... \vee T_n) \supset_{sol} (S_1 \vee ... \vee S_m)$
$(S_1 \vee ... \vee S_m) \supset_{sol} (T_1 \vee ... \vee T_n)$.

Finally, the notation

$$\bigvee_{a \in A} S(a)$$

will be used as the natural generalization of the above disjunctive notation.

The following proposition justifies the generalization of substitutions in n-substitutions. Its proof is out of the scope of the thesis; it can be found in [Lassez et al., 1988].

Proposition 3.49 Let S be a solvable h-system. Suppose S^- is not redundant with S^+ that is $S^+ \approx S$ does not hold. Then, there is no finite set of substitutions $\{\theta_1,...,\theta_m\}$, such that for any solution α of S, one has $\theta_i \leq \alpha$ for some $i \in \{1,...,m\}$.
Proof Admitted result (see [Lassez et al., 1988], for instance). ◊

Hence, substitutions do not provide a finite representation of solutions of h-systems. Some inequations must thus be kept as additional information. This leads us to introduce the concept of n-substitution.

Definition 3.50 An *n-substitution* ν is a pair of the form

$$(\{X_1/t_1,...,X_m/t_m\}, \text{not}\{Y_1/u_1,...,Y_n/u_n\})$$

where $\{X_1/t_1,...,X_m/t_m\}$ is a substitution and $\{Y_1/u_1,...,Y_n/u_n\}$ is a set of bindings such that
  (i) $\text{var}(\{t_1,...,t_m\}) \supset \{X_1,...,X_m\} \cap \{Y_1,...,Y_n\}$,
  (ii) $\text{var}(\{t_1,...,t_m\}) \supset \{X_1,...,X_m\} \cap \text{var}(\{u_1,...,u_n\})$,
  (iii) $u_i \notin \{X_1,...,X_m\}$, for all $i \in \{1,...,n\}$.

The two components are called the *positive part* and the *negative part* of ν, respectively. They are denoted by ν^+ and ν^-, respectively. An n-substitution whose positive part is empty is called an *en-substitution*. It is often represented by omitting the positive part; the n-substitution

$$(\{\}, \text{not}\{Y_1/u_1,...,Y_n/u_n\})$$

is thus rewritten as

$$\text{not}\{Y_1/u_1,...,Y_n/u_n\}.$$

The interpretation of n-substitutions is as follows : X_1, ..., X_m have t_1, ..., t_m as respective values with the constraint that each Y_i must differ from u_i ($1 \leq i \leq n$). Conditions (i), (ii) and (iii) further require that the n-substitutions are presented in a normal form. Basically, conditions (i) and (ii) express the fact that the inequations cannot directly constrain the X_i's but must do this indirectly through their bindings. For instance,

$$X = f(Y) \wedge X \neq f(3)$$

is not allowed to be represented as $(\{X/f(Y)\}, \text{not}\{X/f(3)\})$ but should be represented as $(\{X/f(Y)\}, \text{not}\{Y/3\})$. The latter representation is to our opinion more intuitive and more clear. It is also more concise since inequations are forced to be presented in a simpler form and useless inequations are forced to be removed. Note that non-idempotent substitutions have also been taken into account in the general case. Conditions (i) and (ii) then state that the X_i's can occur in inequations only if they occur in some right-hand side of some bindings. As argued in the following proposition, this has the interesting consequence that no X_i occurs in the negative part of n-substitutions whose positive part is idempotent. Condition (iii) states a weaker property in the general case: the u_i's cannot be used to negate the X_i's. Restated in other terms, the inequality

$X_i \neq Y$

cannot be written as not$\{Y/X_i\}$ but must be expressed as not$\{X_i/Y\}$ (provided this is allowed by Conditions (i) and (ii)).

Proposition 3.51 Let $(\{X_1/t_1,...,X_m/t_m\}, \text{not}\{Y_1/u_1,...,Y_n/u_n\})$ be an n-substitution whose positive part $\{X_1/t_1,...,X_m/t_m\}$ is idempotent. Then no X_i occurs in the negative part not$\{Y_1/u_1,...,Y_n/u_n\}$.

Proof By conditions (i) and (ii) of Definition 3.50, one has

$$\{X_1,...,X_m\} \cap \text{var}(\{t_1,...,t_m\}) \supset \{X_1,...,X_m\} \cap \{Y_1,...,Y_n\},$$
$$\{X_1,...,X_m\} \cap \text{var}(\{t_1,...,t_m\}) \supset \{X_1,...,X_m\} \cap \text{var}(\{u_1,...,u_n\}).$$

The thesis then results from the fact that

$$\{X_1,...,X_m\} \cap \text{var}(\{t_1,...,t_m\})$$

is empty since $\{X_1/t_1,...,X_m/t_m\}$ is idempotent. ◊

The notions of domain, codomain and varcod are extended to n-substitutions in an obvious way.

Definition 3.52 Let $v=(\{X_1/t_1,...,X_m/t_m\}, \text{not}\{Y_1/u_1,...,Y_n/u_n\})$ be an n-substitution.
1) The *domain* and *codomain* of v are defined as the sets $\{X_1,...,X_m,Y_1,...,Y_n\}$ and $\{t_1,...,t_m,u_1,...,u_n\}$, respectively. They are denoted by $var(v)$ and $cod(v)$, respectively. The set of variables of cod(v) is furthermore denoted by $varcod(v)$.
2) The *domain* and *codomain* of v^- are defined as the sets $\{Y_1,...,Y_n\}$ and $\{u_1,...,u_n\}$, respectively. They are denoted by $var(v^-)$ and $cod(v^-)$, respectively. The set of variables of cod(v) is furthermore denoted by $varcod(v^-)$.

N-substitutions and h-systems are related as follows.

Definition 3.53 Let $v = (\{X_1/t_1,...,X_m/t_m\}, \text{not}\{Y_1/u_1,...,Y_n/u_n\})$ be an n-substitution. The *h-system associated with* v, denoted by $hsyst(v)$, is the eh-system composed of the following e-equations and e-inequations

$X_1 = t_1$
...
$X_m = t_m$
$Y_1 \neq u_1$
...
$Y_n \neq u_n$.

The h-system associated with the n-substitutions $v_1, ..., v_m$ is the eh-system composed of the equations and inequations of the h-systems $hsyst(v_1), ..., hsyst(v_m)$. It is denoted by $hsyst(v_1,...,v_m)$. The notation $hsyst(Snsubsts)$ will also be used in order to avoid the listing of the elements of the set of n-substitutions Snsubsts.

Conversely, when the conditions of Definitions 2.22 and 3.50 on substitutions and n-substitutions are satisfied, applying the above transformation in the reverse order associates an n-substitution to any eh-system. This n-substitution is called the *n-substitution associated with the eh-system*.

One important property of h-systems associated with n-substitutions is that they are solvable when the system associated with their positive part is solvable.

Proposition 3.54 Let ν be a n-substitution such that $syst(\nu^+)$ is solvable. Then the h-system $hsyst(\nu)$ is solvable.
Proof This results from the properties (i), (ii), (iii) of Definition 3.50 fulfilled by any n-substitution and from Proposition 3.45. ◊

The association between n-susbtitutions and h-systems allows us to extend the $\leq$ preorder on n-substitutions.

Definition 3.55
1) The n-substitution ν is *more general than* the n-substitution μ iff the following inclusion holds
   $hsyst(\nu) \supset_{sol} hsyst(\mu)$.
   This is denoted by $\nu \leq \mu$. [1]
2) The n-substitutions ν and μ are *variants* iff they verify the inequalities $\nu \leq \mu$ and $\mu \leq \nu$.

This preorder and this equivalence generalizes the $\leq$ and $\equiv$ relations defined in Subsection 2.3.1.

Proposition 3.56 Let σ and τ be two idempotent substitutions. Then the following equivalences hold

1) $\sigma \leq \tau$ iff $(\sigma, not\{\}) \leq (\tau, not\{\})$.
2) $\sigma \equiv \tau$ iff $(\sigma, not\{\}) \equiv (\tau, not\{\})$.

Proof This results from the fact that any idempotent substitution σ is an mgu of its associated system $syst(\sigma)$. ◊

Proposition 3.57 Let ν and μ be two variant n-substitutions. Assume that their positive parts ν^+ and μ^+ are idempotent. Then, they are also variant.
Proof Let us proceed by contradiction. As they are idempotent, the substitutions ν^+ and μ^+ are variant iff the sets $Sol(syst(\nu^+))$ and $Sol(syst(\mu^+))$ are identical. Assume that they are not variant. Then there is a grounding substitution of some set, say $Sol(syst(\nu^+))$, that is not in the other, namely $Sol(syst(\mu^+))$. There is thus a binding Z/ν of μ^+ such that the system composed of the equations of $syst(\nu^+)$ and of the inequation $Z \neq \nu$ is solvable. Therefore, thanks to

---

[1] The remark made for Definition 2.29 about the conflict of the qualification "more general than" and the notation "$\leq$" holds here too.

Propositions 3.45 and 3.54, the systems composed of the equations and inequations of hsyst(ν) and of the inequation Z≠v is solvable. All its solutions are not solutions of syst(μ). However, the n-subsitutions ν and μ are variants ! ◊

Concepts of unifiers and mgus are extended to h-systems thanks to the $\supset_{sol}$ relation.

Definition 3.58
1) An *n-unifier* of a h-system is an n-substitution ν that verifies
   S $\supset_{sol}$ hsyst(ν).
2) An *n-mgu* of S is a set of n-substitutions {ν$_1$,...,ν$_m$} that verifies
   S ≈ hsyst(ν$_1$) ∨... ∨ hsyst(ν$_m$).

A particular class of n-mgu's will often be used in subsequent developments. They are called elementary sets of n-substitutions.

Definition 3.59 An *elementary set of n-substitutions* or *es-nsubst*, for short, is a set of n-substitutions sharing the same positive part.

Notation 3.60 Such an es-nsubst is thus of the form {(θ,ω$_1$),...,(θ,ω$_m$)} where ω$_1$, ..., ω$_m$ are en-substitutions. It is subsequently denoted by the more suggestive form

θ ⊕ {ω$_1$,...,ω$_m$}.

Proposition 3.57 can be generalized to elementary sets of n-substitutions.

Proposition 3.61 Let σ⊕{μ$_1$,...,μ$_m$} and τ⊕{ν$_1$,...,ν$_n$} be variant es-nsubst's. Assume that σ and τ are idempotent. Then, the substitutions σ and τ are variants.
Proof Let us proceed by contradiction, as for Proposition 3.57. Assume, for instance, that Sol(syst(σ)) strictly contains Sol(syst(τ)). Then, as for the proof of Proposition 3.57, one may point out a binding Z/v of τ such that the system composed of the equations of syst(σ) and of the inequation Z≠v is solvable. Therefore, from Propositions 3.45 and 3.54, for any i∈ {1,...,m}, the system composed of the equations and inequations of hsyst((σ,μ$_i$)) and of the inequation Z≠v is solvable. All solutions of these systems are not solutions of any system hsyst(τ,ν$_j$), for any j∈ {1,...,n}. The contradiction then arises from the fact that each one is a solution of one system hsyst((σ,μ$_i$)) and from the fact that the es-nsubst's σ⊕{μ$_1$,...,μ$_m$} and τ⊕{ν$_1$,...,ν$_n$} are variants. ◊

The ≤ preorder and the ≡ equivalence can be extended to sets of n-substitutions in a straightforward way.

Definition 3.62 Let Θ and Ψ be two sets of n-substitutions.
1) The set Θ is *more general than* the set Ψ iff the following inclusion holds

$$\bigvee_{\theta \in \Theta} hsyst(\Theta) \supset_{sol} \bigvee_{\psi \in \Psi} hsyst(\Psi).$$

This is denoted by $\Theta \leq \Psi$.

2) The sets Θ and Ψ are variants iff they verify the inequalities $\Theta \leq \Psi$ and $\Psi \leq \Theta$.

Definition 3.63 The $\leq$ and $\equiv$ relations are finally extended to hold between n-substitutions and sets of n-substitutions by considering n-substitutions as the singletons composed of them. For instance, the n-substitution ν is more general than the sets Θ of n-substitutions iff $\{\nu\}$ is more general than Θ.

The following remarks are worth noting.

1) In contrast with systems of equations, unsolvable systems of equations and inequations have an n-mgu : the empty set of n-substitutions. It is subsequently denoted by $\emptyset_\varepsilon$.
2) The notion of n-mgu is however still a generalization of that of mgu. Any system of equation has a mgu iff, regarded as h-system, it has a non-empty n-mgu. In this case, if θ is an idempotent mgu, then $\{(\theta,\text{not}\{\})\}$ is an n-mgu.
3) N-mgu's are still variants from one another. Such a nice characterization as that of Proposition 2.37 cannot however been established here.

The composition of substitutions is extended to n-substitutions as follows.

Definition 3.64 The composition of the n-substitution

$$\nu=(\{X_1/t_1,\ldots,X_m/t_m\},\text{not}\{Y_1/u_1,\ldots,Y_n/u_n\})$$

by the n-substitution

$$\mu=(\{Z_1/v_1,\ldots,Z_p/v_p\},\text{not}\{T_1/w_1,\ldots,T_q/w_q\})$$

is the set of n-mgu's of the h-system obtained from the h-system

$$\begin{cases} X_1 = t_1\mu^+ \\ \ldots \\ X_m = t_m\mu^+ \\ Y_1\mu^+ \neq u_1\mu^+ \\ \ldots \\ Y_n\mu^+ \neq u_n\mu^+ \\ Z_1 = v_1 \\ \ldots \\ Z_p = v_p \\ T_1 \neq w_1 \\ \ldots \\ T_q \neq w_q \end{cases}$$

by removing any equality $Z_i = v_i$ for which $Z_i \in \{X_1,...,X_m\}$. It is denoted by $\text{Ncomp}(v,\mu)$. By similarity to the composition of substitutions, the notation

$$v \circ \mu$$

will be used to denote one of these n-mgu's.

Example 3.6 Consider the following n-substitutions

$v = (\{X/f(Y,Z)\},\text{not}\{Y/h(3,4)\})$,
$\mu = (\{Y/h(T,U),Z/k(T)\},\text{not}\{T/6,U/7\})$

The set $\text{Ncomp}(v,\mu)$ is formed by the n-mgu's of the h-system

$$\begin{cases} X\mu_1^+ = f(Y,Z)\mu_1^+ \\ Y\mu_1^+ \neq h(3,4)\mu_1^+ \\ Y = h(T,U) \\ Z = k(T) \\ T \neq 6 \\ U \neq 7 \end{cases}$$

that is of the n-mgu's of

$$\begin{cases} X = f(h(T,U),k(T)) \\ h(T,U) \neq h(3,4) \\ Y = h(T,U) \\ Z = k(T) \\ T \neq 6 \\ U \neq 7 \end{cases}$$

One such n-mgu (denoted by $v_1 \circ \mu_1$) is composed of the two following n-substitutions

($\{X/f(h(T,U),k(T)),Y/h(T,U),Z/k(T)\}$, $\text{not}\{T/3,T/6,U/7\}$),
($\{X/f(h(T,U),k(T)),Y/h(T,U),Z/k(T)\}$, $\text{not}\{T/6,U/4,U/7\}$).

The composition of n-substitutions provides us with the possibility of introducing idempotent n-substitutions.

Definition 3.65 An n-substitution v is idempotent iff it verifies $\{v\} \in \text{Ncomp}(v,v)$.

Proposition 3.66 An n-substitution is idempotent iff its positive part is idempotent.
Proof Let v be the n-substitution

$(\{X_1/t_1,...,X_m/t_m\},\text{not}\{Y_1/u_1,...,Y_n/u_n\})$.

Let us first give an equivalent formulation in terms of h-systems to the property $\{v\} \in \text{Ncomp}(v,v)$. The composition $\text{Ncomp}(v,v)$ is defined by the h-system

$$\begin{cases} X_1 = t_1v^+ \\ \ldots \\ X_m = t_mv^+ \\ Y_1v^+ \neq u_1v^+ \\ \ldots \\ Y_nv^+ \neq u_nv^+ \\ Y_1 \neq u_1 \\ \ldots \\ Y_n \neq u_n \end{cases} \qquad (S_1)$$

By definition, saying that v is an element of $\text{Ncomp}(v,v)$ amounts to saying that $\{v\}$ is an n-mgu of (S_1). Hence, the property $\{v\} \in \text{Ncomp}(v,v)$ is equivalent to the two following properties:

1) the equivalence of the h-system (S_1) and the h-system

$$\begin{cases} X_1 = t_1 \\ \ldots \\ X_m = t_m \\ Y_1 \neq u_1 \\ \ldots \\ Y_n \neq u_n \end{cases} \qquad (S_2) \ .$$

2) the fact that the latter system is solvable.

The theorem thus amounts to proving that these h-systems are equivalent and solvable iff v^+ is idempotent.

1° Assume the h-systems S_1 and S_2 are solvable and equivalent. Let us first prove that for any $i \in \{1,\ldots,m\}$, t_iv^+ and t_i are identical. Let us proceed by contradiction. Let $i \in \{1,\ldots,m\}$ be such that $t_iv^+ \neq_s t_i$. There is thus a variable $Z \in \text{var}(t_i)$ such that $Zv^+ \neq Z$. The system composed of the equations and inequations of S_2 and of the inequation $Z \neq Zv^+$ has thus a solution. Let α be such a (grounding) solution. Obviously, one has

$$t_iv^+\alpha \neq_s t_i\alpha.$$

However, from S_1 and S_2, we get

$$X_i\alpha = t_iv^+\alpha$$

and

$$X_i\alpha = t_i\alpha.$$

Hence, the contradiction.

Summing up, we thus have,

$X_i v^+ v^+ = t_i v^+ = t_i = X_i v^+$, for any $i \in \{1,...,m\}$,
$X v^+ v^+ = X v^+$, for any variable $X \notin \text{dom}(v^+)$

so that

$v^+ \circ v^+ = v^+$

holds. The substitution v^+ is thus proved to be idempotent.

2° Assume now v^+ is idempotent. It thus verifies the equality

$\text{dom}(v^+) \cap \text{varcod}(v^+) = \emptyset$,

thanks to Proposition 2.40. Then, the following equalities hold too :

$t_i v^+ = t_i$, for all $i \in \{1,...,m\}$,
   (since $\text{varcod}(v^+) \supset \text{var}(t_i)$, by definition of varcod)
$Y_j v^+ = Y_j$, for all $j \in \{1,...,n\}$,
   (since $\text{varcod}(v^+) \supset \text{var}(\{t_1,...,t_m\}) \supset \{Y_1,...,Y_n\}$, by definitions of varcod and of n-substitutions)
$u_j v^+ = u_j$, for all $j \in \{1,...,n\}$,
   (since $\text{varcod}(v^+) \supset \text{var}(\{t_1,...,t_n\}) \supset \{X_1,...,X_n\} \cap \text{var}(\{u_1,...,u_n\})$, by definitions of varcod and of n-substitutions).

In these conditions, the h-system S_1 rewrites as S_2. Both h-systems are thus equivalent. Thanks to Proposition 3.54, they are also solvable. ◊

Finally, idempotence is extended to sets of n-substitutions as follows.

Definition 3.67 A set of n-substitutions is said to be idempotent iff all its n-substitutions are idempotent.

3.2.3 Definition

Let us now turn back to reconciliation.

Definition 3.68 The n-substitutions $v_1, ..., v_m$ are *n-reconcilable* iff the h-system hsyst($v_1,...,v_m$) is solvable. In this case, any n-mgu of this h-system is called an *n-reconciliation* of $v_1, ..., v_m$. It is called an *en-reconciliation* if it is of the es-nsubst form.

Notation 3.69 The set of n-reconciliations of the n-substitutions $v_1, ..., v_m$ is denoted by

$Nreconc(v_1,...,v_m)$

The notation

$\rho_N(v_1,...,v_m)$

is used to denote one of them. Finally, the notations

Nreconc(Snsubsts) and $\rho_N(Snsubsts)$

are sometimes used instead of the above ones to avoid the listing of the n-substitutions of the set Snsubst.

Example 3.7 Consider the n-substitutions

$v = (\{X/Y\}, \text{not}\{Y/f(1,2)\}$,
$\mu = \{(X/f(U,V)\}, \text{not}\{U/a, V/b\})$.

They are n-reconcilable since the h-system

$$\begin{cases} X = Y \\ X = f(U,V) \\ Y \ne f(1,2) \\ U \ne a \\ V \ne b \end{cases}$$

is solvable. One n-reconciliation is given by the n-mgu

$\{ \ (\{X/f(U,V), Y/f(U,V)\}, \text{not}\{U/1, U/a, V/b\})$
$\quad (\{X/f(U,V), Y/f(U,V)\}, \text{not}\{U/a, V/2, V/b\}) \ \}$.

Defining the n-reconciliation on n-substitutions only is theoretically sufficient for subsequent developments. However, it will be useful to group n-substitutions before reconciling them and speak about the n-reconciliation of sets of n-substitutions. Such an n-reconciliation amounts to the n-reconciliation of all tuples of n-substitutions formed from the sets. It will not be used as a new concept on its own but rather as a shorthand for the n-reconciliation of many n-substitutions, especially when en-mgu's are involved.

Definition 3.70 Let $\Theta = \{\theta_1,...,\theta_m\}$, $\Psi = \{\psi_1,...,\psi_n\}$, ..., $\Omega = \{\omega_1,...,\omega_p\}$ be sets of n-substitutions. They are n-reconcilable iff at least one of the h-systems

$\text{hsyst}(\theta_i, \psi_j,...,\omega_k) \qquad (1 \le i \le m, \ 1 \le j \le n, \ ..., \ 1 \le k \le p)$

is solvable. In this case, let S be the set of tuples $(\theta, \psi,...,\omega)$ of n-reconcilable n-substitutions of $\Theta \times \Psi \times ... \times \Omega$. One n-reconciliation of $\Theta, \Psi, ..., \Omega$ consists of one union

$$\bigcup_{(\theta,\psi,...,\omega) \in S} \rho_N(\theta,\psi,...,\omega) \ .$$

Notation 3.71 The above Nreconc(...) and ρ_N(...) notations are extended to the n-reconciliation of sets of n-substitutions to denote the set of n-reconciliation of those sets and any n-reconciliation, respectively.

3.2.4 Properties

The properties of the n-reconciliation of sets of n-substitutions directly result from the properties of the n-reconciliation of n-substitutions. Development of the latter properties is thus sufficient. We will therefore limit to them in this subsection.

One important property to prove is that the n-reconciliation is a generalization of the reconciliation introduced in Section 3.1.

Proposition 3.72 The substitutions σ and τ are reconcilable iff the n-substitutions $(\sigma,\text{not}\{\})$ and $(\tau,\text{not}\{\})$ are n-reconcilable. In this case, the singleton $\{(\rho(\sigma,\tau),\text{not}\{\})\}$ is one n-reconciliation of $(\sigma,\text{not}\{\})$ and $(\tau,\text{not}\{\})$.
Proof The h-system hsyst$((\sigma,\text{not}\{\}),(\tau,\text{not}\{\}))$ contains no inequations and reduces to the equations of syst(σ,τ). Both systems are thus simultaneously solvable. As a consequence, the substitutions σ and τ are reconcilable iff the n-substitutions $(\sigma,\text{not}\{\})$ and $(\tau,\text{not}\{\})$ are n-reconcilable. In this case, $\rho(\sigma,\tau)$ sums up all solutions of syst(σ,τ) so that all solutions of hsyst$((\sigma,\text{not}\{\}),(\tau,\text{not}\{\}))$ are summarized by the n-substitution $(\rho(\sigma,\tau),\text{not}\{\})$. Hence, $\{(\rho(\sigma,\tau),\text{not}\{\})\}$ is an n-reconciliation of $(\sigma,\text{not}\{\})$ and $(\tau,\text{not}\{\})$. ◊

The basic properties of Subsection 3.1.4 can be extended to the n-reconciliation of n-substitutions. The same scheme of reasoning is essentially used because systems of equations need basically to be generalized to systems of equations and inequations.

Idempotent n-substitutions are proved unchanged by the application of the reconciliation operation.

Proposition 3.73 Every idempotent n-substitution ν constitutes an n-reconciliation $\rho_N(\nu)$.
Proof As ν and ν^+ (see Proposition 3.66) are idempotent, the singleton $\{\nu\}$ is an n-mgu of the h-system hsyst(ν). ◊

The reconciliation of n-substitutions increases with the number of n-substitutions that are reconciled. In other terms, it becomes more and more specific as more and more n-substitutions are reconciled. In particular, Proposition 3.73 implies that every idempotent n-substitution is more general than any n-reconciliation in which it participates.

Proposition 3.74 Let $\nu_1,...,\nu_m$ be substitutions. For any subset $\{\mu_1,...,\mu_k\}$ of $\{\nu_1,...,\nu_m\}$, one has

$$\rho_N(\mu_1,...,\mu_k) \leq \rho_N(\nu_1,...,\nu_m).$$

In particular, for any idempotent n-substitution v_i, one has

$$v_i \leq \rho(v_1,...,v_m).$$

Proof The inequality

$$\rho_N(\mu_1,...,\mu_k) \leq \rho_N(v_1,...,v_m)$$

results from the fact that the h-system $hsyst(\mu_1,...,\mu_k)$ is included in the h-system $hsyst(v_1,...,v_m)$. Thus any n-mgu of $hsyst(\mu_1,...,\mu_k)$ (that is any n-reconciliation $\rho_N(\mu_1,...,\mu_k)$) is more general than any n-mgu of $hsyst(v_1,...,v_m)$ (that is any n-reconciliation $\rho_N(v_1,...,v_m)$).

Taking $\{v_i\}$ as subset of $\{v_1,...,v_m\}$, we obtain

$$\rho_N(v_i) \leq \rho_N(v_1,...,v_m)$$

and thus, thanks to Proposition 3.73,

$$v_i \leq \rho_N(v_1,...,v_m). \lozenge$$

Reconciling the composition $v \circ \mu$ of two substitutions v and μ with other substitutions amounts to reconciling directly the whole set of substitutions, provided the domains of their positive parts are disjoint.

Proposition 3.75 Let $\{\theta_1, ..., \theta_m\}$ be a possibly empty set of n-substitutions. Let v and μ be two idempotent n-substitutions such that $dom(v^+) \cap dom(\mu^+) = \emptyset$.
1) For any n-mgu $v \circ \mu = \{\alpha_1,...,\alpha_n\}$, the n-substitutions $v, \mu, \theta_1, ..., \theta_m$ are reconcilable iff, for all $i \in \{1,...,n\}$, the n-substitutions $\alpha_i, \theta_1, ..., \theta_m$ are reconcilable.
2) In this case, one has
$$\rho_N(\alpha_1,\theta_1,...,\theta_m) \cup ... \cup \rho_N(\alpha_n,\theta_1,...,\theta_m) \equiv \rho_N(v,\mu,\theta_1,...,\theta_m).$$

Proof By definition of the composition of two n-substitutions and thanks to the hypothesis on v and μ, any n-mgu $v \circ \mu = \{\alpha_1,...,\alpha_n\}$ verifies the equality

$$hsyst(\alpha_1) \vee ... \vee hsyst(\alpha_n) \approx hsyst(v,\mu)$$

The proposition then results from the equality

[$Sol(hsyst(\alpha_1,\theta_1,...,\theta_m)) \cup ... \cup Sol(hsyst(\alpha_n,\theta_1,...,\theta_m))$]

= [$Sol(hsyst(\alpha_1)) \cup ... \cup Sol(hsyst(\alpha_n))$] $\cap Sol(hsyst(\theta_1,...,\theta_m))$

and the equality

$Sol(hsyst(v,\mu)) \cap Sol(hsyst(\theta_1,...,\theta_m))$

= $Sol(hsyst(v,\mu,\theta_1,...,\theta_m))$. $\lozenge$

The n-reconciliation turns out to be monotonic in some situations.

Proposition 3.76 Let $v_1, ..., v_m$ be idempotent n-substitutions and $\mu_1, ..., \mu_m, \theta_1, ..., \theta_n$ be n-substitutions. Assume the inequalities $v_i \leq \mu_i$ hold ($1 \leq i \leq m$) and the n-substitutions $v_1, ..., v_m, \theta_1, ..., \theta_n$ are n-reconcilable. Then the n-substitutions $\mu_1, ..., \mu_m, \theta_1, ..., \theta_n$ are n-reconcilable as well. Furthermore, one has

$$\rho_N(v_1,...,v_m,\theta_1,...,\theta_n) \leq \rho_N(\mu_1,...,\mu_m,\theta_1,...,\theta_n).$$

In particular, for any idempotent n-substitution λ and any n-substitution $\mu \geq \lambda$, one has $\rho_N(\mu) \geq \rho_N(\lambda)$.

Proof The theorem results from the fact that any solution of the h-system $\text{syst}(\mu_1,...,\mu_m,\theta_1,...,\theta_n)$ is a solution of the h-system $\text{hsyst}(v_1,...,v_m,\theta_1,...,\theta_n)$. Thus, the n-substitutions $\mu_1, ..., \mu_m, \theta_1, ..., \theta_n$ are n-reconcilable when the n-substitutions $v_1, ..., v_m, \theta_1, ..., \theta_n$ are n-reconciliable. Furthermore, one has

$$\rho_N(v_1,...,v_m,\theta_1,...,\theta_n) \leq \rho_N(\mu_1,...,\mu_m,\theta_1,...,\theta_n).$$

The monotonicity of the n-reconciliation directly results by taking n=0. ◊

N-reconciliation is also idempotent.

Proposition 3.77 Let $\{\alpha_1,...,\alpha_m\}, ..., \{\gamma_1,...,\gamma_n\}$ be sets of n-substitutions.
1) The n-substitutions $\alpha_1,...,\alpha_m, ..., \gamma_1,...,\gamma_n$ are n-reconcilable iff
   - the n-substitutions of each set are n-reconcilable,
   - for any n-reconciliations $\rho_N(\alpha_1,...,\alpha_m), ..., \rho_N(\gamma_1,...,\gamma_m)$, the n-substitutions $v, ..., \lambda$ are n-reconcilable, for all $v \in \rho_N(\alpha_1,...,\alpha_m), ..., \lambda \in \rho_N(\gamma_1,...,\gamma_n)$.
2) In this case, if $\rho_N(\alpha_1,...,\alpha_m) = \{v_1,...,v_p\}, ..., \rho_N(\gamma_1,...,\gamma_m) = \{\lambda_1,...,\lambda_q\}$, one has
$$\rho_N(\alpha_1,...,\alpha_m, ..., \gamma_1,...,\gamma_n) \equiv \rho_N(v_1,...,\lambda_1) \cup ... \cup \rho_N(v_1,...,\lambda_q) \cup ...$$
$$\cup \rho_N(v_p,...,\lambda_1) \cup ... \cup \rho_N(v_p,...,\lambda_q).$$

Proof The theorem results from the following facts
- the h-systems
    $\text{hsyst}(\alpha_1,...,\alpha_m), ..., \text{hsyst}(\gamma_1,...,\gamma_n)$
    are parts of the system $\text{syst}(\alpha_1,...,\alpha_m, ..., \gamma_1,...,\gamma_n)$;
- the disjunction
    $\text{hsyst}(v_1,...,\lambda_1) \vee ... \vee \text{hsyst}(v_1,...,\lambda_q) \vee ...$
    $\vee \text{hsyst}(v_p,...,\lambda_1) \vee ... \vee \text{hsyst}(v_p,...,\lambda_q)$
    is equivalent to the system
    $\text{hsyst}(\alpha_1,...,\alpha_m, ..., \gamma_1,...,\gamma_n)$
    when the n-substitutions $\{\alpha_1,...,\alpha_m\}, ..., \{\gamma_1,...,\gamma_n\}$ are separately n-reconcilable.
◊

The n-reconciliation of n-substitutions can in some case be characterized in terms of the n-substitutions themselves.

Proposition 3.78 Let ν and μ be two idempotent n-substitutions such that

$$[\, dom(\nu^+) \cup varcod(\nu^+) \,] \cap dom(\mu^+) = \emptyset$$

The n-substitutions are n-reconcilable and $\mu \circ \nu$ is an n-reconciliation.

Proof Let ν and μ be

$$(\{X_1/t_1,\ldots,X_m/t_m\}, not\{Y_1/u_1,\ldots,Y_n/u_n\})$$

and

$$(\{Z_1/v_1,\ldots,Z_p/v_p\}, not\{T_1/w_1,\ldots,T_q/w_q\}),$$

respectively. The h-system $hsyst(\nu,\mu)$ is

$$\begin{cases} X_1 = t_1 \\ \ldots \\ X_m = t_m \\ Y_1 \neq u_1 \\ \ldots \\ Y_n \neq u_n \\ Z_1 = v_1 \\ \ldots \\ Z_p = v_p \\ T_1 \neq w_1 \\ \ldots \\ T_q \neq w_q \end{cases}$$

It is equivalent to the h-system

$$\begin{cases} X_1 = t_1 \\ \cdots \\ X_m = t_m \\ Y_1 \neq u_1 \\ \cdots \\ Y_n \neq u_n \\ Z_1 = v_1 v^+ \\ \cdots \\ Z_p = v_p v^+ \\ T_1 v^+ \neq w_1 v^+ \\ \cdots \\ T_q v^+ \neq w_q v^+ \end{cases}$$

for which, thanks to the hypothesis on v and μ, $\mu \circ v$ is one n-mgu ◊

Finally, Proposition 3.20 can be extended as follows.

Proposition 3.79 Let
- t and u be two unifiable terms sharing no variables
- θ be an idempotent mgu of t and u
- λ be an idempotent n-substitution such that
  - λ and $(\theta,\text{not}\{\})$ are n-reconcilable
  - $t\lambda^+$ and u are unifiable
- μ be an idempotent mgu of $t\lambda^+$ and u such that the n-substitutions $(\sigma,\text{not}\{\})$ and λ are n-reconcilable.

Then, the n-substitutions $(\theta,\text{not}\{\})$, λ and $(\mu,\text{not}\{\})$ are n-reconcilable and verify

$$\rho_N((\theta,\text{not}\{\}),\lambda) \equiv \rho_N((\theta,\text{not}\{\}),(\mu,\text{not}\{\}),\lambda) \equiv \rho_N((\mu,\text{not}\{\}),\lambda) \ .$$

Proof Establishing the proposition amounts to proving that the systems

hsyst$((\theta,\text{not}\{\}),\lambda)$,
hsyst$((\theta,\text{not}\{\}),(\mu,\text{not}\{\}),\lambda)$,
hsyst$((\mu,\text{not}\{\}),\lambda)$,

are equivalent. This results from the following equivalences.

1° By elementary system manipulation, the following systems are equivalent

$\{t=u\} \cup \text{hsyst}(\lambda)$
$\{t=u\} \cup \{t\lambda^+=u\} \cup \text{hsyst}(\lambda)$

$\{t\lambda^+=u\} \cup hsyst(\lambda)$.

2° Thanks to the idempotent mgu character of θ, the system $\{t=u\}$ is equivalent to the system $syst(\theta)$ i.e. to the system $hsyst((\theta,not\{\}))$. It follows that the systems

$\{t=u\} \cup hsyst(\lambda)$
$\{t=u\} \cup \{t\lambda^+=u\} \cup hsyst(\lambda)$

are equivalent to the systems

$hsyst((\theta,not\{\}),\lambda)$
$\{t\lambda^+=u\} \cup hsyst((\theta,not\{\}),\lambda)$,

respectively.

3° In a similar way, the system $\{t\lambda^+=u\}$ is equivalent to the system $syst(\mu)$ i.e. the system $hsyst((\mu,not\{\}))$. The systems

$\{t\lambda^+=u\} \cup hsyst(\lambda)$
$\{t\lambda^+=u\} \cup hsyst((\theta,not\{\}),\lambda)$

are thus equivalent to the systems

$hsyst(\mu,not\{\}),\lambda)$,
$hsyst((\mu,not\{\}),(\theta,not\{\}),\lambda)$,

respectively.

Summing up, one has

1° $hsyst((\theta,not\{\}),\lambda)$
    $\approx$ $\{t=u\} \cup hsyst(\lambda)$
    $\approx$ $\{t=u\} \cup \{t\lambda^+=u\} \cup hsyst(\lambda)$
    $\approx$ $\{t\lambda^+=u\} \cup hsyst((\theta,not\{\}),\lambda)$
    $\approx$ $hsyst((\mu,not\{\}),(\theta,not\{\}),\lambda)$

2° $hsyst((\mu,not\{\}),\lambda)$
    $\approx$ $\{t\lambda^+=u\} \cup hsyst(\lambda)$
    $\approx$ $\{t=u\} \cup \{t\lambda^+=u\} \cup hsyst(\lambda)$
    $\approx$ $\{t\lambda^+=u\} \cup hsyst((\theta,not\{\}),\lambda)$
    $\approx$ $hsyst((\mu,not\{\}),(\theta,not\{\}),\lambda)$.

Hence, the following equivalences hold

$hsyst((\theta,not\{\}),\lambda) \approx hsyst((\theta,not\{\}),(\mu,not\{\}),\lambda) \approx hsyst((\mu,not\{\}),\lambda)$. ◊

3.2.5 Algorithm

Let us finally present an algorithm to reconcile n-substitutions. In view of Definition 3.68, this amounts to constructing an algorithm for solving systems of equations and inequations. The one we will present takes profit of the algorithm developed in Subsection 3.1.5. It is stated in the more general context of systems of multi-equations and multi-inequations.

3.2.5.1 Basic concepts

Let us first introduce some basic concepts on systems of multi-equations and multi-inequations.

Definition 3.80 A *multi-inequation* is a construction of the form

$$V \neq T$$

where V is a non-empty set of variables and T is a (possibly empty) multi-set of terms.

Notation 3.81 The LHS and RHS of a multi-inequation I are denoted by I_{left} and I_{right}, respectively.

The interpretation placed in multi-inequations is that all variables of V must be equal and must differ from each term of T. With this interpretation in mind, systems of multi-equations and systems of multi-inequations may be proved to provide a generalization of h-systems. This is quite straightforward for eh-systems : it is sufficient to rewrite

- each e-equation X=t as eq({X,T}),
- each inequation X≠t as {X}≠{t}.

This transformation can be generalized to general h-systems but require the introduction of auxiliary variables and auxiliary multi-equations:

- rewrite each equation t=u as eq({V,t,u}) with V a variable appearing nowhere else
- rewrite each inequation t≠u by the multi-equation {V}={t} and by the multi-inequation {V}≠{u}, with V a variable appearing nowhere else.

It will be useful to distinguish the positive and negative information of a system of multi-equations and multi-inequations. This is achieved by generalizing Notation 3.43.

Notation 3.82 Let S be a system of multi-equation and multi-inequations. The notation

$$S^+$$

denotes the set of multi-equations obtained by associating the multi-equation $I_{left} = \emptyset$ with each multi-equation I of S and by adding them to the multi-equations of S. Moreover, the notation

$$S^-$$

denotes the set of inequations obtained by associating the elementary inequations

$X_1 \neq t_1$
...
$X_1 \neq t_n$

with each multi-inequation $\{X_1,...,X_m\} \neq \{t_1,...,t_n\}$ of S.

The choice of X_1 in $\{X_1,...,X_m\}$ may appear to be arbitrary. It is in fact of no concern since the multi-equation $\{X_1,...,X_m\} = \emptyset$ is included in S^+.

Finally, the notions of solution, n-unifier and n-mgu are extended to systems of multi-equations and multi-equations in an obvious way.

Definition 3.83 Let S be a system of multi-equations and multi-inequations.
1) A *solution* of S is a grounding substitution for the variables of S that solves S^+ and that satisfies each inequation of S^-. The set of these solutions is subsequently denoted by Sol(S).
2) An *n-unifier* of S is an n-substitution ν such that $Sol(S) \supset Sol(hsyst(\nu))$.
3) An *n-mgu* of S is a set of n-substitutions $\{\nu_1,...,\nu_m\}$ such that
   $Sol(S) = Sol(hsyst(\nu_1,...,\nu_m))$.

3.2.5.2 Solving systems of multi-equations and multi-inequations

The algorithm for solving systems of multi-equations and multi-inequations is quite intuitive. Let S be such a system. It basically consists of the three following steps :

1) solving the system S^+ (by using, for instance, Algorithm Solve_syst_meq); let $\theta = \{X_1/t_1,...,X_m/t_m\}$ be the produced mgu;
2) replacing the variables X_i by their corresponding values t_i in S^-, let $S^-\theta$ denote the resulting instance of S^-;
3) simplifying $S^-\theta$ so as to obtain elementary inequations.

Failure may be reported at steps 1 or 3. In this case, the system S may be proved unsolvable and $\emptyset_\varepsilon$ is returned as n-mgu.

Step 1 has been discussed in detail in Subsection 3.1.5. Step 2 should be quite clear. Step 3 remains to be explained. It is based on two algorithms of simplification. The first one aims at simplifying an inequation in an equivalent set of e-inequations. The last one performs this operation on a system of inequations.

Algorithm Simplify_ineq(I).

Specification

Let I be an inequation. The algorithm simplify_ineq(I) succeeds iff I is solvable. In this case, it returns a set of sets of e-inequations, say $\{Sineq_1,...,Sineq_m\}$, such that

$Sineq_1 \vee ... \vee Sineq_m \approx \{I\}$.

Code

Case I of
    $X \neq X$: do report failure od;
    $X \neq Y$: do return $\{\{X \neq Y\}\}$ od;
    $X \neq c$ or $c \neq X$: do return $\{\{X \neq c\}\}$ od;
    $X \neq f(t_1,...,t_m)$ or $f(t_1,...,t_m) \neq X$ with X appearing in one t_i : do return $\{\emptyset\}$ od;
    $X \neq f(t_1,...,t_m)$ or $f(t_1,...,t_m) \neq X$ with X appearing in no t_i :
        do return $\{\{X \neq f(t_1,...,t_m)\}\}$ od;
    $c \neq c$: do report failure od;
    $c \neq d$: do return $\{\emptyset\}$ od;
    $c \neq f(t_1,...,t_m)$ or $f(t_1,...,t_m) \neq c$: do return $\{\emptyset\}$ od;
    $f(t_1,...,t_m) \neq g(u_1,...,u_n)$ with $f \neq_s g$ or $m \neq_s n$: do return $\{\emptyset\}$ od;
    $f(t_1,...,t_m) \neq f(u_1,...,u_m)$:
        do
            Parfor Simplify_ineq($t_1 \neq u_1$) || ... || Simplify_ineq($t_m \neq u_m$) parend;
            If all Simplify_ineq($t_i \neq u_i$) fail
            then report failure
            else
                { Let $S_1, ..., S_p$ be the sets of inequations returned by the successful
                Simplify_ineq($t_i \neq u_i$) }
                If one S_i is $\emptyset$
                    then return $\{\emptyset\}$
                    else return $\{S_1,...,S_p\}$
                fi
            fi
        od
    endcase .

Proposition 3.84 The algorithm Simplify_ineq meets its specification.
Proof The proof consists of a simple verification. ◊

Algorithm Simplify_syst(S)

Specification

Let S be a non-empty system of inequations. The algorithm simplify_syst(S) succeeds iff S is solvable. In this case, it returns a set of systems of e-inequations, say $\{Sineq_1,...,Sineq_m\}$, such that

$Sineq_1 \vee ... \vee Sineq_m \approx Sol(S)$.

Code

{ Let $S = \{I_1,...,I_n\}$ }
Fparfor Simplify_syst(I_1) || ... || Simplify_syst(I_n) **fparend**;
If one Simplify_syst(I_j) fails
  then report failure
  else
    { Let Ssineq$_1$, ..., Ssineq$_p$ be the systems of e-inequations returned by the Simplify_syst(I_j) }
    return $\{S_1 \cup ... \cup S_p : S_i \in$ Ssineq$_i$, $1 \leq i \leq p\}$
fi

Proposition 3.85 The algorithm Simplify_ineq meets its specification.
Proof The proposition results from Proposition 3.84. ◊

We are now in a position to describe our algorithm for solving systems of multi-equations and multi-inequations.

Algorithm Solve_syst_meq_mineq(S)

Specification

Let S be a system of multi-equations and multi-inequations. Then the algorithm Solve_syst_meq_mineq returns an n-mgu for S.

Code

Solve_syst_meq(S^+);
If failure occurs
  then return $\emptyset_\varepsilon$
  else
    { Let θ be the idempotent mgu returned by Solve_syst_meq(S^+) }
    Simplify_syst($S^-\theta$);
    If failure occurs
      then return $\emptyset_\varepsilon$
      else
        { Let Sineq$_1$, ..., Sineq$_m$ be the e-systems returned by Simplify_syst($S^-\theta$)
        Let σ_i be the set of bindings associated with Sineq$_i$ by rewriting each inequation $X \neq t$ as X/t ($1 \leq i \leq m$) }
        Return $\{(\theta, \text{not } \sigma_1), ..., (\theta, \text{not } \sigma_m)\}$
    fi
fi

Proposition 3.86 The algorithm Solve_syst_meq_mineq meets its specification.
Proof Let S be the treated system of multi-equations and multi-inequations.

1° Let us first prove that the theorem holds when S is solvable. In this case, the systems S^+ and S^- are solvable as well as any instance $S^-\theta$ of S^-. The call Solve_syst_meq(S^+) then succeeds and produces an idempotent substitution θ (see Proposition 3.40). The call Simplify_syst($S^-\theta$) also succeeds and delivers h-systems, say $Sineq_1, \ldots, Sineq_m$, such that

$$S^-\theta \approx Sineq_1 \vee \ldots \vee Sineq_m.$$

(see Proposition 3.85). Let, for any $i \in \{1,\ldots,m\}$, v_i be the n-substitution $(\{\}, \text{not } \sigma_i)$ with σ_i the set of bindings associated with $Sineq_i$ as above. The following equivalence results from the previous one

$$S^-\theta \approx \text{hsyst}(v_1) \vee \ldots \vee \text{hsyst}(v_m). \qquad (1)$$

The thesis then results from the following equivalences :

$S \quad = S^+ \cup S^-$
    by definition of S^+ and S^-
$\approx \text{syst}(\theta) \cup S^-\theta$
    thanks to the fact that θ is an idempotent mgu of S^+
$\approx [\text{syst}(\theta) \cup \text{hsyst}(v_1)] \vee \ldots \vee [\text{syst}(\theta) \cup \text{hsyst}(v_m)]$
    thanks to equivalence (1)
$\approx \text{hsyst}((\theta,\text{not } \sigma_1)) \vee \ldots \vee \text{hsyst}((\theta,\text{not } \sigma_m))$
    by definition of the systems $\text{hsyst}((\theta,\text{not } \sigma_1)),\ldots,\text{hsyst}((\theta,\text{not } \sigma_m))$.

2° Assume now S is not solvable. Let us prove that the n-mgu $\varnothing_\varepsilon$ is indeed delivered; that is one of the calls

Solve_syst_meq(S^+);
Simplify_syst($S^-\theta$)

fails. Let us proceed by contraposition. If these two calls succeed, then the systems S^+ and $S^-\theta$ are solvable (thanks to Propositions 3.40 and 3.85). Furthermore as θ is an idempotent mgu of S^+, one has

$$\text{syst}(\theta) \approx S^+.$$

In these conditions, the system $\text{syst}(\theta) \cup S^-\theta$ is solvable. Indeed, let α be a solution of $S^-\theta$. Then, as θ is idempotent and no variable of $\text{dom}(\theta)$ occurs in $S^-\theta$, $\theta\alpha\gamma$ is a solution of the system $\text{syst}(\theta) \cup S^-\theta$ for any grounding substitution γ for the variables of $\text{syst}(\theta) \cup S^-\theta$. Hence, the inequality

$$\text{Sol}(\text{syst}(\theta) \cup S^-\theta) \neq \varnothing$$

holds. The following equivalences then establish that S is solvable

$S \quad = S^+ \cup S^-$
    $\approx \text{syst}(\theta) \cup S^-\theta . \quad \Diamond$

3.2.5.3 The n-reconciliation algorithm

The n-reconciliation algorithm is now quite straightforward. Given the n-substitutions v_1, ..., v_m, it simply consists of the call

solve(S)

with S the h-system hsyst(v_1,...,v_m) rewritten as a system of multi-equations and multi-inequations. An unfolding transformation allows to explicit it a little bit. The multi-equations and multi-inequations of S comes from the positive and negative parts of the n-substitutions. Hence,

- solving S^+ amounts to reconciling v_1^+, ..., v_m^+,
- simplifying $S^-\theta$ amounts to simplifying hsyst(v_1^-, ..., v_m^-)θ

The algorithm can thus be rewritten as follows :

Algorithm N_reconciliation(v_1,...,v_m)

Specification

Let v_1,...,v_m be n-substitutions (m>0). The algorithm N_reconciliation(v_1,...,v_m) succeeds iff v_1,...,v_m are n-reconcilable. In this case, it produces an idempotent en-reconciliation.

Code

Reconcile(v_1^+, ..., v_m^+);
<u>If</u> failure occurs
   <u>then</u> report failure
   <u>else</u>
      { Let θ be the idempotent mgu returned by Reconcile(v_1^+, ..., v_m^+)}
      Simplify_syst(hsyst((v_1^-, ..., v_m^-)θ);
      <u>If</u> failure occurs
         <u>then</u> report failure
         <u>else</u>
            { Let Sineq$_1$, ..., Sineq$_m$ be the eh-systems returned by
               Simplify_syst(hsyst((v_1^-, ..., v_m^-)θ)
            Let σ_i be the set of bindings associated with Sineq$_i$ by rewriting each
            inequation X≠t as X/t (1≤i≤m)   }
            Return {(θ,not σ_1), ..., (θ,not σ_m)}
      <u>fi</u>
<u>fi</u>

Proposition 3.87 The algorithm N_reconciliation meets its specification.
Proof The thesis directly results from Proposition 3.86. ◊

Proposition 3.88 The algorithm N_reconciliation applied to the idempotent en-substitutions $(\theta,\omega_1), \ldots, (\theta,\omega_m)$ succeeds and determines an en-mgu $\sigma \oplus \{\mu_1,\ldots,\mu_n\}$ such that σ is a variant of θ.

Proof Success of the algorithm results from Propositions 3.45, 3.54 and 3.87. The form of any en-reconciliation results from the fact that, as it is idempotent, θ is an mgu of the system $syst(\theta)$. ◊

The algorithm for n-reconciling sets of n-substitutions can be directly deduced from this n-reconciliation algorithm. Given the sets of n-substitutions $\Theta=\{\theta_1,\ldots,\theta_m\}$, $\Psi=\{\psi_1,\ldots,\psi_n\}$, ..., $\Omega=\{\omega_1,\ldots,\omega_p\}$, it is sufficient to apply the following algorithm :

Concurrently perform the m×n×...×p n-reconciliation N_reconciliation($\theta_i,\psi_j,\ldots,\omega_k$);
If all of them fail
    then report failure
    else return the union of the n-mgu's produced by the successful n-reconciliations.

This algorithm is not so much interesting for the general n-reconciliation of sets. However, when en-mgu's are involved the algorithm may be simplified in a (globally) more efficient one. The reconciliation of the positive parts is indeed common to the m×n×...×p n-reconciliations. It is thus sufficient to perform it once. Simplification may then be applied in a concurrent manner to the m×n×...×p systems of inequations. The algorithm is thus as follows :

Algorithm Gen_N_reconciliation($\Theta,\Psi,\ldots,\Omega$)

Specification

Let $\Theta, \Psi, \ldots, \Omega$ be en-mgu's. The algorithm Gen_N_reconciliation($\Theta,\Psi,\ldots,\Omega$) succeeds iff $\Theta, \Psi, \ldots, \Omega$ are n-reconcilable. In this case, it produces an en-reconciliation of $\Theta, \Psi, \ldots, \Omega$ composed of idempotent n-substitutions.

Code

{ Let $\Theta = \theta \oplus \{\theta_1^-,\ldots,\theta_m^-\}$,
    $\Psi = \psi \oplus \{\psi_1^-,\ldots,\psi_n^-\}$,
    ...
    $\Omega = \omega \oplus \{\omega_1^-,\ldots,\omega_p^-\}$ }
Reconcile($\theta,\psi,\ldots,\omega$);
If failure occurs
    then report failure
    else
        { Let μ be the idempotent mgu returned by Reconcile($\theta,\psi,\ldots,\omega$) }
        Parfor i=1 to m, j=1 to n, k=1 to p do
            Simplify_syst(hsyst($\theta_i^-,\psi_j^-,\ldots,\omega_k^-$)$\mu$)
        od

>> If all Simplify_syst calls fail
>> then report failure
>> else
>>> { Let Sineq$_1$, ..., Sineq$_m$ be the eh-systems returned by the successful ones
>>> Let σ$_i$ be the set of bindings associated with Sineq$_i$ by rewriting each
>>> inequation X≠t as X/t (1≤i≤m)   }
>>> Return {(μ,not σ$_1$), ..., (μ,not σ$_m$)}
>> fi
> fi

Proposition 3.89 The algorithm Gen_N_reconc meets its specification
Proof The thesis results from Proposition 3.87 and the definition of en-mgu's. ◊

3.3 Application : a parallel unification algorithm through reconciliation

3.3.1 Description

The reconciliation approach suggests a parallel unification algorithm. Given two compound terms, say f(t$_1$,...,t$_n$) and f(u$_1$,...,u$_n$), it seems natural to unify the terms t$_i$, u$_i$, 1≤i≤n, in a concurrent manner and to reconcile the produced mgu's. This is embodied in the following algorithm.

Algorithm Par_Mgu(t,u)

Specification

Let t and u be two terms. The algorithm succeeds iff the terms t and u are unifiable. In this case, it produces an mgu for t and u made from the variables of t and u only.

Code

> If t is a variable
>> then
>>> If u =$_s$ t
>>>> then return { }
>>>> else
>>>>> If u is a compound term containing t
>>>>>> then report failure
>>>>>> else return {t/u}
>>>>> fi
>>>> fi
>>> else

>   **If** u is a variable
>   **then**
>   **If** t is a compound term containing u
>   **then** report failure
>   **else** return {u/t}
>   **fi**
>   **else** {t and u are compound terms say
>   t = f(t_1,...,t_m) (m≥0)
>   u = g(u_1,...,u_n) (n≥0)}
>   **If** f $=_s$ g, m $=_s$ n
>   **then**
>   **If** m = 0
>   **then** return {}
>   **else**
>   **Fparfor** i:=1 **to** m **do** Par_Mgu(t_i,u_i) **od** ;
>   **If** one of the unification fails
>   **then** report failure
>   **else**
>   { Let θ_i be Par_mgu(t_i,u_i) for i∈ {1,...,m} }
>   Reconciliation(θ_1,...,θ_m)
>   **fi**
>   **fi**
>   **else** report failure
>   **fi**
>   **fi**
>   **fi**

The following propositions justify this approach.

Proposition 3.90 Let t_1, ..., t_n and u_1, ..., u_n be terms. Assume each pair t_i, u_i is unifiable with the idempotent mgu θ_i (made of variables of t_i and u_i, only). For any n-ary functor f, the terms f(t_1,...,t_n) and f(u_1,...,u_n) are unifiable iff the system syst(θ_1,...,θ_n) is unifiable. Furthermore, a substitution is an mgu of f(t_1,...,t_n) and f(u_1,...,u_n) iff it is an mgu of the system syst(θ_1,...,θ_n).
Proof The terms f(t_1,...,t_n) and f(u_1,...,u_n) are unifiable iff the system [1]

---

[1] For the sake of clarity, multi-equations are here also noted as if the terms t_i, u_i, $t_i\theta_i$ and $u_i\theta_i$ were not variables. To obtain a rigorous demonstration, it is sufficient to write eq(V_i,t_i,,u_i) and eq(V_i,$t_i\theta_i$,,$u_i\theta_i$) instead of {V_i}={t_i,u_i} and {V_i}={$t_i\theta_i$,$u_i\theta_i$}, respectively (1≤i≤n).

$$\begin{cases} \{V_1\} = \{t_1, u_1\} \\ \ldots \\ \{V_n\} = \{t_n, u_n\} \end{cases}$$

is unifiable, where the V_i's ($i = 1, \ldots, n$) are distinct auxiliary variables that do not appear in $f(t_1,\ldots,t_n)$ and in $f(u_1,\ldots,u_n)$. Thanks to the hypotheses made on the mgu θ_i, this system is equivalent to the system formed of the multi-equations of $\text{syst}(\theta_1), \ldots, \text{syst}(\theta_n)$ and of the multi-equations

$\{V_1\} = \{t_1\theta_1, u_1\theta_1\},$
$\ldots$
$\{V_n\} = \{t_n\theta_n, u_n\theta_n\}$

that is to the system

$$\begin{cases} \{V_1\} = \{t_1\theta_1, u_1\theta_1\} \\ \ldots \\ \{V_n\} = \{t_n\theta_n, u_n\theta_n\} \end{cases}$$

$\cup$

$\text{syst}(\theta_1,\ldots,\theta_n).$

The theorem then results from the fact that, for any i, $t_i\theta_i$ and $u_i\theta_i$ are identical and from the fact that the variables V_i do not appear in $\theta_1,\ldots,\theta_n$. ◊

Proposition 3.91 The algorithm Par_Mgu verifies its specification.
Proof The theorem is proved by a structural induction on t and u. Obviously, if t is a variable, the term t only unifies

- with itself, with idempotent mgu {}
- with terms not containing it, with idempotent mgu {t/u}.

Note that the mgu's are made from the variables of the terms t and u, only. A similar situation occurs in case u is a variable. Otherwise, t and u must be compound terms, possibly of arity 0. In this case, they unify iff they have the same functor, the same arity and, when this arity is strictly positive, if their corresponding subterms unify with the same unifier. Assuming the first two conditions hold, the last one amounts to the fact that the system $\text{syst}(\theta_1,\ldots,\theta_n)$ is unifiable (see Proposition 3.90) that is the substitutions $\theta_1,\ldots,\theta_n$ are reconcilable. The correctness of Par_Mgu then results from Proposition 3.41 and from the fact that the number of functor symbols in t and u strictly decreases at each recursive call to Par_Mgu. ◊

The extension of the algorithm Par_Mgu to a multi-set of terms involves one more parallel step. The case where the multi-set is empty or reduces to an element is obvious. The case where it contains two terms has just been treated. Assume then it is $\{t_1,\ldots,t_n\}$ with n>2. One way to unify the terms t_i in a parallel context is to partition $\{t_1,...,t_n\}$ into two non-empty sets $\{t_1,...,t_k\}$, $\{t_{k+1},...,t_n\}$, to unify them recursively and to reconcile the resulting mgu's. This is embodied in the following algorithm.

Algorithm Gen_par_unif($\{t_1,...,t_n\}$)

Specification

Let $\{t_1,...,t_n\}$ be a multi-set of terms. The algorithm succeeds iff the terms t_i are unifiable. In this case, it delivers an idempotent mgu formed of the variables of $t_1, ..., t_n$ only.

Code

Case n of
    n=1 : do return {} od
    n=2 : do return Par_mgu(t_1,t_2) od
    n>2 :
        do
        partition $\{t_1,...t_n\}$ into two non-empty sets, say $\{t_1,...t_k\}$ and $\{t_{k+1},...t_n\}$
        Fparbegin
            Gen_par_unif($\{t_1,...t_k\}$) || Gen_par_unif($\{t_{k+1},...t_n\}$) || Par_Mgu(t_1,t_n)
        fparend
        If one of the unifications fails
            then report failure
            else
                { Let θ_1 = Gen_par_unif($\{t_1,...t_k\}$)
                Let θ_2 = Gen_par_unif($\{t_{k+1},...t_n\}$)
                Let θ_3 = Par_Mgu(t_1,t_n}) }
                Return the result of Reconciliation($\theta_1,\theta_2,\theta_3$).
        fi
        od
endcase

Proposition 3.92 The algorithm Gen_par_unif verifies its specification.
Proof The proposition is established by induction on the number n of elements of the multi-set parameter.

1) If n=1 : the proposition is obvious .

2) If n=2 : the proposition results from Proposition 3.91.

3) If n>2 : the proposition is established by first noting the following equivalences. For every partition of $\{t_1,...,t_n\}$ into two non-empty sets $\{t_1,...,t_k\}$ and $\{t_{k+1},...,t_n\}$,

iff the terms $t_1, \ldots, t_n$ are unifiable

the terms
$h(h_1(t_1,\ldots,t_k),h_2(t_{k+1},\ldots,t_n),t_1)$ and
$h(h_1(t_1,\ldots,t_1),h_2(t_n,\ldots,t_n),t_n)$

are unifiable, for some 3-ary functor h, k-ary functor h_1 and (n-k)-ary functor h_2
iff, thanks to Proposition 3.90,

every idempotent mgu θ_1 of $t_1,\ldots,t_k$, made of the variables of $t_1,\ldots,t_k$ only, and
every idempotent mgu θ_2 of $t_{k+1},\ldots,t_n$, made of the variables of $t_{k+1},\ldots,t_n$ only, and
every idempotent mgu θ_3 of t_1 and t_n, made of the variables of t_1 and t_n only,
are reconcilable.

The proposition then results from Propositions 3.41, 3.91 and the fact that the number of the set parameter decreases at each recursive call to Gen_par_unif. ◊

It is worth noting that, in the algorithm Triangularisation, computing the mgu θ for the multi-set of terms E_{right} can be done directly by calling the Par_gen_unif algorithm (rather than by computing its frontier and common part). No infinite loop is introduced since

- the number of variables strictly decreases at each call to Par_gen_unif in the algorithm Triangularisation
- the number of terms strictly decreases at each recursive call to Par_gen_unif in the algorithm Par_gen_unif.

3.3.2 Discussion

The performance of the algorithm Gen_unif may greatly be affected by the way its partition operation is achieved. The simplest and probably the best one consists in partitioning the set into two subsets of similar number of elements. Assuming a random distribution of the terms, it ensures a well-balanced execution of the unification of the two subsets. More complicated methods could attempt

- to detect failure as soon as possible,
- to produce mgu's that are easily reconcilable.

This would however imply an analysis of the terms i.e., in some way, tests for unification. The design of the algorithm precisely excludes such an analysis since it attempts to be an alternative method to the computation of the frontier and common part.

Nevertheless, whatever the way partition is achieved, the algorithms Par_Mgu and Gen_par_unif are less efficient than the parallel version of Martelli and Montanari's algorithm. Reasons for this inefficiency are mainly the following :

unified terms	PMM	PM
h(a(X1,X2), b(Y1,Y2,Y3), c(Z1)) h(a(1,1), b(1,2,3), c(1))	24.49	31.40
h(a(1,1), b(1,2,3), c(1)) h(a(X1,X2), b(X1,X2,Y3), c(Y3))	1	1.8
h(a(X,X), b(Y,Y,Y), c(Z)) h(a(X1,X2), b(X1,X2,Y3), c(Y3))	15.21	18.92
h(h1(h2(h3(X4),3)), h1(h2(h3(Y2)),Y2)) h(h1(h2(h3(X4),Y2)), h1(h2(h3(Y2)),Y2))	30.51	48.74
h(X,X) h(h1(X2,X2), h1(1,1))	18.93	23.22
h(h1(h2(h3(X4),Y2)), h1(X4, Y2)) h(h1(h2(h3(X4),3)), h1(h2(h3(Y2)),Y2))	35.49	56.64
h(X,X) h(h1(h2(h3(X4),3)), h1(h2(h3(Y2)),Y2))	25.68	45.039
h(X1, f(g(X3),X4,X3)) h(g(X2), f(X1,h(X1),X2))	59.16	91.16

Table 3.1

- calls to the algorithms Par_Mgu and Gen_par_unif are mutually recursive,
- reconciliation is involved after each partition.

The real situation where a gain could be expected is when no conflicting bindings are made in the parallel unification, for instance when unification restricts to simple pattern-matching. In this case, parallel execution is already obtained in two ways :

- by parallel executions in the computation of the frontier and common part
- by parallel executions of the corresponding multi-equations (that are independent).

Tables 3.1 and 3.2 confirm this analysis by experimental measures. They compare parallel executions of (the parallel version of) Martelli and Montanari's algorithm (PMM), of the Par_mgu algorithm (PM) and the Gen_par_unif algorithm. Two measures are given for the latter : one corresponds to the partitioning leading to the faster execution (FGPM) and the other to the slower one (SGPM). These measures have been obtained by executing Prolog programs coding these algorithms on a VAX 750 under a C-Prolog interpreter. Parallelism has been simulated by taking the minimum of the execution time of its concurrent subexecutions as the execution time of a parallel statement . Related measures are in fact given. They can then be considered as independent from the VAX computer and the C-Prolog interpreter.

unified terms	PMM	FGPM	SGPM
h(a(X1,X2), b(Y1,Y2,Y3), c(Z1)) h(a(1,1), b(1,1,1), c(1)) h(a(X1,X2), b(X1,X2,Y3), c(Y3)) h(a(X,X), b(Y,Y,Y), c(Z))	1	1.54	3.18
h(h1(h2(h3(X4),3)), h1(h2(h3(Y2)),Y2)) h(h1(h2(h3(X4),Y2)), h1(h2(h3(Y2)),Y2)) h(h1(h2(h3(X4),3)),Y) h(X,h1(h2(h3(Y2)),Y2))	2.87	4.73	11.25

Table 3.2

3.4 Comparison with related work

Notions similar to the reconciliation of substitutions or n-substitutions can be found in three other trends of work. The concept of reconciliation of substitutions has first appeared in [Pollard, 1981]. It has then been extended to study negation in [Khabaza, 1984]. Finally, it is used in [Palamidessi, 1988], [de Boer et al., 1989a], [de Boer et al., 1989b] to design semantics of Guarded Horn Clauses and Parlog, and, recently, in [Palamidessi, 1990] to formulate algebraic properties of idempotent substitutions.

All these versions are compared to the Conclog one in this section. This is achieved in two steps. First, the work of [Pollard, 1981], [Palamidessi, 1988], [de Boer et al., 1989a], [de Boer et al., 1989b], [Palamidessi, 1990] are discussed. They only deal with substitutions. The work of [Khabaza, 1984], including negative information, is then tackled.

3.4.1 Reconciling substitutions

3.4.1.1 Reconciliation of bindings through P-substitutions

A. Description

Pollard reexamines the notion of substitution in order to reconcile them. According to him, the concept of substitution is meaningful only through its application to an arbitrary expression. Hence, the conventional definition of a substitution (see Definition 2.22) which stipulates that there can be no more than one component in the substitution for any given variable is too restrictive. The necessary restriction is that if more than one component for any variable exists in the substitution then, by applying its bindings as many times as possible to an arbitrary expression, the selection order of the components is immaterial : the same instance of the expression must always be computed. Such a set of bindings is subsequently referred to as *P-substitution*. For example, {X/1,X/U,U/1} is a P-substitution whereas {X/a,X/b} is not.

The concept of reconciliation is defined in this framework as follows. Let P_1, ..., P_m be P-substitutions.

- They are reconcilable iff the set of their bindings can be extended to a P-substitution, say P.
- Reconciling P_1, ..., P_m consists in determining an equivalent P-substitution σ that contains only one binding per variable, that is a substitution (in the conventional sense). By equivalent, it is understood that, for any term t, the above application of P to t leads to the term tσ.

Of course, the test for reconciliation of P_1, ..., P_m results from the attempt to construct σ. This is achieved as follows. If every variable of P appears no more than once in the left position of a binding then P is both a P-substitution and the substitution σ. Alternatively, if a variable, say X, appears in the left position of two bindings, say in X/t_1 and X/t_2, and if it is possible to unify t_1 and t_2, say by means of the unifier θ, then it is immaterial which of the two bindings is chosen when P ∪ θ is applied to some expression involving X. The process is then applied to the set of bindings composed of θ, $\{X/t_1\theta\}$ and P cut off the bindings X/t_1 and X/t_2. Manifestly, an equivalent substitution θ is produced when the process converges. It is worth noting that it does so iff the P-substitutions are reconcilable (in Pollard sense).

B. Comparison

Although correct at first sight, this reconciliation process is not fully satisfactory. Consider, for instance, the equality h(X,Y) = h(f(Y),f(X)) or, to obtain a conjunction, the equalities X = f(Y), Y = f(X). The independent reductions of these subgoals deliver the substitution {X/f(Y)} and {Y/f(X)}. According to Pollard, they reconcile since there is only one binding for X and Y though the terms h(X,Y) and h(f(Y),f(X)) cannot be unified.

In fact, the bindings manipulated are not only substitutions but also unifiers. Hence, it is not sufficient to obtain the same instance whatever bindings are chosen but the occur check problem has also to be considered in some way. This character is not taken into account in [Pollard, 1981]. What is done is, in reality, very similar to the resolution of algebraic equations by the substitution method. To be more specific, let us consider the P-substitutions {X/1} and {X/U,U/1}. To be a P-substitution, their union {X/1,X/U,U/1} must deliver, for any expression, the same instance, whatever binding for X is chosen. For this purpose, the verification on the expression X is sufficient. We obtain, on the one hand, 1 (thanks to X/1) and, on the other hand, U (thanks to X/U) and then 1 (thanks to U/1). This, in fact, amounts to simplifying {X/1,X/U,U/1} in one real substitution. Replacing X/U by its value U/1, we obtain {X/1,X/1,U/1} that is {X/1,U/1}. Stated in equational terms, what we do is to write the following system

$$\begin{cases} X = 1 \\ X = U \\ U = 1 \end{cases}$$

and to reduce it into

$$\begin{cases} X = 1 \\ U = 1 \end{cases}$$

However, this is possible because the manipulated system is triangularized! It is worth noting that this condition is not always satisfied!

Guided by this idea of solving equations by substitutions, we adopted an equational point of view and found the merits of idempotent substitutions and of Martelli and Montanari's unification algorithm. Our originality is to adopt it here not in the context of term unification but in the context of substitution unification. Furthermore, as we are particularly interested in parallel executions, we gave a parallel version, too. We were then able to prove the validity of our approach, which is not done in [Pollard, 1981].

3.4.1.2 Parallel composition of substitutions

Concurrently and independently to our research, a recent work on semantics of GHC and Parlog ([Palamidessi, 1988], [de Boer et al., 1989a], [de Boer et al., 1989b]) and on algebraic properties of idempotent substitutions ([Palamidessi, 1990]) has introduced a concept equivalent to our reconciliation of substitutions under the name parallel composition of substitutions. It also refers to an equational interpretation of substitutions. Most of the properties proved in this chapter as well as the extension to n-substitutions are however peculiar to our work.

3.4.2 Reconciling n-substitutions

A. Description

The idea of coupling negative information with bindings has been used in [Khabaza, 1984], too. The philosophy behind this introduction of negative information is however different from ours. It is not motivated by the desire of describing systems of equations and inequations in a finite structure but rather by the following intuitive idea : if the set of bindings Sbind represents the conditions under which the s-goal G is solvable, then (not Sbind) represents the conditions under which not(G) is solvable. This leads Khabaza to introduce constructs of the form

$\sim \{X_1/t_1,...,X_m/t_m\}$.

They are called *negative unifiers*. Their interpretation is as follows :

(not X_1/t_1) or ... or (not X_m/t_m).

They are generally coupled with other unnegated bindings as well as other negative unifiers. This gives rise to constructs of the form

$\{ P, \sim N_1, ..., \sim N_p \}$ ($p \geq 0$)

All unegated bindings have been grouped in P. It is called *positive unifier*. The whole structure is called *complex solution*.

A reconciliation-based approach is also adopted in [Khabaza, 1984] so that complex solutions have to be reconciled. This is achieved by assuming the existence of some means of reconciling sets of bindings. Reconciliation of complex solutions is then defined as follows. Let

$C = \{ P, \sim M_1, ..., \sim M_p \}$ and $D = \{ Q, \sim N_1, ..., \sim N_q \}$

be two complex solutions. They reconcile iff

1) the positive unifiers P and Q reconcile; let P* be the reconciliation produced by the assumed means of reconciliation
2) any of the M_i's and N_j's, say N, verifies the following property :
   if N binds any variable that P* binds and if N reconcile with P*, then new bindings are produced by the reconciliation.

In case C and D are reconcilable, the reconciliation of C and D is defined as

$$P^* \cup N^*$$

where N* is $\{\sim M_1, ..., \sim M_p, \sim N_1, ..., \sim N_q\}$ where negative unifiers, say ~N, such that P* and N does not reconcile are removed.

B. Comparison

Complex solutions and n-substitutions may be closely connected. Any complex solution, say

$$\{ P, \sim\{X_1/t_1,...,X_m/t_m\}, \sim\{Y_1/u_1,...,Y_n/u_n\}, ..., \sim\{Z_1/v_1,...,Z_p/v_p\} \},$$

can be code into m×n×...×k n-substitutions, namely

$(P, \text{not}\{X_i/t_i, Y_j/u_j, ..., Z_k/v_k\})$ with $i \in \{1,...,m\}$, $j \in \{1,...,n\}$, ..., $k \in \{1,...,p\}$.

Conversely, any n-substitution, say $(\theta, \text{not}\{X_1/t_1,...,X_m/t_m\})$, may be coded in one complex solution, namely

$(\theta, \sim\{X_1/t_1\}, ..., \sim\{X_m/t_m\})$.

Complex solutions and n-substitutions may thus be viewed as two different ways of handling negative information. Their respective merits will be discussed in Chapter 5 when their use will be completely defined. Their similarity makes however the comparison of the reconciliation processes pertinent here. The same scheme is in fact employed :

- positive information are first reconciled,
- the result (when any) is then coupled with negative information and tested for compatibility.

The version presented in [Khabaza, 1984] is however not fully satisfactory. Test for compatibility, explicited in point 2 of the above definition, is too weak. Consider, for instance, the complex solutions

$C = \{ \{X/1, Y/2\} \}$
$D = \{ \{\}, \sim\{X/1\} \}$.

They are reconcilable in Khabaza's sense although the formula

$(X=1 \wedge Y=2) \vee (X \neq 1)$

does not hold. To highlight the problem, let us reeaxmine the definition proposed above. The example particularizes the parameters P, Q, p, q, M_i's and N_j's as follows : P={X/1,Y/2}, p=0, Q={}, q=1, N_1={X/1}. The verification of the definition is thus the following : C and D are reconcilable iff

1) P and Q are reconcilable. This is indeed the case; the substitution {X/1,Y/2} can be moreover considered as the result P* of the reconciliation.
2) the only negated unifier N_1 verifies the following condition :
    if N_1 (i.e. {X/1}) binds any variable that P* (i.e. {X/1,Y/2}) binds and if N_1 reconciles with P*, then new bindings are produced by the reconciliation.
    This condition manifestly holds since N_1 does not bind any variable bound by P*.

Point 2 should have however detected that N_1 is not compatible with P*. One remedy could be to strengthen 2) and replace the condition "N binds any variable that P* binds" by the stronger one that dom(P*)∩dom(N)≠∅. This does not work either, as illustrated by the complex solutions

C = { {X/Y} }
D = { {}, ~{Y/X} }.

The real solution is to interpret bindings as equalities and handle systems of equations and inequations. The merits of this approach has already been argued in Subsection 3.4.1.1. Among others, reconciliation then amounts to the (clear and unintricate) resolution of such systems.

The reconciliation algorithm of [Khabaza, 1984] lacks from another point : no simplification of the M_i's and N_j's in N* is performed. This has two major drawbacks :

1° complex solutions resulting from reconciliation are cluttered with useless negated bindings (X/1 is an example of such a binding in the complex solution {{X/1},~{X/1,Y/2}});
2° as a result, further reconciliation are made more expensive.

It should finally be noted that the efficiency of the reconciliation due to the synthetic feature of complex solutions[1] is reached in the Conclog model by means of en-mgu's.

3.5 Conclusion

This chapter has introduced the basic concepts of reconciliation of substitutions and n-reconciliation of n-substitutions. It is composed of three major parts.

---

[1] Complex solutions are more synthetic than n-mgus explicited as sets of n-substitutions (see for instance the above rewriting of complex solutions).

In a first part, the reconciliation of substitutions has been studied. It rests on an equational interpretation of substitutions and is defined in terms of the resolution of systems of equations. Some theory of the reconciliation of substitutions has been elaborated. In particular, the relationship between the unification of substitutions and the reconciliation of substitutions has been established in the context of idempotent substitutions. One interesting consequence is that the definition given in equational terms is proved to meet one interpretation of reconciliation : finding the most general common instance of the substitutions. Algorithmic issues have also been addressed. Precisely, it has been shown how the algorithm of [Martelli and Montanari, 1982], initially developed for the unification of terms, can be exploited for reconciliation purposes. Finally, the merits of the equational approach have been argued through the comparison with other reconciliation schemes.

In a second part, the above theory of reconciliation has been extended to a generalization of substitutions, called n-substitutions. This generalization issues from the introduction of negation by negating equations, thus producing inequations. Negative information must then be introduced in substitutions in order to provide a finite representation of the solutions of systems of equations and inequations. This leads to the concept of n-substitution. The interpretation of the n-substitutions is thus equational, too. Also, the reconciliation of n-substitutions, called n-reconciliation, is defined in terms of the resolution of systems of equations and inequations. Composition of substitutions and idempotence of substitutions have been extended to the n-substitutions. Properties established for the reconciliation of substitutions could then be extended to the n-reconciliation of n-substitutions. Finally, an algorithm of n-reconciliation has been constructed.

In the third part, parallel unification algorithms, based on reconciliation, have been developed as an application. Their performance has also been compared with that of the algorithm of [Martelli and Montanari, 1982].

This reconciliation calculus will be used as an auxiliary calculus in the design of Conclog. First, reconciliation of substitutions will be integrated in a more general reconciliation process, developed for our parallel execution model of Horn clauses. Later, n-reconciliation of n-substitutions will be employed to incorporate negation. How this is achieved is precised in the two following chapters.

Chapter 4

A basic scheme for concurrent logic programming

4.1 Introduction

The first step of the design of Conclog is to construct a parallel execution model for Horn clauses. Just pure Horn clauses, free from extra-logical features/primitives and negation, are thus considered here.

4.1.1 Intuition

As announced, the major operational features of the model are :
- the use of or-parallelism and full and-parallelism
- the use of a reconciliation calculus (developed in the previous chapter) to handle conflicting bindings.

One rough approximation is as follows :
- make the and/or search tree (for the computed query and the considered program) grow until its completion, by using and-parallelism and or-parallelism to develop concurrently subtrees issued from sibling nodes;
- extract thereafter solutions for the query by using the reconciliation calculus of Chapter 3.

This model is however unacceptable, essentially for two reasons.
- Firstly, solutions will then be produced altogether when all of them have been found.
- Secondly, in case the and/or search tree is infinite, no solution will be delivered although some might be discovered. This might be even worse if infinite branches do not contribute to any solution.

One could however expect that parallel executions deliver solutions gradually as they arise, even in the presence of infinite branches.

Some improvements are thus needed. They are achieved in Conclog essentially in two ways :

1° Generation and reconciliation are performed concurrently. As a result, solutions may be produced while others are still under execution or while infinite branches are generated.

2° The and/or search tree is conceptually constructed slice by slice and purged after each generation of a slice. As a result,
- the and/or search tree is pruned from useless branches in a earlier way (that is as soon as they are detected as such by reconciliation),
- bindings are communicated from some subtrees to other subtrees.

The precise definition of the Conclog model is progressively revealed in Section 4.3. It is introduced in this section with the aim of providing an intuitive support for subsequent developments. An overview is thus just presented here.

4.1.2 Overview

The Conclog model of execution can be explained at two levels :

- at a more conceptual level in terms of and/or search trees,
- at a more executable level in terms of processes.

The resulting views of the computations are complementary. The first one gives a more global perception. It is more abstract but also less detailed. In contrast, the second one provides a more local perception. It is more specific and more complete. In particular, it allows a detailed explanation of the various sources of parallelism. Both of these views will be used in the following.

4.1.2.1 The tree view

The tree perception of the Conclog model has already been suggested in the previous subsection. Conceptually, the computation consists of a sequence of cycles. Each one is composed of a generation phase followed by a reconciliation phase.

A The generation phase

The aim of the generation phase is to extend the already constructed part of the and/or search tree of one slice. This corresponds to reducing goals in all possible ways but up to a given R-depth.

Precisely, some R-depth, say D, is given as a parameter of the model. Each generation phase is started with a non-empty set of goal-nodes as input. The effect of its execution is to construct the first slice of R-depth D of the and/or search tree for the input goal-nodes. Each top node of a slice is thus a goal-node. Each tip node is either a s-goal-node marked by ⊗ or a goal-node.

The first generation phase particularizes this scheme by taking the singleton composed of the query-node as input set. Subsequent generation phases particularize it as follows. Assume the ith generation phase is under consideration (i>1). Then, its input set of nodes is composed of the tip-nodes of the part of the and/or search tree resulting from the $(i-1)^{th}$ cycle.

B. The reconciliation phase

The aim of the reconciliation phase is twofold :

R_1. to produce discovered solutions,
R_2. to prevent the execution from useless computations of trees by
- cutting off branches that are detected to participate in no solution subtree,
- communicating bindings from one subtree to others.

The last operation is subsequently called *binding publication* since it essentially consists of making public, inside the and/or search tree, the bindings produced in some of its subtrees.

The input of each reconciliation phase is the tree resulting from the previous generation phase. Its output is twofold. Let T denote the input tree and T^* denote T cut off its last slice of R-depth D. The outputs are

- solutions contained in solution subtrees of T that are not solution subtrees of T^*;
- the subtree T modified as follows :
    * nodes of T that are in no candidate solution of T are removed,
    * for any variable V registered in one Vc set of T, if the binding V/t is common to all the reconciliations of the candidate-solution subtrees of T, then the goal or s-goal of each node of T is instantiated by V/t.

C. The computation

Summing up, the and/or search tree is progressively constructed and modified by the generation and reconciliation phases. The R-depth of the generated slices is taken as a parameter of the model. The term *approximation* will be used to denote the successive trees constructed after the generation phases.

4.1.2.2 The process view

The real computation is far more dynamic. It is subsequently expressed in terms of the behavior of processes of a so-called and/or process model.

Those processes are organized into a hierarchy reflecting the and/or search tree. Precisely, a one-to-one correspondence is established between the nodes of the and/or search tree and the processes of the and/or process model. Each node is associated with exactly one process and vice-versa.

There are thus three kinds of processes, corresponding to the three kinds of nodes introduced in Chapter 2 : the query-process, the goal-processes and the s-goal-processes. The task attached to them is quite clear : to solve the corresponding query, goals and s-goals, respectively.

Another distinction of processes will be useful. It refers to the tip nodes of the approximation under consideration. According as they correspond to them or not, the processes are qualified of tip-processes or non-tip processes. Precisely, given one approximation, tip-processes may be of three kinds :

1) s-goal-processes associated with a s-goal that unifies with no clauses of the considered program;
2) goal-processes associated with a □-node;
3) goal-processes
   - associated with a non-empty conjunction of atoms,
   - corresponding to the tip nodes of the approximation under consideration.

Note that the first two kinds of tip-processes do not depend of one approximation. In contrast, processes of the last kind vary from one approximation to another. As approximations will be successively considered in the computation, the notion of tip-processes is thus made temporal. Processes mentioned in 3) will be considered as tip-processes at some moment and as non-tip-processes later on. Some stability is however ensured : processes of types 1) and 2) are permanent tip-processes.

A final point of terminology will be useful. Thanks to the one-to-one correspondence of the and/or search tree and the process model, notions defined for nodes are subsequently extended to the processes. We will thus, for instance, subsequently speak of the goal associated with a goal-process to denote the goal associated with the goal-node associated with the goal-process.

This terminology precised, let us turn back to the computation. Processes behave so as to achieve (in some way to be precised) the conceptual characterization given in Section 4.1.2.1. In general, the life of a process is organized as follows :

S_1. it creates its children and launches them as parallel processes,
S_2. it waits for them to report solutions,
S_3. it combines these solutions to form solutions for the associated s-goal or goal,
S_4. it sends the latter solutions to its father
S_5. it performs some operations on the descendant processes to achieve operation R_2 above.

Two kinds of processes make however exceptions :

- 1° the query-process has no father and thus does not send any solutions. Rather, these solutions are delivered as results of the computation;
- 2° tip processes of the current approximation have no child (in the considered approximation) and so do not create them nor wait for solutions. Rather, they directly send some solutions (to be determined).

The following terminology will be used to qualify operations S_1, S_3, S_4 and S_5. It is chosen to make an analogy with the generation and reconciliation phases. The procedure employed to perform S_1 is subsequently called the *generation procedure*. That employed to perform S_3, S_4 and S_5 is called the *reconciliation procedure*. It is also said that a process *enters generation or reconciliation* as a synonym to designate the fact that the generation or the reconciliation procedure of this process is activated, respectively.

A. The generation procedure

The generation procedure of a process is activated only if it is a non-tip process. The response differs from goal-processes to s-goal-processes.

(i) Non-tip goal-processes

With respect to non-tip goal processes, the generation procedure consists of the following operations

- create a s-goal-process for each s-goal of their associated conjunction;
- activate the generation procedure for each of them,
- launch these s-goal-processes as parallel processes.

(ii) Non-tip s-goal-processes

With respect to non-tip s-goal-processes, the generation procedure consists of the following operations :

- search all the clauses unifiable with their associated s-goal;
- for each of them, create a goal-process and activate its reconciliation or the generation procedure according as it is a tip-process or not;
- launch all these goal-processes as parallel processes.

B. The reconciliation procedure

The reconciliation procedure is slightly more complicated. Two cases must be considered according to the nature of the considered process.

(i) Tip-processes

The reconciliation procedure of a tip-process is activated just after its creation. Three cases must be considered.

(i.1) S-goal-processes whose associated s-goal unifies with no clause

Manifestly, the s-goal associated with such a process fails. Failure must thus be reported. This is translated in terms of the process behavior by the sending of the empty set of solutions to its father process. The s-goal process is then useless and commits suicide.

(i.2) Goal-processes associated with an empty conjunction of atoms

Such a process corresponds to the end of a successful reduction. Success must thus be reported. Intuitively, the associated mgu must be sent as a solution. Its clause subset is however of no interest. The singleton composed of its atom subset is therefore only sent.

(i.3) Goal-processes associated with a non-empty conjunction of atoms and that correspond to the tip nodes of the approximation under consideration

Such a process does not correspond to failure or success. The only thing to be said is that any of its solutions is some instance of the associated mas. The singleton composed of this mas is therefore sent to its father process.

An auxiliary piece of information is added to the sent substitutions. It consists of

- the set of tip processes associated with the substitution (here the goal-process),
- a label of value "completed" or "incompleted" according as all the tip nodes of the corresponding subtree are □-nodes. It is "completed" for case (i.2) and "incompleted" for case (i.3).

This information will be employed in further treatments. A first use is to distinguish solutions resulting from cases (i.2) (the label is "completed") and (i.3) (the label is "incompleted"). Such triplet composed of a substitution, a set of process identifiers and a label is subsequently referred to by *R-triplet*.

(ii) Non-tip processes

The reconciliation procedure of non-tip processes is activated each time a R-triplet is received. As processes behave in an unsynchronized way, the triplets are received incrementally by non tip processes. The reconciliation procedure also acts in an incremental way so that solutions are sent in an incremental way too. Special end delimitors are sent to indicate that all solutions to be sent have indeed been sent.

Three kinds of processes must be considered here.

(ii.1) Non-tip s-goal-processes

The reconciliation procedure is performed in a very simple way at a s-goal-process. Substitutions issued from its children constitute as many solutions to the associated goal. Computationally, such substitutions are simply incrementally communicated to the goal-process father. Hence, the R-triplets are simply passed.

(ii.2) Non-tip goal-processes

The reconciliation procedure is performed in a more elaborate way for a goal-process. Let P be such a process and let m denote the number of children of P. Furthermore, let F be the process father of P. Intuitively speaking, the substitutions issued from the children of P must be and-conjoined and composed with the mgu associated with P, say θ. Restated in more precise terms, this means that a solution for the goal associated with P is the result of the reconciliation of substitutions $\sigma_1, ..., \sigma_m$, each σ_i being reported by one child. Consequently, no solution is reported by P in the following two cases :
- one of the child of P sends no solution; this situation corresponds to the failure of one goal implied by the failure of one of its s-goals;
- each child sends some solutions but no tuple of reconcilable substitutions can be formed from them; this situation corresponds to the case where s-goals of a goal are solvable but by means of incompatible bindings.

Restated in process terms, the following operations are undertaken at the receipt of each R-triplet. Assume the received R-triplet is R=<σ,Procs,Label> and suppose it has been sent by the child C^* of P. The following tuples are first formed. They are obtained by associating σ with, for each child C of P different from C^*, one substitution of one R-triplet sent by C. For each such tuple, say <$\sigma_1,...,\sigma_m$>, the substitutions $\sigma_1, ..., \sigma_m$ are tested for reconciliation. If they are not reconcilable then nothing results from this tuple. Otherwise, the following substitution is sent to F. It may intuitively be suggested as follows. It is certainly formed from $\rho(\sigma_1,...,\sigma_m)$. Composition with θ must also be performed since, for F, any solution arising from P must combine the result of the unification leading to the goal associated with P, namely θ, with one solution of this goal. Finally, bindings for the variables that are introduced in the computation at the creation of P or of one of its descendants (that is those registered in one Vc set of these processes) are useless for F and other ancestors of P because they are not referred to by them. These bindings for them may thus be removed. Summing up, the substitution

$$[\theta \circ \rho(\sigma_1,...,\sigma_m)]_{|Vars \setminus Var\_vc}$$

is sent; the notation Var_vc is used to denote the union of the Vc sets referred to above. The auxiliary information attached to it is quite easy to determine :
- the set of processes component is composed of the processes associated with the substitutions σ_i;

- the label component takes the value "completed" or "incompleted" according as all the labels associated with the σ_i's are "completed" or not.

The following operations are finally performed when all children have completely sent their R-triplets. They achieve the operation R_2 at the process level. Let Srtriplets be the set of R-triplets sent by P and Ssubsts be the set of the substitutions $\theta \circ \rho(\sigma_1,...,\sigma_m)$ from which the substitutions of the R-triplets of Srtriplets are issued.
- Processes that are referred to in no R-triplet sent by P are ordered to kill themselves. This killing is furthermore backward communicated so that processes kill themselves when all children are killed. All these killed processes are subsequently proved to participate to no solution.
- Processes of the subtree attached to P, including P itself, say ST, are modified as follows:
    for any variable V of Var_vc, if the binding V/t is common to all substitutions of Ssubsts then, for any process Proc of ST, the goal or the s-goal associated with Proc is bound by V/t (or, in processes terms, such process are ordered by P to perform such operation).

(ii.3) The query-process

The reconciliation procedure of the query-process is essentially performed in the same way. The following differences are made. They result from the particular role of the query-process. Let Q denote the query-process.
- No mgu is associated with Q so that the above composition $\theta \circ \rho(\sigma_1,...,\sigma_m)$ is to be reduced to $\rho(\sigma_1,...,\sigma_m)$. No simplification is furthermore made : bindings for the variables occurring in the query are precisely those expected from the computation.
- No substitution is transmitted to some process. Rather the restriction to the variables of the query of those corresponding to completely constructed subtrees are delivered as the results of the computation.
- Finally, a new cycle may be launched when all R-triplets from the children of Q have reported all their solutions. This is performed iff the two following conditions are verified:
    * there exist tip-processes of the form (i.3) above,
    * at least one reconciliation $\rho(\sigma_1,...,\sigma_m)$ succeed.

In this case, the generation procedure of the tip-processes of form (i.3) is activated. Otherwise, the computation is simply halted. Failure results from the computation if no substitution has been produced.

4.1.2.3 Relating the tree and process views

Summing up, the Conclog execution model has been described thanks to two views. The former, the tree view, has presented it in terms of the generation and modification of trees. It has provided a global perception of the computations. The latter, the process view, has presented the dual perception in terms of processes. Up to now, just one aspect of the relationship of these views has been exploited : the tree view has been employed to introduce the more specific process view. We now highlight the tree view back thanks to the process view. As a result, the description of the generation and reconciliation phases made in Section 4.1.2.1 is completed by some features arising from the behavior of the processes. The alternance between the two phases is then reexamined.

A. The generation phase

The two following characteristics of the generation phase should be stressed.

1) As processes generate their children as soon as they are created, the generation phase consists of a forward creation of a slice of the and/or search tree with a forward creation of substitutions.
2) Parallelism is achieved in two ways :
   - Full and-parallelism results from the simultaneous generation of children of the query-process and the goal-processes.
   - Or-parallelism is obtained thanks to the simultaneous generation of the children of goal-processes.

B. The reconciliation phase

The two same points can be stressed too.

1) The reconciliation procedures of the processes are activated in a backward way from the tip-processes to the (root) query-process. Substitutions are also propagated in this way. With respect to this point, the reconciliation phase thus takes a dual approach to the generation phase.
2) Parallelism is achieved during the reconciliation phase in two ways, too.
   - The reconciliation procedure of each process is operated incrementally.
   - The reconciliation procedures of distinct processes may be performed in a quasi-independent way. The only synchronizing point is that, to perform its reconciliation procedure, any process must wait that its children have sent some R-triplets. Precisely,
      - s-goal-processes must wait until at least one child process has (partially) sent a R-triplet;
      - goal-processes and the query-process must wait either

- until one child has reported failure to report failure
- or until all of their children have sent one substitution to perform reconciliation.

C. Alternating the generation and reconciliation procedures

The generation and reconciliation procedure have been presented as alternating in Subsection 4.1.2.1. This is in fact not exactly the case. A new source of parallelism can now be pointed out. The reconciliation procedure of any tip-process (of the considered slice) is activated as soon as it is created. This is furthermore performed with complete discard for other non-ancestor processes. In particular, at this time, other non-ancestor processes may be creating their children. This fact combined with the two sources of parallelism of the reconciliation phase and the parallel behavior of processes ensure that some substitutions may be output from the computation whereas others are still under computation.

The strict interleaving of the generation and reconciliation phases is thus, in fact, relaxed. The only remaining synchronization constraint is that a new cycle can only start at the end of the reconciliation phase of the previous cycle. This is however quite natural since one interest of this reconciliation phase is to prevent the generation phase of the next cycle from generating useless branches.

4.1.3 Example

Let us illustrate the computation on a simple example. Consider the query

$\leftarrow$ p(X).

and the program

   (1)   p([1]) $\leftarrow$ q(Y), r(Y,Z).
   (2)   p([Y,Z]) $\leftarrow$ s(Y,Z), t(Y).
   (3)   q(X) $\leftarrow$ q(X).
   (4)   s(3,X) $\leftarrow$ u(X).
   (5)   s(X,Y) $\leftarrow$ v(X), w(Y).
   (6)   t(2).
   (7)   u(3).
   (8)   v(2).
   (9)   v(3).
   (10) v(4).
   (11) w(4).

Assume the R-depth parameter of the model has been fixed to 2.

The computation is described hereafter. It is drawn in Figures 4.1, 4.2, 4.3 and 4.4 . We suggest the reader refers to them while reading the following description. Numbers between brackets are used to refer to the nodes. Thanks to the one-to-one correspondence of processes and nodes, the following misuse is furthermore used : we will subsequently speak of the process (i) rather than the process associated with the node referred to by (i).

A. First cycle

A.1 First generation phase

The computation begins by executing the first generation phase. It consists of generating the nodes of Figure 4.1 in the forward manner explained above. Specifically, assuming unlimited resources and reduction steps of constant time whatever atoms and clause are involved, nodes or their associated processes are created by layers as follows.

1) First layer

The first generation is started with the query-process (1) associated with the query ←p(X) as conjunction of atoms.

2) Second layer

The s-goal-process (2) is created as soon as process (1) is launched. It is associated with the s-goal p(X).

3) Third layer

Children of the process (2) are then created. Clauses that unify with p(X) are first searched. There are two : the clauses (1) and (2) with idempotent mgu's $\{X/[1]\}$, $\{X/[Y_2,Z_2]\}$, respectively. They introduce the renamings Y_1, Z_1 and Y_2, Z_2, respectively. Two goal-processes are thus created. The first one - process (3) - is associated with the conjunction ←$q(Y_1)$, $r(Y_1,Z_1)$. Its corresponding Mas and Vc sets are $\{X/[1]\}$ and $\{Y_1,Z_1\}$, respectively. The other one - process (4) - is associated with the conjunction ←$s(Y_2,Z_2)$, $t(Y_2)$. Its corresponding Mas and Vc sets are $\{X/[Y_2,Z_2]\}$ and $\{Y_2,Z_2\}$, respectively. Processes (3) and (4) are launched as truly parallel processes.

4) The fourth layer

Children for these goal-processes are created as soon as the processes are launched. They consist of four s-goal-processes associated with the s-goals $q(Y_1)$, $r(Y_1,Z_1)$, $s(Y_2,Z_2)$, $t(Y_2)$, respectively. All these four processes are also parallel processes.

BASIC SCHEME

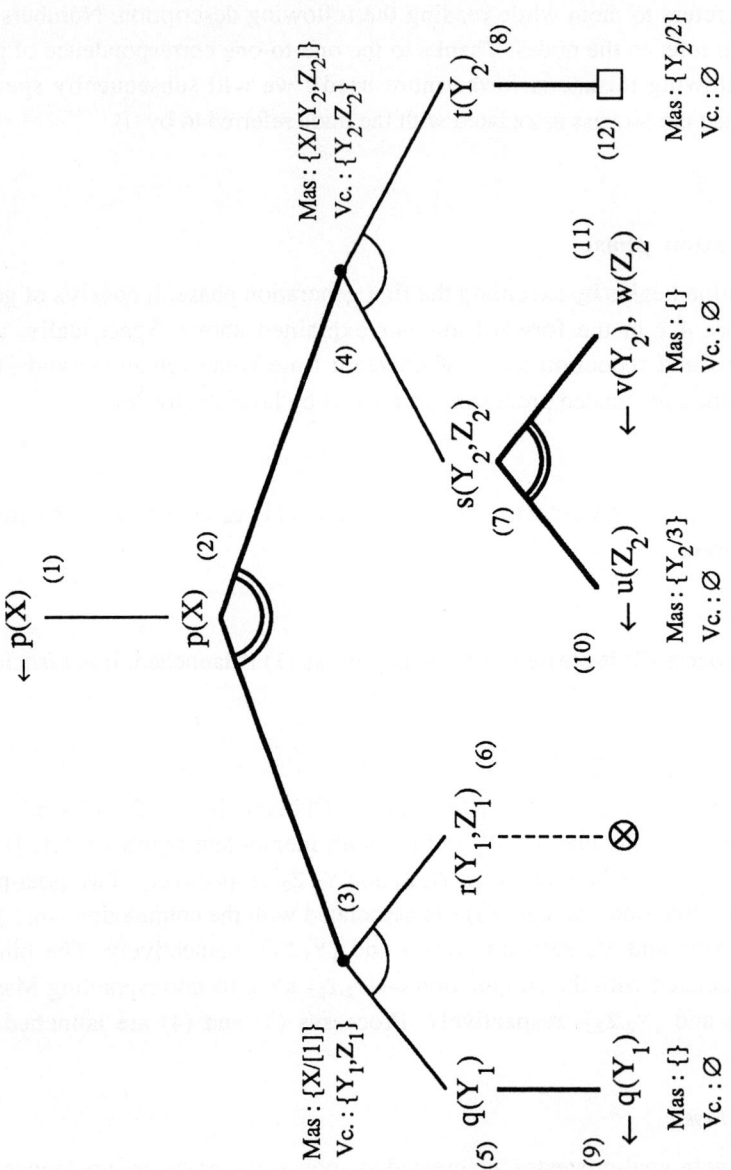

Figure 4.1

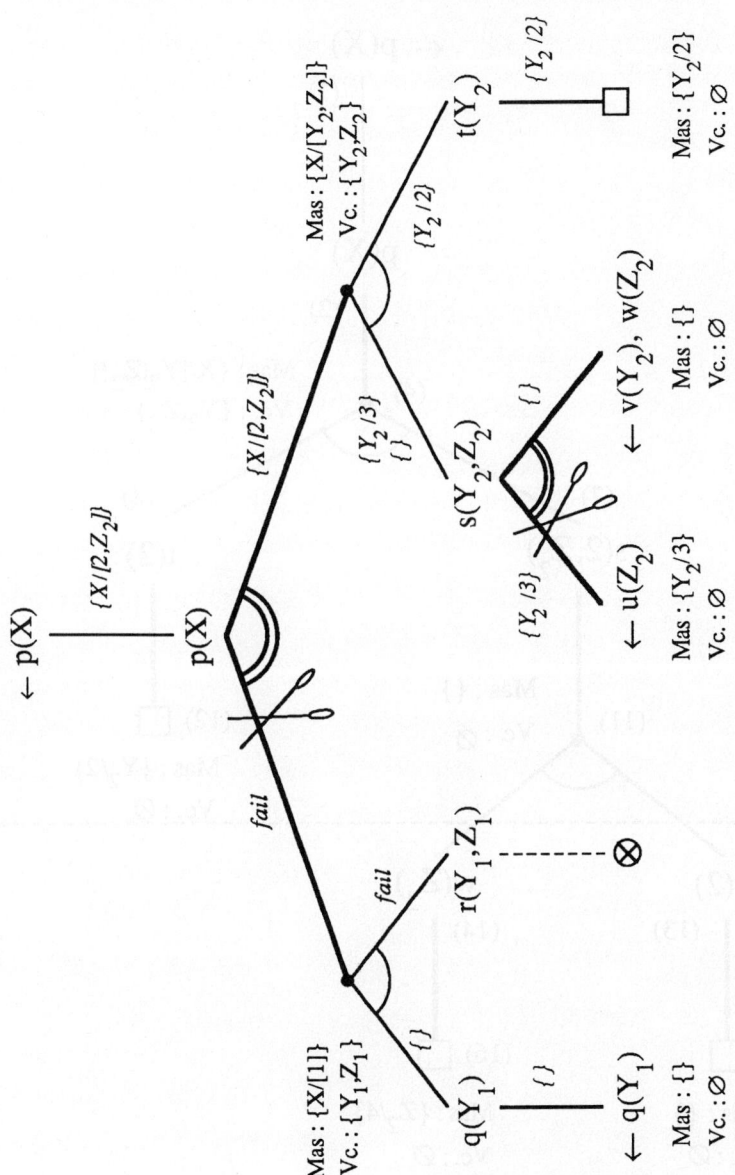

Figure 4.2

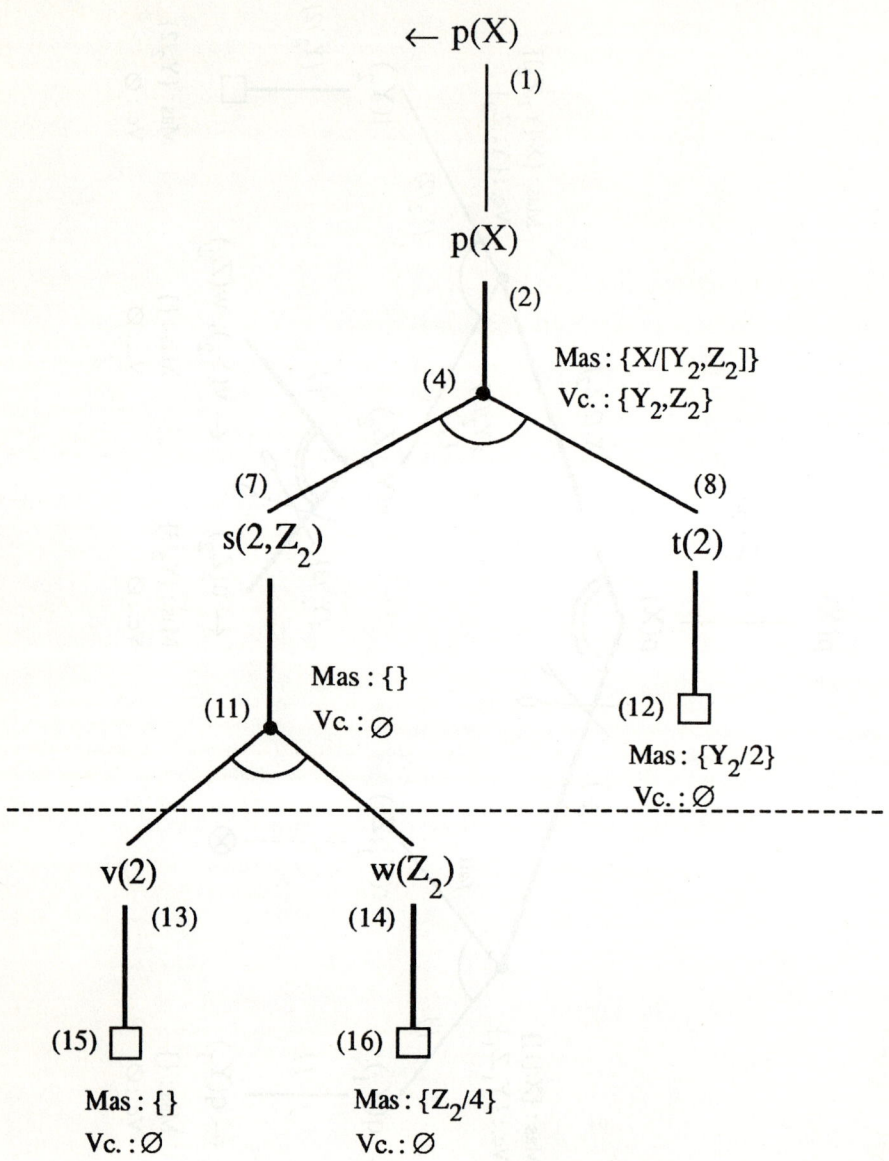

Figure 4.3

INTRODUCTION

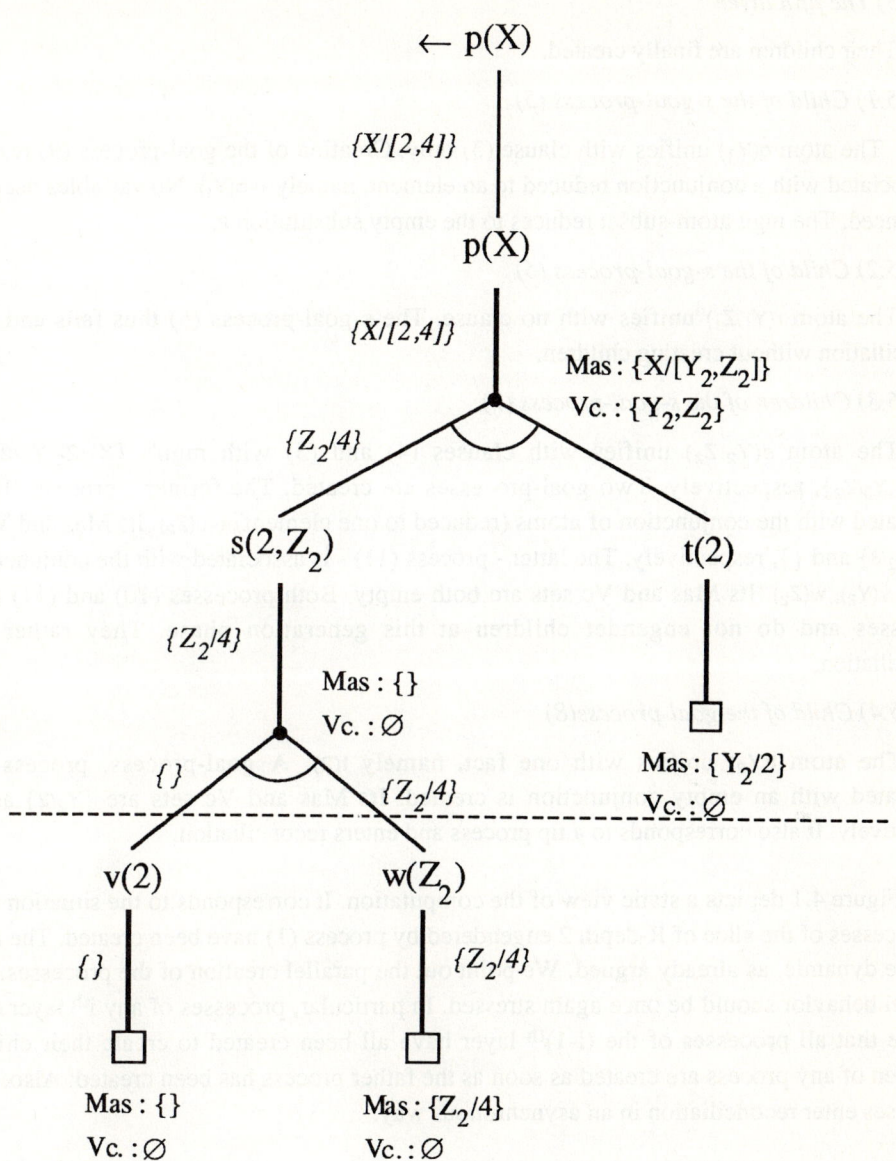

Figure 4.4

5) The fifth layer

Their children are finally created.

5.1) Child of the s-goal-process (5)

The atom $q(Y_1)$ unifies with clause (3) only. Creation of the goal-process (9) results. It is associated with a conjunction reduced to an element, namely $\leftarrow q(Y_1)$. No variables need to be introduced. The mgu atom-subset reduces to the empty substitution ε.

5.2) Child of the s-goal-process (6)

The atom $r(Y_1,Z_1)$ unifies with no clause. The s-goal-process (6) thus fails and enters reconciliation without creating children.

5.3) Children of the s-goal-process (7)

The atom $s(Y_2,Z_2)$ unifies with clauses (4) and (5) with mgu's $\{X_1/Z_2,Y_2/3\}$ and $\{X_2/Y_2,Y_3/Z_2\}$, respectively. Two goal-processes are created. The former - process (10) - is associated with the conjunction of atoms (reduced to one element) $\leftarrow u(Z_2)$. Its Mas and Vc sets are $\{Y_2/3\}$ and $\{\}$, respectively. The latter - process (11) - is associated with the conjunction of atoms $v(Y_2)$, $w(Z_2)$. Its Mas and Vc sets are both empty. Both processes (10) and (11) are tip processes and do not engender children at this generation phase. They rather enter reconciliation.

5.4) Child of the goal-process(8)

The atom $t(Y_2)$ unifies with one fact, namely $t(2)$. A goal-process, process (12), associated with an empty conjunction is created. Its Mas and Vc sets are $\{Y_2/2\}$ and $\varnothing$, respectively. It also corresponds to a tip process and enters reconciliation.

Figure 4.1 depicts a static view of the computation. It corresponds to the situation where all processes of the slice of R-depth 2 engendered by process (1) have been created. The reality is more dynamic, as already argued. We point out the parallel creation of the processes. Their parallel behavior should be once again stressed. In particular, processes of any i^{th} layer do not require that all processes of the $(i-1)^{th}$ layer have all been created to create their children. Children of any process are created as soon as the father process has been created. Also, all tip processes enter reconciliation in an asynchronous way.

A.2 First reconciliation phase

The reconciliation phase is operated from tip processes to the query-process. For ease of presentation, we analyze each layer successively and perform reconciliation when all results from their children are known. The real (more parallel) computation is suggested by pointing out how these restrictions are removed in practice.

1) Reconciliation at the fifth level

1.1) Reconciliation at the tip process (9)

The goal-process (9) corresponds to an incomplete derivation. At the time the first reconciliation occurs, nothing is known about the subtree it engenders. The associated conjunction of atoms does not fail and does not succeed. The maximal information that can be sent consists of the mgu atom subset { }. The auxiliary information is composed of
- the set of process identifiers from which the substitution is made i.e. {(9)},
- the label "incompleted" that indicates that the corresponding subtree is incompletely constructed.

The R-triplet

$< \{\}, \{(9)\}, \text{incompleted} >$

is thus sent to the father process (5). More precisely, it is the singleton composed of this R-triplet which is sent to process (5). For simplicity of the presentation, the set level will however be generally omitted hereafter and its sending will generally be replaced by the sending of its elements.

1.2) Reconciliation at the tip process (10)

Reconciliation at process (10) is performed in a similar manner. The mgu atom-subset is here $\{Y_2/3\}$ so that the R-triplet

$< \{Y_2/3\}, \{(10)\}, \text{incompleted} >$

is sent to process (7).

1.3) Reconciliation at the tip process (11)

Similarly, the R-triplet

$< \{\}, \{(11)\}, \text{incompleted} >$

is sent to process (7) by process (11).

1.4) Reconciliation at the tip process (12)

The goal-process (12) is associated with an empty conjunction. It is thus known to succeed. The mgu atom-subset $\{Y_2/2\}$ is sent to process (8). This time, it is associated with the label "completed" to indicate that the subtree engendered by process (12) is completely constructed. The R-triplet

$< \{Y_2/2\}, \{(12)\}, \text{completed} >$

is thus sent to process (8).

2) Reconciliation at the fourth layer

2.1) Reconciliation at the s-goal-process (5)

Reconciliation at the s-goal-process (5) is quite simple : it consists in transmitting the R-triplets sent by its child. The R-triplet

$< \{\}, \{(9)\}, \text{incompleted} >$

is thus sent to process (3).

2.2) Reconciliation at the s-goal-process (6)

The atom $r(Y_1,Z_1)$ unifies with no clause. Failure is thus simply communicated to the father process (3) by sending the empty set of R-triplets. The s-goal-process (6) furthermore commits suicide.

2.3) Reconciliation at the s-goal-process (7)

The s-goal-process (7) has two children. The set of substitutions for the associated s-goal $s(Y_2,Z_2)$ is conceptually the union of the sets of substitutions coming from its children. The lists of R-triplets from its children are then simply transmitted to process(4). The R-triplets

$< \{Y_2/3\}, \{(10)\}, \text{incompleted} >,$
$< \{\}, \{(11)\}, \text{incompleted} > .$

are thus communicated to s-goal-process (4). Note that the ordering of the R-triplets is not significant. They can thus be sent incrementally at the rate the R-triplets are produced by the children.

2.4) Reconciliation at the s-goal-process (8)

Reconciliation at the s-goal-process (8) is done in the same way as at process (5). The R-triplet

$< \{Y_2/2\}, \{(12)\}, \text{completed} >$

is sent to process (4) as a result.

3) Reconciliation at the third layer

3.1) Reconciliation at the goal-process (3)

The goal-process (3) receives :

- the R-triplet $< \{\}, \{(9)\}, \text{incompleted} >$ from process (5),
- no R-triplet from process (6).

Restated in more conceptual terms, the s-goal $q(Y_1)$ has for the moment not made bindings whereas the s-goal $r(Y_1,Z_1)$ has failed. The conjunction $\leftarrow q(Y_1), r(Y_1,Z_1)$ must thus fail. This is indeed what happens by performing the reconciliation procedure of process (3). The empty set of R-triplets is effectively sent to process (2). Furthermore, processes (3), (5) and (9) are killed as they become useless. Note that, in our parallel context, killing of these processes may be achieved as soon as process (6) reports failure. This may avoid some computation and process creation. For instance, process (9) may, in reality, not be created, provided failure is reported at sufficient time.

3.2) Reconciliation at the goal-process (4)

The goal-process (4) receives the following R-triplets from its children
- the R-triplets
    $< \{Y_2/3\}, \{(11)\}$, incompleted $>$,
    $< \{\}, \{(11)\}$, incompleted $>$
  from process (7);
- the R-triplet
    $< \{Y_2/2\}, \{(12)\}$, completed $>$
  from process (8).

The set of R-triplets to be sent is obtained by coupling each R-triplet from one child with each R-triplet from the other child and by making a common instance of the substitutions in each pair. The pairs are

($<\{Y_2/3\},\{(10)\}$,incompleted$>$, $<\{Y_2/2\},\{(12)\}$,completed$>$),
($<\{\},\{(11)\}$,incompleted$>$, $<\{Y_2/2\},\{(12)\}$,completed $>$).

Obviously, no common instance of the substitutions $\{Y_2/3\}$ and $\{Y_2/2\}$ can be made since Y_2 cannot be bound to 2 and 3 simultaneously. The first pair thus fails to reconcile. In contrast, a common instance of the substitutions $\{\}$ and $\{Y_2/2\}$ of the second pair can be pointed out. It is $\{Y_2/2\}$. The substitution sent to the father process (2) is derived from it. Two modifications are operated. First, the mgu atom-subset $\{X/[Y_2,Z_2]\}$ is composed with it, this giving rise to $\{X/[2,Z_2],Y_2/2\}$. Then this substitution is simplified from the bindings for the variables introduced in the computation from process (4), namely Y_2 and Z_2. Such bindings are indeed of no concern for the s-goal p(X). The sent substitution is thus

$\{X/[2,Z_2]\}$.

The set of process identifiers is composed of the identifiers occurring in the second pair. The label is "incompleted" since the first label of the pair is incompleted. It reflects the fact that the subtree associated with the processes is incompletely constructed. The R-triplet

$< \{X/[2,Z_2]\}, \{(11),(12)\}$, incompleted $>$

is thus sent to process (2).

The following operations are furthermore achieved.

1) Process (10) is not referred to in any R-triplet sent to process (2). It can thus participate in any solution and is killed.

2) The binding $Y_2/2$ is common to all R-triplets that reconcile. It is thus common to any substitution that can be extracted from the subtree engendered by process (4). It is made public in this subtree. Note that there is no need to propagate the binding $X/[2,Z_2]$ since the variable X does not appear in the subtree.

It is worth noting that parallelism can be introduced in the reconciliation procedure. The above pairs can indeed be incrementally computed. Operations 1) and 2) above must however be achieved at the end of the reconciliation procedure.

4) Reconciliation at the second layer

The s-goal-process (2) receives
- no R-triplet from process (3),
- the R-triplet $<\{X/[2,Z_2]\},\{(11),(12)\},\text{incompleted}>$ from process (4).

As processes (3) and (4) represent different ways of reducing $p(X)$, failure of process (3) does not imply failure of the s-goal-process (2). The subtree engendered by process (3) is simply discarded. Process (3) has already been killed and so does not need to be killed once more. The R-triplet sent by process (4) is thus the only one to be transmitted to process (1).

5) Reconciliation at the query-process

The R-triplet

$< \{X/[2,Z_2]\},\ \{(11),(12)\},\ \text{incompleted}>$

is thus transmitted to the query-process (1). It is the only one. There is consequently no need to make a full reconciliation (involving formation of pairs, ...) as described for process (4). No substitution is output since the R-triplet corresponds to an incompletely constructed subtree. No process is killed. Finally, the binding $X/[2,Z_2]$ is common to all the R-triplets resulting from the reconciliation and is thus propagated in the tree of processes. This is for generality of the model but is useless here. The and/or search tree reduces to part of the and/or search tree engendered by process (4) where this binding is already known.

The reconciliation ends by launching a new cycle on the mutilated subtree corresponding to the upper part of Figure 4.3. Note that useless computations that may be engendered by processes (9) and (10) are avoided thanks to reconciliation. The publication of the binding $Y_2/2$ furthermore prevents from useless reduction of $v(Y_2)$ (in (11)) with clauses (9) and (10).

The reconciliation is summarized in Figure 4.2. The substitutions of R-triplets sent by each process have been written on the edge that links it to its father. Killed subtrees of processes are indicated by pairs of scissors.

B. Second cycle

B.1 Second generation phase

The second generation phase is started by activating the generation-procedure of process (11). Its child processes are first created. They consist of the s-goal-processes associated with the s-goals v(2) and w(Z_2), respectively. Their children (15) and (16) are then created. Both are goal-processes associated with an empty conjunction. Thus they have no child and enter reconciliation as soon as they are created.

Figure 4.3 pictures the and/or process model when both processes have been created. The remark made in A.1 on the static character of the figure vs the real dynamic behavior of the computation holds here too.

B.2 Second reconciliation phase

The second reconciliation phase is achieved by following essentially the same principles as those explained in the first reconciliation phase. It is drawn in Figure 4.4 using the same conventions as those employed in Figure 4.2.

The R-triplets

< {}, {(15)}, completed >,
< {Z_2/4},{(16)}, completed >

are sent from processes (15) and (16) to processes (13) and (14), respectively. They are passed to process (11). There, reconciliation is made on the pair formed from the two R-triplets and delivers the R-triplet

<{Z_2/4},{(15),(16)},completed> .

It is transmitted to process (7) and then to process (4). Process (4) thus receives the R-triplet

<{Z_2/4},{(15),(16)},completed>.

It does not receive a R-triplet from process (8) at this reconciliation phase. Such a R-triplet would be redundant with the R-triplet sent at the first reconciliation phase. The R-triplet already corresponds to a completely developed subtree and so does not need to be precised by further computations. It is, in fact, stored at process (4) so that reconciliation can occur. It delivers the R-triplet

<{Y_2/2,Z_2/4},{(12),(15),(16)},completed>.

It is modified as in the first reconciliation phase. The mgu atom-subset {X/[2,Z_2]} is first composed with the substitution {Y_2/2,Z_2/4}. Bindings for the variables Y_2 and Z_2 (referred to in the Vc set at process (4)) are then eliminated in the resulting substitution. The R-triplet

<{X/[2,4]},{(12),(15),(16)},completed>

results. It is propagated as before to the query-process. The substitution {X/[2,4]} is now output since its associated label is completed. Note that this substitution indeed corresponds to a completely developed subtree. The computation is then halted because all tip processes are associated with ⊗-nodes or □-nodes, respectively.

4.2 Basic concepts

At this point, many details of the model remain unprecised. We now progressively precise them. Basic concepts need first to be introduced. They are presented according to our tree level and process level of discussion.

For ease of the presentation, the following convention will be taken in the remainder of this design part.

Convention 4.1 Very often concepts, properties or explanations refer to a program and an initial query. This reference will generally be kept implicit in order to avoid repetition. Without an explicit contrary notice, the referred program and query are those for which the considered computation is made. Therefore, we will generally speak, for instance, of and/or search trees without specifying the programs nor the queries under consideration.

4.2.1 Tree related concepts

As suggested in Section 4.1, and/or search trees are not developed in their pure form by the computation. Subtrees may be removed or instantiated after each reconciliation phase. Furthermore, the and/or search tree is only made apparent slice by slice. This evolution is captured by the notion of computed and/or search tree.

Definition 4.2 Let P be a Horn clause program and Q be a query. A *computed and/or search tree for P and Q* is a tree derived from the and/or search tree for P and Q

- by removing some subtrees attached to some s-goal-nodes, the s-goal-nodes included;
- by instantiating the goal or s-goal associated with the nodes of subtrees attached to goal-nodes, the goal-nodes included;
- by limiting the and/or search tree to some R-depth (possibly infinite).

Note that any and/or search tree is a computed and/or search tree.

Solution subtrees are computed in a similar way. At some moment, some subtrees may appear as the top part of a solution subtree. Partial solution subtrees capture this notion. We introduce it in the more general context of a subtree of a computed and/or search tree. By the way, candidate solution subtrees and solution subtrees are also generalized to this context.

Definition 4.3 Let T be a computed and/or search tree. Let ST be a subtree of T and let N be its root node.

1) *Partial candidate solution subtrees* are finite subtrees defined as follows :
   (i) If N is a s-goal-node then
      (i.1) if it is a $\otimes$-node then ST has no partial candidate-solution subtree;
      (i.2) if it has no child and is not a $\otimes$-node then $\{N\}$ is the only partial candidate-solution subtree of ST;
      (i.3) if it has children, say $C_1, ..., C_m$, then a partial candidate-solution subtree of ST is a finite subtree composed of
         - the node N
         - one partial candidate-solution subtree of one subtree of ST attached to one C_i.
   (ii) If N is a goal-node then
      (ii.1) if it is a $\square$-node then $\{N\}$ is the only partial candidate-solution subtree of ST;
      (ii.2) if it has no child and is not a $\square$-node then $\{N\}$ is the only partial candidate-solution subtree of ST;
      (ii.3) if it has children, say $C_1, ..., C_m$, then the partial candidate-solution subtrees of ST are finite subtrees composed of
         - the node N
         - one partial candidate-solution subtree from each subtree of ST attached to each C_i.

2) A *candidate-solution subtree* is a partial candidate solution subtree whose tips are $\square$-nodes.

3) A *partial solution subtree* of ST is a partial candidate solution subtree of ST whose involved mas reconcile.

4) A *solution subtree* of ST is a partial solution subtree of ST whose tips are $\square$-nodes.

Note that when T is a (conventional) and/or search tree (as defined in Chapter 2), the candidate-solution subtrees and solution subtrees for ST=T defined above are precisely those defined in Definitions 2.51 and 2.52 (with direct reference to the and/or search tree).

The following convention is subsequently taken.

Convention 4.4 (Partial) candidate-solution subtrees and (partial) solution subtrees with no explicit reference to a subtree are implicitly related to the lastly mentioned computed and/or search tree.

The nature of the tip nodes thus distinguishes the partial (candidate) solution subtrees from the (candidate) solution subtrees. The completion of the subtrees generalizes this distinction.

Definition 4.5 A subtree of a computed and/or search tree is *completed* iff any tip node is either a $\otimes$-node or a $\square$-node. It is *incompleted* otherwise.

It will be convenient to speak of the results introduced by the last slice of a computed and/or search tree. The notion of *tree or subtree cut off its last slice of some R-depth* is introduced for this purpose.

Definition 4.6 Let T be a computed and/or search tree. Let D be some strictly positive integer or the infinite.
- (i) If T is infinite then T cut off its last slice of R-depth D is T.
- (ii) If T is finite then let L be the length of the longest path of T connecting the root of T to one tip. The tree T cut off its last slice of R-depth D is formed of the nodes of T reachable from the root of T by a path of length less than L-2*D.

The reconciliation is extended to (partial) solution subtrees in the following way.

Definition 4.7 The *reconciliation-substitution* of a (partial) solution subtree ST is the reconciliation of the mgu atom subsets occurring in ST.

Finally, the following notations will be useful.

Notation 4.8 Let T be a computed and/or search tree and N be a node in T.
- (i) the notation *ST(N,T)* denotes the subtree of T attached to N (this including N too);
- (ii) the notation *Vc(N,T)* denotes the set composed of all the variables of the Vc sets of ST(N,T);
- (iii) the notation *Var(N,T)* denotes the following set of variables :
  - it is the union of the Vc sets of ST(N,T) if N is not the query-node of T
  - it is the union of the Vc sets of T augmented by the set of variables of the query if N is the query-node of T.

Reference to the computed and/or search tree T is furthermore kept implicit when there is no doubt about it.

Example 4.1 Trees of Figures 4.1 and 4.3 are examples of computed and/or search trees. Let us call the former T_1. The subtree $\{(7),(10)\}$ is an example of partial solution subtree of the subtree generated by (7) for T_1, namely the subtree $\{(7),(10),(11)\}$. The subtree $\{(4),(7),(8),(10),(12)\}$ is an example of a partial candidate solution subtree for the subtree attached to (4) in T_1, namely the subtree $\{(4),(7),(8),(10),(11),(12)\}$. It is incompleted. It is not a partial solution subtree since the bindings Y/2 and Y/3 do not reconcile. The subtree $\{(11),(13),(14),(15),(16)\}$ is an example of a (candidate) solution subtree for the subtree attached to (11) in T_2. It is completed. Finally, the substitution $\{Z_2/4\}$ is the reconciliation-substitution of this subtree.

4.2.2 Processes

Processes have been presented in a quite intuitive manner in Section 4.1. We now precise them somewhat. They are subsequently looked at as abstract objects that communicate through message passing. Their contents is described hereafter. Communication between them is then presented. Finally, concepts on trees are extended to processes.

4.2.2.1 Process parts

Processes are composed of two parts, respectively called the data information part and the program information part. Both parts are presented hereafter from an abstract point of view.

A. The data information part.

The data information part captures data about the process and its children. It essentially consists of five components :

- an identifier component,
- an nb_child component,
- a state component,
- a R-depth tag component,
- a qualification component.

These components were suggested in Section 4.1. Their name are quite meaningful.

(i) The identifier component

The identifier component is used to identify the process. Two related functions are assumed. Let Id be the identifier of some process, say Proc, and let N denote the associated node in the and/or search tree. The first function, referred to by *id_child(I,Id)*, is the partial function that returns, when any, the identifier of the process corresponding to the Ith child of N in the and/or search tree. The second function, referred to as *id_father(Id)*, is the partial function that delivers, when any, the identifier of the father process of Proc.

(ii) The nb_child component

The nb_child component simply counts the number of children of the process.

(iii) The state component

The state component is used to characterize the state of the process. As previously suggested, processes move between three states : active, waiting and dead. A process is in the active state in one of the following situations :

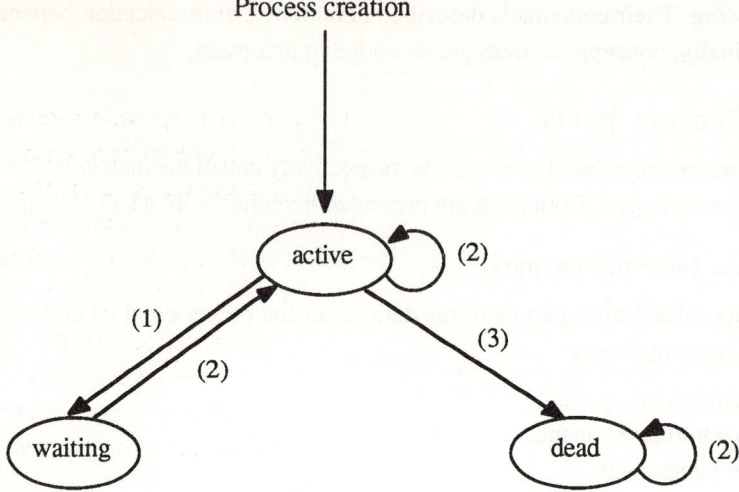

(1) Children have been created and all received messages have been treated
(2) Arrival of messages
(3) A kill message has been treated

Figure 4.5

- the process has been created, is not a tip process and has not yet created its children,
- the process is performing reconciliation,
- the process has been told to die,
- the process has been transmitted bindings.

A process is in the dead state after it has committed suicide. It is in the waiting state when it cannot be active or dead. Figure 4.5 summarizes the conditions under which a process moves from one state to another. It will progressively be commented in the next sections.

(iv) The R-depth tag component

The R-depth tag is used to control the process generation according to the slice by slice generation of the and/or search tree. Precisely, it indicates how many reductions the associated node can engender in the slice under construction. For ease of the presentation, it is viewed as an integer or the infinite (∞). No profit will be taken from this representation except the ease of presentation one. Adaptation to other representations is thus possible in a straightforward way.

The following property is worth noting : at any moment, tip goal-processes associated with a non-empty goal are those whose R-depth tag component is nul.

(v) The qualification component

Finally, the information component contains information specific to each kind of processes. This constitutes the qualification component.

- As far as s-goal-processes are concerned, it is composed of two parts :
    - a s-goal component,
    - a reconciliation component.
- As far as goal-processes are concerned, it is composed of four components :
    - a goal component,
    - a Cv component,
    - a Mas component,
    - a reconciliation component.
- As far as the query-process is concerned, it is composed of two components :
    - a goal component,
    - a reconciliation component.

The s-goal and goal components represent the s-goal and goal associated with the processes. The Cv and Mas components are the previous sets of variables and mas. The reconciliation component varies from one process to another. It is used by the reconciliation procedure. Its precise contents is of no interest for the moment. It is described in Subsection 4.3.2.

Notation 4.9 We subsequently denote the components of a process by suffixing the process name by the component name or one abbreviation. For instance,

Proc.Id, Proc.State, Proc.Goal, Proc.Reconc

refer to the identifier, the state, the goal and the reconciliation components of the process Proc. The process name is furthermore omitted each time the context identifies it without ambiguity. Note that, for ease of notation, intermediate components are omitted. This is allowed by the fact that subcomponent names are identifiers on their own.

B. The program information part

The program information provide the process with program segments that perform appropriate actions and adequately give values to the data information part. Two of them are devoted to the generation and reconciliation procedures. Others aim at handling of messages. The contents of this part is progressively described in the remainder of this chapter, too.

4.2.2.2 Process communication

Communication between processes is achieved through message passing. Most of the communication is due to reconciliation. It only occurs between a father process and its children processes. Other messages are used for killing processes, for making bindings public and for waking up processes. They occur this time between ancestor processes and descendant processes.

Some means of achieving this communication is assumed. The process hierarchy fits well to transmit messages between fathers and their children. It can also be used to pass on messages from ancestors to descendants. An overhead is then induced in the computation because intermediate processes handle messages that are, in fact, irrelevant to them. We left other efficient communication protocols for the implementation phase and only assume at this stage that there is some one. It is also assumed that messages arrive at processes in the order they are sent in the whole system of processes.

4.2.2.3 Trees of processes

It will be useful to extend the notions developed in Section 4.2.1 to trees composed of processes. This is achieved thanks to the one to one correspondance between nodes and processes. Thanks to it, Definitions 4.3, 4.6, 4.7 and Notation 4.8 are extended by replacing nodes by their corresponding processes. We will thus, for instance, speak of solution subtrees of processes to designate the trees of processes corresponding to the solution subtrees (made of nodes). Also, the notations ST(P,T), Vc(P,T) and Var(P,T) will be used to denote the processes associated with the nodes of ST(N,P) and the sets of variables Vc(N,T) and Var(N,T), where N is the node associated with the process P.

By abuse of language, we will also speak of the instantiation of a process by some substitution to refer to the process obtained from the former by instantiating its s-goal or goal by the considered substitution.

4.3 The Conclog model

We are now in a position to the define the Conclog model. There are essentially two ways to proceed. The first one is to state an operational semantics, then to characterize it in terms of static descriptions and finally to establish that the operational semantics meets the descriptions. The latter is more constructive. Descriptions are first given and the model is progressively designed while establishing its adequacy to the description.

We choose the second approach, more explanatory and, to our opinion, more elegant. Our methodological construction is furthermore achieved in two steps. The model is first constructed in the case the R-depth parameter D of the generated slices is finite. It is then discussed when this parameter takes an infinite value. Both cases are moreover explained according to our tree and process levels of discussion.

Convention 4.10 We will subsequently reserve the appellation *Conclog(D)* to refer to the Conclog model with a *finite* value of the R-depth parameter. The notation $Conclog(\infty)$ will be used to denote the Conclog model with an *infinite* value of this parameter.

4.3.1 Finite value of the R-depth parameter

4.3.1.1 The tree view

I Specification

A. Cycles

Computations under the Conclog(D) model are most easily depicted by taking a photo of the and/or search tree after each cycle. This results in the following specification. It characterizes the successively computed and/or search trees.

Specification 4.1

Initial situation

Two inputs are given :
- a non null integer D,
- a finite computed and/or search tree T_in that contains at least one tip node associated with a non-empty goal.

Final situation
1) The tree T_in is transformed into a new computed and/or search tree T_out obtained from T_in as follows.
   Let $N_1, ..., N_m$ be the tip nodes of T_in that are not $\otimes$-nodes or $\square$-nodes. Let furthermore T_aux be the tree T_in augmented by the first slices of R-depth D attached to nodes $N_1, ..., N_m$. Then T_out is T_aux where
   - each node that is not a member of any partial solution subtree of T_aux is removed;
   - for every goal-node N, for every variable V of Vc(N,T_aux), for every non-variable term t, if the binding V/t is common to all reconciliation-substitutions of partial solution subtrees of ST(N,T_aux), then the label of the nodes of T_aux is bound by V/t.
2) The following substitutions are delivered as results. Let T_cut be T_out cut off its last slice of R_depth D. For every solution subtree SS of T_out that is not a solution subtree of T_cut, the restriction of the reconciliation-substitution of SS to the variables of the query is output.

B. Computations

Any computation then basically consists of repeating the algorithm, say cycle, that computes Specification 4.1. The initial tree T_in is composed of the only query-node. The tree taken at the ith iteration is the tree T_out resulting from the $(i-1)^{th}$ cycle. The iteration is repeated until a tree T_out that only contains ⊗-nodes and □-nodes as tip nodes is produced.

Some exception must however be made to this iterative scheme in order to handle the case where the query-node is associated with an empty conjunction of atoms. In this case, the empty substitution {} is simply output.

Definition 4.11 Any substitution produced by the above execution is called a *computed answer substitution*.

C. A parametrized model

The computation thus consists of a (possibly empty) sequence of cycles. The rate at which they succeed is determined by the R-depth of the slices to be constructed at each cycle. As argued in Section 4.4, it impossible to determine a universal value of this R-depth. We thus integrate it as a parameter of the model. One interesting side effect is that several kinds of computations, such as coroutining or unrestricted computations, result as instances. A quite general model is thus pointed out.

Convention 4.12 Thanks to its parameter status, we subsequently take the convention of using the R-depth parameter without re-precising it at each development. It will thus be declared implicitly in the initial situation of the following specifications as well as in the list parameters of subsequent algorithms. Recall that it is considered to be finite in this Section 4.3.1 and will take the infinite value in Section 4.3.2.

II Design of the execution model

The algorithm cycle is constructed in two steps :

- the computation of the tree T_aux from T_in
- the computation of the tree T_out from the tree T_aux and the production of the computed answer substitutions.

These steps correspond to the generation and reconciliation phases, respectively. We therefore call the algorithms developed hereafter to compute them, generation_phase and reconciliation_phase, respectively. The algorithm cycle may thus be expressed as follows :

Algorithm Cycle(T)

Specification : see Specification 4.1

Code

T_aux := generation_phase(T)

Return the results of reconciliation_phase(T_aux).

A. The algorithm generation_phase

The algorithm generation_phase should meet the following specification.

Specification 4.2

Initial situation

A finite computed and/or search tree T containing at least one tip node different from a ⊗-node or a □-node is given.

Final situation

Let $N_1, \ldots, N_m$ be the tip nodes of T_in that are not ⊗-nodes or □-nodes. The tree T is augmented by the first slices of R-depth D attached to the nodes $N_1, \ldots, N_m$.

Obviously, constructing the algorithm generation_phase amounts to creating an algorithm, say develop_node, that generates for any node N and any integer D, the slice of R-depth D it engenders. Precisely such an algorithm should meet the following specification.

Specification 4.3

Initial situation

A node N and an integer I are given.

Final situation

The first slice of R-depth I of the and/or search tree for N is created.

Assuming its existence, the algorithm generation_phase is as follows.

Algorithm generation_phase(T)

Specification : see Specification 4.2.

Code

{ Let $N_1, \ldots, N_m$ be the tip nodes mentioned in Specification 4.2 }

<u>Parbegin</u> develop_node(D,N_1) || ... || develop_node(D,N_m) <u>parend</u> .

Such an algorithm indeed meets Specification 4.2. Note that no interference between the parallel calls develop_node is to be feared since children of nodes of $N_1, \ldots, N_m$ are independent by nature.

The algorithm develop_node is quite easy to construct. Two cases must be considered.

(i) I = 0

In this case, nothing at all must be done.

(ii) I > 0
In this case, the following algorithm need simply to be computed :
- create the children of N, say $C_1, ..., C_m$,
- recursively call the algorithm develop_node for each C_i with the following integer I* :
    - if N is a goal-node then I* is I-1
    - if N is a s-goal-node then I* is I.

The difference of these values for I* is explained by the fact that one reduction must be counted or not according as N is a goal-node or not. Note furthermore that the recursive calls can be performed in parallel since subtrees attached to the C_i's are independent by nature.

The algorithm develop_node is thus as follows :

Algorithm develop_node(I,N)

Specification : see Specification 4.3.

Code

If I>0 then
   create_children(N)
   {Let $C_1, ..., C_m$ be the created children }
   Case N of
     goal-node : do I* := I od;
     s-goal-node : do I* := I-1 od
   endcase;
   Parbegin develop_node(I*,C_1) || ... || develop_node(I*,C_m) parend
fi .

The create_children(N) procedure corresponds to the creation of the child nodes of nodes of and/or search trees as explained in Section 2.33 (see Definition 2.46). We thus do not recall it here. The following convention is however added to this process of creation.

Convention 4.12 In view of the particular role of idempotent substitutions in the reconciliation calculus (see properties developed in Chapter 3), we will only restrict to idempotent unifiers in the following. In particular, idempotent mgu's will only be considered to create children of s-goal-nodes (or, in other terms, to unify atoms with clauses). Also, we will take the convention of taking only idempotent substitutions as reconciliation.

The forward construction of the and/or search tree coupled with the forward production of substitutions, claimed in the introductive Section 4.1, are finally worth noting. They result from the following characteristics of the generation_phase algorithm and of the develop_proc procedure:

- the generation_phase algorithm consists of parallel calls to the develop_proc procedure
- any call to the develop_proc procedure consists of creating children of the node argument and of calling this procedure recursively for these children.

B. The algorithm reconciliation_phase

B.1 Specification

The algorithm reconciliation_phase should meet the following specification.

Specification 4.4

Initial situation

A finite computed and/or search tree T not reduced to its query-node is given.

Final situation

1) The tree T is transformed into a new computed and/or search tree T* as follows :
   - each node that is not a member of any partial solution subtree of T is removed;
   - for every goal-node N, for every variable V of Vc(N,T), for every non-variable term t, if the binding V/t is common to all reconciliation-substitutions of partial solution subtree of ST(N,T), then the label of the nodes of T_aux is bound by V/t.
2) The following substitutions are delivered as results. Let T_cut be T* cut off its last slice of R_depth D. For every solution subtree SS of T* that is not a solution subtree of T_cut, the restriction of the reconciliation-substitution of SS to the variables of the query is output.

B.2 The algorithm

The algorithm reconciliation_phase is constructed by using a recursive approach, too. Roughly speaking, it is as follows. Let $C_1, ..., C_m$ be the children of Q.

- Perform the reconciliation_phase job on the tree attached to each C_i.
- Combine the returned results and perform some induced manipulations on the resulting tree.

The first operation is achieved through the gen_reconc procedure. The last one is achieved by means of a reconciliation-like procedure, called reconc_query.

B.2.1 The gen_reconc procedure

The gen_reconc procedure thus basically consists of doing the job of the reconciliation phase but for strict subtrees of the computed and/or search tree. Precisely, it takes the form gen_reconc(ST,R) and meets the following specification.

Specification 4.5

Initial situation

A non-empty finite subtree T of some computed and/or search tree A that does not contain the root of A is given.

Final situation
1) The subtree T is transformed as follows :
   P_1. each node that is a member of no partial solution subtree of T is removed;
   P_2. for every goal-node N, for every variable V of Vc(N,T), for every non-variable term t, if the binding V/t is common to all reconciliation-substitutions of partial solution subtrees of ST(N,T), then the label of the nodes of T is bound by V/t.
2) Let Rn be the root node of T. The parameter R is bound to a set of triplets of the form <Subst,Nodes,Label> obtained by associating with each partial solution subtree SS of T, the triplet
   - whose Subst component is the restriction of the reconciliation-substitution of SS to the set of variables that are not in Vc(Rn,SS);
   - whose Nodes component is the set of nodes of SS;
   - whose Label component is
     - "completed" if SS is a solution subtree;
     - "incompleted" otherwise.

Note that, as announced in Section 4.1, substitutions have been enriched by auxiliary information composed of sets of nodes and labels. It is slightly more general than that announced there since all nodes (not only the tip ones) of partial solution subtrees are registered in the Nodes component. This generalization is made for the ease of the construction. It will be abandoned later to improve the computation.

The construction of the gen_reconc procedure results from the examination of the following two cases.

(i) The subtree T reduces to one node {Rn}

In this case, Rn is a tip node of the considered computed and/or search tree. The gen_reconc procedure then directly results from the nature of Rn. As already said, the tip node Rn may be of three forms.

(i.1) The node Rn is a s-goal-node whose associated atom unifies with no clause

In this case, Rn does not participate to any partial solution subtree of ST. The following operations must thus be performed :
- the node Rn is removed and T is transformed into the empty subtree;
- the parameter R is bound to the empty set $\emptyset$.

(i.2) The node Rn is a goal-node associated with an empty goal

In this situation, Rn constitutes the only solution subtree of ST. The following operations are thus performed :
- the tree T is kept unchanged;
- the parameter R is bound to the singleton $\{<\sigma,ST,completed>\}$ where σ is the mas associated with Rn.

(i.3) The node Rn is a goal-node associated with a non-empty goal

In this case, Rn constitutes the only partial solution subtree of ST. It is however not a solution subtree. The following operations are thus performed :
- the tree T is kept unchanged;
- the parameter R is bound to the singleton $\{<\sigma,ST,incompleted>\}$ where σ is the mas associated with Rn.

(ii) The subtree T contains more than one node

Let $C_1, ..., C_m$ be the children of Rn and $ST_1, ..., ST_m$ be the subtrees attached to $C_1, ..., C_m$, respectively. Intuitively, most of Specification 4.5 can be achieved by recursively applying the procedure gen_reconc to $ST_1, ..., ST_m$, this producing $R_1, ..., R_m$. The remaining job depends on the nature of the root node Rn. Thanks to the hypothesis made on T, it can only be a s-goal-node or a goal-node distinct from the query-node. We will subsequently call the procedure performing this remaining job as reconc_s_goal or reconc_goal according as Rn is a s-goal node or a goal-node distinct from the query-node.

The algorithm gen_reconc is thus in this case

<u>Parbegin</u> gen_reconc(ST_1,R_1) || ... || gen_reconc(ST_m,R_m) <u>parend</u>;
<u>Case</u> Rn <u>of</u>
    s-goal-node : <u>do</u> reconc_s_goal($R_1,...,R_m$) <u>od</u>
    goal-node : <u>do</u> reconc_goal($R_1,...,R_m$) <u>od</u>
<u>endcase</u>.

Note that the concurrent recursive calls are allowed since they act on distinct structures.

(ii.1) The root node Rn is a s-goal-node

In this case, the subtrees ST_i's essentially represent various possibilities to reduce the atom associated with Rn. Restated in more precise terms, any partial solution subtree of ST is a partial solution subtree of one ST_i augmented by Rn. Specification 4.5 is then quite easy to satisfy :
- Property P_1 is almost satisfied by the recursive calls. All nodes of ST to be removed, Rn excepted, have indeed been removed by them, thanks to the above characterization of partial solution subtrees. The only remaining node to examine is Rn. Obviously, it

participates in no partial solution subtree iff none of the ST_i's contains a partial solution subtree. It is thus removed in this case and only in it.
- As any goal-node of ST is a goal-node of one ST_i, Property P_2 is also established by the recursive calls gen_reconc(ST_i,R_i).
- Finally, the triplets of R are nearly formed too. The set R indeed consists of the union of the R_i where reference to Rn has been added.

It is worth noting that R is empty iff all R_i's are empty that is iff all subtrees ST_i's contain no partial solution subtree. The reconc_s_goal procedure is thus as follows

Algorithm reconc_s_goal($R_1,...,R_m$) :

R := { <σ,Nodes∪{Rn},Label> : <σ,Nodes,Label>∈ R_1∪...∪R_m },

If R=∅ then T := T\{Rn} fi.

(ii.2) The node Rn is a goal-node

In this case, the node Rn is associated with a non-empty conjunction of atoms of same number as the subtrees ST_i's. Let A_1, ..., A_m be these atoms. Roughly speaking, each subtree ST_i contains the solutions for the s-goal A_i. Partial solution subtrees for T are then obtained by combining the partial solution subtrees of ST_1, ..., ST_m. Fortunately, the triplets associated with them need not be computed from the involved substitutions but may be computed directly from the triplets resulting from the examination of the ST_i's. Roughly speaking, the substitutions of these triplets need simply to be reconciled. The reconciliation is however modified, as suggested in Section 4.2. It is first composed with the mas associated with Rn and then restricted to the variables that are not in Vc(Rn,T).

The computation of the value of R turns out to be central in the construction of the reconc_goal procedure. It is precisely performed as follows.
- If one of the R_i is empty, then R is set to the empty set. Emptyness of some set R_i indeed means that the associated subtree ST_i contains no partial solution subtree. Hence, no partial solution subtree of T can be constructed. This intuitively corresponds to the fact that if one A_i is not solvable then so is the whole conjunction ← A_1, ..., A_m.
- Otherwise, R is assigned the set obtained by associating a triplet <σ,Nodes,Label> to all tuples

(<$σ_1$,Nodes$_1$,Label$_1$>,...,<$σ_m$,Nodes$_m$,Label$_m$>)

of triplets of R_1, ..., R_m, respectively, for which the substitutions $σ_1$, ..., $σ_m$ reconcile. The triplet <σ,Nodes,Label> is defined as follows.

1° The substitution σ is defined as

[μ ο ρ($σ_1,...,σ_m$)] $_{|Vars\backslash Vc(Rn,T)}$

where μ is the mas associated with Rn.

This formula means that the mgu atom subset resulting from the reduction that leads to Rn is first composed with the most general common instance of the substitutions $\sigma_1, ..., \sigma_m$. The resulting substitution is then pruned of the bindings for the variables introduced at this reduction or at subsequent reductions.

2° The Nodes component is defined as

$Nodes_1 \cup ... \cup Nodes_m \cup \{Rn\}$.

That is the nodes associated with the substitution σ are the nodes associated with $\sigma_1, ..., \sigma_m$ coupled with Rn.

3° The Label component is
- completed if all the labels L_i are completed
- incompleted, otherwise.

This is quite intuitive too. The subtree formed of the nodes of the "Nodes" set is completely constructed iff each subtree formed of the nodes of "$Nodes_i$" is completely constructed.

It may not appear obvious that the substitution σ is the restriction of the reconciliation substitution of the subtree registered in "Nodes" to the set of variables that are not in Vc(Rn,T). This is however the case. This property is demonstrated in Section 4.5. Nevertheless, some conviction of its validity can be obtained by referring to Proposition 3.18 and by noting the three following properties of any and/or search tree

- no variable of a Vc set of a goal-node is referred to by ancestor nodes of this node;
- no variable of the LHS of a binding registered in the mas of a goal-node appears in the descendant nodes of this node;
- all the mas's are idempotent.

Given this value of the R parameter, the reconc_goal procedure is quite easy to construct.

- Nodes that participate in no partial solution subtree are of three kinds :
  * nodes already identified as such in the subtrees ST_i ;
  * nodes of the partial solution subtrees of ST_i's that cannot be associated with partial solution subtrees of other subtrees ST_j to form a partial solution subtree of T;
  * the node Rn itself in case no partial solution subtrees of T can be formed that is no partial solution subtrees of $ST_1, ..., ST_m$ can be combined.

  Nodes of the first class have already been detected and removed by the recursive calls gen_reconc(ST_i, R_i). Nodes of the second class are the nodes registered in one R_i and do not appear in R. Finally, the node Rn constitutes the third class when R is empty. Property P_1 of Specification 4.5 is thus fulfilled by removing the nodes of the last two classes.

- Property P_2 is already established by the recursive calls too, except, may be, for Rn itself. To make it hold, it is sufficient
  * to examine the above reconciliations $\rho(\sigma_1,...,\sigma_m)$;
  * to collect the bindings $V_1/t_1, ..., V_n/t_n$

- that are common to all these reconciliations
- that verifies the constraint that each V_i is a variable of $Vc(Rn,T)$ and that each t_i is a non-variable term;
* to bind the goal or s-goal of the nodes of T by the substitution $\{V_1/t_1,...,V_n/t_n\}$.

Note that, as all reconciliations are idempotent, the bindings V_1/t_1, ..., V_n/t_n can be applied in any order, either sequentially or simultaneously.

Summing up, the reconc_goal procedure is as follows. Parallel executions have been introduced thanks to the independence of the objects manipulated or of the order in which sets are united. Atomicity of the assignment instruction is assumed. Finally, the notation Sbinds is used to (conceptually) represent the whole sets of bindings. [1]

Algorithm reconc_goal($R_1,...,R_m$) :
{ Computation of R }
R := ∅;
Subst := Sbinds;
Parfor all <σ_1,Nodes$_1$,Label$_1$>∈ R_1, ..., <σ_m,Nodes$_m$,Label$_m$>∈ R_m do
    Reconciliation($\sigma_1,...,\sigma_m$);
    If failure does not occur then
        {Let θ be the returned reconciliation
            θ$_r$ be the set of bindings of θ whose LHS's are variables of $Vc(Rn,T)$ and
            RHS's are non-variable terms }
        If Label$_1$=completed & ... & Label$_m$=completed
            then Label := completed
            else Label := incompleted
        fi;
        Subst := Subst ∩ θ$_r$;
        R := R ∪ {< $[\mu_0\theta]_{|Vars\backslash Vc(Rn,T)}$, Nodes$_1$ ∪ ... ∪ Nodes$_m$ ∪ {N}, Label > }
    fi;
{ Making Property P_1 hold }
{ Let Nodes_in be the set of all nodes mentioned in the R_i's
    Nodes_out be the set of all nodes mentioned in R }
Remove all nodes of Nodes_in \ Nodes_out;
If R=∅ then remove Rn;
{ Making Property P_2 hold }
Parfor all nodes N of T do
    bind the goal or s-goal of N by Subst
    od.

---

[1] In fact, the only property that Sbinds∩θ = θ, for any substitution θ, is used. More efficent representation than the listing of all bindings can thus be used.

B.2.2 The reconc_query procedure

The reconc_query procedure is essentially the same as the reconc_goal procedure. It has to make Specification 4.4 hold in view of the delivered R_i. This is in fact very similar to what is performed at a goal-node in (ii.2) above to make Specification 4.5 hold, thanks to the similarity of the two specifications. The only differences are the following.

1) The substitutions obtained by reconciling substitutions of R_1, ..., R_m (i.e. those referred to by σ above) are no more composed with some mas. They are restricted differently, too. This time, they are restricted to the variables of the query, the only ones of interest. They can be proved, as before in point (ii.2), to be the restrictions to these variables of the reconciliation-substitutions of the associated solution subtrees.

2) Reconciliation-substitutions restricted in this way are not passed as R parameter. Those corresponding to a label of value "completed" and to a set of nodes not included in the tree T_cut are output as results of the computation. Their associated trees are indeed completely constructed thanks to the interpretation placed in the Label component.

B.3 Property

In addition to those specified in Specification 4.4, the following property of the algorithm reconciliation_phase should be pointed out. It is due to our design approach of it and of the gen_reconc procedure, consisting, for each non-tip node,

- of performing reconciliation for the subtrees attached to the children of the node
- of combining the returned results thereafter.

Thanks to it, the backward approach of performing reconciliation and the backward propagation of substitutions, claimed in Section 4.1, is indeed achieved in the reconciliation_phase algorithm.

4.3.1.2 The process view

We now turn to the description of the computation in terms of processes. To this end, profit will be taken from the description in tree terms of Section 4.3.1.1. The algorithms there presented are indeed not completely extraneous to the behavior of the processes. For instance, our use of recursivity is closely connected to the basic life of a process : create children, wait for them to report results, produce and send new results, and modify the process tree in consequence. Roughly speaking, what has been performed at a node when this node has been considered as a root node (see the develop_node and gen_reconc procedures) is now performed during the life of the associated process. More precisely, the expressions of the computation in terms of trees and processes are related as follows :

(i) the generation phases

- the creation part of the algorithm develop_node is performed by the generation program segment of any process,
- the forward character of the generation phases, achieved by the recursive develop_node calls in the tree expression, is achieved by the forward creation of processes in the process expression : the generation program segment of a process is activated just after it has been created.

(ii) the reconciliation phases

- the real reconciliation part of the reconciliation_phase algorithm and the gen_reconc procedure, performed by the procedures reconc_query, reconc_goal and reconc_s_goal, is performed by the reconciliation program segment of the processes;
- the backward approach of the reconciliation phases, achieved by the gen_reconc calls in the tree expression, is achieved by the bottom up way in which reconciliation affects the processes in the process expression : the reconciliation program segment of a tip process is activated just after its creation and that of a non-tip process is activated each time a child process reports the results of the execution of its reconciliation program segment.

Some computational details are of course changed. For instance, there is no more a R parameter. Rather, equivalent R-triplets are sent from child processes to their father process by means of so-called reconciliation messages. The communication of these R-triplets is made incrementally so that some information are conserved in the processes and auxiliary ending reconciliation messages are used.

Also, processes are not fixed but move between three states : active, waiting, dead. Examples of processes in these states are as follows. Removing one node consists in placing the associated process in the dead state. Activating the program segments of one process results in placing this process in the active state. Receipt of messages act in the same way. Finally, idleness of one process (waiting for solutions to be reported, for instance) is translated by its waiting state.

As a last computation detail, killing of nodes and bindings publication are achieved by processes by sending related messages of killing and of binding propagation.

4.3.1.2.1 A simplified model

Given this correspondence, the real challenge of this section is to show how the creative part of the develop_node procedure and the reconciliation work of the procedures reconc_query, reconc_goal, reconc_s_goal can be performed incrementally by the (parallel) execution of the program segments of the processes. Stress is thus subsequently put on the auxiliary data and procedures that make this possible. The program segment then basically consists of rephrasing the above procedures thanks to these auxiliary mechanisms. They are however presented in two steps. A simplified version, more easy to understand, is first described. It is then improved to determine the real version.

I Specification

A. Cycles

The computation is also described by taking photos of the computation after each cycle, but now in terms of processes. This results in the following specification.

Specification 4.6

Initial situation

A non-empty set of processes, say $\{P_1,...,P_m\}$, that verifies the following properties is given :

- the processes $P_1,...,P_m$ form a process tree corresponding to a finite computed and/or search tree T_in;
- there is at least one tip process associated with a non-empty goal; let $P'_1, ..., P'_p$ be these tip processes;
- the R-depth tags of all the tip processes P'_i have the same non null value, say D;
- the processes P_i are set in the active state and their generation procedure is activated.

Final situation

1) Let $N_1, ..., N_p$ be the nodes associated with the tip processes $P'_1, ..., P'_p$. Let $Snodes_1, ..., Snodes_p$ be the set of nodes of the first slice of R-depth D attached to the nodes $N_1, ..., N_p$, respectively. The processes associated with the nodes of $Snodes_1 \cup ... \cup Snodes_p$ are created.
2) These processes as well as the processes $P_1, ..., P_m$ verify the following properties. Let T_aux denote the computed and/or search tree corresponding to all these processes.
    2.1) Processes associated with nodes that are member of no (partial) solution subtree of T_aux are set in the dead state.
    2.2) Tip goal-processes associated with a non-empty goal are moved in the active state with D as R-depth tag component. Their generation procedure is furthermore activated.
    2.3) Other processes are moved in the waiting state.
    2.4) For every goal-process P, the non dead processes of the subtree ST(P,T_aux) are instantiated by the substitution composed of the bindings V/t that verify

- $V \in Var(P,T\_aux)$
- t is a non-variable term
- V/t is common to all reconciliation-substitutions of partial solution subtrees of ST(P,T_aux).

3) For every solution subtree SS of T_aux that is not a solution subtree of T_in, the restriction $\sigma_{|Vg}$ of the reconciliation-substitution σ of SS to the set of variables Vg of the query is output.

Constraints

1) Tip goal-processes associated with a non-empty goal are set in the ready state only when all other properties of the final situation are fullfilled.
2) The final situation is reached after a finite time.

The similarity of this specification with Specification 4.1 is worth noting. It establishes, in fact, the correspondence of the expression of the computation in terms of trees and that in terms of processes.

B. Computations

One consequence of the similarity of Specifications 4.1 and 4.6 is that any computation expressed in process terms also consists of the repetition of cycles. Also, the Conclog model is still parametrized by the R-depth D of the slices to generate. One difference should however been stressed. As each cycle ends with the generation procedure of tip processes associated with a non-emtpy goal being activated, there is here no need to reactivate explicitly a new cycle at the end of each one. Computing a non-empty query then consists of activating the generation program segment of the query-process associated with this query and whose R-depth component is D. Generation and reconciliation program segments will furthermore be constructed to handle empty queries, which forces exception in the tree expression. As a result, any computation does consist of launching the query-process in the above conditions.

II Design of the execution model

The simplified model is constructed in three phases. Program segments are first constructed in order to make Specification 4.6 hold thanks to some assumptions of the initial contents of the processes. It is then shown how the program segments can be adapted in order to make the above properties hold at the beginning of each cycle of a computation. Finally, ending the computation is addressed.

II.1 Making Specification 4.6 holds

The first task is itself achieved in three steps :

- program segments corresponding to the generation and reconciliation procedures are first presented;
- auxiliary messages are then treated;
- the interleaving of the generation and reconciliation phases is addressed thereafter.

A. The generation procedure

The generation procedure is achieved through the generation program segment of any process. Its aim is twofold :

- to launch the reconciliation program segment if the process is a tip one;
- to create the process children otherwise.

It is thus essentially a reformulation in the process context of the develop_node algorithm of Section 4.3.1.1.2. Tests to detect the tip nature need only to be included in addition. It is activated at any process at the end of its creation.

The generation program segment is most easily presented according to the nature of the processes. As agreed in Notation 4.9, the notations S-goal, Goal, Nb_child, Reconc and State refer to the corresponding components of the process under consideration.

(i) s-goal-processes

Generation program segment
Find the clauses unifiable with S-goal, say $C_1, ..., C_m$.
If there are none
    then activate the reconciliation program segment with "tip process" as entry
    else
        Nb_child := m;
        update Reconc;
        Parfor i=1 to m do
            create the goal-process children associated with C_i
        od;
        State := waiting
    fi .

(ii) goal-processes

Generation program segment
If Goal is empty
    then activate the reconciliation program segment with "tip process" as entry
    else

{ Let Goal be ← $A_1, ..., A_m$ }.
Nb_child := m;
update Reconc;
<u>Parfor</u> i=1 <u>to</u> m <u>do</u>
    create the s-goal-process children associated with A_i
<u>od</u>;
State := waiting
<u>fi</u>.

The creation of the child processes may involve many details of refinements. We will here limit to an abstract description given by the following specification.

Specification 4.7

Precondition

Let Proc be a process such that
- its associated node is not a □-node nor a ⊗-node
- its R-depth tag component is not null.

Postconditions

1) If Proc is a s-goal-process then the following processes are created. Let $C_1, ..., C_m$ be the clauses unifiable with the s-goal associated with Proc with idempotent mgu's $\theta_1, ..., \theta_m$, respectively. Assume they are listed in the same order as they appear in the considered program. The child processes of Proc are the processes obtained by associating the following goal-process with each clause C_i :
   - its Id component is id_child(i,Proc.Id),
   - its Nb_child component is 0,
   - its State component is active,
   - its R-depth tag component is Proc.R-depth - 1,
   - its Mas component consists of the atom-subset of the idempotent mgu θ_i,
   - its Goal component is the instantiation of the body of C_i by θ_i,
   - its Vc argument is the set of variables introduced by C_i in the computation,
   - its reconciliation component receives an initial value, precised later on,
   - its program segments are those of the goal-processes.

2) If Proc is a goal-process, then the following processes are created. Let ← $A_1, ..., A_m$ be the associated goal. The child processes of Proc are the processes obtained by associating the following s-goal-process with each G_i
   - its Id component is id_child(i,Proc.Id),
   - its Nb_child component is 0,
   - its State component is active,
   - its R-depth component is Proc.R-depth,
   - its S-goal component is G_i,

- its reconciliation component receives an initial value, precised later on,
- its program segments are those of the s-goal-processes.

All child processes are created as parallel processes. Their generation program segment is furthermore activated.

Note that the creation of children of a process may imply the updating of its reconciliation component. The initial value of this component as well as its updating is postponed to the following subsection, where the reconciliation context is more precisely defined.

The forward character of the generation procedure should finally be stressed. As processes create their children, when any, as soon as they are created, the forward character of generation and the forward production of bindings, claimed in Section 4.1, is achieved at the process level too.

B. The reconciliation procedure

The reconciliation program segment of any process is activated by three events:

- the detection by the process of its nature of tip process
- the arrival of R-triplets by means of the reconciliation messages
- the arrival of ending reconciliation messages.

The reaction to the first two events directly results from the tree description of Subsection B of Section 4.3.1.1.II. Precisely, for the first one, it corresponds to the sending of the R-triplets mentioned in point B.2.1(i). With respect to the second one, it consists of rephrasing the reconc_query, reconc_goal and reconc_s_goal procedures.

The treatment of ending-reconciliation messages consists of the ending operations of these procedures, namely sending new ending-reconciliation messages, killing processes and publishing bindings.

Of course, the reconciliation program segments are designed so that R-triplets can be incrementally communicated. In addition to the reconciliation messages (transporting R-triplets and indicating the end of the communication), some information must be conserved at the processes. Storing this information is the role assigned to the reconciliation component.

This component is defined in the next subsection. The reconciliation messages are then precised. Both structures enable us to present the reconciliation program segment in the last subsection.

B.1 The reconciliation component

B.1.1 Definition

The reconciliation component varies from s-goal-processes to goal-processes.

(i) Goal-processes

The reconciliation component of any goal-process is composed of a S_d structure, a set of identifiers and a set of bindings.

1° The S_d structure is used to conserve, for each child process, the R-triplets it sends. It is furthermore useful to indicate whether the subtree engendered by the process is completely reconciled or not and, in the first case, whether it contains no node to be developed or not.

The S_d structure will be subsequently denoted as follows :
- in case the considered process has no child, it is denoted by $\emptyset_{S\_d}$;
- otherwise, the information corresponding to the child C is referred to by S_d[C]. It consists of the pair
  <Srtriplets,Label>
  where
  - Srtriplets is of the form of the above R parameter but where references to nodes are replaced by references to the corresponding processes,
  - Label is either completed, completed_step, no_end.

2° Some trace of whether or not R-triplets have been sent by the goal-process is conserved. It is stored in a so-called Proc_sol structure. Its value is either 0 or 1. The first value corresponds to the situation where the goal-process has sent no R-triplets. The last one corresponds to the case where it has sent at least one.

3° Processes killing and binding publication requires some additional information. They were previously based on the value of R. Hence, the set R cannot just be incrementally communicated. Some trace must be kept too. This is done by managing a set of process identifiers and a set of bindings. They are subsequently denoted by Set_procs and Set_binds. Roughly speaking, they correspond respectively to the set of processes that participate to one sent R-triplet and the set of bindings that would be transmitted in view of the actual value of R.

(ii) S-goal-processes

As s-goal-processes basically transmit the R-triplets sent by their children, the useful information to conserve is far shorter. It is composed of two parts.

1° The status of the tree engendered by the s-goal-process is just needed for sending appropriate ending-reconciliation messages. This is stored in a so-called elementary S_d structure. It is denoted by E_s_d and takes the following form
- if the s-goal-process has no child, then it is $\emptyset_{e\_s\_d}$;
- otherwise, the information corresponding to the child C, referred to by E_s_d[C], consist of a Label of the above form and meaning.

2° Some trace of whether or not the s-goal-process has sent R-triplets is also conserved in a Proc_sol structure of the above form and meaning.

B.1.2 Invariant properties

The following properties precisely characterize the values of the reconciliation component. They are kept invariant for non dead processes after execution of each program segment. They are furthermore assumed to hold for these processes at the beginning of each cycle.

I_1. For every goal-process P, for every child C of P, the triplet P.S_d[C] = <Srtriplets$_c$,Label$_c$> verifies the following properties :
- its Srtriplets$_c$ part contains the following R-triplets :
  - the R-triplets corresponding to solution subtrees of ST(C,T_in),
  - the R-triplets received at P from C corresponding to partial solution subtrees of ST(C,T_aux) that are not partial solution subtrees of ST(C,T_in).
- Label$_c$ is
  - completed if the two following conditions hold:
    - the subtree ST(C,T_aux) is completely constructed and is completed,
    - the set Srtriplets$_c$ memorizes all R-triplets corresponding to partial solution subtrees of ST(C,T_aux) that are not partial solution subtrees of ST(C,T_in),
  - completed_step if the two following conditions hold :
    - the subtree ST(C,T_aux) is completely constructed but is not completed,
    - the set Srtriplets$_c$ memorizes all R-triplets corresponding to partial solution subtrees of ST(C,T_aux) that are not partial solution subtrees of ST(C,T_in),
  - no_end, otherwise

I_2. For every s-goal-process P, for every child C of P, the label P.E_s_d[C] verifies the following properties : it is
- completed if the two following conditions hold:
  - the subtree ST(C,T_aux) is completely constructed and is completed,
  - the process P has received all the R-triplets corresponding to partial solution subtrees of ST(C,T_aux) that are not partial solution subtrees of ST(C,T_in),
- completed_step if the two following conditions hold :
  - the subtree ST(C,T_aux) is completely constructed but is not completed,
  - the process P has received all the R-triplets corresponding to partial solution subtrees of ST(C,T_aux) that are not partial solution subtrees of ST(C,T_in),
- no_end, otherwise

I₃. For every goal-process P, the sets P.Set_procs and P.Set_binds verify the following properties. Let Spsol be the set of partial solution subtrees of ST(P,T_aux) that can be formed from the solution subtrees stored in the S_d structure of P.
- the set P.Set_procs is the set of process identifiers of partial solutions of Spsol,
- the set P.Set_binds contains the set of bindings
  - of the form V/t with t a non-variable term and V a variable of Var(P)
  - common to the substitutions of the R-triplets of partial solution subtrees of Spsol.

I₄. For every process P, the P.Proc_sol structure has
- 0 as value if Spsol is empty
- 1 otherwise.

B.1.3 Values of the reconciliation components

We are now in position to determine the initial value of the reconciliation components and the way in which they must be updated by the generation program segment.

1° Initial values

The initial values of the reconciliation components of any process P are set as follows :

- the S_d and E_s_d components are set to $\emptyset_{S\_d}$ and $\emptyset_{e\_s\_d}$, respectively;
- the Sproc set is set to the empty set $\emptyset$;
- the set Sbind is set to the set of bindings of the form V/t with V a variable of Var(P,T_aux) and t a non-variable term [1]. This set is subsequently denoted by Sbind_var(P).
- the Proc_sol component is set to 0.

2° Updating by the generation program segment

Updating of the reconciliation structure is quite straightforward too. For any process P, it simply consists of setting, the S_d[C] and E_s_d[C] components to <$\emptyset$,no_end> and "no_end", respectively.

B.2 Reconciliation messages

Three types of messages are needed to send R-triplets incrementally.

1° One form is used to really communicate the solutions. It explicitly refers to

---

[1] As noted in Subsection 4.3.1.2.B.2.1, this set does not need to be explicitly represented. The only used property is that, for any substitution θ, the intersection Sbind_var(P)∩θ is the subset of θ of bindings of the form V/t with V a variable of Var(P) and t a non-variable term.

- the sent triplet,
- the sending child.

It is subsequently denoted by

reconciliation(Child_id,R-triplet)

where Child_id is the identifier of the child and R-triplet is the sent triplet. They are also called *triplet-reconciliation messages* to stress their containing of R-triplets.

2° The two other forms are employed to close the communication that is to indicate that processes of the subtree engendered by the process under consideration in T_aux have completely performed reconciliation. They correspond to the cases where this subtree is completed or not. Both of them just make explicit reference to the sending child. They are subsequently denoted by

end_reconciliation(Child_id),
end_step_reconciliation(Child_id),

respectively (with the above meaning for Child_id), and are referred to as ending-reconciliation messages.

B.3 Auxiliary primitives

Two auxiliary primitives will be useful for further discussion.

1) The first one deals with the updating of the reconciliation component induced by the reception of a reconciliation message. It will be implied in all reconciliations at non-tip processes to preserve the invariance of properties I_1 and I_2. It essentially consists

- of adding the R-triplets of triplet-reconciliation messages in the S_d[C] structure corresponding to the child C referred to in these messages, for any goal-process
- of modifying the value of the label part of this S_d[C] structure, for any goal-process, or E_s_d[C] structure, for any s-goal-process, according to the ending-reconciliation messages received.

Precisely, the update procedure is defined by the following specification. It is only presented in the more complete case of the reconciliation components of goal-processes. Adaptation to E_s_d structure follows as a particular case.

Specification 4.8

Precondition

Let Reconc_mess be a reconciliation message related to some child Child_mess of some goal-process P.

Postcondition

The procedure update(S_d,Reconc_mess) modifies the contents of the S_d structure of the reconciliation component Reconc of P, as follows. Let Old_s_d and New_s_d be the initial and final values of the S_d structure.

- if Reconc_mess is reconciliation(Child_mess,R-triplet_mess) then New_s_d is Old_s_d where R-triplet_mess has been added in the set of R-triplets of Old_s_d[Child_mess];
- if Reconc_message is end_step_reconciliation(Child_mess) then New_s_d is Old_s_d where the label of Old_s_d[Child_mess] is set to "completed_step";
- if Reconc_message is end_reconciliation(Child_mess) then New_s_d is Old_s_d where the label of Old_s_d[Child_mess] is set to "completed".

2) The second auxiliary procedure is used to analyze the completion of the construction and the reconciliation of the subtree generated by one process. In view of properties I_1 and I_2, this amounts to looking at the label parts of the S_d[C] or E_s_d[C] components of the reconciliation component of the process. The following auxiliary primitive is used for this purpose. It takes the form

status_tree(S_d) (resp. status_tree(E_s_d))

and obeys the following specification. It is subsequently only presented for the S_d structure. Adaptation to the E_s_d structure follows as a special case.

Specification 4.9

Precondition

Let S_d be a S_d structure of some process P.

Postcondition

The procedure status_tree(S_d) returns

- completed if for every child C of P, the label part of S_d[C] is completed;
- completed_step if for every child C of P, the label part of S_d[C] is either completed or completed_step, but at least one of them is of the last form;
- no_end, otherwise

B.4 The reconciliation program segments

Let us now turn to the reconciliation program segments. The newly aspects of the computation need only to be taken into account at this point of the dissertation. We will thus only present them. An informal presentation results. It is however sufficiently precise to define the process model without ambiguity.

The design of the program segments is facilitated by assuming that properties I_1 to I_4 hold when the computation of the cycle (specified in Specification 4.6) is started that is for the processes of the tree T_in as they are given before the execution of the cycle. The following Subsection II.2 will show how the program segments can be slightly adapted in order to ensure that this indeed occurs at the beginning of each cycle in the whole computation. Recall that the program segments are expected to keep the properties I_1 to I_4 invariant.

The following rule is furthermore adopted. Intuitively speaking, it states that any process sends any information of interest to its father. Precisely, it states as follows :

R. for any process P different from the query-process,
- any R-triplet corresponding to a partial solution subtree of ST(P,T_aux)
    - that is not a partial solution subtree of ST(P,T_in)
    - that can be computed in view of the information received by P
    is eventually sent to the process father of P
- any information of the completion of ST(P,T_aux) and of its reconciliation that can be computed in view of the information received by P is eventually sent to the process father of P.

The following notations will be used all along it :

- the process under consideration is denoted by Proc;
- its father, if any, is denoted by F_proc.

Finally, it is here worth recalling that the reconciliation program segments are activated by three events :

- the detection by the process of its quality of tip process
- the arrival of the R-triplets by means of the reconciliation messages
- the arrival of ending-reconciliation messages.

Their correspondence with algorithms of Subsection B.2 of Section 4.3.1.1.II should also be kept in mind all along this subsection.

The remainder of this subsection is organized with respect to the nature of the processes. Reconciliation program segments of s-goal-processes are first described. Those of the goal-processes are then examined. Finally, the reconciliation program segment of the query-process is presented.

B.4.1 S-goal-processes

Two cases must be considered here.

(i) Tip s-goal-processes

The case of tip s-goal-processes is quite clear. The empty set of R-triplets is simply reported by such a process Proc and the process Proc then commits suicide. This is achieved by sending the end_reconciliation(Proc.Id) message to F_proc and by moving Proc to the dead state.

(ii) Non tip s-goal-processes

The case of non-tip s-goal-processes is quite easy to treat too. Such processes indeed basically transmit the R-triplets sent by their children to their father. Computationally, the following operations are performed at any such process Proc:
- at the receipt of any reconciliation message, the reconciliation component of Proc is updated as specified in Specification 4.8;
- at its receipt, any R-triplet is augmented by a reference to Proc (in the set of process identifiers) and sent to F_proc;
- each time a R-triplet is sent, the Proc_sol component is set to 1, if need be;
- at the receipt of an ending-reconciliation message, the end_reconciliation(Proc.Id) message or end_step_reconciliation(Proc.Id) message is sent to F_proc as answer if the Status_tree procedure returns the value completed or completed_step, respectively.

The process Proc is moved to the following states each time the received reconciliation messages have been completely treated :
- it is moved to the dead state iff Status_tree returns completed as value and the Proc_sol component has 0 as value;
- it is moved to the waiting state otherwise.

Note that properties I_1 to I_4 are kept invariant in the two cases (i) and (ii).

B.4.2 Non query goal-processes

Two cases must be considered here too : tip goal-processes and non-tip goal-processes.

(i) Tip goal-processes

Tip goal-processes may be of two kinds. A distinct reconciliation procedure corresponds to them.

(i.1) Tip goal-processes associated with an empty goal

Tip goal-processes associated with an empty goal correspond to tip □-nodes of point B.2.1(i.2) of Section 4.3.1.1.II. The following operations must thus be performed. Any such process Proc first sends the R-triplet < Proc.Mas,{Proc.id},completed > to F_proc. It thereafter sends the end_reconciliation(Proc.Id) message to close the communication. It finally moves to the waiting state.

(i.2) Tip goal-processes associated with a non-empty goal

Tip goal-processes associated with a non empty goal correspond to tip nodes of point B.2.1(i.3) of Section 4.3.1.1.II. The following operations are then performed. Any such process Proc first sends the R-triplet < Proc.Mas,{Proc.id},completed_step > to F_proc. It thereafter sends the end_step_reconciliation(Proc.Id) message to close the communication. It finally moves to the waiting state.

(ii) Non tip goal-processes

The execution of the part of a reconciliation program segment corresponding to a non-tip goal-process requires more attention. In fact, it consists of the reformulation, in incremental terms, of the operations performed in the algorithm Reconc_goal of Subsection B.2.1 of Section 4.3.1.1.II. It may be interesting to recall the general scheme of computation but here in terms of processes. As explained in that subsection, the reconciliation procedure of a goal-node basically consists of forming all possible tuples of R-triplets from $R_1 \times ... \times R_m$ (where R_i is the set of R-triplets sent by the ith child), of reconciling the substitutions of each tuple and of sending R-triplets resulting from successful reconciliations. Operations of process killing and bindings publication are furthermore performed in view of the sent R-triplets.

The tuples of $R_1 \times ... \times R_m$ are here incrementally constructed and treated at the arrival of each R-triplet. In contrast, the operations of process killing and of bindings publication can be made only when all tuples have been found that is after all children have sent an ending-reconciliation message for the computation cycle under consideration. The reconciliation program segment is presented with respect to this timing of events. The answer to the triplet-reconciliation messages is first analyzed. The influence of ending-reconciliation messages is then presented.

1° Triplet-reconciliation messages

Let

- reconciliation(Id_child,Rt) be the received reconciliation message
- $C_1, ..., C_m$ be the children of Proc
- <Srtriplets$_i$,Label$_i$> be Proc.S_d[C_i] for any child C_i of Proc.

Assume furthermore that Id_child identifies C_j.

The exact reaction to the receipt of Rt is guided by properties I_1 to I_4 and the rule R. Keeping properties I_1 and I_4 invariant first requires to update the S_d structure. Furthermore, partial solution subtrees of the Spsol set, newly introduced by Rt, should be considered. They correspond to the subtree obtained by associating the nodes registered in Rt with each partial solution subtree of each R-triplet already registered for each child C_i distinct from C_j. Restated in other terms, the step of the incremental computation of $R_1 \times ... \times R_m$ induced by the receipt of Rt consists of making the cartesian product

Srtriplets$_1$ × ... × Srtriplets$_{j-1}$ × {Rt} × Srtriplets$_{j+1}$ × ... × Srtriplets$_m$

Tuples of this cartesian product are then treated as indicated in point B.2.1.(ii.2) of Section 4.3.1.1.II. This has two issues :

- R-triplets corresponding to tuples whose substitutions reconcile are sent to F_proc
- the sets Proc.Set_proc and Proc.Set_bind structures are updated accordingly.

Summing up, the correct answer to the receipt of the reconciliation message is as follows :

- update the S_d structure and more generally the reconciliation component thanks to the update procedure of Subsection B.3 above; let, for any $i \in \{1,...,m\}$, New_srtriplets$_i$ be the set of R-triplets component of S_d[C_i];
- operate the reconciliation process developed in the reconc_goal procedure (see Subsection B.2.1 of Section 4.3.1.1.II) on each tuple of the cartesian product
$$Srtriplets_1 \times ... \times Srtriplets_{j-1} \times \{Rt\} \times Srtriplets_{j+1} \times ... \times Srtriplets_m;$$
- send the resulting R-triplets to F_proc through reconciliation messages
- if at least one R-triplet is sent then update the Proc.Proc_sol component to 1
- update the Proc.Set_proc and Proc.Set_bind structure as follows. Let $Rt_1 = <\sigma_1, Procs_1, Label_1>$, ..., $Rt_m = <\sigma_m, Procs_m, Label_m>$ be the sent R-triplets and $\theta_1, ..., \theta_m$ be the reconciliation of the substitutions from which the σ_i's are issued (see algorithm Reconc_goal in Subsection B.2.1 of Section 4.3.1.1.II). Then, perform
Proc.Set_procs := Proc.Set_procs $\cup$ Procs$_1$ $\cup$ ... $\cup$ Procs$_m$;
Proc.Set_binds :=
Proc.Set_binds $\cap [\theta_1]_{|Var(Proc,T\_aux)} \cap ... \cap [\theta_m]_{|Var(Proc,T\_aux)}$

Note that nearly all the information necessary to perform this answer operation are known by the process :
- the tuples can be formed from the value of the S_d component and from the sent R-triplet,
- the substitutions to reconcile are those of the R-triplets of the tuples,
- the mas to be composed with the resulting reconciliations is registered in a component of the process.

The only missing information is the set of variables Var(Proc,T_aux) employed to restrict the composition from which the σ_i's are issued and to update the set Proc.Set_binds. We will here assume some means of determining it in view of the process identifier (for example, by an adequate naming of the variables).

2° Ending-reconciliation messages

The receipt of an ending-reconciliation message also leads to the updating of the reconciliation component (as obtained by the update procedure of Subsection B.3 above). No further treatment is necessary to maintain properties I_1 to I_4 invariant. In contrast, achieving Specification 4.6 requires to kill some processes and to publish some bindings. Finally, rule R forces to send the ending-reconciliation messages when the exact status of ST(P,T_aux) is known. This is achieved as follows.

- If the status_tree procedure applied on the updated value of S_d returns "completed", then the end_reconciliation(Proc.Id) message is sent to F_proc.
- If the status_tree procedure applied on the updated value of S_d returns "completed_step", then the end_step_reconciliation(Proc.Id) message is sent to F_proc.
- In these two cases, processes referred to in S_d and not in Set_procs are sent kill messages. In view of property I_3, they indeed correspond to the nodes killed in the reconc_goal procedure. Assuming the receipt of kill messages forces the receiving process to move to the dead state, killing required in Specification 4.6 is achieved.
- In these two cases too, provided Binds differs from Sbinds_var(Proc), child processes of Proc are sent an instantiation message with Binds as substitution. Assuming the treatment of such a message at any process consists of binding its s-goal or its goal component and of transmitting the message to its children when any, the instantiation required in Specification 4.6 is achieved.

Finally, the process Proc is moved to the following states each time the received reconciliation messages have been completely treated :

- it is moved to the dead state iff Status_tree returns completed as value and the Proc_sol structure is 0;
- it is moved to the waiting state otherwise.

Note that properties I_1 to I_4 are indeed kept invariant either by the reconciliation procedure of cases (i) and (ii).

B.4.3 The query-proces

The reconciliation procedure attached to a query-process is that of a goal-process modified with respect to the differences explained in Subsection B.2.2 of Section 4.3.1.1.II. Two cases need to be considered here according as the query-process is a tip one or not.

(iii.1) Tip query-process

Because the R-depth D of the slice to be generated is non null, the query-process is a tip one only if it is associated with an empty goal. In this case, the empty substitution is output. The execution is stopped since there are no more processes to create or to activate.

(iii.2) Non-tip query-process

The reconciliation is also induced by the arrival of a reconciliation message. It is here also described by distinguishing the triplet-reconciliation messages from the ending ones.

(iii.2.1) Triplets reconciliation messages

The tuples of the cartesian product

$$Srtriplets_1 \times \ldots \times Srtriplets_{j-1} \times \{Rt\} \times Srtriplets_{j+1} \times \ldots \times Srtriplets_m$$

are also formed and reconciled as in the previous subsection but with the adaptations stated in Subsection B.2.2 of Section 4.3.1.1.II. R-triplets are furthermore not sent. Rather, for every R-triplet <R,Ids,L> such that L=completed, the restriction $\sigma_{|VQ}$ of the substitution σ to the set VQ of variables of the query is output.

Nevertheless, the structures S_d, Set_binds, Set_procs and Proc_sol are updated as indicated in the previous subsection. The query-process is moved in the same states, too.

It is here worth noting that such substitutions σ correspond to solution subtrees of the tree T_aux but not of T_in (that is to the substitutions that Specification 4.6 requires to output). They indeed arise from substitutions sent by the tip processes of the newly produced slice and progressively transmitted up to the query-process.

(iii.2.2) Ending-reconciliation messages

The treatment of ending-reconciliation messages is more different. The same instantiation and killing messages are sent. The query-process is moved in the same states too. However, the following operations make difference.

- No ending-reconciliation message is sent.
- When all instantiation and killing messages have been sent, tip goal-processes associated with a non-empty goal are woken up. This is achieved here by the sending of a wake_up message to the children of the query-process that is progressively transmitted to the tip processes.

  Such a method is chosen to make constraint 1 of Specification 4.6 holds. In fact, the only (simple) means that ensures that wake_up messages will be treated after instantiation messages is to use the process communication convention of Section 4.2.2.2 that messages are treated by processes in the order they are communicated. Therefore, as instantiation messages are transmitted in the above progressive way, the easiest way to achieve constraint 1 of Specification 4.6 is to make the wake_up messages in this way. More efficient methods will be presented in Section 4.4.

It is finally worth noting that properties I_1 to I_4 are kept invariant both in cases (i) and (ii).

B.5 Property

In addition to the properties specified in Specification 4.6, the backward character of reconciliation should also be pointed out here. It results from the fact that the reconciliation procedure is started at tip processes first and is activated at a non-tip process each time a R_triplet is received from a child.

C. Handling auxiliary messages

The reconciliation program segments presented in the above Subsection B have used three kinds of auxiliary messages : kill, instantiation and wake_up messages. Their handling has been roughly sketched. We now precise them.

(i) Handling kill messages

Kill messages aim at eliminating the receiving processes from the computation. They are handled in a very simple way. Receiving processes simply move to the dead state. They are then completely deaf to subsequent messages.

(ii) Handling instantiation messages

Instantiation messages aim at instantiating the receiving process as well as its descendants. They are handled in a direct way too. Receiving processes simply replace their s-goal or goal by the instantiation induced by the sent instantiation message. They then transmit the message to their children when any.

(iii) Handling wake_up messages

Wake_up messages aim at reactivating tip processes associated with non empty goals. They are handled in the following manner :
- a receiving non tip process (i.e. a process whose Nb_child component is non null) transmits the wake_up messages to its children;
- a receiving tip process associated with a □-node or a ⊗-node (i.e. a goal-process whose Goal component is empty or a s-goal-process whose Nb_child component is null) ignores the messages;
- a receiving tip process associated with a non-empty goal (i.e. a process whose Goal component is empty and whose Nb_child component is null), updates its R-depth component by the R-depth mentioned in the wake_up message, moves to the active state and activates its generation program segment.

D. Correctness of the program segments

The correctness of the program segments results from
- the correctness of the expression of the execution model made in Section 3.4.1.2,
- the properties I_1 to I_4 made hold after and before the execution of each program segment,
- the rule R that ensures that information is always communicated.

E. Interleaving the generation and reconciliation phase

As a conclusion of this first design part, let us argue that the interleaving of the generation and reconciliation phases is indeed relaxed as noted in Section 4.1. Indeed, processes are concurrent and their reconciliation procedure works incrementally, thus treating R-triplets (received incrementally) in an incremental manner and sending the resulting R-triplets in an incremental manner too. Some processes might thus be generating children whereas others are already performing reconciliation. Also, solutions of some solution subtrees might be computed whereas other solution subtrees are still under computation. Hence, the strict interleaving between generation and reconciliation phases is relaxed as noted in Section 4.1.

II.2 From cycles to cycles

The design of the above Subsection II.1 has ensured that any tree of processes T_in, that verifies the input situation of Specification 4.6 and whose (internal) reconciliation components verify properties I_1 to I_4, is transformed into a tree of processes that verifies the final situation of Specification 4.6. Restated in other terms, we have shown how to establish the final situation of a cycle of any computation from the initial one, provided properties I_1 to I_4 holds initially. The complete computation is not however, in general, composed of only one cycle but of a succession of cycles, the input of the initial one being reduced to the only query-process and the input of any other cycle being the output of the previous one. Two points thus remain to be established :

- P_1. The reconciliation component of the query-process verifies properties I_1 to I_4 at the beginning of the first cycle;
- P_2. The reconciliation components of non dead processes as they are output by one cycle verify properties I_1 to I_4 provided they do so at the beginning of the cycle.

A final point should furthermore be considered in order to make a complete correspondence between the tree expression and the process expression. Let $T_1, ..., T_n, ...$ be the computed and/or search trees formed of nodes pointed out in the tree expression of Section 4.3.1.1. For any i, the tree of processes corresponding to T_i is transformed into a tree of processes that does not exactly correspond to T_{i+1} : T_{i+1} only corresponds to the tree of the non dead processes. This fact might appear to be of no concern since processes do not act as soon as they are dead and can thus be discarded. It turns out however to be significant in the verification of P_2.

Let us now establish points P_1 and P_2. Point P_1 is already achieved thanks to the definition of the initial contents of the reconciliation components of processes. Point P_2 seems to be obvious too. It is in fact not achieved in general for the three following reasons D_1, D_2 and D_3. Consider the transition from the ith cycle to the $(i+1)^{th}$ one. Let T_i_aux be the tree T_aux defined in Specification 4.6 by taking T_i as tree T_in.

D_1. Some R-triplets of partial solution subtrees that are not solution subtrees in T_{i+1} are still stored in S_d structures whereas this is forbidden by property I_1.

D_2. Because some nodes of T_i_aux have been removed in T_{i+1}, some subtrees engendred by some processes might be referred as incompleted in T_i_aux whereas they are completed in T_{i+1}.

D_3. Other completed_step labels are obsolete and do not fit properties I_1 and I_2.

These defficiencies can be removed by extending somewhat the program segments and reconciliation structures just presented.

(i) Eliminating D_1

Defficiency D_1 can be solved by reinitializing the Srtriplets sets of the S_d structures. Practically, this is achieved by making the query-process send a reinitialize_s_d message just before it sends a wake_up message. This message is progressively propagated from father process to child processes as is the wake_up message. Its treatment at any process takes profit of the following property. For any process P, partial solution subtrees of T_i_aux that are not solution subtrees of T_{i+1} exactly correspond to those associated with an "incompleted" label. Indeed, removal of nodes cannot make a partial solution subtree of T_i_aux, that is not a solution subtree of T_i_aux, a solution subtree of T_{i+1}. Furthermore, any solution subtree of T_i_aux is a solution subtree of T_{i+1} since none of its nodes is removed (see I_3). Reinitialize_s_d messages are thus handled at any process P by the following two operations :

- R-triplets with "incompleted" label are removed
- the messages are then passed to the child processes of P, when any.

The removal of R-triplets induces the violation of property I_3. The sets Set_procs and Set_binds need thus furthermore to be recomputed in view of the new contents of S_d. This is achieved simply by recomputing, at any process P, the solution subtrees of $ST(P,T_{i+1})$ in view of the R-triplets registered in S_d and by deducing therefrom the new values for the P.Set_procs and P.Set_binds sets. Note that a far more efficient method will be proposed in the real model of Section 4.3.1.2.2.

(ii) Eliminating D_2

Defficiency D_2 is solved by extending process killing. Subtrees that move from the incompleted status in T_i_aux to the completed one in T_{i+1} because of process killing may be characterized in the following recursive way. Let us call them newly completed subtrees.

- Subtrees engendered by killed processes are newly completed.
- Subtrees
  - engendered by a non tip process P
  - such that all the subtrees engendered by the children of P are either completed in T_i_aux or newly completed in T_{i+1}, with at least one subtree of the last kind,

are newly completed.

Definiciency D_2 can then be handled as follows.

- Killed processes inform their father of the newly completed characterization of the subtree they engender thanks to a new kind of message, called completion message.
- Program segments are extended to handle completion messages as follows. Let P be the receiving process and Child be the sending child.
  - The label of the S_d and E_s_d structure of C is set to completed.
  - If the status_tree function reports completed after such an updating then the subtree engendered by P has become a newly completed one. Such information is passed to the father of P by sending a completion message.

The query-process makes exception to this treatment : it does not send a completion message to its non-existing father in the last case.

Note that this does not ensure that properties I_1 and I_2 hold at the beginning of the $(i+1)^{th}$ cycle. Tip processes may indeed be woken up before completion messages reaches the query-process. However, it is ensured that properties I_1 and I_2 hold for any process the first time it is activated in the $(i+1)^{th}$ cycle. This is what is really required.

(iii) Eliminating D_3

Definiciency D_3 is solved by extending a little bit the handling of initialize_s_d messages. In addition to the operations performed in (i) above, the labels of the S_d and E_s_d structures that are completed_step are set to the no_end value.

Note that the induced interference with the above treatment is of no concern since in any way the final value of the S_d or E_s_d label will be completed.

II.3 Ending the computation

Ending of the computation just remains to be discussed in order to conclude the design of the simplifed model. Intuitively speaking, the computation should halt when there is no more useful job to be done. This occurs in the two following cases :

- the computed and/or search tree under consideration contains no partial solution subtree;
- the computed and/or search tree is completed i.e all its tip nodes are either ⊗-nodes or □-nodes.

They are covered by the following computational situation : all the tip processes associated with a non empty goal are in the dead state. The termination is thus already ensured in the process model since only non-dead processes are activated for a new cycle by wake_up messages.

4.3.1.2.2 The real model

Let us now turn to the real Conclog model. It keeps all the features of the simplified model but improves it in seven points :

- handling reinitialize_s_d messages
- handling completion messages
- handling of the Set_binds structure
- process referencing in R-triplets
- storing of R-triplets in the S_d structure
- handling failure at goal-processes
- handling of the Set_procs structure.

The third improvement induces a slight modification in Specification 4.6. It concerns the instantiation of the processes and leads to Specification 4.10. This modification will be motivated in the following Subsection II.C. It will also be argued there that, as far as the computed answer substitutions are concerned, an equivalent model is provided. Nevertheless, we state Specification 4.10 before it for uniformity purposes.

I Specification

The new specification is defined from Specification 4.6 as follows.

Specification 4.10 is Specification 4.6 where point 2.4 is replaced by the following point 2.4' :

2.4') For every goal-process P, the non dead processes of the subtree ST(P,T_aux) are instantiated by the substitution composed of bindings V/t that verify
- $V \in Var(P, T\_aux)$
- t is a non-variable term
- V/t is common to all reconciliation-substitutions of incompleted partial solution subtrees of ST(P,T_aux).

The only difference is thus that bindings selected for publication arise only from the incompleted partial solution subtrees and not from all partial solution subtrees, as in Specification 4.6. A more specific substitution is thus published.

II Design of the execution model

A. Handling reinitialize_s_d messages

As it is performed by reinitialize_messages, S_d structures are updated in a quite costly way. All the S_d structures, even the one to be kept unchanged, are examined after each reconciliation phase. A more efficient method would be to update the S_d structures when need be. It turns out that this is indeed possible by extending somewhat the handling of reconciliation messages.

S_d structures can in fact be updated in two ways :

1° in an early and systematic way after each reconciliation phase, as the simplified model does by means of reinitialize_s_d messages

2° in a lazy and "on demand" way in the next reconciliation phase at the receipt of the first reconciliation message.

The second solution is employed in the real Conclog model. In addition to the gain of performance explained above, a gain of messages results. As a counterpart, however, some extension of the reconciliation components, of their updating and of the reconciliation messages is needed.

(i) Reconciliation components and reconciliation messages

Adopting the "on demand" updating leads to the possibility of having, in one reconciliation phase, information of the preceeding one. Some piece of information is thus necessary to identify the reconciliation phase to which the information of the reconciliation components refer. It is registered in a new subcomponent of the reconciliation component, denoted by *Reconc_ph*. It is regarded as an integer for ease of the presentation. We will thus speak of the Proc.Reconc_ph th phase. Adaptation to other representation is however straightforward. Note that, as each cycle is composed of one generation and one reconciliation phase, Reconc_ph is also an identifier for the cycles.

Reconciliation messages are also extended by a Reconc_ph identifier in order to determine to which reconciliation phase they refer.

As expected, the real adaptation induced by "on demand" updating concerns the updating of the reconciliation component caused by reconciliation messages. It is now in charge of performing two tasks

- the previous updating of the S_d structure identified by Specification 4.6
- the updating tasks of the reconciliation components attached to the reinitialize messages, this including the updating of the newly introduced Reconc_ph component.

The last tasks are performed at the receipt of the first reconciliation message. This message is determined by the disequality of the Reconc_ph identifiers of the Reconc_ph subcomponent and of the reconciliation message.

Precisely, the update procedure is defined by the following procedure. It is only presented in the more complete case of the reconciliation components of goal-processes. Adaptation to s-goal-processes follows as a particular case.

Specification 4.11

Precondition

Let Reconc_mess be a reconciliation message related to some child C of some goal-process P.

Postcondition

The procedure update(Reconc,Reconc_mess) modifies the contents of the reconciliation component Reconc of P, as follows.

Let Old_s_d and New_s_d be the initial and final values of the S_d component
   Old_set_procs and New_set_procs be the initial and final values of the Set_procs component
   Old_set_binds and New_set_binds be the initial and final values of the Set_binds component
   Old_reconc_ph and New_reconc_ph be the initial and final values of the Reconc_ph component
   Reconc_ph_mess and Child_mess be the identifier of the reconciliation phase of Reconc_mess and Child component of Reconc_mess.

1° If Old_reconc_ph ≠ Reconc_ph_mess then
  * New_reconc_ph is Reconc_ph_mess
  * New_s_d is as follows. Let Aux_s_d be Old_s_d modified as follows : for any child C of P,
      - any R-triplet whose label is "incompleted" is removed from the set of R-triplets of the Old_s_d[C] component,
      - the label component of Old_s_d[C] is changed to no_end if it was completed_step.
   Then, New_s_d is Aux_s_d except that New_s_d[Child_mess] takes the following value :
      • if Reconc_mess is reconciliation(Child_mess,R-triplet_mess,Reconc_ph_mess) then New_s_d[Child_mess] is Aux_s_d[Child_mess] where R-triplet_mess has been added in the set of R-triplets;
      • if Reconc_message is end_step_reconciliation(Child_mess,Reconc_ph_mess) then New_s_d[Child_mess] is Aux_s_d[Child_mess] whose label is changed to "completed_step";
      • if Reconc_message is end_reconciliation(Child_mess,Reconc_ph_mess) then New_s_d[Child_mess] is Aux_s_d[Child_mess] whose label is changed to "completed".
  * New_set_procs and New_set_binds are recomputed from New_s_d as determined in point II.2.(i) of Section 4.3.1.2.1.

2° If OLd_reconc_ph = Reconc_ph_mess then
  * New_reconc_ph is Old_reconc_ph
  * New_set_procs is Old_set_procs
  * New_set_binds is Old_set_binds
  * New_s_d is determined as in 1° above by taking Old_s_d as Aux_s_d structure.

(ii) Handling reconciliation messages

Reconciliation messages are handled essentially in the same way as in the simplified model. This is due to the fact that most of the modification has been reported in the update procedure. Two points should however be noted.

- Reconciliation messages are now augmented by the identifier of the reconciliation phase in which they are sent. Such a piece of information is supposed to be public as the program is. It is set to 0 at the beginning of the computation and is updated by the query-process at the beginning of each cycle.
  It is used by tip processes to initiate the launching of reconciliation messages. Other non-tip processes can also refer to it to fill in their sent reconciliation messages. We will however not use it in this way. Rather, the identifier of the reconciliation phase will be taken from the received messages. As we will see later, this solution is more flexible.
- R-triplets used in the incremental construction of the $R_1 \times \ldots \times R_m$ set of tuples at goal-processes should be selected with care. Updating of the S_d structure should be performed before the construction of the cartesian product
  $Srtriplets_1 \times \ldots \times Srtriplets_{j-1} \times \{Rt\} \times Srtriplets_{j+1} \times \ldots \times Srtriplets_m$,
  as we did in the simplified model.

B. Handling completion messages

The work performed by completion messages in some cycle can also be performed by means of reconciliation messages of the next cycle. This is suggested by the way in which completion messages are treated. They indeed behave as end_reconciliation messages but of a next reconciliation phase. Now that reconciliation components are correctly handled with respect to the reconciliation phases, completion messages of one cycle are replaced in the real model by end_reconciliation messages but for the next cycle. In order to identify this next reconciliation phase precisely, kill messages are now augmented by a reference to the reconciliation phase in which they are ordered.

Handling completion messages this way leads to a simplification of the model and, in particular, of messages handling.

C. Handling the Set_binds structure

Binding publication may also be made in a simpler way. The gain achieved by binding publication arises in fact from the instantiation of the tips of the only incompleted partial solution subtrees. This suggests that the set of bindings to be published could be determined by limiting to the only incompleted partial solution subtrees computed in one cycle. A more specific substitution results. It prunes the computed and/or/not search tree in a more efficient way but still in a correct way, as proved in Section 4.5. It is also more efficiently handled. It does not require the expensive reinitialization of Subsection II.2 of Section 4.3.1.2.1; the Set_binds set needs here simply to be reinitialized to the set Sbind_var(P). It is furthermore updated when a R-triplet whose label is "incompleted" is determined.

D. Referencing processes in R-triplets

The fourth improvement concerns the contents of R-triplets. Any R-triplet is attached the task of summing up the information contained in a partial solution subtree. In the simplified model, each R-triplet refers, in its set of processes part, to all the processes of its corresponding solution subtree. Such a reference is however quite expensive for most solution subtrees. Fortunately, reference to these processes may be considerably reduced. In fact, any partial solution subtree is completely determined by its tip processes. Their memorization is thus sufficient. It is, in reality, performed in Conclog.

This improvement is achieved by two modifications to the simplified scheme. One affects the reconciliation procedure of non-tip processes. The other results from it and concerns the handling of kill messages.

The reconciliation procedure of non-tip processes is adapted as follows. They no longer refer themselves in the R-triplets they sent and thus are no more referred to in the S_d and Set_procs structures. No other alteration is made to R-triplets handling and sending as well as to binding publication and process killing. In particular, just tip processes are now ordered to kill since they are the only ones to be manipulated. Killing of intermediary processes (killed in the simplified model) is however still achieved by adapting the handling of kill messages and of new reconciliation structures.

The handling of kill messages is extended by the following operation : any tip process reports failure to its father by entering a new reconciliation phase but this time by sending a reconciliation message of a new type. It is called fail message. In contrast with other reconciliation messages, it just makes explicit reference to the sending child. It essentially plays the role of previously sent end_reconciliation messages. It acts however somewhat differently because it implicitly induces the suppression of previously sent R-triplets.

The extension of the reconciliation component and of the reconciliation procedure results from the introduction of this new reconciliation message. As some R-triplets may be removed, the only information that a s-goal-process has sent some ones is not sufficient to distinguish the case where all its children remove their sent R-triplets (this forcing the s-goal-process to do so) from the case where some of them remove their sent R-triplets but other R-triplets sent by other children remains valid. The Proc_sol structure should thus be changed and split into similar structures, each one reporting to one child. The E_s_d component is extended to this end in the following manner : for each child C, the E_s_d[C] subcomponent is now formed of

- a label, namely the previous contents of the E_s_d[C] subcomponent, with same meaning;
- a Child_sol structure, of value either 0 or 1. Its interpretation transposes and generalizes that of the Proc_sol to children. It is 1 if the the corresponding child is not in the dead state and has sent at least one R-triplet. It is 0 otherwise.

Note that such an extension is not needed for goal-processes since, for any goal-process, failure of one of its child implies the failure of the goal-process whatever the status of the other children is.

The introduction of a new reconciliation message induces an extension of the reconciliation procedure. Two cases should be considered : goal-processes and s-goal-processes.

1° goal-processes

As just noted, for any goal-process, reception of a fail message from one child directly implies the failure of the goal-process. The following operations are thus performed at the receipt of a message at a goal-process :

- a fail message is sent to the father process of the goal-process
- the goal-process is then moved to the dead state.

2° s-goal-processes

The reception of a fail message at a s-goal-process does not necessarily imply the failure of the s-goal-process but just that the R-triplets from the sending child must be removed. R-triplets from other children may thus remain valid. It is only when all children have removed their sent R-triplets that the s-goal-process should fail.

Fail messages are handled in consequence : at the receipt of any fail message, the following operations are performed :

- the Child_sol structure of the E_s_d[C] structure corresponding to the sending child is moved to 0,
- if the Child_sol structure of every child is 0 then a fail message is sent to the father of the s-goal-process and the s-goal-process is moved to the dead state,
- otherwise, an end_reconciliation message is sent to the father of the s-goal-process if any child verifies one of the following conditions :

- its corresponding Child_sol structure is 0,
- its completion label is completed.

The extension of the reconciliation component also requires an extension of the reconciliation procedure. It is quite limited since the newly introduced information (i.e. the Child_sol structures) is not really influenced by the arrival of the reconciliation messages. The only perturbations are :

- when a triplet-reconciliation message is received at a s-goal-process, then the Child_sol structure of the E_s_d[C] structure corresponding to the sending child is updated to 1 if need be;
- when a R-triplet is sent from the s-goal-process, the (no more existing) Proc_sol structure is not updated.

The following property should finally be remarked. Handling fail-messages consists in fact of performing a new reconciliation phase in a earlier way. Interaction with the current reconciliation phase might thus be feared. Other processes are indeed, in general, still performing generation/reconciliation for the current cycle.

The two reconciliation phases do not however interfere in practice. To argue this thesis, let us establish the following property.

P.   Let Proc be a goal-process. Then the fail-messages induced by the kill message sent by Proc only act on the subtree ST(Proc).

As Proc has completely performed its reconciliation procedure when it launches the kill messages and thus has reported its last results at that time, the two reconciliation phases cannot then interfere.

Let us now establish property P. Fail messages are progressively transmitted up from the tip processes of ST(Proc). Processes that are not in ST(Proc) are thus affected by them only if Proc sends a fail message at its turn. However, this would happen iff one child process of Proc has failed that is, no R-triplet from one child can be used to form a R-triplet sent by Proc. In this situation, no R-triplet at all is sent by Proc (recall that a R-triplet is formed from one R-triplet of each child) and Proc is thus moved to the dead state. Summing up, when a fail message reaches Proc, it reaches a dead process completely deaf to any message. Hence, no fail message is thus sent by Proc.

E. Storing R-triplets in the S_d structure

Another optimization can be coupled to process killing. Thanks to the conditions in which they are killed, R-triplets referring to killed processes are useless. Some of them might however be still registered in the S_d component of intermediary processes. They could thus be removed. In addition to the gain of place, a gain of computation is achieved too. If not removed, such R-triplets would indeed be employed in subsequent computation cycles to form tuples from which new R-triplets may be formed. As the former R-triplets were detected to be of no help to produce solutions, the resulting latter R-triplets are doomed to the same diagnostic too.

The removal of such useless R-triplets is achieved thanks to the introduction of a new type of messages. They are called *removal messages*. They just take one argument, namely a list of process identifiers. Handling of such messages is quite easy :

- s-goal-processes simply transmit the removal messages to their children, when any;
- goal-processes remove the R-triplets referring to one process mentioned in the removal messages and then transmit these messages to their children, when any.

This removal of processes is initiated by any goal-process for the process it kills, when any.

F. Handling failure at goal-processes

Another improvement concerns the early propagation of failure from goal-processes. In the simplified model, failure is reported by a goal-process to its father only when all its children have completely performed reconciliation. However, failure of one child forces the failure of the goal-process whatever the R-triplets reported by other children are. The reconciliation procedure of goal-processes can thus be optimized as follows :

> as soon as one child reports failure then
> report failure
> kill other children and their descendants
> commit suicide

or, in more precise terms,

> at the receipt of any ending-reconciliation message from one child C,
> if the updated version of the S_d[C] contains no R-triplets,
> then
> send an ending-reconciliation message to the father process
> send a kill message to all children different from C
> move to the dead state.

To ensure a correct behavior, it is expected that kill messages are progressively transmitted from father processes to child processes. This is achieved by generalizing the handling of kill messages at non-tip processes as follows : for any such process, handling of any kill message involves the two following operations :

> send a kill message to all children
> commit suicide.

Note that fail messages returned by tip processes in answer to kill messages are of no importance since father processes are previously set in the dead state and are thus deaf to these messages.

G. Handling the Set_procs structure

Finally, the handling of the processes to kill may be simplified. Processes from the partial solution subtrees computed in the current reconciliation phase need only to be considered. Processes of other partial solution subtrees have indeed been killed in the previous reconciliation phases. Hence, the previous expensive Set_procs set can be avoided. As a counterpart, two auxiliary lists are needed to determine the processes to kill in a safe and complete way.

- The first one is used to collect all the processes of received R-triplets that have not been identified in the previous cycles as participating in solution subtrees (for the subtree engendered by the considered process). It is called In_proc.
- The second one is used to collect the processes that are determined in the current reconciliation phase to be of a solution subtree. It is called Set_procs_ss. The Set_procs then only serves to memorize the processes associated with incompleted partial solution subtrees.

These sets are then handled as follows :

- all of them are initialized to $\emptyset$;
- the set Set_procs and Set_procs_ss are re-initialized to $\emptyset$;
- the set In_proc is re-initialized to its old value where the processes referred in Set_proc_ss have been removed.

Process killing is then ordered at the same time as before but for the processes of In_proc that are not in Set_procs nor in Set_proc_ss.

4.3.2 Infinite value of the R-depth parameter

So far, and/or search trees have been constructed by finite slices. We now turn to the limit case where slices are allowed to grow up to an infinite R-depth. The resulting model is called Conclog(∞). It is described in this section as the Conlog(D) model were in Section 4.3.1, namely according to the tree and process views and, for each of these views, by first specifying the model and then by designing it.

4.3.2.1 The tree view

I Specification

As slices are allowed to grow up to an infinite R-depth, any computation under the Conclog(∞) model is composed of only one cycle : the and/or search tree is constructed in its pure form and is reconciled thereafter. The computation may thus be described directly without calling the auxiliary cycles. This leads to the following specification.

Specification 4.12

Initial situation

A tree limited to the query-node is given.

Final situation

1) The and/or search tree T generated by the query and the program under consideration is constructed.
2) The restriction of the reconciliation-substitution of any solution subtree of T to the variables of the query is output.

The notion of computed answer n-substitution is extended to these substitutions.

Definition 4.13 Any substitution produced in point 2 above is called *computed answer substitution*.

II Design of the execution model

The model developed in Section 4.3.1 for finite values of the R-depth parameter applies in fact for an infinite value of this parameter. Computations involving finite and/or search trees are the same that those computed in the Conclog(D) models with D finite and greater than the R-depth of the considered and/or search trees. Problems can thus only arise from infinite and/or search trees. They indeed occur from the sequentialization of the generation and reconciliation phases presented in Section 4.3.1.1. According to it, substitutions are only computed when the and/or search tree is completely constructed, that is never. This problem is however circumvented when this sequentialization is relaxed in such a way that the reconciliation phase may treat solution subtrees progressively at the rate they are completed, thus without waiting for the completion of the entire and/or search tree. This is what is precisely achieved in the process expression of the computation. Processes behave concurrently and incrementally treat the reconciliation messages. Furthermore, sending of these messages is initiated by tip processes as soon as they are created. This given, it is easy to check that the construction described in Section 4.3.1.2 can be directly applied to the case where the R-depth parameter takes the ∞ value. As the process expression describes the real dynamic computation, we will not develop further the explanation of the Conclog(∞) model in terms of trees but rather turn directly to the process view of the computation.

4.3.2.2 The process view

I Specification

The following specification re-expresses Specification 4.12 in terms of processes.

Specification 4.13

Initial situation

The process associated with the query is given with the following properties :
- its R-depth tag is infinite,
- its state is active
- its generation procedure is activated.

Final situation
1) The processes of the process model associated with the and/or search tree T for the considered query and program are created.
2) If T is finite then
   - processes associated with nodes of any solution subtree are set in the dead state;
   - other processes are set to the waiting state.
3) The restriction of the reconciliation-substitution of any solution subtree of T to the variables of the query is output.

Constraints
1) Any answer substitution is eventually computed.
2) In case T is finite, the final situation is reached after a finite time.

II Design of the execution model

As argued in the previous Subsection II, the execution model of Section 4.3.1.2 explained in process terms for finite values of the R-depth parameter also applies for an infinite value of this parameter. The Conclog(∞) model is thus in fact already constructed. It may be however be simplified in several ways.

1° First, the R-depth tag is no more needed. It was employed in the Conclog(D) model just to ensure the construction of the and/or search tree slice by slice. It is thus obsolate in Conclog(∞) and can be omitted.

2° Second, binding publication and pruning of the and/or search tree performed in the Conclog(D) model after each reconciliation phase has no interest too. They would indeed occur when the tree is completely constructed and reconciled.

3° As a result, the associated Set_procs and Set_binds structures have no grounds for existence. The Conclog(∞) model may thus also be simplified from their management.

4° As a further consequence, there is no need to reference processes in R-triplets. Furthermore, as their substitution always refer to completed solution subtree, their label is also useless. R-triplets may thus be just reduced to substitutions. Consequently, their management also reduces to the management of these substitutions.

5° Finally, as there is only one cycle, there is no need to handle Reconc_ph identifiers in the reconciliation components and in the reconciliation messages.

4.4 Variants of the model

Several choices made in the design of Conclog could be questioned. Alternatives are now examined. They lead to variants or extensions of the Conclog model. All of them are both sound and complete and thus only differ by the efficiency of the induced computations.

By the way, instances of the Conclog model are discussed. In particular, the choice of the value to give to the R-depth parameter is examined. As for the above models, it should also be stressed that all these instances are both sound and complete and thus differ by the efficiency of the induced computations.

4.4.1 The R-depth parameter of the model

The most apparent manner of making variant execution models is to change the value of the R-depth D parameter of the Conclog model. Two of them are worth pointing out.

On the one hand is coroutining. It is obtained by instantiating D to 1. It is furthermore worth noting that, in this case, early detection of failure is achieved too. An example is given by the following square procedure. Its aim is to produce the sequence of square numbers. Recalling the formula

$$k^2 = (k-1)^2 + (2k-1),$$

a square number can be computed by adding its predecessor to some odd number. The successive odd numbers furthermore increase by 2. Therefore, in order to compute the sequence of square numbers, it is sufficient to coroutine the square procedure itself with a process in charge of computing the odd numbers. This is what is achieved by the following clauses.

```
squares([0|L])  ←  sq([0|L],[1|L_odds_rem]),  odd(1,L_odds_rem).

odd(Old_odd,[New_odd|L_odds_rem])  ←
     New_odd is Old_odd + 2,
     odd(New_odd,L_odds_rem).
```

sq([Old_square,New_square|L_squares_rem],[Odd|Odds_rem]) ←
    New–square is Old_square + Odd,
    sq([New_square|L_squares_rem],Odds_rem).

Figure 4.6 pictures the result of the first alternations of the generation and reconciliation phases. Note that for one reconciliation over two, an odd number is passed to the sq procedure and a square number can be delivered as a partial result.

On the other hand are unconstrained computations. They are obtained by instantiating D to ∞. The qualification of the computation results from the fact that no provoked reconciliation occurs in this situation. Generation is thus unconstrained. As a counterpart, no branches are cut off and no bindings are transmitted. One example is given by the append procedure called for the query ←append(L1,L2,[a,b,c]). Recall that it is defined by the clauses

append([],L,L).
append([H|T],L,[H|L_rem]) ← append(T,L,L_rem).

The and/or search tree constructed by the generation phase is drawn in Figure 4.7a). The reconciliation phase is summarized in Figure 4.7b). Note that no conflicting bindings occur.

Other computation models range between these two extremes by giving intermediate values to the R-depth parameter D. It is here worth recalling that the value of D only influences the efficiency of the computation. All resulting models are complete and sound whatever D takes as value. (The reader is referred to Section 4.5 for a proof.) Given this efficiency context, the value to give to D is in fact not universal and varies from one desired execution to another. This might be surprising at first sight. It might indeed appear that the only function to minimize is the execution time. However, what should we consider to measure it? The first produced solution? All of them? Should we also consider the time spent to detect failure? There is thus, at the basis already, a choice of criterias to determine D, all of which do not necessarily favour the same computations. Moreover, this choice is made more difficult by the availability of the resources. They are generally limited so that one choice of D, adequate for one query, may be unacceptable for another query of greater height.

The choice of D results, in reality, from a compromize to be made between two mechanisms:

- computing solution subtrees as rapidly as possible
- detecting and removing useless branches as rapidly as possible and preventing as much as possible the computation from them.

These two mechanisms may be conflicting since the latter needs reconciliation to be performed and thus generation to be constrained. This is however not necessarily done at the expense of generation. Resources are generally finite and computation of useless branches (not killed) delay the generation of useful ones.

BASIC SCHEME

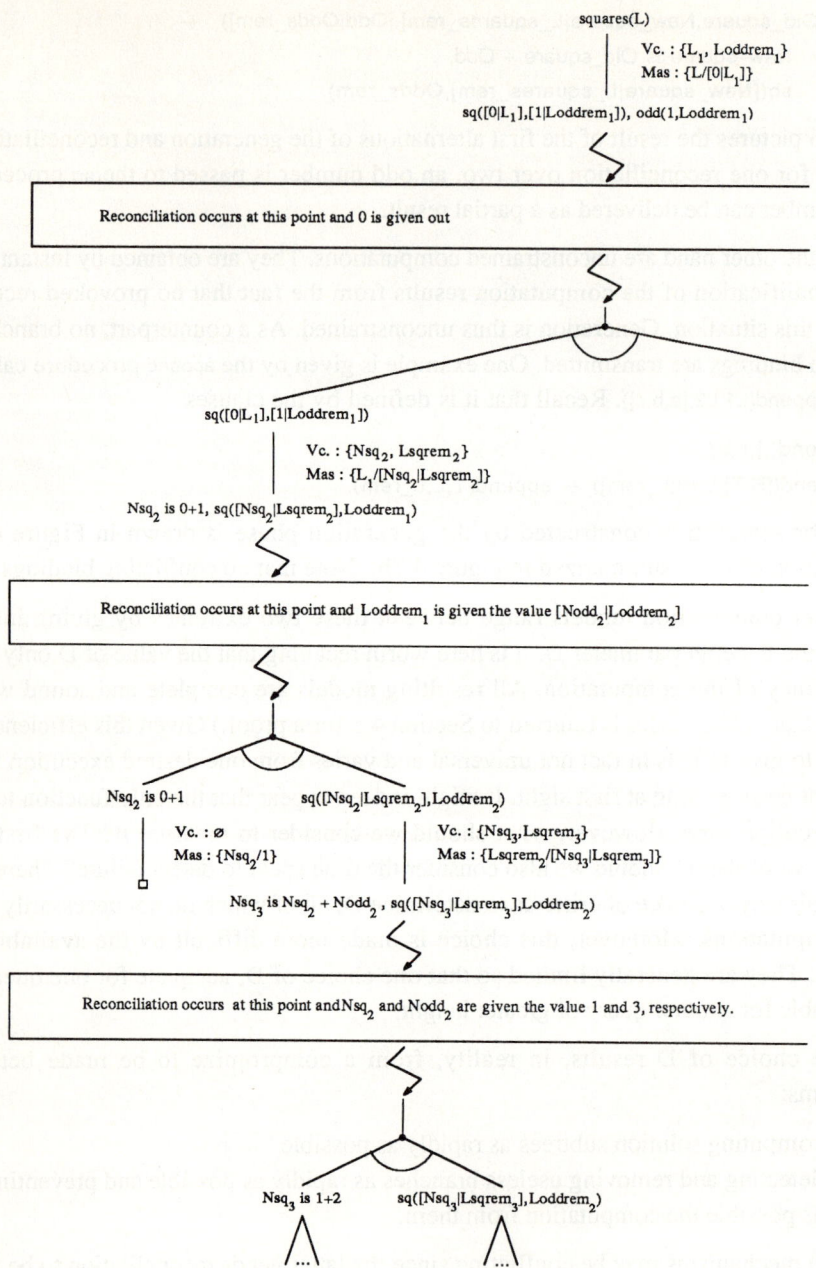

Figure 4.6

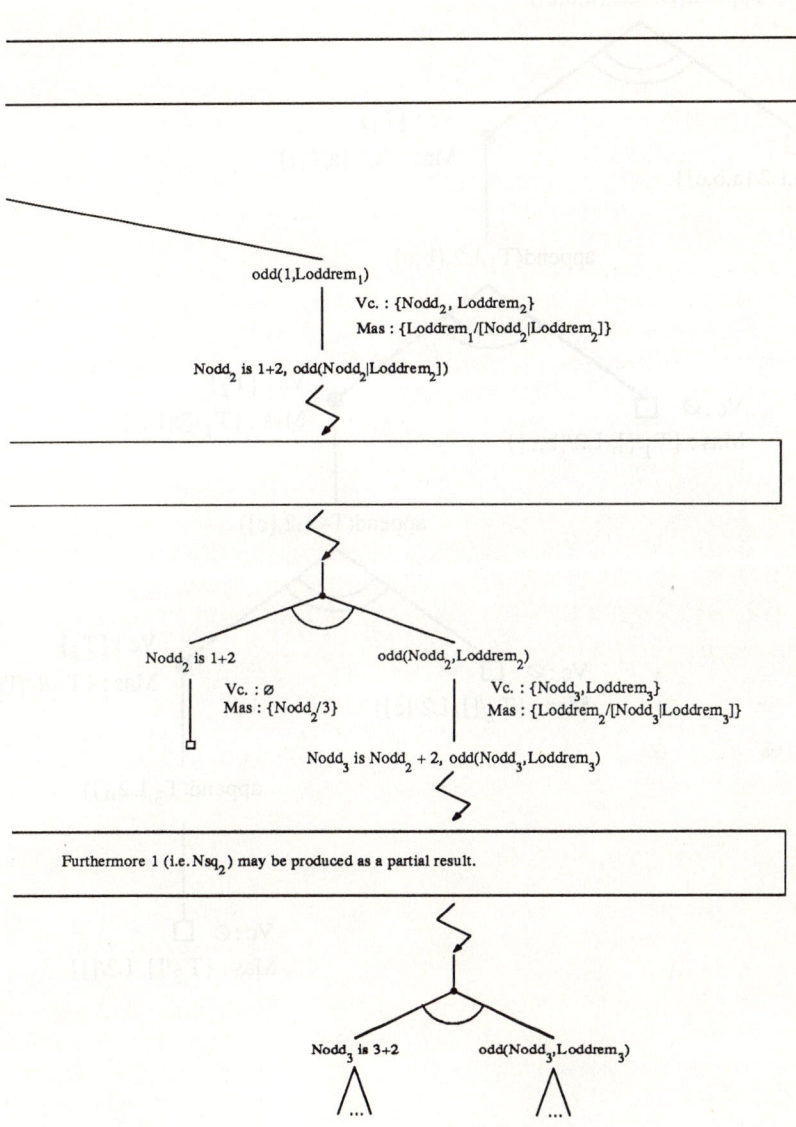

Figure 4.6 continued

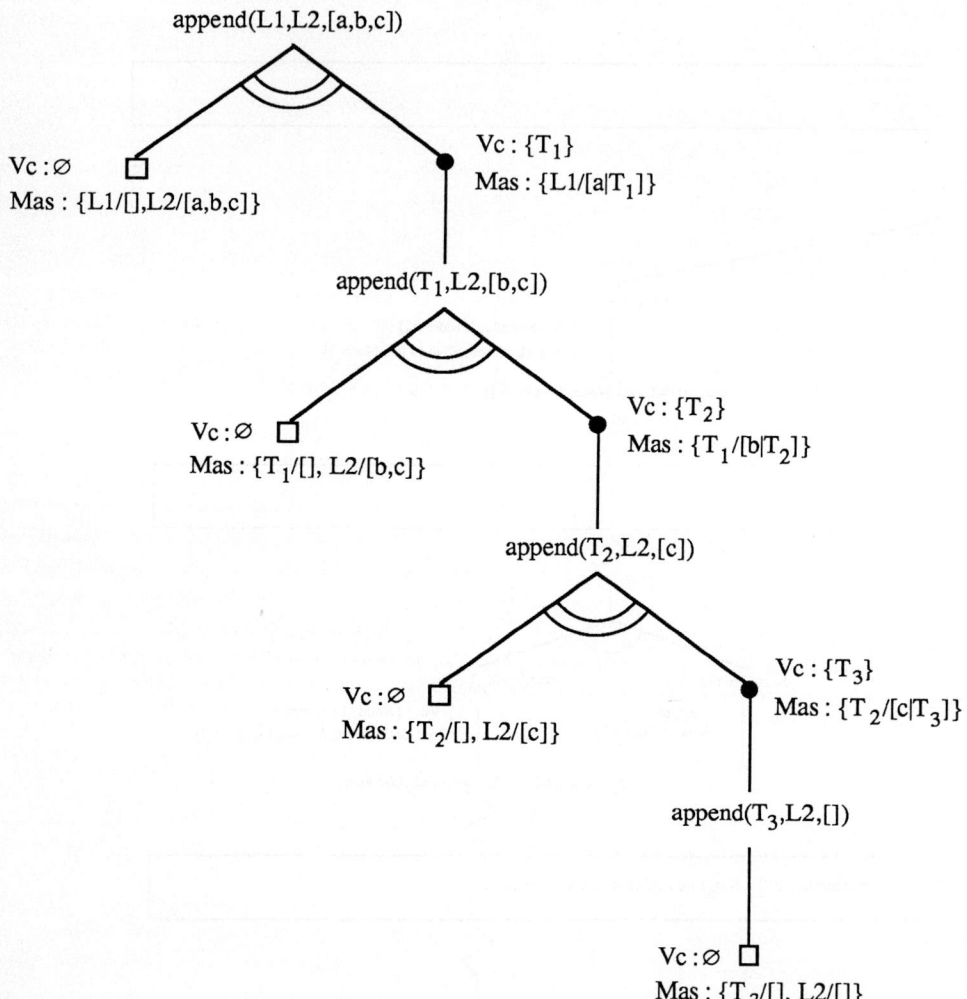

Figure 4.7a)

VARIANTS OF THE MODEL

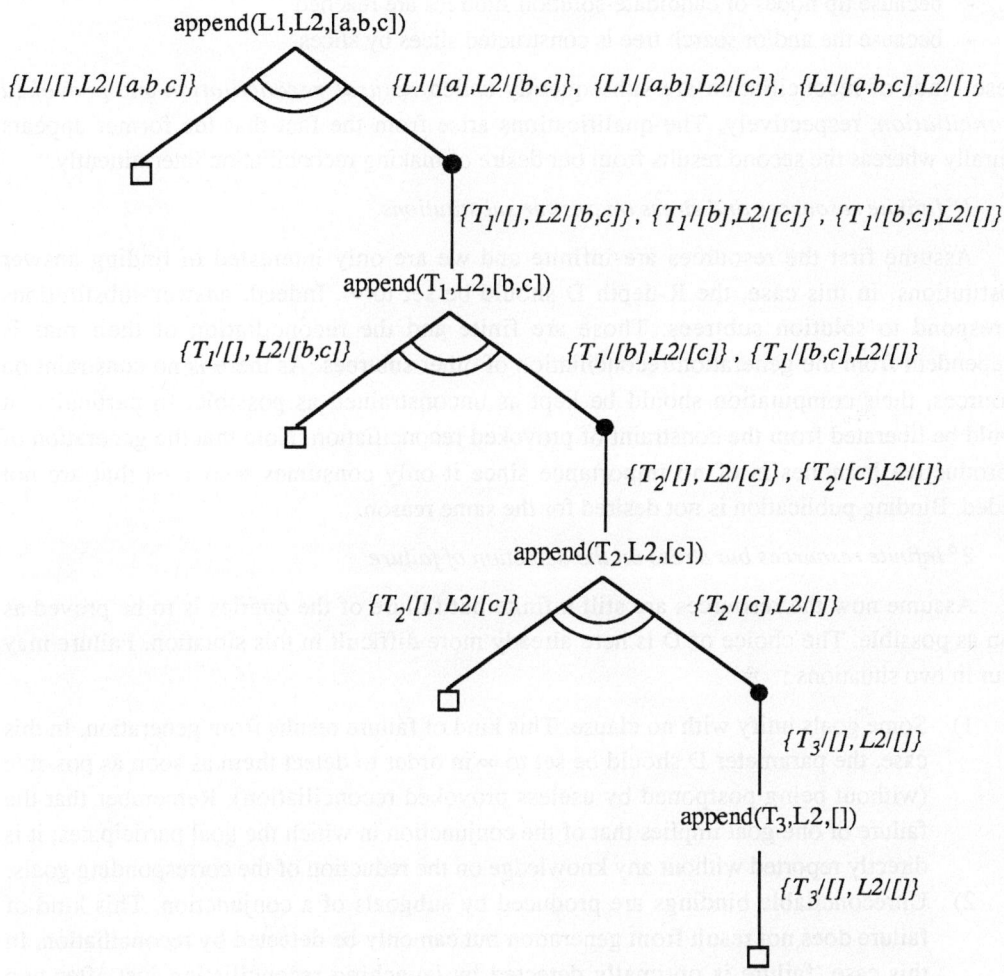

Figure 4.7b)

The three following situations further suggest the difficulty of the choice. For ease of their presentation, the following terminology is adopted. Recall that reconciliation occurs in two ways :
- because tip nodes of candidate-solution subtrees are reached
- because the and/or search tree is constructed slices by slices

These kinds of reconciliation are subsequently called *natural reconciliation* and *provoked reconciliation*, respectively. The qualifications arise from the fact that the former appears naturally whereas the second results from our desire of making reconciliation intermittently.

1° Infinite resources and stress on answer substitutions

Assume first the resources are infinite and we are only interested in finding answer substitutions. In this case, the R-depth D should be set to ∞. Indeed, answer substitutions correspond to solution subtrees. Those are finite and the reconciliation of their mas is independent from the generation/reconciliation of other subtrees. As there is no constraint on resources, their computation should be kept as unconstrained as possible. In particular, it should be liberated from the constraint of provoked reconciliation. Note that the generation of unproductive branches is of no importance since it only consumes resources that are not needed. Binding publication is not desired for the same reason.

2° Infinite resources but stress on the detection of failure

Assume now the resources are still infinite but failure of the queries is to be proved as soon as possible. The choice of D is here already more difficult in this situation. Failure may occur in two situations :

1) Some goals unify with no clause. This kind of failure results from generation. In this case, the parameter D should be set to ∞ in order to detect them as soon as possible (without being postponed by useless provoked reconciliation). Remember that the failure of one goal implies that of the conjunction in which the goal participates; it is directly reported without any knowledge on the reduction of the corresponding goals.

2) Unreconcilable bindings are produced by subgoals of a conjunction. This kind of failure does not result from generation but can only be detected by reconciliation. In this case, failure is optimally detected by launching reconciliation just after two conflicting bindings have been produced. The parameter D should thus be set to the minimal R-depth in which these bindings are known. Note that the precise knowledge of this value requires a pre-execution of the computation in some way. Consequently, only one approximation can generally be considered.

3° Finite resources

More realistic computations involve only finite resources. The choice of D is still more difficult in this case. It must, in fact, vary from one couple program-query to another. How far it could vary is suggested by the two following extreme kinds of computation.

1) *Deterministic computation.* The former is exemplified by deterministic computations. In this case, the generation phases create no useless branches. It is then better to let the and/or search tree grow and let the reconciliation appear naturally. The D parameter should thus be set to ∞.
2) *Generate and test computations.* The latter is exemplified by generate and test computations. In this case, many branches that do not participate to any solution subtree are generated. It is here more interesting to cut them as soon as possible. The computation should generate the and/or search tree little slices by little slices and reconcile the resulting bindings thereafter. The rough way to do this is to set D to 1. In this configuration, bindings are tested as soon as they are generated. Inconsistent bindings are thus discovered as soon as possible. But an overhead of testing is induced so that other small integer values may be more adequate.

Other computations range from these two extremes and the value for D varies from one case to another. There is unfortunately no computable function to determine this value in view of the program and the query. The above programs excepted, there is futhermore no general rule to guide its choice. It must be made from some guess on each particular situation.

Our solution to this problem has been to make D a parameter of the model. The user of the model is thus made responsible for this choice. Some value may however be fixed as a standard in order to liberate him from it. Section 4.5 will prove the soundness and completeness of the model whatever D is. Hence, users only interested in the logical aspects may be totally liberated from the existence of the parameter by assuming some standard value. The only perceptible consequence is some performance of execution in comparison with the optimal execution.

4.4.2 Binding publication

Let us now turn to one design decision implicitly taken in Section 4.3. It concerns the way in which the bindings are selected in order to be made public. Our choice has here been guided by efficiency purposes and is, to our opinion, the best one. Note again here that this is not achieved at the expense of the soundness and completeness properties (as argued in Section 4.5).

Recall the way in which bindings are selected for publication :

For every goal-process P, for every variable V of the set Vc(P), for every non-variable term t, if the binding V/t is common to all reconciliation-substitutions of partial solution subtrees of the subtree ST(P), then

- the s-goal or goal of any descendant process of P is bound by V/t,
- the goal of P is bound by V/t.

(see Specification 4.6 or Specification 4.1 for an expression in tree terms).

The way in which the bindings are selected may be criticized in two points :

1° *The restriction to variables of the Var(P) set of goal-processes.* Publication for all variables - and not only to those mentioned above - seems more powerful. This publication process has however not been adopted for two reasons.

- It is an improvement only in cases where the publication of a binding V/t is only possible in a strict subtree of ST not reduced to one branch. Our experience however suggests that such cases reduce to the examples specially created for this purpose.
- It induces the repetition of the publication of any binding V/t in all subtrees of ST whereas this publication is only made once in the actual Conclog model.

All in all, we believe that such a publication is not an improvement but rather leads to a decrease of efficiency.

2° *The restriction to bindings common to all reconciliation-substitutions.* Let $\theta_1, ..., \theta_m$ be the involved reconciliation-substitutions. In the Conclog model, a binding V/t is selected only if $V\theta_i$ is the same term for all i. A more powerful method could be to make public, for any variable $V \in Vc(P)$, the binding V/t where t is the inf of $V\theta_1, ..., V\theta_m$. We do not adopt this optimization for the following reasons.

- Bindings to be published are generally of one of the two following categories
    * Ground terms. They are already treated in our approach.
    * Lists for which some prefix is known. In this case, the prefix has been denoted by a variable and this variable has been bound to a term. The prefix is thus also communicated.
- The computation of the inf value for most other terms $V\theta_1, ..., V\theta_m$ gives a variable; this variable is of no use for our reconciliation purposes.

All in all, we believe that such an inf computation leads to a decrease rather than an increase of efficiency.

4.4.3 Restriction of substitutions

Another design choice is related to the simplification of substitutions operated at goal-processes. Remember that the substitutions sent by one goal-process, say P, are of the form

$$[\mu \circ \rho(\sigma_1,...,\sigma_n)]_{|Vars \setminus Vc(P)}$$

where μ is the mas associated with P and σ_i is one substitution transmitted by the ith child of P (see Subsection B.2.1 of Section 4.3.1.2. The restriction to the set Vars\Vc(P) is, in fact, a pure matter of simplification too. Performing it or not does not affect the soundness and completeness properties of the model. This property has already been suggested. It may be strengthened in that simplification can be made with respect to any subset of Vc(P) (see Section 4.5 for a proof). This result may greatly simplify implementations. We choose the stronger simplification to present our model. This choice may however be harmful for some referencing mechanisms to variables. In this case, weaker simplifications (of easier implementations) may be taken into account.

4.4.4 Instantiation of intermediary processes

Another possible simplification in some implementations context arises from instantiation messages. Their handling at any process requires the instantiation of the s-goal or goal associated with the process. Although this is required in Specification 4.6, the s-goal or goal associated with non-tip processes does not need to be instantiated in reality. Indeed, these s-goals or goals are not directly used to produce computed substitutions. Furthermore, the slices generated from tip processes only depend on the tip processes and not on their ancestors. One possible improvement of the Conclog model is thus for non-tip processes to transmit the received instantiation messages without altering them.

4.4.5 Activating tip processes only

The Conclog model can be further optimized in cases where the existence of a procedure, that, given two process identifiers, determines whether the former is a descendant of the latter, may be assumed. If so, instantiation and waking up of tip processes may be performed directly. This is achieved by handling an auxiliary list of process identifiers, called Tips. It is accessible by all processes as the computed Horn clause program is. It is attached the following invariant property :

> at any time, the processes registered in Tips are tip processes of the approximation of the and/or search tree under computation.

It is manipulated as follows :

- it is initialized to the empty list at the beginning of each cycle by the query-process;
- any goal-process registers itself in it each time it identifies itself as a tip process associated with a non-empty goal (recall that these are the only tip processes to be woken up).

The instantiation and the waking up of processes is then achieved as follows.

- The instantiation of tip processes consists of sending an instantiation message to the processes of Tips that are descendants of the sending process. Note that, as instantiation is ordered by a process when it has completely performed reconciliation

(for the cycle under consideration), all descendant tip processes (for the cycle under consideration) are indeed registered in Tips.
- The waking up of tip processes consists of sending wake up messages to processes referred to in Tips. Note that, as the waking up is performed in the above condition, all tip processes (for the cycle under consideration) have indeed been registered in Tips.

Care must furthermore be taken for process killing. As killing may be progressively ordered (see Subsection II.F of Section 4.3.1.2.2), nothing prevents logically killed descendants of killed processes to be woken up before they are effectively killed. This may be ensured by coupling a new list of process identifiers with the Tips list. It is called Deads. It is initialized to the empty list at the beginning of each cycle by the query-process. It is then updated by each failing goal-process : any such process adds a reference to itself before it commits suicide. Wake up messages are then only sent to tip processes that are not descendants of a process registered in Deads.

4.4.6 Early relaunch of tip processes

A possible extension of the Conclog model would be to relax the strict succession of cycles and reactivate tip processes associated with non-empty goals in the following manner : given some level of the and/or search tree (specified in some way), for any process P of this level, the tip processes of ST(P) that are associated with non-empty goals are relaunched once the reconciliation procedure of P is completely performed. One way to specify this level could be to add a new parameter to the model, say a relaunch parameter R. Processes of the specified level would then be the goal-processes, ancestors of such tip processes and situated at a R-depth R of them. The Conclog model would thus be obtained by instantiating R to ∞.

The Conclog model so extended is called *er-model* in the following. Its merits can be depicted as follows. Compared with the Conclog model of same R-depth parameter, the advantage of the er-model is that the generation of children of tip processes is no more constrained by the whole reconciliation of the tree of processes. As a counterpart, however, prevention from useless reductions is decreased : tip processes killed or whose goal or s-goal are instantiated as a result of the reconciliation procedure of higher level processes in the Conclog model only receive such messages when their children are created.

Compared with the Conclog model with infinite R-depth parameter, the advantage of the er-model is that process killing and binding publication still occur. The drawback is that, as a result, the generation of processes is constrained by reconciliation procedures.

The er-model can thus be situated between the Conclog model with same R-depth parameter and the Conclog model with an infinite R-depth parameter. All in all, we believe that it is worth interesting only in the following situations :

- some goal or s-goal perform some subcomputation, call them of type I, that has no other interference with other subcomputations, call them of type II, than the production of bindings for some variables;
- intermittent reconciliation of bindings coupled with process killing and binding publication is desired to manage the subcomputations of type II.

These situations will be addressed in Chapter 7 and suitable annotations will be provided to handle them. The interest of our approach is that the early relaunch of tip-processes can be located to the subtrees (e.g. the subtrees associated with subcomputations of type I) without altering subtrees of type II (as in the er-model). Hence, in contrast with the er-model, the interest of the prevention of process killing and binding publication can thus be coupled with the interest of the early relaunch of processes. For this reason, we do not incorporate the relaunch parameter in our basic model of execution.

4.4.7 Reconciliation provoked by events

A final extension of the Conclog model could be to provoke reconciliation by the occurrence of some events (to be defined). For ease of presentation, this extension is further discussed in Chapter 7. There, the dissertation will have reached a point that allows a more complete discussion.

4.5 Theoretical properties

The soundness and completeness properties of the Conclog execution model are now proved. They are established in two steps. Branches killing and binding instantiation are firstly discarded. The properties are thus established for models of execution involving only one generation phase and one reconciliation phase i.e. for the model whose R-depth parameter is infinite. They are then proved for general models of execution. Soundness and completeness properties of variants of Section 4.4 are finally established.

4.5.1 Preliminary results

The following proposition will be used all over this section to simplify the exposition of the proofs. It states the results claimed in Section 4.3 without proof, namely

any partial solution subtree ST, say of root node N, verifies the following properties

(i) the restriction of the reconciliation-substitution of ST can be made either progressively, as reconciliation is operated, or after the reconciliation-substitution is completely constructed;

(ii) whatever subsets of the Vc(ST) sets are taken for the intermediate computation, the same restriction to the variables of N is computed.

Furthermore, it establishes that mgu's can be taken instead of their corresponding mas's to compute this restriction.

Simplification of the exposition results. The way in which this restriction is operated can be abstracted. Furthermore, mgu's of more suggestive use for our proofs can be employed, too.

Proposition 4.14 Let

- ST be a (partial) solution subtree whose root Rn is a non-empty goal $\leftarrow G_1, ..., G_m$
- σ be the reconciliation-substitution of ST
- μ be
  - the mas associated with the root of Rn if Rn is not a query-node
  - the identity substitution { } if Rn is a query-node
- θ be the reconciliation of the mgu's of ST
- ST_i be the subtree generated by the child of G_i ($1 \leq i \leq m$);
- σ_i be the reconciliation-substitution of ST_i ($1 \leq i \leq m$).

For any subset Subvars_ST_i of Vc(G_i) and for any subset Sub_vc_q of var($G_1,...,G_m$), one has

(i) $\sigma_{|Sub\_vc\_q} = [\mu \circ \rho((\sigma_1)_{|Vars \backslash Vc(ST_1)},...,(\sigma_m)_{|Vars \backslash Vc(ST_m)})]_{|Sub\_vc\_q}$

(ii) $\sigma_{|var(G_1,...,G_m)} = \theta_{|var(G_1,...,G_m)}$.

Proof The equalities result from Proposition 3.18 and from the following properties of any and/or search tree. Let Cvars and Gvars be the variables of the domain of clause subset and the atom subset of the mgu's of ST.

- No variable of some Vc set of some node N is referred to in ancestor nodes of N.
- No variable of the LHS of a binding registered in the Mas of some node appears in the subtree attached to this node.
- All mas's and mgu's are idempotent
- Variables of Cvars never give conflicting bindings since the only variables of Gvars may be bound to conflicting bindings. ◊

The following point should also be stressed here. According to Definition 4.10 and Specification 4.1, the computed answer substitutions are defined in terms of the reconciliation of the mas of solution subtrees. Subsequent proofs can thus be explained in terms of trees rather than in terms of processes. The operational behavior of processes can then be abstracted. Particularly notice that this is due in fact to our constructive design with respect to Specifications 4.1 and 4.6.

Finally, subsequent proofs can limit to computations made with respect to non-empty queries. The Conclog model is indeed trivially sound and complete for the empty ones.

4.5.2 Execution model with infinite R-depth parameter

Computations under a model with an infinite R-depth parameter further ease the characterization of computed answer substitutions. In this model, and/or search trees are constructed in their pure form. The computed answer substitutions thus simply consist of the restriction to the variables of the query of the reconciliation-substitutions of the solutions subtrees of the and/or search tree under consideration (and not general computed and/or search trees). The soundness and completeness properties can then be stated as follows. Remember that, for any substitution θ and for any term t, the terms $t\theta$ and $t\theta_{|var(t)}$ are identical.

Let P be a program, Q a query and T be the resulting and/or search tree.

(i) *soundness* : For every solution subtree ST of T, its reconciliation-substitution θ verifies

$P \models Q\theta$ [1]

(ii) *completeness* : For every substitution σ such that $P \models Q\sigma$, there is a solution subtree of T, whose reconciliation-substitution θ verifies $Q\theta \leq Q\sigma$.

A. Soundness

The soundness property can be directly established.

Theorem 4.15 Let P be a Horn clause program and $\leftarrow G_1, ..., G_m$ be a goal. Then every computed answer solution θ for the query $G_1, ..., G_m$ verifies $P \models (G_1 \wedge ... \wedge G_m)\theta$.
Proof The theorem is established by induction on the R-depth Rd of the subtree ST associated with θ.

1° Rd = 0

If Rd=0, then no reduction occurs and the conjunction $\leftarrow G_1, ..., G_m$ is empty. In this case, the only computed substitution is the identity substitution $\{\}$ and one obviously has

$P \models (G_1 \wedge ... \wedge G_m)\{\}$.

2° Rd > 0

If Rd>0, then the conjunction $G_1, ..., G_m$ is not empty and the subtree ST is of the form drawn in Figure 4.8. Let $H_i \leftarrow B_i$ be the clause used to reduce G_i and let θ_i be the idempotent mgu used in the unification ($1 \leq i \leq m$). Let Vc_i be the set of variables introduced by this reduction. Let ST_i be the subtree generated by $B_i\theta$. Let furthermore Svc_i be the set

---

[1] If Q represents the conjunction $\leftarrow G_1, ..., G_m$, we write $P \models Q\theta$ as a shorthand for $P \models (G_1 \wedge ... \wedge G_m)\theta$.

$Vc(ST_i)\backslash Vc_i$. Let finally ρ_i be the reconciliation-substitution of ST_i and τ_i be $(\theta_{i,atom} \circ \rho_i)$ restricted to the variables that are not in $Vc(ST_i)$.

The computed answer substitution θ is obtained by restricting the reconciliation $\rho(\tau_1,...,\tau_m)$ to the variables of $G_1, ..., G_m$. As it is applied to $G_1, ..., G_m$, the theorem amounts to proving the relation

$$P \models (G_1 \wedge ... \wedge G_m)\rho(\tau_1,...,\tau_m) .$$

The induction hypothesis implies, for all $i \in \{1,...,m\}$,

$$P \models (B_i\theta_i) \, (\rho_i)_{|Vars\backslash Svc_i} .$$

As the variables of $B_i\theta_i$ are included in $Vars\backslash Vc(ST_i)$, we thus also have, for all $i \in \{1,...,m\}$,

$$P \models (B_i\theta_i)\rho_i$$

that is,

$$P \models (G_i\theta_{i,atom})\rho_i .$$

and, consequently, as the variables of G_i are in $Vars\backslash(Vc(ST_i) \cup Vc_i)$,

$$P \models G_i\tau_i$$

($1 \le i \le m$). Proposition 3.15 then establishes, for all $i \in \{1,...,m\}$,

$$P \models G_i\rho(\tau_1,...,\tau_m)$$

and, consequently,

$$P \models (G_1, ..., G_m)\rho(\tau_1,...,\tau_m) . \lozenge$$

B. Completeness

Completeness is more difficult to prove. We will proceed as in [Lloyd, 1987] and establish weaker results first. Similar names have been given to our lemmas although our proofs are not simple transpositions of those of [Lloyd, 1987].

The notion of solution subtree needs to be generalized to subtrees of same skeletons but where idempotent unifiers instead of mgu's have been taken to perform reduction. Those trees are called unrestricted solution subtrees.

Definition 4.16 An *unrestricted solution* subtree is a solution subtree involving idempotent unifiers (instead of mgu's).

Convention 4.17 We will nevertheless keep the convention that unifiers are formed from the variables of the computation. Hence, no auxiliary variable is introduced by unification.

Let us first prove that the existence of unrestricted solution subtrees implies that of solution subtrees.

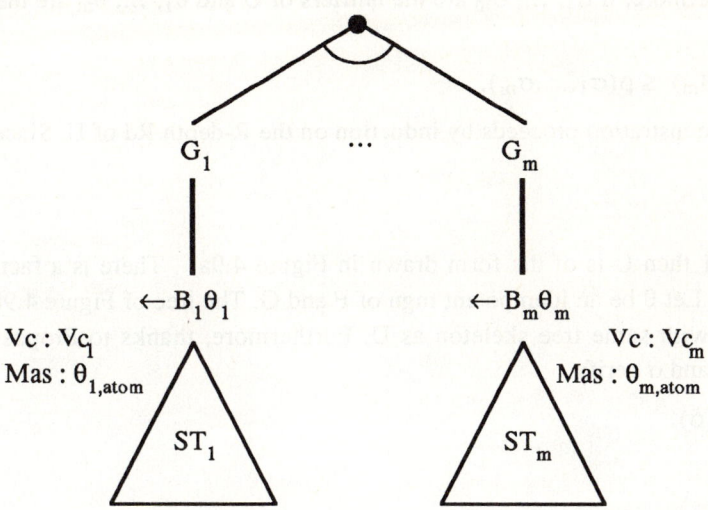

Figure 4.8

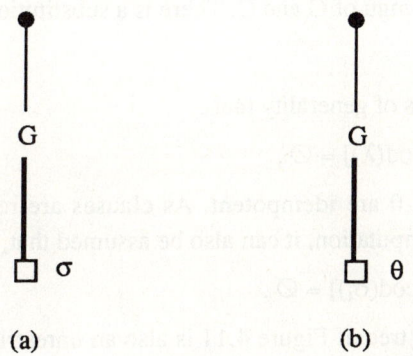

Figure 4.9

Mgu lemma 4.18 Let P be a Horn clause program and G be a s-goal. Suppose there is an unrestricted solution subtree U for ←G. Then there is a solution subtree T with same tree skeleton. Furthermore, if σ_1, ..., σ_m are the unifiers of U and θ_1, ..., θ_m are the mgu's from T then

$$\rho(\theta_1,...,\theta_m) \leq \rho(\sigma_1,...,\sigma_m).$$

Proof The demonstration proceeds by induction on the R-depth Rd of U. Since G is a s-goal, it is at least 1.

1° Rd=1

If Rd is 1 then U is of the form drawn in Figure 4.9a). There is a fact, say F, which unifies with G. Let θ be an idempotent mgu of F and G. The tree of Figure 4.9b) is a solution subtree for G with same tree skeleton as U. Furthermore, thanks to Proposition 3.17, the substitutions θ and σ verify

$$\rho(\theta) \leq \rho(\sigma).$$

2° Rd>1

Assume now Rd>1 and the lemma holds for any unrestricted solution subtree of R-depth strictly less than Rd. In case Rd>1, the tree U has the form given in Figure 4.10. The C, C_1, ..., C_m symbols refer to the clauses used to reduce the top level s-goals and the substitutions σ, σ_1, ..., σ_m refer to the involved (idempotent) unifiers. The body of C is denoted by G_1, ..., G_m. The subtree generated by the instantiation of the body of C_i with σ_i is designated by S_i ($1 \leq i \leq m$). Finally, the set of unifiers of S_i is referred to by Λ_i.

Let θ be an idempotent mgu of G and C. There is a substitution λ such that

$$\sigma = \theta\lambda.$$

It can be assumed without loss of generality that

$$\text{dom}(\theta) \cap [\text{dom}(\lambda) \cup \text{vcod}(\lambda)] = \emptyset,$$

thanks to the fact that σ and θ are idempotent. As clauses are renamed with new variables appearing nowhere in the computation, it can also be assumed that, for any $i \in \{1,...,m\}$,

$$\text{dom}(\sigma) \cap [\text{dom}(\sigma_i) \cup \text{vcod}(\sigma_i)] = \emptyset.$$

In these conditions, the tree of Figure 4.11 is also an unrestricted solution subtree for G. Furthermore, for all $i \in \{1,...,m\}$, the subtree composed of $G_i\theta$, its child and S_i is an unrestricted solution subtree for $G_i\theta$ with $\{\lambda\sigma_i\} \cup \Lambda_i$ as associated set of unifiers. Thanks to the induction hypothesis, it corresponds a solution subtree (for $G_i\theta$), say T_i, of same skeleton whose associated set of mgu's Θ_i verifies the inequality

$$\rho(\Theta_i) \leq \rho(\{\lambda\sigma_i\} \cup \Lambda_i). \tag{1}$$

The tree of Figure 4.12 is thus a candidate-solution subtree for G with same skeleton as U. To conclude the proof, it remains to be proved that the substitutions of $\{\theta\}\cup\Theta_1\cup\ldots\cup\Theta_m$ are reconcilable and verify the inequality

$$\rho(\{\theta\}\cup\Theta_1\cup\ldots\cup\Theta_m) \leq \rho(\{\sigma,\sigma_1,\ldots,\sigma_m\}\cup\Lambda_1\cup\ldots\cup\Lambda_m) . \tag{2}$$

Let γ_i be a substitution such that

$$\rho(\{\lambda\sigma_i\}\cup\Lambda_i) = \rho(\Theta_i) \circ \gamma_i \quad (1\leq i\leq m) \tag{3}$$

(see inequality (1)). The inequaliy (2) results from the following inequalities

$\rho(\{\sigma,\sigma_1,\ldots,\sigma_m\}\cup\Lambda_1\cup\ldots\cup\Lambda_m)$

$= \rho(\{\theta\lambda\} \cup (\{\sigma_1\}\cup\Lambda_1) \cup \ldots \cup (\{\sigma_m\}\cup\Lambda_m))$
  thanks to the equality $\sigma=\theta\lambda$

$= \rho(\{\theta,\lambda\} \cup (\{\sigma_1\}\cup\Lambda_1) \cup \ldots \cup (\{\sigma_m\}\cup\Lambda_m))$
  thanks to Proposition 3.16

$= \rho(\{\theta\} \cup (\{\lambda,\sigma_1\}\cup\Lambda_1) \cup \ldots \cup (\{\lambda,\sigma_m\}\cup\Lambda_m))$

$= \rho(\{\theta\} \cup \{\rho(\{\lambda,\sigma_1\}\cup\Lambda_1),\ldots,\rho(\{\lambda,\sigma_m\}\cup\Lambda_m)\})$
  thanks to Proposition 3.18

$= \rho(\{\theta\} \cup \{\rho(\{\lambda\sigma_1\}\cup\Lambda_1),\ldots,\rho(\{\lambda\sigma_m\}\cup\Lambda_m)\})$
  thanks to Proposition 3.16

$= \rho(\{\theta\} \cup \{\rho(\Theta_1) \circ \gamma_1\} \cup \ldots \cup \{\rho(\Theta_m) \circ \gamma_m\})$
  thanks to the equalities (3)

$\geq \rho(\{\theta\} \cup \{\rho(\Theta_1)\} \cup \ldots \cup \{\rho(\Theta_m)\})$
  thanks to Proposition 3.17

$= \rho(\{\theta\} \cup \Theta_1 \cup \ldots \cup \Theta_m)$
  thanks to Proposition 3.18 . ◊

As a corollary, we can now establish the existence of a solution subtree for a conjunction $\leftarrow G_1, \ldots, G_m$ from the existence of a solution subtree for $\leftarrow G_1\theta, \ldots, G_m\theta$, for some substitution θ.

Lifting lemma 4.19 Let P be a Horn clause program, $\leftarrow G_1, \ldots, G_m$ be a goal and σ be a substitution. Suppose there is a solution subtree U for $\leftarrow G_1\sigma, \ldots, G_m\sigma$. Then there is a solution subtree T for $\leftarrow G_1, \ldots, G_m$ with same tree skeleton. Furthermore, if $\sigma_1, \ldots, \sigma_n$ are the mgu's of U and $\theta_1, \ldots, \theta_n$ are those of T, then one has

$$\rho(\sigma,\sigma_1,\ldots,\sigma_n) = \sigma \circ \rho(\sigma_1,\ldots,\sigma_n) \geq \rho(\theta_1,\ldots,\theta_n).$$

212 BASIC SCHEME

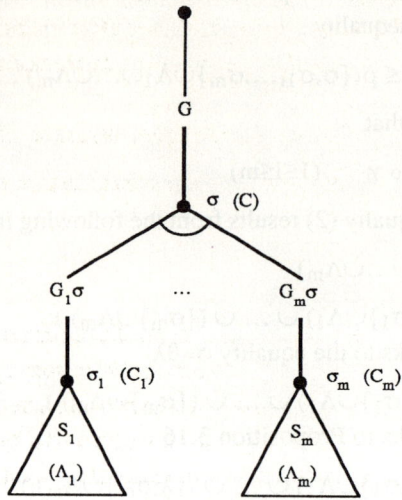

Figure 4.10

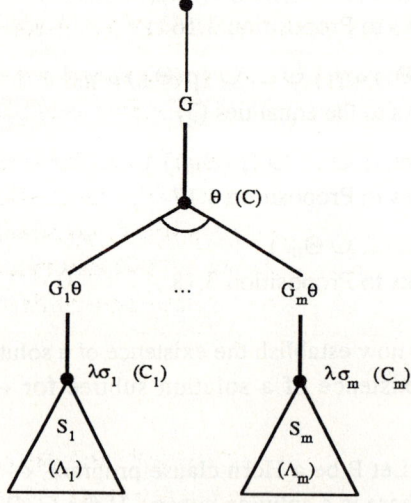

Figure 4.11

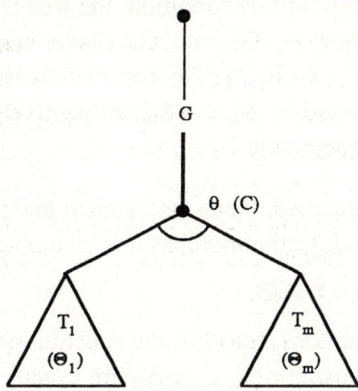

Figure 4.12

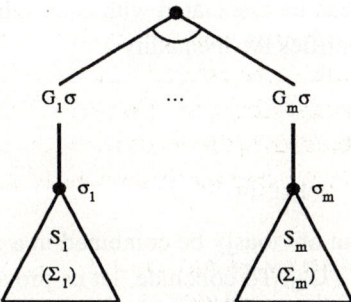

Figure 4.13

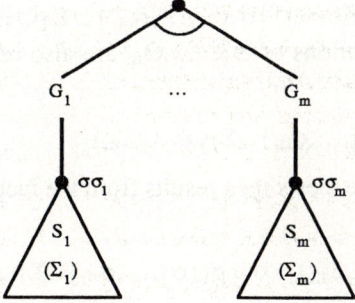

Figure 4.14

Proof The lemma is obviously verified in case the conjunction $\leftarrow G_1, ..., G_m$ is empty. Let us thus assume that it is not empty. In this condition, the tree U has the form given in Figure 4.13. The mgu's used to reduce $\leftarrow G_1, ..., G_m$ have been denoted by $\sigma_1, ..., \sigma_m$, respectively. Let $H_1 \leftarrow B_1, ..., H_m \leftarrow B_m$ be the involved clauses. The subtrees generated by $B_1\sigma_1, ..., B_m\sigma_m$ have been denoted by $S_1, ..., S_m$, respectively. The involved set of mgu's are designated by $\Sigma_1, ..., \Sigma_m$, respectively.

As the clauses have been renamed, it can be assumed that the substitution σ does not act on any variables of $B_1, ..., B_m$ and, furthermore, as it is idempotent, that

$$\text{dom}(\sigma) \cap [\text{dom}(\sigma_i) \cup \text{vcod}(\sigma_i)] = \emptyset,$$

for all $i \in \{1,...,m\}$. In these conditions, for all i, the substitution $\sigma\sigma_i$ is a unifier of G and H_i and the subgoals generated by G using $\sigma\sigma_1, ..., \sigma\sigma_m$ are exactly those generated by $G\sigma$ using $\sigma_1, ..., \sigma_m$, respectively. The tree of Figure 4.14 is thus an unrestricted solution subtree for $G_1, ..., G_m$ which looks like U except that the top goals and unifiers differ. Thanks to Lemma 4.18, a solution subtree, say T_i, can be associated with each subtree generated by each G_i. Its associated set of mgu's, say Θ_i, verifies the inequality

$$\rho(\Theta_i) \leq \rho(\{\sigma\sigma_i\} \cup \Sigma_i).$$

that is, thanks to Proposition 3.16,

$$\rho(\Theta_i) \leq \rho(\{\sigma,\sigma_i\} \cup \Sigma_i) \qquad (1 \leq i \leq m). \tag{1}$$

The subtrees $T_1, ..., T_m$ can obviously be combined in a candidate-solution subtree for the whole conjunction $\leftarrow G_1, ..., G_m$. To conclude, let us prove that the substitutions of $\Theta_1, ..., \Theta_m$ are reconcilable and verify the inequality

$$\rho(\Theta_1 \cup ... \cup \Theta_m) \leq \rho(\{\sigma,\sigma_1,...,\sigma_m\} \cup \Sigma_1 \cup ... \cup \Sigma_m) \equiv \sigma \circ \rho(\{\sigma_1,...,\sigma_m\} \cup \Sigma_1 \cup ... \cup \Sigma_m)$$

Indeed, the substitutions of the set $\{\sigma,\sigma_1,...,\sigma_m\} \cup \Sigma_1 \cup ... \cup \Sigma_m$ are, by hypothesis, reconcilable. Hence, the substitutions of $\Theta_1, ..., \Theta_m$ are also reconcilable. They furthermore verify the inequality

$$\rho(\Theta_1 \cup ... \cup \Theta_m) \leq \rho(\{\sigma,\sigma_1,...,\sigma_m\} \cup \Sigma_1 \cup ... \cup \Sigma_m)$$

thanks to the inequalities (1). The thesis then results from the fact that, thanks to the hypothesis made on σ, one has

$$\rho(\{\sigma,\sigma_1,...,\sigma_m\} \cup \Sigma_1 \cup ... \cup \Sigma_m) = \sigma \circ \rho(\{\sigma_1,...,\sigma_m\} \cup \Sigma_1 \cup ... \cup \Sigma_m). \ \Diamond$$

A characterization of the successful computations in terms of subsets of the Herbrand base will be useful. We subsequently introduce the sets of such atoms, called the success set, and prove that it is equal to the least Herbrand model of the considered program.

Definition 4.20 The *success set* of a Horn clause program P is the set of all ground atoms $A \in B_P$ such that there is a solution subtree for A.

Proposition 4.21 The success set of a Horn clause program is equal to its least Herbrand model.

Proof Let P be a Horn clause program. In view of Theorem 4.15, the success of P is in its least Herbrand model. It thus remains to prove that the least Herbrand model of P is contained in the success set of P. Let A be an element of the least Herbrand model of P. By the least fix point characterization Theorem 2.21, it is sufficient to establish that $T_P\uparrow n$ is in the success set of P, for all n. Let us proceed by induction on n. Suppose n=1 and let $A \in T_P\uparrow 1$. The atom A is a ground instance of a unit clause of P and clearly there is a solution subtree for A given P. Assume now n>1 and the result holds for n-1. Let $A \in T_P\uparrow n$. By definition, $A \in B_H$ and there are $A_1, ..., A_m \in T_P\uparrow(n-1)$ such that $A \leftarrow A_1, ..., A_m$ is a ground instance of a clause of P. The induction hypothesis provides each A_i with a solution subtree. All of them can be combined in a solution subtree for A since the A_i's are ground. The thesis then results from Lemma 4.18. ◊

The following lemma is a first completeness result.

Lemma 4.22 Let P be a Horn clause program and $\leftarrow G_1, ..., G_m$ be a non-empty goal. Suppose $P \models G_1 \land ... \land G_m$. Then there is a solution subtree for $\leftarrow G_1, ..., G_m$ given P with identity substitution as computed answer substitution.

Proof Let $X_1, ..., X_n$ be the variables of $G_1, ..., G_m$ and $a_1, ..., a_n$ be constants not appearing in $G_1, ..., G_m$ or P. Let furthermore θ be the substitution $\{X_1/a_1,...,X_m/a_m\}$. Obviously, the term $(G_1,...,G_m)\theta$ is ground and verifies the relation $P \models (G_1 \land ... \land G_m)\theta$. Proposition 4.21 then ensures the existence of a solution subtree for $\leftarrow (G_1,...,G_m)\theta$. Since the a_i's do not appear in $G_1, ..., G_m$ or P, a solution subtree for $\leftarrow G_1, ..., G_m$ can be obtained by replacing a_i by X_i in the solution subtree; the identity substitution is the corresponding computed answer substitution. ◊

We are now in a position to demonstrate the completeness property.

Completeness theorem 4.23 Let P be a Horn clause program and $\leftarrow G_1, ..., G_m$ be a goal. For every substitution σ such that $P \models (G_1 \land ... \land G_m)\sigma$ there exists a solution subtree for $\leftarrow G_1, ..., G_m$ with θ as computed answer substitution such that $Q\theta \leq Q\sigma$.

Proof Since $P \models (G_1 \land ... \land G_m)\sigma$, there exists, thanks to Lemma 4.22, a solution subtree T_1 for $\leftarrow (G_1,...,G_m)\sigma$ with the identity substitution as computed answer substitution. It corresponds, by Lemma 4.19, a solution subtree T_2 for $\leftarrow G_1, ..., G_m$ such that, if $\sigma_1,...,\sigma_n$ are the mgu's of T_1 and $\theta_1, ..., \theta_n$ are those of T_2, one has

$$\sigma \circ \rho(\sigma_1,...,\sigma_n) \geq \rho(\theta_1,...,\theta_m) .$$

The thesis then results from the equality

$$(G_1,...,G_m)(\sigma \circ \rho(\sigma_1,...,\sigma_m)) = (G_1,...,G_m)\sigma$$

obtained from the property of T_1 and Proposition 4.14.   ◊

4.5.3 General models

Soundness and completeness properties for unrestricted models (i.e. those with an arbitrary R-depth parameter) result from the previous ones provided the two following properties hold :

(i) no solution subtree is eliminated by process killing
(ii) the reconciliation-substitutions of such subtrees are not made less general by instantiations of goals or s-goals due to binding publications.

To be more precise, let us adopt the following terminology. Fix some R-depth D for the slices generated by the executions. Assume some query

←$G_1, ..., G_m$

and some Horn clause program P are given. Let T be the and/or search tree associated with the query.

The execution under general models results, in general, in the computation of an arbitrary number (possibly infinite but always denumerable) of computed and/or search trees. Let us denote by CT_i the computed and/or search tree delivered at the end of the ith reconciliation phase.

Given these conventions, the two above properties can be restated as follows:

For all integer Rd, any solution subtree ST of T of R-depth Rd verifies the two following properties

(I) for all $j \geq Rd/D$, the computed and/or search tree CT_j contains a solution subtree (for CT_j) of same skeleton as ST;
(II) the reconciliation-substitutions of such subtrees is the same and equals the reconciliation-substitution of ST.

A. Instance subtrees

The proofs of these properties will make use of instance subtrees. This concept is precisely defined as follows.

Definition 4.24 Let S be a (partial) solution subtree of T. Then an *instance subtree* of S is any subtree

- obtained from S by instantiating the s-goal or goal of nodes of some subtrees of S attached to some goal-nodes (these goal-nodes included) by any idempotent

substitution more general than the corresponding reconciliation-substitutions and formed of the same variables,
- whose unifiers are more general than the corresponding mgu's in S.

Instantiations corresponding to the description of the first item above are subsequently called *adequate*.

B. Proof of property I

Property I is proved by establishing the following stronger result.

Lemma 4.25 For any integer Rd, any solution subtree ST of T of R-depth Rd verifies the following properties.

(i) For any $j<Rd/D$, the computed and/or search tree C_j contains an instance subtree of the top part of R-depth $j*D$ of ST.

(ii) For any $j \geq Rd/D$, the computed and/or search tree C_j contains an instance subtree of ST. Moreover, all these instance subtrees share the same set of mgu's.

Proof Let Rd and ST be such integer and solution subtree, respectively. The lemma is proved by induction on the set of computed and/or search trees $\{CT_1, ..., CT_n, ...\}$.

1° for $\{CT_1\}$

The computed tree CT_1 is the top part of R-depth D of T where some nodes may be killed and others may be instantiated. The part of ST corresponding to this top part, say ST(1), has been created during the first generation phase. It is

- ST if $D \geq Rd$,
- some strict top part if $D < Rd$.

In both cases, the mgu's of ST_1 constitute a subset of the mgu's of ST. They are reconcilable, thanks to Proposition 3.18. No node of ST are thus removed at the reconciliation phase (see Specification 4.4). All that can occur at this phase is that some nodes are adequately instantiated. Summing up, the tree CT_1 contains an instance subtree of ST.

2° for $\{CT_1,...,CT_m\}$ with $m>1$

Assume now the property holds for $\{CT_1,...,CT_{m-1}\}$. Let us prove that it also holds for $\{C_1,...,C_m\}$. Two cases must be considered.

2.1 $Rd \leq (m-1)*D$

In this case, by induction hypothesis, an instance of ST, say ST(m-1), is already present in CT_{m-1}. Its leaves are □-nodes, as ST is a solution subtree. Hence, the mth generation phase does not modify it. Moreover, the mth reconciliation phase does not kill any of its nodes (thanks to Specification 4.4 and given the fact that ST is a solution subtree) but may further instantiate some of them adequaly. Summing up, a new instance of ST is thus created. It furthermore shares the same set of mgu's as ST(m-1).

2.2 Rd>(m-1)*D

In this case, by induction hypothesis, an instance subtree, say ST(m-1), of the top part of R-depth (m-1)*D is present in CT_{m-1}, too. Tip nodes that are not □-nodes are given for the mth generation phase and the slice of R-depth D they engender is created (see Specification 4.4). Let them be Tn_1, ..., Tn_t. Let Sn_1, ..., Sn_t be the corresponding nodes in ST. Because ST is a solution subtree and because of the adequate quality of the instantiations in ST(m-1), the clauses employed to construct the slices of R-depth D attached to Sn_1, ..., Sn_t in ST can also be used for building the slices of R-depth D attached to Tn_1, ..., Tn_t. Let N_1, ..., N_k denote the nodes of the latter slices. They are manifestly instances of the corresponding nodes in ST. Furthermore, the associated mgu's are also instances of the corresponding mgu's of ST since they result from the unification of an instance of s-goals with the same clauses. The subtree ST(m-1) augmented by the nodes N_1,..., N_k is thus an instance of ST or of its top part of R-depth m*D according as Rd is less than m*D. None of its nodes is removed during the mth reconciliation phase since the associated unifiers are a subset of instances of those of ST. All that can occur is that some nodes may be instantiated and this in an adequate way. Summing up, an instance subtree of ST has been pointed out. ◊

C. Proof of property II

Proving property II requires the following lemma.

Lemma 4.26 Let

- ← G_1, ..., G_m be a goal,
- σ be an idempotent substitution such that dom(σ) only contains variables of G_1, ..., G_m
- U be a solution subtree for ← $G_1σ$, ..., $G_mσ$ such that if $σ_1$, ..., $σ_n$ are the involved mgu's, the equality
    dom(σ) ∩ [dom($σ_i$)∪varcod($σ_i$)] = ∅
  holds for all i∈ {1,...,n}.

There is a solution subtree T of ← G_1, ..., G_m of same skeleton as U and such that the involved mgu's, say $θ_1$, ..., $θ_n$, verify

ρ(σ,$θ_1$,...,$θ_n$) = ρ(σ,$σ_1$,...,$σ_n$) .

Proof The lemma is again established by induction on the R-depth R of U.

1° R=0

If R=0, the conjunctions ← $G_1σ$, ..., $G_mσ$ and ← G_1, ..., G_m are empty and the tree U reduces to the only node □. In this case, T=U verifies the thesis.

$2° R > 0$

Assume now the thesis holds for any query, substitution and solution subtree of R-depth strictly less than R. Let us prove that it holds for any query $\leftarrow G_1, ..., G_m$, substitution σ and solution subtree of R-depth R.

Obviously, if R>0, then the query $\leftarrow G_1, ..., G_m$ is not empty. The tree U is furthermore of the form given in Figure 4.15. The clause and the mgu used to reduce each $G_i\sigma$ are denoted by $H_i \leftarrow B_i$ and λ_i, respectively ($1 \leq i \leq m$). The subtree generated by $B_i\lambda_i$ is referred to by S_i ($1 \leq i \leq m$). Finally, the set of mgu's included in S_i is denoted by Λ_i ($1 \leq i \leq m$).

Lemma 4.19 establishes the existence of a solution subtree for $G_1, ..., G_m$ of same skeleton as U such that the involved mgu's $\theta_1, ..., \theta_n$ verify

$$\rho(\sigma, \sigma_1, ..., \sigma_n) \equiv \sigma \circ \rho(\sigma_1, ..., \sigma_n) \geq \rho(\theta_1, ..., \theta_n).$$

We make the result stronger and prove that

$$\rho(\sigma, \theta_1, ..., \theta_n) \equiv \rho(\sigma, \sigma_1, ..., \sigma_n)$$

or, in view of the redistribution of $\sigma_1, ..., \sigma_n$ in $\lambda_1, ..., \lambda_m, \Lambda_1, ..., \Lambda_m$, that

$$\rho(\{\sigma, \theta_1, ..., \theta_n\}) \equiv \rho(\{\sigma, \lambda_1, ..., \lambda_m\} \cup \Lambda_1 \cup ... \cup \Lambda_m).$$

The proof is constructed in a very similar way to that of Lemma 4.19. Let us first examine the subtree generated by each G_i. Let us fix some i in $\{1, ..., m\}$. Obviously, the s-goal G_i can be reduced by the clause $H_i \leftarrow B_i$. Let θ_i be an idempotent mgu. As $\sigma\lambda_i$ is a unifier of G_i and H_i, the substitutions σ, λ_i and θ_i verify the inequality

$$\theta_i \leq \sigma\lambda_i$$

and, as θ_i is idempotent and thanks to Proposition 2.40, the equality

$$\sigma\lambda_i = \theta_i\sigma\lambda_i. \tag{1}$$

Moreover, the sets var(B_i) and dom(σ) are disjoint, thanks to the renaming of the clauses. The terms B_i and $B_i\sigma$ are thus equal and, consequently, thanks to equality (1), the equalities

$$B_i\lambda_i = B_i\sigma\lambda_i = B_i\theta\sigma\lambda_i$$

hold.

Summing up, the tree of Figure 4.16 is an unrestricted solution subtree of G_i. Its subtree S_i is of R-depth less than Rd-1 and can play the role of the U tree for the conjunction $\leftarrow (B_i\theta_i)\sigma\lambda_i$. By induction hypothesis, there is thus a solution subtree T_i for $\leftarrow B_i\theta_i$, whose set of idempotent mgu's Θ_i is such that

$$\rho(\{\sigma\lambda_i\} \cup \Theta_i) = \rho(\Lambda_i)$$

and consequently, thanks to the hypothesis made on σ and Proposition 3.16, such that

$$\rho(\{\sigma, \lambda_i\} \cup \Theta_i) = \rho(\Lambda_i). \tag{2}$$

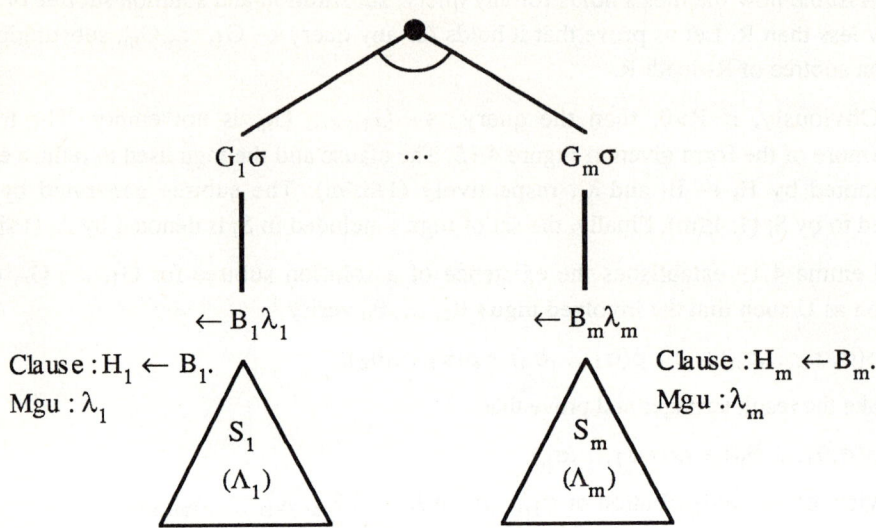

Figure 4.15

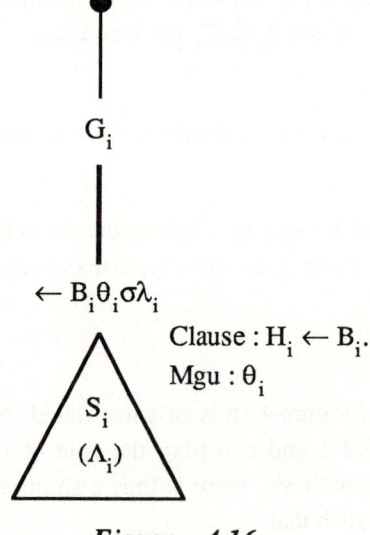

Figure 4.16

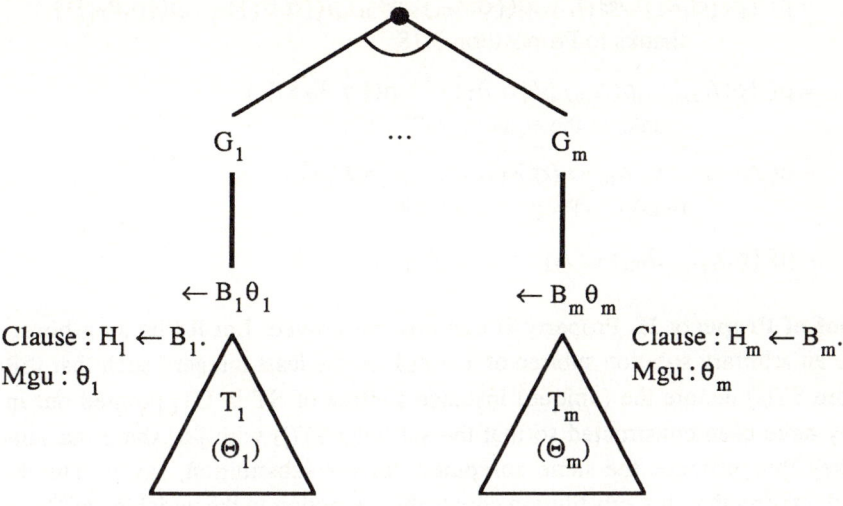

Figure 4.17

Assembling those subtrees T_i (see Figure 4.17) provides a good candidate solution subtree for $\leftarrow G_1, ..., G_m$. It has the same skeleton as U and only includes idempotent mgu's. To conclude, it remains to be proved that they are reconcilable and verify the equality

$$\rho(\{\sigma\}\cup\{\theta_1,...,\theta_m\}\cup\Theta_1\cup...\cup\Theta_m) = \rho(\{\lambda_1,...,\lambda_m\}\cup\Lambda_1\cup...\cup\Lambda_m).$$

We will only prove the equality. The reconcilable character results from it. Let us first note that Proposition 3.20 establishes the equalities

$$\rho(\sigma,\theta_i) = \rho(\sigma,\theta_i,\lambda_i) = \rho(\sigma,\lambda_i). \tag{3}$$

The thesis results from the following equalities

$\rho(\{\sigma\}\cup\{\theta_1,...,\theta_m\}\cup\Theta_1\cup...\cup\Theta_m)$

$= \rho(\{\sigma,\theta_1\}\cup...\cup\{\sigma,\theta_m\}\cup\Theta_1\cup...\cup\Theta_m)$

$= \rho(\{\rho(\{\sigma,\theta_1\}),...,\rho(\{\sigma,\theta_m\})\} \cup \Theta_1 \cup ... \cup \Theta_m)$
    thanks to Proposition 3.18

$= \rho(\{\rho(\{\sigma,\theta_1,\lambda_1\}),...,\rho(\{\sigma,\theta_m,\lambda_m\})\} \cup \Theta_1 \cup ... \cup \Theta_m)$
    thanks to equality (3)

$= \rho(\{\sigma,\theta_1,\lambda_1\}\cup...\cup\{\sigma,\theta_m,\lambda_m\}\cup\Theta_1\cup...\cup\Theta_m)$
    thanks to Proposition 3.18

$= \rho(\ (\{\sigma,\lambda_1\}\cup\Theta_1) \cup ... \cup (\{\sigma,\lambda_m\}\cup\Theta_m) \cup \{\sigma,\theta_1\}\cup ... \cup \{\sigma,\theta_m\})$

$$= \rho(\ \{\rho(\{\sigma,\lambda_1\}\cup\Theta_1),...,\rho(\{\sigma,\lambda_m\}\cup\Theta_m),\rho(\{\sigma,\theta_1\}),...,\rho(\{\sigma,\theta_m\})\}\ )$$
thanks to Proposition 3.18

$$= \rho(\ \{\rho(\Lambda_1),...,\rho(\Lambda_m),\rho(\{\sigma,\theta_1\}),...,\rho(\{\sigma,\theta_m\})\}\ )$$
thanks to the equalities (2) and (3)

$$= \rho(\ \Lambda_1 \cup ... \cup \Lambda_m \cup \{\sigma,\lambda_1\}\cup ... \cup \{\sigma,\lambda_m\})$$
thanks to Proposition 3.18

$$= \rho(\ \{\sigma,\lambda_1,...,\lambda_m\} \cup \Lambda_1 \cup ... \cup \Lambda_m\ )\ . \quad \Diamond$$

Proof of Property II Property II can now be proved. Let Rd be an arbitrary integer and ST be an arbitrary solution subtree of T. Let k be the least integer j such that j≥Rd/D. Let furthermore ST(i) denote the (unique) instance subtree of ST in CT_i pointed out in Lemma 4.25. They have been constructed so that the subtrees ST(j) with j≥k share the same sets of mgu's. They thus produce the same computed answer substitution, say υ. The thesis then amounts to proving that this substitution equals the restriction to the variables of G_1, ..., G_m of the reconciliation-substitution of ST. The subtree ST(k) may furthermore be considered to determine υ. We will establish this result by an induction on k.

1° k=1

In case k is 1, the mgu's of ST(1) are exactly those of ST and the equality is obviously established.

2° k>1

Assume Property II is established for solution subtrees whose R-depth R is such that R/D<k and let us establish it for the subtree ST. Let us first adopt the following terminology. Let

- FST be the top slice of R-depth D of ST,
- Θ be the set of mgu's of Fst
- Q_1, ..., Q_n be the tip nodes of Fst that are not □-nodes
- σ_1, ..., σ_n be the idempotent substitutions that instantiate Q_1, ..., Q_n at the end of the first reconciliation phase, respectively
- S_1, ..., S_n be the subtrees generated by Q_1, ..., Q_n in ST, respectively
- Θ_1, ..., Θ_n be their corresponding sets of mgu's
- U_1, ..., U_n be the corresponding subtrees in ST(k)
- Λ_1, ..., Λ_n be their sets of mgu's.

The subtrees ST and ST(k) are suggested in Figure 4.18. Remember that, for all i, the substitution σ_i is a subset of the reconciliation $\rho(\Theta)$.

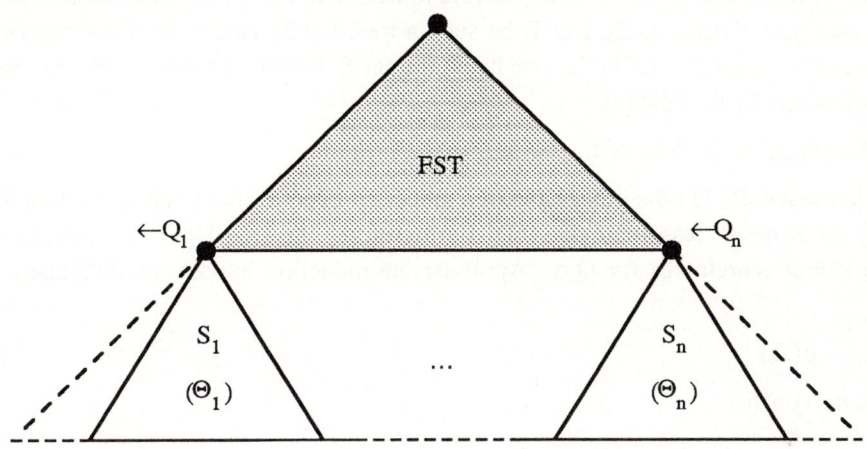

Subtree ST

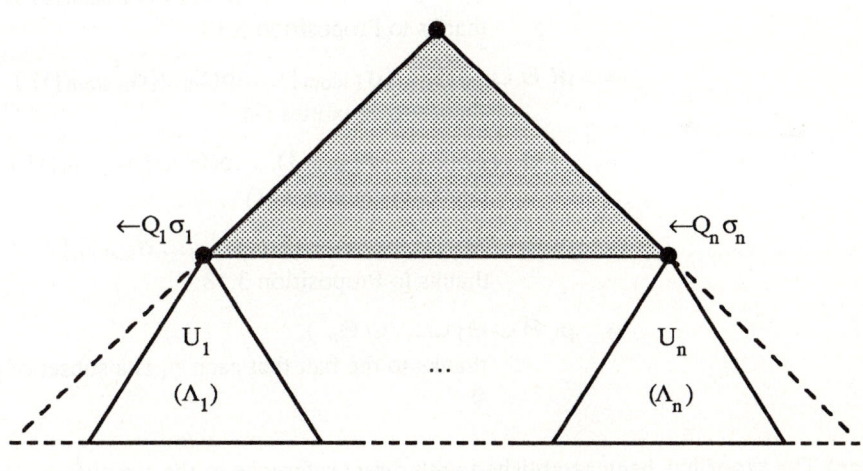

Subtree ST(k)

Figure 4.18

The induction reasoning is applied as follows. Fix arbitrarily i in $\{1,\ldots,n\}$ and consider $Q_i\sigma_i$. Since σ_i is a subset of $\rho(\Theta)$, it is possible to derive from S_i a solution subtree for $Q_i\sigma_i$ that uses the same clauses as S_i. Let T_i be such a tree. Let Σ_i be the involved mgu's. Two properties can be pointed out. On the one hand, the set Σ_i is related to the set Θ_i and the mgu atom subset $\sigma_{i,atom}$ by the equality

$$\rho(\Theta_i \cup \{\sigma_{i,atom}\}) = \rho(\Sigma_i \cup \{\sigma_{i,atom}\}), \tag{1}$$

thanks to Lemma 4.26. On the other hand, the induction hypothesis can be applied on T_i. It is manifestly of R-depth less than $(k-1)*D$. Furthermore, the tree U_i is the corresponding computed and/or search tree for $Q_i\sigma_i$. Applying the induction hypothesis thus leads to the equality

$$\rho(\Lambda_i) = \rho(\Sigma_i). \tag{2}$$

and thus to the equality

$$\rho(\Lambda_i \cup \{\sigma_{i,atom}\}) = \rho(\Sigma_i \cup \{\sigma_{i,atom}\}).$$

The thesis then results from the following equalities

$$\begin{aligned}
\rho(\Theta \cup \Lambda_1 \cup \ldots \cup \Lambda_n) &= \rho(\Theta \cup \{\sigma_{1,atom},\ldots,\sigma_{n,atom}\} \cup \Lambda_1 \cup \ldots \cup \Lambda_n) \\
&\qquad \text{thanks to the fact that each } \sigma_i \text{ is a subset of } \rho(\Theta) \\
&= \rho(\Theta \cup \{\rho(\Lambda_1 \cup \{\sigma_{1,atom}\}),\ldots,\rho(\Lambda_n \cup \{\sigma_{n,atom}\})\}) \\
&\qquad \text{thanks to Proposition 3.18} \\
&= \rho(\Theta \cup \{\rho(\Sigma_1 \cup \{\sigma_{1,atom}\}),\ldots,\rho(\Sigma_n \cup \{\sigma_{n,atom}\})\}) \\
&\qquad \text{thanks to equalities (2)} \\
&= \rho(\Theta \cup \{\rho(\Theta_1 \cup \{\sigma_{1,atom}\}),\ldots,\rho(\Theta_n \cup \{\sigma_{n,atom}\})\}) \\
&\qquad \text{thanks to equalities (1)} \\
&= \rho(\Theta \cup \Theta_1 \cup \ldots \cup \Theta_n \cup \{\sigma_{1,atom},\ldots,\sigma_{n,atom}\}) \\
&\qquad \text{thanks to Proposition 3.18} \\
&= \rho(\Theta \cup \Theta_1 \cup \ldots \cup \Theta_n) \\
&\qquad \text{thanks to the fact that each } \sigma_i \text{ is a subset of } \rho(\Theta).
\end{aligned}$$

◊

Remark The proof has been established with direct reference to the simplified Conclog model for ease of comprehension. It is however worth noting that it holds in fact for idempotent substitutions σ_i verifying

$$\sigma_i \leq \rho(\Theta)$$

$$\bigcup_{\theta \in \Theta} [\mathrm{dom}(\theta) \cup \mathrm{varcod}(\theta)] \supset [\mathrm{dom}(\sigma_i) \cup \mathrm{varcod}(\sigma_i)].$$

Moreover, it also holds for binding publication as it is described in Section 4.3.1.2.2 (which makes the only differences between the simplified and real models). Indeed, any tip node associated with a non empty goal is still instantiated by the bindings issued from all the partial solution subtrees in which it participates.

4.5.4 Variants of the model

Soundness and completeness of the variant models introduced in Section 4.4 are now proved. They can be directly derived from the results of the previous subsections.

- It is manifestly the aim of Section 4.5.2 to establish that the Conclog model is sound and complete whatever the R-depth parameter takes as value.
- Proposition 4.14 and the results of Section 4.5.3 establish that the model is kept sound and complete by adapting binding publication as suggested in Section 4.4.2.
- Proposition 4.14 also allows substitutions to be restricted as indicated in Section 4.4.3.
- As solution subtrees and their reconciliation-substitutions are not modified by adapting instantiation messages as indicated in Section 4.4.4, the resulting model is also sound and complete.
- Soundness and completeness of the model of Section 4.4.5 result from the soundness and completeness of the model of Section 4.4.4.
- Finally, soundness and completeness of the er-model of Section 4.4.6 are consequences of the results of Section 4.5.3.

4.6 Comparison with related work

Let us now compare the Conclog basic model with other parallel execution models. These models are presented according to the two approaches for handling and-parallelism :

(i) reconciliation of conflicting bindings resulting from the independent resolutions of subgoals ([Pollard, 1981]).

(ii) determination of a producer subgoal for each shared variable ([Conery and Kibler, 1981], [Conery, 1983], [Lin et al., 1986], [Li and Martin, 1986], [Conery, 1987b], [Kalé, 1987])

The comparison with other work, more related to parallel logic programming languages or parallel implementations of logic programming languages, is pursued in Chapters 6 and 7 (where Conclog is treated as a (complete) language rather than a pure parallel execution scheme, as here).

Our model is more closely related to the first approach. We thus first point out its specific differences.

4.6.1 Independent resolution with reconciliation

The principle of solving subgoals independently and of reconciling substitutions was first proposed in [Pollard, 1981]. It is, to our best knowledge, the only one today to use such an approach. Our scheme is very similar. It differs however by the way bindings are reconciled and and/or search trees are managed. Reconciliation of bindings has already been treated in Chapter 3. We thus now only turn to the and/or search tree management.

A. Description

A.1 Terminology

The management of and/or search trees in [Pollard, 1981] is based on the notions of scope and filter. They themselves use the notions of primary unifiers and auxiliary unifiers :
- The mgu's of the and/or search tree constitute the *primary unifiers*.
- The unifiers resulting from reconciliation (such as the substitution θ in Subsection A of Section 3.4.1.1) constitute the *auxiliary unifiers*.

The notion of scope is defined as follows.

(i) The *scope of a primary unifier* at the node N is the singleton {N}.
(ii) The *scope of an auxiliary unifier* resulting from the reconciliation of unifiers with scopes S_1 and S_2 is formed from the union of S_1 and S_2 by deleting the nodes which are ancestors of others in the union.

The interpretation Pollard places in scopes is that if a scope S of a unifier θ is a subset of any particular solution then θ is a member of the corresponding substitution.

The notion of scope is extended to the case where reconciliation fails. If so, the notion of *filter* which is computed in the same way as the scope of an auxiliary unifier is produced. The filter interpretation is that no candidate solution which includes a filter is a solution.

The notion of subsumption is finally required. A set of nodes S_1 is said to *subsume* another set of nodes S_2 if every node in S_1 is an ancestor of some node in S_2.

A.2 Computation principles

With these concepts, Pollard builds up several principles in order to avoid wasting time in useless manipulations of the and/or search tree. Two of these principles are quite intuitive; they are based on the following remarks.

P_1. A candidate solution subtree must not necessarily be fully computed in order to determine whether a given filter is a subset of it. Hence, partially complete computations can be abandoned under appropriate circumstances.

P_2. Reconciliations are relevant if and only if the scope of the resulting auxiliary unifier or the filter is a subset of some candidate solution subtree. Consequently, a rule for determining whether or not a set of nodes is a subset of some candidate solution subtree is of importance. It should be apparent that the following works : for each pair of nodes in the set, their nearest common ancestor is a goal-node. In practice, however, given two unifiers with scope $S_1 = \{N_1, ..., N_n\}$ and $S_2 = \{M_1, ..., M_m\}$, it is not necessary to compute the scope of the auxiliary unifier or the filter and then to test each pair of nodes for conjointness, the n*m tests with one node coming from each scope are sufficient.

(P3) A filter F_1 is redundant when it is subsumed by another filter F_2. In this case, it can be removed.

Finally, some principles are directed to the filtering and pruning of the and/or search tree. They are based on three operations : promotion, reduction and pruning.

i) Promotion

This operation creates a filter owing to the existence of other ones. A set of filters $F_1, ..., F_n$ is promoted to form a filter $(F_1 \cap ... \cap F_n) \cup \{N\}$ if for each F_i ($1 \le i \le n$), $F_i \setminus (F_1 \cap ... \cap F_n)$ is a singleton, say $\{N_i\}$, and if $N_1, ..., N_n$ are all the children of a child of the node N.

Promotion of filters is justified as follows. Let F' be $(F_1 \cap ... \cap F_n)$ and N' be the father of $N_1, ..., N_n$. Recall that both $F_1, ..., F_n$ only contain goal-nodes so one representation may be as in Figure 4.19.

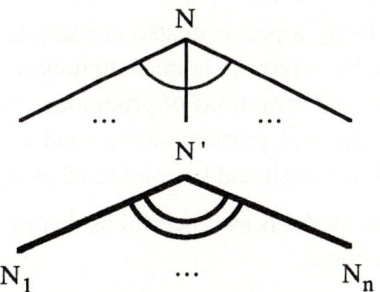

Figure 4.19

The justification results from the fact that no solution includes the set $F' \cup \{N\}$. Indeed, any candidate solution subtree that contains N must contain one child of N'. Therefore, any candidate solution subtree including $F' \cup \{N\}$ also contains one of the filters $F_1, ..., F_n$ and cannot correspond to a solution.

ii) Reduction

Promotion raises the possibility that the node N is an ancestor of some other nodes of F'. More generally, it may happen that filters contain nodes which are ancestors of others. In this case, such filters may be made simpler by deleting these ancestral nodes. This process is called *reduction* and is easily justified from the definition of a filter.

iii) Pruning

Deletion in a filter may reduce it to a singleton. Appealing to the interpretation placed in filters, the remaining node cannot be included in any solution subtree; hence, it can be removed from the and/or search tree as well as the subtree it generates. Pollard calls this operation the *pruning* of the and/or search tree.

More precisely, pruning involves the following aspects : let {N} be the considered filter,
- deletion of filters subsumed by {N};
- killing of all computations whose projected unifiers or filters are subsumed by {N}. In particular, this includes computations which seek to extend the subtree generated from node N.

B. Comparison

Conserving the spirit of equation manipulation, our model takes another approach for managing the and/or search tree. The most apparent difference is its simplicity, which makes it, to our opinion, very attractive. Every aspect is treated in a simple uniform framework (based on multi-equations manipulation). No reference is made to notions of primary and auxiliary unifiers, scope, filter, subsumption and operations of promotion, reduction and pruning. In particular, we found the distinction between primary unifiers and auxiliary unifiers unskilful since bindings resulting from reconciliations should be considered as identical to those reconciled.

Despite its simplicity, our model is as powerful as that of [Pollard, 1981]. This claim is argued from the following four points.

(i) Principle P_1 is also taken into account in our model. Indeed, we do not wait for a candidate solution subtree to be completely constructed to reject it if it cannot contribute to a solution. We do this as soon as reconciliation establishes such an impossibility.

(ii) Principle P_2 is of no concern for our computation model. In fact, we do not have to worry whether a set of nodes is a subset of a candidate solution subtree since, by construction, we only consider such subsets.

(iii) Principle P_3 as well as the promotion and reduction operations are irrelevant to our model too, since we do not manipulate filters.

(iv) The pruning operation corresponds, in our model, to the cutting of child nodes that do not participate to any partial solution subtree.

Finally, our model is also as efficient as that of [Pollard, 1981]. The two models differ by two features : filter handling and binding communication.

(i) *Filter handling.* In [Pollard, 1981], the role of filters is to memorize the associations of nodes that are known to be of no solution. This memorization is handled in our model for nodes that are of no solution subtrees. Such nodes are removed and thus are thereafter completely discarded. However, pairs of nodes that are incompatible are not memorized and thus are still handled. Nevertheless, in this case, our experience suggests that filter memorization increases the computation time rather than it improves it. On the one hand, the added work in our model is just one unnecessary reconciliation per filter but, as bindings generally involve terms of simple structure, failure in the reconciliation process occurs, in general, rapidly. On the other hand, employing filters increases the normal reconciliation by the test whether the associated set of nodes is a filter or not. Furthermore, some extra manipulations on filters have to be made. All in all, we believe that filter memorization induces an increase in time rather than a decrease.

(ii) *Binding publication.* In [Pollard, 1981], no binding publication is performed. Our model contrasts by making some bindings public at the reconciliation phases. For any subtree ST, those bindings correspond to the common part of the reconciliation-substitutions of the partial solution subtrees of ST. This results in the instantiation of nodes of ST. The importance of the publication of bindings should be stressed. It prevents the execution from developing branches that are a priori known as unproductive. Hence, communicating bindings decreases the overall cost of the computation.

Summing up, our model appears to be simpler than that of [Pollard, 1981]. This simplicity is not at the expense of computation power or efficiency. On the one hand, our model supports the same computation principles and is even more powerful by ensuring binding communication. On the other hand, the two major differences, viz. filter memorization and binding communication, appear to make Pollard's scheme less efficient than ours.

4.6.2 Determination of producer subgoals

As discussed earlier, another way to manage and-parallelism consists in determining a producer subgoal for each shared variable of a goal. This scheme has been first proposed in [Conery and Kibler, 1981] and [Conery, 1983]. The backtracking algorithm there presented has been proved to be false and has been corrected in [Lin et al., 1986]. It has thereafter been improved in [Conery, 1987b]. Other work ([Li and Martin, 1986], [Kalé, 1987]) has been concerned with eliminating the necessity to backtrack by including more or-parallelism in Conery's scheme.

The models of [Conery, 1983], [Li and Martin, 1986] and [Kalé, 1987] are discussed hereafter. They are subsequently referred to as D-models. The modifications brought in [Lin et al., 1986] and [Conery, 1987b] are not described since they do not add anything to our comparison. Of course, the following section is limited to our purposes. More details can be found in the above references.

4.6.2.1 General principles

As already said, D-models determine a producer subgoal for each shared variable of a goal. This subgoal is the only one allowed to generate bindings for the variable. Other subgoals containing it can just use these bindings and are thus evaluated only after the producer subgoal has computed some bindings. Those subgoals are called consumer subgoals or, simply, consumers.

D-models differ in the ways bindings are communicated and are consumed. These range from sequential ones in [Conery, 1983], parallel for communication and sequential for consumption in [Li and Martin, 1986] and parallel ones in [Kalé, 1987]. Nevertheless, two components are shared by the three D-models with, of course, some adaptation in each one.

(i) An *ordering algorithm* is used to determine the producer subgoals for shared variables.

(ii) A *forward execution component* is used to monitor the execution of subgoals in view of their ordering and the computed substitutions.

A. The ordering algorithm

The ordering algorithm takes a conjunction of s-goals (i.e. a goal) as input and delivers an ordering of them as output. This ordering is expressed in a graph, called the dataflow graph. It links, for each shared variable, the producer of the variable to its consumers.

The precise way in which the ordering is done is out of purpose for our discussion. Nevertheless, the simplest form, due to [Conery, 1983] is quite illustrative of some problems that may be involved in the D-models approach. It uses the four following rules in the subsequent order.

1. The head of the clause is the generator for all the variables that are instantiated when the clause is invoked;
2. Annotations may be used. They specify that certain atomic formulae must be or cannot be a producer for some arguments;
3. A so-called connection rule states that among the subgoals sharing a variable, those which have the larger number of instantiated variables may be the producer for that variable.

4. In case these three rules are not sufficient to designate a single producer, the leftmost subgoal of the conjunction is chosen as producer.

B. The forward execution component

The forward execution component aims at solving an ordered conjunction of s-goals. It essentially consists of a graph reduction algorithm. S-goals of the dataflow graph with no predecessor are launched first. When solved, they are removed from the graph as well as the arcs leaving them. The ordering algorithm is then applied to the instance (by the produced bindings) of the remainder of the conjunction. The process is thereafter repeated until the current dataflow graph is empty.

It is worth noting that applying the ordering algorithm is necessary to handle cases where a variable, say X, is bound to a non-variable term, say t. In this case, all consumer subgoals of X are candidate producers of the variables contained in t. The dataflow graph is thus in reality precised dynamically.

As already said, the ways in which the s-goals are reduced and the resulting bindings are transmitted differ from one model to another. We now examine them one by one and point out the specific treatments implied by the employed strategies.

4.6.2.2. Conery's and/or process model

As usual, clauses unifying with s-goals are first searched and then tried in parallel. As soon as one of the clauses has been completely reduced, the generated bindings (constituting one solution for the s-goal) are passed to the consumer subgoals. Other solutions are conserved and used when failure occurs. Failure is reported at the forward execution component if no unifying clause can be found or if all the unifying clauses lead to failure. In this case, previously solved subgoals are re-solved.

Some form of backtracking is thus needed. Conery provides an algorithm, called the backward execution algorithm for this purpose. It is this algorithm that has been revised in [Lin et al., 1986] and [Conery, 1987b]. It is quite elaborated and is out of purpose for our discussion. The interested reader is referred to the above references for further details.

4.6.2.3 The Sync model

In the Sync model ([Li and Martin, 1986]), producer subgoals do not transmit generated bindings one by one but as soon as they are generated. They are however still sequentially treated by consumer subgoals.

An important consequence of this strategy of communication is that backtracking is no more needed. As a counterpart, special markers must be used to separate solutions obtained from distinct bindings. A join operator is furthermore needed to combine solutions of (independently solved) subgoals coherently.

4.6.2.4 The Reduce-or process model

In the Reduce-or process model ([Kalé, 1987]), producer subgoals also communicate bindings as soon as they are produced. The novelty is that these bindings are concurrently consumed : given a shared variable X, a producer subgoal G and the consumer subgoals of X, say $G_1, ..., G_m$, a process is created for each instance of $(G_1, ..., G_m)$ by each transmitted binding.

No backtracking is thus also needed in this model. There is furthermore no need to separate solutions resulting from distinct bindings since this is ensured by the concurrent executions of processes associated with the transmitted bindings.

4.6.2.5 Comparison

A. Completeness

In contrast with the Conclog model, the models of [Conery, 1983] and of [Li and Martin, 1986] are not complete. This is due to the ordering strategy and is not really surprising since incompleteness is on a par with depth first search strategies. As an example, let us consider the following program

    p([]).
    p([a]).
    q([],[]).
    q(X,[Y|Z]) ← q(X,Z).

and the query ←p(X),q(X,Y) with X and Y unbound. The ordering algorithm designates p(X) as the producer of X and q(X,Y) as the consumer of X and the producer of Y. Let us suppose that the evaluation of p(X) yields the binding X/[a] first. Then the query evaluation never terminates. Indeed, reducing q([a],Y) implies exploring an infinite branch of the and/or search tree. It is only after q([a],Y) fails, for Conery's model, or terminates, for the Sync model, (none of the two situations occurs) that the other binding X/[] for X would be considered. It is furthermore worth noting that there is no means such as clause ordering to prevent X/[a] to be produced before X/[].

Kalé (1987) provides another interesting example of incompleteness. Suppose the query

    ← p(X), q(Y), t(X,Y)

is asked. Assume p and q are infinite relations and t(X,Y) is a test only predicate. According to Conery's ordering algorithm (and any intuitive one), processes p and q are respectively producers of X and Y. Assume the solutions generated by p(X) and q(Y) are $x_1, ..., x_m, ...$ and

$y_1, ..., y_n, ...$, respectively. Assume finally that $t(x_1,y_j)$ does not hold for any y_j. Then the solution (x_2,y_2) will never be found since the choice of x_1 for X will be called into doubt after all the y_j have been tested with it.

Note that the Reduce-or model is complete. This is due to the fact that all bindings are treated in parallel. Restated in other terms, a breadth first search strategy takes place here instead of the above depth first search one.

B. Rigidity of the dataflow

All the D-models suffer from other problems arising from the rigidity of the static dataflow determined.

1) In those models, there are no means of killing unproductive branches of producer processes. To be more specific, let us consider the query

$\leftarrow$ a(X,Y), b(X,T), c(Y,S), d(T,S).

Assume the relation c(Y,S) only holds for some value of Y, say y*. The involved dataflow graph is depicted in Figure 4.20. Bindings for X and Y are produced by the evaluation of a(X,Y). Many bindings of Y to terms different from y* may be produced. None of the D-models however provides some means of stopping their production. In particular, in case the bindings involve complex terms, their progressive construction cannot be stopped when their generated parts make them different from y*. The Conclog model contrasts by intermittently suppressing them.

2) None of the D-models can handle more structured dataflows, such as those involved in the back communication mechanism. This consists of making a consumer instantiate a variable generated by some producer. Let us consider the following example to illustrate this dataflow. Suppose the query

$\leftarrow$ gen1(X), cons1(X)

is given with the program

gen1([S,T,U]) $\leftarrow$ gen2(S), cons2(T,U).
cons1([a,t_1,_]).
...
cons1([a,t_p,_]).
...
cons1([c,t_q,_]).
...
cons1([c,t_m,_]).
gen2(a).
cons2 $\leftarrow$ infinite relation

The computation should ideally proceed as follows. The subgoal gen1(X) (of the query) should be evaluated first. The s-goal gen2 should then start to reduce whereas cons2 should suspend. Thereafter, in view of the value "a" delivered for S, the subgoal cons1 should instantiate T and transmit the bindings to cons2 to continue the computation of U.

All the D-models are obviously unable to deal with such a situation. The Conclog model contrasts by making such communication through reconciliation phases. A very simple form of back communication has already been given in Section 3.6 through coroutining. More elaborated forms will be made later thanks to annotations in Chapter 5.

C. The ordering algorithm

It is worth noting that determining the appropriate producer subgoal automatically is impossible in all cases. Indeed, a basic requirement for this subgoal is that it finds its solutions or any finite incremental part in a finite time. However, this is an undecidable problem. We furthermore believe that it is not possible to find a sufficiently general class of problems for which the automatic detection of the appropriate producer subgoal would be possible. Restated in other terms, any ordering algorithm fails to determine the appropriate producer subgoal in some cases. The D-models are thus limited by nature. To further substantiate our claim, let us prove that Conery's ordering algorithm, although intuitive, fails in elementary situations. Consider the following matrix multiplication :

    matrix_mult(A,B,Res) ← inner_matrix_mult(A,B_transposed,Res),
                                          transpose(B,B_transposed).

Assume the procedure matrix_mult is used with arguments A and B ground and Res to be found. The proper sequence is first to reduce the transpose subgoal, instantiating B_transposed and then to compute the inner products by evaluating the inner_matrix_mult subgoal. However, the ordering algorithm applies its 4th rule and selects the inner_matrix_mult subgoal as the generator of B_transposed!

D. Dataflow directed computations

It must nevertheless be recognized that the Conclog scheme is computationally more expensive in situations where a dataflow can be identified. This is particularly the case for producer/consumer schemes. To be specific, let us consider the one clause procedure

    r(X,Z) ← p(X,Y), q(Y,Z).   1

Let ←r(V,t), where t is a ground term, be the query to be solved. The dataflow usually induced is to produce instantiations for Y by evaluating q(Y,t) and then to determine bindings for X by means of the evaluation of p(X,Y).

---

[1] A classical instance is the grand-father definition : grand_father(X,Z) ← father(X,Y), parent(Y,Z).

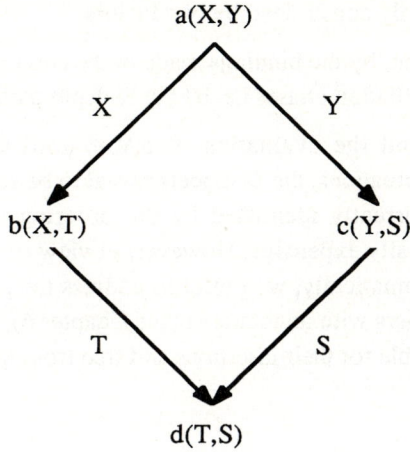

Figure 4.20

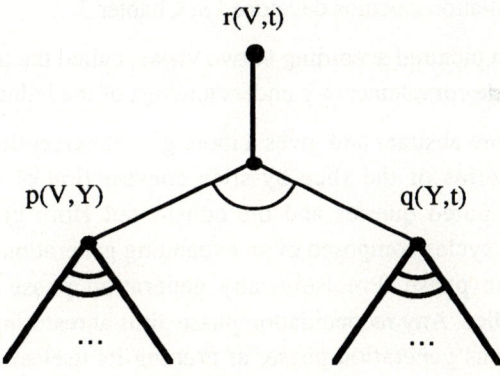

Figure 4.21

The Conclog model does not care for this dataflow and constructs the and/or search tree given by Figure 4.21. The subtree generated by p(V,Y) is, in some cases, computationally expensive and its growth is only constrained by two factors

- through reconciliation, by the bindings made in the subtree generated by q(Y,t),
- by the rate of reconciliation phases i.e. by the R-depth parameter of the model.

Often, it is better to suspend the evaluation of p(V,Y) until that of q(Y,t) has produced instantiations for Y. In these situations, the D-models reveal to be superior to the Conclog model provided the dataflow is correctly identified by the ordering algorithm and the ordering algorithm is not computationally expensive. However, in view of the difficulty of designating the right dataflow graph automatically, we prefer to address the problem at the programming level by providing programmers with annotations (see Chapter 6). This has the twofold advantage of making them responsible for their insertions and free from incorrect automatic detection.

4.7 Conclusion

This chapter has presented a parallel execution model of Horn clauses. It uses a reconciliation-based approach and embodies both or-parallelism and full and-parallelism. In particular, subgoals of any goal are reduced in a purely concurrent manner even if they do share variables. Conflicting bindings may result. They are handled in a reconciliation procedure making use of the reconciliation calculus developed in Chapter 3.

The model has been pictured according to two views, called the tree view and the process view. Both of them provide complementary understandings of the induced computations.

The tree view is more abstract and gives a more global perception of the computation. It has described them in terms of the slice by slice construction of the and/or search trees associated with the computed queries and the considered Horn clause programs. Such a construction results from cycles composed of an expanding generation phase followed by a re-organizing reconciliation phase. Precisely, any generation phase aims at extending the constructed part by one slice. Any reconciliation phase aims at restoring consistency in the part resulting from the previous generation phase, at pruning its useless branches, at publishing bindings and at delivering newly produced solutions.

The process view is more specific and gives a more local perception of the computations. It has described them in terms of the behavior of processes. Roughly speaking, any computation consists of activating one process associated with the considered query. Any created process then spends its life in creating children processes as parallel processes, in waiting for them to report substitutions, in performing some reconciliation procedure and in sending substitutions to its father process or, for the query process, in delivering some substitutions. Processes associated with the last step of a successful or failed derivation make exception. They create no child but directly report success or failure to their father, respectively.

As already said, the two views are not conflicting but complementary. They correspond through a one to one correspondence associating a process to each node of the computed and/or search tree. Their complementarity is best stressed by the two following facts.

1° Cycles engendered by the generation and reconciliation phases (tree view) force the basic life of the processes to be refined (process view) as follows.

- The slice by slice generation of the and/or search tree constrains the generation of processes. Processes are also created slice by slice. Assume the ith cycle is under execution. Processes that
    - correspond to tip nodes of the ith slice of the and/or search tree
    - are not associated with successful or failed derivations

  create no child in this i^{th} generation phase but directly report some substitution. They are reactivated to resume their children creation once the query-process has completely performed its ith reconciliation phase.
- Reconciliation phases further induce two operations on processes. On the one hand, a process may be told to die because it cannot contribute to any answer substitution to the query. On the other hand, it may be communicated bindings made public by reconciliation.

2° The apparent strict interleaving of the generation and reconciliation phases (tree view) is in fact relaxed by the parallel behavior of processes (process view). Indeed, as processes behave concurrently and perform their reconciliation procedure incrementally, parts of and/or search trees may be under reconciliation whereas others are still under generation. One important consequence is that solutions may be produced whereas others are still under computation.

Nevertheless, one synchronization point remains : a new generation phase can only be started when the previous reconciliation phase is ended. The rate at which these synchronization points occur may greatly influence the efficiency of the computations. It is in fact determined by the value of the depth of the generated slices. This value has been discussed. Among others, two computations result from it : coroutining with early detection of failure and unrestricted computations.

The depth of the slices has been incorporated as a parameter of the model. A family of execution models is thus in fact presented. All of them have been proved to be both sound and complete. They thus constitute a good basis for a concurrent language stressing the declarative aspect of logic programming. Negation remains to be incorporated. This is the purpose of the next chapter.

Chapter 5

Incorporating negation

5.1 Introduction

Although not theoretically necessary, negation is, in practice, a very convenient feature. To convince the skeptical readers, let us show how far it naturally appears. Consider the delete relation with the following specification :

> delete(L,El,L_filtered) holds iff the list L_filtered is the list L where all occurrences of El have been removed.

It can be defined constructively by means of the following equivalence :

$$\begin{aligned}
\text{delete(L,El,L\_filtered)} \Leftrightarrow \ & L = [] \wedge \text{L\_filtered} = [] \\
& \vee \\
& L = [H|T] \wedge (\ H = El \wedge \text{delete(T,El,L\_filtered)} \\
& \qquad \vee \\
& \qquad H \neq El \wedge \text{L\_filtered} = [H|\text{L\_filtered\_rem}] \\
& \qquad \wedge \text{delete(T,El,L\_filtered\_rem)}\ )
\end{aligned}$$

or equivalently by

$$\begin{aligned}
\text{delete(L,El,L\_filtered)} \Leftrightarrow \ & L = [] \wedge \text{L\_filtered} = [] \\
& \vee \\
& L = [El|T] \wedge \text{delete(T,El,L\_filtered)} \\
& \vee \\
& L = [El|T] \wedge H \neq El \wedge \text{L\_filtered} = [H|\text{L\_filtered\_rem}] \\
& \qquad \wedge \text{delete(T,El,L\_filtered\_rem)}\ .
\end{aligned}$$

The first two conjunctions are easily translated into Horn clauses, namely

delete([],_,[]).
delete([El|T],El,L_filtered) ← delete(T,El,L_filtered).

The last conjunction contains a negation and cannot be directly expressed in the Horn clause framework. However, one is naturally tempted to write a clause of the form delete([H|T],El,[H|L_filtered_rem]) ← H≠El, delete(T,El,L_filtered_rem).

This difficulty is circumvented in logic programming by introducing the special predicate not/1 in Horn clauses, thus extending them. Thanks to it, the above clause is then rewritten as

delete([H|T],El,[H|L_filtered_rem]) ← not(H=El), delete(T,El,L_filtered_rem).

To complete the remedy an operational semantics has to be defined. To that effect, let us first note that negation can, in general, take three places : at the head of a clause, in the body of a clause and in a query. Negation in clause heads provides the full power of first order logic and needs a more expensive form of resolution than ours. In contrast, one of the very attractive features of Horn clauses with the resolution principle recalled in Chapter 2 is precisely that it can be implemented very efficiently. Hence, the only places where the not predicate is usually allowed to appear are in queries and clause bodies. It follows that there is no means of deriving negative information from the computational model. The following trick is generally employed for that purpose. It consists of solving not(p) by first solving p and inverting the answers delivering yes if no is found and vice versa. This is known as *negation as failure*. Its great advantage is that it can be implemented with essentially no extra cost to the resolution system. Its main drawback is that it is not "real" negation. More specifically, variables have to be carefully manipulated as the result generally depends on the reduction strategies. For instance, with Prolog depth first search strategy and with regards to the following one clause program

p(a).

not(p(X)) fails whereas not(p(b)) succeeds. In fact, not(p($\bar{X}$)), with $\bar{X}$ the variables occurring in p, is interpreted as $\neg (\exists \bar{X}\ p(X))$ instead of $\exists \bar{X}\ (\neg p(X))$. These, of course, are not always the same. Nevertheless, works ([Apt et al., 1988], [Barbuti and Martelli, 1986], [Cavedon and Lloyd, 1990], [Clark, 1978], [Dahl, 1980], [Jaffar et al., 1983], [Lloyd and Topor, 1985], [Lloyd and Topor, 1986], [Shepherderson, 1984]) have been done to identify situations where there is equivalence. It appears therefrom that negation as failure rule can be considered as viable.

5.1.1 Intuition

Negation is introduced in Conclog by means of the negation as failure rule too. It takes benefit from the basic model to bring out a form of negation very close to the real negation. On the one hand, or-parallelism provides a means of collecting all solutions at the same time and to avoid the wrong interpretation $\neg (\exists \bar{X}\ p(X))$. On the other hand, as suggested in Section 3.2, the equational framework is extended to incorporate inequations. This turns out to be very adequate to characterize values for $\bar{X}$ such that $\neg p(X)$ holds. By combining these two features with the negation as failure rule, a form of negation very close to the real negation is obtained. The only differences between these two forms of negation arise from infinite computations. Although some query or some instance can be proved or disproved, infinite computations may prevent the

Conclog model to conclude. However, in contrast with most languages, the floundering problem is here of no concern : negated atoms are reduced in a sound way even if they are not ground.

5.1.2 Overview

The introduction of negation in Conclog is achieved thanks to four major extensions. They affect both the generation and reconciliation phases or, in (equivalent) processes terms, the generation and reconciliation procedures. They are essentially presented, in the following, according to these phases. Nevertheless, they are also described in terms of processes when a local view is more suited for explanation. The effect on the interleaving of the two phases is finally examined.

A. Impact on the generation phase

Generation phases are computed in essentially the same way as in the basic model. Two extensions are moreover operated. They arise from the introduction of the not predicate and from the explicit introduction of negative information in substitutions and atoms. The effect of the not predicate is first examined. A generalization of and/or search trees into so-called and/or/not search trees follows. The effect of negative information is then studied. It induces a review of the and/or/not search trees as well as the extension of the classical notions of unification and instantiation.

A.1 Introducing the not predicate

The most appearing extension results from the introduction of negative literals. As already suggested, they are introduced by means of the not/1 predicate. This predicate is designed in Conclog so as to take a goal as argument, some of its subgoals being possibly of the not(...) form. The resulting construction is called a *negative simple goal* or *ns-goal*, for short. By analogy, previous s-goals corresponding to positive literals are now called *positive simple goals* or *ps-goals*, for short. The term *general s-goal* is used to refer either to a ps-goal or to an ns-goal. Goals formed of ps-goals and ns-goals are called *general goals*. Following the similar extension of language, any query and program are now called *general query* and *general program*, respectively. As a final terminology suggar, the qualifier "general" will generally be omitted when there is no doubt about the general context of negation.

Any generation phase is extended in consequence. It is expressed in terms of nodes associated with general goals, ps-goals and ns-goals, subsequently called *general goal-nodes*, *ps-goal-nodes* and *ns-goal-nodes*, respectively.

- Each general goal-node engenders a node for any subgoal of its representing goal. It is a usual s-goal-node, here called ps-goal-node, if the subgoal is a ps-goal. It is a ns-

goal-node if the subgoal is a ns-goal. Nodes of these two kinds are called *general s-goal-nodes*.
- Any ps-goal-node engenders its children, here called (general) goal-nodes, as in the basic model.
- The real novelty comes from ns-goal-nodes. As negation is introduced in the form of negation as failure, the general goal-node C is created as the only child node of the ns-goal-node not(C). Any ns-goal thus basically acts as a ps-goal that fictively unifies with one clause. However, special treatments will be required at the reconciliation phase so that ps-goals and ns-goals (and consequently ps-goal-nodes and ns-goal-nodes) need to be differentiated. Note that, the alternance of goal-nodes and s-goal-nodes of the basic model is preserved here. It directly results from our choice of designing the argument of the not predicate as a goal.

An extended version of the and/or search tree is thus created. The novelty is the presence of nodes labelled by the not predicate. For this reason, the extended version is subsequently called *and/or/not search tree*.

The translation in process terms is made in an obvious way. An *and/or/not process model* is associated with the and/or/not search tree. It is composed of a *(general) query-process*, of *(general) goal-processes*, of *ps-goal-processes* and of *ns-goal-processes* corresponding to the (general) query-node, to (general) goal-nodes, to ps-goal-nodes and to ns-goal-nodes, respectively.

A.2 Incorporating negative information in substitutions and s-goals

The final extensions are induced by the explicit introduction of negative information. Section 3.2 has already justified the incorporation of negative information in substitutions, this giving rise to n-substitutions. Thus n-substitutions are now manipulated. In particular, binding publication performed in the basic model will be generalized in the publication of n-substitutions. It follows that general goals and s-goals will have to be instantiated by n-substitutions. What this means can be defined in two ways :

- by ignoring the negative parts of n-substitutions and by calling instantiation of general goals or s-goals their usual instantiation by the positive parts of the n-substitutions;
- by keeping the negative parts and by calling instantiation of general goals and s-goals the above instantiation coupled with the negative parts of the n-substitutions.

The second solution is adopted in Conclog to detect useless reductions as early as possible. This has two consequences :

- general s-goals must be coupled with negative information;
- unification, instantiation and and/or/not search trees must be extended to such generalized atoms.

On a point of terminology, the association (E,Θ) of an expression E with a set of en-substitutions Θ verifying the following property P is called an *extended expression*.

P: any Y/u of any en-substitution of Θ verifies the following conditions:
  i) Y occurs in E;
  ii) if u is a variable then it should appear in E.

The E part is called the positive part of the extended expression whereas the Θ part is called its negative part. They are also denoted by F^+ and F^-, respectively, when the general expression is referred to by F.

The intuition behind the extended expression $(E, \{\omega_1, \ldots, \omega_m\})$ is to constrain E to at least one ω_i with the variables of ω_i not in E universally quantified. For instance, $(h(X,Y), \{\text{not}\{X/f(Y)\}, \text{not}\{X/g(Z)\}\})$, represents the term $h(X,Y)$ restricted by one of the following constraints:
  i) X differs from $f(Y)$ (i.e. $X \neq f(Y)$),
  ii) X differs from an 1-ary term whose functor is g (i.e. $X \neq g(Z)$, for all Z).

It is worth noting that, as for n-substitutions, the condition P is used to force extended expressions to be presented in a normalized form. In contrast with n-substitutions, however, quantification has been introduced on "free variables" appearing only in the negative part of extended terms. The reason for this difference is that n-substitutions are just employed to sum up the solutions of h-systems (representing unification or reconciliation) whereas terms are involved more closely in the reduction process where variables are quantified. Notice, by the way, that one could have quantified the variables of extended terms existentially rather than universally. The existential quantification is however less expressive and constraining than the latter one since any inequation $X \neq f(Y)$ for some Y can always be satisfied even if X takes the form $f(t)$ for some t.

Let us now analyze the consequences of the introduction of extended expressions more precisely.

1° Unification is first extended as follows.

Definition 5.1 Two extended expressions (E,Θ) and (F,Ψ) are said to be unifiable iff the two following conditions hold :

- E and F are unifiable, say with the idempotent mgu μ
- the sets of n-substitutions $\{(\mu, \text{not}\{\})\}$, Θ and Ψ are n-reconciliable with taking care of the quantification of the variables i.e. there are some $\theta \in \Theta$, $\psi \in \Psi$ such that
   i) $(\mu, \text{not}\{\})$, θ and ψ are n-reconcilable,
   ii) for any idempotent en-reconciliation $\lambda \oplus \Lambda$, there is $\nu \in \Lambda$, such that any binding Y/u of ν verifies the following properties

1° Y is a variable of E, of F or of λ,
2° if u is a variable, then it is a variable of E, of F or of λ.

In this case, let, for any such en-reconciliation $\lambda \oplus \Lambda$, Λ_r denote the subset of Λ composed of the n-substitutions ν verifying 1° and 2° above. Any set of n-substitutions obtained by associating any such $\lambda \oplus \Lambda_r$ with each pair (θ,ψ) such that μ, θ, ψ are n-reconcilable in the above sense is called an n-mgu of (E,Θ) and (F,Ψ). As Θ and Ψ are composed of en-substitutions, it can be expressed in the form $\mu \oplus \{\nu_1,...,\nu_m\}$ with $\nu_1, ..., \nu_m$ en-substitutions (see Section 3.2). Let, for any $i \in \{1,...,m\}$, μ_i denote the restriction of ν_i to the variables of $E\mu$ obtained by removing any binding Y/u that verifies one of the following conditions:

- Y $\notin$ var(Eμ)
- u is a variable and u $\notin$ var(Eμ).

The extended term $(E\mu,\{\mu_1,...,\mu_m\})$ is called a *most general instance* of (E,Θ) and (F,Ψ). As before, we will often abuse language and speak of *the* most general instance of (E,Θ) and (F,Ψ) to denote one of them.

Such a unification will subsequently be referred to as *extended unification*. Thanks to Proposition 3.76, it is independent of the selected idempotent mgu μ. Furthermore, it is worth noting that we will prove that property ii) above holds if it holds for one arbitrary idempotent en-reconciliation (see Proposition 5.14). Note finally that the extended unification subsumes the usual unification: the former indeed reduces to the latter by taking the singleton $\{not\{\}\}$ as sets Θ and Ψ.

2° Any computation starts with general goals and s-goals as described in the above Subsection A.1 that is associated with no negative information. During the first reconciliation phase however, binding publication forces them to be decorated with sets of en-substitutions. Nodes produced in subsequent cycles are then progressively touched by it too. The extended unification is indeed used in order to take as much profit as possible from the negative information. It results that s-goals will generally be coupled with sets of en-substitutions. Such s-goals are subsequently called *extended s-goals*. Goals formed by conjuncting such extended s-goals are called *extended goals*. Notice particularly that any pure usual s-goal G may be presented in the equivalent extended form $(G,\{not\{\}\})$ associating a null negative information.

The generation scheme presented in Subsection A.1 above needs thus to be precised in terms of extended s-goals. This is performed as follows.

- Any extended ps-goal-node, say (G,Θ), creates its child nodes by first searching clauses whose head, considered in their extended form, unifies with (G,Θ). For each of them the following extended goal-node is created. Let

  H $\leftarrow$ G_1, ..., G_m

  be such a clause. Assume the corresponding idempotent en-mgu is $\psi \oplus \Psi$. Let for any $i \in \{1,...,m\}$, Ψ_i denote the set of the restrictions of the n-substitutions of Ψ to the

variables of $G_i\psi$, as defined in Definition 5.1. Let furthermore λ denote the restriction of the substitution ψ to the variables of G and Λ denote the set of restrictions of the n-substitutions of Ψ to the variables of varcod(λ) (as defined in Definition 5.1 by taking varcod(λ) instead of var(Eμ)). Then the corresponding goal-node is associated with the conjunction of extended s-goals

$(G_1\psi, \Psi_1), \ldots, (G_m\psi, \Psi_m)$.

Such a node is called an *extended (general) goal-node*. The es-nsubst $\lambda \oplus \Lambda$ is registered as the counterpart of the mas in the basic model. It is called *nmas*.

- Any extended goal-node creates an extended s-goal node for each of its extended s-goal.
- Any extended ns-goal node (not$(G_1,\ldots,G_m),\Theta$) creates the extended goal-node associated with the conjunction

$(G_1,\Theta), \ldots, (G_m,\Theta)$

as child node. For purposes of uniformity, it is implicitly associated the $\{\}\oplus\{$not$\{\}\}$ nmas and the empty Vc set.

3° Finally, as s-goals now appear in the extended form, binding publication requires extended expressions to be instantiated by n-substitutions. The resulting instantiations are fortunately extended expressions so that no further extension of expressions, their unification and their instantiation will be needed. It is defined by taking into account a set of variables aiming at allowing some variables to be considered as existentially quantified.

Definition 5.2

1) An extended expression (E,Ω) is *instantiable by an n-substitution* ν wrt the set of variables Svars iff the sets Ω and $\{\nu\}$ are n-reconcilable wrt the variables of E and Svars i.e. iff some $\omega \in \Omega$ verifies the two following conditions:
   i) ω and ν are n-reconcilable
   ii) for any idempotent en-reconciliation $\lambda \oplus \Lambda$, there exist $\varphi \in \Lambda$ such that any binding Y/u of φ verifies the following properties
      1° Y is a variable of E, of Svars or of λ,
      2° if u is a variable, then it is a variable of E, of Svars or of λ.

2) In this case, let for any such en-reconciliation $\lambda \oplus \Lambda$, Λ_r denote the subset of Λ composed of the n-substitutions verifying 1° and 2° above. Any set of n-substitutions obtained by associating any such $\lambda \oplus \Lambda_r$ with each $\omega \in \Omega$ such that ω and ν are n-reconcilable in the above sense is called an *instantiation es-nsubst* of (E,Ω) by ν wrt Svars.

3) Let $\lambda \oplus \{\lambda_1,\ldots,\lambda_r\}$ be such an es-nsubst. Let furthermore for any i, μ_i be the restriction of λ_i obtained by removing any binding Y/u that verifies one of the following properties:
   i)   Y is not a variable of Eλ,
   ii) Y is a variable of Eλ, u contains a variable of Svars not occurring in Eλ.

The extended expression $(E\lambda, \{\mu_1,...,\mu_r\})$ is defined as the *instance* of (E,Ω) by ν wrt the instantiation es-nsubst $\lambda \oplus \{\lambda_1,...,\lambda_r\}$ and the set Svars. By abuse of language, we will often omit to mention the instantiation es-nsubst and the set of variables Svars.

The concept of term restriction is introduced as a generalization of the above restriction.

Definition 5.3 Given a set Ψ of en-substitutions, a (non-extended) expression E and a set of variables Svars, the set Ψ_r determined from Ψ as in point 3) of Definition 5.2 but by taking E instead of Eλ is called the *term restriction* of Ψ to E wrt Svars.

A major departure with the usual instantiation is thus that the extended one is not always possible. What happens when instantiation induced by binding publication is possible or not is related to reconciliation and is treated in the following subsection.

B. Impact on the reconciliation phase

Reconciliation phases are affected in four ways by the introduction of negation. The generalization of substitutions into n-substitutions is the first one. The reconciliation procedure of goal-processes and ps-goal-processes needs then to be adapted to this context. Also, the reconciliation procedure of ns-goal-processes need to be defined. Finally, because instantiation can now fail, the treatment of binding publication needs to be extended.

B.1   N-substitutions

Ns-goals are designed with the negation as failure rule interpretation in mind. They thus act essentially as "negators" of the solutions of their child. Roughly speaking, this means that bindings are negated in some way. Restated in our equational interpretation of bindings, this means that systems of equations and inequations are now manipulated. As a first consequence, as argued in Section 3.2, substitutions need to be generalized into n-substitutions. Hence, in order to provide a finite representation of the solutions of ns-goals, n-substitutions are now introduced in place of substitutions in the computations. The consequences on the generation phases have been examined above. The consequences on the reconciliation procedures is examined hereafter.

B.2   The reconciliation procedures of goal-processes and ps-goal-processes

The reconciliation procedure of ps-goal-processes is adapted in a quite natural way : substitutions are simply replaced by n-substitutions in the treatments. The same adaptation is basically required for goal-processes. Three treatments require some further attention.

1° Extending reconciliation to n-reconciliation is not sufficient. The restriction of the n-substitution is no more a simple matter of efficiency. It must be performed at any goal-process to ensure correctness. Furthermore, some care must be taken for the quantification of variables. To that effect, a formula is associated with any n-substitution resulting from the n-reconciliation performed at any goal-process. It is stated as follows. Let

$$v=(\{X_1/t_1,\ldots,X_m/t_m\},not\{Y_1/u_1,\ldots,Y_n/u_n\})$$

be the n-substitution under consideration and G be the treated goal. Then, the formula Form(v,var(G)) associated with v is :

$$X_1=t_1\wedge\ldots\wedge X_m=t_m\wedge Y_1\neq u_1\wedge\ldots\wedge Y_n\neq u_n$$

where variables are quantified as follows :

- variables of v^+ that are not in G are quantified existentially,
- variables of v^- that do not occur in G nor in v^+ are quantified universally.

The n-substitution v is interpreted at G as the set of grounding substitutions for the variables of G that makes the Form(v,var(G)) true. Because of the universal quantification, some n-substitutions may be associated with unsatisfiable formulae. Those n-substitutions should thus be removed. This is achieved by discarding any n-substitution v such that a binding Y/u of v^- verifies one of the following conditions :

(i) Y is not a variable of G nor a variable of v^+,
(ii) if u is a variable, then u is not a variable of G nor a variable of v^+.

2° N-reconciliations of distinct tuples of n-substitutions may deliver the same results. Hence, one feature of the basic model cannot be ensured here : at any goal-process, the n-reconciliation of different solutions reported by its children may give rise to duplicates. Such duplicates are removed in two ways :

- at the query-process, by memorizing them and by discarding any newly computed n-substitution already registered;
- at any other goal-process, by means of the S_d structure of its grand-father process. R-triplets are not registered if they correspond to an already sent R-triplet.

3° Binding publication needs to be extended to n-substitutions. The way this is achieved is presented in the following Subsection B.4.

B.3 The reconciliation procedure of ns-goal-processes

The reconciliation procedure of a ns-goal process needs of course to be precised. It consists of the second extension to the basic reconciliation phases. It is performed according to our intuitive understanding of negator. Consider an ns-goal-process Proc associated with the ns-goal not(G). Let $v_1, \ldots, v_m$ be the n-substitutions produced by its child goal-process C. To simplify the exposition, assume the following hypothesis :

H. The n-substitutions v_i's correspond to completely constructed subtrees.

Then the set of n-substitutions $\{\mu_1,\ldots,\mu_n\}$ returned by Proc is one set of n-substitutions that fulfills the following property : the set of grounding substitutions for the variables of G that makes the formula

$$\neg\ (\ \text{Form}(v_1,\text{var}(G)) \vee \ldots \vee \text{Form}(v_m,\text{var}(G))\ )$$

true is exactly the set of such grounding substitutions that makes the formula

$$(\ \text{Form}(\mu_1,\text{var}(G)) \vee \ldots \vee \text{Form}(\mu_n,\text{var}(G))\ )$$

true.

Two particular cases are worth noting :

1) if one v_i is ({},not{}) then the above formula reduces to ¬(true) and the empty set of n-substitutions is reported;
2) if no v_i is reported (i.e. if the child goal-process C fails) then the treated ns-goal succeeds and the only ({},not{}) n-substitution is reported.

N-substitutions are also sent in R-triplets. The auxiliary information attached to the μ_i's is as follows :

- the set of process identifiers part reduces to Proc. This is justified by the fact that, as shown by the formula $\neg\ (F_1 \vee \ldots \vee F_m)$, the n-substitutions μ_i's involve all the processes of the subtree generated by Proc. Reference to Proc is thus a synthetic way of referring to them.
- the label part is either "completed" or "incompleted". Its interpretation is similar to that employed in the basic model. One difference is however made here. It is motivated by case 1) above. As illustrated there, the subtree engendered by Proc needs not be completely generated to determine all the solutions contained in it. The label part is thus "completed" if this subtree is sufficiently constructed i.e.constructing the remainding part would not bring further information. It is "incompleted" otherwise. A more precised definition will be given in Section 5.2.

Let us now come back to more concrete situations where hypothesis H does not hold. In such cases, just the n-substitutions v_i's that are completely constructed (i.e. whose associated label is "completed") are retained to form the above set $\{v_1,\ldots,v_m\}$. The substitutions μ_j's are then determined as explained above. The reason of such a restriction of the n-substitutions v_i's is justified later on. For the moment, it is sufficient to say that this preserves the following feature of the basic model : sent n-substitutions are never replaced in subsequent reconciliation phases but simply precised.

Note finally that the set of n-substitutions $\{\mu_1,\ldots,\mu_n\}$ cannot be incrementally constructed as the n-substitutions v_i's become available. R-triplets from C must thus be conserved in Proc in its reconciliation structure. This structure is manipulated as that of any goal-process with only one child.

B.4 Handling instantiation messages

A final extension is induced by binding publication. Precisely, it is due to the following fact. Consider a goal-process Proc and the binding publication it produces. In the basic model the induced instantiations are always coherent with the goals or s-goals to which they are applied. The instantiating substitution is indeed a subset of any solution of Proc. Processes which are incoherent with it thus participate to no solution solution subtree and have been removed by the reconciliation procedure of Proc. This property does no longer hold in the extended model mainly for processes of subtrees engendered by ns-goal-processes. Inconsistencies may be involved in two cases :

- the extended instantiation does not succeed
- the instantiating n-substitution is not n-reconcilable with the associated mas.

Binding publication should thus be extended. The following operations are now performed when an instantiation message is received. Let P be the considered process and ν be the n-substitution of the message.

- If P is an (extended) goal-process then the two following tests are operated. Let G be the goal associated with P and Svars be its associated Vc set of variables.
    - The n-susbtitution ν is tested for n-reconciliation with the nmas of P with respect to the variables of G and Svars (as defined in Definition 5.2).
    - Each s-goal of G is tested for instantiability with ν wrt the variables of Svars.
  Two different behaviors arise from the issues of the tests.
    - If the two tests succeed then G is replaced by the conjunction of the instantiation of its s-goals. The instantiation message is thereafter passed to the child processes of P.
    - If one of the tests fails, then a fail message is sent to the father process of P. Process P then sends a kill message to its child processes and commits suicide. Note that the instantiation of Proc with ν will be always guarenteed to succeed.
- If P is a(n) (extended) s-goal-process then instantiation of its (extended) s-goal with ν is ensured by the previous instantiation of its father process. The s-goal is then replaced by the corresponding instantiation and the instantiation message is transmitted to the child processes of P.

Fail messages are handled by goal-processes and ps-goal-processes as explained in Section 4.4. The report of failure at an ns-goal-process is interpreted as the confirmation of success thanks to its "negator" interpretation. Previously sent n-substitutions are thus confirmed. Furthermore they do not need to be precised. This is explicited by the sending of a special end-reconciliation message for the new reconciliation phase. It is treated by the father process as the re-sending of the n-susbtitutions but with "completed" as label. Precisely, the label of the n-substitutions sent by the ns-goal-process is just changed to "completed" if need be and new tuples of R-triplets are formed if possible for the new reconciliation phase.

C. Impact on the interleaving of generation and reconciliation phases

The reconciliation procedure of ns-goal-processes introduces a new synchronization point. It is due to the impossibility of constructing, in general, the set of output n-substitutions from the input ones incrementally. Thus, any ns-goal-process generally waits that its child has completely reported its R-triplets to perform its reconciliation procedure. Note that this is not a real constraint since, to be produced, any solution involving an ns-goal-node generally needs that the subtree attached to this node is entirely constructed. Furthermore exceptions to this property correspond to the cases where the above waiting can be relaxed.

This incremental property excepted, all the features of the basic model are conserved. In particular, processes behave in the same quasi-independent way and n-substitutions are still transmitted incrementally by goal-processes and ps-goal-processes. Hence, solutions might be produced whereas others are still under computation.

5.1.3 Example

The following example illustrates the extended Conclog model. Consider the query

$\leftarrow$ p(X,Y)

and the program

(c_1) p(X,Y) $\leftarrow$ not(q(X,Y)), r(X,Y).
(c_2) q(1,f(a)).
(c_3) q(2,g(b)).
(c_4) q(3,h(X)) $\leftarrow$ s(X).
(c_5) r(1,X) $\leftarrow$ t(X).
(c_6) s(b).
(c_7) s(c).
(c_8) t(f(X)) $\leftarrow$ u(X).
(c_9) u(a).
(c_{10}) u(b).

Assume the R-depth parameter of the Conclog model is 3. The resulting computation is depicted in Figures 5.1 to 5.4. It is composed of two cycles, as we will see in a moment.

Two remarks are worth noting before describing it.

1) On the one hand, the remark of Section 4.1 on the dynamicity of the computation with respect to the relative staticity of the exposition should be retained here too.

2) On the other hand, s-goals produced in the first generation phase are associated with the null negative information part i.e. the set {not{}} of en-substitutions. They can thus be considered in their primitive form of literal. As a result, the extended unification amounts to the

normal unification. All nmas's involved in the first generation phase have thus a null negative information part too. Therefore, they can also be considered in their basic mas form. We will indeed consider s-goals and nmas's this way during the exposition of the first cycle. This is made in the twofold aim of easing the exposition and of stressing other novelties of the model. A rigourous exposition can be obtained by replacing any s-goal G by its extended form (G,{not{}}) and any mas θ by its corresponding θ⊕{not{}}form. Nevertheless, n-substitutions will be propagated in their general form since some of them involve negative information. Furthermore, the second cycle will be explained using the general form, thus using extended s-goals and nmas's.

A. The first cycle

A.1 The first generation phase

The computation is started by launching the query-process with the query as goal component and the R-depth parameter, namely 3, as R-depth component. The first generation phase then consists in generating the processes associated with the nodes of the and/or search tree of Figure 5.1. Precisely, the following processes are created as soon as their father is created. As in Section 4.1, numbers are used to refer to the nodes and consequently to the processes.

- The query-process (1) creates the ps-goal-process (2) associated with the ps-goal p(X,Y).
- The s-goal-process (2) creates the goal-process (3) associated with the goal
  ← not(q(X,Y)), r(X,Y).
  It results from the unification of p(X,Y) with the clause c_1. The associated mas is {}. No variable needs to be introduced at this point.
- The goal-process (3) creates two s-goal-processes. One, process (4), is associated with the ns-goal-process not(q(X,Y)). The other, process (5), is associated with the s-goal-process r(X,Y).
- The ns-goal-process (4) creates the s-goal-process (6) associated with the goal
  ← q(X,Y).
- The ps-goal-process (5) creates the goal-process (7) associated with the goal ← t(Y). It results from the unification of r(X,Y) with the clause c_5. The associated mas is {X/1}. No variables need to be introduced at this point.
- The goal-process (6) creates the ps-goal-process (8) associated with the ps-goal q(X,Y).
- The goal-process (7) creates the ps-goal-process (9) associated with the ps-goal t(Y).

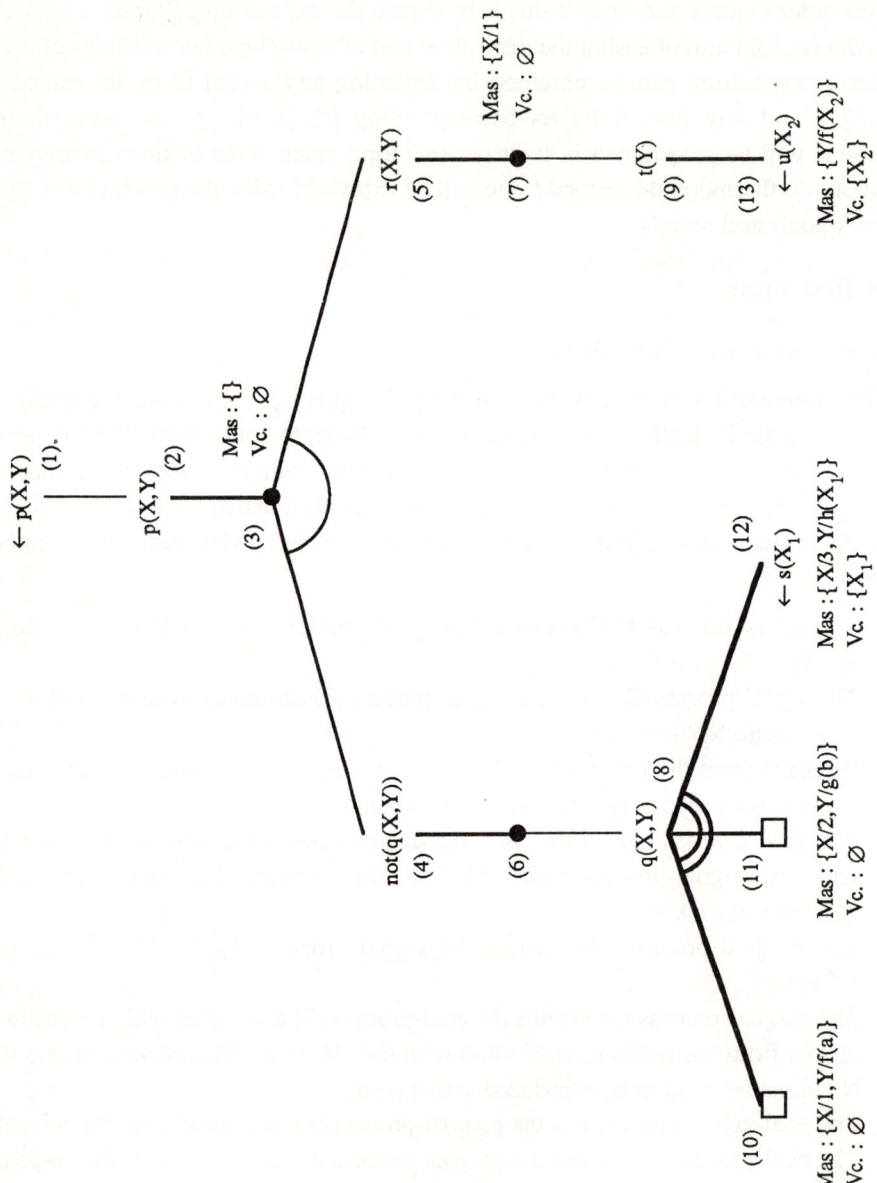

Figure 5.1

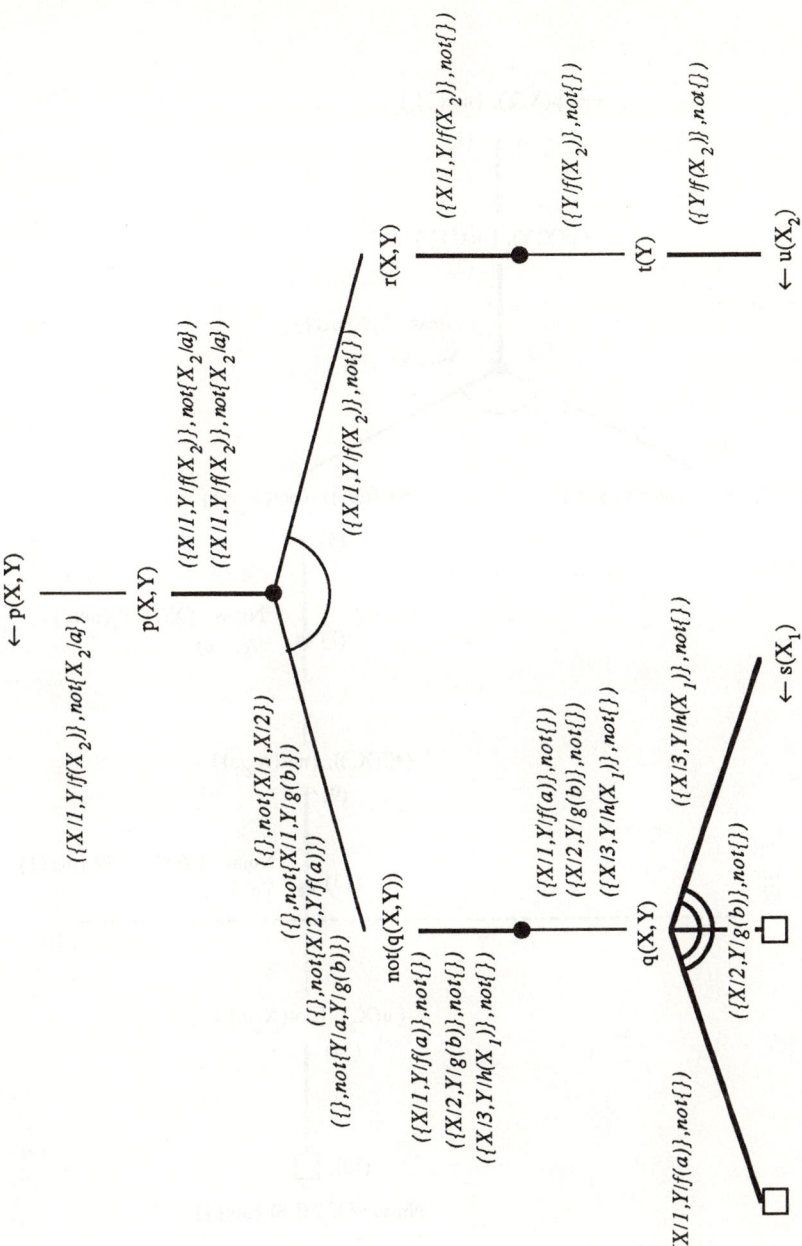

Figure 5.2

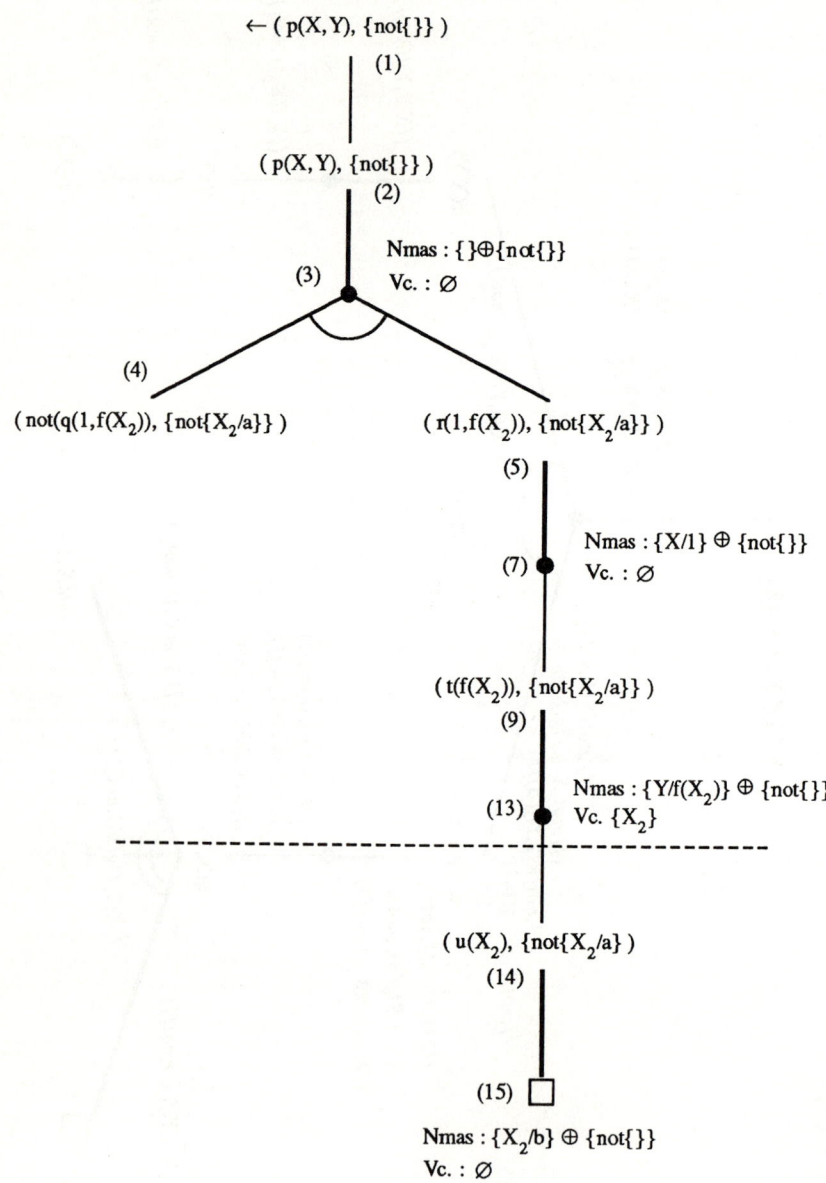

Figure 5.3

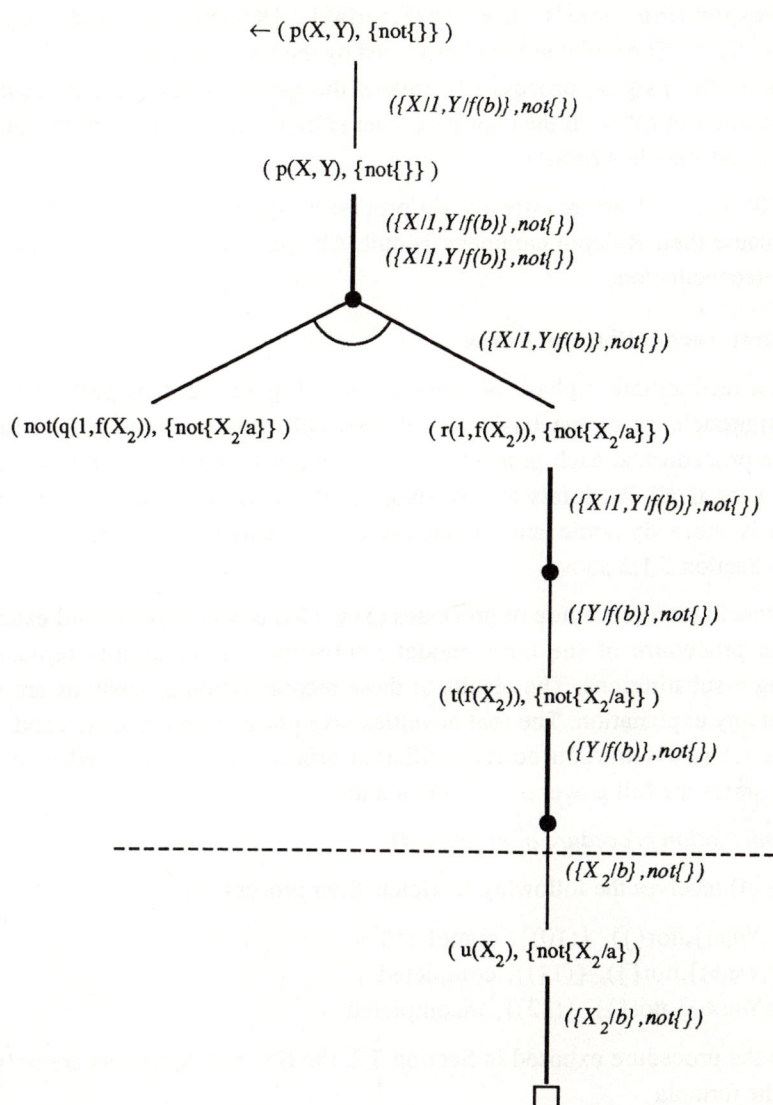

Figure 5.4

- The ps-goal-process (8) creates three goal-processes, namely processes (10), (11) and (12). They correspond to the unification of q(X,Y) with the clauses c_2, c_3 and c_4. The corresponding mas's are {X/1,Y/f(a)}, {X/2,Y/g(b)} and {X/3,Y/h(X_1)}, respectively. The variable X_1 is introduced by the last unification.
- Finally, the ps-goal-process (9) creates the goal-process (13). It results from the unification of t(Y) with the clause c_8. One variable is introduced here, namely X_2. The produced mas is {Y/f(X_2)}.

Processes (10) and (11) are manifestly tip processes. Processes (12) and (13) are also tip processes because their R-depth parameter is null. All these processes thus create no child but directly enter reconciliation.

A.2 The first reconciliation phase

The first reconciliation phase is summed up in Figure 5.2. It is performed by using a bottom up approach, as in the basic model. We will thus describe it by examining the reconciliation procedure at each process. As in Section 4.1, for ease of the presentation, we will present it as if all R-triplets are available at the same time at any process. The real computation is more dynamic and conserves the incremental treatment of R-triplets as mentioned in Section 5.1.2 above.

The reconciliation procedure of processes (5) to (13) is a straightforward extension of the reconciliation procedure of the basic model : substitutions are simply replaced by their corresponding n-substitutions. The results of these reconciliation procedures are thus simply given without any explanation. The real novelties take place at processes (3) and (4). Process (4) illustrates the newly introduced reconciliation procedure of an ns-goal-process whereas process (3) requires the full power of n-reconciliation.

(i) Reconciliation procedure of process (4)

Process (4) receives the following R-triplets from process (6) :

< ({X/1,Y/f(a)},not{}), {(10)}, completed >
< ({X/2,Y/g(b)},not{}), {(11)}, completed >
< ({X/3,Y/h(X_1)},not{}), {(12)}, incompleted >

According to the procedure exposed in Section 5.2, the first two R-triplets are only taken into account and the formula

$$\neg (X=1 \land Y=f(a)) \land \neg (X=2 \land Y=g(b)) \qquad (F)$$

is formed. Output n-substitutions are then searched such that they cover all grounding substitutions making it hold. This formula amounts to the formula

$$(X \neq 1 \land X \neq 2) \lor (X \neq 1 \land Y \neq g(b)) \lor (Y \neq f(a) \land X \neq 2) \lor (Y \neq f(a) \land Y \neq g(b)).$$

so that all grounding substitutions are covered by the n-susbtitutions

({},not{X/1,X/2}), ({},not{X/1,Y/g(b)}), ({},not{X/2,Y/f(a)}),
({},not{Y/f(a),Y/g(b)}).

Four R-triplets are formed from them and are sent by process (4) to process (3). Each one associates one of the above n-substitutions with the following auxiliary information :

- {(4)} as set of process identifiers
- "incompleted" as label.

(ii) The reconciliation procedure of process (3)

Process (3) thus receives

- the above four R-triplets from process (4)
- the R-triplet < ({X/1,Y/f(X_2)},not{}), {(13)}, incompleted > from process (5).

They are treated as usual in a goal-process but here the full power of n-reconciliation is needed. The following four tuples are thus first formed

(< ({},not{X/1,X/2}), {(4)}, incompleted >,
     < ({X/1,Y/f(X_2)},not{}), {(13)}, incompleted >),

(< ({},not{X/1,Y/g(b)}), {(4)}, incompleted >,
     < ({X/1,Y/f(X_2)},not{}), {(13)}, incompleted >),

(< ({},not{X/2,Y/f(a)}), {(4)}, incompleted >,
     < ({X/1,Y/f(X_2)},not{}), {(13)}, incompleted >),

(< ({},not{Y/f(a),Y/g(b)}), {(4)}, incompleted >,
     < ({X/1,Y/f(X_2)},not{}), {(13)}, incompleted >),

Just the last two pairs contain reconcilable n-substitutions. The resulting R-triplets are identical :

< ({X/1,Y/f(X_2)},not{X_2/a}), {(4),(13)}, incompleted >.

Both of them are however transmitted to process (2). Binding publication can furthermore be done : the n-substitution ({X/1,Y/f(X_2)},not{X_2/a}) is indeed common to all sent R-triplets. It is communicated progressively to the processes (4) to (13). The induced instantiation succeeds at each process except at the tip processes (10), (11) and (12). Fail messages are sent in response to process (8). Failure is then is progressively communicated to process (4). There, as indicated previously, a special end-reconciliation message is sent to process (3) to state that the set of answer n-substitutions limits to the four previously sent n-substitutions. Such operations might appear surprising. They are justified in the following sections. Nevertheless, the validity of these operations can be tested on this simple example. This is rather technical and is operated at the end of the example.

The instantiation performed at tip process (13) is worth noting since generation will be restarted from it. Let us recall the components of the instantiation :

- the goal associated with process (13) is ← $u(X_2)$;
- the Nmas associated with process (13) is $(\{Y/f(X_2)\}, not\{\})$.
- the instantiating n-substitution is $(\{X/1, Y/f(X_2)\}, not\{X_2/a\})$.

The Nmas and instantiating n-substitution are test for n-reconciliation. Obviously, they n-reconcile and the n-substitution $(\{X/1, Y/f(X_2)\}, not\{X_2/a\})$ can be considered as the n-reconciliation. Therefore, the instantiation succeeds and the goal ← $u(X_2)$ is replaced by the instance

← ($u(X_2)\{X/1, Y/f(X_2)\}$, $\{not\{X_2/a\}\}$)

that is

← ($u(X_2)$, $\{not\{X_2/a\}\}$).

(iii) Reconciliation at processes (2) and (1).

Let us now turn back to the two (same) R-triplets sent by process (3):

< $(\{X/1, Y/f(X_2)\}, not\{X_2/a\})$, $\{(4),(13)\}$, incompleted > .

Both of them are transmitted by process (2) to process (1). Process (1) is a goal-process that registers them as they arrive. The R-triplet first received is memorized. No result is delivered since the R-triplet correspond to an incompletely constructed subtree. At its receipt, the second received R-triplet is registered too. However, as it is identical to the first one, no real updating is operated and no real memorization is performed. It can thus be considered as discarded: if process (1) had a father then only the first received R-triplet would be transmitted.

B. The second cycle

Once the second R-triplet is treated at process (1), the only remaining tip process (13) is woken up. A new computation cycle is started. It is depicted in Figure 5.3 and Figure 5.4.

B.1 The second generation phase

Process (13) creates its descendants as follows:

1° Its child ps-goal-process (14) is first created. It is associated with the (extended) ps-goal $(u(X_2), \{not\{X_2/a\}\})$.

2° Process (14) then creates its children. Clauses that unify (in the extended sense) with $(u(X_2), \{not\{X_2/a\}\})$ are first searched. Clauses c_9 and c_{10} are the only ones that unify with $u(X_2)$. However, the former binds X_2 to "a", which is forbidden by the negative information $\{not\{X_2/a\}\}$ of the extended ps-goal. Clause c_{10} is then just retained. It gives rise to process (15). Its associated Nmga is $\{X_2/b\} \oplus \{not\{\}\}$. Its associated goal is empty. It is thus a tip process. Consequently, it creates no child but directly enters reconciliation.

B.2 The second reconciliation phase

The reconciliation procedure of process (15) is quite short : the R-triplet

< ({X_2/b},not{}), {(15)}, completed >

is simply sent to process (14). The induced reconciliation at processes (14), (13), (9), (7) and (5) is now quite familiar and is omitted. The R-triplet

< ({X/1,Y/f(b)},not{}), (15), completed >

is transmitted to process (3). On the other hand, process (3) registers two R-triplets from process (4) for this reconciliation phase, namely

< ({},not{X/1,X/2}), {(4)}, completed >
< ({},not{X/1,Y/g(b)}), {(4)}, completed >
< ({},not{X/2,Y/f(a)}), {(4)}, completed >,
< ({},not{Y/f(a),Y/g(b)}), {(4)}, completed >.

They are issued from the four R-triplets sent at the first reconciliation phase; their labels were moved to "completed" as a result of the above binding publication.

The following tuples are formed at process (3) :

(< ({},not{X/1,X/2}), {(4)}, completed >,
   < ({X/1,Y/f(b)},not{}), {(15)}, completed >),

(< ({},not{X/1,Y/g(b)}), {(4)}, completed >,
   < ({X/1,Y/f(b)},not{}), {(15)}, completed >),

(< ({},not{X/2,Y/f(a)}), {(4)}, completed >,
   < ({X/1,Y/f(b)},not{}), {(15)}, completed >),

(< ({},not{Y/f(a),Y/g(b)}), {(4)}, completed >,
   < ({X/1,Y/f(b)},not{}), {(15)}, completed >).

As in the first reconciliation phase, only the last two have n-reconcilable n-substitutions. Two identical R-triplets result, namely

< ({X/1,Y/f(b)},not{}), {(4),(15)}, completed >.

They are treated as in the first reconciliation phase so that only the R-triplet received first is considered. Its n-substitution ({X/1,Y/f(b)},not{}) is associated with a label "completed" and is output as a computed answer n-substitution. Note that it indeed corresponds to a solution. The computation is then halted since there remains no tip process associated with a non-empty goal.

C. Appendix

Let us establish our claim on binding publication made on point (ii) of Subsection A.2. Assume process (12) completely generates its attached subtree of processes. The returned n-substitutions would be $(\{X/1,Y/h(b)\},not\{\})$ and $(\{X/1,Y/h(c)\},not\{\})$. As a consequence, the formula F computed by process (4) would be

$$\neg (X=1 \wedge Y=f(a)) \wedge \neg (X=2 \wedge Y=g(b)) \wedge \neg (X=1 \wedge Y=h(b)) \wedge \neg (X=1 \wedge Y=h(c)).$$

It is equivalent to the following ones:

$$(X \neq 1 \vee Y \neq f(a)) \wedge (X \neq 2 \vee Y \neq g(b)) \wedge (X \neq 1 \vee Y \neq h(b)) \wedge (X \neq 1 \vee Y \neq h(c)).$$

or

$$(X \neq 1 \wedge X \neq 2 \wedge X \neq 1 \wedge X \neq 1) \vee (X \neq 1 \wedge X \neq 2 \wedge X \neq 1 \wedge Y \neq h(c)) \vee$$
$$(X \neq 1 \wedge X \neq 2 \wedge Y \neq h(b) \wedge X \neq 1) \vee (X \neq 1 \wedge X \neq 2 \wedge Y \neq h(b) \wedge Y \neq h(c)) \vee$$
$$(X \neq 1 \wedge Y \neq g(b) \wedge X \neq 1 \wedge X \neq 1) \vee (X \neq 1 \wedge Y \neq g(b) \wedge X \neq 1 \wedge Y \neq h(c)) \vee$$
$$(X \neq 1 \wedge Y \neq g(b) \wedge Y \neq h(b) \wedge X \neq 1) \vee (X \neq 1 \wedge Y \neq g(b) \wedge Y \neq h(b) \wedge Y \neq h(c)) \vee$$
$$(Y \neq f(a) \wedge X \neq 2 \wedge X \neq 1 \wedge X \neq 1) \vee (Y \neq f(a) \wedge X \neq 2 \wedge X \neq 1 \wedge Y \neq h(c)) \vee$$
$$(Y \neq f(a) \wedge X \neq 2 \wedge Y \neq h(b) \wedge X \neq 1) \vee (Y \neq f(a) \wedge X \neq 2 \wedge Y \neq h(b) \wedge Y \neq h(c)) \vee$$
$$(Y \neq f(a) \wedge Y \neq g(b) \wedge X \neq 1 \wedge X \neq 1) \vee (Y \neq f(a) \wedge Y \neq g(b) \wedge X \neq 1 \wedge Y \neq h(c)) \vee$$
$$(Y \neq f(a) \wedge Y \neq g(b) \wedge Y \neq h(b) \wedge X \neq 1) \vee (Y \neq f(a) \wedge Y \neq g(b) \wedge Y \neq h(b) \wedge Y \neq h(c))$$

or finally

$$(X \neq 1 \wedge X \neq 2) \vee (X \neq 1 \wedge X \neq 2 \wedge Y \neq h(c)) \vee$$
$$(X \neq 1 \wedge X \neq 2 \wedge Y \neq h(b)) \vee (X \neq 1 \wedge X \neq 2 \wedge Y \neq h(b) \wedge Y \neq h(c)) \vee$$
$$(X \neq 1 \wedge Y \neq g(b)) \vee (X \neq 1 \wedge Y \neq g(b) \wedge Y \neq h(c)) \vee$$
$$(X \neq 1 \wedge Y \neq g(b) \wedge Y \neq h(b)) \vee (X \neq 1 \wedge Y \neq g(b) \wedge Y \neq h(b) \wedge Y \neq h(c)) \vee$$
$$(Y \neq f(a) \wedge X \neq 2 \wedge X \neq 1) \vee (Y \neq f(a) \wedge X \neq 2 \wedge X \neq 1 \wedge Y \neq h(c)) \vee$$
$$(Y \neq f(a) \wedge X \neq 2 \wedge Y \neq h(b) \wedge X \neq 1) \vee (Y \neq f(a) \wedge X \neq 2 \wedge Y \neq h(b) \wedge Y \neq h(c)) \vee$$
$$(Y \neq f(a) \wedge Y \neq g(b) \wedge X \neq 1) \vee (Y \neq f(a) \wedge Y \neq g(b) \wedge X \neq 1 \wedge Y \neq h(c)) \vee$$
$$(Y \neq f(a) \wedge Y \neq g(b) \wedge Y \neq h(b) \wedge X \neq 1) \vee (Y \neq f(a) \wedge Y \neq g(b) \wedge Y \neq h(b) \wedge Y \neq h(c)).$$

Each component of the disjunction corresponds to an n-substitution that should normally be sent to process (3). There it will be combined with the n-substitutions returned by process (5), that is some instances of the n-substitution $(\{X/1,Y/f(X_2)\},not\{\})$. Let us introduce this substitution in the above disjunction and verify that no more or no other n-substitutions are produced. The validity of our approach then follows. The disjunction becomes

$$(1 \neq 1 \wedge 1 \neq 2) \vee (1 \neq 1 \wedge 1 \neq 2 \wedge f(X_2) \neq h(c)) \vee$$
$$(1 \neq 1 \wedge 1 \neq 2 \wedge f(X_2) \neq h(b)) \vee (1 \neq 1 \wedge 1 \neq 2 \wedge f(X_2) \neq h(b) \wedge f(X_2) \neq h(c)) \vee$$
$$(1 \neq 1 \wedge f(X_2) \neq g(b)) \vee (1 \neq 1 \wedge f(X_2) \neq g(b) \wedge f(X_2) \neq h(c)) \vee$$
$$(1 \neq 1 \wedge f(X_2) \neq g(b) \wedge f(X_2) \neq h(b)) \vee (1 \neq 1 \wedge f(X_2) \neq g(b) \wedge f(X_2) \neq h(b) \wedge f(X_2) \neq h(c)) \vee$$
$$(f(X_2) \neq f(a) \wedge 1 \neq 2 \wedge 1 \neq 1) \vee (f(X_2) \neq f(a) \wedge 1 \neq 2 \wedge 1 \neq 1 \wedge f(X_2) \neq h(c)) \vee$$

$(f(X_2){\neq}f(a) \wedge 1{\neq}2 \wedge f(X_2){\neq}h(b) \wedge 1{\neq}1) \vee (f(X_2){\neq}f(a) \wedge 1{\neq}2 \wedge f(X_2){\neq}h(b) \wedge f(X_2){\neq}h(c)) \vee$
$(f(X_2){\neq}f(a) \wedge f(X_2){\neq}g(b) \wedge 1{\neq}1) \vee (f(X_2){\neq}f(a) \wedge f(X_2){\neq}g(b) \wedge 1{\neq}1 \wedge f(X_2){\neq}h(c)) \vee$
$(f(X_2){\neq}f(a) \wedge f(X_2){\neq}g(b) \wedge f(X_2){\neq}h(b) \wedge 1{\neq}1) \vee$
$(f(X_2){\neq}f(a) \wedge f(X_2){\neq}g(b) \wedge f(X_2){\neq}h(b) \wedge f(X_2){\neq}h(c)).$

As $1{\neq}1$ cannot hold, it is equivalent to the following formula

$(f(X_2){\neq}f(a) \wedge 1{\neq}2 \wedge f(X_2){\neq}h(b) \wedge f(X_2){\neq}h(c)) \vee$
$(f(X_2){\neq}f(a) \wedge f(X_2){\neq}g(b) \wedge f(X_2){\neq}h(b) \wedge f(X_2){\neq}h(c)).$

which, in turn, can be simplified to

$(X_2{\neq}a) \vee (X_2{\neq}a)$

that is $X_2{\neq}a$. Summing up, solutions retained by process (3) are instances of the n-substitution $(\{X/1, Y/f(X_2)\}, \text{not}\{X_2/a\})$. This is indeed what has been pointed above. Hence, the operations made by process (4), (6), (8), (10), (11) and (12) do not destroy the completeness of the model.

5.2 Basic concepts

The extended model is now made more precise. Basic concepts are first defined for this purpose. Some notions, like ps-goal, ns-goal, general goal, general query, extended s-goal, extended goal, extended unification and extended instantiation have already been defined in Section 5.1. We consequently do not reformulate them here but directly foccus on new notions related to trees and processes. Other notions related to programs and n-substitutions will be necessary and are also presented here.

To ease the presentation, the following conventions will be taken all along this chapter.

Convention 5.4 Many properties or explanations refer to a general program and an initial extended query. This reference will generally be kept implicit in order to avoid repetition. Without explicit contrary notice, the referred program and query should thus be considered as those for which the considered computation is made.

Convention 5.5 To facilitate the notation, extended expressions with {not{}} as negative part are generally just denoted by their positive parts. We will thus write subsequently p(3) instead of (p(3),{not{}}).

5.2.1 Program related concepts

Subsequent explanations will require to interpret the programs in some way. One immediate interpretation is to consider each general Horn clause as an implication. However, it is impossible to derive negative information from any set of Horn clauses. Restated in more precise terms, whatever the general Horn clause program P and the conjunction of literals $\leftarrow L_1, ..., L_m$ are, the relation

$$P \models \neg \exists (L_1 \wedge ... \wedge L_m)$$

can never be established. This problem is circumvented by interpreting the program P as its so-called completion (as usual in logic programming). Intuitively, this corresponds to look at each relation p the program P defines as the disjunction of the body of the clauses of the corresponding procedure p. Special treatment has to be made for variables occurring in the clauses. The precise definition due to [Clark, 1979] is as follows.

Definition 5.6 Let p be a procedure of a general program P. Each clause defining p is first transformed in the following implication. Let

$$p(t_1,...,t_m) \leftarrow L_1, ... , L_n$$

be such a clause. The associated implication is

$$p(X_1,...,X_m) \Leftarrow (\exists Y_1, ..., Y_d) (X_1 = t_1 \wedge ... \wedge X_m = t_m \wedge L'_1 \wedge ... \wedge L'_n)$$

where $X_1, ..., X_m$ are variables that do not appear in the clauses defining p, $Y_1, ..., Y_d$ are the variables of the clause considered and the L'_i's are the L_i's where the *not* predicates are replaced by the $\neg$ symbol. K implications, corresponding to the k clauses defining p, are thereby obtained. They take the form

$$p(X_1,...,X_m) \Leftarrow E_1.$$

...

$$p(X_1,...,X_m) \Leftarrow E_k.$$

The completed definition of p is then defined by the equivalence

$$\forall X_1,...,X_m (p(X_1,...,X_m) \Leftrightarrow E_1 \vee ... \vee E_k).$$

The completed definition of a predicate q of arity m in P which does not occur in the head of a clause is defined as

$$\forall X_1,...,X_m (\neg q(X_1,...,X_m)).$$

Finally, the *completion* of P, denoted by *comp(P)*, is the collection of the completed definitions for each predicate in P together with the equality theory defined by the following axioms

(1) $\forall (f(X_1,...,X_m) \neq g(Y_1,...,Y_n))$ for all pairs f, g of distinct functions.
(2) $\forall (t[X] \neq X)$ for each non-variable term t[X] containing X.
(3) $\forall (X_1 \neq Y_1 \vee ... \vee X_m \neq Y_m \Rightarrow f(X_1,...,X_m) \neq f(Y_1,...,Y_m))$, for each function f.
(4) $\forall (X=X)$.
(5) $\forall (X_1 = Y_1 \wedge ... \wedge X_m = Y_m \Rightarrow f(X_1,...,X_m) = f(Y_1,...,Y_m))$, for each function f.
(6) $\forall (X_1 = Y_1 \wedge ... \wedge X_m = Y_m \Rightarrow p(X_1,...,X_m) = p(Y_1,...,Y_m))$, for each predicate p.

This equality theory is subsequently denoted by $Ax_=$.

5.2.2 N-substitution related concepts

A. The Form(v;Svars) interpretation

Interpreting n-substitutions will also be necessary in the following. One equational interpretation has already been given in Chapter 3. However it completely ignores the quantification of variables. It is extended to this aim according to the intuition given in Section 5.1.

Definition 5.7 Let $v=(\{X_1/t_1,\ldots,X_m/t_m\},\text{not}\{Y_1/u_1,\ldots,Y_n/u_n\})$ be an n-substitution. Let furthermore Svars be a set of variables. The notation

Form(v;Svars)

denotes the formula

$$\exists Z_1\ldots\exists Z_p \forall V_1\ldots\forall V_q : (X_1=t_1 \wedge \ldots \wedge X_m=t_m \wedge Y_1 \neq u_1 \wedge \ldots \wedge Y_n \neq u_n)$$

where

- $Z_1, \ldots, Z_p$ are the variables occurring in v^+ and not in Svars
- $V_1, \ldots, V_q$ are the variables occurring in v^- but neither in v^+ nor in Svars.

In particular, it is reduced to the empty conjunction (interpreted as true) if v is ({},not{}).

The notation

Form*(v;Svars)

denotes the formula Form(v;Svars) without any quantifier i.e. the formula

$$X_1=t_1 \wedge \ldots \wedge X_m=t_m \wedge Y_1 \neq u_1 \wedge \ldots \wedge Y_n \neq u_n .$$

The equational interpretation

$$X_1=t_1 \wedge \ldots \wedge X_m=t_m \wedge Y_1 \neq u_1 \wedge \ldots \wedge Y_n \neq u_n$$

is quite expected. Quantification of the variables is perhaps less clear. The following example should help to understand it.

Example 5.1 Consider the query $\leftarrow p(X)$ and the program

$p(f(Y)) \leftarrow Y \neq 3$.

The natural answer is $X=f(Y)$ for some Y different from 3. The n-substitution $v=(\{X/f(Y)\},\text{not}\{Y/3\})$ will indeed be given as the result of the computation. Obviously, the quantification of X should be kept out of the scope of v and v should be interpreted as

$\exists Y : X=f(Y) \wedge Y \neq 3$.

This is precisely what is achieved by Form(v;{X}).

Consider now the same query but together with the program

p(X) ← not(q(X)).
q(f(Y)).

In this case, the natural answer is X≠f(Y) whatever Y is. The n-substitution μ=({ },not{X/f(Y)}) will indeed be given as the result of the computation. The quantification of X should also be kept out of the scope of μ. Furthermore, the interpretation of μ should be

$\forall Y : X \neq f(Y)$.

This is precisely what is achieved by Form(μ;{X}).

Consider as a final example the query ←p(X,Y) with the program

p(f(Z),Z) ← Z≠3.

The natural answer is X=f(Y) and Y≠3. The n-substitution λ=({X/f(Y)},not{Y/3}) will indeed be computed as a result. Obviously, the quantification of the variables X and Y should be kept out of the scope of λ and λ should be interpreted as

X=f(Y) ∧ Y≠3.

This is precisely what is achieved by Form(λ;{X,Y}).

The Form interpretation is extended to sets of n-substitutions as follows.

Definition 5.8 Let $v_1, ..., v_m$ be n-substitutions and Svars be a set of variables. The notation

Dform($v_1,...,v_m$;Svars)

is used as a shorthand to denote the disjunction

Form(v_1;Svars) ∨ ... ∨ Form(v_m;Svars).

Given a set of n-substitutions, the notation

Dform(Snsubst;Svars)

is also used in order to avoid the listing of all the n-substitutions of Snsubst.

The Form* notation is extended to sets of n-substitutions in the same way. The notation

Dform($v_1,...,v_m$;Svars)*

thus denote the disjunction

Form*(v_1;Svars) ∨ ... ∨ Form*(v_m;Svars).

Given a set of n-substitutions, the notation

Dform(Snsubst;Svars)*

is also used in order to avoid the listing of all the n-substitutions of Snsubst.

Finally, the following notation gives a conjunctive counterpart.

Definition 5.9 Let $v_1, \ldots, v_m$ be n-substitutions and Svars be a set of variables. The notation

$Cform^*(v_1,\ldots,v_m;Svars)$

denotes the conjunction

$Form^*(v_1;Svars) \wedge \ldots \wedge Form^*(v_m;Svars)$.

The notation

$Cform(v_1,\ldots,v_m;Svars)$

denotes the conjunction $Cform^*(v_1,\ldots,v_m;Svars)$ quantified as follows :

$\exists Z_1 \ldots \exists Z_p \, \forall V_1 \ldots \forall V_q : Cform^*(v_1,\ldots,v_m;Svars)$

where

- $Z_1, \ldots, Z_p$ are the variables occurring in the v_i^+'s and not in Svars
- $V_1, \ldots, V_q$ are the variables occurring in one v_i^- but neither in one v_i^+ nor in Svars.

Given a set of n-substitutions Snsubst, the notation

$Cform^*(Snsubst;Svars)$
$Cform(Snsubst;;Svars)$

is also used in order to avoid the listing of all the n-substitutions of Snsubst.

B. The ground(E;v) set of substitutions

It will also be convenient to give an interpretation of n-substitutions in terms of substitutions. Referring to the equational interpretation of Chapter 3, this interpretation should be regarded as the counterpart of the solutions of the set Sol(hsyst(v)). It is defined here as the ground(E;v) set.

Definition 5.10 Let t be a term and v be an n-substitution. The notation

$ground(t;v)$

denotes the set of grounding substitutions α such that

(i) $dom(\alpha) = var(t)$,
(ii) $Ax_= \models Form(v;var(t))\alpha$.

The notation

$ground(t)$

is used as a shorthand for $ground(t;(\{\},not\{\}))$. Note that it designates all the grounding substitutions whose domains are $var(t)$.

Example 5.2 Returning to the n-substitutions ν, μ and λ of Example 5.1, one has

ground(p(X);ν) = { {X/f(t)} : t∈ B_H, t≠3 }
ground(p(X);μ) = { {X/t} : t∈ B_H, t is not a compound term with f/1 as functor }
ground(p(X,Y);λ) = { {X/f(t),Y/t} : t∈ B_H, t≠3 } .

Note that this indeed corresponds to the interpretation placed in ν, μ and λ.

For purposes of generality, it will be useful to extend the ground(t;Svars) notation to extended expressions.

Definition 5.11 Let E=(t,{ν_1,...,ν_m}) be an extended expression and ν be an n-substitution. The notation

ground(E;ν)

denotes the set of grounding substitutions α such that

(i) dom(α) = var(t),
(ii) $Ax_= \models$ Cform(ν,ν_i;var(t))α holds for some i∈ {1,...,m}.

Similarly, the notation

ground(E)

is used as a shorthand for ground(E;({},not{})).

Any n-substitution ν computed for some goal G can thus be interpreted as representing the grounding substitutions of ground(G;ν). Another interpretation might also be plausible : the n-substitution ν represents the grounding substitutions α verifying (i) above and that n-reconcile with ν. This interpretation is however not consistent with the Form(ν;Svars) interpretation. Consider for instance the n-substitution μ of Example 5.1. According to the last interpretation, μ would represent the substitution {X/f(2)}. It can however in no case be considered as a solution to the program and query for which μ was computed! Note that it is indeed not in ground(p(X);μ).

The notion of instance of an extended expression/term can be defined from the ground(E) set.

Definition 5.12 The extended expression or term E is an *instance* of the extended or term expression F iff it verifies

{$F^+\alpha$: $\alpha\in$ ground(F)} $\supset$ {$E^+\alpha$: $\alpha\in$ ground(E)}.

Note that this definition indeed generalizes Definition 2.25 to the extended expressions.

Example 5.3 The term p(3) is an instance of the extended expression (p(X);{not{X/f(Y)}}).

C. N-reconciliation and consistency

The introductory Section 5.1 has suggested the need of generalizing n-reconciliation in order to take care of the quantification of variables. To further illustrate this need, let us consider the query

← not(p(X)),q(X).

and the program

p(f(Y)).
q(f(3)).

Assume the R-depth parameter of the model is infinite. The corresponding and/or/not search tree is drawn in Figure 5.5. As indicated there, the query-process will receive the n-substitution ({},not{X/f(Y)}) from the ns-goal-process (2) and the n-substitution ({X/f(3)},not{}) from the ps-goal-process (3). Referring to the above interpretation, the first n-substitution reports the fact that X must differ from any f(Y) whatever Y is and the second requires that X must be equal to f(3). The two n-substitutions should thus not be n-reconcilable. They are however n-reconcilable according to Definition 3.68. This is because all variables are manipulated as existentially quantified in this n-reconciliation scheme. The two n-substitutions are indeed n-reconcilable iff there are some values for X and Y such that the system

$$\begin{cases} X = f(3) \\ X \neq f(Y) \end{cases}$$

is solvable.

N-reconciliation needs thus to be extended to handle universally quantified variables too. This is achieved by means of the notion of consistency.

Definition 5.13 An n-substitution v is *consistent with respect to a set of variables* Svars iff any binding Y/u of v^- verifies the following properties :

(i) Y is a variable of Svars or of v^+;
(ii) if u is a variable then u is a variable of Svars or of v^+.

Example 5.4 The n-substitution ({X/f(Z)},not{Y/3,Z/4,U/V}) is consistent with respect to the set {X,Y,U,V}. However, the n-substitution ({X/f(3)},not{Y/3}) is not consistent with respect to the set {X}.

The following property identifies, among the idempotent n-substitutions, the n-substitutions v consistent wrt Svars as those satisfying the formula Form(v;Svars).

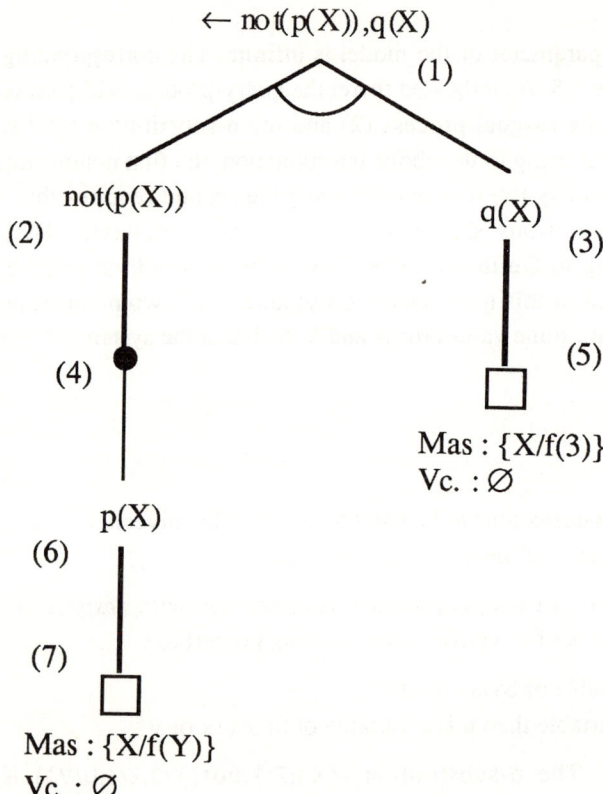

Figure 5.5

BASIC CONCEPTS 269

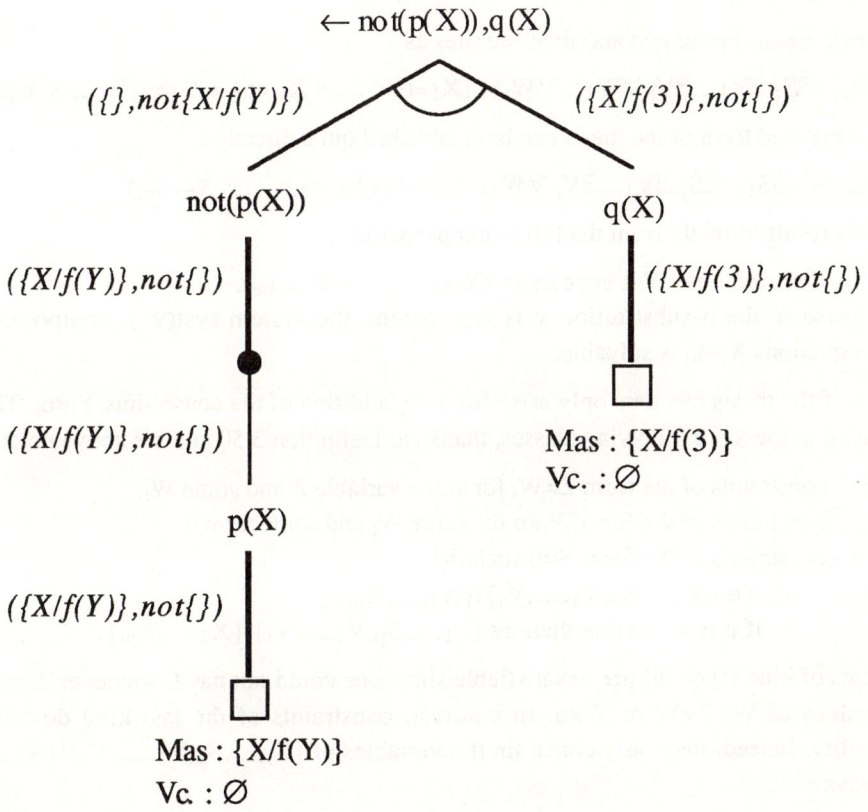

Figure 5.5 continued

Proposition 5.14 Let Svars be a set of variables and ν be an idempotent n-substitution. Then ν is consistent wrt Svars iff the relation $Ax_= \models \exists_{Svars}(Form(\nu;Svars))$ holds.[1]

Proof To ease the demonstration, let us first adopt the following notational conventions. Let

- ν be $(\{X_1/t_1,...,X_m/t_m\}, not\{Y_1/u_1,...,Y_n/u_n\})$,
- Svars be $\{S_1,...,S_p\}$,
- $\{V_1,...,V_r\}$ be $var(\nu^+)\backslash Svars$,
- $\{W_1,...,W_s\}$ be $var(\nu^-)\backslash\{S_1,...,S_p,V_1,...,V_r\}$.

The formula $\exists_{Svars} Form(\nu;Svars)$ then rewrites as

$$(\exists S_1...\exists S_p \exists V_1...\exists V_r \forall W_1...\forall W_s) : (X_1=t_1 \wedge ... \wedge X_m=t_m \wedge Y_1 \neq u_1 \wedge ... \wedge Y_n \neq u_n).$$

A weakened form of the thesis can be established quite directly :

$$Ax_= \models (\exists S_1...\exists S_p \exists V_1...\exists V_r \forall W_1...\forall W_s) : (X_1=t_1 \wedge ... \wedge X_m=t_m)$$

holds. This results directly from the following properties :

- by definition, no W_i's appears in $(X_1=t_1 \wedge ... \wedge X_m=t_m)$,
- because the n-substitution ν is idempotent, the system $syst(\nu^+)$, composed of the equations $X_i=t_i$, is solvable.

Violation of the thesis can thus only arise from the addition of the constraints $Y_i \neq u_i$. They can be classified in the three following classes, thanks to Definition 3.50 and the above notations :

(i) constraints of the form $Z \neq W_i$ for some variable Z and some W_i,
(ii) constraints of the form $W_i \neq u$ for some W_i and some term u,
(iii) constraints of the form $Y \neq u$ such that
  - $Y \in \{S_1,...,S_p,V_1,...,V_r\}\backslash\{X_1,...,X_m\}$
  - if u is a variable then $u \in \{S_1,...,S_p,V_1,...,V_r\}\backslash\{X_1,...,X_m\}$.

Constraints of kind (i) or (ii) are unsatisfiable since one could not have, whatever Z and u are, for all values of W, $Z \neq W$ or $W \neq u$. In contrast, constraints of the last kind do not imply unsolvability. Indeed, they only constrain the variables of $\{S_1,...,S_p,V_1,..., V_r\}\backslash\{X_1,...,X_m\}$ in two ways :

- by excluding a finite number of (non-variable) terms (for the u_i's that are not variable)
- by excluding the sharing of values for some of them (for the u_i's that are variable).

These variables are not constrained by the equalities $X_i=t_i$. Moreover, they range in a universe that cannot be completely covered by a finite number of (non-variable) terms thanks to the definition of $\mathcal{L}$ (see Section 2.1). The exclusion of the first kind can thus be always satisfied.

---

[1] The notation $\exists_{Set}$ (F) (resp. $\forall_{Set}$ (F)) is used as a shorthand to denote the formula $(\exists X_1...\exists X_m)$ (F) (resp. $(\forall X_1...\forall X_m)$ (F)), where $X_1, ..., X_m$ are the variables of Set.

The exclusion of the second kind is always achievable for the same reason, for instance, by progressively assigning values for the variables that are not excluded by previously assigned ones.

Summing up, the addition of the constraints $Y_i \neq u_i$ in the formula

$$(\exists S_1 ... \exists S_p \, \exists V_1 ... \exists V_r \, \forall W_1 ... \forall W_s) : (X_1 = t_1 \wedge ... \wedge X_m = t_m)$$

induces unsatisfiability iff constraints of kinds (i) and (ii) above are involved that is, thanks to Definition 5.13, ν is not consistent wrt to Svars. $\Diamond$

One desired property is that consistency is simultaneously achieved by variant n-substitutions. This is indeed the case for idempotent n-substitutions.

Proposition 5.15 Let Svars be a set of variables. All variant idempotent n-substitutions are simultaneously consistent wrt Svars.
Proof Let

$$\nu = (\{X_1/t_1, ..., X_m/t_m\}, \text{not}\{Y_1/u_1, ..., Y_n/u_n\})$$

and

$$\mu = (\{X'_1/t'_1, ..., X'_{m'}/t'_{m'}\}, \text{not}\{Y'_1/u'_1, ..., Y'_{n'}/u'_{n'}\})$$

be two variant n-substitutions. Furthermore, let Svars be $\{S_1, ..., S_p\}$.

The thesis is established by proving first that ν and μ share the same variables and that they are quantified in the same manner in Form(ν;Svars) and Form(μ;Svars). The first part of this claim results from the fact that ν and μ are variants. Hence they can only differ from non significant equations of the form U=U that are not memorized in the n-substitutions. The second part is issued from the fact that, thanks to Proposition 3.57, the positive parts ν^+ and μ^+ are also variants and thus involve also the same sets of variables.

Let $\{V_1, ..., V_r\}$ and $\{W_1, ..., W_s\}$ be the sets of variables that are existentially and universally quantified in Form(ν;Svars), respectively. Note that, thanks to what preceeds, they also represent the sets of variables that are existentially and universally quantified in Form(μ;Svars). In these conditions, thanks to the variance of ν and μ, the two sets

$$\{(s_1,...,s_p,v_1,...,v_r,w_1,...,w_s) \in B_H :$$
$$Ax_= \models (X_1 = t_1 \wedge ... \wedge X_m = t_m \wedge Y_1 \neq u_1 \wedge ... \wedge Y_n \neq u_n)\theta\} \},$$

$$\{(s_1,...,s_p,v_1,...,v_r,w_1,...,w_s) \in B_H :$$
$$Ax_= \models (X'_1 = t'_1 \wedge ... \wedge X'_{m'} = t'_{m'} \wedge Y'_1 \neq u'_1 \wedge ... \wedge Y'_{n'} \neq u'_{n'})\theta\} \},$$

where θ denotes the substitution $\{S_1/s_1, ..., S_p/s_p, V_1/v_1, ..., V_r/v_r, W_1/w_1, ..., W_s/w_s\}$, are equivalent. The thesis then directly results from Proposition 5.14. $\Diamond$

N-reconciliation generally involves more than one n-substitution. Consistency should thus be extended to sets of n-substitutions to be fully taken into account. Restriction to en-substs is however sufficient for our purposes.

Definition 5.16 A set of n-substitutions $\{v_1,...,v_m\}$ is *consistent wrt to a set of variables* Svars iff, at least, one v_i is consistent wrt to Svars.

Propositions 5.14 and 5.15 may be extended to es-nsusbt's quite directly.

Proposition 5.17 Let Svars be a set of variables and $\theta \oplus \{\omega_1,...,\omega_m\}$ be an idempotent es-nsubst. Then $\theta \oplus \{\omega_1,...,\omega_m\}$ is consistent wrt to Svars iff the relation

$$Ax_= \models \exists_{Svars} (Dform(\theta \oplus \{\omega_1,...,\omega_m\}; Svars)$$

holds.

Proof The proof is established by taking profit of the results established in the proof of Proposition 5.14. Let

- θ be $\{X_1/t_1,...,X_m/t_m\}$,
- $\omega_1, ..., \omega_m$ be $not\{A_1/a_1,...,A_k/a_k\}, ..., not\{C_1/c_1,...,C_\ell/c_\ell\}$, respectively,
- Svars be $\{S_1,...,S_p\}$,
- $\{V_1,...,V_r\}$ be $var(\theta) \backslash Svars$,
- $\{W_1,...,W_s\}$ be $[var(\omega_1) \cup ... \cup var(\omega_m)] \backslash \{S_1,...,S_p,V_1,...,V_r\}$.

The formula $\exists_{Svars} (Dform(\theta \oplus \{\omega_1,...,\omega_m\}; Svars)$ then rewrites as

$(\exists S_1...\exists S_p \exists V_1...\exists V_r \forall W_1...\forall W_s)$:
$\quad\quad (X_1=t_1 \wedge ... \wedge X_m=t_m \wedge \ [\ (A_1 \neq a_1 \wedge ... \wedge A_k \neq a_k)$
$\quad\quad\quad\quad\quad\quad\quad\quad\quad\quad\quad\quad \vee ... \vee$
$\quad\quad\quad\quad\quad\quad\quad\quad\quad\quad\quad\quad (C_1 \neq c_1 \wedge ... \wedge C_\ell \neq c_\ell)\ ]\ )$

The weakened form

$$Ax_= \models (\exists S_1...\exists S_p \exists V_1...\exists V_r \forall W_1...\forall W_s) : (X_1=t_1 \wedge ... \wedge X_m=t_m)$$

results directly from the proof of Proposition 5.14. Furthermore, thanks to the above description, violation of $\exists_{Svars} (Dform(\theta \oplus \{\omega_1,...,\omega_m\}; Svars)$ occurs iff all the following relations are violated :

$(\exists S_1...\exists S_p \exists V_1...\exists V_r \forall W_1...\forall W_s) : (X_1=t_1 \wedge ... \wedge X_m=t_m \wedge A_1 \neq a_1 \wedge ... \wedge A_k \neq a_k)$,
...
$(\exists S_1...\exists S_p \exists V_1...\exists V_r \forall W_1...\forall W_s) : (X_1=t_1 \wedge ... \wedge X_m=t_m \wedge C_1 \neq c_1 \wedge ... \wedge C_\ell \neq c_\ell)$.

That is, as shown in the proof of Proposition 5.14, iff all n-substitutions $(\theta,\omega_1), ..., (\theta,\omega_m)$ are not consistent wrt to Svars. ◊

Proposition 5.18 Let Svars be a set of variables. All variants idempotent en-subst's are simultaneously consistent wrt to Svars.

Proof Once again, profit will be taken of the demonstration of the corresponding Proposition 5.15 for n-substitutions. Let $\theta \oplus \{\omega_1,...,\omega_m\}$ and $\theta' \oplus \{\omega'_1,...,\omega'_{m'}\}$ be two variant en-nsubst's. As the two es-nsubst's are variant, the two substitutions θ and θ' are variants too, thanks to Proposition 3.61. They thus share the same set of variables. Hence, the same variables are existentially and universally quantified in Dform($\theta \oplus \{\omega_1,...,\omega_m\}$;Svars) and Dform($\theta' \oplus \{\omega'_1,...,\omega'_{m'}\}$;Svars). Let them be $\{V_1,...,V_r\}$ and $\{W_1,...,W_s\}$, respectively. The variance of the two es-nsusbt's then makes the two following sets identical :

$$\{(s_1,...,s_p,v_1,...,v_r,w_1,...,w_s) \in B_H :$$
$$Ax_= \models (\text{Dform*}(\theta \oplus \{\omega_1,...,\omega_m\};\text{Svars}))\theta\},$$

$$\{(s_1,...,s_p,v_1,...,v_r,w_1,...,w_s) \in B_H :$$
$$Ax_= \models (\text{Dform*}(\theta' \oplus \{\omega'_1,...,\omega'_{m'}\};\text{Svars}))\theta\}.$$

The thesis then directly results from Proposition 5.17. ◊

We are now in a position to generalize the n-reconciliation in order to handle quantified variables.

Definition 5.19 Let Svars be a set of variables. The n-substitutions v_1, ..., v_m are *qn-reconcilable wrt Svars* iff

(i) they are n-reconcilable
(ii) any idempotent en-reconciliation is consistent wrt Svars.

Proposition 5.18 ensures that all idempotent en-reconciliations simultaneously verify condition (ii). When this is the case, any such idempotent en-reconciliation, restricted to its consistent n-substitutions, is called a *qn-reconciliation* of v_1, ..., v_m.

Qn-reconciliation is extended to sets of n-substitutions as follows.

Definition 5.20 Let Svars be a set of variables. The sets of n-substitutions Ψ_1, ..., Ψ_m are qn-reconcilable wrt to Svars iff there exist m n-substitutions $\psi_1 \in \Psi_1$, ..., $\psi_m \in \Psi_m$ qn-reconcilable wrt to Svars. In this case, a qn-reconciliation of Ψ_1, ..., Ψ_m consists of a set of n-substitutions obtained by associating the consistent n-substitutions of one qn-reconciliation with each tuple $(\psi_1,...,\psi_m) \in \Psi_1 \times ... \times \Psi_m$ qn-reconcilable wrt to Svars.

Note that Definitions 5.19 and 5.20 re-express in the new terminology the n-reconciliation wrt the quantification of variables introduced in Definitions 5.1 and 5.2.

D. Negation of n-substitutions

Section 5.1 suggests that n-substitutions will have to be negated in some way. What this means is captured by the concepts of negation of n-substitutions and of negation of sets of n-substitutions.

Definition 5.21 The *negation of the n-substitution*

$$v=(\{X_1/t_1,...,X_m/t_m\},\text{not}\{Y_1/u_1,...,Y_n/u_n\})$$

is the set of n-substitutions obtained by associating

- the n-substitution $(\{\},\text{not}\{X_i/t_i\})$ with each binding X_i/t_i, $1 \le i \le m$,
- the n-substitution $(\{X_1/t_1,...,X_m/t_m\} \circ \{Y_j/u_j\},\text{not}\{\})$ with each binding Y_j/u_j, $1 \le j \le n$.

It is denoted by *neg(v)*.

Referring to our equational interpretation of n-substitutions, it might seem quite natural to define the negation of the n-substitution $(\{X_1/t_1,...,X_m/t_m\},\text{not}\{Y_1/u_1,...,Y_n/u_n\})$ as the set of n-substitutions

$$\{ (\{\},\text{not}\{X_1/t_1\}), ..., (\{\},\text{not}\{X_m/t_m\}), (\{Y_1/u_1\},\text{not}\{\}), ..., (\{Y_n/u_n\},\text{not}\{\}) \}.$$

Once again, this does completely ignore the quantification of variables. Consider, for instance, the n-substitution $v=(\{X/f(Y)\},\text{not}\{Y/3\})$ of the first query $\leftarrow p(X)$ of Example 5.1. Its associated interpretation was pointed as

$$\exists Y : X=f(Y) \land Y \ne 3.$$

Negating this n-substitution as above would lead to the two n-substitutions $(\{\},\text{not}\{X/f(Y)\})$ and $(\{Y/3\},\text{not}\{\})$ with the interpretation

$\forall Y : X \ne f(Y),$
$\exists Y : Y=3,$

respectively. Assigning the value $f(2)$ to X would thus make the negation of

$\neg\ (\exists Y : X=f(Y) \land Y \ne 3)$!

hold. The problem is that the variable Y has lost its relation with X in the second n-substitution. This is circumvented by Definition 5.21.

According to this critic, it may then be strange that the variables X_1, ..., X_m receive no special treatment. This is indeed not necessary for our purposes since we will always assume that the quantification of the X_i's is out of the scope of the considered n-substitutions.

Ns-goals will generally have to negate sets of n-substitutions rather than single n-substitutions. Negation should thus be extended to sets of n-substitutions. This is achieved by referring to the set understanding already developed in Chapter 3: n-substitutions of the set to negate are considered as as many alternatives. The set is then negated by negating each n-substitution separately and by combining the resulting n-substitutions. The last operation implies reconciliation. This induces two possible acceptations according as quantification is taken into account or not. We could then define two negations, one involving quantification and the other not. The latter is however useless for our purposes. We thus only describe the former.

Definition 5.22 A set of n-substitutions $\{v_1, ..., v_m\}$ is *negatable wrt the set of variables Svars* iff one of the two following conditions holds :
- the set is empty
- the set is not empty and the sets of n-substitutions $neg(v_1), ..., neg(v_m)$ are qn-reconcilable wrt to Svars.

In the first case, the n-substitution ($\{\}$,not$\{\}$) is called the *negation* of the empty set. In the last case, any qn-reconciliation is called a *negation of* $\{v_1, ..., v_m\}$ *wrt Svars*. It is denoted by

$sneg(\{v_1, ..., v_m\}; Svars)$.

Reference to Svars will often be omitted when the context designates it without ambiguity.

The following property relates the negation of an n-substitution with the negation of the singleton composed of this n-substitution.

Proposition 5.23 Let Svars be a set of variables and v be an n-substitution such that the set

$dom(v^+) \cup \{Xv^+ : Xv^+ \text{ is a variable}\}$

is included in Svars. Then, the singleton composed of v is negatable wrt to Svars. Furthermore, the set $neg(v)$ is a negation of $\{v\}$ wrt to Svars.
Proof The proposition directly results from Definitions 5.21 and 5.22. ◊

E. Restriction of n-substitutions

The restriction of substitutions needs finally to be extended to our general context.

Definition 5.24 Let $v=(\{X_1/t_1,...,X_m/t_m\}, not\{Y_1/u_1,...,Y_n/u_n\})$ be an n-substitution and Svars be a set of variables. The restriction $v_{/Svars}$ of v to Svars is the n-substitution μ
- whose positive part μ^+ is obtained from $\{X_1/t_1,...,X_m/t_m\}$
    1. by removing any binding X_i/t_i such that $X_i \notin$ Svars,
    2. by removing any binding X_i/t_i such that $X_i \in$ Svars and $t_i \notin$ Svars
    3. by replacing any occurrence of any t_i pointed out in 2 by one of the X_j such that X_j/t_i is of the form pointed out in 2.
- whose negative part μ^- is obtained from the version of $\{Y_1/u_1,...,Y_n/u_n\}$, updated as indicated in 3. above, by removing any binding Y_i/u_i that verifies one of the two following conditions :
    (i) $Y_i \notin$ Svars, $Y_i \notin varcod(\mu^+)$
    (ii) u_i is a variable, $u_i \notin$ Svars, $u_i \notin varcod(\mu^+)$.

Example 5.5 Let $v=(\{X_1/f(Z), X_2/Y_1, X_3/g(Y_1), X_4/h(Y_2)\}, not\{Y_1/1, Y_2/2\})$. Let Svars be $\{X_2, X_3, X_4, Z\}$. The restriction $v_{|Svars}$ is

$(\{X_3/g(X_2), X_4/h(Y_2)\}, not\{X_2/1, Y_2/2\})$.

Note that it sums up the solutions of the system

$$hsyst(v) = \begin{cases} X_1 = f(Z) \\ X_2 = Y_1 \\ X_3 = g(Y_1) \\ X_4 = h(Y_2) \\ Y_1 \neq 1 \\ Y_2 \neq 2 \end{cases}$$

where occurrences of the variables that are not in Svars have been removed as much as possible i.e. without altering the set of solutions of the system to such an extend that the set of 4-tuples $<X_2,X_3,X_4,Z>\theta$ for the solutions θ is not altered.

It is worth noting that the restriction of n-substitutions does not exactly generalize the restriction of substitutions as stated in Definition 2.23 : bindings X_i/t_i such that t_i is a variable of Svars are not removed in the restriction defined in Definition 2.23. The above restriction is thus slightly stronger. This difference is explained by the fact that Definition 5.24 results from an equational perception of substitutions and n-substitutions whereas Definition 2.23 results from a functional one. For this reason, the restriction of Definition 5.24 is subsequently called *equational restriction*.

Although our model manifestly rests on equational foundations, the functional interpretation of restriction makes also sense. It is defined as follows.

Definition 5.25 Let $v=(\{X_1/t_1,...,X_m/t_m\},\text{not}\{Y_1/u_1,...,Y_n/u_n\})$ be an n-substitution and Svars be a set of variables. The *functional restriction* of v to Svars is the n-substitution μ
- whose positive part μ^+ is obtained from $\{X_1/t_1,...,X_m/t_m\}$ by removing any binding X_i/t_i such that $X_i \notin$ Svars;
- whose negative part μ^- is obtained from $\{Y_1/u_1,...,Y_n/u_n\}$ by removing any binding Y_i/u_i that verifies one of the two following conditions :
    (i) $Y_i \notin$ Svars, $Y_i \notin \text{varcod}(\mu^+)$
    (ii) u_i is a variable, $u_i \notin$ Svars, $u_i \notin \text{varcod}(\mu^+)$.

It is subsequently denoted as *f_restriction(v;Svars)*.

Note that this indeed generalizes the restriction defined in Definition 2.23 for substitutions.

Example 5.6 The functional restriction of the n-substitution v of Example 5.5 to the same set $\{X_2,X_3,X_4,Z\}$ is

$(\{X_2/Y_1,X_3/g(Y_1),X_4/h(Y_2)\},\text{not}\{Y_1/1,Y_2/2\})$.

As suggested above, it is different from the restriction obtained in Example 5.5.

A classical use of restriction takes place in the context of the unification of an atom with a clause. It was indeed well suited to distinguish the atom part and the clause part of an mgu in Chapter 2. It refers to a functional framework and so is defined with respect to the f_restriction operator.

Definition 5.26 Let $\{v_1,...,v_m\}$ be the n-mgu unifying (in the extended sense) the extended atom A with the clause C. The atom and clause subsets of $\{v_1,...,v_m\}$ are the sets

$$\{f\_restriction(v_1;var(A)),...,f\_restriction(v_m;var(A))\}$$

and

$$\{f\_restriction(v_1;var(C)),...,f\_restriction(v_m;var(C))\},$$

respectively. They are denoted as $\{v_1,...,v_m\}_{atom}$ and $\{v_1,...,v_m\}_{clause}$. The atom subset is furthermore referred to as *nmas*.

Another use of the functional restriction is to extract bindings related to some variables from n-substitutions. These bindings are called general bindings.

Definition 5.27
1) Let v be an n-substitution v and X be a variable of $dom(v^+)$. Then, the *general binding* of v for X is the functional restriction of v to $\{X\}$.
2) Let $\{v_1,...,v_m\}$ be a set of n-substitutions and X be a variable of $dom(v_1^+) \cap ... \cap dom(v_m^+)$. The *general bindings* of $\{v_1,...,v_m\}$ for X are the general bindings of the v_i's for X.

5.2.3 Tree related concepts

Let us now turn to tree related concepts.

A. And/or/not search trees

The concept of and/or/not search tree has been intuitively introduced in Section 5.1. It is precised as follows.

Definition 5.28 Let $\leftarrow L_1, ..., L_m$ be an extended goal and P be a general program. The and/or/not search tree T for $\leftarrow L_1, ..., L_m$ and P is the tree of nodes defined by the following rules :

(i) Its root is the node labelled by the query $\leftarrow L_1,...,L_m$.
(ii) Any node labelled by an extended goal has as many child nodes as the extended s-goals contained in the extended goal. They are associated with the s-goals in a one-to-one fashion. Each child node is labelled by the corresponding s-goal.
(iii) Any node labelled by an extended ps-goal (G,Θ) has as many child nodes as clauses of P are unifiable (in the extended sense) with G. They are associated with

these unifiable clauses in a one-to-one fashion. Each child node is labelled by the goal

$\leftarrow (G_1\psi,\Omega_1), ..., (G_m\psi,\Omega_m)$

where
- $H \leftarrow G_1, ..., G_m$ is the clause corresponding to the node
- $\psi \oplus \Psi$ is the en-mgu of H and (G,Θ)
- Ω_i is the functional restriction of Ψ to the variables of $G_i\psi$ for all $i \in \{1,...,m\}$.

(iv) Any node labelled by an extended ns-goal $(not(G),\Theta)$ has only one child node. It consists of the node labelled by the extended s-goal (G,Θ).

The following property gives a recursive characterization of and/or/not search trees. As for and/or search trees, it should be noted that non-decrease of the value of some well-founded function forbids to use it as a definition.

Proposition 5.29 Let $\leftarrow L_1, ..., L_m$ be an extended goal and P be a general program. The and/or/not search tree T for $\leftarrow L_1, ..., L_m$ and P verifies the following properties.

i)   If m=0 (i.e. the conjunction is empty) then T is formed of the only node labelled by □.

ii) If m>0, then T is composed of
- a node, labelled by $\leftarrow L_1, ..., L_m$, as root node
- m subtrees $ST_1, ..., ST_m$ attached to the m extended s-goals $L_1, ..., L_m$, respectively. Each ST_i is defined as follows ($1 \leq i \leq m$). Fix some i in $\{1,...,m\}$.
    - If L_i is an extended ns-goal, say $(not(G),\Theta)$, then ST_i is composed of
        - a node, labelled by $(not(G),\Theta)$, as root node
        - the and/or/not search tree for $\leftarrow G$ and P.
    - If L_i is an extended ps-goal, say (G,Θ), then let
      $H_1 \leftarrow Cl_1$.
      ...
      $H_n \leftarrow Cl_n$.
      be the clauses unifiable (in the extended sense) with (G,Θ), say with en-mgus $\psi_1 \oplus \Psi_1, ..., \psi_n \oplus \Psi_n$, respectively.
        - If there is none, then ST_i reduces to a node, labelled by L_i.
        - Otherwise, let, for any $j \in \{1,...,n\}$, Cl_inst$_j$ be the extended goal obtained from the (non extended goal) Cl_j as follows. Assume Cl_j is the conjunction $G_1, ..., G_p$. Let furthermore, for any $k \in \{1,...,p\}$, Ω_k be the functional restriction of Ψ_j to the variables of $G_k\psi_j$ ($1 \leq j \leq p$). Then, Cl_inst$_j$ is the extended goal $\leftarrow (G_1\psi_j,\Omega_1), ..., (G_p\psi_j,\Omega_p)$.
          With this notation in mind, the subtree ST_i is composed of

- a node, labelled by L_i, as root node
- the n and/or/not search trees for the extended goals Cl_inst_j and the program P.

Definition 2.48 and Conventions 2.49 and 2.50 on and/or search trees are extended to and/or/not search trees. The following resulting points are particularly worth noting.

- Nodes labelled by an extended goal, an extended ps-goal, an extended ns-goal or an extended s-goal are called extended goal-node, extended ps-goal-node, extended ns-goal-node, extended s-goal-node, respectively. They are also usually confused with their respective goal, ps-goal or ns-goal. We will thus speak, by abuse of language, of the goal-node ← G instead of the goal-node labelled by ← G.
- The appellation □-node is conserved for nodes labelled by the empty goal □. Similarly, the appellation ⊗-node is reserved to nodes associated with any ps-goal that unifies with no clause. Such nodes are also decorated in and/or/not search trees by a ⊗ pending mark.
- Goal-nodes, children of ps-goal-nodes, are labelled by an additional piece of information. Recall that such goal-nodes are issued from the unification of their father ps-goal with some clauses. The additional piece of information is precisely associated with this origin. It is as follows :
  - the set of variables introduced by the corresponding unifiable clause. It is signalled by the Vc abbreviation;
  - the atom subset of the corresponding n-mgu. It is referred to by the Nmas abbreviation.

The following convention is furthermore taken. As illustrated in Section 5.1, the negative piece of information associated with an extended goal, an extended s-goal or an nmas is sometimes null. In case this occurs in the whole and/or/not search tree, we will subsequently ease the drawing of and/or/not search trees by omitting this null negative piece of information. The extended goals and s-goals will thus be presented, in these cases, in their shorter non-extended form. Similarly, nmas's of the es-nsubst form will, in these cases, be presented in their mas form.

Note furthermore that the alternance between goal-nodes and s-goal-nodes of the basic model is conserved in and/or/not search trees. It follows that the notion of R-depth and related ones (like the notion of slice of R-depth of an and/or search tree limited to some R-depth) directly extend to and/or/not search trees.

As a final point of terminology, the qualifier "extended" will also be generally omitted when the context clearly states it implicitly.

Example 5.7 Figure 5.6 draws the and/or/not search tree for the extended goal

$\leftarrow$ (p(X,Y),{not{X/3,Y/f(a)}})

and the program of Section 5.1.3.

B. Computed and/or/not search trees

As suggested in Section 5.1, and/or/not search trees are not developed in their pure form by the computations. Subtrees may be removed here too or instantiated after each reconciliation phase. Furthermore, the and/or/not search tree is only made apparent slice by slice. This is captured by the notion of computed and/or/not search tree. The meaning of the instantiation of a node is first precised. The notions of computed and/or/not search tree and instantiation subtree of such a search tree are then defined.

Definition 5.30 Let N be a s-goal-node or a goal-node and v be an n-substitution. *The node N is instantiable by the n-substitution v* iff the following conditions are fulfilled :

(i) If N is a s-goal-node then the (extended) s-goal associated with N is instantiable by v;

(ii) If N is a goal-node then
- the n-substitution v and the nmas of N are qn-reconcilable wrt the variables of N and of its associated set Vc; let μ be a qn-reconciliation;
- each s-goal of the goal associated with N are instantiable by μ.

When these conditions are fulfilled, an *instantiation of N by v* is the following node N_inst :

(i) If N is a s-goal-node then N_inst is the node formed of the instantiation by v of the s-goal associated with N.

(ii) If N is a goal-node then N_inst is attached the same Vc set and Nmas as N but its goal is composed of the instantiation of the s-goals of N by μ.

Note that as usual now, such a concept is defined up to some variant. This justifies the expression "an instantiation" a posteriori.

The expression *"instantiating a node"* is used to designate the action of replacing a node by one instantiation.

Example 5.8 Referring to the example of Section 5.1.3, the s-goal-node (r(X,Y),{not{}}) (node (5)) is instantiable by the n-substitution ({X/1,Y/f(X_2)},not{X_2/a}). One instantiation is the s-goal node

(r(1,f(X_2)), {not{X_2/a}}).

Similarly, the goal-node (node (13))

$\leftarrow$(u(X_2), {not{}})

is instantiable by the same n-substitution. However, the goal-node (node (12))

← (s(X_1), {not{}})

is not since the n-substitution ({X/3,Y/h(X_1)},not{}) and ({X/1,Y/f(X_2)},not{X_2/a}) are not n-reconcilable.

We are now in a position to define the notion of computed and/or search tree.

Definition 5.31 Let P be a program and Q be an extended query. A computed and/or/not search tree for P and Q is a tree derived from the and/or/not search tree for P and Q

- by removing some subtrees attached to some ps-goal-nodes, the ps-goal-nodes included;
- by removing some subtrees attached to some ns-goal-nodes, the ns-goal-nodes excluded;
- by instantiating the goals or s-goals associated with the nodes of subtrees attached to goal-nodes, the goal-nodes included;
- by limiting the and/or search tree to some R-depth, possibly infinite.

Example 5.9 Trees of Figures 5.1 and 5.3 are examples of computed and/or/not search trees for the program and query of Section 5.1.3.

Proposition 5.32 Any and/or/not such tree is a computed and/or/not search tree.
Proof This is immediate. ◊

Notation 5.33 The notations ST(N,T), Var(N,T) and Vc(N,T), introduced in Notation 4.8, are extended to computed and/or/not search trees by means of the same definitions.

Instantiation subtrees are defined as follows.

Definition 5.34 Let ST be a finite subtree of some computed and/or/not search tree and ν be an n-substitution. Let furthermore N be the root node of ST and ST_1, ..., ST_m be the subtrees associated with the children of N, if any. As for nodes, *instantiation subtrees* ST_inst of *ST by* ν are defined up to variants. They are defined by means of the following auxiliary subtrees ST_aux; a subtree ST_inst is associated with each subtree ST_aux in the following manner :

- if N is not an ns-goal, if ST is not reduced to N and if ST_aux is reduced to N then the associated subtree ST_inst is ∅;
- otherwise, the associated subtree ST_inst is simply ST_aux.

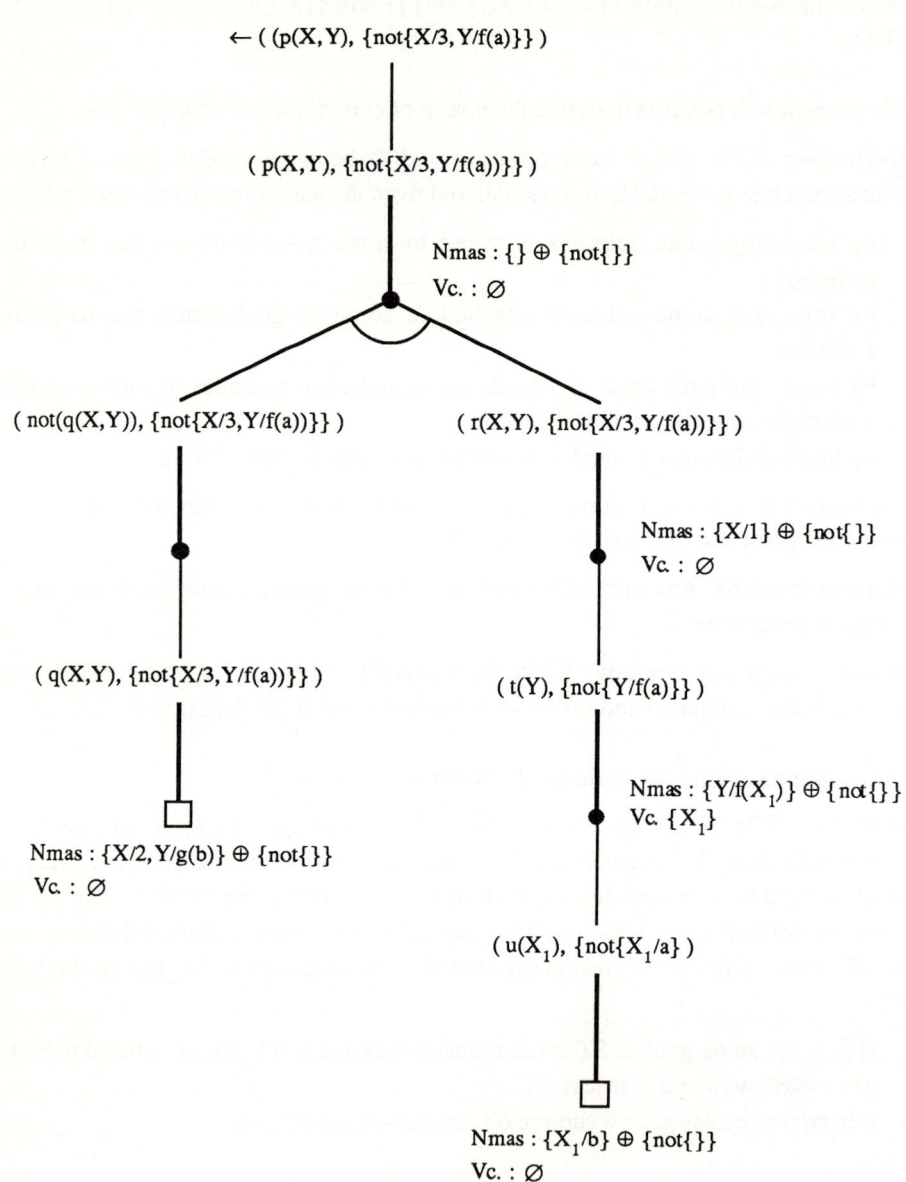

Figure 5.6

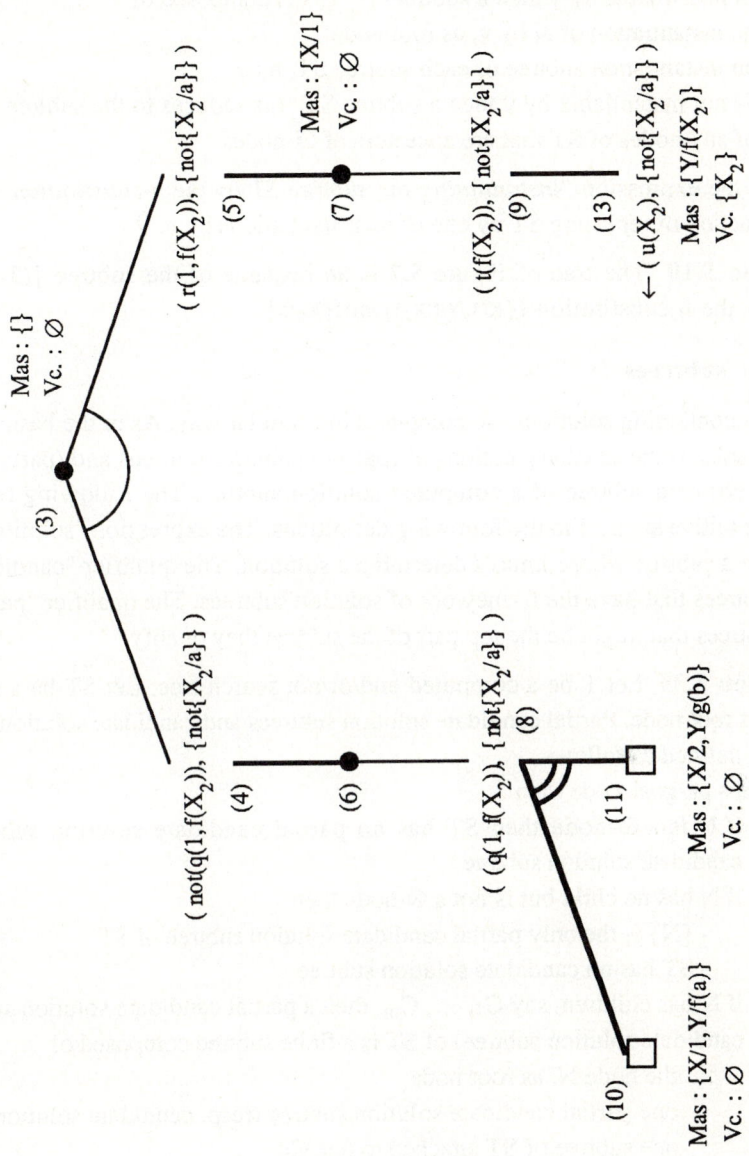

Figure 5.7

The subtrees ST_aux are defined as follows.

- If N is instantiable by ν then a subtree ST_aux is composed of
    - an instantiation of N by ν, as root node
    - an instantiation subtree of each subtree ST_i by ν.
- If N is not instantiable by ν then a subtree ST_aux reduces to the subtree formed of N and of any nodes of ST that are ancestors of □-nodes.

Finally, the expression *"instantiating the subtree ST by the n-substitution ν"* is used to designate the action of replacing ST by one of its instantiations by ν. ◊

Example 5.10 The tree of Figure 5.7 is an instance of the subtree {(3),...,(13)} of Figure 5.1 by the n-substitution ({X/1,Y/f(X_2)},not{X_2/a}).

C. Solution subtrees

Subtrees containing solutions are computed in a similar way. As in the basic model, they are defined thanks to the auxiliary notions of (partial) solution subtrees and (partial) candidate solution subtrees of a subtree of a computed solution subtree. The following interpretation provides the intuitive support to the following definitions. The expression "solution subtree" is used to denote a subtree whose nmas's determine a solution. The qualifier "candidate" is used to identify subtrees that have the framework of solution subtrees. The qualifier "partial" is used to identify subtrees that might be the top part of the subtree they qualify.

Definition 5.35 Let T be a computed and/or/not search tree. Let ST be a subtree of T and let N be its root node. Partial candidate solution subtrees and candidate solution subtrees are finite subtrees defined as follows.

(i) If N is a ps-goal-node then

(i.1) if N is a ⊗-node then ST has no partial candidate solution subtree and no candidate solution subtree

(i.2) if N has no child but is not a ⊗-node then
- {N} is the only partial candidate solution subtree of ST
- ST has no candidate solution subtree

(i.3) if N has children, say C_1, ..., C_m, then a partial candidate solution subtree (resp. candidate solution subtree) of ST is a finite subtree composed of
- the node N, as root node
- one partial candidate solution subtree (resp. candidate solution subtree) of one subtree of ST attached to one C_i.

(ii) If N is an ns-goal-node, say not(G), then

(ii.1) if N has no child then ST is its only partial candidate solution subtree and candidate solution subtree

(ii.2) otherwise
- any partial candidate solution subtree of ST consists of a finite subtree composed of
  - the node N
  - some partial solution subtrees for the subtree ST(G,ST).
- ST is its only candidate solution subtree but provided it is finite and its tip nodes are either ⊗-nodes or □-nodes.

(iii) If N is a goal-node then
  (iii.1)   if N is a □-node then {N} is the only partial candidate solution subtree and candidate solution subtree of ST
  (iii.2)   if N has no child and is not a □-node then
    - {N} is the only partial candidate solution subtree of ST,
    - ST has no candidate solution subtree
  (iii.3)   if N has children, say $C_1, ..., C_m$ then the partial candidate solution subtrees (resp. candidate solution subtrees) of ST are finite subtrees composed of
    - the node N, as root node
    - one partial candidate solution subtree (resp. candidate solution subtree) from each subtree of ST attached to each C_i.

Example 5.11 The subtree {(2),(3),(4),(5),(6),(8),(10),(12)} of Figure 5.1 is an example of partial candidate solution subtree for the subtree attached to node (2). It is not a candidate solution subtree. The subtree {(3),(4),(5),(7),(9),(13),(14),(15)} of Figure 5.3 is a candidate solution subtree for the subtree attached to node (3).

Partial solution subtrees and solution subtrees were defined in Section 4.2 as partial candidate solution subtrees and candidate solution subtrees whose mas's reconcile. The counterparts in computed and/or/not search trees are defined in a more complicated way because of the presence of ns-goals. They are defined together with the generalization of the notion of reconciliation-substitution, namely the notion of set of n-reconciliation-substitutions, in the inductive way used above.

Definition 5.36 Let T be a computed and/or/not search tree. Let ST be a subtree of T and let N be its root node. Partial solution subtrees, solution subtrees and their n-reconciliation-substitutions are defined as follows.
(i) If N is a ps-goal-node then
  (i.1)   if N is a ⊗-node then ST has no partial solution subtree, no solution subtree and no n-reconciliation-substitution;
  (i.2)   if N has no child but is not a ⊗-node then
    - {N} is the only partial solution subtree of ST. Its set of n-reconciliation-substitution reduces to the n-substitution ({},not{}),
    - ST has no solution subtree;

(i.3) if N has children, say $C_1, ..., C_m$, then a partial solution subtree (resp. solution subtree) of ST is a finite subtree composed of
- the node N, as root node,
- one partial solution subtree (resp. solution subtree), say ST_child, of one subtree of ST attached to one C_i.

Its set of n-reconciliation-substitutions is the set of n-reconciliation-substitutions of ST_child.

(ii) If N is an ns-goal-node, say not(G), then

(ii.1) if N has no child then ST is its only partial solution subtree and candidate solution subtree. Its set of n-reconciliation-substitution reduces to the n-substitution ({},not{}).

(ii.2) otherwise
- the only potential partial solution subtree of ST is the finite subtree formed of the partial solution subtrees of ST(G,ST). It is a partial solution subtree iff it verifies the following property.

Let $S_1,...,S_m$ be the solution subtrees of ST(G,ST). Then, the set of the n-reconciliation-substitutions of the S_i's, say Θ, is negatable wrt to var(G).

In this case, its set of n-reconciliation-substitutions is composed of the restriction to the variables of G of the negation of Θ.

- This partial solution subtree is a solution subtree of ST iff its tip nodes are either ⊗-nodes, ☐-nodes or ns-goal-nodes.

(iii) If N is a goal-node, let
- G be the goal associated with N,
- Cvc(N,ST) be the set of variables of ST that are not in Vc(N,ST),
- Θ be
  - the nmas associated with N, if any
  - { ({},not{}) }, otherwise.

Then,

(iii.1) if N is a ☐-node then {N} is the only partial solution subtree and solution subtree of ST. Its set of n-reconciliation-substitutions is the equational restriction to the variables of Cvc(N,ST) of the n-substitutions of Θ.

(iii.2) if N has no child and is not a ☐-node then
- {N} is the only partial solution subtree of ST; its set of n-reconciliation-substitutions is formed of the equational restriction to the variables of Cvc(N,ST) of the n-substitutions of Θ.
- ST has no solution subtree

(iii.3) if N has children, say $C_1, ..., C_m$ then the partial solution subtrees (resp. solution subtrees) of ST are finite subtrees composed of

- the node N, as root node
- one partial solution subtree ST_i (resp. solution subtree) from each subtree of ST attached to each C_i

such that the sets of n-reconciliation-substitutions of the ST_i's, say Ψ_1, ..., Ψ_m, qn-reconcile wrt the variables of the G.

The set of n-reconciliation-substitutions, say Σ, of such a partial solution subtree (resp. solution subtree) is defined as follows. Let Λ be the qn-reconciliation of Ψ_1, ..., Ψ_m wrt the variables of G. Let furthermore Ω be the set of n-substitutions obtained by the compositions $\theta \circ \lambda$, for θ and λ varying in Θ and Λ, respectively. Then, Σ is composed of the equational restriction to the variables of Cvc(N,ST) of the n-substitutions of Ω.

Example 5.12 The subtree {(3),...,(13)} of Figure 5.1 is an example of a partial solution subtree for the subtree attached to node (3). Its set of n-reconciliation-substitution is composed of the only n-substitution

$(\{X/1,Y/f(X_2)\},not\{X_2/a\})$.

The subtree {(3),(4),(5),(7),(9),(13),(14),(15)} of Figure 5.3 is a solution subtree. Its set of n-reconciliation-substitutions is composed of the n-substitution $(\{X/1,Y/f(b)\},not\{\})$.

Remark This definition might be quite unnatural. Let us justify it in some words. It differs from the equivalent definition in the basic model (see Definition 4.3) in four points :
- by the recursive and progressive way in which n-reconciliation-substitutions are defined;
- by the restriction operated at the goal-node steps;
- by the implicit use of consistency through the qn-reconciliation and negation operations;
- by the elimination of some partial solution subtrees to compute n-reconciliation-substitutions (see point (ii)).

The progressive way of determining the n-reconciliation-substitutions is explained by the fact that nmas's of (partial) solution subtrees cannot be just n-reconciled. As ns-goals act as negators, some of the nmas's must first be negated before being composed with other nmas's. The progressive and recursive approach is quite suited to handle such negations clearly and correctly.

Restriction must furthermore be performed in order to ensure some correctness of the n-reconciliation-substitutions. It is again due to the presence of ns-goals. As they act as negators, some care must be taken for the existential and universal quantifications of the manipulated variables. It turns out that the above restriction ensures a correct handling of these quantifications. The use of consistency is justified in the same way. It is worth noting that it ensures that all n-reconciliation-substitutions cover solutions (see Propositions 5.14 and 5.17).

Finally, the elimination of partial solution subtrees that are not solution subtrees in the determination of the set of n-reconciliation-substitutions of a subtree rooted by an ns-goal is explained by the negation role of ns-goals too. By discarding them, it is ensured that the sets of n-reconciliation-substitutions of closer and closer partial approximations of any solution subtree become more and more specific and closer and closer to the set of n-reconciliation-substitutions of the solution subtree. ◊

Besides n-reconciliation-substitutions, n-substitutions of another kind will be associated with subtrees attached to goal-nodes. They intend to extract the information common to the n-reconciliation-susbtitutions of all partial solution subtrees of the considered subtree.

Definition 5.37 Let T be a computed and/or/not search tree and ST be a subtree of T rooted by a goal-node N. The *partial solution subtree n-substitution* - or *pss-n-substitution*, for short - of ST is defined as the n-substitution $(\{X_1/t_1,...,X_m/t_m\}, \text{not}\{Y_1/u_1,...,Y_n/u_n\})$

- whose positive part collects the bindings X_i/t_i that verify the following properties :
  - they are common to the positive parts of the n-reconciliation-substitutions of all partial solution subtrees of ST
  - their LHS variable X_i is in Vars(N,T)
  - their RHS term t_i is a non-variable term.
- whose negative parts collects the bindings Y_j/u_j that verify the following properties
  - they or their inversion u_j/Y_j are common to the negative parts of the n-reconciliation-substitutions of all partial solution subtrees of ST
  - their LHS variable Y_j is in Vars(N,T)
  - they are not registered with their inversion i.e. there are no bindings Y_p/u_p and Y_q/u_q such that $Y_p=u_q$ and $u_p=Y_q$.

Example 5.13 The pss-n-substitution of the subtree $\{(3),...,(13)\}$ of Figure 5.1 is the n-substitution $(\{X/1, Y/f(X_2)\}, \text{not}\{X_2/a\})$.

Proposition 5.38 Let T be a computed and/or/not search tree and ST be a subtree of T rooted by a goal-node. Then any instance subtree of ST by its pss-n-substitution has the skeleton of ST possibly modified by the removal of subtrees of the subtree engendered by ns-goal-nodes.
Proof This results from the definition of computed and/or/not search tree, partial solution subtree and pss-n-substitution. ◊

D. Completed subtrees

Finally completed subtrees are extended to and/or/not search trees as follows.

Definition 5.39 A subtree of a computed and/or/not search tree is *completed* iff all its tip nodes are either ⊗-nodes, □-nodes or ns-goal-nodes. It is *incompleted*, otherwise.

Example 5.14 The subtree {(2),(3),(4),(6),(8),(10),(11)} of Figure 5.1 is an example of a completed subtree. The subtree {(2),(3),(4),(5),(6),(8),(10),(11),(12)} of the same figure is an example of an incompleted subtree.

5.2.4 Process related concepts

As in the basic model, processes are associated with nodes in a one-to-one correspondence and are named according to their corresponding node. Hence, goal-processes, s-goal-processes, ps-goal-processes, ns-goal-processes and query-processes correspond to goal-nodes, s-goal-nodes, ps-goal-nodes, ns-goal-nodes and query-nodes, respectively. They are essentially the same as those of the basic model. In particular, processes move between the same states and communicate through messages. The only perturbations induced by the introduction of negation are the following :

- the substitutions appearing in the data part of goal-processes and ps-goal-processes must be generalized to n-substitutions;
- similarly, the goal and s-goals of this data part must be generalized to extended goal and extended s-goals, respectively;
- the data information part of the query-process must be extended to register some R-triplets;
- a new kind of processes, corresponding to ns-goal-nodes, must be introduced.

The two first extensions are obvious and not detailed. The extension of the data information part of the query-process simply consists of a set of R-triplets. Finally, ns-goal processes are defined as follows :

- the data information part of any ns-goal-process is composed of the following components:
    - an identifier component, as defined in Section 4.2.2.1
    - a nb_child component, as defined in Section 4.2.2.1
    - a state component, as defined in Section 4.2.2.1
    - a R-depth component, as defined in Section 4.2.2.1
    - a qualification component, composed of
        - a ns-goal subcomponent, corresponding to the ns-goal associated with the ns-goal process;
        - a reconciliation component, precised later on;
- the program information part of any ns-goal-process is composed of the program segments defined later on.

As a final point, notions developed in Section 5.2.1 are extended to processes thanks to the one-to-one correspondence between nodes and processes by replacing nodes by their corresponding processes. We will thus, for instance, speak of solution subtrees of processes to designate the trees of processes corresponding to solutions subtrees (of nodes).

The instantiation of trees of processes is also defined thanks to the corresponding instantiation of the corresponding trees of nodes. Precisely, an instantiation of a tree of processes by an n-substitution ν is the tree of processes obtained

- by moving to the dead state the processes corresponding to removed nodes in the instantiation by ν of the nodes corresponding to the processes,
- by instantiating the goal or s-goal of any other process as is the goal or s-goal of the corresponding nodes in an instantiation by ν.

5.3 The Conclog model

We are now in position to precise the Conclog model extended to handle negation. As for the basic model, the model is first described for a finite value of the R-depth parameter and then for an infinite one. Both tree point of view and process point of view are used as well.

Convention 5.40 We will extend Convention 4.10 and reserve the appellation extended Conclog(D) to the refer to the extended Conclog model with a *finite* value of the R-depth parameter. The appellation extended Conclog(∞) will be used to denote the extended Conclog model with an *infinite* value of the R-depth parameter. As announced above, the qualifier extended will often be omitted when it is unambiguously understood.

5.3.1 Finite value of the R-depth parameter

5.3.1.1 The tree view

I Specification

A. Cycles

The computation under the Conclog(D) model is also most easily described here by taking a photo of the and/or/not search tree after each cycle. This results in the following specification. It characterizes the successively computed and/or/not search trees.

Specification 5.1

Initial situation

Two inputs are given :
- a non null integer D
- a finite computed and/or/not search tree T_in that contains at least one tip node associated with a non-empty goal.

Final situation

1) The tree T_in is transformed into a new computed and/or/not search tree T_out obtained from T_in as follows.

    Let $N_1, ..., N_m$ be the tip nodes of T_in that are associated with a non-empty goal. Let furthermore T_aux be the tree T_in augmented by the first slices of R-depth D attached to the nodes $N_1, ..., N_m$. Then T_out is T_aux where
    - each node that is not a member of any partial solution subtree of T_aux is removed;
    - for every goal-node N, the subtree ST(N,T_aux) is instantiated by the its pss-n-substitution.

2) The following substitutions are delivered as results. For every solution subtree SS of T_out that is not a solution subtree of T_in, the restriction of the n-reconciliation-substitutions of SS to the variables of the query is output.

B. Computations

Any computation also basically consists of repeating an algorithm, say cycle, that computes Specification 4.1. The initial tree T_in is composed of the only query-node. The tree taken at the ith iteration is the tree T_out resulting from the $(i-1)^{th}$ cycle. The iteration is repeated until a tree T_out, that contains no tip nodes associated with non-empty goals, is produced. Some exception is moreover made to this iterative scheme in order to handle the case where the query-node is associated with an empty query. In this case, the n-substitution ({},not{}) is simply output.

Definition 5.41 Any n-substitution produced by the above execution is called a *computed answer n-substitution*.

C. A parametrized model

Any computation in the extended model thus consists of a (possibly empty) sequence of cycles. The rate at which they succeed is determined by the R-depth of the slices to be constructed at each cycle. Such a R-depth is kept as a parameter of the extended model, as it was in the basic model. Thanks to this status, we will also declare it implicitly in the following developments - in particular, in the following specifications. It is worth remembering that, through this section, it is assumed to take a finite value. The infinite value case will be discussed in Section 5.3.2.

II Design of the execution model

The design of the extended model is not started from scratch. In contrast, profit is taken from the design of the basic model and the extensions required for the extended model are just presented here.

The algorithm cycle implementing Specification 5.1 is also constructed in two steps, reflecting the generation and reconciliation phases, namely

- the computation of the T_aux from T_in (generation phase)
- the computation of the tree T_out from the tree T_aux and the production of the computed answer n-substitutions (reconciliation phase).

They are called generation_phase and reconciliation_phase and obey the following Specifications 5.2 and 5.3, respectively.

Specification 5.2

Initial situation

A finite computed and/or/not search tree T that contains at least one tip node associated with a non-empty goal is given.

Final situation

Let $N_1, ..., N_m$ be the tip nodes associated with non-empty goals. The tree T is augmented by the first slices of R-depth D attached to nodes $N_1, ..., N_m$.

Specification 5.3

Initial situation

A finite computed and/or/not search tree T not reduced to its query-node is given.

Final situation

1) The tree T is transformed into a new computed and/or/not search tree T* as follows:
   - each node that is not a member of any partial solution subtree of T is removed;
   - for every goal-node N, the subtree ST(N,T) is instantiated by the its pss-n-substitution.
2) The following substitutions are delivered as results. Let T_cut be T* cut off its last slice of R_depth D. For every solution subtree SS of T* that is not a solution subtree of T_cut, the restriction of the n-reconciliation-substitutions of SS to the variables of the query is output.

A. The algorithm generation_phase

The algorithm generation_phase is the straightforward adaptation of the basic model as described in Section 5.1.2. It is not detailed here. Notice that the main features of the basic model are conserved. In particular, any generation phase is characterized by the forward procedure explained in Subection II.A of Section 4.3.1.1 with the forward production of n-substitutions.

B. The algorithm reconciliation_phase

The algorithm reconciliation_phase is also inspired by that presented in Subsection II.B of Section 4.3.1.1 for the basic model. The recursive approach is therefore adopted here too. Hence, if $C_1, ..., C_m$ denote the children of the query-node, the reconciliation-phase algorithm basically consists of performing the following operations :

- O_1. perform the reconciliation_phase job on each subtree attached to each C_i; this returns some results and modifies the subtrees;
- O_2. combine the returned results and perform some manipulations on the resulting subtrees; this delivers new results and performs the final modifications to obtain the tree T^*.

This is transposed for every subtree at every level of the computed and/or/not search tree, except for subtrees composed of one node. With respect to them, operations O_1 and O_2 are not performed; some adequate operations are rather performed to determine the R-triplets that should be returned and the way in which the subtree should be modified .

To precise further the extended model, the exact meaning of the expression "perform the reconciliation_phase job on each subtree attached to each C_i" should be explained. This is achieved by the following specification. It gives the counterpart in the extended model of Specification 4.5 of the gen_reconc(T,R) procedure of the basic model. The two following points are particularly worth noting :

- some optimizations are not performed here, as we did in the basic model. For instance, subtrees are not referenced in the more efficient way;
- R-triplets are extended in two ways :
    - substitutions are generalized into n-substitutions;
    - the label can now take the "incompleted(...)" value.

The first extension is expected. The second one is less intuitive. It is suggested by the fact that the instantiation of subtrees may modify the completion of subtrees. Hence, incompleted partial solution subtrees may move to (completed) solution subtrees.

Specification 5.4

Initial situation

A non-empty subtree T of some computed and/or/not search tree A that does not contain the root of A is given.

Final situation

1) The subtree T is transformed in the following tree T^* :
    - each node that is not a member of any partial solution subtree of T is removed;

- for every goal-node N, the subtree ST(N,T) is instantiated by its pss-n-substitution.
2) Let Rn be the root node of T. The parameter R is bound to a set of triplets of the form <Nsubst,Nodes,Label> obtained by associating with each partial solution subtree SS of T*, the triplet
    - whose Nsubst component is the restriction of one n-reconciliation-substitution of SS to the set of variables that are not in Vc(Rn,SS);
    - whose Nodes component is the set of nodes of SS;
    - whose Label component is
        - "completed" if SS is a solution subtree of T;
        - "incompleted(Nsgnodes)", where Nsgnodes is a list of ns-goal-nodes, iff
            - SS is a partial solution subtree of T;
            - SS is not a solution subtree of T but would be if all subtrees attached to the ns-goal-nodes of Sngnodes were completed;
        - "incompleted" otherwise.

This given, two questions remain to be answered in order to define the extended model in a precise way :

- how is the gen_reconc procedure performed for subtrees formed of only one node ?
- how is operation O_2 performed (for subtrees formed of more than one node) ?

B.1. Subtrees formed of only one node

Thanks to the definition of computed and/or/not search trees, four kinds of subtrees formed of only one node should only be considered : those composed of

- a □-node
- a ⊗-node
- a goal-node associated with a non-empty goal
- an ns-goal node.

The first three kinds correspond to the tip nodes of the basic model. The last kind results from the introduction of negation.

The gen_reconc procedure for the first three kinds of tip nodes directly results from that developed in the basic model. Indeed, Specification 5.4 simply rephrases Specification 4.5 in our extended context and partial solution subtrees are shared by the basic and extended models (see Definitions 4.3 and 5.18). The gen_reconc procedure is thus performed as follows.

- Subtrees are modified only if they are composed of a ⊗-node. Such nodes cannot participate to any partial solution subtree and are thus removed.

- As far as the value to give to the R parameter is concerned, delivered R-triplets need simply to be rephrased in our extended context. The only extension is in fact that nmas's, consisting of n-substitutions, are now handled instead of mas's, consisting of one substitution. The adaptation is thus quite straightforward. Whenever a R-triplet was placed for one mas substitution in the R parameter, a R-triplet is now placed, with the same label and the same set of nodes, for each n-substitution of the nmas.

A subtree formed of only one ns-goal corresponds to a solution subtree. Such a subtree is thus kept unchanged and its R parameter is set to the singleton composed of the R-triplet

- whose n-substitution part is the n-substitution ({},not{})
- whose set of nodes is reduced to the ns-goal
- whose label is completed.

B.2 Subtrees formed of more than one node

The second question is answered by the description of four procedures : the reconc_query, reconc_goal, reconc_ps_goal procedures - corresponding to the reconc_query, reconc_goal and reconc_s_goal procedures of Subsection II.B.2 of Section 4.3.1.1, respec-tively - and the reconc_sn_goal procedure - corresponding to the newly introduced ns-goal. The last three aim at making Specification 5.4 hold for a subtree rooted at a goal-node, ps-goal-node and ns-goal-node, respectively and this on the basis of the recursive call gen_reconc on the sub-trees attached to their children. The former acts similarly but this time to make Specification 5.3 hold.

B.2.1 The reconc_goal and reconc_ps_goal procedures

The reconc_goal and reconc_s_goal procedures result essentially from their corresponding procedures of Subsection II.B.2 of Section 4.3.1.1. The only adaptations are the following :

- n-substitutions are now manipulated instead of substitutions
- they are restricted in the equational sense of Definition 5.24
- qn-reconciliation (wrt the variables of the treated goal) is employed instead of reconciliation
- instantiation of subtrees is made in the more elaborated way explained in Definition 5.34
- the determination of labels of R-triplets determined by the reconc_goal procedure are generalized as follows. Let $<v_1,Nodes_1,Label_1>, ..., <v_n,Nodes_n,Label_n>$ be the tuple from which the considered R-triplet $<v,Nodes,Label>$ is issued. Then, Label takes the value
    - "completed" iff all the $Labels_i$'s are "completed";
    - "incompleted(Sngnodes)" iff all the $Label_i$'s are either "completed" or "incompleted($Sngnodes_i$)" with at least one of the last form. In this case,

- Sngnodes is the union of the Sngnodes$_i$ sets of the "incompleted(Sngnodes$_i$)" labels;
- "incompleted", otherwise.

B.2.2 The reconc_query procedure

As in the basic model, the reconc_query procedure here also results from the reconc_goal procedure by following the adaptations stated in Subsection II.B.2 of Section 4.3.1.1. An additional adaptation is moreover required to output correctly the computed answer n-substitutions. It results from the relationship between partial solution subtrees of T and partial solution subtrees of T*, made somewhat more complicated by instantiation. Thanks to Definition 5.37 and Proposition 5.38, it can be claimed that

- any partial solution subtree of T is, after removal of nodes due to instantiation, a partial solution subtree of T*;
- two distinct partial solution subtrees of T give rise to two distinct partial solution subtrees in T*.

However, some incompleted partial solution subtrees of T may be, after removal of nodes due to instantiation, (completed) solution subtrees in T*. Such subtrees correspond to partial solution subtrees registered in R-triplets of the R parameter (as it is computed with the adaptations of Subsection II.B.2.2 of Section 4.3.1.1) such that

- their label is "incompleted(Sngnodes)"
- for any node N of Sngnodes, the subtree ST(N,T) is completed.

Summing up, the output of n-substitutions must be generalized as follows :

- n-substitutions of R-triplets of R whose label is "completed" are output;
- n-substitutions of R-triplets of R whose label is "incompleted(Sngnodes)" and whose list Sngnodes verifies the above property are output in addition.

B.2.3 The reconc_ns_goal procedure

The reconc_ns_goal procedure is new. It is performed in the following way. Let

- N be the ns-goal under consideration
- ST be the subtree engendered by N in T
- C be the child of N
- ST_C be the subtree engendered by C
- $\{<v_1,Nodes_1, Label_1>, ..., <v_m, Nodes_m, Label_m>\}$ be the set of R-triplets returned by the gen_reconc procedure applied to ST_C. Assume furthermore that these R-triplets are numbered in such a way that the R-triplets $<v_1, Nodes_1, Label_1>$, ..., $<v_p, Nodes_p, Label_p>$ are all the R-triplets whose labels verify one of the following properties :

- they are "completed",
- they are of the "incompleted(L)" form and all subtrees attached to the nodes of L have become completed thanks to instantiations.

Thanks to Specification 5.4, the following property can be claimed : the n-substitutions $v_1, ..., v_p$ are the only n-reconciliation-substitutions of solution subtrees in T* of the subtree ST_C. According to Definition 5.35, the subtree formed of N and of the nodes of the Nodes$_i$'s is the only potential partial solution subtree of ST. It is furthermore indeed a partial solution subtree iff the set of n-substitutions $\{v_1,...,v_m\}$ of the solution subtree of ST_C are negatable wrt to the variables of N. Finally, it is a solution subtree iff any tip nodes of the partial solution subtree of ST are □-nodes or ns-goal-nodes that is iff any Label$_i$ (1≤i≤m) is "completed" or p equals m. Otherwise, it is a partial solution subtree that will turn to be a solution subtree when it will become completed. Hence, in this case, the label of the sent R-triplets is "incompleted(N)".

The reconc_ns_goal procedure is now straigthforward :

Test the set $\{v_1,...,v_p\}$ for negatibility wrt to the variables of N
If it is negatable
   then
      { let Σ be a negation }
      make a R-triplet <μ,Nodes,Label> for each n-substitution σ of Σ with
        - $\{N\} \cup Nodes_1 \cup ... \cup Nodes_m$ as set of nodes Nodes
        - completed (resp. incompleted({N})) as label Label iff p=m (resp. p<m);
      set R as the set of such R-triplets
   else
      set R := ∅;
      remove the node N
fi .

5.3.1.2 The process view

Let us now re-express the computation in terms of processes. This is achieved once again by analogy to the basic model. Precisely, the expressions of the computation in tree terms and in process terms are related by using the correspondence of the basic model :

- the creation part of the generation_phase algorithm is performed by the generation program segment of processes,
- the real reconciliation part of the reconciliation_phase algorithm and the gen_reconc procedure is performed by the reconciliation program segment of the processes.

Note furthermore that, as in the basic model, the forward and backward characterization of the generation phases and reconciliation phases is conserved here too :

- the forward character of the generation phases is achieved by the forward creation of processes : the generation program segment of a process is activated just after it has been created;
- the backward character of the reconciliation phases is achieved by the bottom up way in which reconciliation affects processes : the reconciliation program segment of a tip process is activated just after its creation and the reconciliation program segment of a non-tip process is activated each time a child process reports the results of the execution of its reconciliation program segment.

Finally, the same computation details are changed here too :

- There is here no R parameter. The R-triplets (where reference to nodes is replaced by reference to the corresponding processes) are rather sent incrementally by means of real-reconciliation messages. End-reconciliation messages are then used to signal the end of the transmission of these R-triplets as well as to indicate whether the corresponding tree is completely constructed or not.
- Processes are also not fixed but move between the three states : active, waiting and dead.
- Killing and binding publication are achieved by sending the related messages of killing and binding publication.

The program segments of the processes are thus derived in a very similar way to that exposed in Chapter 4 for the basic model. We will then only foccus here on the real novelties. As in the basic model, a simplified model is first proposed. It directly results from the design operated in Section 5.3.1.1.II. The correspondence with the model expressed in tree terms in Section 5.3.1.1 is thus achieved in a quite easy way. It is in fact an extension to our extended context of the model presented in Section 4.3.1.2.1. It thus contains some inefficiencies. They are removed in a second version. As in the basic model, it does not exactly obey the same specification though it delivers the same results. The difference is here also induced by instantiation. Each model is thus subsequently described with its own specification.

5.3.1.2.1 A simplified model

I Specification

A. Cycles

As in the tree expression, the computation is also described by taking photos after each cycle but now in terms of processes. This results in the following specification.

Specification 5.5

Initial situation

A non-empty set of processes, say $\{P_1,...,P_m\}$, that verifies the following properties is given :

- the processes $P_1,...,P_m$ form a process tree corresponding to a finite computed and/or/not search tree T_in,
- there is at least one tip process associated with a non-empty goal; let P'_1, ..., P'_p be these tip processes,
- the R-depth component of all the tip processes P'_i have the same non null value, say D,
- the processes P'_i are set in the active state and their generation procedure is activated.

Final situation

1) Let N_1, ..., N_p be the nodes associated with the tip processes P'_1, ..., P'_p. Let $Snodes_1$, ..., $Snodes_p$ be the set of nodes of the first slice of R-depth D attached to the nodes N_1, ..., N_p, respectively. The processes associated with the nodes of $Snodes_1 \cup ... \cup Snodes_p$ are created.

2) These processes as well as the processes P_1, ..., P_m verify the following properties. Let T_aux denote the computed and/or/not search tree corresponding to all these processes.
    - Processes associated with nodes that are member of no (partial) solution subtree of T_aux are set in the dead state.
    - For every goal-process P, the process subtree ST(P,T_aux) is instantiated by its pss-n-substitution.
    - Tip goal-processes associated with a non-empty goal are moved in the active state with D as R-depth tag component. Their generation procedure is furthermore activated.
    - Other processes are moved in the waiting set.

3) Let T_out be T_aux cut off the nodes corresponding to dead processes. For every solution subtree SS of T_out that is not a solution subtree of T_in, the restriction $\sigma_{|Vg}$ of the reconciliation-substitution σ of SS to the set of variables Vg of the query is output.

Constraints

1) Tip goal-processes associated with a non-empty goal are set in the ready state only when all other properties of the final situation are fullfilled.
2) The final situation is reached after a finite time.

The similarity of this specification with Specification 5.1 is worth noting. It establishes in fact the correspondence of the expression of the computations in terms of trees and that in terms of processes. Note furthermore that Specification 5.5 extends Specification 4.6 to our extended context.

B. Computations

The similarity of Specifications 5.1 and 5.5 induces several similarities in the computations.

1. First, any computation expressed in process terms also consists of the repetition of cycles in the extended model.
2. The extended Conclog model is also parametrized by the R-depth D of the slices generated by each cycle.
3. As each cycle ends with the generation procedure of tip processes associated with a non-emtpy goal being activated, there is here no need to explicitly reactivate a new cycle at the end of each one. Computing a non-empty query then consists of activating the generation program segment of the query-process associated with this query and whose R-depth component is D.
4. Generation and reconciliation program segments will furthermore be constructed to handle empty queries, which forces exception in the tree expression. As a result, as in the basic model, any computation does consist of launching the query-process in the above conditions.

II Design of the execution model

The similarity of Specifications 4.6 and 5.5, on the one hand, and the equivalence of Specifications 5.1 and 5.5, on the other hand, allow to derive quite directly the reconciliation program segments of processes. The situation can be depicted by the graph of Figure 5.8. It suggests two ways to derive the program segments :

- to extend the derivation process of Section 4.3.1.2.II to our extended context
- to transpose the extension of Section 5.3.1.1.II.

We will in fact use both of them but will adopt the derivation scheme for the uniformity of the presentation. The necessary extensions are furthermore only presented here. They are classified as in Chapter 4 in three subsections :

- the first one aims at making Specification 5.5 hold thanks to some assumptions of the initial contents of the processes;
- the second one aims at making these properties hold at the beginning of each cycle
- the third one aims at ending the computation.

Basic model

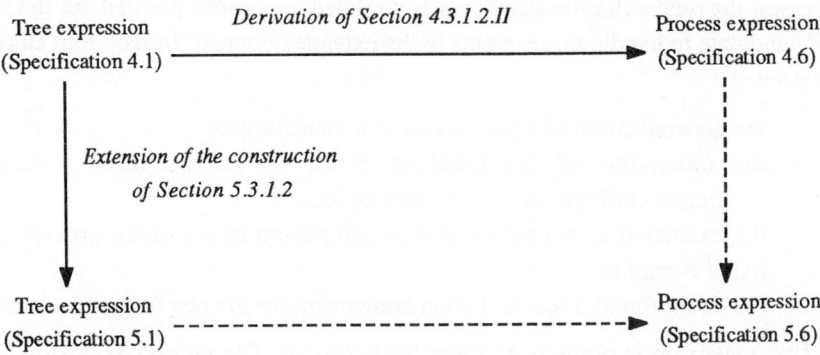

Extended model

Figure 5.8

II.1 Making Specification 5.5 holds

As in the basic model, program segments achieving Specification 5.5 are addressed in three steps. Generation program segments of the processes are first sketched. Reconciliation ones are then described. Finally, program segments handling auxiliary messages are examined.

A. Generation program segments of processes

Generation program segments of processes are extended in the straightforward way described in Sections 5.1 and 5.3.1.1.II. They are not detailed here and we refer the reader to the above sections if need be.

B. Reconciliation program segments of processes

B.1 Reconciliation components

As suggested above too, the reconciliation program segments of processes is activated by three events :

- the detection by the process of its nature of tip process
- the arrival of R-triplets by means of real reconciliation messages
- the arrival of end reconciliation messages.

These events exactly correspond to the sources of activation of the reconciliation program segments in the basic model of Chapter 4. As R-triplets are configured in the same manner, are sent in the same manner and are treated in the same manner at goal-processes and s-goal-processes, the reconciliation structures and related operations pointed out in Chapter 4 are thus good candidate to handle these events in the extended context. In fact, four slight extensions are only needed :

- the generalization of substitutions in n-substitutions;
- the extension of the label of R-triplets to the three values "completed", "incompleted(Sngnodes)" and "incompleted";
- the extension of the reconciliation component of the query-process, including a new list of R-triplets
- the definition of a reconciliation component for the newly introduced ns-goals.

The first extension is obvious and now well-known. The second extension has already been detailed in Section 5.3.1.1. The third extension simply consists of adding a new list of R-triplets, called Part_sol, in the reconciliation component of the query-process. Finally, the fourth extension is motivated by the reconciliation philosophy of the ns-goal processes. As already argued, the n-substitutions sent by any ns-goal process cannot be incrementally determined at the rate the input n-substitutions are received from its child. Any ns-goal process must thus store all the R-triplets sent by its child before it computes the R-triplets it will send. This is the only constraint imposed by ns-goal processes. It is quite easy to achieve since such a memorization is in fact already performed at any goal-process that has only one child. The reconciliation component of any ns-goal process is thus composed of one part : a S_d structure that has one of the two following values

- either the empty structure $\emptyset_{S\_d}$
- or a pair <Srtriplets,Label>, where Srtriplets is a set of R-triplets and Label has either "completed", "incompleted" or "no_end" as value;

The S_d structure takes the value $\emptyset_{S\_d}$ at the time of the creation of the ns-goal process only. It is definitively converted to a pair <Srtriplets,Label> once its child process has been created.

Invariant properties I_1, I_2, I_3 and I_4 (handling the values of the reconciliation components of goal-processes and ps-goal processes) are also maintained here, with the following adaptations :

- substitutions and reconciliation-substitutions should be generalized to n-substitutions and n-reconciliation-substitutions;
- completion of a subtree should be understood in the generalized way of Definition 5.39.

An invariant property I_5 is added for ns-goals :

I_5.   For every ns-goal-process P, P.S_d = <Srtriplets,Label> verifies the following properties.

- If P has no child process in T_in then
    - Srtriplets is $\emptyset$,
    - Label is completed
- If P has a child process, say C, then
    - Srtriplets contains the following R-triplets :
        - the R-triplets corresponding to solution subtrees of ST(C,T_in),
        - the R-triplets received at P from C corresponding to partial solution subtrees of ST(C,T_aux) that are not partial solution subtrees of ST(C,T_in).
    - Label is
        - "completed" if the following two conditions hold:
            - the subtree ST(C,T_aux) is completely constructed and is completed;
            - the set Srtriplets memorizes all the R-triplets corresponding to partial solution subtrees of ST(C,T_aux) that are not partial solution subtrees of ST(C,T_in),
        - "completed_step" if the two following conditions hold:
            - the subtree ST(C,T_aux) is completely constructed and is incompleted;
            - the set Srtriplets memorizes all R-triplets corresponding to partial solution subtrees of ST(C,T_aux) that are not partial solution subtrees of ST(C,T_in),
        - "no_end", otherwise.

It determines the values of the reconciliation component of any ns-goal process. In particular, the initial value <$\emptyset$,no_end> of the pair <Srtriplets,Label> results.

The two auxiliary operations of Subsection II.1.B.3 of Section 4.3.1.2.1 are conserved here with the same intentions :

- updating the reconciliation components of processes after the receipt of a reconciliation message and with regards to properties I_1 to I_5
- testing the completion of the construction and the reconciliation of the subtree generated by one process.

The adaptation to our extended context directly results from the two above adaptations as far as goal-processes and s-goal-processes are concerned. Extension to ns-goal-processes is achieved by assimilating the ns-goal-processes as goal-processes having only one child.

B.2 Reconciliation program segments of goal processes and ps-goal processes

As stated at the beginning of this section, designing the reconciliation program segments of the processes amounts to applying the adaptations operated in Subsection II of Section

5.3.1.1 in the derivation process of Subsection II of Section 4.3.1.2.1. Hence, program segments should be extended as follows :

- n-substitutions should be treated in place of substitutions;
- qn-reconciliation of n-substitutions should be employed instead of the simple reconciliation of n-substitutions;
- restriction is performed in the equational sense of Definition 5.24;
- instantiation should be generalized according to Definition 5.30;
- labels of R-triplets should be treated as indicated in Subsection II of Section 5.3.1.1;
- substitutions of R-triplets should be output as indicated in this subsection.

Let us briefly comment on these extensions.

(i) Tip processes

Tip processes send the induced extension of R-triplets mentioned in the basic scheme (see Subection 5.3.1.1.II for a rough description of the contents of these R-triplets). They are moved in the same states as in the basic model after having sent the corresponding reconciliation messages.

(ii) Non tip ps-goal-processes

Non-tip ps-goal-processes simply transmit (with addition of the process reference) the R-triplets sent by their child ps-goal processes. End-messages determined in the basic model are sent in the same way in response to end-reconciliation messages.

(iii) Non tip goal-processes

Non-tip goal processes now treat reconciliation messages as follows :

- R-triplets are also combined here into tuples and are qn-reconciled (wrt the variables of the treated goal) to determine the R-triplets to send. Two technical extensions are here needed.
    - 1° The first one is to handle es-nsubsts resulting from qn-reconciliation. In this simplified model a R-triplet is sent for each of their qn-substitutions. It is sent in the incremental way used in the basic model.
    - 2° The second one is induced by the generalization of the label value of the R-triplets. The label of the R-triplet resulting from a tuple of R-triplets is determined in the generalized way exposed in Subsection II.B.1 of Section 5.3.1.1.
- Handling of processes to be killed is performed in the same way as in the basic model.
- The n-substitution to be made public is constructed progressively as the R-triplets are sent, with the method pointed out in the basic model and the extensions precised in Definition 5.37.

- Process killing and binding publication are ordered at the same time as in the basic model (i.e. just before the goal-process sends an ending-reconciliation message) thanks to the same kill and instantiation messages. Their handling is somewhat more elaborated. It is presented in the following Subsection C.

(iv) The query-process

The query-process behaves essentially as any goal-process with the usual adaptations on the computed n-substitutions, as transposed from Subsection II.1.B.4.3 of Section 4.3.1.2.1. A particular adaptation is furthermore required here. It has already been suggested by the particular production of the computed answer n-substitutions. In the dynamic context of processes, R-triplets with a "incompleted(Snsgprocess)" label are computed incrementally. At the time they are computed, there is no need to determine whether or not the subtrees attached to the processes referred to in Snsgprocess have moved from the incompleted status in T_aux to the completed one in T_out. These R-triplets should thus be memorized until further information. This is achieved thanks to the Part_sol list introduced in Subsection B.1 above. Precisely, this list is attached the following invariant property:

I_6. At any time, the list Part_sol contains the R-triplets
- corresponding to partial solution subtrees of T_aux that are not partial solution subtrees in T_in;
- whose label is of the "incompleted(Sngprocess)" form
- which can be computed in view of the contents of the R-triplets registered in the S_d structure.

This invariant property determines the updating of the list :

- it is set to ∅ at the beginning of the cycle
- it is augmented by any R-triplet computed as in the basic model but whose label takes the "incompleted(Sngprocess)" form.

Specification 5.5 is then achieved by assuming the existence of some events that eventually report the moving from the incompleted state to the completed one. This is indeed achieved as a consequence of the handling of killing and instantiation messages. Practically, the so-called completion messages are received to indicate this moving. At the receipt of each one, the label of R-triplets of the Part_sol list are progressively updated in consequence. Furthermore, their n-substitutions are output when all trees engendered by the processes of its associated Snsgprocess list (in the "incompleted(Snsgprocess)" label) have been informed of being completed. The exact handling of completion messages is closely related to the transition from one cycle to another. It is precised in the following Subsection II.2 where this transition is discussed.

B.3 Reconciliation program segment of ns-goal processes

Although they may correspond to nodes considered as tip-nodes in the tree expression, ns-goal-processes are never considered as tip processes. Any ns-goal process, once created, directly creates a child goal-process for the goal negated in its ns-goal. This process then evolves in the computation but always remains a child process. Tip ns-goal-nodes correspond in fact to ns-goal-process whose child processes have moved in the dead state (see Specification 5.5). The reconciliation program segments of ns-goal-processes thus need only to be explained in the non-tip case. Note that such a difference in the treatment of reconciliation expressed in tree terms and in process terms is also present in the basic model. All the processes of the considered computed and/or search tree are indeed not touched by reconciliation but just the tip process of the newly created slice as well as their ancestors are.

The reconciliation program segment of an ns-goal-process is directly inspired from the reconc_ns_goal procedure of Subsection II.B of Section 5.3.1.1. It is performed as follows.

- R-triplets of real reconciliation messages are simply registered using the auxiliary update procedure of the above Subsection B.1. All of them must indeed be registered before the R-triplets, to be output by the ns-goal-process, can be computed.
- This is signalled by the arrival of an end-reconciliation message. At that time, all completion messages are received to indicate the moving of incompleted partial solution subtrees to the completed state. The negation stated in Subsection II.B of Section 5.3.1.1 is then computed and the resulting R-triplets are sent to the father process of the considered ns-goal-process. An end-reconciliation message of the same kind as the one received is thereafter transmitted.

C. Handling auxiliary messages

Four kinds of auxiliary messages have been required in the simplified model. Three of them namely the kill, instantiation and wake_up messages, are inherited from the basic model. The latter, namely the completion messages, result from the special treatment of the instantiation messages. As already justified, the treatment of these messages will be precised in the next section.

(i) Handling wake_up messages

Wake_up messages are treated as indicated in Subsection II.1.C of Section 4.3.1.2.1.

(ii) Handling instantiation messages

Instantiation messages need to be handled in a more elaborated manner than that of Subsection II.1.C of Section 4.3.1.2.1. Fundamentally speaking, the extensions result from the fact that, in contrast with the instantiation by a substitution, the instantiation by an n-substitution does not necessarily succeed. This fact has lead to define the instantiation of subtrees in a more elaborated way than the simple instantiation of processes of the subtrees. This has been specified in Definition 5.34. It is this task that the handling of the instantiation messages should perform.

The version presented hereafter is directly inspired from Definition 5.34. It is developed with the aim of proving the feasibility of the approach and without care for performance. It will be improved in a more efficient version in the real model of Section 5.3.1.2.2.

Definition 5.34 is, in fact, well suited for a direct implementation. Once a process P receives an instantiation message, it tests itself for instantiability with the n-substitution registered in the message (see Definition 5.34). Two cases may occur.
- The process P is instantiable. In this case, the process instantiates its goal or s-goal component and transmits the instantiation message to its children, if any.
- The process P is not instantiable. In this case, processes of the subtree ST(P,T_aux), P excluded, that are not $\Box$-processes or ancestor of such processes should be killed. This is achievable, for instance, by means of three new auxiliary messages :
    - one ordering such a killing
    - two others for determining whether a non tip process has at least one $\Box$-process as descendant (one is used for asking the descendant processes and another is used from tip processes for answering).

Finally, in both cases, according to Definition 5.34, any non ns-goal-process is killed in the case descendants, previously non dead, are killed. This might be achieved as an answer to process killing. Deafness of the child processes is now registered explicitly in the reconciliation components of processes. Any process then commits suicide when all its children become dead.

Such a method may appear to be quite complicated. However we recall that our purpose is here just to prove the feasability of the approach. More efficient treatments are pointed out in the next section.

(iii) Handling kill messages

Handling kill messages is performed in a somewhat more elaborated manner than that of the simple basic model of Subsection II of Section 4.3.1.2.1. This is necessitated by the above handling of instantiation messages. In contrast with the reconciliation that specifies (in this simple model) all the processes to be killed, handling of instantiation messages now requires to kill all descendants of some processes, these descendants being not explicitly referred to. Furthermore, killed processes explicitly report their death to their father. This suggests the way in which kill messages are handled : any process receiving a kill message

- transmits the message to its childen, if any,
- reports its death to its father process (by means of the fail-messages of Section 4.3.1.2.2)
- moves to the dead state.

II.2 From cycles to cycles

The design of the above Subsection II.1 has ensured that any tree of processes, that verifies the input situation of Specification 5.5 and such that the reconciliation components of the processes verify properties I_1 to I_6, is transformed into a tree of processes that verifies the final situation of Specification 5.5. As the computation is generally composed of more than one cycle, two points thus remain to be established :

P_1. the reconciliation component of the query-process verifies properties I_1 to I_6 at the beginning of the first cycle;

P_2. the reconciliation components of non dead processes as they are output by a cycle verify properties I_1 to I_6 provided they do so at the beginning of the cycle.

They correspond to the two points P_1 and P_2 pointed out in the Subsection II.2 of Section 4.3.1.2.1 (corresponding to this section in Chapter 4). As there too, the following point should also be stressed in order to ensure a complete correspondence between the tree expression and the process expression of the computation. Let $T_1, ..., T_n, ...$ be the computed and/or/not search trees formed of nodes pointed out in the tree expression of Section 5.3.1.1. For any i, the tree of processes corresponding to T_i is transformed into a tree of processes that does not exactly correspond to T_{i+1} : T_{i+1} only corresponds to the tree of non dead processes. Although this might appear of no importance since processes do not act once they are dead, it is significant in the verification of P_2.

Let us now turn to points P_1 and P_2. Point P_1 is also achieved in our extended context thanks to the definition of the initial reconciliation components of the processes. In contrast, point P_2 is not achieved, essentially for the same three reasons as those pointed out in the basic model. A fourth one results from the Part_sol extension of the query-process. Consider the transition from the ith cycle to the $(i+1)^{th}$ one. Let T_i_aux be the tree T_aux defined in Specification 5.5 by taking T_i as tree T_in.

D_1. Because some nodes of T_i_aux have been removed in T_{i+1}, some subtrees, in particular the partial solution ones, might be referred to as incompleted in T_i_aux whereas they are completed in T_{i+1}.

D_2. R-triplets of partial solution subtrees are desirable at the beginning of the $(i+1)^{th}$ cycle iff they correspond to solution subtrees of T_{i+1}. Some of them are thus useless.

D_3. Completed_step labels are obsolate in all cases.

D$_4$. Finally, R-triplets registered in Part_sol are obsolate when the $(i+1)^{th}$ cycle is undertaken.

These defficiencies are mostly solved by the procedures proposed in the basic model. Two extensions are needed. One of them embodies the core of the required extensions. It is presented first. The other concerns the reinitialization of newly introduced structures. It is presented next.

A. First extension

The first extension results from the fact that, because of the particularity of the (extended) instantiation, two kinds of subtrees may now move from the incompleted status in T_i_aux to the completed one in T_{i+1}, namely

K$_1$. subtrees engendered by processes,
K$_2$. partial solution subtrees.

Subtrees of kind K$_1$ have already been identified in the basic model. They were called newly completed subtrees and were described as follows :

- subtrees engendered by killed processes are newly completed
- subtrees
    - engendered by a non tip process P
    - such that all the subtrees engendered by the children of P are either completed in T_i_aux or newly completed in T_{i+1}, with at least one subtree of the last kind
  are newly completed.

Subtrees of kind K$_2$ are new and result from the moving of completeness of subtrees engendered by ns-goal processes, only. Definition 5.36 characterizes them as follows. A partial solution subtree ST, incompleted in T_i_aux, is completed in T_{i+1} iff the two following conditions holds :

(i) ST is not reduced to one process;
(ii) let N_1, ..., N_m be the ns-goal-processes of ST that are not descendant of one ns-goal process in ST and whose engendered subtrees $ST(N_i,ST)$ are incompleted. Then,
    - all tip processes of ST that are not descendant from one N_i are associated with □-nodes, ⊗-nodes or ns-goal-nodes;
    - for any i, the subtree corresponding to $ST(N_i,ST)$ in T_{i+1} is completed.

The moving of subtrees of both kinds K$_1$ and K$_2$ only affects the two kinds of labels of the reconciliation components:

L$_1$. the moving of subtrees of kind K$_1$ affects the label components of the S_d and E_s_d structures;
L$_2$. the moving of subtrees of kind K$_2$ affects the labels of the R-triplets.

Affectation of the first kind is already handled in the basic model and does not require special treatments here. In contrast, affectation of the second kind is new and requires some adaptations.

The following fact should be noted in order to discover the necessary extensions. In the basic model, R-triplets that do not have "completed" as value are removed by the reinitialization messages. Such an alteration may be conserved here too but provided that the reinitialization messages are sent only when the moving of the completion status described above is completely treated. This synchronization is useless in the basic model and is not ensured. It is however of importance here.

The correct answer to the moving of the completion status of subtrees of both of the above kinds is described hereafter. It first requires an extension of the completion messages of the basic model. This results in extending the related treatments, which, in turns, requires the reconciliation components to be extended.

A.1 Extension of the completion messages

Two kinds of completion like messages are now needed.

1° Messages of the first kind are devoted to the report of the completion of subtrees engendered by ns-goal-processes. They are called nsg_completion messages. They take the form nsg_completion(Id) where Id is the identifier of the ns-goal-process for which completion is reported.

2° Messages of the second kind are devoted to the report of the status of the subtree engendered by any process after this subtree is completely modified by process killing and binding publication. They are called status messages. One of their argument has "completed" or "incomplete" as value according to the completion status. As any process may be touched by several process killings and binding publications ordered by several ancestor goal-processes, another argument is required to determine to which ordering process the status message refers. Status messages are thus of the form status(Label,Id) where Label is either completed or incompleted and Id is a process identifier.

Nsg_completion messages and Status messages may appear to be somewhat redundant. They are indeed in their semantics but not in subsequent treatments, as we will see in a moment.

A.2 Extension of the reconciliation components

The reconciliation components need to be extended too. As mentioned above, the status of any subtree may be changed by different processes. In order to avoid the interleaving of the status information induced by process killing and binding publication by several (ancestor) processes, a new E_s_d like structure is added to any reconciliation structure. It is called Status component. Its value at the time of the creation of the process is $\emptyset_{e\_s\_d}$. It is then moved to a non-empty E_s_d like structure. Precisely, each Status[C] component takes one of the two following values

>   <incompleted,Id>
>   "completed",
>   "none".

The first value indicates that, after the handling of process killing and binding publication induced by the process identified by Id, the subtree engendered by the child C is incompleted. The second value indicates that the subtree engendered by the child C is completed. Recall that process killing and binding publication can not alter the completion of a subtree by making incompleted a completed subtree. It is useless to signal which process makes a subtree completed. Hence, no Id identifier is coupled with the "completed" value. Finally, the third value is used as a neutral value.

We will ensure in a moment that process killing and binding publication ordered by one process do never act simultaneously with that ordered by any ancestor of the process. One E_s_d structure is thus sufficient to handle the status moving of subtrees. It could even be removed by generalizing the existing S_d and E_s_d structures. We do not adopt this solution here because this generalization will be proved to be itself useless in the real model. We then prefer keeping these existing E_s_d and S_d structures free from the handling of the defficiencies and simply augment them by an additional structure that will be removed in a moment.

A.3 Extensions of the treatments

Given these extensions of structures, the correct updating of the labels referred to in L_1 and L_2 (see above) is achieved in five extensions of the program segments. The last two extensions really perform these tasks. They necessitate the first three extensions.

1° Ending reconciliation messages are sent by a goal process only when the process killing and the binding publication it orders have been completely treated i.e. when the status of the subtree it engenders has been reported through the status message. This synchronization ensures that process killing and binding publication ordered by ancestor processes never act simultaneously.

2° Process killing and binding publication are ordered as before but the process that ordered them is now identified explicitly in the killing and instantiation messages. This identifier will be necessary in a moment to indicate to which process the process killing and binding publication refer.

3° Killing of one process is augmented by the following operations:
- any process sends a status(completed,Id) message to its father when it commits suicide because of the reception of a kill message from the process Id;

- it furthermore sends a nsg_completion message to its father before the status(completed,Id) message if it corresponds to an ns-goal process.

4° Handling of nsg_completion messages performs the updating of the labels of R-triplets required in L_1. This is achieved as follows.

4.1 Nsg_completion messages are passed from child processes to father processes.

4.2 Nsg_completion messages are handled by goal-processes distinct from the query-process in two operations. Fix some goal-process P. Let C be the child that sends the treated nsg_completion message and let Nsg be the ns-goal-process referred to in it.
- The nsg_completion message is first passed to the father process of P.
- It then acts on the labels of the R-triplets of the P.S_d structure as follows. Just those of S_d[C] whose label is of the incompleted(Snsgprocess) form are in fact touched. Let <σ,Nodes,incompleted(Snsgprocess)> be such a R-triplet. Its label is modified as follows.
    - Reference to Nsg is first removed from Snsgprocess. Given the information that the subtree engendered by Nsg is completed, the subtree referred to in the considered R-triplet is indeed completed iff, for every remaining process of Snsgprocess, the subtree it engenders is completed.
    - If the set Snsgprocess becomes empty then the subtree associated with the considered R-triplet is proved completed and the incompleted(Snsgprocess) label is changed to completed. Otherwise, it is conserved in the incompleted(Snsgprocess) form but with the updated value for the set Snsgprocess.

4.3 Nsg_completion messages are handled by the query process by analogy to the goal-processes.
- The R-triplets of the S_d structure are updated in the same way;
- the R-triplets of the Part_sol list are updated in the same way too. Additional actions are furthermore performed on the R-triplets whose label becomes completed. The n-substitutions contained in them is first output, as suggested in point (iv) of the above Subsection B.2. They then become useless and are removed.

4.4 Nsg_completion messages are simply passed by ps-goal-processes.

4.5 Finally, nsg_completion messages are absorbed by ns-goal-processes. They are indeed useless to ancestor processes of ns-goal-processes since, as indicated by the reconciliation program segments of the ns-goal processes (see the above Subsection B.3), no ns-goal-process, descendant from an ns-goal-process, say Nsg, is referred to in the R-triplets sent by Nsg. This corresponds to the fact that the only useful piece of information for the father process of Nsg is that the subtree engendered by Nsg has become completed. This results from the handling of the status messages.

5° Handling of status messages performs the updating of the labels of E_s_d and S_d structures required in L_2. This is achieved as follows. Let status(Label,Id) be the status message received from the child Child_mess at the process P.

5.1 The reception of the status message first leads to the updating of the Status structure: the completed or <incompleted,Id> value is registered in Status[Child_mess] according as Label is completed or incompleted.

5.2 Let $Cond_1$ and $Cond_2$ denote the following conditions.
$Cond_1$. For any child C of P, one of the two following conditions holds :
- S_d[C] or E_s_d[C] has "completed" as label,
- Status[C] is "completed" or <incompleted,Id>.

$Cond_2$. For any child C of P, one of the two following conditions holds :
- S_d[C] or E_s_d[C] has "completed" as label,
- Status[C] is "completed".

The following operations are furthermore undertaken when the above condition $Cond_1$ is verified.
- If P is an ns-goal-process and if condition $Cond_2$ is verified then the nsg_completion(P.Id) is first sent.
- If P is the goal-process identified by Id then
  - the ending-reconciliation message pointed out in the above Subsection II.1 is sent to the father process of P provided P is not the query-process,
  - reinitialize and wake_up messages are sent in case P is the query-process.
- Otherwise, a status message is sent to the father process of P. Its label component is completed or incompleted according as $Cond_2$ holds or not. Its identifier component is Id.

B. Second extension

Most of the reinitialization of the components have been described in the basic model. They hold here too. The reinitialization of the newly introduced Part_sol and Status structures just remains to be precised. The value to give to them directly results from their definitions :
- the Part_sol is reinitialized to the ∅ set;
- the Status[C] components are reinitialized to the "none" value iff they are not "completed".

II.3 Ending the computation

As in the basic model, we conclude the design of the simplified model by addressing the termination of the computation. Here too, the computation should halt when there is no more useful job to be done that is in one of the two following situations :

- the computed and/or/not search tree under consideration contains no partial solution subtree;
- the computed and/or/not search tree is completed i.e. all its tip nodes are either ⊗-nodes, □-nodes or ns-goal-nodes.

Those situations are covered by the following computational situation : all the tip processes associated with a non empty goal are in the dead state. Termination is thus ensured here too. Non-dead processes are indeed the only processes activated for a new cycle by wake up messages.

5.3.1.2.2 The real model

The simplified process model just presented fits quite directly the model expressed in tree terms in Section 5.3.1.1. The drawback is that it contains several sources of inefficiencies. They are now removed. As in the basic model, this however requires some departure from Specification 5.5. The reason is the way in which subtrees are instantiated. This is now achieved in a simpler and more efficient way thanks to the information stored in the reconciliation components of the processes.

This section is organized in two parts. The first part is devoted to the specification level. It is articulated in two subsections presenting respectively the new instantiation of subtrees, called optimal instantiation, and the new specification of the cycles, resulting from the replacement of the instantiation defined in Definition 5.34 by the optimal one. The second part then discusses the optimizations of the simplified model leading to the real Conclog model.

I Specification

The optimal instantiation is defined as follows.

Definition 5.42 Let ST be a finite subtree of some computed and/or/not search tree and ν be an n-substitution. Let furthermore N be the root of ST and ST_1, ..., ST_m be the subtrees associated with the children of N, if any. As for the instantiation of Definition 5.34, *optimal instantiations* ST_inst of subtrees are defined up to variants. They are defined by means of the following auxiliary subtrees ST_aux; a subtree ST_inst is associated with any subtree ST_aux as follows :

- if N is not an ns-goal, if ST is not reduced to N and if ST_aux is reduced to N then the associated subtree ST_inst is the empty subtree $\varnothing$;
- otherwise, the associated subtree ST_inst is simply ST_aux.

The subtrees ST_aux are now defined as follows :

- if N is instantiable by ν then a subtree ST_aux is composed of
   - an instantiation of N by ν, as root node
   - an instantiation subtree of each subtree ST_i by ν;
- if N is not instantiable, the empty subtree is the only subtree ST_aux.

Note that all instantiation subtrees have the same tree skeleton.

The optimal instantiations of a subtree of processes are defined by analogy to the above optimal instantiation of a subtree of nodes. Precisely, optimally instantiating a subtree of processes by an n-substitution ν consists of

- moving any process corresponding to a removed node to the dead state;
- replacing the s-goal or goal component of other processes by one instantiation by ν of the s-goal or goal of the corresponding nodes.

Compared to the instantiation defined in Definition 5.34, the optimal instantiation differs by the treatment of the subtrees whose top nodes are not instantiable. They are simply removed in the optimal version whereas the ancestor nodes of □-nodes were conserved in the basic version of Definition 5.34. This optimization is possible in the process context, without influencing the computed answer n-substitutions, because all the information kept in the above ancestor nodes are already stocked in the reconciliation components of non dead ancestor processes of the processes under instantiation. Replacing the basic instantiation by the optimal one thus leads to two equivalent models.

Specification 5.5 is modified in consequence. The optimization of the completion messages further modifies it : it will not be guaranteed that waking up of processes will be performed only after all the computed answer n-substitutions produced in the considered cycle (see property 3 of Specification 5.5) are ouptut. Nevertheless, their computation is ensured but may occur in the next cycle. Hence, constraint 1 is also relaxed. Summing up, Specification 5.5 is modified to the following Specification 5.6.

Specification 5.6

Initial situation

A non-empty set of processes, say $\{P_1,...,P_m\}$, that verifies the following properties is given :

- the processes $P_1,...,P_m$ form a process tree corresponding to a finite computed and/or/not search tree T_in;

- there is at least one tip process associated with a non-empty goal; let P_1', ..., P_p' be these tip processes;
- the R-depth components of all the tip processes P_i' have the same non null value, say D;
- the processes P_i' are set in the active state and their generation procedure is activated.

Final situation

1) Let N_1, ..., N_p be the nodes associated with the tip processes P_1', ..., P_p'. Let $Snodes_1$, ..., $Snodes_p$ be the set of nodes of the first slice of R-depth D attached to the nodes N_1, ..., N_p, respectively. The processes associated with the nodes of $Snodes_1 \cup ... \cup Snodes_p$ are created.

2) These processes as well as the processes P_1, ..., P_m verify the following properties. Let T_aux denote the computed and/or search tree corresponding to all these processes.
   - Processes associated with nodes that are member of no (partial) solution subtree of T_aux are set in the dead state.
   - Tip goal-processes associated with non-empty goals are moved in the active state with D as R-depth tag component. Their generation procedure is furthermore activated.
   - Other processes are moved in the waiting set.
   - For every goal-process P, the subtree ST(P,T_aux) is optimally instantiated by its pss-n-substitution.

3) Let T_out be T_aux cut off the nodes corresponding to the dead processes. For every solution subtree SS of T_out that is not a solution subtree of T_in, the restriction $\sigma_{|Vg}$ of the n-reconciliation-substitution σ of SS to the set of variables Vg of the query is output.

Constraints

1) Tip goal-processes associated with a non-empty goal are set in the ready state only when properties 1) and 2) of the final situation are fullfilled.
2) The final situation is reached after a finite time.

II Design of the execution model

The simplified model, just presented (see Section 5.3.1.2.1), has been built as an extension of the simplified version of the basic model (see Section 4.3.1.2.1). It thus inherits the seven inefficiencies of this basic simplified model pointed out in Subsection II of Section 4.3.1.2.2. Four other optimizations arise from the extensions. We now turn to these optimizations. The real Conclog model results. It meets Specification 5.6 but conserves the main computational features of the simplified model.

A. Improvements inherited by the basic execution model

Three of the seven sources of optimization used in the real basic model (see Subsection II of Section 4.3.1.2.2) may be directly used in our extended context. They concern the handling of the Set_bind and Set_procs structures as well as the early detection of failure. The other four sources may also be employed but with some adaptations. We now rexamine them one by one and indicate the required adaptations for each one.

(i) Handling reintialize messages

Handling reintialize messages in one cycle may also be achieved here in an "on demand" fashion by means of reconciliation messages of the next cycle. The auxiliary Reconc_ph components should also be added to the reconciliation messages and the reconciliation components for this purpose but with the following adaptation for goal-processes. It results from the two following facts

- in contrast with the basic model, R-triplets may be moved from the incompleted state to the completed one;
- the only synchronization we will ensure is that, for any child C of a goal-process P, nsg_completion messages from the subtree ST(C) in one cycle reach P before any reconciliation message from C in the next cycle. (S)

Hence, it is incorrect to eliminate all R-triplets whose labels are not "completed" at the receipt of the first reconciliation message of a cycle. This can only be done on each structure S_d[C] with respect to the first reconciliation message sent by C. The following extensions are then made.

- Reinitialization of the S_d structure is then now made separately on each S_d[C] when C sends its first reconciliation message.
- To determine it, one Reconc_ph identifier is introduced in each S_d[C] component.
- As a final adaptation, the reconciliation procedure is modified as follows :
   - the receipt of a R-triplet Rt induces the construction of the tuples of the cartesian product
   $Srtriplets_1 \times \ldots \times Srtriplets_{j-1} \times Rt \times Srtriplets_{j+1} \times \ldots \times Srtriplets_m$
   (see point (iii.2.1) of Subsection II.1.B of Section 4.3.1.2.1) only when, after updating of the S_d structure induced by the receipt of Rt, all the Reconc_ph identifiers of S_d refer to the same reconciliation phase;
   - the receipt of an ending-reconciliation message results similarly in the sending of an ending-reconciliation message only when all the children corresponding to non completed subtrees have reported an ending-reconciliation message for the same reconciliation phase.

To conclude the handling of reintialize messages, the reinitialization of the newly introduced Status and Part_sol structures should be precised. The first one is not discussed since it will be removed in a moment. The second one cannot just consist of affecting $\emptyset$ to Part_sol at the receipt of the first reconciliation message from some child in any phase. Because of the weak synchronization mentioned above, nsg_completion may indeed be reported by other children. Our solution takes profit of the following property. Let, for any i, Part_sol$_i$ be the contents of the Part_sol structure when process killing and binding publication are ordered by the query-process in the ith cycle. Thanks to the synchronization S above, for any i, nsg_completion messages can only affect the R-triplets of Part_sol$_{i-1}$ and Part_sol$_i$. Furthermore, any R-triplet of Part_sol$_{i-1}$ is obsolate with respect to any R-triplet of Part_sol$_i$ mentioning the same list of ns-goal-processes. Our solution is thus to split the Part_sol structure into two sets : New_part_sol and Old_part_sol. Assuming the ith cycle is under computation, the first one aims at storing the R-triplets of Part_sol$_i$ and the second those of Part_sol$_{i-1}$ whose lists of ns-goal-processes are not referred to in an incompleted(...) label of a R-triplet of Part_sol$_i$. This semantics suggests their treatment. Both of them are modified as discussed before by nsg_completion messages. They are initialized to the empty set at the creation of the query-process. Finally, they are reinitialized as follows. Assume the receipt of the first reconciliation message of the jth reconciliation phase is under consideration. At this time, they are as follows :

- New_part_sol
    - contains the R-triplets of Part_sol$_{j-1}$ if j>1
    - is $\emptyset$ otherwise,
- Old_part_sol,
    - contains the R-triplets of Part_sol$_{j-2}$ whose lists of ns-goal-processes are not refered to in an incompleted(...) label of one R-triplet of New_part_sol, if j>2,
    - is $\emptyset$ otherwise;

Hence, to conserve their meaning, the reception of the first reconciliation message of a phase induces the following reinstantiation :

- the New_Part_sol set is reinitialized to the empty set.
- the Old_part_sol set is reinitialized to the contents of New_part_sol;

(ii) Handling completion messages

Two types of completion messages must be considered here : nsg_completion messages and status messages. The first ones are not altered in the real model. In contrast, the last ones are suppressed in the real model. They were assigned two roles in the simplified model :

- to indicate the end of the moving of the completion status of subtrees induced by process killing and binding publication;
- to inform about this completion.

The first task is abandoned here. This has two consequences :

- the synchronization required in constraint 1 cannot be guaranteed
- the process killing and instantiation bindings ordered by two ancestor processes may interfere.

The first consequence is however not significant. What is really of importance in Specification 5.6 is that nsg_completion messages sent by one child in one reconciliation phase reach its father before any reconciliation message sent by this child in the next reconciliation phase. This is indeed ensured because nsg_completion messages and reconciliation messages are propagated in the same bottom up way.

The second consequence is not significant too. The same result is achieved even if the process killing and binding publication ordered by two ancestors intefere, thanks to the following facts.

- As already said, the only thing that can be induced by process killing and binding publication is that subtrees may move from the incompleted state to the completed one. No completed subtree is altered in its completion by process killing or binding publication.
- Instantiation and killing can be interchanged because dead processes are completely deaf to sent messages. Sending an instantiation message to a killed process or killing an instantiated process has no affect. Similarly, instantiation leading to report completion to a dead process has no effect.
- Killings ordered by two processes are order independent for the same deafness reason.
- Instantiations ordered by two processes are not interleaved because they are propagated in the same top to bottom way.

Suppressing the status messages has two important consequences. First, the computation is made more dynamic since a goal-process does no more wait until its descendant processes to report the termination of the operations induced by the process killing and binding publication it orders. Second, the Status structure of the reconciliation components becomes useless. It is thus removed in the real model. A gain of place and of computation time is thus achieved by avoiding its storing and handling.

(iii) Referencing processes in R-triplets

Referencing of processes of partial solution subtrees can also be strongly optimized. This is achieved by identifying the partial solution subtrees by

- the processes corresponding to ☐-nodes and that are not descendant of ns-goal processes,
- ns-goal-processes that are not descendant of other ns-goal-processes.

Note that this indeed identifies the partial solution subtrees. The modifications induced by this optimal referencing of processes directly result from those described in Subsection II.D of Section 4.3.1.2.2. The two following extensions are just needed.

1° The killing of processes includes, as decribed in Subsection II.1.C of Section 5.3.1.2.1, the killing of descendant processes when any;

2° The handling of fail messages (introduced in Subsection II.D of Section 4.3.1.2.2) is extended to nsg-processes as follows. They do not induce the failure of the nsg-processes but rather its completion. Hence, an nsg_completion message for the considered ns-goal-process is simply sent to its father process as an answer.

(iv) Storing R-triplets in the S_d structure

Storing R-triplets in S_d structures can be achieved thanks to essentially the same modifications as in the basic model (see Subsection II.E of Section 4.3.1.2.2). The following adaptation is just needed. R-triplets that become useless in S_d structures also correspond to those referring to killed processes. However, killing may be ordered either by direct process killing or by instantiation. It follows that the top to bottom propagation of the removal messages used in the basic model must be abandoned here. R-triplets made useless by the second source of killing are indeed not removable in this way. We thus adopt an alternative here. It consists of making killed □-processes and ns-goal-processes send a removal message. Such messages are treated as in the basic model with the adaptation that they are propagated from children to fathers. A further optimization is achieved by limiting this propagation. Thanks to Definition 5.37, properties I_1 to I_6 and the above optimal referencing of processes, for any goal-process P, process killing and binding publication P orders do not kill processes referred to in R-triplets sent by P. Hence, removal messages may be limited to the goal-processes. This is easily achieved by extending the kill, instantiation and removal messages by a process identifier (practically, the identifier of the goal-process that orders the process killing or the instantiation).

B. Instantiating subtrees

Instantiating subtrees of processes is improved by performing it in the optimal way of Definition 5.42. This definition is in fact well suited for implementation. The following scheme is thus employed. When a process receives an instantiation message, it tests its goal or s-goal for instantiability. If it is instantiable, then it replaces its goal or s-goal by an instantiation and sends the instantiation message to its children. Otherwise, it kills itself (this including the sending of the associated completion and the fail messages).

C. N-substitutions and en-mgus

Another optimization is obtained by reconsidering the n-reconciliation. As described in Chapter 3, n-reconciliation produces en-mgus. This fact is employed by goal-processes and leads to adapt the following feature of the basic model : a R-triplet is associated with each n-substitution of the produced en-mgus (see point (iii) of Subsection II.1.B.2 of Section 5.3.1.2.1). This feature was actually made to ease the presentation but induces inefficiencies. They result from the following fact. As pointed out in Section 3.2.5.3, reconciling pairs of n-substitutions issued from two en-mgus in an independent way causes the same reconciliation of the positive parts to be performed for each pair. It is then better to directly n-reconcile the en-mgus, as this is achieved by Algorithm Gen_N_reconciliation (see Section 3.2.5.3). Associating a R-triplet with each n-substitution of produced en-mgus leads to the above inefficiencies. As R-triplets are combined into tuples at goal-processes - with one R-triplet arising from each child -, the (same) reconciliation of the positive parts is computed many times. This is avoided in the real model by replacing n-substitutions by en-mgus in R-triplet. The en-mgu's are then n-reconciled by using the dedicated Algorithm Gen_N_reconciliation. They are however considered as sets of n-substitutions to negate them, to determine the n-substitutions to be made public as well as to output the computed answer n-substitutions. Note that the transformation of n-substitutions to en-mgus is always possible since any information contained in the n-substitution v may be rewritten in the en-mgu form $v^+ \oplus \{v^-\}$.

D. Avoiding duplicates

As a further optimization, duplicates of R-triplets are avoided at a very slow cost. As noted in the introductory Section 5.1, combining the n-substitutions (of a negation) produced by an ns-goal-process with n-substitutions of sibling s-goal-processes may lead to duplicates of the same R-triplets. Such duplicates are highly undesirable because they induce duplicates in the reconciliation procedure of any ancestor processes. They can be removed in a straightforward way by any goal-process P : for any child C, the S_d[C] structure behaves as a set so that any duplicate produced by one child of C may be removed by P. Hence, duplicates produced by a goal-process are removed by its grandfather process. Duplicates produced by the query-process, remains to be handled. This can be achieved at a slow cost by adding a set, called Sol, to the reconciliation structure. Considering the ith cycle, it aims at collecting the R-triplets corresponding to the completed solution subtrees produced during the ith cycle. It is thus instantiated to the $\emptyset$ set at the beginning of each cycle. Furthermore, a computed answer n-substitution is produced only if it is issued of one R-triplet that is not already registered in Sol. If so, the R-triplet is furthermore added to it. Note that two sets do not need to be managed here as it is the case for the Part_sol sets. This is because duplicates are always produced in a same phase and are simultaneously touched by nsg_completion messages.

E. Early propagation of failure

The final optimisation consists of making ns-goal-processes report failure in an early way. In the simplified model, any ns-goal-process first collects the R-triplets from its child and then negate them. However, if the n-substitution ({},not{}) is returned with the "completed" label, it is no use waiting for other R-triplets. Whatever they are, failure will be reported. The final optimization consists precisely of making ns-goal-processes report failure as soon as one of the two following events happens :

- they receive a R-triplet whose n-substitution is ({},not{}) and whose label is "completed",
- the label of a R-triplet whose n-substitution is ({},not{}) is moved to "completed".

5.3.2 Infinite value of the R-depth parameter

So far, and/or/not search trees have been constructed by finite slices. We now turn to the limit case where slices are allowed to grow up to an infinite R-depth. By analogy to the models of Chapter 4, the resulting model is also called the extended Conclog(∞) model or, more simply, Conclog(∞) when the qualifiers "extended" and "model" are understood. It is described in this section as the other models were previously, namely according to the tree and process views and for each of these views, by first specifying the model and then by designing it.

5.3.2.1 The tree view

I Specification

As slices are allowed to grow up to an infinite R-depth, any computation under the basic model results in the construction of an and/or/not search tree in its pure form followed by its reconciliation. Therefore, as in the basic model, any computation under the Conclog(∞) model is composed of one cycle. The computation may thus also be described directly without calling the auxiliary cycles. This leads to the following specification.

Specification 5.7

Initial situation

The and/or/not search tree limited to the query-node is given.

Final situation

1) The and/or/not search tree T generated by the query and the program under consideration is constructed.
2) The restriction of the n-reconciliation-substitution of any solution subtree of T to the set of variables of the query is output.

The notion of computed answer n-substitution is extended to these n-substitutions.

Definition 5.43 Any n-substitution produced in point 2 above is called *computed answer n-substitution*.

II Design of the execution model

The extended Conclog(∞) model can in fact be directly derived from the extended Conclog(D) model, as the basic Conclog(∞) were from the basic Conclog(D) model. Indeed, computations under the extended Conclog(∞) that involve finite and/or/not search trees are the same that those computed under the extended Conclog(D) model with D finite and greater than the R-depth of the considered and/or/not search tree. As for the basic model, problems can thus also only arise from infinite and/or/not search trees. They indeed occur since, when infinite and/or/not search trees are involved, the strict sequentialization of the generation and reconciliation phases (inherited in the tree expression of Section 5.3.1.1 from that of the basic model) postpones at infinite the production of answer n-substitutions. Fortunately, as for the basic model, this problem is circumvented when the sequentialization of the phases is relaxed in such a way that the reconciliation phase is allowed to treat solution subtrees progressively, at the rate they are computed. This is what is precisely achieved in the process expression of the computation. As this expression describes the real dynamic computation, we will not develop further the explanation of the extended Conclog(∞) model in terms of trees but rather turn directly to its expression in terms of processes.

5.3.2.2 The process view

I Specification

The following specification re-expresses Specification 5.7 in terms of processes.

Specification 5.8

Initial situation

The process associated with the query under consideration is given with the following properties :
- its R-depth tag is infinite
- its state is active
- its generation procedure is activated.

Final situation

1) The processes of the process model associated with the and/or/not search tree T for the considered query and program are created.
2) If T is finite then
    - processes associated with nodes of any solution subtree are set in the dead state;
    - other processes are set in the waiting state.
3) The restriction of the n-reconciliation-substitution of any solution subtree of T to the set of variables of the query is output.

Constraints

1) Any answer n-substitution is eventually computed.
2) If T is finite, the final situation is reached after a finite time.

II Design of the execution model

As just argued in the above Subsection II, the execution model of Section 5.3.1.2 explained in process terms for finite values of the R-depth parameter also applies for the infinite value of this parameter. The extended Conclog(∞) model is thus in fact already constructed. Simplifications may furthermore be operated thanks to this special value. Some of them correspond to the simplifications performed for the basic model. Others issue from the handling of negation.

1° As for the basic model, process R-depth tag, employed to ensure the construction of the and/or/not search tree slice by slice, has no more ground for existence. It can thus be omitted as well as its management.

2° Binding publication and pruning of the and/or /not search tree has no ground for existence too. Indeed, they would only occur in Conclog(∞) when the and/or/not search tree is completely constructed. They can thus be eliminated.

3° As a result, the associated Set_procs and Set_binds have no ground for existence. The Conclog(∞) model can thus be simplified from their management as well.

4° As a further consequence, it is useless to reference processes in R-triplets. Furthermore, as their n-substitutions always refer to completed solution subtrees, their labels are also useless. R-triplets may thus be just reduced to their n-substitution component. Consequently, their management can be reduced to the management of these n-substitutions.

5° As there is only one cycle, the and/or/not search tree is computed in its pure non-extended form. Goals and s-goals are thus manipulated in the conventional literal format without any negative information. As a further consequence, unification is performed in the conventional way (see Section 2.3.1) and not in the extended one.

6° Another consequence of the one-cycle computation is that there is no more need to handle Reconc_ph identifiers in the reconciliation components and in the reconciliation messages.

7° As a final consequence, only one Part_sol set needs to be manipulated.

5.4 Variants of the model

The model just constructed has been developed as an extension of the basic model of Chapter 4 and has inherited its main features. All the design choices questioned in Section 4.4

may thus be questioned here too. They are discussed hereafter in a first subsection. Results of Section 4.4 exempt us from a completely detailed description. The only adaptation to our extended framework are thus only presented. Other design choices, related to the newly introduced ns-goal-processes, are then discussed in a second subsection.

5.4.1 Variants inherited from the basic model

5.4.1.1 The R-depth parameter of the model

The extended model has inherited the R-depth parameter from the basic model. Discussion about its choice remains valid here too. An additional dimension introduced by negation should furthermore be stressed. Handling negation has the effect of mixing the search for the positive and negative information. The success of an ns-goal results from the failure of its associated ps-goal and conversely. Hence, early detection of the success and failure of an ns-goal takes profit of the early detection of the failure and of the success of the associated ps-goal. Therefore, when a negation is effectively treated in the computation, the R-depth parameter should be chosen to combine both the search for positive information (computed answer n-substitutions) and for negative information (detection of failure). Remember that the two cases were separated in the basic model.

5.4.1.2 Binding publication

The way in which bindings to published are selected may be criticized in the same two points as in Section 4.4 with the same answers. The following point should furthermore be added against the (unretained) inf optimization. Although the inf optimization applies safely to substitutions, i.e. the positive parts of the n-substitutions, computing it for the negative parts of n-substitutions leads to inconsistencies. Assume, for instance, that the two n-substitutions ($\{X/f(Y)\}$,not$\{Y/g(1)\}$), ($\{X/f(Y)\}$,not$\{Y/g(2)\}$) are computed by a goal-process P. It is true that X must be equal to f(Y) in ST(P). However, adding the constraint not$\{Y/g(Z)\}$ (with g(Z) the inf of g(1) and g(2)) is too strong : Y must in fact differ from g(1) or from g(2). Note that, in contrast, our selection of bindings applies safely (and uniformally) to both parts of n-substitutions.

5.4.1.3 Restriction of n-substitutions

The restriction of substitutions at goal-processes was a simple matter of efficiency in the basic model. However, it is here also a matter of correctness. Consider the query

← not(p(X)).

and the program

```
p(X) ← q(X,Y).
q(X,Y) ← not(r(X)),s(Y).
r(1).
s(2).
```

Assume the R-depth parameter is infinite. The computed and/or/not search tree is drawn in part (a) of Figure 5.9. The computed answer n-substitutions are depicted in parts (b) and (c) of Figure 5.9. Part b) uses the Conclog scheme with restriction. Only one n-substitution results : $\nu=(\{X/1\},\text{not}\{\})$. Part c) makes no restriction. Two n-substitutions result : $\nu=(\{X/1\},\text{not}\{\})$, $\mu=(\{\},\text{not}\{Y/2\})$. The n-substitution ν is quite correct. The set ground(p(X);ν) reduces to the only substitution $\{X/1\}$ and one has

$$\text{comp}(P) \models (\text{not}(p(X))\{X/1\}.$$

In contrast, the n-substitution μ is not correct. The substitution $\{X/2\}$ is a ground substitution of ground(p(X);μ) that does not verify

$$\text{comp}(P) \models \text{not}(p(X))\{X/2\}.$$

Restriction is both a matter of efficiency and a matter of correctness. Nevertheless, Section 5.5 will enable the freedom on the restriction of substitutions achieved in Section 4.4.3 but provided that

- those uncomputed restrictions are effectively made by ns-goal-processes before any operations on the received n-substitutions;
- n-substitutions are restricted before being delivered as computed answer n-substitutions.

In a similar way, consistency tests do not need to be performed by goal-processes provided

- this is effectively performed by ns-goal-processes before any operations on the received n-substitutions;
- n-substitutions are tested for consistency before being delivered as computed answer n-substitutions.

5.4.1.4 Instantiation of intermediary processes

Another possible extension of the Conclog model concerns the instantiation of non-tip processes. As in the basic model, tip processes only determine the slice they engender in a new generation phase. It follows that non-tip processes do not need to be effectively instantiated. However, they should still be tested for instantiability.

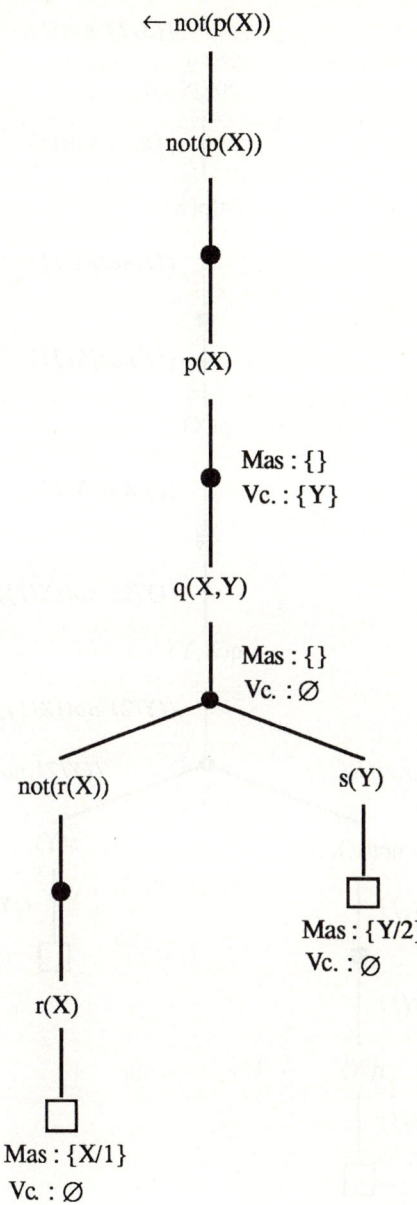

Figure 5.9 (a) : generation phase

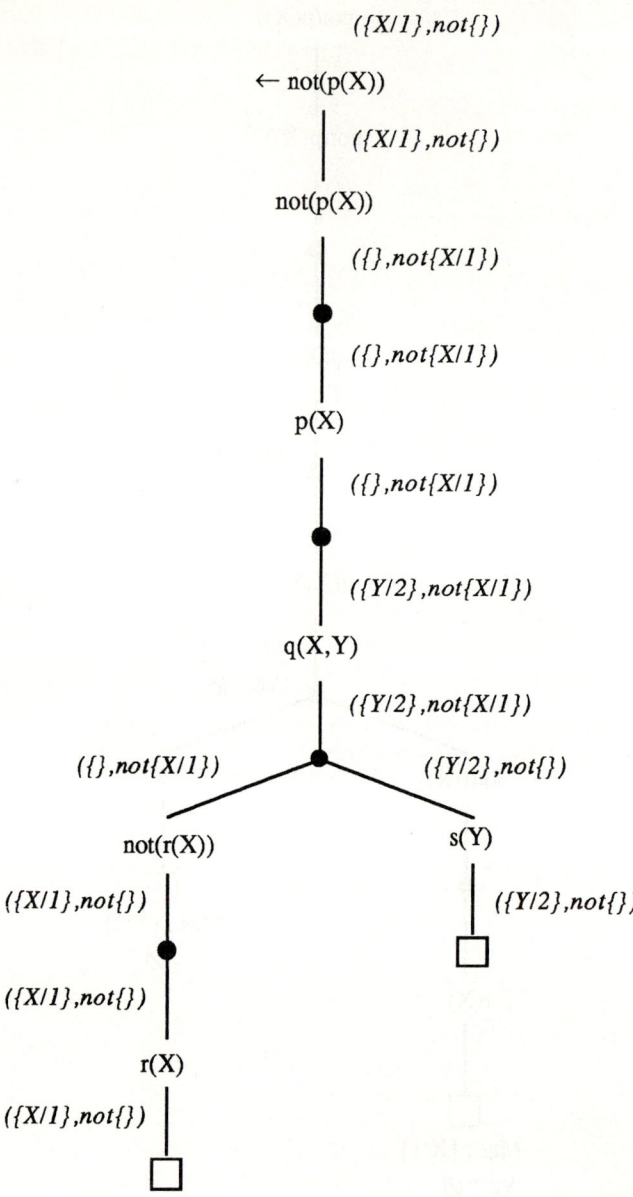

Figure 5.9 (b) : reconciliation phase with restriction

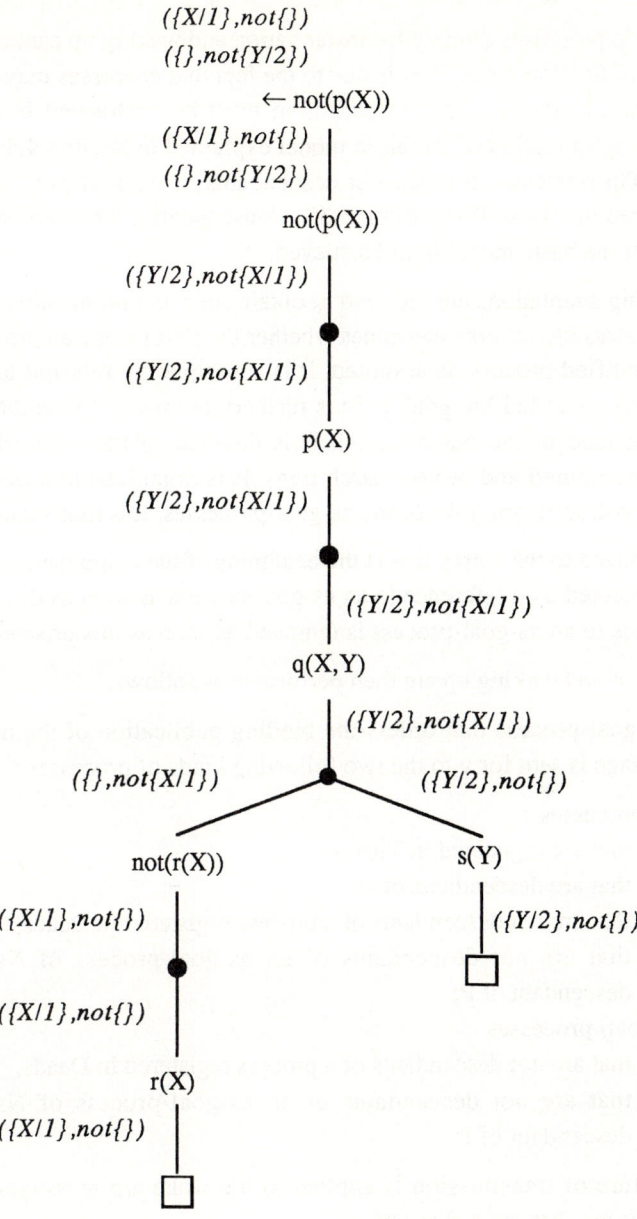

Figure 5.9 (c) : reconciliation phase without restriction

5.4.1.5 Activating tip processes directly

Activating tip processes directly for instantiation and waking up cannot be achieved in the so direct manner of Section 4.4.5. This is due to the fact that processes may be killed as a result of instantiation and to the fact that instantiation must be performed in a progressive way. Nevertheless, the optimization of the basic model explained in Section 4.4.5 can be somewhat preserved here. Tip processes that are not descendants of ns-goal-processes may indeed be directly instantiated thanks to Proposition 5.38. Consequently, when no negation is involved, the optimization of the basic model is still achieved.

The following adaptations are required to obtain such an optimization. First, some means, that given two process identifiers determines whether the first identified process is a descendant of the second identified process, is assumed. It is subsequently referred to as the "anc_desc" procedure. A structure called Sn_goal_proc is furthermore needed in addition to the Tips and Deads lists introduced in the basic model. It is devoted to the memorization of ns-goal-processes of the computed and/or/not search trees. It is organized in a tree structure so as to reflect the ancestor-descendant links of the ns-goal-processes. It is thus managed as follows :

- it is initialized to the empty tree at the beginning of the computation,
- it is augmented by a reference to an ns-goal-process as soon as this process is created,
- a reference to an ns-goal-process is removed as soon as this process is killed.

Binding publication and waking up are then performed as follows.

Let P be a goal-process that orders the binding publication of the n-substitution v. An instantiation message is sent for v to the two following kinds of processes :

(i) (tip) processes
   - that are registered in Tips,
   - that are descendants of P,
   - that are not descendants of a process registered in Deads,
   - that are not descendants of an ns-goal-process of Ns_goal_proc, itself descendant of P;

(ii) (ns-goal) processes
   - that are not descendants of a process registered in Deads,
   - that are not descendants of an ns-goal-process of Ns_goal_proc, itself descendant of P.

The same procedure of transmission is applied to the wake_up messages. Instantiation and wake_up messages are then treated as before.

5.4.2 Extensions of ns-goal-processes

The reconciliation program segments of the ns-goal-processes can be criticized in two points:

- the non incremental way in which n-substitutions are produced,
- the discarding of incompleted partial solution subtrees to determine them.

5.4.2.1 Computing n-substitutions incrementally

As described in Subsection II.1.B.3 of Section 5.3.1.2.1, any ns-goal-process waits that its child has completely reported its R-triplets to compute the R-triplets it sends. This does not destroy the incremental production of computed answer n-substitutions, as argued in Subsection 5.1.2.C. Nevertheless, it might seem attractive to preserve uniformity in the model and thus to compute the output R-triplets incrementally at the rate the input ones are received. The induced consequences are analyzed hereafter.

Consider an ns-goal-process P, say associated with the ns-goal not(C). Assume all the R-triplets received by P are $<v_1,Nodes_1,Label_1>$, ..., $<v_m,Nodes_m,Label_m>$ and suppose the first p ones correspond to solution subtrees. Finally, let, for any $i \in \{1,...,m\}$, F_i be Form(v_i;Svars) where Svars is the set of variables of the ns-goal associated with P. Then, the n-substitutions μ_1, ..., μ_n sent by P are such that

$$\text{ground}(C;\mu_1) \cup ... \cup \text{ground}(C;\mu_n) = \{\alpha \in \text{ground}(C) : Ax_= \models \neg(F_1 \vee ... \vee F_p)\alpha\}.$$

Assume now that, among v_1, ..., v_p, only v_{k_1}, ..., v_{k_r} are known. Let μ'_1, ..., μ'_s be the n-substitutions computed from them. They verify the following equality

$$\text{ground}(C;\mu'_1) \cup ... \cup \text{ground}(C;\mu'_s) = \{\alpha \in \text{ground}(C) : Ax_= \models \neg(F_{k_1} \vee ... \vee F_{k_r})\alpha\}.$$

and thus the inclusion

$$\text{ground}(C;\mu'_1) \cup ... \cup \text{ground}(C;\mu'_s) \supset \{\alpha \in \text{ground}(C) : Ax_= \models \neg(F_1 \vee ... \vee F_p)\alpha\}.$$

Hence, μ'_1, ..., μ'_s cover more substitutions than μ_1, ..., μ_n. This fits well our model where the exact solutions are approximated by greater approximations (see for instance the substitutions covered by the n-reconciliation-substitutions of partial solution subtrees). There is thus a priori no reason to refuse to compute the output n-substitutions μ_i at the rate the input n-substitutions v_i's are received. Nevertheless, such an incremental computing leads to an overhead of reconciliations. It is due to the fact that we found no simple relation between the various sets $\{\mu'_1,..., \mu'_s\}$ resulting from various approximations of $\{v_1,...,v_p\}$. Hence, at any ancestor goal-process and ns-goal-process, the only way to obtain the reconciliation results corresponding to the sent approximations $\{\mu'_1,..., \mu'_s\}$ of $\{\mu_1,..., \mu_n\}$ is to re-compute the reconciliation for each approximation. What is the gain? It rests in the detection of failure. As the sets of substitutions covered by the approximation $\{\mu'_1,..., \mu'_s\}$ of $\{\mu_1,..., \mu_n\}$ are greater than the set of substitutions covered by $\{\mu_1,..., \mu_n\}$, if the reconciliation at an ancestor goal-process of P rules out P as an member of a solution subtree, then the same diagnosis is given when $\{\mu_1,..., \mu_n\}$ is implied in the reconciliation. Process P could thus be killed as well as its descendants before all of them have reported their R-triplets.

All in all, the gain is not evident, especially since no computed answer n-substitution could result from the approximations $\{\mu'_1,..., \mu'_s\}$. We then do not incorporate this incremental sending of the sets $\{\mu'_1,..., \mu'_s\}$ on the basis on the incremental receipt of the v_i's. This possibility will however be provided by means of annotations in the following chapter.

5.4.2.2 Using incompleted partial solution subtrees

Discarding incompleted partial solution subtrees might appear quite surprising. This is however necessary to ensure one of the basic properties of the Conclog model : n-reconciliation-substitutions of solution subtrees are approximated by greater and greater[1] approximations, by the n-reconciliation-substitutions of the corresponding subtrees in the successively computed and/or/not search trees. This property is essential to justify the binding publication and the process killing.

Using incompleted partial solution subtrees would destroy this property. To be more specific, consider the query

    ← p(X).

together with the program

    p(X) ← not(q(X)).
    q(X) ← r(X).
    r(1).
    r(2).

Assume the R-depth parameter is fixed to 2. The and/or/not search tree for this query and this program is drawn in Figure 5.10. The first computed and/or/not search tree is drawn in part (a) of the figure. At the first reconciliation phase, no solution subtree of q(X) is known but one partial solution subtree composed of the only node (5) can be determined. The R-triplet <({},not{}),{5},incompleted({5})> is thus sent to the ns-goal-process (4). Making the ns-goal-process take incompleted partial solution subtrees into account would force process (4) to negate ({},not{}). Failure would follow and would be transmitted to process (3). This does not however constitute a greater approximation to the n-reconciliation-substitution of the solution subtree attached to process (4), namely ({},not{X/1,X/2}). It is furthermore worth noting that reporting failure is unintuitive. Indeed, intuitively speaking, the ns-goal-process (4) does not fail at the first reconciliation phase but should rather report no constraint at all.

---

[1] according to the meaning just explained in Section 5.4.2.1.

VARIANTS OF THE MODEL

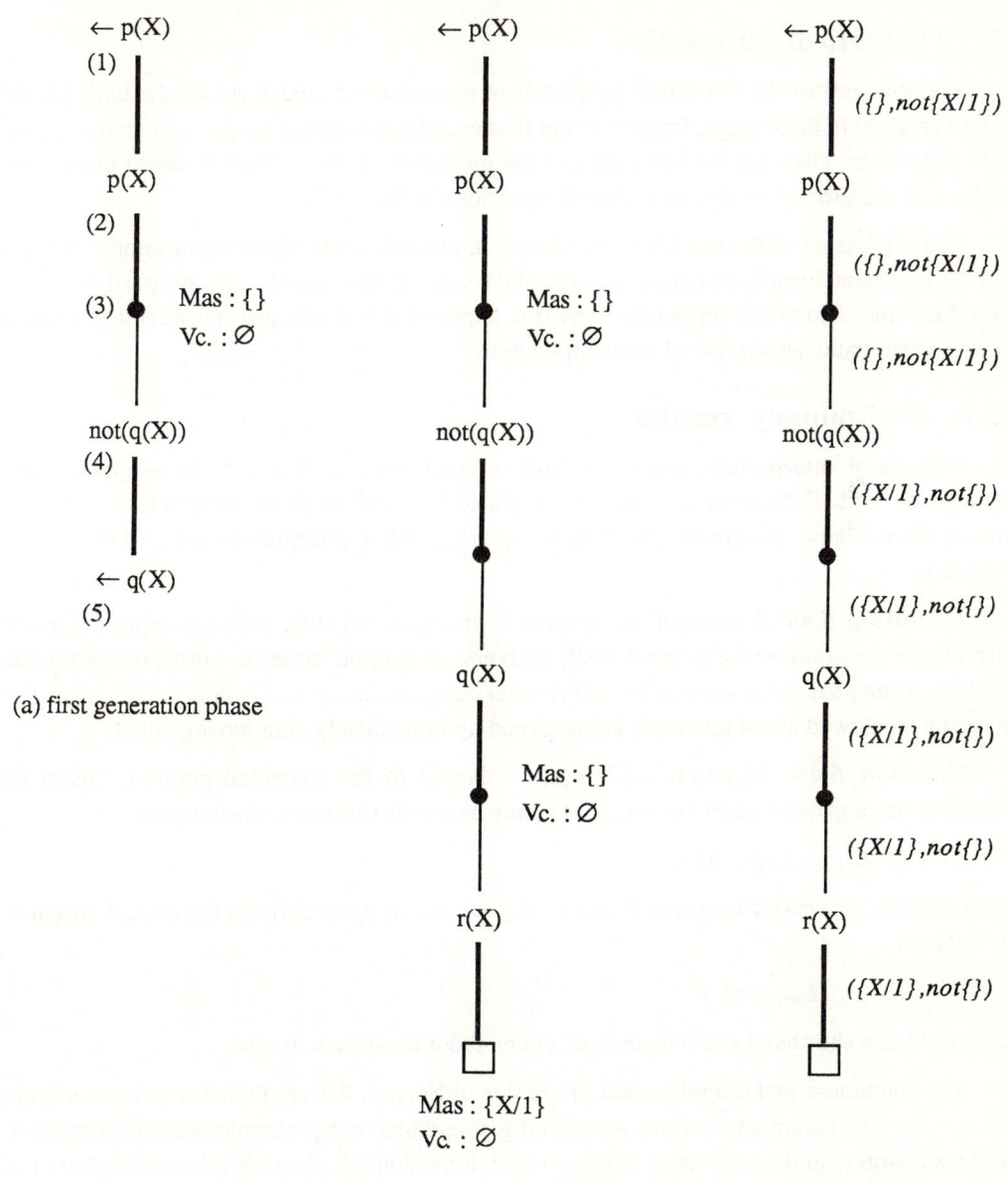

Figure 5.10

5.5 Theoretical properties

We now turn to the theoretical properties of the extended model. As for the basic model we will proceed in three steps. Properties are first established for the model with an infinite R-depth parameter. They are then extended to the models with an arbitrary R-depth parameter. Finally they are proved for the variants and extensions of Section 5.4.

The expression of the models in tree terms, in process terms, either in the simplifed form or in the real form, have been argued as equivalent. One of them can then be arbitrarily selected to establish the theoretical properties. The tree expression has retained our attention since it allows a more static description of the computation.

5.5.1 Preliminary results

Notions of interpreters, soundness and completeness need first to be adapted to the extended context. Definition 2.56 is first extended in order to allow interpreters to handle general Horn clause programs and general queries. Such interpreters are called general intepreters.

Definition 5.44 A *general interpreter* is an algorithm that, given as input a general Horn clause program and a general goal, delivers, as output, either n-substitutions for the variables of the goal or the answer no. In the latter case, the interpreter is said to fail. A general interpreter is allowed to not terminate but must end up immediately after having failed.

Notation 5.45 Notation 2.57 is also adapted to the extended context. Given an interpreter Int, a general query $\leftarrow L_1, ..., L_m$ and an n-substitution v, the notation

$$P \mid\text{-}_{Int} (L_1, ..., L_m) \text{ with } v$$

means that the interpreter Int given P and $\leftarrow A_1, ..., A_m$ as input delivers the n-substitution v. The notation

$$P \mid\text{-} (L_1, ..., L_m) \text{ with } v$$

is also used as a shorthand when there is no doubt about the interpreter Int.

The soundness and completeness properties of Section 2.4 are then extended in a quite similar way. The extended versions are called g-soundness and g-completeness properties to avoid confusion with the basic ones. As motivated in Section 5.2, they appeal the completion of the programs as the interpretation of the general Horn clause programs.

Definition 5.46 A general interpreter Int is
1) *g-sound* iff for every general Horn clause program P, every conjunction of literals $\leftarrow L_1, ..., L_m$, if the property

$$P \mid\text{-}_{Int} (L_1, ..., L_m) \text{ with } v$$

holds, then so does the property
$$\text{comp}(P) \models (L_1 \land ... \land L_m)\alpha$$
for any substitution α of ground$((L_1, ..., L_m); \nu)$.

2) *g-complete* iff for every general Horn clause program P, every conjunction of literals $\leftarrow L_1, ..., L_m$, if
$$\text{comp}(P) \models (L_1 \land ... \land L_m)\alpha$$
holds for some substitution $\alpha \in$ ground$(L_1, ..., L_m)$, then there is an n-substitution ν such that the following properties hold
1) $P \vdash_{\text{Int}} (L_1, ..., L_m)$ with ν;
2) $\alpha \in$ ground$((L_1,...,L_m);\nu)$.

Convention 2.60 is finally extended to the negated context.

Convention 5.47 By language misuse, we will subsequently say that a language is g-sound and g-complete whenever these properties hold for all general interpreters induced by the language.

5.5.2 Execution model with infinite R-depth parameter

The execution model with an infinite R-depth parameter provides a very simple characterization of computed answer n-substitutions. Under this model, and/or/not search trees are generated in their pure form with the additional characterization that no negative information is associated with their s-goals and goals. Furthermore, as all tip nodes are either $\otimes$-nodes or $\square$-nodes, instantiation do not remove any solution subtree. Hence, referring to Definition 5.34 and Specification 5.1, computed answer n-substitutions correspond to n-reconciliation-substitutions of solution subtrees of and/or/not search trees.

The g-soundness and g-completness properties can then be stated as follows.

Let P be a general Horn clause program, $\leftarrow L_1, ..., L_m$ be a general query and T be the and/or/not search tree for P and Q.

(i) *G-soundness*. Any n-reconciliation-substitution ν of any solution subtree of T is such that
$$P \models (L_1,...,L_m)\alpha$$
holds, for any substitution $\alpha \in$ ground$((L_1,...,L_m);\nu)$.

(ii) *G-completeness*. For any substitution $\alpha \in$ ground$(L_1,...,L_m)$ such that $P \models (L_1,...,L_m)\alpha$, there is a solution subtree of T with a n-reconciliation-substitution ν such that $\alpha \in$ ground$((L_1,...,L_m);\nu)$.

A. Characterization of solution subtrees

Establishing the g-soundness and g-completeness properties will thus essentially result from the properties of the solution subtrees. The following proposition constitutes a first step in this direction. It is stated in the more general context of computed and/or/not search trees.

Proposition 5.48 Let T be a computed and/or/not search tree.
1) For any s-goal N of T, any n-reconciliation-substitution ν of ST(N;T) verifies the following properties :
    (i) $var(N) \supset dom(\nu^+)$;
    (ii) ν is consistent wrt the variables of $var(N)$.
2) For any goal N of T, any qn-reconciliation computed from the n-reconciliation-substitutions of its children is consistent wrt to the variables of $var(N)$.

Proof The proposition is easily demonstrated by an induction on the R-depth of the subtree ST(N;T). It results from the restriction operated at each goal-node as well as from the incorporation of consistency tests in the qn-reconciliation and the negation operations. ◊

B. Lemma

The following lemma is the core of our discussion about the g-soundness and g-completness properties. It issues from the fact that soundness and completeness cannot be dissociated in the so clear way used in the basic model. Reducing ns-goals in a sound way indeed implies computing their associated ps-goal in a complete way. Hence, soundness and completeness must be interconnected in some way. This is precisely what is done in the following lemma.

Lemma 5.49 Let P be a general Horn clause program and $\leftarrow L_1, ..., L_m$ be a general query. Assume the and/or/not search tree T for P and $\leftarrow L_1, ..., L_m$ is finite. Let $\nu_1, ..., \nu_n$ be the n-reconciliation-substitutions of the solution subtrees of T. Then, the following holds :

$$comp(P) \models \forall_{var(L_1,...,L_m)} [(L_1 \wedge ... \wedge L_m) \Leftrightarrow Dform(\{\nu_1,...,\nu_n\}; var(L_1,...,L_m))] .$$

Proof The proof is established by induction on the R-depth D of the and/or/not search tree T.

1° D is 0

If D is 0, then the query $\leftarrow L_1, ..., L_m$ is empty and the only n-reconciliation substitution is $(\{\},not\{\})$. The thesis then results from the fact that $Dform(\{(\{\},not\{\})\})$ and $(L_1,...,L_m)$ are tautologies.

2° D is strictly positive

If D is strictly positive, then the query $\leftarrow L_1, ..., L_m$ is not-empty and the and/or/not search tree T does not reduce to the only query-node. Let, for any $i \in \{1,...,m\}$,

- ST_i denote the subtree of T attached to L_i
- Σ_i denote the set of n-substitutions of the n-reconciliation substitutions of ST_i.

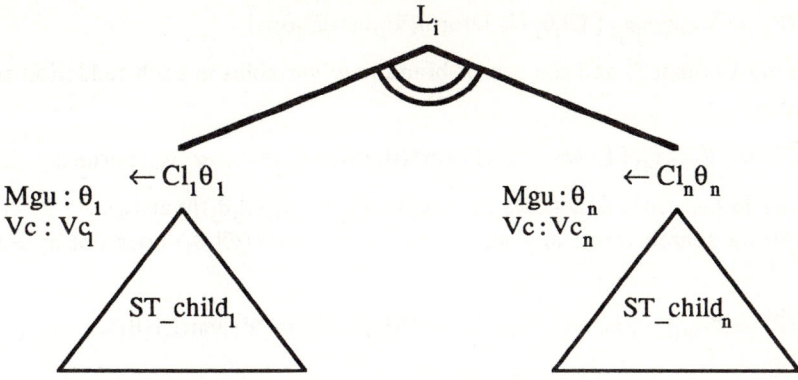

Figure 5.11

The demonstration is constructed in two steps. First, the following property is proven :

(P) for any $i \in \{1,...,m\}$, one has $\text{comp}(P) \models \llbracket L_i \Leftrightarrow \text{Dform}(\Sigma_i) \rrbracket$.

Second, the thesis is demonstrated therefrom.

2.1° Proving assertion P

Fix some $i \in \{1,...,m\}$. Assertion P is proved by distinguishing ns-goals from ps-goals.

2.2.1 The literal L_i is a ps-goal

In case L_i is a ps-goal (i.e. an atom), the subtree ST_i is formed by means of all the clauses of P that unifies with L_i. Let them be

$H_1 \leftarrow Cl_1$.
...
$H_n \leftarrow Cl_n$.

where the H_i's are atoms and the Cl_i's are conjunctions of literals. Let furthermore
- $\theta_1, ..., \theta_n$ be idempotent mgu's used in T for these clauses;
- $Vc_1, ..., Vc_n$ be the sets of variables introduced by them;
- ST_child_j be the subtree attached to $Cl_j\theta_j$ (the Vc_j and θ_j information excluded), for any $j \in \{1,...,n\}$,
- Ψ_j be the set of qn-reconciliations formed at node $Cl_j\theta_j$, for any $j \in \{1,...,n\}$,
- Π_j be the set of n-substitutions resulting from the compositions $\theta_j \circ \psi_j$ for ψ_j varying in Ψ_j, for any $j \in \{1,...,n\}$.

Summing up, the subtree ST_i takes the form of Figure 5.11. Each subtree ST_child_j has a R-depth strictly less than D. The induction hypothesis can then be applied to them. It follows that, for any j,

$$\text{comp}(P) \models \forall_{\text{var}(Cl_j\theta_j)} [\ Cl_j\theta_j \Leftrightarrow \text{Dform}(\Psi_j;\text{var}(Cl_j\theta_j))]$$

The definition of comp(P) and the use of brand new variables at each reduction step lead to another relation :

$$\text{comp}(P) \models \forall_{\text{var}(L_i)} [\ L_i \Leftrightarrow [\ \exists_{S_1}(\text{Form}^*(\theta_1) \wedge Cl_1\theta_1) \vee \ldots \vee \exists_{S_n}(\text{Form}(\theta_n) \wedge Cl_n\theta_n)\ ]\ ]$$

where, for any $j \in \{1,\ldots,n\}$, S_j denotes the set $[\text{var}(\theta_j) \cup \text{var}(Cl_j\theta_j)] \backslash \text{var}(L_i)$. As by construction of the and/or/not search trees, any variable of $\text{var}(\theta_j) \backslash \text{var}(Cl_j\theta_j)$ does not appear in Ψ_j, it follows that

$$\text{comp}(P) \models \forall_{\text{var}(L_i)} [\ L_i \Leftrightarrow [\ \exists_{S_1}(\text{Form}^*(\theta_1) \wedge \text{Dform}(\Psi_1;\text{var}(Cl_1\theta_1) \cup \text{var}(L_i)))$$

$$\vee \ldots \vee$$

$$\exists_{S_n}(\text{Form}^*(\theta_n) \wedge \text{Dform}(\Psi_n;\text{var}(Cl_n\theta_n) \cup \text{var}(L_i)))\ ]\ ] .$$

The definition of the Π_j's and Proposition 5.48 then lead to

$$\text{comp}(P) \models \forall_{\text{var}(L_i)} [\ L_i \Leftrightarrow [\ \exists_{S_1}(\text{Dform}(\Pi_1;\text{var}(Cl_1\theta_1) \cup \text{var}(L_i)))$$

$$\vee \ldots \vee$$

$$\exists_{S_n}(\text{Dform}(\Pi_n;\text{var}(Cl_n\theta_n) \cup \text{var}(L_i)))\ ]\ ] .$$

As Proposition 5.48 ensures consistency, restriction operated to obtain the n-substitutions of Σ_i from the n-substitutions from the Π_j's can be done safely. Referring to the disjunctive definition of Dform, the desired relation results:

$$\text{comp}(P) \models \forall_{\text{var}(L_i)} [\ L_i \Leftrightarrow \text{Dform}(\Sigma_i)\ ] .$$

2.2.2 The literal L_i is a ns-goal

In case L_i is a negative literal, say not(A), the subtree ST_i is formed of the ns-goal-node not(A) and the and/or/not search tree, say T', for A and P. Let Λ be the set of n-substitutions of the solution subtrees of T'. The tree T' is of R-depth strictly less than D. The induction thus applies to it and delivers

$$\text{comp}(P) \models \forall_{\text{var}(A)} [\ A \Leftrightarrow \text{Dform}(\Lambda;\text{var}(A))]$$

and, thus,

$$\text{comp}(P) \models \forall_{\text{var}(A)} [\ \neg A \Leftrightarrow \neg \text{Dform}(\Lambda;\text{var}(A))]$$

that is, as $\text{var}(A) = \text{var}(L_i)$,

$$\text{comp}(P) \models \forall_{\text{var}(L_i)} [\ L_i \Leftrightarrow \neg \text{Dform}(\Lambda;\text{var}(L_i))]$$

Assertion P then results from the relation of Λ and Σ_i.

- If Λ is negatable wrt var(L_i) then Σ_i is, by construction, one negation of Λ wrt var(L_i). In this case, the definition of the negation and consistency of the n-substitution of Λ wrt to var(L_i) delivers

    comp(P) $|= \forall_{\text{var}(L_i)}$ [$\neg$Dform(Λ;var(L_i)) $\Leftrightarrow$ Dform(Σ_i)].

    It results that

    comp(P) $|= \forall_{\text{var}(L_i)}$ [$L_i \Leftrightarrow$ Dform(Σ_i)].

- If Λ is not negatable, then
    - Dform(Λ) is a tautology, thanks to Definitions 5.8 and 5.22
    - Σ_i is empty, by construction, and Dform(Σ_i) is unsatisfiable.

    The relation

    comp(P) $|= \forall_{\text{var}(L_i)}$ [$L_i \Leftrightarrow$ Dform(Σ_i)].

    holds thus in this case too.

2.2° Proving the thesis from P

Summing up the results of point 2.1, we have, for any $i \in \{1,...,m\}$,

comp(P) $|= \forall_{\text{var}(L_i)}$ [$L_i \Leftrightarrow$ Dform(Σ_i;var(L_i))].

Since, for any i, one variable of any L_i appears in Dform(Σ_j) iff it appears in L_j (thanks to the definition of and/or/not search trees), it follows that

comp(P) $|= \forall_{\text{var}(L_1,...,L_m)}$ [($L_1 \wedge ... \wedge L_m$) $\Leftrightarrow$ (Dform(Σ_1;var($L_1,...,L_m$))

$$\wedge ... \wedge$$

Dform(Σ_m;var($L_1,...,L_m$)))].

Proposition 5.48 and the consistency ensured by qn-reconciliation then deliver the relation

comp(P) $|= \forall_{\text{var}(L_1,...,L_m)}$ [($L_1 \wedge ... \wedge L_m$) $\Leftrightarrow$ Dform($\{v_1,...,v_n\}$,var($L_1,...,L_m$))] . $\Diamond$

C. G-soundness

We are now in position to establish the soundness of the extended model with an infinite R-depth parameter.

Theorem 5.50 Let P be a general Horn clause program and $\leftarrow L_1, ..., L_m$ be a general query. Then every computed answer n-substitution v for $\leftarrow L_1, ..., L_m$ and for P is such that

comp(P) $|= (L_1 \wedge ... \wedge L_m)\alpha$

for any substitution α of ground($(L_1,...,L_m);\alpha$).

Proof The theorem is established by induction on the R-depth D of the solution subtree ST from which v is issued.

1° D is null

If D is null, then no reduction occurs and the query $\leftarrow L_1, \ldots, L_m$ is empty. In this case, v is $(\{\}, \text{not}\{\})$ and one obviously has, for the substitution α,

$\text{comp}(P) \models (L_1 \wedge \ldots \wedge L_m)\alpha$.

2° D is strictly positive

If D is strictly positive, then the query $\leftarrow L_1, \ldots, L_m$ is not empty. As the order of the L_i's only influences the left-to-right reading of the subtrees attached to them, it may be assumed that the first p L_i's correspond to ns-goals whereas the other ones correspond to ps-goals. The query can then be rewritten as

$\leftarrow \text{not}(A_1), \ldots, \text{not}(A_p), A_{p+1}, \ldots, A_m$

where the A_i's are atoms. With these notations, the subtree ST can be characterized as composed of

- for any $i \in \{1,\ldots,p\}$, the subtree, say ST_i, formed of
    - the node $\text{not}(A_i)$, as root node,
    - the subtree, say ST_{i_aux}, formed of all the solution subtrees of $ST(A_i, ST)$;
- for any $i \in \{p+1,\ldots,m\}$, the subtree, say ST_i, formed of
    - the node A_i, as root node,
    - one solution subtree attached to one $\leftarrow Cl_i\theta_i$ where Cl_i is the body of a clause unifiable with A_i and θ_i is an idempotent mgu of A_i and the clause.

Moreover, the n-substitution v is obtained by qn-reconciling (wrt the variables of $A_1, \ldots, A_m$) one n-substitution, say v_i, issued from each subtree ST_i.

To establish the thesis, let us first prove that, for any i, the relation

$\text{comp}(P) \models A_i\alpha_i$

holds for any substitution $\alpha_i \in \text{ground}(A_i; v_i)$. This is achieved by distinguishing the ns-goals from the ps-goals.

1° For $i \in \{1,\ldots,p\}$

Fix some i in $\{1,\ldots,p\}$. As ST is finite, the subtree ST_{i_aux} is also finite. Lemma 5.49 can thus be applied. The following relation follows :

$\text{comp}(P) \models \forall_{\text{var}(A_i)} [\ A_i \Leftrightarrow \text{Dform}(\Sigma_i; \text{var}(A_i))\ ]$

where Σ_i denotes all the n-reconciliation-substitutions of ST_{i_aux}. Applying the derivation of point 2.2.2 of the proof of Lemma 5.49 then results in the following relation :

$\text{comp}(P) \models \forall_{\text{var}(A_i)} [\ \neg A_i \Leftrightarrow \text{Dform}(\Lambda_i; \text{var}(A_i))\ ]$

where Λ_i is the set of n-substitutions resulting from the negation of Σ_i. As v_i is a member of Λ_i, any grounding substitution α_i of ground($A_i;v_i$) thus verifies

   comp(P) $|= \neg\ A_i\alpha_i$.

2° For $i \in \{p+1,...,m\}$

As for any $i \in \{p+1,...,m\}$, the subtree ST_i is of R-depth strictly less than D, the induction hypothesis can be applied and directly leads to

   comp(P) $|= Cl_i\theta_i\beta_i$

for any substitution β_i of ground($Cl_i\theta_i;\mu_i$), where μ_i is the n-substitution from which v_i is issued. Applying the reasoning of point 2.2.1 of the demonstration of Lemma 5.49 then leads to

   comp(P) $|= A_i\alpha_i$

for any substitution α_i of ground($A_i;v_i$)

The thesis can now be quite directly proved. It results from the fact that, for any qn-reconciliation of $v_1, ..., v_m$, any substitution α of ground($(L_1,...,L_m);\rho$) is also a substitution of any set ground($A_i;v_i$), for any $i \in \{1,...,m\}$. Therefore, one has, for any such ρ, for any substitution α of ground($(L_1,...,L_m);\rho$) and for any $i \in \{1,...,m\}$,

   comp(P) $|= L_i\alpha$

Hence, using the same notations, the relation

   comp(P) $|= (L_1 \wedge ... \wedge L_m)\alpha$

holds. The thesis then results from the fact that, as any qn-reconciliation-substitution ρ wrt var($L_1,...,L_m$) is consistent wrt to the set var($L_1,...,L_m$), any ground substitution of ground($(L_1,...,L_m),v$) is also a substitution of ground($(L_1,...,L_m);\rho^*$) where ρ^* is the n-substitution from which v is issued by restriction. ◊

D. G-completeness

Although the negation has been introduced to model the real negation as close as possible, the Conclog model is not complete. Consider, for instance, the query

   ← p(X)

and the program

   p(X) ← q(X).
   p(X) ← not(q(X)).
   q(f(X)) ← q(X).

Manifestly, the relation

$$\text{comp}(P) \models \forall X\ p(X)$$

holds. However it is not confirmed by the model. Indeed, the execution goes into an infinite branch when it computes q(X).

In fact, this example points out the limit of the negation as failure. Whatever rule is chosen to reduce the positive s-goals, negation-as-failure cannot be identical to the real negation. In counterpart, it has the advantage to be cheap to integrate : integrating real negation requires the full power of resolution and is generally considered as non viable. This does not however mean that negation as failure is useless. Completeness can be proved in significant situations. The Conclog model is not an exception to this state of affairs. The following proposition gives some g-completeness result.

Proposition 5.51 Let P be a general Horn clause program and $\leftarrow L_1,...,L_m$ be a general query. Assume that P is such that for any ns-goal N involved by $L_1, ..., L_m$, the and/or/not search tree for P and N is finite. Then, for any substitution α of ground($L_1,...,L_m$) such that

$$\text{comp}(P) \models (L_1 \wedge ... \wedge L_m)\alpha,$$

there is a computed answer n-substitution ν such that $\alpha \in \text{ground}((L_1,...,L_m);\nu)$.

Proof The hypothesis of the and/or/not search tree attached to ns-goals ensures that any solution subtree attached to such an ns-goal is finite. Lemma 5.49 then proves that, for any ns-goal N, any solution of N is covered by a computed answer n-substitution of N. The thesis then results from the completeness result of the basic model : any solution for any ps-goal is covered by a solution subtree. ◊

Note that this result states the more general situation where the negation as failure rule can be proved complete. The Conclog negation is thus as complete as possible when the negation as failure rule and the resolution principle are used.

5.5.3 General models

G-soundness and g-completeness properties may be proved to be preserved for general models as for the basic model. All properties used for the reconciliation have indeed been extended to the n-reconciliation in Chapter 3. The demonstrations of Section 4.5.3 need thus basically to be rephrased in our extended context. The only technical point that might appear obscure concerns the instantiation procedure, in particular the node removal. It is justified as follows.

Consider some computed and/or/not search tree T. Consider some goal $\leftarrow L_1,..., L_m$ and the subtree, say ST, it engenders. Let Ψ be the set of n-reconciliation-substitutions produced at the goal and ψ be the n-substitution to be made public. It may be proved, by a straightforward adaptation of the proof of Lemma 5.49, that

$$\text{comp}(P) \models \forall_{\text{var}(L_1,...,L_m)}\ [\ (L_1 \wedge ... \wedge L_m) \Rightarrow \text{Dform}(\Psi;\text{var}(L_1,...,L_m))\ ].$$

By construction, the n-substitution ψ verifies the relation

$$\forall_{var(L_1,...,L_m)} [\text{ Dform}(\Psi;var(L_1,...,L_m)) \Rightarrow \text{Form}(\psi;var(L_1,...,L_m))].$$

For any value for the variables of $var(L_1,...,L_m)$, evaluating the conjunction $L_1 \wedge ... \wedge L_m$ thus amounts to evaluating the conjunction

$$L_1 \wedge ... \wedge L_m \wedge \text{Form}(\psi;var(L_1,...,L_m))$$

or the conjunction

$$(L_1 \wedge \text{Form}(\psi;var(L_1,...,L_m))) \wedge ... \wedge (L_m \wedge \text{Form}(\psi;var(L_1,...,L_m))).$$

Restated in other terms, for any value for the variables of $var(L_1,...,L_m)$, unsastifiability of one

$$L_i \wedge \text{Form}(\psi;var(L_1,...,L_m))$$

thus implies the unsatisifiability of the conjunction L_1, ..., L_m. Let us thus turn to the satisfiablility of formula

$$\exists_{var(L_1,...,L_m)} [L_i \wedge \text{Form}(\psi;var(L_1,...,L_m))].$$

1° Literal L_i is a ps-goal

If L_i is a ps-goal, let

$H_1 \leftarrow Cl_1.$

...

$H_n \leftarrow Cl_n.$

be the clauses of the considered program that unify with it, say with idempotent en-mgu's $\theta_1 \oplus \Theta_1$, ..., $\theta_n \oplus \Theta_n$. Then, thanks to our completion understanding of the programs, one has

$\text{comp}(P) \models \forall_{var(L_i)} [L_i \Leftrightarrow \exists_{var(H_1,Cl_1)} (\text{Form}(\theta_1 \oplus \Theta_1;var(L_1) \cup var(H_1,Cl_1)) \wedge Cl_1\_\text{inst}$
$\vee ... \vee$
$\exists_{var(H_n,Cl_n)} (\text{Form}(\theta_n \oplus \Theta_n;var(L_n) \cup var(H_n,Cl_n))$
$\wedge Cl_n\_\text{inst}].$

where each Cl_i_inst denotes the instance of Cl_i by the $\theta_i \oplus \Theta_i$ (rewritten as a conjunction). Thanks to the brand new renaming of the variables at each reduction step, we thus have

$\text{comp}(P) \models \forall_{var(L_i)}$

$[L_i \wedge \text{Form}(\psi;var(L_1,...,L_m)) \Leftrightarrow$

$(\exists_{var(H_1,Cl_1)} (\text{Form}(\theta_1 \oplus \Theta_1;var(L_1) \cup var(H_1,Cl_1)) \wedge Cl_1\_\text{inst})$
$\wedge \text{Form}(\psi;var(L_1,...,L_m))))$

$\vee ... \vee$

$(\exists_{var(H_n,Cl_n)} (\text{Form}(\theta_n \oplus \Theta_n;var(L_n) \cup var(H_n,Cl_n)) \wedge Cl_n\_\text{inst})$
$\wedge \text{Form}(\psi;var(L_1,...,L_m))))].$

Obviously, the contribution of any conjunction

$$(\exists_{var(H_1,Cl_1)} (Form(\theta_j \oplus \Theta_j; var(L_j) \cup var(H_j,Cl_j)) \wedge Cl_{j\_}inst)$$
$$\wedge Form(\psi; var(L_1,...,L_m)))$$

can be removed in case it reveals to be unsatisfiable. This precisely occurs when the (extended) conjunction $Cl_{j\_}inst$ is not instantiable by the n-substitution ψ (see Definition 5.34). The satisfiability problem can furthermore be continued with each s-goal of $Cl_{j\_}inst$. The treatment of any such goal results from a recursive application of the reasoning we are describing.

2° Literal L_i is a ns-goal

Assume now L_i is an ns-goal, say not(G). We have to consider the satisfiability of

$$\exists_{var(L_1,...,L_m)} [L_i \wedge Form(\psi; var(L_1,...,L_m))].$$

that is of

$$\exists_{var(L_1,...,L_m)} [\neg G \wedge Form(\psi; var(L_1,...,L_m))]$$

This formula is identical to the following one

$$\exists_{var(L_1,...,L_m)} (\neg [G \wedge Form(\psi; var(L_1,...,L_m))] \wedge Form(\psi; var(L_1,...,L_m)))$$

Hence, instantiation can be pursued in the subtree attached to the conjunction G by using the recursive reasoning under development.

Some remark must finally be added to this reasoning. It applies well to our scheme but provided that the formula $Form(\psi; var(L_1,...,L_m))$ is indeed fulfilled by the n-reconciliation-substitutions of $\leftarrow L_1,...,L_m$ as they result after instantiation. This is ensured in the model by keeping already discovered solution subtrees free from instantiation (see Definition 5.34).

5.5.4 Variants of the model

Let us finally turn to the g-soundness and g-completeness of the variants and extensions of the model presented in Section 5.4.

- It is manifestly the aim of the previous section to establish that the R-depth parameter of the model does not influence the g-soundness and g-completeness of the model.
- The binding publication may be done according to the variants of Sections 4.4 and 5.4.1.2. All these variants deliver n-substitutions ψ that still verify

$$\forall_{var(L_1,...,L_m)} [Dform(\Psi; var(L_1,...,L_m)) \Rightarrow Form(\psi; var(L_1,...,L_m))].$$

  The developments of the previous section thus hold.
- N-substitutions can be restricted according to the variant proposed in Section 5.4.1.3. N-substitutions can indeed be just n-reconciled by goal-processes and transmitted by ps-goals and this without testing them for consistency nor restricting them. As a result

inconsistent and unrestricted n-subtitutions may be transmitted by ps-goal-processes and goal-processes. This is not of real importance thanks to the following properties :
- all manipulated n-substitutions are idempotent;
- variables introduced in a Vc set of a goal-process P are not manipulated by ancestor processes of P.

They ensure that the test for consistency and restriction can be operated either when all n-reconciliations have been performed or at each n-reconciliation. It is thus sufficient to make them at ns-goal-processes and query-processes.
- Finally, variants proposed in Sections 5.4.1.4, 5.4.1.5. and 5.4.2 have obviously been designed so as to preserve the computed answer n-substitutions and thus the g-soundness and g-completeness properties.

5.6 Comparison with related work

Six kinds of related negation can be pointed out from the literature :
- classical Prolog negation, embodied in Prolog,
- delayed negation, embodied in Prolog dialects such as Nu-Prolog ([Naish, 1986]) and Prolog II ([Giannesini et al., 1986]),
- negation by complex solutions, proposed in [Khabaza, 1984],
- negation by constraints, proposed in [Wallace, 1987],
- constructive negation, proposed in [Chan, 1988] and [Chan, 1989],
- negation by failure substitutions, proposed in [Maluszynski and Näslund, 1989].

We now compare the Conclog form with them. Furthermore, we discuss its relationship with
- work of constraint logic programming ([Giannesini et al., 1986], [Colmerauer, 1987], [Jaffar et al., 1986], [Jaffar and Lassez, 1987], [Jaffar and Michaylov, 1987], [Van Hentenrijck, 1987]),
- work about transformations of programs ([Sato and Tamaki, 1984], [Barbuti et al., 1987], [Barbuti et al., 1990]),
- a deduction procedure for first order programs ([Lugiez, 1989]).

5.6.1 Classical Prolog negation

Prolog negation is a direct application of the negation as failure rule. Any ns-goal, say not(G), is reduced in two steps :
- first, by reducing the goal G,
- second, by inverting the results of this reduction, thus reporting
    - failure if the reduction of G is successful,
    - success if the reduction of G fails.

In both cases, no bindings at all are delivered.

This form of negation leads to two kinds of problems. First, although this might appear to be correct, g-soundness and g-completeness problems can occur. Second, unprecised results are produced by the g-sound computations.

A. G-soundness and g-completeness problems

G-soundness problems are quite easy to illustrate. Consider the simple query

← not(not(X=1)), X=2.

Prolog acts as follows :

- First, the ns-goal not(not(X=1)) is reduced. This is achieved in three steps :
    - X=1 is reduced with success;
    - the success is then negated and failure is reported by the reduction of the ns-goal not(X=1),
    - failure is negated and success is reported by the ns-goal not(not(X=1)).
- Second, the ps-goal X=2 is reduced successfully and reports the substitution {X/2}.

Summing up, the substitution {X/2} is reported whereas the query should manisfestly fail.

Because of negation, the g-soundness problem can be closely related to the g-completeness problem. Consider, for instance, the query

← not(p(X)).

with the one-clause program

p(X) ← not(not(X=1)), X=2.

It is the negation of the above query. Failure is reported whereas p(X) holds for any X.

The problem arises in fact from variables. Any ns-goal not(G) is interpreted as

$\neg (\exists_{var(G)} G)$

whereas it should be interpreted as

$\exists_{var(G)} (\neg G)$.

The two formulae are equivalent only in the two following situations :

- when no variables are present in the ns-goal,
- when, referring to the above notations, $\forall_{var(G)} G$ holds.

Prolog negation is viable in these two situations only. In contrast, the Conclog negation was proved g-sound in all situations in Section 5.5. Furthermore, g-completeness has been proved when the reduction of ns-goals does not go into the computation of infinite subtrees. In particular, in the above example, the n-substitution ({},not{}) is indeed delivered as the only computed answer n-substitution.

B. Problems of precision

G-soundness problems of Prolog are also closely related to problems of precision. Consider for instance, the query

← not(not(X=1)).

Prolog negation simply answers successfully. This can be interpreted in two ways :
- as the fact that not(not(X=1)) holds for any X,
- as the fact that not(not(X=1)) holds for some X.

The first interpretation is the usual one. It obviously leads to problems of g-soundness. The second one results from the negation as failure rule philosophy. In this case however some precision is highly desired. It would avoid the incorrect answer to the query

← not(not(X=1)), X=2.

Note that this does not occur in Conclog. The n-substitution ({X/1},not{}) is indeed produced in answer to the query

← not(not(X=1)).

The problem is that no bindings are output by ns-goals in Prolog. Ns-goals then act passively. In contrast, they act actively in Conclog. This has been made possible thanks to the introduction of negative information in n-substitutions. Although this information results from theoretical reasons of representing solutions of systems of equations and inequations in finite terms, n-substitutions turn out to be a very elegant representation of infinite number of solutions. This has already been suggested by the above example. It is furthermore strengthened by the following efface example ([Deville, 1990]). The specification is as follows :

efface(X,L,L_eff) holds iff X occurs in L and L_eff is L where the first occurrence of X has been removed.

This relation can be defined by the following equivalence

$$efface(X,L,L\_eff)$$

$$\Updownarrow$$

$$\exists\ H,\ T,\ L\_eff\_rem\ :$$
$$L=[H|T] \wedge [\ (H=X \wedge T=L\_eff)\ \vee\ (H \neq X \wedge L\_eff=[H|L\_eff\_rem] \wedge efface(X,T,L\_eff\_rem)\ ]$$

It is thus defined by the following general Horn clauses

efface(X,[X|T],T).
efface(X,[H|T],[H|L_eff_rem]) ← not(X=H), efface(X,T,L_eff_rem).

Consider the query

← efface(X,L,[1,2]).

Intuitively the answers are

L=[X,1,2],
L=[1,X,2] and X≠1,
L=[1,2,X] and X≠1, X≠2.

Conclog indeed finds them, as shown in Figure 5.12. Note that, in contrast, Prolog has a very poor behavior. Indeed it only finds the first answer since, whatever place the ns-goal not(X=H) takes in the above clause, the variable X is never instantiated at the time of the reduction.

5.6.2 Suspended negation

G-soundness problems of Prolog have been solved in some Prolog dialects (e.g. Nu-Prolog ([Naish, 1986]), Prolog II ([Giannesini et al., 1986]) by modifying the left-to-right rule of selection of s-goals inside a goal as follows : the reduction of any ns-goal is delayed until it is ground. G-soundness is then achieved. However, this is not sufficient to solve all the problems mentioned above. Infinite suspension occurs when all literals are unground ns-goals. This is known as the floundering problem. As a result, completeness problems appear in another way. For instance, the same poor behavior is achieved in the above efface example : the evaluation of the ns-goal not(X=H) suspends forever since the variable X, in the ns-goal not(X=H), is never instantiated.

Conclog constrasts with such systems. By making ns-goals act actively, it is manifestly not affected by the floundering problem.

5.6.3 Negation by complex solutions

Negation by complex solutions [Khabaza, 1984] is the closest work to our negation. It is based on the complex solutions introduced in Section 3.4.2. The reconciliation of such structures have already been discussed there. Two points should furthermore be pointed out after the presentation of the Conclog model.

1° Complex solutions are essentially handled in the same way as in Conclog (of course, with the adaptations required by the syntax). Yet, no care is taken for the quantification of variables. In particular, no restriction is operated by any process. This is however crucial for the correctness of the model, as explained in Section 5.4.1.3. Omitting them thus makes the model of [Khabaza, 1984] incorrect !

2° Like the model of [Pollard, 1981], the model of [Khabaza, 1984] does not include any binding publication. This is however quite interesting, as we argued in Section 4.6.1.

The merits of the complex solution and n-substitution/es-nsubst representation should finally be discussed. Section 3.4.2 has revealed the equivalence of the two representations as far as the n-reconciliation is concerned. The negation of complex solutions and of n-substitutions/es-nsusbt's gives an additional criteria of comparison. However, negating complex solutions implies the computation of a similar cartesian product, the same negation of bindings and n-reconciliations. Therefore, negation does not separate the representations. This transposes in all other auxiliary treatments performed by processes. The two representations are thus equivalent as far as the performance of the computation is concerned. Nevertheless, the n-substitutions or their compact es-nsusbt representation constitute a more elegant representation of the information contained in solution subtrees. As this generally necessitates several complex solutions, it is, to our opinion, more natural to represent this information by disjunction of conjunctions of equalities/inequalities (i.e. sets of n-substitutions) than by disjunction of conjunctions, some of them being disjunction of inequalities (i.e. sets of complex solutions).

5.6.4 Negation by constraints

A. Description

Negation by constraints ([Wallace, 1987]) has also some similarities with our form of negation. It replaces the usual negation as failure rule by using the program completion directly. Precisely, if

$$\forall X_1, ..., X_m [p(X_1,...,X_m) \Leftrightarrow E_1 \vee ... \vee E_n]$$

is the completed definition of the procedure p, then the negative literal

$$not(p(t_1,...,t_m))$$

is reduced to

$$\leftarrow (\neg E_1 \wedge ... \wedge \neg E_n)\{X_1/t_1,...,X_m/t_m\}.$$

In general, such a goal is not a conjunction of literals but an arbitrary formula involving the connectives

$\vee$

$\wedge$ (rewriting the usual "," goal separator)

$\neg$ (rewriting the usual not predicate)

and the $\exists$ and $\forall$ quantifiers. It follows that the resolution rule has to be extended to handle such formulas. This is achieved in [Wallace, 1987] by means of ordered sets of constraints.

A constraint is either a so-called finite constraint, of the form $X \in$ Set, or a so-called co-finite constraint of the form $X \notin$ Set. The set

350   INCORPORATING NEGATION

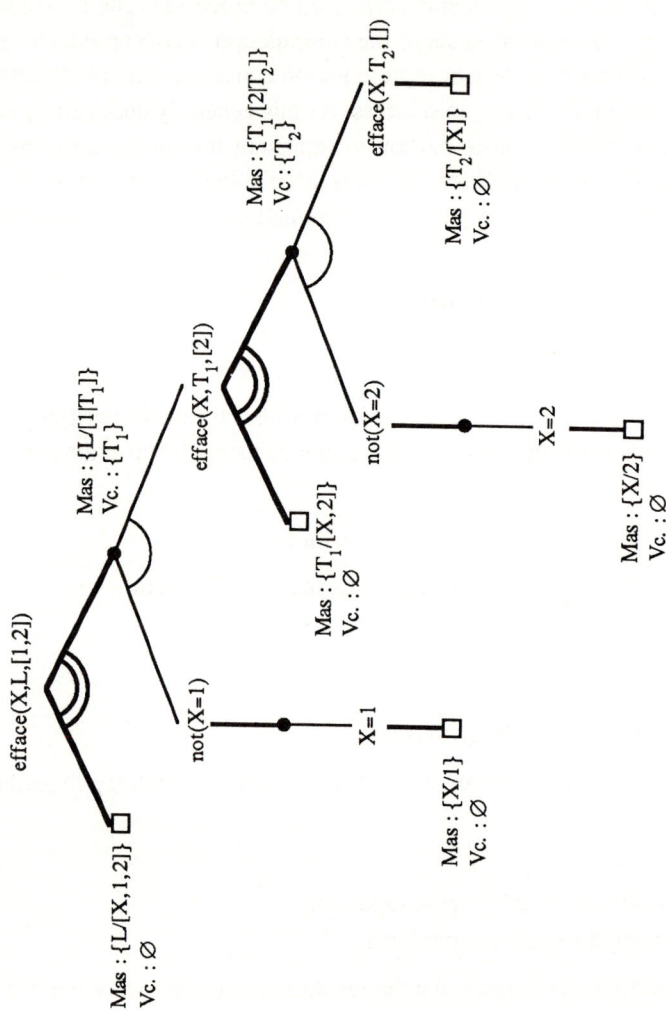

Figure 5.12 (a) : generation phase

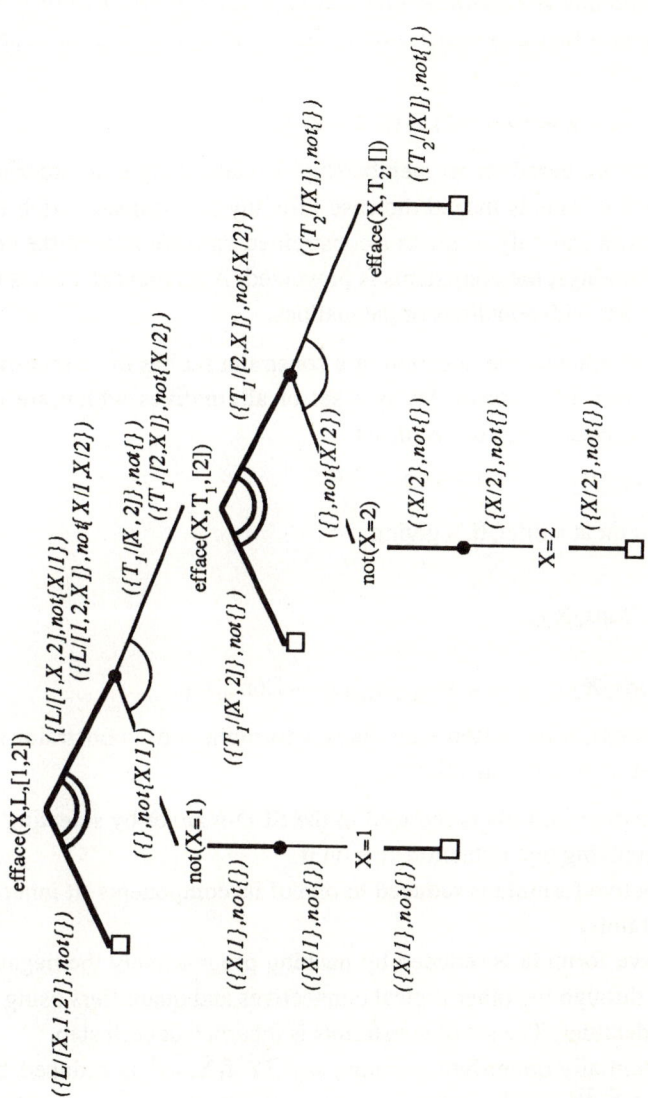

Figure 5.12 (b) : reconciliation phase

$(X \in \{1,Y,2,Z\}, Y \notin \{Z\}, Z \in \{3,4\})$

is an example of constraint sets. The first constraint is a finite one that constrains X to be either 1, Y, 2 or Z. The second one is a co-finite one that imposes Y to differ from Z. The last one is a finite one that expresses that Z is either 3 or 4. Thus, the whole constraint set represents the conjunction

$(X=1 \vee X=Y \vee X=2 \vee X=Z) \wedge (Y \neq Z) \wedge (Z=3 \vee Z=4)$.

This representation -based on set membership- is viable only if an ordering is imposed on the constrained variable. This is indeed the case : for any constrained variable, a constraining variable in its constraint can only occur as a constrained variable later in the constraint set. By this way, circularity amongst the constraints is prevented. A special calculus is then provided to increment constraint sets with equalities or inequalities.

To complete the scheme, the negation of a constraint set has to be specified. This is done by treating the negation of a constraint as a set of alternatives which are evaluated using standard backtracking. Hence the constraint set

$Cons_1 X_1 \wedge Cons_2 X_2 \wedge \ldots \wedge Cons_n X_n$

is negated one constraint at a time, this giving

$\neg Cons_1 X_1,$
$Cons_1 X_1 \wedge \neg Cons_2 X_2,$
$\ldots,$
$Cons_1 X_1 \wedge Cons_2 X_2 \wedge \ldots \wedge Cons_{n-1} X_{n-1} \wedge \neg Cons_n X_n.$

Given this context, a reduction step takes a formula and a constraint set and yields a derived constraint set. It operates as follows.

1) A conjunctive formula is reduced in the SLD-manner by selecting one component and by applying one reduction step on it.
2) A disjunctive formula is reduced to one of its components. It inherits the initial set of constraints.
3) A negative formula is reduced by pushing progressively the negation inwards the formula through the other logical connectives and quantifiers using the well-known logical identities. The set of constraints is inherited at each step.
4) An existentially quantified formula, say $\exists \bar{Y}\ f(\bar{X},\bar{Y})$[1] is reduced by reducing the formula $f(\bar{X},\bar{Y})$ and by conserving the constraints on $\bar{X}$ only. If the reduction is successful, the empty conjunction is returned as the derived formula. The

---

[1] We use the notation $f(\bar{X},\bar{Y})$ to point out the variables of the formula. It is worth stressing that $f(\bar{X},\bar{Y})$ is not necessarily a predicate whose arguments are variable. The vector Y contains the variables that are existentially quantified. The vector X contains the other ones.

constraints computed for X added to the initial ones are furthermore returned as the derived set of constraints. Otherwise, the reduction fails.

5) A universally quantified formula $\forall \overline{Y}\ f(\overline{X},\overline{Y})$ is reduced in two steps:
   - the formula $f(\overline{X},\overline{Y})$ is first reduced, the constraints on the variables of $\overline{X}$ being only conserved;
   - the resulting set of constraints on the variables of $\overline{X}$ is then progressively tightened so that $f(\overline{X},\overline{Y})$ holds for any value of the variables of $\overline{Y}$ (the precise calculus is out of interest for our discussion and is consequently not developed).

   If this reduction is successful then the empty conjunction is returned as the derived formula and the constraints computed for X added to the initial ones are returned as the derived set of constraints. Otherwise, the reduction fails.

6) A negative literal is reduced as indicated at the beginning of this section, the set of constraints being inherited. Inequalities are reduced by simply adding them to the set of constraints.

7) A positive literal is reduced as usual by searching for a unifiable clause and by replacing it by the induced instance of the clause bodies. Consistency with the given set of constraints is furthermore operated. The derived set of constraints is obtained by adding the unifier to the initial set of constraints.

Any computation then consists of a SLD-derivation extended as described above. Backtracking is used to explore the various alternative reductions. To improve the execution, it extends standard backtracking in the following way : at any choice point P, the bindings performed subsequently to P are not only removed but the constraint set corresponding to P is augmented by the negation of the constraints computed after P.

B. Comparison

Negation by constraints manifestly takes place in the usual depth-first logic programming style. As a consequence, no reference is done to a parallel computing scheme and, in particular, to reconciliation.

In fact, the constraint set representation of positive and negative information as well as the negation of (extended) constraint sets do not fit our reconciliation-based approach. This should be clear for the latter point. As far as the former is concerned, let us remember that the reconciliation of {X/Y,Y/Z} with {Y/1} does not only imply to particularize X to 1 but also Z to 1. As we argued in Chapter 3, a more elegant representation to do this is to consider bindings as equalities. Hence, in our model, ordering of the bindings as operated in constraint sets is unusable and even harmful (the time lost to maintain the ordering when inserting an equality or inequality is useless).

Another difference concerns the nature of the formulas handled by the resolution rule. We could integrate negation in Conclog without extending goals to first order logic formulas. In particular, we have kept the quantification of variables implicit in the derivations. Moreover, we have avoided the heavy iterative reduction of the universally quantified formulas.

A final difference of our integration of negation concerns the induced extension of term, substitution, unification and instantiation to deal with negative information. Although constraint sets can be seen as the counterpart of the n-substitutions and although unification of an atom with a clause is extended to take constraints into account, there is, in [Wallace, 1987], no counterpart for the instantiation of terms and for our theory of n-substitutions (developed in Chapters 3 and 5).

5.6.5 Constructive negation

Constructive negation is also close to our work. It has been introduced in [Chan, 1988] and has been extended in [Chan, 1989]. Two main results issue from these works. On the one hand, an extension of the SLD-resolution rule, called SLD-CNF resolution rule, has been pointed out. On the other hand, an incremental evaluation of negative literals has been proposed.

5.6.5.1 The SLD-CNF resolution rule

A. Description

A.1 CONCEPTS

Constructive negation consists basically in reducing any negative literal not(Q) by the two following steps :

1. the query evaluation procedure is first used to simplify the unnegated goal Q to an equality formula,
2. a normalisation procedure and a negation procedure are then applied to it in order to produce answers for not(Q).

As we argued before, positive information (i.e.equations or bindings) is not in general sufficient to express these answers in finite terms. This results, in the SLD-CNF resolution, in a generalization of the goals manipulated in the derivations. They are subsequently called c-goals. They are defined by means of the notion of cs-goal, giving the counterpart of our s-goal, itself defined from the so-called simple cs-goals. [1]

---

[1] Note that this terminology is not the original one of [Chan, 1988] and [Chan, 1989]. We have adapted it for purposes of consistency of our terminology.

1) A *simple cs-goal* is one of the following constructs :
    t = u
    $\forall_{Svars} (t \neq u)$
    $p(t_1,...,t_m)$

    where t, u, t_1, ..., t_m are terms, p is a predicate name and Svars is a (possibly empty) set of variables. By extension, cs-goals of the $\forall_{Svars} (t \neq u)$ form are called inequalities.

2) A *cs-goal* is defined recursively by the two following rules :
    - a simple cs-goal is a cs-goal
    - if Svars is a (possibly empty) set of variables and if Cs_1, ..., Cs_m are cs-goals then $\neg \exists_{Svars} (Cs_1 \wedge ... \wedge Cs_m)$ is also a cs-goal.

3) A *c-goal* is a (possibly empty) conjunction of cs-goals.

The SLD-CNF resolution then consists of deriving a sequence of c-goals from an initial one. Some auxiliary concepts need first to be introduced to further precise what this means.

(i) Satisfiability and validity of inequations.

The inequality $\forall_{Svars} (t \neq u)$ is defined to be *c-unsatisfiable* if t and u can be unified with the binding of variables of Svars only. It is *c-valid* if t and u cannot be unified.

(ii) Normalized answers

Normalized answers present the composition of the substitutions of (possibly incomplete) derivations in a normal way. They are defined as follows. Let
- Svars be a set of variables
- D = ($\leftarrow Cg_1$, ..., $\leftarrow Cg_m$) be a (possibly incomplete) derivation.
- θ be the composition of unifiers from $\leftarrow Cg_1$ to $\leftarrow Cg_m$
- X_1, ..., X_n be the variables of Svars$\cap$dom(θ),
- $\bar{X}$ be the tuple $<X_1,...,X_n>$

Then, the *normalized answer* associated with D and Svars is the following formula.

1) If $\leftarrow Cg_m$ is the empty conjunction, then the normalized answer is the conjunction of equalities
    $X_1 = X_1\theta \wedge ... \wedge X_n = X_n\theta$.

2) If $\leftarrow Cg_m$ is not the empty conjunction, let I_1, ..., I_p be its inequality cs-goals and let Cs_1, ..., Cs_q be the non-inequality cs-goals. Let furthermore SrelVars be the set of variables of Cs_1, ..., Cs_q that do not appear Svars. The normalized answer is obtained from the formula
    $X_1 = X_1\theta \wedge ... \wedge X_n = X_n\theta \wedge I_1 \wedge ... \wedge I_p \wedge Cs_1 \wedge ... \wedge Cs_q$
    by applying the two following simplifications.
    - Redundant variables and equations are first removed.

If Y is a variable that is not in Svars and that is equated to one variable X_i, then all occurrences of Y are replaced by X_i. All redundant equations are furthermore removed.
- Irrelevant inequalities are then removed.

They consist of inequalities containing a free variable that is neither in Svars nor in Srelvars and that does not appear in $X_1 = X_1\theta \wedge ... \wedge X_n = X_n\theta$.

(iii) Negation of normalized answer

Normalized answers are negated in the following way. Let

- $X_1 = X_1\theta \wedge ... \wedge X_n = X_n\theta \wedge I_1 \wedge ... \wedge I_p \wedge Cs_1 \wedge ... \wedge Cs_q$ be the normalized answers to negate
- Svars be the set of variables to which it is associated
- Sxvars be varcod(θ)\Svars
- Simpvars be the set of variables of $X_1 = X_1\theta \wedge ... \wedge X_n = X_n\theta$ and of Svars
- Sexpvars be the free variables of $Cs_1 \wedge ... \wedge Cs_q$ that are not in Simpvars
- $I'_1, ..., I'_r$ be the inequalities of $\{I_1,...,I_p\}$ that contain a variable in Sexpvars
- $I''_1, ..., I''_s$ be the remaining inequalities of $\{I_1,...,I_p\}$
- $Cs'_1, ..., Cs'_v$ be the cs-goals of $\{Cs_1,...,Cs_q\}$ that contain a variable in Sexpvars
- $Cs''_1, ..., Cs''_w$ be the remaining cs-goals of $\{Cs_1,...,Cs_q\}$.

Let furthermore, for any inequation I and non-inequation cs-goal Cs, $\tilde{I}$ and $\tilde{Cs}$ denote the following negation formulas.

- The inequation I is either of the form $t \neq u$ or $\forall_S(t \neq u)$ for some set of variables S. In both cases, $\tilde{I}$ is defined as $t = u$.
- The non-inequation cs-goal Cs can be of three forms :
    $t = u$,
    $p(t_1,...,t_k)$,
    $\neg \exists_S C_1, ..., C_k$.
The negation $\tilde{Cs}$ is defined as
    $t \neq u$,
    $\neg p(t_1,...,t_k)$,
    $C_1, ..., C_k$.
respectively.

The negation of the normalized answer is composed of the following formulas

$\forall_{Sxvars}(\overline{X} \neq \overline{X}\theta)$,

$X_1 = X_1\theta \wedge ... \wedge X_n = X_n\theta \wedge \tilde{I}'_1$,

...

$X_1 = X_1\theta \wedge ... \wedge X_n = X_n\theta \wedge I'_1 \wedge ... \wedge I'_{r-1} \wedge \tilde{I}'_r$

$X_1 = X_1\theta \wedge ... \wedge X_n = X_n\theta \wedge I'_1 \wedge ... \wedge I'_r \wedge \tilde{C}s'_1$

...

$X_1 = X_1\theta \wedge ... \wedge X_n = X_n\theta \wedge I'_1 \wedge ... \wedge I'_r \wedge Cs'_1 \wedge ... \wedge Cs'_{t-1} \wedge \tilde{C}s'_v,$

$X_1 = X_1\theta \wedge ... \wedge X_n = X_n\theta \wedge I'_1 \wedge ... \wedge I'_r \wedge Cs'_1 \wedge ... \wedge Cs'_t$
$\wedge \neg \exists_{Sexpvars} (I''_1 \wedge ... \wedge I''_s \wedge Cs''_1 \wedge ... \wedge Cs''_w).$

(iv) Negation of a disjunction of normalized answers

The negation of a disjunction of normalized answers is obtained by negating each normalized answer and by combining the components.

A.2 THE RESOLUTION RULE

We are now in position to define the SLD-CNF resolution rule. Like the SLD-one, it consists of transforming step by step a given c-goal into other c-goals. Each step is also non-deterministic. It selects arbitrarily one cs-goal that is not a non-valid satisfiable inequality and transforms this input c-goal into one c-goal derivable from it. A reduction then consists of a sequence of such steps. It is completed if no c-goal can be derived from the last one. It is incompleted, otherwise. When completed, it is said to succeed iff its terminal c-goal is either the empty conjunction of cs-goals or a conjunction formed of only non-valid satisfiable inequalities. It is said to fail otherwise.

The class of c-goal derivable from a c-goal $\leftarrow Cs_1, ..., Cs_m$ and a selected cs-goal Cs_i is defined as follows.

1) If Cs_i is the equality $t=u$ then
    - if t and u are unifiable, say with mgu θ, then the only derivable c-goal is
        $\leftarrow (Cs_1,...,Cs_{i-1},Cs_{i+1},...,Cs_m)\theta$
    - otherwise, no c-goal is derivable.

2) If Cs_i is the inequality $\forall_S(t \neq u)$ then
    - if it is c-valid, the only derivable c-goal is
        $\leftarrow Cs_1,...,Cs_{i-1},Cs_{i+1},...,Cs_m$
    - if it is c-unsatisfiable, no c-goal is derivable.

3) If Cs_i is a non-equality positive cs-goal, then one derivable c-goal is associated with each unifiable clause. It is as follows. Let
    $H \leftarrow B_1,...,B_n$
    be the unifiable clause, say with mgu θ. The derived c-goal is the c-goal
        $\leftarrow (Cs_1,...,Cs_{i-1},B_1,...,B_n,Cs_{i+1},...,Cs_m)\theta.$
    There are no other derivable c-goals.

4) If Cs_i is of the form $\neg \exists_{Svars} Q$ then
    - if $\leftarrow Q$ has no successful reductions then the only derivable c-goal is

$\leftarrow Cs_1,...,Cs_{i-1},Cs_{i+1},...,Cs_m$

- otherwise, let $A_1, ..., A_m$ be all the normalized answers associated with the successful reductions of $\leftarrow Q$ and the set of free variables of $\exists_{Svars} Q$.
  - If $A_1 \vee ... \vee A_m$ is equivalent to true then no c-goal is derivable.
  - Otherwise, one derivable c-goal is associated with any formula of the negation of $(A_1 \vee ... \vee A_m)$. Let $B_1 \wedge ... \wedge B_n$ be such a formula. Then, the associated derived c-goal is
    $\leftarrow Cs_1,...,Cs_{i-1},B_1,...,B_n,Cs_{i+1},...,Cs_m$.
    There are no other derivable c-goals.

B. Comparison

Manifestly, the SLD-CNF resolution rule does not also take place in a pure parallel computing context and in particular in our reconciliation based approach. This has two consequences. First, there is no counterpart for the concept of reconciliation of n-substitutions. Second, our negation of answer n-substitutions (corresponding to that of the normalized answers) is performed in a more symmetric way.

Furthermore, inequalities are treated in Conclog in a more uniform way : they are handled as other negative literals without caring for satisfiability and validity.

Another difference with our work is that negative information plays no role during the reduction of a positive literal. Restated in other terms, unification has not been extended to handle negative information (as we did in Conclog). As a related fact, instantiation has also not been extended to deal with negative information.

A fifth difference concerns the handling of quantifiers. They are handled in an implicit way in Conclog and in an explicit way by constructive negation.

Finally, our integration of negative information in substitutions is, to our point of view, a more natural extension of answer substitution than the normalized answer is. This has allowed us to present a more intuitive introduction of negation (compare, for instance, the negation of n-substitutions and the negation of normalized answers). Another interesting consequence is that it has lead us quite naturally to develop some generalization of the usual theory of substitutions as well as some interpretation theory about them. A counterpart does not appear so clearly in the normalized answer approach and is actually not present in [Chan, 1988] and in [Chan, 1989].

5.6.5.2 Incremental constructive negation

A. Description

Reducing a negative literal by first fully reducing the associated positive literal has the drawback of postposing infinitely any answer to the negative literal when the search tree engendered by the reduction of the positive literal is infinite. To circumvent this problem, an incremental evaluation of the negative literal is necessary. It can be provided when constructed negation is used since the normalisation and negation procedures can be applied on incompleted reductions. This has been illustrated in coroutined executions in [Chan, 1989].

B. Comparison

The incremental evaluation of a negative literal is also possible in Conclog but, as Conclog rests in a parallel context, in different ways. Two means are in fact provided for this purpose.

1) On the one hand, the incremental evaluation of the negative literals arises from the slice by slice construction of the and/or/not search trees. Approximations of the answers are produced by each reconciliation phase. Furthermore, coroutining is obtained by taking 1 as the value of the R-depth parameter. Applications of [Chan, 1989] are then obtained quite naturally in the Conclog model as well.

2) On the other hand, the incremental negation of n-substitutions returned by the reduction of the associated positive literals is also possible, as described in Section 5.4.2.

5.6.6 Negation by failure substitutions

A. Description

Negation by failure substitutions ([Maluszynski and Näslund, 1989]) is an extension of the negation-as-failure principle based on the following idea. If γ is a substitution such that the query $\leftarrow G\gamma$ has a finitely failed SLD-tree then, by soundness of the negation-as-failure rule, $\forall \neg G\gamma$ is a logical consequence of the completion of the program under consideration. Therefore, reducing negative literals can be achieved by finding all such substitutions γ, called failure substitutions. Of course, only maximal substitutions need to be found and are indeed computed in [Maluszynski and Näslund, 1989]. The concepts of constrained substitutions and constrained terms, adding inequalities of terms to substitutions and terms, respectively, have been introduced for this purpose.

B. Comparison

Our n-substitutions and extended terms share some similarities with these constrained substitutions and terms. The major differences is that n-substitutions and extended terms are always presented in a normalized form and that n-substitutions may share the empty substitution as positive part. Furthermore, our theory of n-substitutions and extended terms is more elaborated than that of [Maluszynski and Näslund, 1989] where the concept of composition of substitutions is just extended.

Another difference with our work is that negation by failed substitutions only tackles sequential computations and, consequently, provides no counterpart for our concept of reconciliation of n-substitutions, our parallel form of negation and our concept of publication of n-substitutions.

5.6.7 Constraint logic programming

Although it has not been conceived in this framework, it turns out that the Conclog negation has some similarities with work made in concurrent logic programming. We pursue our comparison by relating the Conclog negation to some of them ([Giannesini et al., 1986], [Colmerauer, 1987], [Jaffar et al., 1986], [Jaffar and Lassez, 1987], [Jaffar and Michaylov, 1987], [Van Hentenrijck, 1987]).

5.6.7.1 The CLP scheme

Before turning to particular languages, we first sketch one general scheme developed to capture the semantics of a class of constraint logic languages. It is called CLP. It is issued from [Jaffar et al., 1986] and [Jaffar and Lassez, 1987].

Programs of these languages are definite Horn clauses where some constraints can be used as literals. In contrast with conventional logic programming, the computation domain is however not necessarily the Herbrand universe. It is rather left unspecified. The reduction mechanism is based on the resolution principle but constraints solving is used instead of unification. Any language of this class is defined by specifying the computation domain, the constraints and the constraint solver.

5.6.7.2 Prolog II

Although it has not been presented in this way, Prolog II ([Giannesini et al., 1986]) is a first instance of the CLP scheme. The domain of the computation is the set of finite and infinite trees. Equations and inequations are manipulated as constraints. The algorithm used to solve systems of equations is based on Gaussian elimination and is thus similar to that of [Martelli and Montanari, 1982], and thus to ours. The algorithm used to solve systems of equations and inequations uses a similar approach too : the associated systems of equations are first solved and the inequations are considered thereafter.

A computation in Prolog II then consists of a Prolog like execution extended by the resolution of the systems of equations and inequations at each reduction step. Precisely, each reduction step takes a goal and a system of equations and inequations as input and derive a new goal and a new system of equations as output. The derived goal is obtained by selecting the first literal of the input goal, by searching for a unifiable clause and by replacing this literal by the clause body (without instantiating it). The derived system of equations is the solved form of the system composed of the equations and inequations of the initial system, the equations and inequations appearing in the clause and the equation equaling the selected literal and the clause head. Of course, the reduction can only proceed in the case this system is solvable. Failure of the reduction results in backtracking as in Prolog.

Except for inequalities, negative literals have received no special treatment. They behave basically as in Prolog. Thus they essentially act as tests and produce no substitution, possibly coupled with negative information. Some delay mechanism may furthermore be used. Therefore, critics of Section 5.6.1 and 5.6.2 apply to Prolog II too.

Another difference with our work is that no negative information has been incorporated to substitutions or to terms. There is thus no counterpart for our theory of n-substitutions and to our extended instantiation notion. However, handling of systems of equations and inequations at each reduction step represents the counterpart of our use of extended unification.

A final difference issues from the computing context. As Prolog II rests in the sequential one and consequently not in our reconciliation approach, there is no counterpart of the reconciliation of n-substitutions.

5.6.7.3 Prolog III

Prolog III ([Colmerauer, 1987]) is an extension of Prolog II handling "$\leq$", "$<$", "$\geq$", "$>$" inequalities and boolean calculus. The inequations are solved by a module based on Dantzig's simplex algorithm ([Dantzig, 1963]) whereas the boolean calculus is computed by Siegel's algorithm ([Siegel, 1987]). Manifestly, such techniques are out of the scope of our context of negation handling.

5.6.7.4 The CLP(R) language

The CLP(R) language is another instance of the CLP scheme. Its computation domain is the set of real numbers R. Constraints are formed with the "$=$", "$\leq$", "$\geq$", "$<$", "$>$" operators and may involve any arithmetic functions (sin, log, ...). The equations are also solved by Gaussian elimination whereas linear inequalities are solved by an adaptation of Dantzig's simplex algorithm. A delay mechanism is used to postpone the solving of non-linear inequalities until they become linear. Inferences are performed as in Prolog II by checking the solvability of an associated set of constraints at each reduction step.

In view of its similarities with Prolog II, the comparison made in Section 5.6.6.2 applies to CLP(R) too.

5.6.7.5 The language CHIP

An alternative proposal for inequations solving has been proposed in [Van Hentenrijck, 1987] (from which the language CHIP is issued). It conserves all the features of logic programming, does not use a constraint solver but just makes use of domain declarations. Those are associated with procedures. They are used to constrain the computation domain of argument variables in finite sets. The unificiation algorithm has been extended so as to cope with them. Inequalities are handled by simply updating the computation domain of the involved variables.

Applications addressed by CHIP are mostly those where variables range in finite domains. In this context, the solutions for any query, even those involving negative literals, may be represented in finite terms by substitutions without the help of negative information. It is thus not surprising that no counterpart of our n-substitution is present in [Van Hentenrijck, 1987]. As a further consequence, there is also no notion corresponding to our extended terms and extended instantiation. The CHIP extended unification is however the counterpart of our extended unification.

Another difference with our work is that the language CHIP takes place in the sequential framework. It thus also provides no counterpart of our notion of reconciliation.

Finally, inequalities excepted, there is no treatment of negative literals. They are reduced in the Prolog way. The comparison of Section 5.6.1 thus applies to CHIP too.

5.6.8 Transformations of programs

Another way of handling negation consists of deriving, from a Horn clause program P, a new set of predicates computing the negation of the predicates of P. This approach has been first proposed in [Sato and Tamaki, 1984] in the more general context of the synthesis of logic programs from first order specifications. The synthesis rests however on a negation technique that is worth comparing with our treatment of negation. This negation technique has been extended in [Barbuti et al., 1987] in order to tackle the full class of logic programs and to compute, in more cases, non ground answer substitutions to negative queries. The latter feature has finally been improved in [Barbuti et al., 1990]. The differences in the pieces of work are quite minor for our comparative purposes. We will consquently refer essentially to the most recent work ([Barbuti et al., 1990]) to describe the transformation technique and to substantiate our comparison. Nevertheless, our discussion applies to the two other pieces of work, as well.

A. Description

Basically, the transformation technique consists of negating the completion of the given Horn clause program, of replacing each negative literal $\neg p$ by a new predicate $\tilde{p}$, and of regarding the negation of the completion as the completion defining those predicates $\tilde{p}$. To be more specific, let us recall that any logic program can be transformed in an equivalent factorized form i.e. a form where each predicate p

- is either the predicate eq, defined by the only clause
  eq(X,X).
- or is defined by a clause of one of the following forms
  (i) $p(\bar{X}) \leftarrow r(\bar{X}), s(\bar{X}).$
  (ii) $p(\bar{X}) \leftarrow r(\bar{X}) + s(\bar{X}).$ [1]
  (iii) $p(\bar{X}) \leftarrow r(\bar{X},\bar{Y}).$
  (iv) $p(\bar{t}) \leftarrow r(\bar{u}).$
  (v) $p(\bar{t}).$

where

- $\bar{X}$ and $\bar{Y}$ denote tuples of distinct variables,
- $\bar{t}$ is a tule of terms where any variable occurs at most once,
- $\bar{u}$ is a tuple of terms such that $\text{var}(\bar{t}) \supseteq \text{var}(\bar{u})$
- "+" stands for a disjunction of goals.

Such a transformation is proposed in [Barbuti et al., 1990], for instance. We may thus assume, without loss of generality, that the program P to negate is presented in a factorized form. Let us negate its completion. One gets, for clauses (i) to (v), formulae of the form

$$\forall \bar{X} [\neg p(\bar{X}) \Leftrightarrow \neg r(\bar{X}) \vee \neg s(\bar{X})] \qquad (1)$$
$$\forall \bar{X} [\neg p(\bar{X}) \Leftrightarrow \neg r(\bar{X}) \wedge \neg s(\bar{X})] \qquad (2)$$
$$\forall \bar{X} [\neg p(\bar{X}) \Leftrightarrow \forall \bar{Y} \neg r(\bar{X},\bar{Y})] \qquad (3)$$
$$\forall \bar{X} [\neg p(\bar{X}) \Leftrightarrow \forall \bar{Y} (\bar{X} \neq \bar{t} \vee \neg r(\bar{u}))] \qquad (4)$$
$$\forall \bar{X} [\neg p(\bar{X}) \Leftrightarrow \forall \bar{Y} (\bar{Y} \neq \bar{t})] \qquad (5)$$

respectively. Formula (4) can be further transformed into the equivalent formula

$$\forall \bar{X} [\neg p(\bar{X}) \Leftrightarrow (\forall \bar{Y} (\bar{X} \neq \bar{t})) \vee (\exists \bar{Y} (\bar{X} \neq \bar{t} \wedge r(\bar{u})))] \qquad (6)$$

Moreover, if we restrict the programming language $\mathcal{L}$ to one with a finite number of functions, say $c_1, ..., c_m$ of arity $n_1, ..., n_m$, respectively, and if we only consider models such that the axiom

$$\forall \bar{U} [\exists \bar{V}_1 (\bar{U} = c_1(\bar{V}_1)) \vee ... \vee \exists \bar{V}_m (\bar{U} = c_m(\bar{V}_m))] \qquad (A)$$

holds, then it is possible to find a finite set of tuples of terms $\{\bar{t}_1, ..., \bar{t}_p\}$ such that

$$\forall \bar{Y} (\bar{X} = \bar{t})$$

is equivalent to

---

[1] Actually, this clause is a shorthand for the two clauses
  $p(\bar{X}) \leftarrow r(\bar{X}).$
  $p(\bar{X}) \leftarrow s(\bar{X}).$

$$\exists \bar{Y}_1 (\bar{X} = \bar{t}_1) \vee \ldots \vee \exists \bar{Y}_p (\bar{X} = \bar{t}_p).$$

Hence, in those conditions, formulae (5) and (6) can be equivalently written as

$$\forall \bar{X} [\neg p(\bar{X}) \Leftrightarrow \exists \bar{Y}_1 (\bar{X} = \bar{t}_1) \vee \ldots \vee \exists \bar{Y}_p (\bar{X} = \bar{t}_p) \vee \exists \bar{Y} (\bar{X} = \bar{t} \wedge \neg r(\bar{u}))] \qquad (7)$$

$$\forall \bar{X} [\neg p(\bar{X}) \Leftrightarrow \exists \bar{Y}_1 (\bar{X} = \bar{t}_1) \vee \ldots \vee \exists \bar{Y}_p (\bar{X} = \bar{t}_p)] \qquad (8)$$

respectively. Let us now replace each negative literal $\neg p$ by $\tilde{p}$. Formulae (1), (2), (3), (7) and (8) become

$$\forall \bar{X} [\tilde{p}(\bar{X}) \Leftrightarrow \tilde{r}(\bar{X}) \vee \tilde{s}(\bar{X})] \qquad (9)$$

$$\forall \bar{X} [\tilde{p}(\bar{X}) \Leftrightarrow \tilde{r}(\bar{X}) \wedge \tilde{s}(\bar{X})] \qquad (10)$$

$$\forall \bar{X} [\tilde{p}(\bar{X}) \Leftrightarrow \forall \bar{Y} \tilde{r}(\bar{X},\bar{Y})] \qquad (11)$$

$$\forall \bar{X} [\tilde{p}(\bar{X}) \Leftrightarrow \exists \bar{Y}_1 (\bar{X} = \bar{t}_1) \vee \ldots \vee \exists \bar{Y}_p (\bar{X} = \bar{t}_p) \vee \exists \bar{Y} (\bar{X} = \bar{t} \wedge \tilde{r}(\bar{u}))] \qquad (12)$$

$$\forall \bar{X} [\tilde{p}(\bar{X}) \Leftrightarrow \exists \bar{Y}_1 (\bar{X} = \bar{t}_1) \vee \ldots \vee \exists \bar{Y}_p (\bar{X} = \bar{t}_p)] \qquad (13)$$

respectively. Completion-like formulae are thus obtained. The next step of the transformation consists precisely of considering Formulae (9) to (13) as various completions of the predicate $\tilde{p}$ and of deriving the corresponding clauses for $\tilde{p}$. This is quite easy to achieve for Formulae (9), (10), (12) and (13). The corresponding clauses are

$$\tilde{p}(\bar{X}) \leftarrow \tilde{r}(\bar{X}) + \tilde{s}(\bar{X}).$$
$$\tilde{p}(\bar{X}) \leftarrow \tilde{r}(\bar{X}), \tilde{s}(\bar{X}).$$

for Formulae (9) and (10), respectively,

$$\tilde{p}(\bar{t}_1).$$
$$\ldots$$
$$\tilde{p}(\bar{t}_p).$$
$$\tilde{p}(\bar{t}) \leftarrow \tilde{r}(\bar{u}).$$

for Formula (12) and

$$\tilde{p}(\bar{t}_1).$$
$$\ldots$$
$$\tilde{p}(\bar{t}_p).$$

for formula (13). Treating Formula (11) is more difficult because of the universal quantification of the variables $\bar{Y}$. A weak form of this quantification has first been proposed in [Barbuti et al., 1987]. It consists of computing $\forall \bar{Y} \tilde{r}(\bar{X},\bar{Y})$ in two steps:

(1) evaluate $\tilde{r}(\bar{X},\bar{Y})$ by using the clauses for $\tilde{r}$. Let θ be a computed answer substitution.

(2) evaluate $r(\bar{X}\theta,\bar{Z})$ where $\bar{Z}$ is a tuple of fresh variables replacing the universally quantified variables $\bar{Y}$. If the evaluation finitely fails then return $\theta_{|var(\bar{x})}$ as computed answer substitution for $\forall \bar{Y} \tilde{r}(\bar{X},\bar{Y})$.

This weak form is, in fact, a generate-and-test evaluation. The evaluation of $\tilde{r}(\bar{X},\bar{Y})$ generates candidate substitutions for $\bar{X}$ whereas the evaluation of $r(\bar{X}\theta,\bar{Z})$ checks, under negation as failure, whether the values computed for $\bar{X}$ make the original predicate finitely fail.

Although correct, this weak form is not powerful enough to guarantee completeness. Indeed, the evaluation of $r(\bar{X}\theta,\bar{Z})$ can succeed even if there is a substitution $\gamma \geq \theta$ such that $\forall \bar{Y} \; \tilde{r}(\bar{X}\gamma,\bar{Y})$ holds. A remedy has been proposed in [Barbuti et al., 1990]. It consists of refining the above step (2) as follows

(2') If the evaluation of $r(\bar{X}\theta,\bar{Z})$ has only finitely failed SLD derivations then succeed and return $\theta_{|var(\bar{X})}$ as computed answer substitution.

(2") Otherwise, instantiate further $\bar{X}\theta$, say to $\bar{X}\tau$, and repeat from step (2') for $r(\bar{X}\tau,\bar{Z})$.

The instantiation procedure is essentially achieved by means of the predicate herbrand defined by the clause

herbrand(X).

and the clause

herbrand($c_i(X_1,...,X_{n_i})$) ← herbrand(X_1), ..., herbrand(X_{n_i}).

for each function c_i. The computation induced by the herbrand predicate is however infinite in the case where one n_i is strictly positive. Hence, the actual solution of [Barbuti et al., 1990] is to cut the reduction of herbrand of further instantiations of $\bar{X}\tau$ for the τ's such that $r(\bar{X}\tau,\bar{Z})$ has only finitely failed SLD derivations.

To complete the transformation scheme, it remains to specify how predicates non defined in P and the predicate eq are negated. On the one hand, the predicate $\tilde{p}(\bar{X})$ corresponding to a predicate p not defined in P is simply defined by the clause

$\tilde{p}(\bar{X})$.

On the other hand, the procedure defining $\tilde{eq}$ is composed of the clause

$\tilde{eq}(c_i(\bar{X}),c_j(\bar{Y}))$.

with $\bar{X}$ and $\bar{Y}$ tuples of distinct variables, for each pair of distinct functor symbols c_i and c_j and of the clause

$\tilde{eq}(c_i(\bar{X}_1,...,\bar{X}_{n_i}),c_i(\bar{Y}_1,...,\bar{Y}_{n_i}))$ ← $\tilde{eq}(\bar{X}_j,\bar{X}_j)$. $(1 \leq j \leq n_i)$

for each functor c_i.

B. Comparison

Compared with Conclog, one attractive feature of the transformational approach to negation is that negation is tackled without extending terms and substitutions with negative information while negative literals can compute substitutions as the positive literals do. This is achieved essentially thanks to two restrictions : the restriction of the programming language $\mathcal{L}$ to one with a finite number of function symbols and the restriction of models to those verifying the axiom (A). We believe that the first restriction is quite constraining from a programming point of view. Indeed, the construction of a procedure should not be influenced by the construction of another (possibly unrelated) procedure. This is the reason why we have chosen to consider a universal language $\mathcal{L}$ and to define the interpretations according to it rather than the considered programs. However, in the transformational approach to negation, the terms $\bar{t}_i$ depend on the functions of the program. Hence, the procedures $\tilde{p}$ vary according to the programs containing the procedure p. As another consequence, the procedures $\tilde{p}$ cannot be incrementally derived at the rate the corresponding procedures p are constructed. This situation contrasts with Conclog where the negation of a procedure p depends on the procedure p only. Nevertheless, the transformation can be applied quite nicely as soon as the program is completely written.

Another advantage of the transformational approach to negation is that it is complete whereas that of Conclog is complete in some cases only. Consider, for instance, the program composed of the only even procedure computing the set of even numbers:

```
even(0).
even(s(s(X))) ← even(X).
```

The corresponding procedure $\widetilde{even}$ is derived therefrom as

```
even˜(s(0)).
even˜(s(s(X)))← even˜(X).
```

(see [Barbuti et al., 1987] for the transformation). The query ←not(even(X)) or ←$\widetilde{even}$(X) thus compute the set of odd numbers. In contrast, the Conclog negation falls in the infinite computation of all the solutions of even(X) and never delivers a solution.

A drawback of the transformational approach to negation is the verbosity of the procedures $\tilde{p}$. The number of terms $\bar{t}_i$ and consequently the number of the clauses

$$\tilde{p}(\bar{t}_i).$$

grows with the number of functions of the program. It can be quite important for database applications. Consider, for instance, the one-procedure program

```
parent(john,mary).
parent(john,bill).
parent(mary,paul).
parent(bill,anne).
```

Its negation $\widetilde{parent}$ is composed of 21 clauses

```
parent˜(t,u).
```

where (t,u) ranges over the set of pairs of

({john,mary,bill,paul,anne} × {john,mary,bill,paul,anne})
\ {(john,mary),(john,bill),(mary,paul),(bill,anne)}.

Similarly, the number of clauses defining $\tilde{eq}$ and herbrand is quite large for normal size programs. The memorization of those extra clauses is thus quite expensive! It is furthermore worth noting that the processing necessary to transform a given program in a factorized form introduces additional procedures for which a negative counterpart has to be derived. In contrast, in Conclog, the procedures are used to compute the negated calls to them. This expensive memorization is thus avoided.

A related drawback concerns the conciseness of the computed substitutions. In general, the n-substitutions computed in Conclog cover more soltions than the substitutions computed by the transformational approach. As an example, considering the parent procedure above, four substitutions are returned by the evaluation of $\tilde{parent}$(mary,Y) whereas one n-substitution is computed in Conclog. The comparison is even better for Conclog if procedures introducing new functions are added to the parent procedure. Another example concerns the predicate $\tilde{eq}$. As noted in [Barbuti et al., 1990], the evaluation of $\tilde{eq}$(X,f(X)) produces an infinite set of answer substitutions whereas it should intuitively succeed without binding X. In contrast, the Conclog execution computes the (intuitive) n-substitution ({},not{}).

Finally, the Conclog negation is, to our opinion, more uniform than the negation of the transformational approach. Indeed, the latter uses both a new form of negation by means of $\tilde{p}$ procedures and the negation-as-failure rule.

5.6.9 The ENF deduction procedure

A. Description

The ENF deduction procedure ([Lugiez, 1989]) is a deduction procedure for first order programs which subsumes SLDNF-resolution and which improves the handling of $\forall \overline{Y} \tilde{r}(\overline{X},\overline{Y})$ formulae of [Barbuti et al., 1990]. In a way similar to SLD-derivations, it essentially consists of progressively transforming first order formulae thanks to the clauses of the considered program and of computing, on the way, values for the variables. They are presented here in the form of conjunctions of equations and inequations, subsequently referred to as extended substitutions. This is basically achieved by means of two sets of rules. The first one aims at simplifying a first order formula into a set of canonical formulae. It is an extension of the set of rules developed in [Common and Lescanne, 1988] to transform any first order formula involving the only predicate = into a set of formulae in so-called solved form i.e. formulae that are either true, false or of the form

$$\exists \bar{Z}\ X_1 = t_1 \wedge \ldots \wedge X_m = t_m \wedge Y_1 \neq u_1 \wedge \ldots \wedge Y_n \neq u_n\ ^1$$

where the variables X_i occur only once in the equalities and inequalities and where any variable Y_j is different from any u_j ($1 \leq j \leq n$). The complete description of the rules is out of the scope of our comparison. Nevertheless, the following ones are worth pointing out

(S$_1$) If $Y \in \{Y_1, \ldots, Y_k\}$ then transform
$\forall Y_1 \ldots Y_k\ (p \wedge Y \neq t)$,
$\forall Y_1 \ldots Y_k\ (p \wedge (Y \neq t \vee d))$
into
false,
$\forall Y_1 \ldots Y_k\ (p \wedge d\{Y/t\})$,
respectively.

(S$_2$) If $f \neq g$ then transform
$f(t_1, \ldots, t_n) = g(u_1, \ldots, u_m)$,
$f(t_1, \ldots, t_n) \neq g(u_1, \ldots u_m)$
into
false,
true,
respectively.

(S$_3$) Transform
$f(t_1, \ldots, t_n) = f(u_1, \ldots, u_m)$,
$f(t_1, \ldots, t_n) \neq f(u_1, \ldots u_m)$
into
$t_1 = u_1 \wedge \ldots \wedge t_m = u_m$,
$t_1 \neq u_1 \vee \ldots \vee t_m \neq u_m$,
respectively.

(S$_4$) Transform $\forall \bar{Y}\ p$ into $\forall \bar{Y}\ (p \wedge s = f(Z_1, \ldots, Z_d))$ where the Z_i's are fresh variables. [2]

The following proposition sums up the effect of the extended set of simplification rules: under a suitable reduction strategy, any first order formula F is transformed into a set Solved(F) of formulae such that

- the set of solutions of F is equal to the union of the sets of solutions of the formulae of Solved(F),

---

[1] The notation $\exists \bar{Z}$ is used to denote the existential quantification $\exists Z_1 \ldots \exists Z_p$ over some variables $Z_1, \ldots, Z_p$.
[2] As before, $\bar{Y}$ is used to denote a tuple of variabes and $\forall \bar{Y}$ and $\exists \bar{Y}$ are used as shorthands for the quantification over this vector i.e. for $\forall Y_1 \ldots \forall Y_n$ and $\exists Y_1 \ldots \exists Y_n$, respectively.

- each quantified variable of F occurring in an equality or inequality and in the scope of a universal quantifier does not appear in Solved(F) but each quantified variable not occurring in an equality remains,
- all literals of F but those involving = are instances of literals of Solved(F).

The second set of rules defines the ENF derivation procedure. It is composed of the following rules applied according to the order (SOL)≥(SIMP)≥(R):

(R) Assume $p(\overline{t})$ is the literal selected in the formula F by some given selection function SL. Assume that def(p) is the completed definition[1] of p in the considered program. Let G denote the formula
$$\exists \overline{Z} \,[\, \overline{X} = \exists \overline{t} \wedge \text{def}(p) \,]$$
where $\overline{Z}$, $\overline{X}$ and var(def(p)) are fresh variables and where $\overline{Z}$ is composed of the variables of $\overline{X}$ and of var(def(p)). Then transform F into the formulae obtained by replacing the selected literal $p(\overline{t})$ by G.

(SIMP) Replace F by the disjunction of the formulae of the above Solved(F) set

(SOL) If E is $(X_1=t_1 \wedge \ldots \wedge X_m=t_m \wedge Y_1 \neq u_1 \wedge \ldots \wedge Y_n \neq u_n)$ and is in solved form then replace $E \vee F$ by F and produce E as extended substitution.

(T) Replace in F any tautology $p(\overline{t}) \vee \neg p(\overline{t})$ by true.

The resulting ENF procedure has been proved to be sound and to subsume the SLDNF-refutation procedure in the following sense: if L is a literal and if the goal ←L has a SLDNF-refutation then there is an ENF derivation of ←L to true.

An interesting application of the ENF deduction procedure concerns the transformation of first-order program into sets of Horn clauses. In particular, its has been shown in [Lugiez, 1989] how quantified goals $\forall \overline{Y} \, \tilde{r}(\overline{X},\overline{Y})$ can be eliminated by applying it.

B. Comparison

The ENF deduction procedure presents several similarities with our work. Negative information is also combined with the positive one to sum up solutions and, in fact, the extended substitutions are quite close to our n-substitutions. Furthermore, several rules to obtain them, namely rules (S_1), (S_2) and (S_3), are comparable to those used in Conclog. However, no theory of extended substitutions has been proposed and negative information is not employed to constrain the reduction process. Moreover, as parallel executions are not tackled, there is also no counterpart of our reconciliation concept.

A major departure with Conclog is that first order formulae are handled. Hence, as this may be suggested by the above description, the ENF deduction procedure is computationally

---

[1] This concept is defined as the straightforward extension of that defined in Definition 5.6 for general programs.

more expensive than the Conclog model. With respect to this problem, the main issues of the search strategy, namely the order of the application of the rules of the first set as well as the selection function SL and its efficient implementation, are not precised in [Lugiez, 1989] and are left for future research.

Finally, although its application to program transformation eliminates the goals of the form $\forall \overline{Y} \; \tilde{r}(\overline{X},\overline{Y})$, the ENF deduction procedure still uses the terms $\overline{t}_i$ of [Barbuti et al., 1990], as suggested by rule (S_4). The verbosity problem of the derived Horn clauses thus remains in this new transformation too.

5.7 Conclusion

This chapter has integrated negation in the basic model of Chapter 4. The Conclog negation consists of a new form of the negation as failure rule. It has been designed so as to keep and take profit of the main features of the basic model.

First, the equational framework employed in the basic model has been used here, too. Systems of equations have thus been generalized to systems of equations and inequations. Generalization of substitutions to n-substitutions to integrate negative information results. It is issued from the technical reason of providing a finite representation of solutions of systems of equations and inequations. Nevertheless, n-substitutions have revealed to be very convenient for representing infinite set of solutions of computations.

Second, the reconciliation approach has been used here too. It allows to combine both or-parallelism and full and-parallelism. As a result, subgoals of any goal are reduced in a purely concurrent manner even if they do share variables. Conflicting bindings may thus occur too. They are handled by generalizing the reconciliation procedure of the basic model to n-substitutions. This makes use of the n-reconciliation concept developed in Chapter 3 as well as of the auxiliary concept of consistency of n-substitutions with respect to a set of bindings.

Finally, the features explained by the tree and process views have been conserved. Both views have been explicited here too.

On the one hand, the tree view has extended the abstract and global perception of the basic model to handle negation. It has pointed out the generalization of and/or search trees to and/or/not search trees. Such trees are also constructed slice by slice thanks to cyles, each one composed of an expending generation phase followed by a re-organizing reconciliation phase. The aims of these phases have been kept. In particular, bindings are also published but here through n-substitutions. This has induced four successive extensions.

  1° The instantiation of terms is extended in order to take profit of the negative information stored in the n-substitutions.

2°   Coupling of this negative information to s-goals and goals results. It induces the generalization of s-goals and goals to so-called extended s-goals and extended goals;

3°   The unification of terms is then generalized to capture the unification of such extended s-goals with clauses.

4°   Finally, the instantiation of terms is extended to the extended s-goals and goals; one of its main characteristics is that, in contrast with the instantiation of s-goals and goals by substitutions, the extended instantiation of extended s-goals and extended goals by an n-substitution does not always succeed. This further adds to the task of binding publication of preventing the computation from the generation of useless branches.

On the other hand, the process view has extended the local perception of the basic model to incorporate negation. It has conserved the dynamic and quasi-independent behavior of processes of the basic model. Hence, the strict interleaving of the generation and reconciliation phases is relaxed here too. It follows that the n-substitutions may be delivered as results of the computations whereas others are still under computation.

It is here worth noting that the tree and process perceptions have been extended so as to guarantee that the model reduces to the basic one when no negation is involved in the computations.

The combination of all the above features results in a negation very close to real negation. It has been proved sound with respect to the completion interpretation of the programs. It has also been argued to be as complete as possible when the negation as failure rule and the resolution principle are used. Very general situations of completeness have furthermore been pointed out. Finally, the floundering problem has been showed to be of no concern.

Chapter 6

Adding extra-logical features

So far, we have only faced with purely logical programs. We now introduce extra-logical features. This is motivated by two reasons : optimization and practicability.

1° *Optimization*. Very often, the construction process of programs reveals that it is useless to perform some reductions before the results of some other reductions are known or before some conditions are fulfilled. Although these useless reductions have been argued to be harmless in Sections 4.4 and 5.4 provided the computing resources are infinite, it is, in practice, quite interesting to remove them. These resources are indeed generally finite. Removing the useless reductions allows to dedicate them to useful work. As we will see later, this may lead to a substantial increase of the performance of the computation. Annotating the programs provides a means of achieving this goal.

It is here worth stressing that such an incorporation of annotations is made only for efficiency purposes and not for soundness or completeness aims. Transformations that allow to achieve the incorparation will furthermore be given in Part III.

2° *Practicability*. To be practical, any language must incorporate some "extra-logical" built-in primitives such as input/output primitives. An interesting side effect of point 1° is that a framework suitable to manipulate the built-in primitives will result. For instance, sequentialization annotations will be developed for optimization purposes. They will then be available to force the writing of a solution after it has effectively been computed.

Given these annotations and built-in primitives, Conclog can be argued to be as powerful and as practical as other concurrent logic programming languages such as Guarded Horn Clauses ([Ueda, 1986a]), Concurrent Prolog ([Shapiro, 1983]), Parlog ([Gregory, 1985]), P-Prolog ([Yang, 1986]).

The remainder of this chapter is organized as follows. Section 6.1 explores the various sources of inefficiencies. It gives the basis for the second section. There, the Conclog annotations and built-in primitives are defined. Moreover, the gain induced by the annotations is characterized and the set of annotations and built-in primitives is argued to be "reasonably complete" and minimal. Section 6.3 further precises the incorporation of the annotations in the

Conclog model. Section 6.4 addresses the impact of the annotations on the soundness and completeness properties. Section 6.5 compares the Conclog extra-logical features with related ones. Finally, Section 6.6 gives the conclusion of the chapter.

6.1 Sources of inefficiencies

As it results from Chapters 4 and 5, the Conclog model incorporates three potential sources of inefficiencies :

- the simultaneous reduction of subgoals of goals,
- the simultaneous use of clauses to reduce a subgoal,
- the parameters of the model.

These sources cover, in fact, many situations. They are subsequently called optimizable situations. Analyzing them is a prerequisite for finding suitable annotations to handle them. We now turn to such an analysis. It is organized according to the above sources of inefficiencies.

A. Simultaneous reduction of sibling subgoals

1° A first class of optimizable situations can be depicted as follows : the reduction of some s-goals of goals would better wait until some of their variables have been bound to some terms. Consider, for instance, the usual quicksort procedure (see Section 10.4.1.4 for a precise construction) :

```
q_sort([],[]).
q_sort([H|T],L_sorted) ←
     partition(H,T,Smaller,Greater),
     q_sort(Smaller,Smaller_sorted),
     q_sort(Greater,Greater_sorted),
     append(Smaller_sorted,[H|Greater_sorted],L_sorted).
```

Assume that the append procedure is built to be multi-directional and the q_sort procedure is always called with its first argument ground. Then, the call to the append procedure in the second clause should obviously behave as a consumer of the two lists Smaller_sorted and Greater_sorted. Letting it reduce freely, as in the basic model, would lead it to produce lists of arbitrary length, most of which are incompatible with Smaller_sorted and Greater_sorted.

The remedy to this inefficiency is to constrain the reduction of the append call so that it cannot run ahead the production of the two lists Smaller_sorted and Greater_sorted. This can be done by forcing the unification of the call

```
append(Smaller_sorted,[H|Greater_sorted],L_sorted)
```

with any of the clauses defining append to suspend until the lists Smaller_sorted and Greater_sorted have been bound to some terms[1].

More generally, it may be useful to suspend the reduction of a s-goal until some of its variables have been bound to terms that verify some conditions. The annotations materializing such a condition differ by the place they take as well as the nature of the condition they should embody.

As far as the place is concerned, there are only two places where an annotation can take place : in the clauses defining the procedures or in the call to the procedure. Placing the annotations in both places is desirable. On the one hand, for predicates for which the constraint holds for all calls, it is more natural and more elegant to annotate the clauses defining the predicate. Convincing examples of such predicates are the predicates embodying procedures directed by nature, such as the functions. The above q_sort provides a good instance. On the other hand, the constraints may only hold for some calls. A typical example is the append call in the above definition of the q_sort predicate. In this case, it is better to annotate the calls rather than the procedure clauses.

As far as the conditions to embody are concerned, we believe that the two following conditions constitute the most usefull conditions to express:

- the variable is bound to a term verifying some pattern (in particular, is bound to a non-variable term or to a ground term) or some more complicated condition
- the variable is input i.e. is never constructed by the reduction of the s-goal.

2° A second optimizable situation can be described as follows : reducing s-goals of goals makes only sense when other sibling s-goals successfully reduce. Convincing examples of the latter s-goals are s-goals embodying tests. Consider, for instance, the (classical) definition of the partition predicate

```
partition(_,[],[],[]).
partition(X,[H|T],[H|T_smaller],T_greater) ←
    H<X, partition(X,T,T_smaller,T_greater).
partition(X,[H|T],T_smaller,[H|T_greater]) ←
    H≥X, partition(X,T,T_smaller,T_greater).
```

Consider the conjunction

```
H<X, partition(X,T,T_smaller,T_greater)
```

of the second clause. Manifestly, reducing the recursive call to partition is only profitable if the test

---

[1] We will refine these conditions in a moment. The necessary condition is in fact that the list Smaller_sorted is known to be empty or non-empty and in this case that its head is instantiated.

H<X

holds. Although failure of the test would imply the failure of the whole conjunction and would result in stopping the partition call, it may be useful to conserve (generally limited) resources for reductions that are known to be profitable. Hence, it is generally more interesting to make the test first and, if successful, to compute the partition call.

3° Sequentializing the reduction of conjunctions of s-goals inside a goal may be profitable in another situation : the reduction of the s-goals succeeds in quite restricted situations. Such s-goals can be regarded as tests. Computing other s-goals is relevant only if they succeed. Furthermore, the bindings produced by their reduction considerably limit the reduction of others. Hence, transmitting these values, once they are completely produced, prevents the computation from useless reductions. Constraint satisfactory problems provide good examples. For them, it is better to treat the constraints completely, this producing constraints on the bindings, and then to reduce the other sibling s-goals, those producing s-goals.

B. Simultaneous use of unifiable clauses

Inefficiency can also result from the simultaneous use of unifiable clauses to reduce a goal. This results in the following fourth and fifth situations.

4° It may happen that just some - often just one - solutions need to be computed for a s-goal. The two following situations provide good examples :

- only one solution is expected from the execution of the program;
- the solutions are equivalent with respect to the treatment that is applied on them.

They may of course be generalized to some number of solutions. In such situations, computing all solutions may be quite costly; this is furthermore useless. Optimization can thus take place here, too. There are two ways to achieve it :

- to compute the required solutions (for instance, only one) and then to kill the reductions computing the other ones;
- to select only some clauses to limit the reduction.

The first method has the advantage of being quite declarative. Hence, the annotations that implement it can be introduced quite safely and directly : it is sufficient to state that only n solutions are required. As a counterpart, the exponential explosion of the and/or/not search trees cannot be reduced until the required solutions are produced. The second method has the advantage and the drawback of the former as drawback and advantage, respectively. It has the advantage of drastically limiting the exponential growth of the search tree and even, in some cases, of linearlizing it, for instance when only one clause is retained at each reduction step. However, the selection of the clauses requires generally more attention since it must be ensured that the selected clauses will indeed lead to one solution. Introducing the corresponding annotations is thus more delicate than for the first method. Nevertheless, both are complementary and should be provided.

The place of the corresponding annotations is here worth noting. The annotation corresponding to the first method is manifestly specific to some calls and thus should be placed on the calls. In contrast, the discussion of point 1° above can be transposed for the annotations associated with the second method. Hence, both calls and procedures should be annotated. Note that as a particular case of the latter annotations, partitionning the clauses in some classes may be quite interesting too.

5° It may also happen that the clauses are constructed so that the successful reduction of some s-goals of one clause body excludes that other clauses contribute to solutions to any call. In other terms, some clauses may be discarded once some s-goals of one clause body are successfully reduced. The partition procedure provides an example : once the test H<X is successfully reduced, then the third clause cannot contribute to any solution and the reduction it involves may be removed. Achieving this optimization should manifestly be done by annotating the clauses rather than the calls. In particular, some partition of the clauses seems interesting.

C. Parameters of the model

6° Finally, the parameters of the model may themselves induce some inefficiencies. Reporting to the discussion of Section 4.4.1, the R-depth parameter has been chosen to make a compromize between the effort spent for the useful reductions and the time spent to detect and prevent the useless ones. This choice is fixed for the entire computation. However, it may happen that a greater or a lower value could locally be better. Typical examples are deterministic or generate and test procedures included in more general programs (see Section 4.4.1).

The incremental communication of R-triplets has also been restricted by ns-goal-processes. As argued in Section 5.4.2.1, the solution we proposed in the model of Chapter 5 has the advantage of minimizing the number of R-triplets to be sent and of reconciliations to be performed. However it has the drawback of delaying the detection of failure. Hence, the choice made in Chapter 5 may not be the best one in specific situations, for instance, when many unproductive branches are generated. It however sets the entire computation. Allowing it to be modified for some subcomputations may thus be useful.

Finally, the models of Chapters 4 and 5 embody one synchronization point : the generation phase of one cycle may only be started when the reconciliation phase of the previous one is completely terminated. All the subtrees are thus cycled in the same manner. It might however be useful to make some subtrees be regulated by their own cycle. The generation phase would thus be started in some subtree when the subtree is completely reconciled and without waiting until the reconciliation phase for the whole and/or/not search tree is completely performed. Typical examples of such subtrees include those engendered by s-goals

- that act with the remainder of the computations as the producer of some values,

- that are defined by generate and test procedures.

Summing up annotations to modify such features of the basic model locally should also be provided. As far as their place is concerned, the discussion of point 1° applies quite well. It should thus be possible to annotate both calls and procedures.

6.2 The extra-logical features

The Conclog extra-logical features are presented in this section. As the design space of extra-logical features is rather small, some of the extra-logical features presented in this section will recall other features of existing concurrent languages. Nevertheless, this section is only descriptive. Due comparison is made in Section 6.5.

For the clarity of the presentation, the following terminology is adopted.

(i) Reduction, reduction step, ||-reduction step

The term "reduction" will subsequently be used in various variants. In general, it refers to the replacement of a s-goal by some goals. How this is performed leads to three variants : reduction step, ||-reduction step, reduction.

The term "reduction step" has been introduced in Section 2.3.2. It was defined there in the context of Horn clauses. We now extend it to handle negation and annotations. A *reduction step* now consists of transforming a s-goal Sg into a goal G according to the following rules :

- if the s-goal Sg is an ns-goal, say not(Goal), then G is defined as Goal,
- if the s-goal Sg is a ps-goal, then G is the instance of the body of a clause that unifies with Sg. Precisely, G is the instance by the en-mgu unifying Sg with the clause.

The term *"||-reduction step"* extends the term "reduction step" by using all unifiable clauses to replace a ps-goal. In this case, the result of the ||-reduction is a set of goals.

The expression *"reduction of a s-goal or of a goal"* and the expression *"reducing a s-goal or a goal"* designate the progressive transformation of the considered s-goal or goal according to the Conclog model. The qualifier "parallel" will sometimes be added to strengthen the parallel nature of the reduction.

(ii) Direct and indirect bindings

We will subsequently be interested in the bindings made for the variables. In general, any variable X can be bound in two ways :

1°   directly, by a binding of the form X/t resulting from the unification of a ps-goal with a clause,

2°   indirectly, by successive bindings

$$X/t; Y_1/u_1, ..., Y_m/u_m; Z_1/v_1, ..., Z_n/v_n; ...$$

where the Y_i's are variables of t, the Z_j's are variables of the u_i's, ... This results in a binding X/t' where t' is the instance of t induced by the bindings

$Y_1/u_1, ..., Y_m/u_m; Z_1/v_1, ..., Z_n/v_n; ...$

The first binding X/t is called a *direct binding* for X. The variable X is furthermore said to be bound directly to t. The second binding X/t' is called an *indirect binding* for X. The variable X is then said to be bound indirectly to t'.

(iii) Annotating the extended goals and the extended s-goals

As a result of the introduction of negation, s-goals are now handled in their extended form (G,Ψ). The annotations will however only act on the G part. We will then use the expression "annotating a ps-goal" to denote in reality the action of annotating its G part only.

Moreover, the annotations are designed to annotate s-goals. We will use the expression "annotating a goal" as a shorthand to denote the action of annotating its s-goals.

The remainder of this section is organized in three subsections. Annotations are described in the first subsection. They are designed so as to deal with the optimizable situations of the above Section 6.1. Built-in primitives are then presented in the second subsection with the aim of making the language as practical as possible. Finally, all these extra-logical features are argued to form a complete and minimal set of such features.

6.2.1 The annotations

6.2.1.1 Read-only annotations

A. Motivation

Read-only annotations aim at solving the optimizable situation of point 1° of Section 6.1 by annotating the variables of calls. To be more specific, let us turn back to the q_sort procedure stated there. The call

    append(Smaller_sorted,[H|Greater_sorted],L_sorted).

of this procedure has been identified as a consumer of the lists Smaller_sorted and Greater_sorted. The append procedure is usually defined as follows (see Section 10.3.1 for a precise construction) :

    append([],L,L).
    append([H|T],L,[H|L_app]) ← append(T,L,L_app).

Making the append call a consumer of the lists Smaller_sorted and Greater_sorted can thus be achieved

- by suspending its reduction until the list Smaller_sorted is known to be empty or not;
- by suspending any call to the append procedure (resulting from the recursive append(T,L,L_app) call of the second clause) until its first argument list is known to be empty or not.

This behavior is obtained by annotating the Smaller_sorted list by the read-only annotation "?".

B. Description

More generally, read-only annotations may be employed in the following forms :

"?", "?nv", "?g", "!", "!nv", "!g".

The first three forms are called *global read-only annotations*. The last three forms are called *local read-only annotations*. All of them can annotate only variables of calls.

Roughly speaking, read-only annotations express the constraint that the reduction of the calls cannot bind the annotated variables. Reductions that would do so are suspended until concurrent reductions (of conjoined s-goals) bind the annotated variables to terms such that the former reductions can proceed with the induced instances of the calls without breaking the constraint. For example, the reduction of the s-goal p(X?) by means of the clause

p(1) ← ...

is suspended until X becomes bound to 1. Reducing p(X?) directly would indeed have instantiated X to 1. Similarly, the reductions of the s-goals q(X?,1) and q(Y?,Z?) by means of the clause

q(V,V) ← ...

are suspended since direct reductions would, on the one hand, bind X to 1 and, on the other hand, make Y and Z share the same values.

Read-only annotations differ by the way in which they refine the above constraint. On the one hand, the "nv" and "g" annotations further require that the annotated variables are bound to non variable terms or to ground terms before the reduction can occur. On other hand, the global and local annotations differ by the strength of the constraint in the successive reduction steps. Local read-only annotations act only once for the first reduction step of the call. In contrast, global read-only variables are inherited by the subgoals produced by each reduction steps and are thus propagated.

This intuition given, let us describe the impact of read-only annotations in more precise terms. It is twofold. First, unification of an extended ps-goal and a general Horn clause is extended once more in order to handle suspension. Second, the behavior of processes is extended in order to capture the new unification issue.

B.1 EXTENDING UNIFICATION

Read-only annotations introduce a third issue in the unification of a ps-goal with a clause: the unification can now suspend. Attempting it can thus result in three issues : success with the production of an idempotent en-mgu, failure or suspension.

Definition 6.1 Let

- $(p(a_1,...,a_n),\Theta)$ be an extended ps-goal,
- $X_1, ..., X_m$ be its read-only annotated variables,
- $p(a'_1,...,a'_n)$ be $p(a_1,...,a_n)$ where the read-only annotations have been removed,
- $p(t_1,...,t_n) \leftarrow ...$ be a general Horn clause.

The unification of the extended ps-goal and the general Horn clause

- succeeds iff the three following conditions are fulfilled :
    1) $(p(a'_1,...,a'_n),\Theta)$ and $p(t_1,...,t_n)$ unifies, say with idempotent en-mgu $\psi \oplus \Psi$,
    2) $dom(\psi) \cap \{X_1,...,X_m\} = \varnothing$,
    3) none of the X_i's is annotated by one of the following read-only annotations "?nv", "?g", "!nv", "!g";
- suspends iff condition 1 above is fulfilled but no idempotent en-mgu verifies conditions 2 and 3;
- fails, otherwise.

Remark Note that the equational framework developed in Chapter 3 is also well suited to test condition 2) above from the computation of an idempotent en-mgu $\theta \oplus \Theta$ of $(p(a'_1,...,a'_n),\Theta)$ and of $p(t_1,...,t_n)$. Taking the compact multi-equational representation of θ, condition 2 is indeed fulfilled iff every multi-equation E that contains one variable X_i verifies the two following conditions :

- its right-side member E_{right} is empty,
- its left-side member E_{left} reduces to a singleton or contains one variable distinct from one X_i.

Let us give some examples of unification. The negative information, of no real concern, is not taken into account here for the clarity of the presentation.

Example 6.1 Let us first turn back to the examples of the above Subsection A. The unification of the ps-goal

p(X?)

and the clause

p(1) ← ...

suspends. The only idempotent mgu is {X/1}. It violates the condition 2 of Definition 6.1. Similarly, the unification of the ps-goals

q(X?,1) and q(Y?,Z?)

with the clause

q(V,V) ← ...

suspends. Idempotent mgu's must solve the systems

$$\begin{cases} X = V \\ 1 = V \end{cases}$$

and

$$\begin{cases} Y = V \\ Z = V \end{cases}$$

respectively. This implies binding X to 1 in the first case and either Y or Z in the second case.

In contrast, the ps-goal

q(X?,1)

unifies with the clause

p(V,W) ← ...

The idempotent mgu {V/X,W/1} indeed meets condition 2 and no read-only variable violates condition 3.

Finally, the unification of the ps-goal

q(X?,X,1)

and of the clause

q(2,W,W) ← ...

fails since q(X,X,1) and q(2,W,W) are not unifiable.

B.2 EXTENDING THE REDUCTION OF PS-GOAL

This given, the real impact of the read-only annotations is to suspend some reductions. The process view of the computation is most suited to explain what this exactly means. It is therefore employed in the following. Suspending reductions has then two effects. The essential one concerns the generation of the child processes. Just that of children of ps-goal-processes needs in fact to be extended. This induces the second effect : reconciliation procedures of processes must be extended.

B.2.1 EXTENDING THE GENERATION OF CHILDREN OF PS-GOAL-PROCESSES

Instantiating annotated terms by substitutions will be required to unsuspend some reductions. The way in which read-only annotations are inherited is first precised. It is defined as follows.

Definition 6.2 Let E be an expression possibly read-only annotated and $\theta=\{X_1/t_1,...,X_m/t_m\}$ be a substitution. Then the instance of E by θ is the expression obtained from E by replacing any occurence of any X_i as follows :
- any unannotated occurrence of any X_i is replaced by the corresponding term t_i,
- any occurrence of any X_i, read-only annotated by the "?", "?g", "!" or "!g" symbols is replaced by the corresponding term t_i where every variable is read-only annotated by the "?", "?g", "!" or "!g", respectively,
- any occurrence of any X_i, read-only annotated by the "?nv" or "!nv" symbol is replaced by
    - t_i?nv or t_i!nv, respectively, if t_i is a variable,
    - t_i where each variable is annotated by the "?" or "!" symbol, respectively, if t_i is a non-variable term.

It is denoted as $E\theta$.

The instantiation of an extended expression (E,Θ) by an n-substitution ν only extends the normal unification by testing the n-reconcilability of Θ and $\{\nu\}$. Definition 6.2 can thus be easily extended to extended expressions. In this case, for any read-only annotated expression E, for any en-reconciliation of Θ and $\{\nu\}$, say $\psi\oplus\Psi$, the expression $(E\psi,\Psi_r)$ is defined as the extended instance of (E,Θ) by ν. The Ψ_r set, used there, denotes the restriction of Ψ to the set of variables of $E\psi$.

Let us now turn back to the reduction of s-goals. Let Proc be a ps-goal-process and G be the associated (extended) ps-goal. Clauses unifying with G are first searched. Those for which the unification succeeds or suspends are retained. Each issue of unification induces a different creation of processes.

1) On the one hand, for each clause that successfully unifies with G, a goal-process is created for the corresponding instance of the clause body. The read-only annotations are inherited by the instance as follows : any occurrence of a variable globally read-only annotated in G is annotated by the "?" symbol.

2) On the other hand, for any clause whose unification with G suspends, a so-called *suspended ps-goal-clause-process* is created for the ps-goal and the clause. It is also called *suspended process* for short. It is suspended on each read-only annotated variable and is listening to bindings for them. The following bindings are heard by it. Let, for any variable V,

$\Theta(V)$ be the set of nmas's that bind V and that are referred to by a goal-process P that verifies the following properties :
- P_1.   it is not a descendant of Proc,
- P_2.   its lower (in the and/or/not process hierarchy) common ancestor with Proc is not separated from it by an odd number of ns-goal-processes in the and/or/not process hierarchy.

Then, the heard bindings are the functional restrictions to any read-only annotated variable V of the nmas of $\Theta(V)$. How this is achieved is out of purpose for the moment and will be treated later. It is just assumed that bindings are heard as soon as they are produced.

Unification is re-attempted for each such heard binding that instantiates the extended ps-goal G but this time for the instance of G by the heard binding. This results as before in the creation of a goal-process or a suspended goal-clause-process according as the unification of the instance of G with the clause succeeds or suspends. In case the unification fails, no process is created.

Unification is also re-attempted after each binding publication. The instance (where read-only annotations are inherited as just described) is then taken into account. If the unification succeeds then a goal-process is created as before. If the unification suspends, no suspended goal-clause-process is created but the suspended process indicates its suspension on the variables that are newly read-only annotated. Finally, in case the unification fails, no process is created.

Remarks

1) The choice of the bindings heard by a suspended process may appear to be quite arbitrary. It is justified as follows. The communicated bindings roughly correspond to the bindings made anywhere in the and/or/not search tree or equivalently by the associated goal-processes. They are coupled with the negative information associated with them in the nmas. This justifies the expression of the bindings in the form of the restriction of the nmas's. Two kinds of bindings are however undesirable. On the one hand, bindings made by alternative reductions of any s-goal should be kept independent. Bindings produced by them should be discarded to wake up suspended processes. This justifies the presence of property P_1. On the other hand, bindings produced by the reduction of an ns-goal are relevant for non-descendant processes only through their negation. Property P_2 then results from the fact that negative information does not however produce instances that could force unsuspension.

2) It is worth noting that the unification need not be reattempted from scratch when the multi-equational framework of Chapter 3 is used. Indeed, if the en-mgu $\theta \oplus \Theta$ is represented in its equivalent equational form, it is sufficient to replace the bound variables of the heard bindings by their binding terms and to resolve the obtained system.

3) The inheritance of suspension induced by the "?g" annotation is useless. When the unification succeeds, the annotated variable has indeed become ground. It follows that the "?g"

annotation is redundant with the "!g" one. We will however keep both of them for purposes of symmetry.

B.2.2 EXTENDING THE RECONCILIATION PROCEDURES OF PROCESSES

Introducing read-only annotations also results in extending the reconciliation procedure of processes in three ways.

1) The reconciliation procedure of suspended processes needs first to be precised. Children of such processes manifestly act as many alternatives of reducing the s-goals associated with them. Their reconciliation procedure is thus defined as that of s-goal-processes. They thus basically transmit the n-substitutions computed by their children.

2) Bindings used for unsuspending suspended processes should be taken into account . Let Proc be a process affected by such a binding i.e. a child of a suspended process. Let X/t be the binding heard to create it. Then any n-substitution v that Proc would normally sent is not sent as such. The n-substitution

$$(\{X/t\} \circ v^+, v^-)$$

is sent instead.

3) Bindings are heard as soon as the processes that produce them are created. It may however happen that such a producer process is killed thereafter. In this case, the bindings it produced are obsolate provided they have not been produced by other processes. Therefore, processes created by hearing such bindings are also removed as soon as the producing processes are killed.

C. Example

Figure 6.1 illustrates an execution involving read-only annotations. It refers to the program

p([1|T]) ← r(T).	(1)
p([2|T]) ← r(T).	(2)
q([],0).	(3)
q([H|T],Nb) ← q(T,Nb).	(4)
r([3]).	(5)

and the query

← p(X),q(X?,Y).

The R-depth parameter of the model has been fixed to the infinite value.

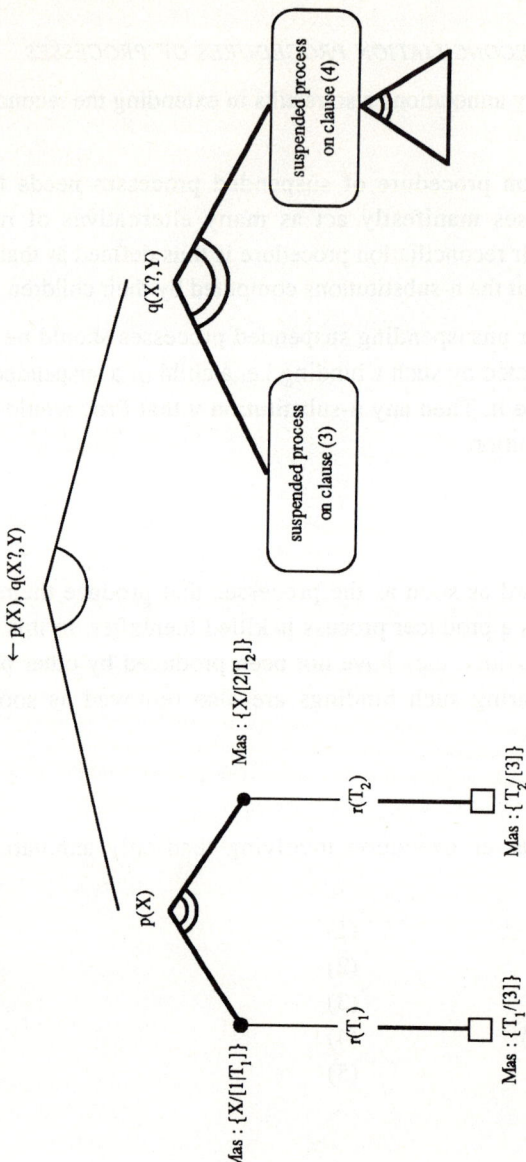

Figure 6.1 (a)

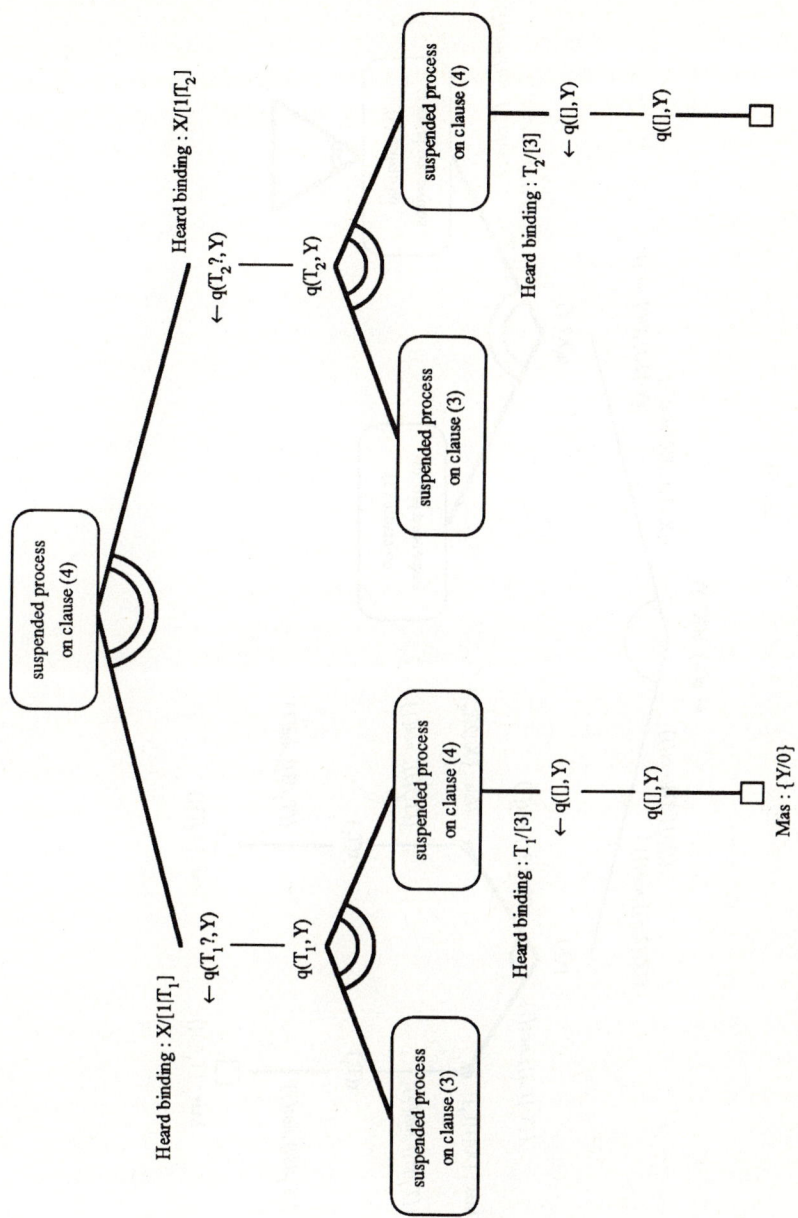

Figure 6.1 (a) continued

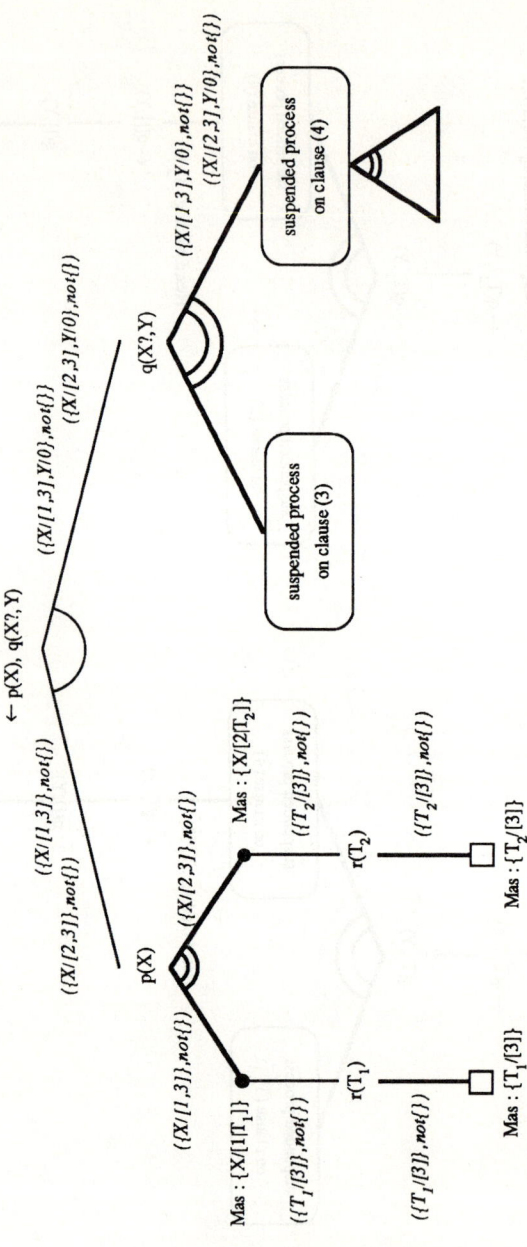

Figure 6.1 (b)

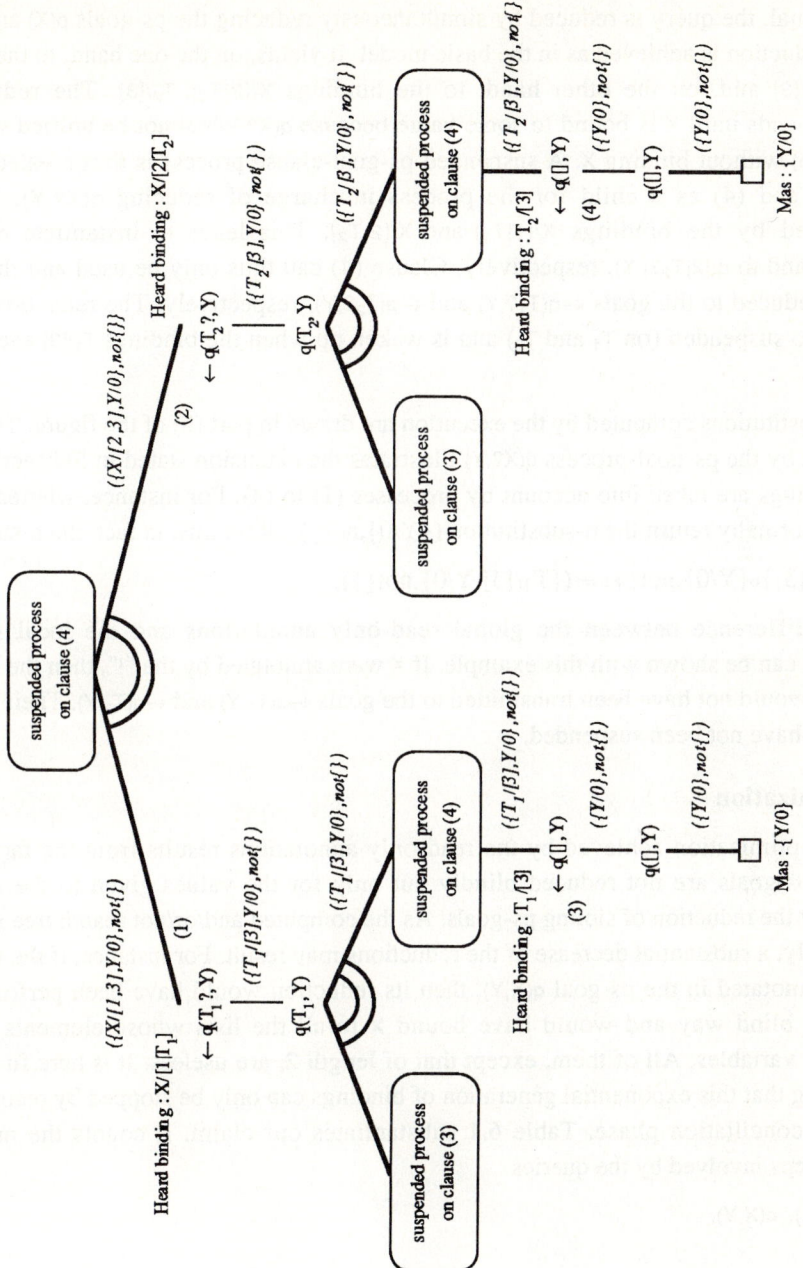

Figure 6.1 (b) continued

As usual, the query is reduced by simultaneously reducing the ps-goals p(X) and q(X?,Y). The first reduction is achieved as in the basic model. It yields, on the one hand, to the bindings X/[1|T_1], T_1/[3] and, on the other hand, to the bindings X/[2|T_2], T_2/[3]. The reduction of q(X?,Y) suspends until X is bound to some value because q(X?,Y) cannot be unified with q([],0) or q([H|T],Nb) without binding X. A suspended ps-goal-clause process is thus created for each clause (3) and (4) as a child for the process in charge of reducing q(X?,Y). They are unsuspended by the bindings X/[1|T_1] and X/[2|T_2]. This leads to instantiate q(X?,Y) to q([1|T_1?],Y) and to q([2|T_2?],Y), respectively. Clause (4) can thus only be used and the ps-goal q(X?,Y) is reduced to the goals ←q(T_1?,Y) and ←q(T_2?,Y), respectively. The reduction of these goals is also suspended (on T_1 and T_2) and is waken up when the bindings T_1/[3] and T_2/[3] are produced.

N-substitutions computed by the execution are drawn in part (b) of the figure. The subtree engendered by the ps-goal-process q(X?,Y) illustrates the extension stated in Subsection B.2.2. Heard bindings are taken into account by processes (1) to (4). For instance, whereas process (3) would normally return the n-substitution ({Y/0},not{}), it returns, in fact, the n-substitution

$$(\{T_1/[3]\} \circ \{Y/0\}, \text{not}\{\}) = (\{T_1/[3], Y/0\}, \text{not}\{\}).$$

The difference between the global read-only annotations and the local read-only annotations can be shown with this example. If X were annotated by the "!", then the read-only annotation would not have been transmitted to the goals ←q(T_1,Y) and ←q(T_2,Y). Their reduction would then have not been suspended.

D. Optimization

The optimization achieved by the read-only annotations results from the fact that the annotated ps-goals are not reduced blindly but only for the values given to the annotated variables by the reduction of sibling ps-goals. As the computed and/or/not search tree may grow exponentially, a substantial decrease of the reductions may result. For instance, if the variable X were not annotated in the ps-goal q(X,Y), then its reduction would have been performed in a completely blind way and would have bound X to all the lists whose elements are non-instantiated variables. All of them, except that of length 2, are useless. It is here furthermore worth noting that this exponential generation of bindings can only be stopped by reconciliation during a reconciliation phase. Table 6.1 substantiates our claim. It counts the number of reduction steps involved by the queries

← p(X), q(X,Y),

and

← p(X), q(X?,Y).

R-depth	Reduction steps for unannotated version	Reduction steps for annotated version
5	14	10
10	24	10
20	44	10
∞	∞	10

Table 6.1

The reduction of the annotated version is optimal. It is the same whatever value the R-depth parameter of the model takes. This is not true for the unannotated version so that measures are given for the following values of the R-depth parameter : 5, 10, 20 and ∞.

The same analysis applies to the append call in the q_sort procedure. The gain is there even more substantial since, in the unannotated version, the blind reduction of an append call is involved by each recursive call to q_sort.

6.2.1.2 Suspension declarations

A. Motivation

Suspension declarations provide in their basic form the counterpart of the read-only annotations at the procedure level. Their general form further handles some arbitrary suspension conditions.

It is here worth recalling that the presence of suspension declarations is justified by procedures for which the suspension constraints hold for any call. Procedures embodying functions provide good examples of such procedures. For instance, the above q_sort procedure is manifestly only used to determine the sorted version of any list. It should thus not construct it. In view of this example, it is tempting to relate modes of use of procedures with the suspension conditions, and, consequently, to call mode declarations the corresponding annotations. However, these annotations are not really mode declarations so that we prefer to call them *suspension declarations*.

B. Description

A suspension declaration is a construct of the following form :

suspend proc_name($Arg_1,...,Arg_n$) until Cond.

where

- proc_name is the functor of an n-ary predicate,
- the Arg_i's are distinct variables, possibly read-only annotated,
- Cond is a non-extended goal.

The until Cond part is optional. The Arg_i arguments of the proc_name(Arg_1,...,Arg_m) part are also optional when they are not referred to in the Cond goal. The read-only annotations, when any, may thus just be conserved. The "*" symbol is then used to replaced non-annotated Arg_i variables. Suspension declarations are called *complex* or *simple* according as they contain a "Cond" part or not.

The read-only annotations of the Arg_i's arguments provide the counterpart of the read-only annotations in the calls. The Cond goal adds a further condition of suspension. One typical use is to force suspension until an argument is known to be of some pattern, for instance, one of the following pattern : [] or [H|T].

One or more suspension declarations can be associated with each procedure. Their effect is very similar to that of the read-only annotations. They first induce a new extension of the unification of ps-goals and of clauses in order to capture them. They then induce an extension of the reduction of ps-goals.

B.1 EXTENDING UNIFICATION

Unification of a ps-goal and a clause with respect to a suspension declaration is achieved essentially as in Definition 6.1. The "Cond" part of more complex declarations complicates it a little bit. Nevertheless, the definition will first be given in the more general context of complex suspension declaration. The (more simple) definition for simple suspension will then be deduced from it.

Definition 6.3 Let
- $(p(a_1,...,a_n),\Theta)$ be an extended ps-goal, possibly read-only annotated,
- $p(t_1,...,t_n) \leftarrow ...$ be a general Horn clause,
- suspend $p(Arg_1,...,Arg_n)$ until Cond, be a suspension declaration for p,
- for any $i \in \{1,...,n\}$, ra_i be
    - a_i where all its variables have been read-only annotated by the "?" symbol, if Arg_i is globally read-only annotated,
    - a_i where all its variables have been read-only annotated by the "!" symbol, if Arg_i is locally read-only annotated,
    - a_i, otherwise.

Then, the unification of the extended ps-goal and the clause with respect to the suspension declaration

- succeeds iff the following conditions are fulfilled
  1) the reduction of
     $\text{Cond}\{\text{Arg}_1/\text{ra}_1,...,\text{Arg}_n/\text{ra}_n\}$
     computes at least one n-substitution
  2) one answer n-substitution computed for it, say ν, verifies the following properties:
     2.1) it instantiates $(p(\text{ra}_1,...,\text{ra}_n),\Theta)$
     2.2) the resulting instantiation, say $(p(\text{ra\_inst}_1,...,\text{ra\_inst}_n),\Psi)$, unifies with $(p(t_1,...,t_n),\{\text{not}\{\}\})$,
  3) for any $i \in \{1,...,n\}$ such that Arg_i is read-only annotated by "?nv" or "!nv", ra_inst_i is a non variable term,
  4) for any $i \in \{1,...,n\}$ such that Arg_i is "?g" or "!g", ra_inst_i is a ground term,
- suspends iff one of the following conditions holds
  - the reduction of $\text{Cond}\{\text{Arg}_1/\text{ra}_1,...,\text{Arg}_n/\text{ra}_n\}$ suspends without having produced answer n-substitutions that verify properties 2.1) and 2.2) above
  - for any computed answer n-substitution ν, the unification of the instance $(p(\text{ra\_inst}_1,...,\text{ra\_inst}_n),\Psi)$ and of $(p(t_1,...,t_n),\{\text{not}\{\}\})$ suspends
  - one of the above conditions 3) or 4) is not verified.
- fails, otherwise.

In the case of success, any n-mgu (resp. en-mgu) of $(p(\text{ra\_inst}_1,...,\text{ra\_inst}_n),\Psi)$ and $p(t_1,...,t_n)$ is defined as an n-mgu (resp. en-mgu) of the ps-goal and the clause with respect to the suspension declaration.

The unification of a ps-goal and of a clause with respect to a simple declaration results from the above definition by taking the empty goal as Cond part. Particularizing this definition is worth noting. This leads to the following definition.

Definition 6.4 Let
- $(p(a_1,...,a_n),\Theta)$ be an extended ps-goal, possibly read-only annotated,
- $p(t_1,...,t_n) \leftarrow ...$ be a general Horn clause,
- suspend $p(\text{Arg}_1,...,\text{Arg}_n)$ be a suspension declaration for p,
- for any $i \in \{1,...,n\}$, ra_i be
  - a_i where all its variables have been read-only annotated by the "?" symbol, if Arg_i is globally read-only annotated,
  - a_i where all its variables have been read-only annotated by the "!" symbol, if Arg_i is locally read-only annotated,
  - a_i, otherwise.

Then, the unification of the extended ps-goal and the clause with respect to the suspension declaration

- succeeds iff the following conditions are fulfilled
    1) the unification of $(p(ra_1,...,ra_n),\Theta)$ and of $(p(t_1,...,t_n),\{not\{\}\})$ succeeds
    2) for any $i \in \{1,...,n\}$ such that Arg_i is read-only annotated by "?nv" or "!nv", a_i is a non variable term,
    3) for any $i \in \{1,...,n\}$ such that Arg_i is "?g" or "!g", a_i is a ground term,
- suspends iff one of the following conditions holds
    - the unification of $(p(ra_1,...,ra_n),\Theta)$ and of $(p(t_1,...,t_n),\{not\{\}\})$ suspends
    - one of the above conditions 2) or 3) is not verified.
- fails, otherwise.

B.2 EXTENDING THE REDUCTION OF PS-GOALS

The reduction process is modified in a way very similar to that exposed in Subsection 6.2.1.1.B. It thus only affects the reduction of ps-goals by suspending them. Let Proc be the process in charge of some (extended) ps-goal G. The clauses are first tested for unification with G without taking into account the read-only annotations and the suspension declarations. Those for which the unification succeeds are retained. Let them be $c_1, ..., c_m$. Each of them is then tested for unification but this time with respect to the read-only annotations and the suspension declarations. The novelty is that here several suspension declarations may be used to unify the same ps-goal and clause. For efficiency purpose, just one of them will however be retained.

Precisely, things are performed as follows.

1) For each clause c_i, a so-called ps-goal-clause process is created. It is in charge of handling the unification of G with c_i according to the suspension declarations associated with the procedure to which c_i belongs. To this aim, it creates, for each suspension declaration a child process in charge of computing effectively the unification as it is stated in Definitions 6.3 and 6.4. Each such child acts as follows. For ease of the exposition, let us denote it by Sp and let us denote by P_G_c_i its father process.

    1.1 If the suspension declaration associated with Sp is a simple one, then, using the notation of Definition 6.3, process Sp just unifies the terms $(p(ra_1,...,ra_n),\Theta)$ and $(p(t_1,...,t_n),\{not\{\}\})$. Note that as $(p(a_1,...,a_n),\Theta)$ and $(p(t_1,...,t_n),\{not\{\}\})$ are known to be unifiable, this just amounts to handling suspension. Suspended processes are created as in Section 6.2.1 to this end. When it succeeds, the n-mgus computed for it are returned to P_G_c_i. Note that, because of suspension, several ones, resulting from several instantiations of $(p(ra_1,...,ra_n),\Theta)$ may in fact be returned.

    1.2 If the suspension declaration associated with Sp is a complex one, then the process Sp creates two child processes. The former, say P_cond, is a goal-process in charge of reducing the Cond part. It acts as an arbitrary process. Using the notations of Definition 6.3, the latter is in charge of testing the unification of $(p(t_1,...,t_n),\{not\{\}\})$ and of each instance $(p(ra\_inst_1,...,ra\_inst_n),\Psi)$ induced by the answer n-substitutions computed by the P_cond and that n-reconcile with Θ. To this end, it is made suspended on these answer n-substitutions. It creates a child process for each computed n-substitution ν that n-reconciles with Θ. This chid process essentially acts as the Sp process of the point 1.1 above. The only difference is that the composition $\nu \circ \mu$ is, in fact, returned for each n-substitution μ that it computes. The process Sp then reports all these compositions to its $P\_G\_c_i$ father process.

2) The Sp processes act as concurrent processes. The suspension declaration of the first one that reports an n-substitution to $P\_G\_c_i$ is selected for reduction. This means that all other Sp processes and their descendant are then killed.

3) Then, a goal-process is created as a child of $P\_G\_c_i$ for each n-substitution ν reported by the selected Sp process. It is in charge of reducing the instance of the body of c_i by ν, each occurrence of a variable globally read-only annotated in $<ra_1,...,ra_n>$ being read-only annotated. It retains the n-substitution ν that engenders it and returns as n-substitution the composition $\nu \circ \mu$ of its creating n-substitution ν by the n-substitutions μ it computes.

Choosing one suspension declaration, as we do in point 2 above, may appear to be quite arbitrary. Why do we not use all of them in parallel as we do for clauses when reducing ps-goals? The reason is that duplicate reductions would then result. Consider, for instance, ground calls. They obviously fulfill all suspension constraints of suspension declarations and all of them lead exactly to the same reduction steps! Duplicating them would be quite disastrous when optimizing computations !

The following property is furthermore worth noting. The choice of the suspension declaration only influences the read-only annotations of the successively derived goals. Precisely, the global read-only annotations induced by the suspension declarations may only vary from the use of one suspension declaration from another. In particular, when local read-only annotations are only involved, the choice of the suspension declaration has no impact on the resulting goal.

C. Example

As an illustration of the impact of suspension declarations, let us consider the following non-multi-directional definition of the append procedure

Def_1 : suspend append(?,*,*). (1)
 suspend append(*,*,?). (2)
 append([],[],[]). (3)
 append([],[H|T],[H|T]). (4)
 append([H|T],[],[H|T]). (5)
 append([H1|T1],[H2|T2],[H1|L_app]) ← append(T1,[H2|T2],L_app). (6)

Consider the query

← append([1,2],[3,4],L).

Its reduction proceeds as follows. Clauses unifiable with the s-goal

append([1,2],[3,4],L)

reduces to clause (4). Because of the third parameter [H|L_app], the second suspension declaration cannot be used. In contrast, employing the first one does not involve suspension. This suspension declaration is thus selected and the above query is reduced to the goal

← append([2],[3,4],L_app$_1$).

The same scheme of computing applies to it. The first suspension declaration and fourth clause are thus once again selected. They engender the goal

← append([],[3,4],L_app$_2$).

Its reduction is also similar but the clause (2) is used here. The empty goal results. The reduction is then terminated.

Consider now the query

← gen(L1), append(L1,[3,4],L)

where the predicate gen(L1) is defined as follows :

gen([1|T]) ← gen_1(T).
gen_1([2]).

The computation involves the parallel reduction of the ps-goals gen(L1) and append(L1,[3,4],L). The reduction of gen(L1) is independent of that of append(L1,[3,4],L) and is not influenced by any annotations. It successively produces the bindings

L1/[1|T],
T/[2].

The reduction of append(L1,[3,4],L) is similar to that of the query ←append([1,2],[3,4],L) but suspends twice because of unsufficient knowledge of L1 and L, in the first reduction step, and of T and L_app, in the second reduction step. It is relaunched, the first time, when the binding L1/[1|T] is produced and, the second time, when the binding T/[2] is produced.

The following example illustrates the impact of the choice of the suspension declaration. Consider the query

← append([1|X],[3|Y],[1|Z]).

It can be reduced by the fourth clause of the append procedure but thanks to the two suspension declarations. One is thus arbitrarily chosen. Using the first declaration leads to the goal

← append(X?,Y,Z).

Using the second one leads to the goal

    ← append(X,Y,Z?).

As claimed above, they indeed only differ by their read-only annotations. Note furthermore that if the suspension declarations were defined as local instead of global, the generated goal would be

    ← append(X,Y,Z)

whatever suspension declaration is retained for the reduction.

Finally, the following query illustrates the use of the Cond part of the suspension declaration. Consider the following definitions of the append procedure :

    Def_2 :   suspend append(L1,L2,L) until list(L1).
              append(L1,L2,L) ← L1 = [], L2 = L.
              append(L1,L2,L) ← L1 = [H|T], L = [H|L_app], append(T,L2,L_app).

    Def_3 :   suspend append(?,*,*).
               append(L1,L2,L) ← L1 = [], L2 = L.
              append(L1,L2,L) ← L1 = [H|T], L = [H|L_app], append(T,L2,L_app).

    Def_4 :   suspend append(?,*,*).
               append([],L,L).
              append([H|T],L2,[H|L_app]) ← append(T,L2,L_app).

where the list condition is defined as follows :

    suspend list(?).
    list([]).
    list([H|T]).

Consider the reduction of the ps-goal

    append(L1,L2,L).

It is suspended until L1 is known to be of the pattern [] or [H|T] if Definitions Def_2 or Def_4 are used. In contrast, it does not suspend if definition Def_3 is used.

It is here worth noting that Definitions Def_2 and Def_4 lead to the same reductions and same suspensions. The test for the list condition of Def_2 is embodied in the head of the clauses in Def_4. Definition Def_2 may thus appear in some sense to be more declarative than Def_4 since the suspension conditions are independent from the heads of the clauses. As an important consequence, suspension constraints may be added without modifying the clauses of the procedure. For instance, the following definition of append is equivalent to Definition Def_1 given at the beginning of this section.

Def_5 : suspend append(L1?,L2,L) until list(L1).
         suspend append(L1,L2,L?) until list(L).
         append([],L,L).
         append([H|T],L2,[H|L_app]) ← append(T,L2,L_app).

No folding of the clauses is thus necessary. As a counterpart however the unification of the arguments is more expensive. Unifications are indeed involved in the reduction of the Cond part. For instance, in the above example, one unification is necessary to reduce the list condition.

D. Optimization

The optimizations achieved by the suspension declarations without Cond condition are the same as those explained in Subsection 6.2.1.1.D for read-only annotations. This is due to the fact that these suspension declarations are exactly the counterpart of read-only variables at the procedure level.

Suspension declarations with Cond part may state stronger conditions. A gain of optimization can result from them. It should however be diminished from the cost of the reduction of Cond. To preserve the optimization gain, they should thus be used only when the equivalent suspension conditions cannot be coded by using the read-only annotations of the suspension declarations and the head of clauses. This has been suggested by the analysis of the above Def_1 and Def_2 definitions. Table 6.2 substantiates this intuition. It compares the reduction steps involved in the reduction of the ps-goal

append(L1,L2,L)

thanks to Definition Def_4 and the following definition Def_6

Def_6 : suspend append(L1,L2,L) until list(L1).
         append([],L,L).
         append([H|T],L2,[H|L_app]) ←append(T,L2,L_app).

The latter definition is Definition Def_2 where the unifications are embodied in the clause head. A concurrent incremental instantiation of L1 to the lists

[1,2,3,4],
[1,2,3,4,5,6,7,8],
[1,2,3,4,5,6,7,8,9,10]

is assumed, respectively. The R-depth parameter of the model has no incidence on the results and so need not be precised.

Def$_4$	Def$_6$
5	10
9	18
11	22

Table 6.2

6.2.1.3 The sequentialization operator

A. Motivation

The sequentialization operator aims at solving the optimizable situations of Points 2° and 3° of Section 6.1. It differs from the read-only annotations and suspension declarations by taking into account bindings that correspond to computed answer substitutions of some goals rather than bindings produced by reduction steps. As a result, the reduction of some s-goals is sequentialized. As a counterpart, the incremental communication of bindings supported by the read-only annotations and the suspension declarations is also lost.

B. Description

The sequentialization operator is a s-goal separator. It is denoted by the "|" symbol. It has a lower prirority than the usual "," ps-goals separator and is defined as right-associative so that, e.g.,

$G_1, G_2 | G_3, G_4, G_5 | G_6, G_7$

is to be interpreted as

$[G_1,G_2] | [(G_3,G_4,G_5) | (G_6,G_7)]$.

Of course, brackets can be used to overcome these priorities.

Introducing the sequentialization operator thus leads to partition the ps-goals of goals into groups. Such subgroups are connected either by one "|" separator or by one or more "," separator. The corresponding goals are subsequently designated as *sequentialized goal* and *complex goals*, respectively. Goals involving no "|" operator are called *parallel goals*. The goals

← p(X,Y) | q(X,Y) ,
← [p(X,Y) | q(X,Y)] , r(X,Y),
← p(X,Y), q(X,Y), r(X,Y)

are examples of sequentialized, complex and parallel goals, respectively.

Parallel goals involve no "|" annotations and are thus reduced as above. In contrast, sequentialized and complex goals involve at least one "|" annotation. Reduction of these goals should thus be extended to them.

1) Complex goals are reduced as if each subgroup of ps-goals were defined by a new predicate. The complex goal

$$\leftarrow C_1(\bar{X}_1), ..., C_n(\bar{X}_n),$$

is thus reduced as the parallel goal

$$\leftarrow p_1(\bar{X}_1), ..., p_n(\bar{X}_n),$$

where, for any $i \in \{1,...,n\}$, $\bar{X}_i$ denotes the variables of C_i ($1 \leq i \leq m$) and p_i is defined as

$$p_i(\bar{X}_i) \leftarrow C_i(\bar{X}_i).$$

2) Sequentialized goals are reduced as follows. Let

$$\leftarrow C_1 \mid C_2$$

be such a goal. The goal $\leftarrow C_1$ is reduced without any concern for C_2. In contrast, the reduction of $\leftarrow C_2$ suspends until answer n-substitutions are computed for $\leftarrow C_1$. For any of them, say v, that instantiates C_2, the reduction of $\leftarrow C_2 v$ is launched. Computed answer n-substitutions for the whole goal

$$\leftarrow C_1 \mid C_2$$

are then defined in the following sequential way. Let Θ denote the set of n-substitutions obtained by composing each answer n-substitution v for $\leftarrow C_1$ instantiating C_2 with the answer n-substitutions for $\leftarrow C_2 v$. Then, the computed answer ns-subtitutions for the whole goal

$$\leftarrow C_1 \mid C_2$$

are defined as the restriction of the n-substitutions of Θ to the variables of this goal.

This given, the evaluation of C_1 and C_2 is indeed sequentialized.

C. Example

As an illustration of the effect of the sequentialization operator, let us consider the following program

p([]).	(1)
p([1|T]) ← r(T).	(2)
q([]).	(3)
q([H|T]) ← q(T).	(4)
r([2]).	(5)

and the query

← p(X) | q(X).

The computed and/or/not search tree is drawn in Figure 6.2. As indicated there, the ps-goal p(X) is reduced in an unconstrained way. It produces the answer n-substitutions ({X/[]},not{}) and ({X/[1,2]},not{}). In contrast, the reduction of the ps-goal q(X) is suspended and relaunched for each of the above n-answer substitutions. The corresponding instances both produce the n-substitution ({},not{}). Computed answer n-substitutions for

← p(X) | q(X).

are thus ({X/[]},not{}) and ({X/[1,2]},not{}).

The difference of the sequentialization operator with the read-only annotations and the suspension declarations is here worth noting. Consider the query

← p(X), q(X?)

Evaluating it also leads to the unconstrained reduction of p(X) and to the suspended reduction of q(X). However, the latter reduction is woken up three times:

- it is first woken up when the bindings X/[] and X/[1|T] are produced,
- this results, for the latter binding, in reducing q(X?) to q(T?),
- the reduction of q(T?) is then suspended,
- it is finally woken up when the binding T/[2] is produced.

Bindings are thus incrementally transmitted and not (as for the query ←p(X)|q(X)) when they are known to be part of a computed anwer n-substitution !

D. Optimization

The optimization induced by the sequentialization operator results from the fact that the goal ←C_2 in ←C_1|C_2 is only reduced for each computed answer n-substitution of ←C_1, if any. This may also be employed to code consumer/producer schemes. Gains similar to those exposed in Subsection 6.2.1.1.B. and 6.2.1.2.B. for the read-only annotations and the suspension declarations is thus achieved too. For instance, in the computation of the query

← p(X) | q(X),

the blind evaluation of q(X) (leading to bind X to all the lists whose elements are uninstantiated variables) is also avoided. The difference with the read-only annotations and the suspension declarations is that bindings that are known to be of part of a computed answer n-substitution are only considered when the answer n-substitution is completely computed. Therefore, reductions cannot be unsuspended by bindings that would reveal later to be useless. As a counterpart, parallelism in the computation is decreased since no incremental communication of bindings can occur!

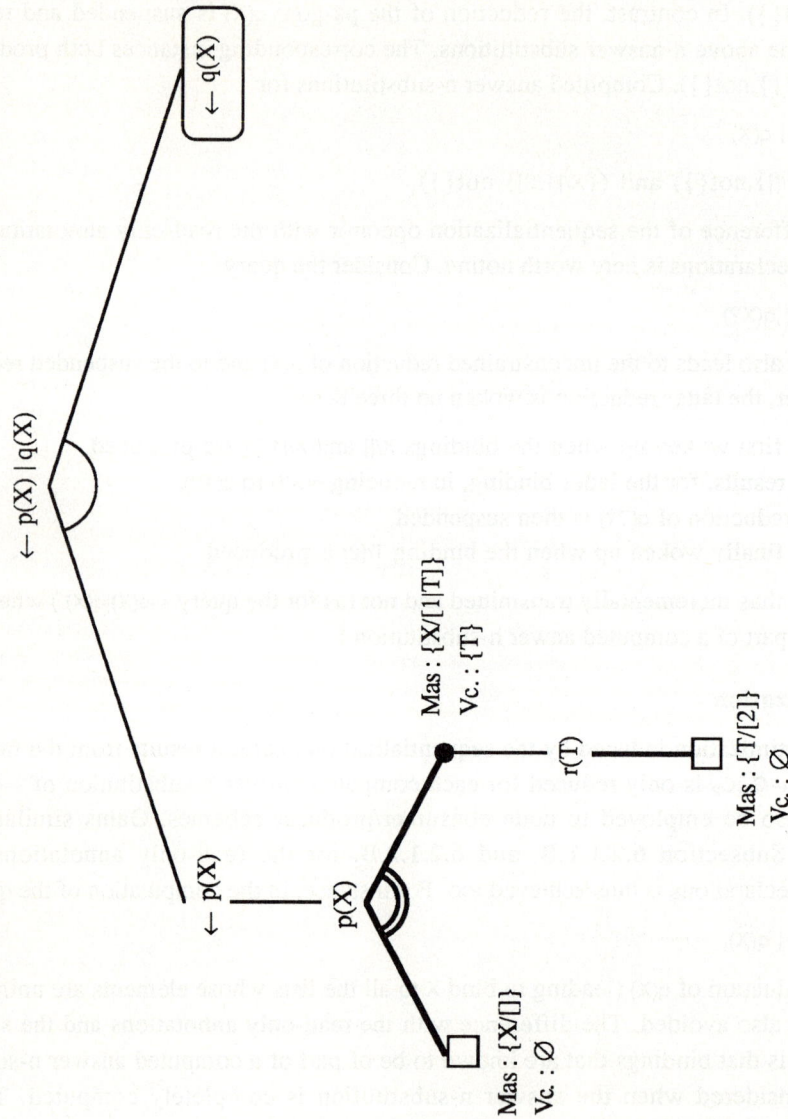

Figure 6.2 (a) : The goal ←p(X) is reduced whereas the reduction of the goal ←q(X) is suspended

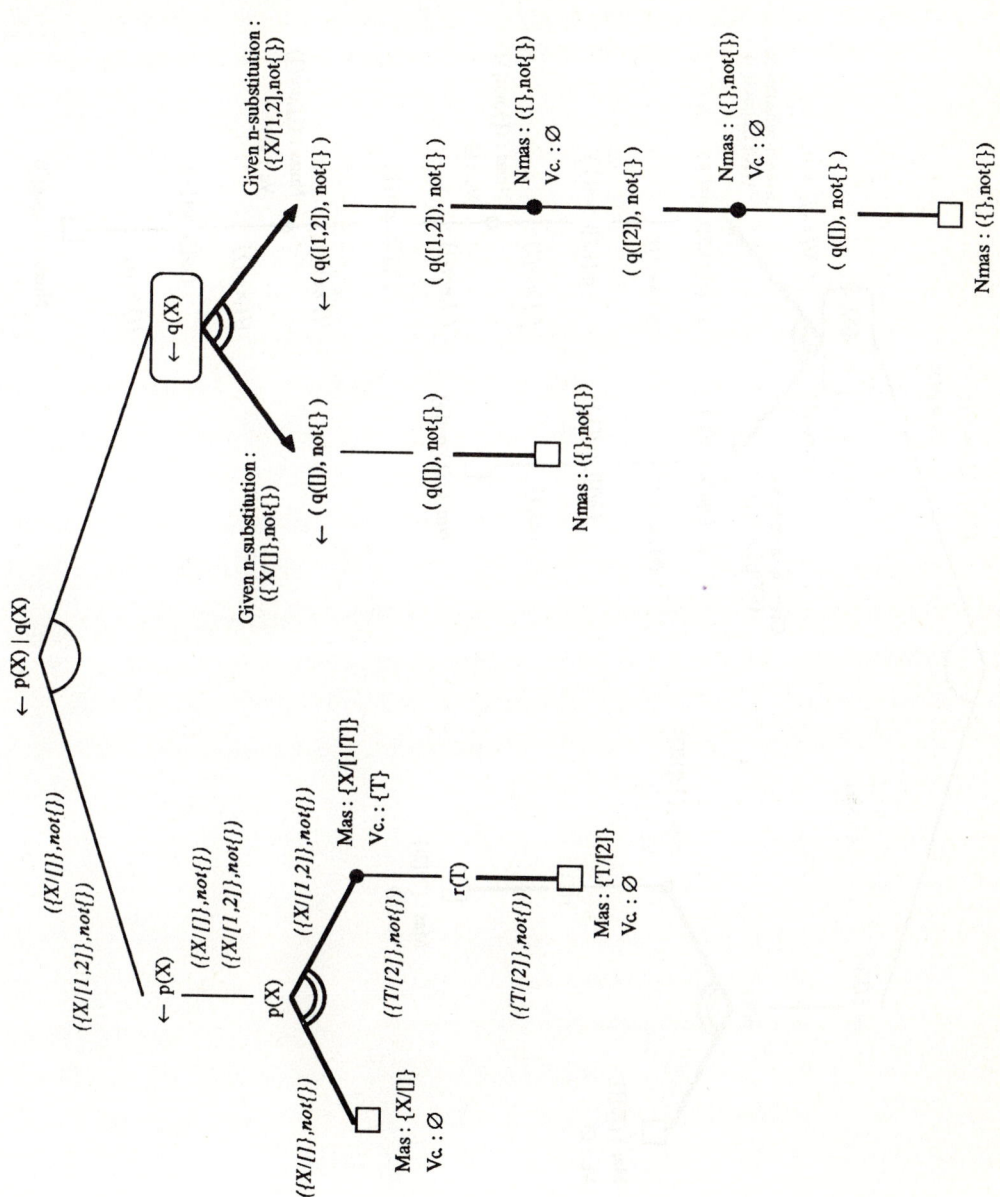

Figure 6.2 (b) : The goal ←q(X) is reduced

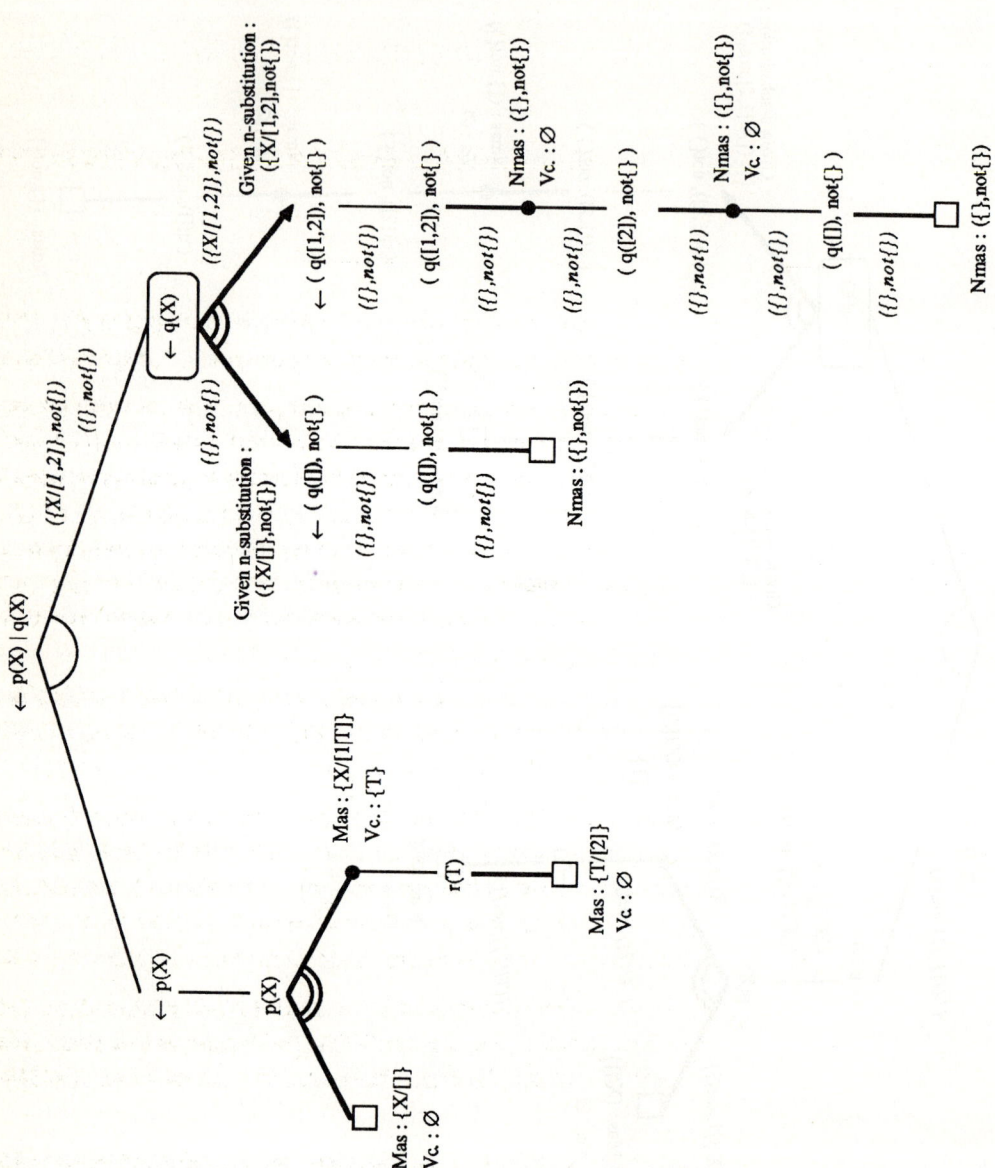

Figure 6.2 (c) : The computed answer n-substitutions

6.2.1.4 The sol and det operators

A. Motivation

The sol(n,G) and det(G) operators aim at solving the situations of Point 4° of Section 6.1 according to the first method presented there. They thus reduce the search space by limiting the reduction of any goal to the production of some solutions only.

B. Description

They apply to s-goals according to the following syntax

sol(n, G),
det(G),

where n is an integer and G is a s-goal. The last form is a shorthand for the annotation

sol(1,G).

Reducing the annotated ps-goal sol(n,G) essentially consists of reducing the ps-goal G as before. The effect induced by the annotation is that the reduction is stopped when n answer n-substitutions have been computed for G.

C. Example

The following example illustrates a typical use of the det operator. Consider the following program :

p(N1,N2,Res) ← prod1(N1,L1), prod2(N2,L2), merge(L1?,L2?,L), cons(L,Res).

where

- prod1(N1,L1) and prod2(N2,L2) are some producers of L1 and L2,
- merge(L1,L2,L) holds iff L lists the elements of L1 and L2 so that the order of the elements of L1 and of L2 are preserved in L,
- cons(L,Res) is a consumer of all elements of L, this producing Res.

The various lists L produced by merge(L1?,L2?,L) often lead to the same result Res. Computing one of them is thus sufficient to solve p(N1,N2,Res). The following instantiation of this scheme is particularly convincing. Let integer and add be the procedures embodying the following relations :

- integer(N,L) holds iff L lists in increasing order the integers of the interval [1,N],
- add(L,Res) holds iff Res is the sum of all the elements of L.

Then take

integer(N1,L1), integer(N2,L2) and add(L,Res)

as

prod1(N1,L1), prod2(N2,L2) and cons(L,Res),

respectively. Obviously, computing all merged versions of L1 and L2 leads to the same sum. The corresponding instantiation of the p(N1,N2,Res) scheme of predicates can thus be annotated as follows

p(N1,N2,Res) ← integer(N1,L1), integer(N2,L2), det(merge(L1?,L2?,L)), add(L,Res).

Remark It might appear that this example has been constructed on purpose in order to illustrate the det annotation. The merge procedure consists, in fact, of a somewhat relaxed version of the append procedure. Using this stronger append version instead of the merge one makes the above discussion obsolate. This opinion is indeed valid in the sequential context. It is however no longer true in the concurrent one. Using append makes any partial knowledge of L2 useless until L1 is completely constructed. In contrast, the merge version allows to consume the produced prefixes of L1 and L2 concurrently.

D. Optimization

The optimization achieved by the sol and det annotations result from the fact that the and/or/not search tree produced by the reduction of the annotated ps-goal is limited to the production of solutions of the required number. This might be quite substantial. As an illustration, Table 6.3 compares the reduction of the ps-goals

merge([1,2,3],[1,2,3,4,5],L),
merge([1,2,3,4,5],[1,2],L)

in their unannotated version and their annotated version by the det operator. Reconciliation has no effect on the generated ps-goals so that the measures have been taken by fixing the R-depth parameter of the Conclog model to ∞. It is assumed that all reduction steps take the same time and that and-parallelism and or-parallelism are applied in their fully parallel sense. Finally, the following classical definition of the merge procedure has been used (see Section 11.4.1 for a construction) :

merge([],L,L).
merge(L,[],L).
merge([H|T],L,[H|T_merged]) ← merge(T,L,T_merged).
merge(L,[H|T],[H|T_merged]) ← merge(L,T,T_merged).

S-goal	Unannotated version	Annotated version
merge([1,2,3],[1,2,3,4,5],L)	418	30
merge([1,2,3,4,5],[1,2],L)	166	14

Table 6.3

6.2.1.5 The commit operators

A. Motivation

The commit operators aim at pruning the computed and/or/not search tree by discarding some unifiable clauses for reduction. As a result, they achieve the optimizable situations of Point 4° of Section 6.1 according to the second method there exposed as well as the situations of Point 5° of this section.

B. Description

Two kinds of commit operators are introduced. The commit operator of the first kind is used to describe some additional constraint to the unification one. It is called *descriptor commit*. As such, it does not force the selection and the discarding of clauses. The commit operators of the second kind provide the complementary information. They are called *activator commits*.

B.1 SYNTACTICAL DESCRIPTION

Syntactically, the commit operators present as follows.

(i) The descriptor commit

The descriptor commit is denoted by the "$|_c$" symbol. It takes place in the body of any clause as s-goals separator. It can however only appears once in any clause. It is defined with a lower priority than the sequentialization operator. As we will see, it acts in some aspects as the sequentialization operator. This justifies the similarities of the notations.

Clauses containing the descriptor commit are called *guarded clauses*. Their general form is thus as follows :

$H \leftarrow G_1,...,G_m |_c B_1,...,B_n.$

where the symbols $G_1, ..., G_m, B_1, ..., B_n$ represent s-goals. The conjunction $G_1,...,G_m$ is called the *guard* of the clause. The conjunction $B_1,...,B_m$ is called its *commit-body*. By definition, the integers m and n must be strictly positive. Nevertheless, the special built-in predicate true can be used to replace the empty conjunction. It has the property to always succeed with the n-substitution ({},not{}).

(ii) The activators commits

Two types of activator commits are provided.

1) Commits of one type are used to annotate s-goals. They are called *call-commit*. They take the form of the following unary operators

"*l_commit(...)*", "*g_commit(...)*".

They are called *global* and *local call-commit*s, respectively. Of course, just one of them can annotate any s-goal.

2) Commits of the other type are used to annotate clauses. They are called *procedure-commits*. Two of them are used as a global declaration of the procedure :

l_commit pred_name,
g_commit pred_name,

where pred_name is the name of the annotated procedure. They also exclude one another. Two others are used in combination with suspension declarations :

suspend pred_name(m_1,...,m_n) with l_commit
suspend pred_name(m_1,...,m_n) with g_commit.

Their presence is constrained by the two following rules :

(i) just one of them can be associated with any suspension declaration
(ii) they are allowed only if no commit has been declared as a global declaration.

The commit operators prefixed by the "l_" and "g_" strings are called *local* and *global procedure-commits*, respectively.

B.2 SEMANTICAL DESCRIPTION

Operationnally, the commit operators modify the reduction of ps-goals as follows. Five cases must be considered. Let G be the ps-goal to reduce (annotated or not), p be the procedure name that corresponds to it and

$H_1 \leftarrow Cl_1$. (c_1)
...
$H_m \leftarrow Cl_m$. (c_m)

be the clauses defining p.

1) The ps-goal G and the procedure p are not annotated by any commit operators. In this case, the reduction of G is done as decribed in the previous sections.

2) The ps-goal G and the procedure p are not annotated by an activator commit but the procedure p is annotated by at least one descriptor commit. In this case, the descriptor commit simply acts as the main sequentiliazation operator the clause bodies where it appears.

3) The ps-goal G is annotated by an activator operator but not the procedure p. In this case, let G' be G without its commit annotation and let us associate with each clause c_i, namely

$$H_i \leftarrow Cl_i,$$

the clause

$$H_i \leftarrow Cg_i \mid_c Cb_i \qquad (c_i')$$

where

- Cg_i and Cb_i are the following annotated versions of the guard and commit-body of c_i if it is a guarded clause :
    - if G is annotated by a local commit then no annotation is added,
    - otherwise, each ps-goal of Cg_i and Cb_i is annotated by the global call-commit
- Cg_i is true and Cb_i is Cl_i annotated as above, if the clause $H_i \leftarrow Cl_i$ is not a guarded clause.

The reduction of G owing to the clauses c_1 to c_m is defined as the reduction of G by means of the clauses c_1' to c_m'. This proceeds as follows. All of c_i' 's are used in a parallel manner to reduce G' with the possible suspensions induced by read-only annotations and suspension declarations as well as the possible induced instantiations of G' (see Sections 6.2.1.1 and 6.2.1.2). When any clause c_i' successfully unifies with one instance of G', the induced instance, say Cl_inst$_i$, of the body of c_i' is evaluated as follows.

1. Its guard part is first reduced.
2. As soon as an n-substitution is computed as an answer, a request is made to commit the reduction of G' to Cl_inst$_i$.
3. It is acknowledged if it is the first request to occur. Otherwise, no acknowledgment is returned.
4. In the case the request is acknowledged, the reduction of G is indeed committed to Cl_inst$_i$. This means that all other concurrent reductions, using the other clauses c_j' or other instances of G', are eliminated. Note that the case where the request is not acknowlegded thus corresponds to the situation where another request has been acknowledged. The evaluation of Cl_inst$_i$ is then killed by the commitment to another alternative of reduction.

4) The procedure p is annotated by an activator commit in the form of a global declaration. The reduction then amounts to a reduction of the above case 3) by omitting the commit annotation of p and by considering G to be annotated as follows :

- if G is not annotated by a call-commit, then it is annotated by a global or local call-commit according as p is globally or locally annotated by the activator commit,
- otherwise,
    - if G is annotated by a global call-commit or if the commit annotation of p is local, then G is considered as such,
    - otherwise, G is annotated by a global call-commit.

5) The procedure p is annotated by some activator commit operators associated with its suspension declarations. In this case, the derivation of G is essentially performed as described in cases 1), 2) or 3) by omitting the commit operators of p. These operators are taken into account as follows. As described in Section 6.2.1.2, any effective reduction of G by a clause necessitates the choice of a suspension declaration. The induced instance of the clause body is reduced as before if no commit annotation is associated with the selected suspension declarations. In the opposite case, the commit annotation is taken into account. The s-goals are annotated by commit operators as decribed in cases 4) and 5). A request for commitment also results, provided the reduction is not killed. Acknowledged, it forces the reduction of G to commit to the reduction of the clause body under consideration.

C. Examples

The following examples illustrate the impact of the commit operators.

1) Consider the ps-goal

merge([1,2],[3,4],L)

and the definition of the merge procedure of Section 6.2.1.4. Without commit annotations, the ps-goal would be reduced by creating two goals corresponding to the last two clauses of the merge procedure, namely

merge([H|T],L,[H|T_merged]) ← merge(T,L,T_merged).
merge(L,[H|T],[H|T_merged]) ← merge(L,T,T_merged).

These two goals would, at their turn, create two goals, and so on, ... The computed and/or/not search tree thus grows in an exponential way.

Annotating the merge ps-goal by a global activator commit forces one clause to be selected at any ||-reduction step. Only one goal thus results from the ||-reduction of each ps-goal. It follows that the computed and/or/not search is reduced to a linear growth.

The same effect is achieved by annotating the merge procedure by the global procedure commit operator.

2) Assume now that the merge procedure is defined with three suspension declarations, two of them being associated with a commit operator :

```
suspend merge(L1,L2,L3) until list(L1) with g_commit.
suspend merge(L1,L2,L3) until list(L2) with g_commit.
suspend merge(L1,L2,L3) until list(L3).
merge([],L,L).
merge(L,[],L).
merge([H1|T1],L2,[H1|L]) ← merge(T1,L2,L).
merge(L1,[H2|T2],[H2|L]) ← merge(L1,T2,L).
```

Consider the three following ps-goals :

P_1 : merge([1,2],[3,4],L).
P_2 : merge(L1,L2,[3,4]).
P_3 : merge([1,2],[3,4],[1,2,3,4]).

Appealing the interpretation of the above Subsection A, P_1 manifestly uses the merge procedure as a function of its two first arguments to produce the last one. Only one value for L is thus expected. This is indeed the case. The two last clauses of the merge procedure are the only ones that unify with P_1. Just the two first suspension declarations may be satisfied. Commitment is thus applied. As a result, only one clause is selected at each ||-reduction step of P_1.

The ps-goal P_2 embodies the dual approach of the merge procedure. It is used to produce all the pairs of lists (L1,L2) for which one merged version is [3,4]. Although commitment is required by the first suspension declaration, all of them are in fact computed. The second suspension declaration is indeed the only one to be fulfilled at each ||-reduction step.

The reduction of the ps-goal P_3 is more subtil. At its ||-reduction step, the three suspension declarations are indeed fulfilled. Commitment may thus be involved or not according as one of the two first suspension declarations is selected or not. This is however of no worry since only one clause can be used at each reduction step.

These ps-goals illustrate one important characteristic of the commit operators associated with suspension declarations. According to the pattern of use, the same procedure definition can be used in two extreme ways :

- either, in a committed one, to produce at most one solution; this results in the computation of a linearlized search tree
- or, in an unconstrained one, to produce all solutions; this results in the computation of a fully (generally exponential) search tree.

D. Optimization

The optimization induced by the commit operators may be quite substantial. It results from the fact that each ||-reduction step may be forced to employ only one clause. Hence, the and/or/not search, inherently of exponential growth, can be linearlized. This optimization has already been illustrated by the above example. Table 6.4 further substantiates it. It compares the number of reduction steps resulting from the reduction of the ps-goals

> g_commit(merge([1,2,3],[1,2,3,4,5],L),
> merge([1,2,3],[1,2,3,4,5],L),

on the one hand, and

> g_commit(merge([1,2,3,4,5],[1,2],L),
> merge([1,2,3,4,5],[1,2],L),

on the other hand. They use the merge definition of the above Subsection C. The R-depth parameter has been fixed to ∞. The results are however independent from it since reconciliation would not alter the reductions.

S-goal	Unannotated version	Annotated version
merge([1,2,3],[1,2,3,4,5],L)	418	6
merge([1,2,3,4,5],[1,2],L)	166	6

Table 6.4

It is interesting to compare Tables 6.3 and 6.4. The optimization of the commit operator is greater than that induced by the det operator. This is expected since, in contrast with the det operator, the commit operators reduce the complexity of the growth of the computed and/or/not search trees. However, commit operators cannot always be manipulated in a so direct way without destroying the soundness of the reductions. To ensure that an answer n-substitution is computed, they must be placed so that, when a clause is selected, the reduction of its induced body indeed leads to such an answer n-substitution. This might be quite difficult to ensure in some cases. In contrast, the "det" operator can be introduced safely since obtaining an answer n-substitution is ensured by its definition.

6.2.1.6 The sequentializing clause separator

A. Motivation

Up till now, the order of the clauses has not been taken into account. The sequentializing clause separator provides a means of ordering them. As we will see in a moment, this is particularly suitable when the sol, det and commit operators are involved in the reductions.

B. Description

The sequentializing clause separator consists of the ";" delimitor of the clauses. It is defined with a lower priority than the usual "." clause delimitor. This results in partitioning the clauses of the procedures. For instance, the clauses

c_1 ;
c_2 .
c_3 ;
c_4 .

are, in fact, partitionned into the following sets $\{c_1\}$, $\{c_2,c_3\}$, $\{c_4\}$. Furthermore, the effect of the ";" delimitor is to introduce an order on the clause sets of the partition. Let them be $Sclause_1$, ..., $Sclause_n$. Then the clauses are employed according to the following two rules :

- for any i, all the clauses of $Sclause_i$ are indeed used in parallel,
- for any i>1, the clauses of $Sclause_i$ are only used when the reductions induced by all clauses of $Sclause_1$, ..., $Sclause_{i-1}$ have been computed.

Restated in other terms, clauses of one clause set are employed only when all the reductions resulting from the clauses of preceeding clause sets are completely computed.

C. Example

To suggest the interest of the ";" delimitor, let us consider the following procedure

$H_1 \leftarrow Cg_1 |_c Cb_1$;
$H_2 \leftarrow Cg_2 |_c Cb_2$.

Furthermore let G be a ps-goal which unifies with both H_1 and H_2. Consider the annotated goal

g_commit(G).

Because of the commitment mechanism and thanks to the ";" delimitor, the second clause is only used when the guard of the first one fails. The above clauses are thus equivalent to the two following ones :

$H_1 \leftarrow Cg_1 |_c Cb_1$.
$H_2 \leftarrow not(Cg_1), Cg_2 |_c Cb_2$.

Hence, using the ";" operator with the commit operator makes the ps-goal $not(Cg_1)$ implicit in the second clause. On the operational point of view, its reduction is thus gained. Note that the same behavior is also achieved by using the "det" operator.

A particular interesting use of this combination of the ";" with the "det" or the commit operator concerns the handling of default cases. To this end, clauses corresponding to exceptions are first stated and are separated from the clause corresponding to the general case by a ";" delimitor. The first clauses are thus first tested for reduction. If they succeed, then the treated ps-goal corresponds to an exception. Otherwise, the last clause is used to reduce the ps-goal. In this case, it corresponds to the general case.

The interest of the above programming is twofold. On the one hand, a procedure very easy to modify results. A clause corresponding to an additional exception can be added without modifying other clauses. On the other hand, some optimization is achieved. Tests to determine whether a call constitutes an exception or not is performed only once.

D. Optimization

In general, the optimization induced by the ";" operator arises from two points :

- from the possibility to postpone some costly evaluations until some other less expensive ones are made. This is particularly interesting when only some solutions are required. Those corresponding to the less costly evaluations are only computed.

- from the possibility to state some conditions implictly. The gain then results from the fact that the same evaluations are not performed twice or (even) more.

6.2.1.7 The reduction operators

A. Motivation

We finally introduce the reduction operators. Their presence result from point 6° of Section 6.1.

B. Description

As the commit operators, the reduction operators can annotate both calls and procedures. They are subsequently described in this order.

B.1 REDUCTION OPERATORS APPLIED TO CALLS

Four reduction operators are provided to annotate calls. They can be combined but provided that only one R-depth operator is used.

(i) The R-depth operators.

The *R-depth operators* annotate s-goals in the following manner :

$G\uparrow n$ or $G\downarrow n$

where G is a s-goal and n is a strictly positive integer or the infinite. They are called *increasing* and *decreasing reduction operators*, respectively. Their effect is to modify the R-depth of the slices generated by the reduction of G to the maximum (resp. minimum) of the current R-depth associated with G and n.

(ii) The reconciler operator

The *reconciler operator* annotates s-goals as follows :

G rec(r_1, r_2, r_3)

where G is a s-goal and the r_i's are either "restricted", "total" or "_". These three arguments refer to the manner in which reconciliation is performed in the following processes of the subtree engendered by G :

1) goal-processes,
2) ps-goal processes and suspended processes,
3) ns-goal-processes,

respectively. The "total" value indicates that reconciliation must be performed in a fully incremental way, as described in Chapters 4 and 5. The "restricted" value indicates that R-triplets whose labels are "complete" (that is those corresponding to (completed) solution subtrees) are only transmitted incrementally. The other R-triplets are transmitted altogether when the considered process has completely performed its reconciliation task for the reconciliation phase under consideration. Finally, the "_" value indicates that the way in which reconciliation is operated by any process is not altered by the annotation.

(iii) The relaunch operator

The *relaunch operator* annotate s-goals as follows :

G▽ .

It makes the s-goal G act as a top level query as far as reconciliation is concerned. Let P be the process associated with G. Processes of the subtree ST engendered by P are relaunched for a new generation phase as soon as reconciliation is completely performed by P and this without waiting that the reconciliation phase under consideration is completely performed. Processes of ST are then completely deaf to instantiation messages ordered by ancestor processes of P.

B.2 REDUCTION OPERATORS APPLIED TO PROCEDURES

Similar operators can be stated at the procedure level. They have essentially the same syntax and are named as their counterparts. As the commit operators, they can be defined for the whole procedure, as in

reconciliation proc_name↑n

or in association with some suspension declarations, as in

suspend proc_name($m_1,...,m_n$)↑n.

In the first case, the reduction is altered as if the call was annotated by the reduction operators. In the second case, the reduction operators only act if the suspension declaration to which they are associated is selected for reduction. In this case, the reduction operators are only applied to the clause body resulting from the reduction step.

C. Optimization

The optimization induced by the reduction operators results from a more adequate choice of the parameter of the model for specific computations. We refer the reader to Sections 4.4.1 and 5.4.2.1 for a detailed discussion of the merits of the different possible values of these parameters.

6.2.2 Built-in primitives

To be practical, any logic programming language must incorporate some built-in primitives. Before describing the Conclog ones, it is first worth noting that the annotations presented in Section 6.2.1 provide a quite suitable framework to introduce the built-in primitives. For instance, a means of sequentialization is provided to force the printing of a solution after it has effectively been computed.

Let us now describe the Conclog built-in primitives. Classical primitives for arithmetic, input/output or to create and access components of general structures are first provided, with their implicit suspension declarations. The following built-in primitives are furthermore provided :

- a three argument meta-call primitive,
- primitives for testing bindings made for variables,
- primitives for waiting until some arguments are bound to non-variable terms or to ground terms.

A. The three-argument meta-call primitive

The Conclog meta-call primitive extends the Prolog counterpart by explicitly handling failure and suspension. It takes the following form :

call(Ps-goal,Status,Control)

where

- Ps-goal is a variable or a ps-goal
- Status and Control are variables.

Its reduction is as follows. Let Proc be the process is charge of it.

#1. If Ps-goal is a variable then the reduction suspends. It is resumed when Ps-goal is bound, directly or indirectly, to a non-variable term in the form of a ps-goal. One of this bounding terms is arbitrarily selected. Let it be T. Step #3 is then undertaken by taking T as value for Ps-goal.

#2. If Ps-goal is not a variable then step #3 is directly undertaken.

#3. The ps-goal Ps-goal is reduced essentially as a normal ps-goal. Its reduction is started as such. It may then be modified as follows.

The process Proc is hearing the direct or indirect bindings for the Control variable. Precisely, a set of variables, say Svars, is progressively constructed :
- it contains the Control variable,
- it contains any variable V appearing in a binding
    - produced in the computed and/or/not search tree
    - of one of the forms X/V or X/[e_1,...,e_m|V], where X is in the set Svars and each e_i is either "suspend", "continue", "stop".

The process Proc then hears the bindings of the above form for the variables of Svars. Reception of bindings of the form X/[e_1,...,e_m|V] induces some action on the descendant processes of Proc (i.e. on the reduction of Ps_goal). The elements "suspend", "continue" and "stop" are interpreted as orders forcing these processes to the following actions, respectively :
- to suspend,
- to resume their work if they are suspended
- to stop engendering their children and to activate reconciliation at the tip processes. In this case, the subtree engendered by Proc is considered as completely constructed. Completeness of the partial solution subtrees is however considered as in Definition 5.29.

These orders are executed according to their order in the bounding list [e_1,...,e_m|V]. As a result, Status is furthermore incrementally bound to a list whose elements are "suspended", "continued", "stopped", according to the sent orders.

#4. R-triplets transmitted by the children of Proc and whose labels are "complete" are transmitted to the father process of Proc. The end-reconciliation messages are also transmitted as if Proc were a simple ps-goal. The following extension is furthermore operated. It is justified by the particularity of the meta-call primitive to succeed in any case. At each reconciliation phase, one R-triplet is sent by Proc if no R-triplets have been transmitted by it. It is
- < ({},not{}), {Proc.id}, incomplete > if the subtree engendered by Proc, say ST, is completely constructed,
- < ({},not{}), {Proc.id}, complete >, otherwise.

#5. Finally, the Status list is ended as follows when ST is completely constructed. At that time, Status is a variable or has the form of an open-ended list [m_1,...,m_n|Tail] where all m_i's are either "suspended", "continued" or "stopped". The following instantiations are operated.
- If Status is of the [m_1,...,m_n|Tail] form with "stopped" as last value m_n then Tail is bound to the empty list.

- Otherwise, if no R-triplets of the children of Proc have naturally been transmitted by Proc,
  - then Status is bound to
    - [failed] if it is a variable
    - $[m_1,\ldots,m_n,\text{failed}]$, otherwise,
  - else Status is bound to
    - [succeeded] if it is a variable
    - $[m_1,\ldots,m_n,\text{succeeded}]$, otherwise.

A simpler form of the meta-call argument is sometimes used. It has only two arguments : Ps-goal and Status. It acts as a three-argument meta-call primitive

   call(Ps–goal,Status_list,Control)

that does not obey any Control variable. The last final value m_i of its Status_list argument is only reported in Status. Note that it can only be "failed" or "succeeded".

B. The "var_syst" and "uvar_syst" primitives

In view of our use of full and-parallelism, variable arguments are always considered as variables even if they are bound to non-variable terms in the and/or/not search tree. To handle such information, the following primitives are provided :

   uvar_syst(T),
   var_syst(T),

where T is some term. The first primitive succeeds iff, at the time of the call evaluation, T is a variable that is not directly bound to a non-variable term by an nmas that could be heard by it[1]. The way in which variables binding X are themselves bound is thus of no importance. The second primitive succeeds iff, at the time of the call evaluation, T is a non-variable term that is not bound directly or indirectly to a non-variable term.

C. The "waitnv" and "waitg" primitives

Finally, the waitnv(T) and waitg(T) calls suspend until their argument T is bound to a non-variable term or to a ground term, respectively. They succeed for each such bindings that could be heard by them.

---

[1] See Section 6.2.1.1 for the definition of heard bindings.

6.2.3 A minimal and "reasonably complete" set of extra-logical features

We believe that one of the wealths of Conclog is to incorporate various forms of annotations : read-only annotations, suspension declarations, sequentialization operator, det and sol operators, commit operators, sequentialization clause separator, reduction operators. It is worth noting that most other concurrent logic programming languages only use a few of these annotations. For instance, Concurrent Prolog ([Shapiro, 1983]) only uses read-only annotations and the commit operators. It is our claim that the extra-logical features provided by Conclog constitute a minimal and reasonably complete set, with the following acceptation :

minimal : for any extra-logical feature, it is practically not convenient to simulate it by a combination of other ones;

reasonably complete : most desirable forms of synchronization, communication or, more generally, computations can indeed be programmed by using the Conclog extra-logical features.

We now turn to substantiate this claim.

A. Minimality

As far as the built-in primitives are concerned, it is quite straightforward to argue that each of them cannot be replaced by a combination of other extra-logical features. This is manifestly the case for the three arguments meta-call. This is also the case for the uvar_syst and var_syst primitives. This is finally the case for the waitnv and waitg primitives. Although they have some counterpart in the "nv" and "g" extension of read-only annotations, they necessitate no unification with a clause to induce suspension. They thus have grounds for existence, too.

The minimality of the annotations essentially results from the analysis of Section 6.1., describing the desired optimization mechanisms, and of the motivation subsections of Section 6.2.1, linking the annotations with the optimization mechanisms they address. Three points should, perhaps, be clarified. All of them concern the read-only annotations.

1° Are the global and local read-only declarations not redundant with each other?
2° Are the "nv" and "g" suffixes of the read-only annotations not redundant with the constraint stated by the read-only annotations "?" and "!" ?
3° Are these "nv" and "g" suffixes not redundant with the sequentialization operator and the waitnv and waitg primitives ?

(i) Global vs local read-only annotations

As already argued, local and global read-only annotations differ by the way in which they are inherited in the reduction. On the one hand, a global read-only annotation acts in the whole reduction of the considered ps-goal and thus forbids any globally read-only annotated variable to be instantiated by this reduction. Such a constraint can thus be stated only once. In contrast, local read-only annotations only act in the first reduction step and thus allow any annotated variable to be instantiated by further reduction steps. In particular, this allows to program what is called back communication. To be more specific, let us consider the query

← prod(X), cons(X).

with the program

prod([H|T]).

suspend cons(!).

cons([H|T]) ← p(H), q(T).

Due to the suspension declaration, the reduction of cons(X) suspends until X becomes bound to [H|T]. At this time, cons(X) is reduced to the ps-goals p(H) and q(T). No read-only annotation is inherited so that p(H) and q(T) can bind H and T, respectively. They can thus create a two-way communication between prod(X) and cons(X). This scheme is called back communication. In contrast, the

suspend cons(?).

would have propagated global read-only annotations in p(H) and q(T). This would have forbidden H and T to be instantiated by the reduction of p(H) and q(T).

(ii) "Nv" and "g" annotations vs "?" and "!" annotations

The "nv" and "g" suffixes of read-only annotations have been introduced as a means of forcing suspension until the annotated variable, for read-only annotations in calls, or the term corresponding to read-only annotated argument, for read-only annotations in suspension declaration, is non-variable or ground, respectively. It may be asked whether this could not be removed by a suitable choice of the clause heads. This is indeed the case when the constrained variable or term can be described by finite patterns. However, this is not always the case for other types. For instance, forcing the reduction of the ps-goal

add(X,Y,Z),

where X, Y, Z are of the integer type, to suspend until the variable X and Y are bound to a non-variable term, cannot be achieved by means of read-only constraint "?" or "!" and by means of head of clauses.

(iii) "Nv" and "g" annotations vs sequentialization operator and waitnv and waitg primitives

The "nv" and "g" annotations can, in all cases, be replaced by a combination of the sequentialization operator and of the waitnv and waitg primitives. For instance, reducing the s-goal

p(X?nv,Y!g)

amounts to reducing the sequentialized goal

    (waitnv(X),waitg(Y)) | p(X?,Y!).

Similarly, the suspension declaration

    suspend p(X?nv,Y!g)

is equivalent to the suspension declaration

    suspend p(X?,Y!) until waitnv(X), waitg(Y).

Such transformations can manifestly be generalized. Hence, from a theoretical point of view, the "nv" and "g" annotations are redundant with respect to the sequentialization operator and the waitnv and waitg primitives. However this is not the case from a practical point of view. Indeed, the equivalent combination of the sequentialization operator and the waitnv and waitg primitives is quite heavy to write. The above examples are particularly convincing to this respect. This contrasts with the "nv" and "g" annotations. Appealing to the practice of programming, they thus have grounds for existence too.

B. Completeness

Completeness of a set of extra-logical features is a quite questionable matter. Whatever rich such a set is, it might certainly be possible to point out a very particular computation that cannot be programmed by using it. Nevertheless, it is our claim that the Conclog extra-logical features constitute a "reasonbly complete" set in the sense that all usual computation schemes can indeed be programmed by using them.

This claim is established in this work in three complementary ways.

1) Firstly, many programs, ranging over a wide variety of applications, are programmed in Part III. This provides a concrete proof of our claim.

2) Secondly, the annotations are compared with success to others embodied in other concurrent logic programming languages. Completeness of the Conclog annotations then also results from the claim that those languages are sufficiently complete to be usable.

3) Thirdly, the Conclog extra-logical features have been designed in order to meet all the optimization mechanisms required by the analysis of Section 5.1. Completeness of the extra-logical features would then result from the completeness of this analysis. We believe that it is indeed complete.

As a final argumentation, we subsequently answer the two following questionable points.

On the one hand, it might be surprising that no output constraint can be specified in Conclog. Would it be useless to annotate producer subgoals explicitly? From a methodological point of view, certainly not. Nevertheless, from an operational point of view, it is better to state input constraints (what we do thanks to the read-only annotations in calls and suspension declarations). Indeed, this has the advantage of designating explicitly the places where suspension must occur. Furthermore we believe that the input constraints are sufficient. Indeed from our point of view, the restriction of the use of a procedure only comes from these input constraints.

On the other hand, it might also be surprising to notice that head clauses cannot be annotated although this is proposed in languages such as IC-Prolog ([Clark et al., 1982]), Relational Language ([Clark and Gregory, 1981]), CP ([Saraswat, 1987]). To our opinion, it is better to annotate the procedure as a whole than the heads of the clauses. We believe that this is also sufficient. These claims are argued by the following two points.

(i) First, suspensions stated in the clause heads are in fact required by the specification of the procedure and should be considered at the same level as the relation defined by the procedure. Conserving these levels in the procedure code is certainly interesting from a methodological point of view. Restated in other terms, it is worth separating the suspension constraints of the procedure and the clauses defining it.

(ii) Second, cases where it would be easier to annotate each clause head separately often reveal a bad formulation of the suspension conditions. To visualize this, let us consider the following clauses :

   plus(X?,Y?,Z) ← Z is X+Y.
   plus(X?,Y,Z?) ← Y is Z-X.
   plus(X,Y?,Z?) ← X is Z-Y.

In fact, the real suspension condition is not that the first clause should be used with X and Y instantiated, the second one with X and Z instantiated and the third one with Y and Z instantiated. Rather, it is that to use a construct of the form

   Res is Exp

the term Exp must be ground. Hence, a better synchronization is achieved by declaring the is predicate with the implicit suspension declaration

   suspend is(*,?g).[1]

6.3 Design of the Conclog model

It now remains to be shown how the Conclog model can be extended to incorporate the extra-logical features just defined. Precising the tree view here is not interesting since the features manifestly addresses the more local perception of the computations. We will thus directly turn to the process view in the following. Consequently, this section will describe the impact of each extra-logical feature on the process model.

---

[1] To ease the notation, we use an equivalent prefix notation.

A. Read-only annotations and suspension declarations

The effect of read-only annotations and suspension declarations on the process model has already been described in Section 6.2.1.1 and 6.2.1.2. Two points have been passed over in silence:

- communication of bindings heard by suspended processes,
- reconciliation of the newly introduced tip suspended processes.

A.1 COMMUNICATION OF BINDINGS HEARD BY SUSPENDED PROCESSES

Communication of bindings heard by suspended processes is achieved thanks to three synergetic operations.

1) Each goal-process registers for any variable V of its Vc set, the functional restriction to V of the nmgas that occurs in some process P' of ST(P) that are separated from P by an odd number of ns-goal-processes.

2) Each ns-goal-process registers the same general bindings but for the variables of its associated ns-goal.

3) Each time a ps-goal-process is created, it communicates to the above processes the general bindings it makes. Those bindings correspond to the general bindings for the variables of the dom(ψ) set of the en-mgu $\psi \oplus \Psi$ associated with the ps-goal-process. Note that this is quite easy to achieve. Such general bindings need simply be transmitted in a backward manner from child processes to father processes according to the two following rules :

   1°   the general bindings are negated by the ns-goal-processes as follows : the negation not($\{X/t\} \oplus \Theta$) is communicated by any ns-goal-process when it receives the general bindings $\{X/t\} \oplus \Theta$. As a result, general bindings and their negation are in fact communicated. This makes the two following points relevant :
- general bindings are delivered as the negation of negation of general bindings by ns-goal-processes,
- processes of 1) and 2) above only hear general bindings and not their negation.

   2°   the communication of any general binding $\{X/T\} \oplus \Psi$ or of its negation is stopped by the goal-process registering X in its Vc set.

These three operations given, the communication of bindings to be heard by suspended processes is quite easy to achieve. Each suspended process indicates its suspension to the following processes. For each variable X that forces suspension, the following processes are informed of the suspension of the suspended process :

- the goal-process that registers X in its Vc set,
- any ancestor ns-goal-process that is not ancestor of the previous processes.

They are called *processes responsible of X for the suspended process*. Any general binding $\{X/t\}\oplus\Theta$ is then communicated to the suspended process as soon as they are known by these processes.

Killing of processes induced by the killing of producing processes has to be handled as a corollary of such binding communication. This can be achieved by extending the above handling of binding communication as follows. Processes registering general bindings further counts the number of times the general binding has been produced. Similarly, suspended processes count the number of times any general binding is communicated to them. Then, when a producing process fails, it communicates the removal of the general bindings it produces as it communicates their production. Processes registering the general bindings then simply updates the number of times the general bindings have been produced. When all productions of a same bindings have been removed, the obsolateness of the general bindings is communicated to the suspended processes. Similarly, these processes decrease the number of times they have received the general bindings. Finally, the child processes of a suspended process resulting from a general binding are killed when all communications of it have been removed.

A.2 RECONCILIATION OF TIP SUSPENDED PROCESSES

Suspended processes constitute a new class of tip processes. In contrast with the other tip processes (issued from the basic model of Chapter 4 and the extended model of Chapter 5), they do not however enter reconciliation once they are created. It follows that any reconciliation phase does no longer end naturally. To achieve this, tip suspended processes must be activated explicitly when no binding can be communicated to them. This occurs when all tip processes have been created. Signalling this event is performed thanks to two additional structures accessible by any process. The first one is a list of process identifiers. It aims at recording suspended processes that have no child. It is updated in an obvious way :

- at its creation, each suspended process registers in this list,
- it removes from it when it creates a child.

The second one acts as a semaphore. It aims at indicating whether or not there remain active processes. It is set at the beginning of each phase to the number of processes without child that are not suspended. It is then updated as follows:

- each time such a process creates children, say in number n, the semaphore is increased by n-1,
- each time a tip process is created, it is decreased by 1.

Suspended tip processes registered in the above list are then activated for reconciliation when the semaphore becomes null.

B. The sequentialization operator

The introduction of the sequentialization operator results in the following modifications of the process model.

1) Complex goals are treated as follows. Let P be the process in charge of the complex goal

$$\leftarrow C_1(\overline{X}_1), ..., C_n(\overline{X}_n).$$

Then, a child goal-process is created for any $C_i(\overline{X}_i)$ with $\varnothing$ as Vc set and $\{\}\oplus\{not\{\}\}$ as nmas.

2) Sequentialized goal-processes are handled in a similar way. Let P be the goal-process in charge of the goal

$$\leftarrow Cl_1 \mid Cl_2.$$

Two processes, say P_1 and P_2, are created for the goals Cl_1 and Cl_2. The first one is a normal goal-process. The last one is a suspended process of a special kind. It does not wait for general bindings produced for variables but for answer n-substitutions computed for Cl_1 by P_1. For any such n-substitution ν, it creates a child goal-process in charge of computing the instance of Cl_2 by ν. This child process has an empty Vc set and registers $\nu^+\oplus\{\nu^-\}$ as nmas. This given, it returns for any n-substitution μ it computes the composition $\nu\circ\mu$, as required in Section 6.2.1.3. Process P_2 then acts as a normal suspended process and thus simply transmits any n-substitution to P. Finally, the reconciliation procedure of the goal-process P is particularized as follows. It does not combine the n-substitutions produced by P_1 and P_2. Rather each n-substitution computed by P_1 is transmitted to P_2 provided it corresponds to a completed subtree (i.e. is a computed answer n-substitution for Cl_1). Furthermore, each n-substitution issued from P_2 is transmitted without any reconciliation to the father process of P. Ending-reconciliation messages are however handled as for normal goal-processes.

C. The det and sol operators

The det and sol operators need a minor adaptation of the process model. S-goal-processes associated with s-goals annotated by them are modified as follows. They count the number of answer n-substitutions associated with completed subtrees they compute. Then they send end_reconciliation messages to their father processes and freeze any descendant processes when the quota required by the annotation has been reached.

D. The commit operators

Commitment is handled by augmenting any ps-goal-process by a structure to register whether or not some child has been selected for commitment. Commitment requests are then handled in the following obvious way :

- if this structure indicates that a child has already been selected for commitment, then the request is discarded;
- otherwise, the structure is updated and all children distinct from the requesting child are killed, as well as their descendants.

E. The sequentializing clause separator

The sequentializing operator is handled by modifying the generation procedure of ps-goal-processes in a straightforward way. When they are searched for unifiability, clauses are considered in the order indicated by the sequentializing clause separator. Restated in more precise terms, if $Sclause_1$, ..., $Sclause_n$ are the clause sets induced by the sequentializing operator, then the following happens :

- goal-processes or suspended processes issued from clauses of $Sclause_1$ are first created,
- goal-processes or suspended processes, resulting from the clauses of some set $Sclause_i$, are created only after all processes resulting from the clauses of set $Sclause_{i-1}$ have returned an ending-reconciliation message, provided this is not forbidden by a commitment acknowledgement.

F. The reduction operators

The reduction operators are handled as follows.

1) The R-depth operators are handled by creating processes with a R-depth component corresponding to them.

2) Reconciler operators are handled in two steps :
- by extending the reconciliation component of any process by two subcomponents. The first one, say "param_comp", aims at memorizing the way in which the descendant processes perform reconciliation. It is inherited from that of the father process and modified, when need be, as required by the reconciler operators. The second subcomponent is introduced if the process under consideration is required to perform reconciliation in an non-incremental way. In this case, a structure is introduced in order to stock R-triplets that will be sent at the end of the reconciliation procedure of the process.
- by extending the reconciliation procedure in order to incorporate the incremental and non-incremental sending of R-triplets.

3) Finally, the relaunch operator modifies the reconciliation procedures of processes as follows. Let P be a process whose associated s-goal is annotated by the relaunch operator. Then, just before it sends an ending-reconciliation message, process P sends a wake_up message to its descendant tip processes that are not descendant of s-goal-processes, themselve

descendant of P and whose associated s-goal is annotated by the relaunch operator. This may be achieved in two ways :

- by sending a wake_up message to each child of P, that is progressively communicated and stopped by any s-goal-process whose s-goal is annotated by a relaunch operator;
- by sending the wake_up messages to the tip processes directly. In this case, an auxiliary structure is used to test whether or not a tip process is a descendant of s-goal-processes, themselves descendant of P and whose associated s-goal is annotated by the relaunch operator. It simply consists of a tree-like structure memorizing the s-goal-process annotated by the relaunch operator.

G. The three arguments meta-call primitive

Handling the three argument meta-call primitive just requires to extend the process model in order to force some processes to suspend their activity, to resume them and to abandon them definitively. This is basically achieved by the sending of appropriate messages and appropriate reactions to them. Furthermore some auxiliary mechanisms need to be added. Progressively propagating the messages is not sufficient. Processes that have no child at the time of the sending of the messages may, for instance, have created children so that a stop message could infinitively run after tip processes. To avoid this, an auxiliary structure is required. At any moment, it registers the processes that have no child and that are descendants of the process associated with the call. Suspend, continue and stop messages are then sent to them directly.

I. The u_var_syst and var_syst primitives

Handling the u_var_syst and var_syst primitives is quite direct. Let P be the s-goal-process in charge of reducing a call to one of these primitives and let T be the term tested by the primitives. If T is a non-variable term, then the answer is immediate : process P fails. Otherwise, the following happens.

1) As far as the u_var_syst primitive is concerned, processes responsible of T for P are questioned. If all of them register no bindings to non-variable term for T, then process P succeeds. It fails, otherwise.

2) As far as the var_syst primitives are concerned, processes responsible of T for P are questioned. If one of them reports the binding of T to some non-variable term then process P fails. Otherwise, for any binding T/V they register, processes responsible of the variable V for P are questioned too. The above process then repeats for variables binding these variables V until one of the two following conditions is fulfilled :

- one of the above variables is bound to a non-variable term. In this case, T is indirectly bound to a non-variable term and process P fails.
- no variable needs to be tested. In this case, process P succeeds.

J. The waitnv and waitg primitives

The waitnv and waitg primitives are handled in a similar way. Let P be the s-goal-process in charge of a call to them and T be the argument of the call. If T is non-variable or is ground then the waitnv or waitg call succeeds and returns the ({},not{}) n-substitution. Process P thus succeeds and returns this n-substitution. Otherwise, P is suspended on the variables of T. It behaves as processes suspended because of read-only annotations but uses the heard general bindings in a slightly different way. They are not used for unification but tested to determine whether or not they make T non variable or ground, respectively. Each time this is the case, P succeeds and reports the composition of the heard general bindings. Each time this is not the case, it re-suspends on the newly introduced variables.

6.4 Theoretical properties

Introducing the sequentializing and reduction operators has no effect on the theoretical properties of Sections 4.5 and 5.5, as proved by the results of these sections. In contrast, introducing other annotations may alter them :

- read-only annotations and suspension declarations may introduce infinite suspensions and thus deadlocks;
- the det, sol and commit operators may eliminate solutions of sub-computations required for the complete evaluation of the whole computation or for its soundness, when negation is involved;
- the sequential clause delimiter may infinitely postpone the computation of solutions.

Guaranteeing the soundness and completion properties is thus not immediate when annotations are involved. Chapter 9 will provide transformations to introduce them safely.

6.5 Comparison with related work

Some of our extra-logical features have similar counterparts in other concurrent logic programming languages. This is, in fact, not surprising since, as pointed out in [Saraswat, 1986], the design space of extra-logical features is rather small. Nevertheless, a first interest of the ones over others has been argued in Section 6.2.3 : they form a more extensive set. This section goes further in their comparison. Each one is subsequently taken at its turn and compared with related ones.

A. Read-only annotations

Our read-only annotations (of calls) resemble that of Concurrent Prolog ([Shapiro, 1983]). However, the semantics has been made clearer and takes profit of multi-equations manipulation. This makes the Conclog read-only annotations different from the Concurrent

Prolog ones in three points. The first two of them result from problems firstly pointed out in [Saraswat, 1986].

1) First, unification is order-dependent in Concurrent Prolog. That is the result of the unification varies in Concurrent Prolog according to the order the arguments are unified. To be more specific, let us try to unify the terms f(X?,X) and f(1,1) ([Saraswat, 1986]). If the unification of the arguments is done in a left-to-right order, deadlock may occur since, while X is not instantiated elsewhere, the unification of X? and 1 infinitely suspends. At the opposite, if the unification order is right-to-left, the unification succeeds because, thanks to the unification of the last argument, X is bound to 1 and the unification of the first argument then succeeds. Manifestly, our definition (see Definition 6.1) does not suffer from this problem. Furthermore, thanks to the manipulation of multi-equations, propagation of read-only annotations is very easy and early detection of failure can be made. This last point also contrasts with the Concurrent Prolog model. Indeed, failure is detected in this model when unification can proceed without being suspended.

Concerning the order of unification, it might be surprising to find out that, in Conclog, the unification of f(X?,X) and f(1,1) suspends though the evaluation of

$\leftarrow$ X?=1, X=1

does not suspend. Hence, although one could expect a parallel evaluation of the arguments during the unification and although Section 3.1 has claimed that the unification of f(X,X) and of f(1,1) is equivalent to the reduction of the conjunction $\leftarrow$X=1,X=1, the unification of f(X?,X) and of f(1,1) is not equivalent to the reduction of $\leftarrow$X?=1,X=1. The justification is that read-only annotations address a non-declarative issue, namely the statement of constraints. It is thus not, in fact, strange that the goals

$\leftarrow$ f(X?,X)=f(1,1)

and

$\leftarrow$ X?=1, X=1

behave differently although they are identical on an declarative point of view (i.e. by discarding the extra-logical read-only annotations).

2) Other problems with the Concurrent Prolog read-only annotation come from the possibility of unifying two terms containing read-only annotations. What should happen for the unification of X? and X, of X? and X?, of X? and Y?, respectively? These problems are irrelevant in the Conclog model since the variables of goals are the only terms to be read-only annotated and read-only annotations only affect the reduction of a goal owing to a clause.

3) Finally, the inheritance of our read-only annotations is clearer than the Concurrent Prolog one. In Concurrent Prolog, a variable unified with a read-only variable is made read-only; the read-only annotation thus behaves as our strong read-only annotation. In contrast, for

compound read-only annotated terms, inner variables are not considered as read-only. Read-only annotations may thus be inherited or not. This has surprising consequences when read-only annotations are involved in the reduction of s-goals. For instance, the reduction of the ps-goal

    p(X?)

with the clause

    p(t(1,2)) ← ...

suspends whereas that of the instance p(t(Y,Z)?) of p(X) succeeds!

In fact, Concurrent Prolog read-only annotations prevent any variable of a call to be constructed by the reduction but not to be instantiated. Suspension is thus ensured when any read-only variable would be instantiated but is removed once the main functor of a binding term is known. Forbidding the instantiation of inner variables must thus be ensured explicilty. This may lead to some tricky code. For instance, to ensure that the reduction of the ps-goal p(X) never instantiates X, the above clause must be rewritten as

    p(t(Y,Z)) ← Y?=1, Z?=2, ...

B. Suspension declaration

Concepts similar to the suspension declarations have also been proposed in the literature, either to design languages or to conceive methodologies of programming. As the Conclog design is only discussed here, we will subsequently limit our comparison to the concepts related to the design of languages.

(i) Prolog mode declarations

Mode declarations introduced in some Prolog dialects ([Bowen et al., 1982]) have some syntactic similarities to our suspension declarations. Their aim of use is however different : they are used for ease of the compilation whereas in Conclog they are used to express suspension constraints. Therefore, the violation of a mode declaration results in an error in such Prologs whereas it forces suspension in Conclog.

(ii) Parlog mode declaration

Parlog mode declaration is very similar to our suspension declaration, too. One difference is that a Parlog procedure must always been accompanied by one and only one mode declaration. Hence, in Parlog, it is impossible to declare multi-directional procedures i.e. procedures without mode declaration. The fact that more than one mode declaration cannot be associated with a procedure can appear as syntatic sugar since the use of auxiliary procedures can circumvent the restriction. For instance, in Parlog, if append is restricted to two patterns of use, separate definitions have to be given with a different relation name for each mode of use although the definitions are, in fact, the same. Hence, from a declarative point of view and for sake of space, our proposal looks better.

Another difference is that, in Parlog, the only alternatives to annotate an argument of a procedure is to declare it either as input or as output. The input constraint corresponds to our "!" annotation. The output constraint is denoted by the "o" symbol. It requires that, at the time of the execution, the corresponding argument is a variable. If not, an error occurs. We already argued in Section 6.2.3 why such an "o" annotation is not provided in Conclog. The above description has another consequence : no "*" argument can thus occur in a mode declaration in Parlog. As it does not impose any restriction, the "*" argument allows to group several elementary mode declarations in one simple mode declaration. This is not possible in Parlog, which is a pity in view of the restriction to one mode declaration per procedure. More importantly, a three argument procedure built to be used with its first two arguments declared as input must be declared with one of the modes (i,i,o) or (i,i,i). This means that this procedure can only be used in one mode as the generator of the third argument or as a test although the real restriction and the gain engendered from the mode declaration comes from the input restriction of the first two arguments. Furthermore, in no case, such a procedure can be used with the third argument partially instantiated!

Finally, it should be pointed out that no global read-only annotations, "nv" or "g" constraints or "Cond" part can be used in mode declarations of Parlog despite of the merits stated in Sections 6.1 and 6.2.

(iii) Mu-Prolog wait declaration

The Mu-Prolog wait declaration ([Naish, 1985a]) is also closely related to our suspension declaration. It is optionally associated with a procedure and can be combined with other ones. Each wait declaration declares a set of input arguments corresponding to our "!" constraint. As in our model, an attempt to bind the corresponding arguments of the call results in a suspension. Nevertheless, no "?", "nv" and "g" annotations and no "Cond" part are provided.

(iv) Trigger

Triggers ([Warren, 1979]) are also related to our suspension declaration. They consist of declarations associated with procedures that state the set of arguments which must be non-variable for the call to proceed. Hence, they cause delay if arguments in the call are variables rather than if they get constructed. They are easier to implement because their effect is independent of the clause heads and of the unification algorithm. However, they are also less powerful. For instance, the recursive call ord([Y|T]) of the following ord procedure cannot be delayed using triggers since the argument is not a variable.

ord([]).
ord([X]).
ord([X,Y|T]) ← X≤Y, ord([Y|T]).

Nevertheless, such suspensions are useful and have also been embodied in our suspension declaration by the "nv" annotation. We also deal with suspension until the argument is ground by means of the "g" annotation.

(v) Threshold

Wise proposes an even simpler concept, called threshold ([Wise, 1982]). This states the number of arguments of a call that must be bound to non-variable terms. If fewer arguments are non-variable, the call is delayed. Clearly, this is less powerful and less useful than our suspension declarations.

(vi) When declaration

Naish tries to combine most of the advantages of wait declarations and triggers by allowing more complex terms in the declarations. This leads to declarations of the form

```
ord_merge(L1,L2,L) when L1 and L2 or L.
ord([H|T]) when T.
```

The first declaration states that ord_merge can be called if the two first arguments or the last argument are non variable. The second declaration states to call ord when the argument is a list with a non-variable tail. The flexibility of such declarations is argued in [Naish, 1985a].

Our suspension declaration can express such synchronizations. For instance, the above when declaration (handling list arguments) are equivalent to the following suspension declarations and clauses :

```
suspend merge(!,!,*).
suspend merge(*,*,!).
merge([],[Y|Ys],[Y|Ys]).
merge([X|Xs],[],[X|Xs]).
merge([X|Xs],[Y|Ys],[X|Zs]) ← X<Y | merge(Xs,[Y|Ys],[X|Zs]).
merge([X|Xs],[Y|Ys],[X,Y|Zs]) ← X=Y | merge(Xs,Ys,Zs).
merge([X|Xs],[Y|Ys],[X|Zs]) ← Y<X | merge(Xs,[Y|Ys],[Y|Zs]).

smode ord(i).
ord([H1,H2|T]) ← ...
```

It should furthermore be noted that because of their complexity when-declarations are more expensive to implement than read-only annotations and suspension declarations in their shortest form without "Cond" conditions.

(vii) Global declarations

Curiously, despite their interest pointed out in Section 6.2, global declarations have received little attention in the literature. Besides Conclog, inheritance of annotations has only be employed in IC-Prolog ([Clark and Mac Cabe, 1979]).

C. The commit operators

Commitment is a notion central to so-called committed-choice languages (Concurrent Prolog ([Shapiro, 1983], GHC ([Ueda, 1985], [Ueda,1986a]), Parlog ([Gregory, 1985]), P-Prolog ([Yang, 1986]), CP ([Saraswat, 1987])). The descriptor commit operator is however just provided by these languages. The activator operators are original to our approach. As proved in Section 6.2.1.5, combining both operators provides a powerful means of optimization : using this combination allows the same procedure to be used either to produce just one solution, by using the commitment mechanism, or to produce all solutions, by not using it. Such procedures cannot be coded in the committed-choice languages. To substantiate this claim, let us turn to a more detailed analysis of the languages.

(i) Concurrent Prolog, Guarded Horn Clauses and Parlog

The commitment mechanism is performed at each ||-reduction step in Concurrent Prolog, GHC and Parlog. At most one solution may thus be produced from the reduction of any call. This restriction is particularly strong. It is somewhat relaxed in Parlog by means of the set built-in primitive acting on particular clauses, excluding commitment in all cases. Hence, in contrast with Conclog, a same procedure cannot be used by involving or not the commitment mechanism.

(ii) P-Prolog

P-Prolog circumvents the "strong commitment" of the previous languages by using the concept of "exclusively commitable clauses". The committable Horn clauses

$H_1 \leftarrow Cg_1 |_c Cb_1$.

...

$H_n \leftarrow Cg_n |_c Cb_n$.

are said to be *exclusively commitable for the (non-extended) ps-goal G* iff only one of them verifies the following property :

(P) its head H_i unifies with G, say with idempotent mgu π_i, and the instance $Cg_i\pi_i$ of its guard can be successfully reduced.

They are called *non-exclusively committable for G* otherwise.

This concept is used as follows. Suppose that the n above clauses have been declared as exclusively committable for any ps-goal. Assume that reducing G points out that more than one clause verifies the above property P. Then suspension occurs and the reduction of G is postponed until more instantiation of the variables allows only one clause to verify property P.

Clauses can also be declared as non-exclusively committable. In this case, all of them are used in parallel to reduce any ps-goal. Or-parallelism still occurs.

However, the exclusively committable character is a property of the clauses. It is thus impossible to declare them as exclusively committable for some patterns of use and non-exclusively committable for other ones. This is a pity since this is precisely what could be required. Consider, for instance, the append procedure. Using it with its first arguments ground and the third to be determined requires the clauses to be declared as exclusively committable. In contrast, using it with its third argument ground and the two first arguments to be determined requires them to be declared as non-exclusively committable. Hence, in contrast with Conclog, the same procedure cannot be used either by forcing commitment or not.

(iii) The CP family of languages

The CP family of languages introduces two descriptor operators, called the don't care commit and the don't know commit. The first one forces commitment to be employed. Thus it acts as our descriptor commit activated by an activator commit. The second acts as our sequentiliazation operators or, in other terms, as our descriptor commit unactivated by an activator commit. Both commits are however distinct so that, once more, the same procedure cannot be used either by forcing commitment or not.

D. The reduction operators

The reduction operators are obviously peculiar to the Conclog model and are thus original to our approach.

E. The sequentialization operator, the sequential clause delimiter and the three-argument meta call primitive

The Conclog sequentialization operator and the sequential clause delimiter are identical to the Parlog "&" ps-goal separator and ";" clause separator. Our three-argument meta-call primitive is furthermore an adaptation of the Parlog meta-call primitive to our model.

F. Other annotations

We finally conclude this section by examining two other control mechanisms not directly related to Conclog ones : freeze ([Colmerauer, 1982]) and delay mask ([Vasak, 1986]).

The Prolog II freeze primitive is a control information placed on goals. It takes the form

freeze(V, Ps-goal).

Its effect is to delay the ps-goal Ps-goal until the variable V is bound to a non-variable term. The interest of extending this freeze annotation in order to incorporate a list of variables rather than a simple one is furthermore advocated in [Naish, 1985a]. However, even this extended form cannot provide an adequate control when terms with more than one level functor are involved. Furthermore, it cannot be used to force the suspension constraint to be propagated all along the reduction. One remedy would be to require suspension until all variables becomes bound to ground terms. However this is manifestly too strong for a parallel scheme where stream-parallelism is desired. As an alternative, a weakened form, called delay mask, has been presented in [Vasak, 1986]. It consists of describing the most general forms of the arguments for which resolution can occur. Suspension happens when call arguments are more general than one of these forms. For instance, the ps-goal append(X,Y,Z) annotated as

    append(X,Y,Z) delaying{append(_,_,[_|_]),append([_|_],_,_)}

suspends until X or Z becomes bound to a list of at least one element. Variables can also be used to indicate the equality between arguments or some of their subterms. For example,

    {append([],X,X)}

expresses that at least the first argument must be the empty list and the two last arguments must be equal.

It is worth noting that theses suspensions may be coded in Conclog, too. On the one hand, the suspension required by the freeze primitive, even in its extended form, can be achieved thanks to the "?nv", "!nv" annotations or the wait primitive. On the other hand, the delay mask can be coded by means of a combination of the sequentialization operator, the suspension declaration and head unification constraints. For instance, the delay mask of the append procedure

    append([],L,L).
    append([H|T],L,[H|T_rem]) ←
           append(T,L,T_rem) delaying {append(_,_,[_|_]),append([_|_],_,_)}

can be simulated as follows :

    append([],L,L).
    append([H|T],L,[H|T_rem]) ← delay(T,L,T_rem) | append(T,L,T_rem).
    suspend delay(?,?,?).
    delay(_,_,[]).
    delay([_|_],_,_).

Note that the annotation corresponding to the delay mask at the procedure level is also provided in Conclog by the Cond part of the suspension declaration. For instance, stating the above delay for the whole append procedure is achieved by the declaration

    suspend append(X,Y,Z) until delay(X,Y,Z).

where delay is defined as above.

As a final remark, let us note that thanks to the sequential operator or the Cond condition of the suspension declaration, most complex delaying condition can be programmed in Conclog. For instance, given a predicate p of variables $\overline{X}$ submitted to a delay condition C, it is sufficient

- to add the C condition in the Cond part of the suspension declarations, if there are some,
- to add the suspension declaration

    suspend p($\overline{X}$) until C,

    otherwise.

If the delay condition were to hold on some calls only, it is sufficient to replace any such call p(...) by the complex goal

(C' | p(...))

where C' is the condition C where the variables $\overline{X}$ have been replaced by their corresponding value in (...).

Pursuing this idea, special built-in predicates insuring exclusive access to variables or more complicated synchronizations (to be realized at a meta-programming level) can take place in C. The definition of such predicates is however out of the scope of this book.

6.6 Conclusion

This chapter has introduced the Conclog extra-logical features both for purposes of optimization and of practicability. Built-in primitives that make a language practical are quite well-known : input/output primitives, arithmetic related primitives, ... We add to them a three-argument meta-call primitive, inspired by that of [Gregory, 1985]. The creative part of the work thus rests essentially on the design of the annotations to optimize pure logic programs. This has been achieved in a quite rational way. Needs of optimization have first been pointed out. Annotations ensuring these optimizations have then been designed and the induced optimizations have been characterized. An interesting side effect is that a framework well-suited for handling built-in primitives has resulted. As another nice property, the whole set of extra-logical features has been argued to be minimal and "reasonably complete", in the sense that

- it is practically not convenient to simulate any extra-logical feature by a combination of other ones (minimality);
- most desirable forms of synchronization, communication or, more generally, computations can indeed be programmed by using the Conclog extra-logical features ("reasonable completion").

The introduction of extra-logical features is the last step of the design of Conclog. It is here worth noting that, for pure logical programs (i.e. free from side effect primitives), the Conclog annotations are not introduced to ensure soundness and completeness, as this is the case for committed-choice languages. They are only introduced for purposes of optimization. Chapter 9 will moreover provide correctness preserving transformations to insert them in programs.

Chapter 7

Event-driven reconciliation

So far, reconciliation is only activated in a rigid manner by the creation of tip processes. This results from the Conclog strategy of computing and/or/not search trees slice by slice and of reconciling each slice after it has been generated. The induced interleaving of generation and reconciliation phases has been shown to be less rigid than it appears at first sight. Furthermore, reduction operators have been provided in order to modify locally the R-depth of the slices as well as the incremental way in which reconciliation is operated. Nevertheless, it might be attractive to start reconciliation more dynamically when some events (to be made precise later) occur. This way of performing reconciliation is subsequently called *event-driven reconciliation*. It is analyzed in this chapter.

7.1 Description

7.1.1 Event-driven reconciliation without annotations

The difficulty of obtaining such a reconciliation without annotations should first be mentioned. There seems indeed to be no safe way to decide when some subtree should stop growing and begin to reconcile by using only general Horn clauses. Note that because conjoined subgoals are solved independently even if they share variables, the instantiations of some variables by conflicting bindings is not an interesting kind of event to trigger reconciliation. Adopting it would destroy an attractive property of the basic model : the possibility of treating disjoint subtrees in a purely independent way. Moreover, it should be reminded that conflicting bindings do not necessarily occur directly but may result from the reconciliation of bindings for other variables. The only possibility to use event-driven reconciliation without annotations would thus be to add heuristics to the interpreter to stop the generation of branches which seem to be infinite or which, a priori, seem to lead to failure. For instance, a branch where a subgoal appears repeatedly in a renamed form may be suspected to generate an infinite reduction. Also, a ps-goal of the form append(L1,L2,L3) where L1 is a priori known to be of length strictly superior to the length of L3 is certainly an unsuccessful ps-goal. Nevertheless, such infinite incorrect branches are already killed in our model with a finite R-depth parameter because reconciliation occurs after a finite time. Moreover, determining safe heuristics seems very difficult, especially when a gain of efficiency is expected.

7.1.2 Event-driven reconciliation with annotations

The only alternative is then to incorporate such heuristics in the program, thereby adding redundancy as proposed in [Bruynooghe, 1982] and [Vasak, 1986]. The idea is to annotate goals or clauses with some invariant to be maintained during the reductions. When the invariant is violated in some subtree, the generation of this subtree is stopped and reconciliation begins. Consider, for instance, the append3 procedure. It obeys the following specification :

append3(L1,L2,L3,L) holds iff L is the list obtained by concatenating the lists L1, L2 and L3.

It can be defined by using the append procedure as follows :

append3(L1,L2,L3,L) ← append(L1,L2,L12),
                          append(L12,L3,L) with length(L12)≤length(L).

The annotation "with length(L12)≤length(L)" allows the reduction of append(L12,L3,L) until the inequation is no longer satisfied. This seems very attractive but, as we will see, introduces two undesirable extra-logical features for little profit.

To adopt this method, a language for expressing such annotations has first to be chosen. Manifestly, there are two possible approaches : annotations can be expressed either relationally or functionally. The first one has the advantage over the latter of providing a desirable homogeneity between clauses and annotations. However, as noted in [Vasak, 1986], all the constraints that need to be expressed have a definite functional flavour. Expressing them in a relational framework leads to complicated expressions essentially because nesting function calls must be done by means of auxiliary variables. The following example should be convincing ([Vasak, 1986]). Suppose we manipulate a tree T and a list L and we want to express that the number of nodes of T must be kept less than the number of elements of L. In a functional approach, we write

Nb_nodes(T) ≤ Nb_elm(L)

whereas in a relational one, we should write

nodes(T,Nb_nodes), length(L,Nb_elm), Nb_nodes ≤ Nb_elm.

To conclude definitively in favour of the functional approach, we add the following argument. For efficiency purposes, it is out of question to manipulate a new and/or search tree at each node of the original constrained and/or search tree. Summing up, annotations should be expressed in a functional style!

Annotations have now to be evaluated efficiently. To be more specific, let us consider the (second) subgoal append(L12,L3,L) of append3(L1,L2,L3,L) for the query ←append3(L1,L2,L3,[a,b,c]). It is associated with the annotation

length(L12) ≤ length([a,b,c]).

The function length is defined as

length([],0).
length([H|T]) = 1 + length(T).

The evaluation of length([a,b,c]) is straightforward. In contrast, the evaluation of length(L12) is more difficult since it involves a variable. In fact, the inequation can be verified iff the minimum of values for expressions of the form length(L12) is less than 3. We will thus evaluate length(L12) as this minimum when verifying the inequation. Similarly, for inequations of the form

...≤ length(L12),

the maximum of length(L12) is taken as value. Hence, information about the range of variation of functions, such as minimum and maximum, has to be associated with the definition of the functions. Furthermore, built-in relational operators such as ≤, ≥, +, - have to be coupled with a qualification of their arguments to decide whether the minimum or the maximum has to be taken when evaluating expressions containing variables.

To sum up, dynamic reconciliation based on event detection leads to the necessary introduction of function definitions associated with domain information. What could be the gain ?

7.2 Analysis

7.2.1 Samples analysis

A potential gain can occur only when various uses of a same query would require conflicting read-only annotations. Otherwise, using them leads to better performances since no extra evaluation is involved.

To be more specific, assume that the append procedure is built to be multi-directional and suppose that append3 is to be used in mode (i,i,i,o) i.e. with the three first arguments as input and the latter as output. As the two first parameters are input, the first call to append behaves deterministically. In contrast, since append(L12,L3,L) proceeds independently and with the second argument only as input, many useless reductions are performed. Some of them further contribute to an infinite branch. These unproductive computations can be eliminated by a read-only annotation. The procedure append3 could thus be rewritten as

```
suspend append3(?,?,?,*).
append3(L1,L2,L3,L) ← append(L1,L2,L12), append(L12?,L3,L).
```

This solution can unfortunately not be adopted when two (or more) modes induce conflicting dataflows. For example, if append3 were to be used also with the first argument to be determined and the others being input i.e. in mode (o,i,i,i), the ps-goal append(L1,L2,L12) would now create many useless reductions (in the same way as append(L12,L3,L) did previously). If we remedy as before by read-only annotating L12 in append(L1,L2,L12), deadlock results because none of the two subgoals append(L1,L2,L12?) and append(L12?,L3,L) is able to construct L12.

Suppose thus append3 is to be multi-directional. Because L12 cannot be constrained in the body by read-only annotations and because append is multi-directional too, many useless computations are to be feared. Let us employ the event-driven reconciliation and associate, with each mode of use, the most appropriate constraint to reduce the unproductive computations. The results are given in Table 7.1. They can be summed up in the following append3 procedure.

```
append3(L1,L2,L3,L) ←  append(L1,L2,L12) with length(L12) ≤ length(L) - length(L3).
                       append(L12,L3,L) with length(L12) ≤ length(L1) + length(L2).
```

Let us now compare the execution of this annotated append3 procedure under the event-driven reconciliation method and the execution of the unannotated version under the Conclog model. Those executions are subsequently referred to as E_{event} and $E_{Conclog}$.

1° mode (i,i,i,i)

In mode (i,i,i,i), the $E_{Conclog}$ execution is superior to the E_{event} execution. This is verified by analyzing the number of reduction steps involved by the evaluation of the two calls append(L1,L2,L12) and append(L12,L3,L).

1) Two cases must be distinguished to analyze the reduction of append(L1,L2,L12).

    1.1) Failure occurs because, during the reduction of append(L1,L2,L12), the lists L12, L and L3 violate the inequation

        length(L12) ≤ length(L) - length(L3).

    (case C_1). In this case, no ps-goal may be generated in E_{event} if the inequation

        0 ≤ length(L) - length(L3).

    does not hold. The number of reduction steps involved in E_{event} is thus at least that involved in the computation of

        length(L) - length(L3)

    i.e. |L|+|L3|+3 [1]. Moreover, the reduction of append(L1,L2,L12) in $E_{Conclog}$ involves at most |L1|+1 reduction steps.

---

[1] The |L| notation is used to denote the length of the list L understood as the number of elements L contains.

mode	append(L1,L2,L12)	append(L12,L3,L)
(i,i,i,i)	—	—
(i,i,i,o)	—	length(L12)≤length(L1)+length(L2)
(i,i,o,i)	—	—
(i,i,o,o)	—	length(L12)≤length(L1)+length(L2)
(i,o,i,i)	length(L12)≤length(L)-length(L3)	—
(i,o,i,o)	—	—
(i,o,o,i)	—	—
(i,o,o,o)	—	—
(o,i,i,i)	length(L12)≤length(L)-length(L3)	—
(o,i,i,o)	—	—
(o,i,o,i)	length(L12)≤length(L)-length(L2)	length(L12)≤length(L)-length(L2)
(o,i,o,o)	—	—
(o,o,i,i)	length(L12)≤length(L)-length(L3)	—
(o,o,i,o)	—	—
(o,o,o,i)	length(L12)≤length(L)	—
(o,o,o,o)	—	—

Table 7.1

1.2) In the alternative case (case C_2), the number of reduction steps involved in $E_{Conclog}$ and E_{Event} to reduce append(L1,L2,L12) are the same, say Nb1. The E_{Event} method further requires the evaluation of length(L)-length(L3) i.e. |L|+|L3|+3 reduction steps.

2) A similar analysis can be made for the reduction of append(L12,L3,L).
   2.1) Failure occurs because the inequation

   length(L12) ≤ length(L1) + length(L2).

   is violated (case C_3). In this case, |L1|+|L2|+1 reduction steps are involved in E_{Event} to reduce append(L12,L3,L). Evaluating the RHS of the above inequation further requires |L1|+|L2|+|L12|+4 reduction steps. In total, 2|L1|+2|L2|+|L12|+5 reduction steps are thus involved in E_{Event}. Moreover, the number of reduction steps involved in $E_{Conclog}$ is |L|+1.

   2.2) In the alternative case (case C_4), the number of reduction steps employed in E_{Event} and $E_{Conclog}$ are the same. Let us call it Nb2. The E_{Event} execution further requires |L12|+|L1|+|L2|+4 reduction steps to evaluate the inequation

   length(L12) ≤ length(L1) + length(L2).

cases	E_{event}	$E_{Conclog}$
$C_1 \wedge C_3$	$\geq (2|L1|+2|L2|+|L3|+|L|+8)$	$\leq (|L1|+|L|+2)$
$C_1 \wedge C_4$	$\geq (|L1|+|L2|+|L3|+|L12|+|L|+Nb2+7)$	$\leq (|L1|+Nb2+1)$
$C_2 \wedge C_3$	$\geq (2|L1|+2|L2|+|L3|+|L|+Nb1+8)$	$\leq (|L|+Nb1+1)$
$C_2 \wedge C_4$	$|L1|+|L2|+|L3|+|L12|+|L|+Nb1+Nb2+7$	$Nb1+Nb2$

Table 7.2

Table 7.2 sums up this analysis. The $\leq Nb$ and $\geq Nb$ notations indicate that less than or more than Nb reduction steps are involved. This table proves our initial claim that the $E_{Conclog}$ execution is superior to the E_{event} one.

2° Other modes

Evaluating the performance of E_{Event} and $E_{Conclog}$ is more difficult in other modes. Nevertheless, the merits of the two executions can be depicted as follows.

1) In favour of the E_{Event} execution, some ps-goals may not be generated because of the violation of inequations. Note that the difference between the ps-goals generated in $E_{Conclog}$ and in E_{Event} is at most the maximal number of ps-goals generated in a slice.

2) In favour of the $E_{Conclog}$ execution, the following reduction steps are required in the E_{Event} execution and not in the $E_{Conclog}$ one :
    - for each reduction step of any ps-goal, a reduction step and an extra-evaluation of the associated inequation is involved,
    - for each known prefix of the lists, a number of reduction steps equivalent to their length is involved.

All in all, the gain induced by the event-driven reconciliation does not seem to be significant! The following measures confirm this idea. They compare the four following append3 procedures.

A. The event annotated version

append3(L1,L2,L3,L) ←
    append(L1,L2,L12) with [length(L12) ≤ length(L) - length(L3)],
    append(L12,L3,L) with [length(L12)≤length(L1) + length(L2)].

event_annotation length(0,∞). [1]
length([]) → 0.
length([H|T]) → 1+length(T).

B. *The unannotated Conclog version*

append3(L1,L2,L3,L) ←
    append(L1,L2,L12),
    append(L12,L3,L).

C. *The read-only annotated Conclog version for append(L12,L3,L) to run in stream-parallelism after append(L1,L2,L12).*

append3(L1,L2,L3,L) ←
    append(L1,L2,L12),
    append(L12?,L3,L).

D. *The read-only annotated Conclog version for append(L1,L2,L12) to run in stream-parallelism after append(L12,L3,L).*

append3(L1,L2,L3,L) ←
    append(L1,L2,L12?),
    append(L12,L3,L).

The following queries have been asked :

Q_1 : ← append3([1,2,3,4,5],[6,7,8,9,10],[11,12,13,14,15],L).
Q_2 : ← append3(L1,L2,L3,[1,2,3,4,5]).
Q_3 : ← append3(L1,[6,7,8,9,10],[11,12,13,14,15],
              [1,2,3,4,5,6,7,8,9,10,11,12,13,14,15]).
Q_4 : ← append3([1,2,3,4,5],L2,[11,12,13,14,15],
              [1,2,3,4,5,6,7,8,9,10,11,12,13,14,15]).
Q_5 : ← append3([1,2,3,4,5],[6,7,8,9,10],L3,[1,2,3,4,5,6,7,8,9,10,11,12,13,14,15]).

Queries Q_1, Q_3, Q_4 and Q_5 lead to only one solution. For each of them, the number of reduction steps involved in the computation of the solution subtree has been measured under a R-depth parameter fixed to 20 and 30, respectively. Query Q_2 leads to 10 different solutions. Therefore, two numbers of reduction steps are given. The first one, referred to in regards with Q_2 (1st sol), measures the number of reduction steps required for the computation of the solution subtree corresponding to the first answer substitution. The last one, referred to in regards with Q_2, gives the number of reduction steps involved for the computation of the solution subtree of the last solution. The number of reduction steps involved in the solution subtrees is furthermore indicated for each query. The results are listed in Table 7.3.

---

[1] The (0,∞) pair represents the minimum and maximum values of the function length.

Query	Involved	Version A	Version B	Version C	Version D
Q_1	12	61 (61)	35 (55)	17 (17)	∞ (∞)
Q_2 (1st sol.)	3	15 (15)	5 (5)	7 (7)	5 (5)
Q_2	25	56 (56)	49 (69)	∞ (∞)	47 (47)
Q_3	18	105 (105)	55 (75)	∞ (∞)	32 (32)
Q_4	18	78 (78)	23 (23)	23 (23)	23 (23)
Q_5	18	89 (89)	38 (38)	18 (18)	32 (32)

Table 7.3

Another benchmark is given by the compress procedure ([Vasak, 1986]). Its specification and construction are out of concern for the moment. They can be found in Chapter 10. The four following versions are compared here :

A. Unannotated Conclog program

compress([],[]).
compress([C|T],[C,Lg|Tail_CL]) ←
 first_max_seq([C|T],F_seq,Suff),
 length(F_seq,Lg),
 compress(Suff,Tail_CL).

first_max_seq([],[],[]).
first_max_seq([C],[C],[]).
first_max_seq([C1,C2|T],[C1],[C2|T]) ← C1≠C2.
first_max_seq([C,C|T],[C|TF_seq],Suff) ← first_max_seq([C|T],TF_seq,Suff).

length([],0).
length([H|T],s(N)) ← length(T,N).

B. Annotated Conclog program for the (i,*) mode of use

suspend compress(!,*).
compress([],[]).
compress([C|T],[C,Lg|Tail_CL]) ←
 first_max_seq([C|T],F_seq,Suff),
 length(F_seq,Lg),
 compress(Suff,Tail_CL).

suspend first_max_seq(!,*,*).
first_max_seq([],[],[]).
first_max_seq([C],[C],[]).
first_max_seq([C1,C2|T],Seq,Suffix) ← C1≠C2 | Seq=[C1], Suffix=[C2|T].
first_max_seq([C,C|T],[C|TF_seq],Suff) ← first_max_seq([C|T],TF_seq,Suff).

suspend length(!,*).
length([],0).
length([H|T],s(N)) ← length(T,N).

C. Annotated Conclog program for the mode (*,i).

suspend compress(*,!).
compress([],[]).
compress([C|T],[C,Lg|Tail_CL]) ←
    first_max_seq([C|T],F_seq,Suff),
    length(F_seq,Lg),
    compress(Suff,Tail_CL).

suspend first_max_seq(*,!,!).
first_max_seq([],[],[]).
first_max_seq([C1],[C2],[]) ← C1=C2.
first_max_seq([C1,C2|T],[C3],[C2|T]) ← C1=C3, C1≠C2.
first_max_seq([C1,C2|T],[C3|TF_seq],Suff) ←
    C1=C2, C1=C3, first_max_seq([C1|T],TF_seq,Suff).

suspend length(*,!).
length([],0).
length([H|T],s(N)) ← length(T,N).

D. The event annotated version

compress([],[]).
compress([C|T],[C,Lg|Tail_CL]) ←
    first_max_seq([C|T],F_seq,Suff) with length(T)≥Lg-1,
    length(F_seq,Lg),
    compress(Suff,Tail_CL).

first_max_seq([],[],[]).
first_max_seq([C],[C],[]).
first_max_seq([C1,C2|T],[C1],[C2|T]) ← C1≠C2.
first_max_seq([C,C|T],[C|TF_seq],Suff) ← first_max_seq([C|T],TF_seq,Suff).

length([],0).
length([H|T],s(N)) ← length(T,N).

event_annotation length(0,∞).
length([]) → 0.
length([H|T]) → 1+length(T).

They have been compared on the following queries :

Q_1 : ← compress([a,a,e,e,e,i,i,i,i,i,i],L).
Q_2 : ←compress(L,[a,s(s(0)),e,s(s(s(0))),i,s(s(s(s(s(0))))))]).

Both of them have only one solution. Table 7.4 delivers for each of them the number of reduction steps required by each method with the R-depth parameter of the model fixed to a value of 20 and 30, respectively. The number of reduction steps involved in the solution subtree is furthermore indicated.

Query	Involved	Version A	Version B	Version C	Version D
Q_1	35	364 (1419)	44 (44)	∞ (∞)	378 (1433)
Q_2	35	124 (274)	∞ (∞)	59 (59)	91 (91)

Table 7.4

7.2.2 More general analysis

From a more general point of view, it is worth noting that the event-driven reconciliation is attractive for clauses containing a variable local to their body and that must be instantiated by a different subgoal according to the mode of use of the clause. Such clauses can be efficiently handled in Conclog in two ways.

1) In a direct manner, the s-goals can be annotated by reduction operators to decrease the R-depth of the slices generated before reconciliation occurs. The append3 procedure could, for instance, be redefined as

append3(L1,L2,L3,L) ← append(L1,L2,L12)↓3, append(L12,L3,L)↓3.

2) In a less direct way, all problems of useless computations can generally be ruled out by transforming the procedure in order to eliminate the local variable. For instance, the list L12 of the append3 procedure can be ruled out as follows. It is always L2, possibly preceded by a prefix. If L12 is L2 then L1 is [] and

append3(L1,L2,L3,L) = append(L2,L3,L).

If L12 is the concatenation of some prefix list with L2 then L1 is of the form [H|T] and

append3(L1,L2,L3,L) = append3([H|T],L2,L3,[H|T_rem]) with append3(T,L2,L3,T_rem).

Using the definition of append, we then obtain, by unfolding,

    append3([],[],L,L).
    append3([],[H|T],L3,[H|T_rem]) ← append3([],T,L3,T_rem).
    append3([H|T],L2,L3,[H|T_rem]) ← append3(T,L2,L3,T_rem).

7.2.3 Infinite trees and even-driven reconciliation

One could hope that reconciliation would only be activated in an even-driven way. As a result, there would then be no need to force generation and reconciliation to be alternated by computing and/or/not search trees slice by slice. This is however not the case since event-driven reconciliation does not ensure that infinite branches killed in the Conclog model would indeed be removed. A convincing example is given by the query

    ← append3([1,2],L2,[5],[3,4|L]).

7.3 Conclusion

Summing up, the event-driven reconciliation has several drawbacks : it pollutes the programs with function declarations and domain information and complicates the execution model. Morevover, the induced improvements are quite minor, when any. Finally, the event-driven reconciliation is not sufficient to ensure on its own the pruning of the computed and/or/not search trees performed by the Conclog reconciliation. In view of these drawbacks and (small) advantages, we do not include it in our scheme.

Chapter 8

Comparison with related work

As a final step in this design part, Conclog is compared with other parallel logic schemes and other parallel logic languages. Those works are subsequently classified into five categories, according to the trends of research to which they belong:
- *parallel Prologs*, group parallel implementations of Prolog and Prolog dialects incorporating primitives to express parallel executions;
- *parallel execution models of Horn clauses*, address the parallel interpretation of Horn clauses in their pure form, essentially;
- *guarded Horn clause languages*, compute guarded Horn clauses;
- *distributed logic languages*, extend logic programming to distributed programming;
- *constraint concurrent logic programming languages*, generalize concurrent logic languages.

8.1 Parallel Prologs

Parallel implementations of Prolog programs and Prolog dialects incorporating primitives to express parallel executions are closely connected. The first ones generally incorporate primitives of the second ones and the second ones generally involve parallel implementations. They are however distinguishable since the first ones essentially arise from implementation considerations whereas the last ones arise from language considerations. This given, these two trends of research are treated in the same section but two subsections are, nevertheless, devoted to them.

8.1.1 Parallel implementations of Prolog

Compared with Conclog, we claim that Prolog - and, consequently, any parallel implementation - suffers from four drawbacks.

1° Because clauses are selected from top to bottom, Prolog can fall into the exploration of infinite subtrees engendered by top clauses. This prevents it from finding solutions although the and/or search tree may contain some. This is typical of tail recursive clauses placed in first position. For instance, if member were defined as

member(X,[H|T]) ← member(X,T).
member(X,[X|T]).,

queries of the form ←member(t,L), with L a variable and t a non-variable term, would never terminate and succeed.

2° The second drawback is a consequence of the left-to-right reading of goals. Because of it, unacceptable performance can result. Generate and test programs provide good examples. As noted in 4.4.1, most candidate solutions can be rejected before they are entirely computed. They are however completely computed in Prolog before being tested. Recall that this is avoided in Conclog through reconciliation.

It should furthermore be noted that for independent s-goals, say

p(X), q(Y)

with m solutions for p(X) and n solutions for q(Y), finding all the solutions for ←p(X),q(Y) is achieved with a complexitiy m*n whereas, in Conclog, this is achieved with a complexity m+n (see Section 2.3.4 for more details).

3° The third drawback is also a consequence of the left-to-right reading of goals. Because of it, problems of multi-directionality may result too. This is particularly the case when ns-goals are involved. As proved in [Deville, 1990], it is impossible to program a fully multi-directional Prolog procedure for the efface relation of Section 5.6.1. Recall that, in contrast, such multi-directional procedures are supported in Conclog.

4° Finally, the rigidity of the depth first search strategy should be emphasized. A first direct consequence is that no cooperating processes can be executed in Prolog. It is thus a poor language to code applications requiring the expression of concurrency. More generally, Prolog embodies little sources of parallelism. The only ones are :

- clauses can be used in parallel, providing the results are still produced in the order required by Prolog,
- independent subgoals of goals can be reduced in parallel,
- bindings can be transmitted incrementally but according to a left-to-right data flow.

This lack of parallelism is furthermore strengthened by the presence of typically sequential features such as the cut. This is not surprising since Prolog is sequential by nature.

All these drawbacks lead us to reject the parallel implementation of Prolog trends of research at the beginning of our work. It is furthermore worth noting that this approach is somewhat conflictory. The logic programming framework, inherently parallel (as discussed in Chapter 2), is first sequentialized to obtain Prolog. This sequentialization is then tried to be parallelized when designing parallel implementations. Why do we not start from the beginning and avoid the intermediate sequentialization step?

Nevertheless, it makes sense to improve the performance of existing Prolog programs by using computers with parallel architectures. This is at the basis of projects at Argonne National Laboratory (see e.g. [Butler et al., 1986], [Overbeek et al., 1985]), ECRC ([Whesphal et al., 1987]), Manchester University ([Shen, 1986], [Calderwood and Szeredi, 1989], [Szeredi, 1989]) and SICS ([Hausman et al., 1987], [Ali, 1988]). Another argument can be advanced in favour of this approach. Parallel reasoning is generally felt to be more complicated than sequential reasoning. This approach has precisely the advantage of liberating programmers from the complicated parallel reasoning while still offering the efficiency of parallel executions. The argument is however not completely true for the two following reasons.

i) On the one hand, parallel implementations are generally coupled with the introduction of parallel features and even the replacement of sequential features by parallel ones. Examples of the former parallel features are the strict commit and cavalier commit, extension of Prolog cut in [Warren, 1987a], or-parallel declaration in the Argonne Model, parallel modules in PEPSys. An example of the replacement of sequential features by parallel ones is that of the cut by the cut-clause and cut-goal cuts of [Shapiro, 1987a].

ii) On the other hand, procedures as declarative and even more declarative can be programmed in Conclog without taking parallel executions into consideration. Annotations may then be introduced to improve the executions (without being mandatory). Part III will furthermore give transformations to introduce them in a safe way. We believe that one wealth of Conclog is precisely its ability to support the programming of programs written in a declarative style (with the execution made as transparent as possible) as well as the programming of algorithms built in an intrisically parallel framework.

8.1.2 Augmenting Prolog with parallel features

Let us now examine three Prologs dialect incorporating parallel features : Prism ([Kasif et al., 1983]), IC-Prolog ([Clark and Mac Cabe, 1979]) and Epilog ([Wise, 1984], [Porto, 1984a]). The two first ones share the characteristics of conserving the sequential strategy of Prolog at their basis. They are described and compared with Conclog in a first subsection. The latter language takes some departure from them by taking a parallel scheme at the basis. It is still described in this section since its author himself refers to reinterpreting and extending Prolog. It is treated in a second subsection.

8.1.2.1 Basic sequential strategy

A. Prism

Prism provides two features to express parallel executions in Prolog. The first one is the possibility to relax the strict left-to-right order of conjoined subgoals by using brackets for parallel executions. Precisely, a conjunction of subgoals is formed of groups delimited by parantheses or brackets. Each group can contain other groups. The elements of a group delimited by parantheses are to be executed in a left-to-right sequence. In contrast, the elements of a group delimited by brackets are executed independently. This first feature thus provides the counterpart of the well-known fork and join parantheses of imperative parallel programming. The execution of

   (G1,[G2,(G3,G4),G5],[G6,G7])

is particularly examplative. It is drawn in Figure 8.1. When G1 has terminated, three parallel executions begin : that of G2, of G5 and that of the sequence G3, G4. When these three executions are finished, the parallel execution of G6 and G7 begins. The whole computation teminates when both G6 and G7 are finished.

The second parallel features of Prism concerns the ordering of the clauses. Two orders can be specified. One acts as a recommanded ordering; it is materialized by integers. The other acts as an obligatory ordering; it is represented by asterisked integers. The following clauses illustrate these two orderings :

   1:    P ← G1, G2.
   1:    P ← G3.
   2:    P ← G4, G5, G6.
   *3:   P ← G7.
   4:    P ← G8, G9.

They are to be understood as follows. The two first clauses (with priority 1) may be executed simultaneously. The third one (with priority 2) and the fifth one (with priority 4) may also be executed in parallel with them. However, the fourth clause cannot be executed unless the three first clauses have been completely executed.

B. IC-Prolog

IC-Prolog incorporates more powerful features, some of which have been included in recent concurrent languages. Annotations for clause selection have first been introduced. Their syntax is "?" and "^"; they are placed in the head of clauses. Their meaning is that the annotated term must be used as input and as output, respectively. A clause can be selected to reduce a ps-goal only if the input and output constraints are satisfied. For example, the r(X,Z) relation of Subsection D of Section 4.6.2.5 is redefined as

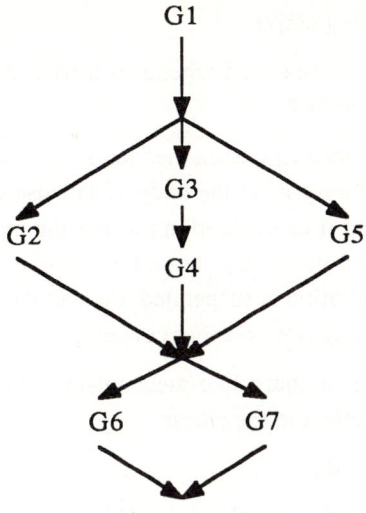

Figure 8.1

r(X?,Z) ← p(X,Y), q(Y,Z).
r(X^,Z?) ← p(X,Y), q(Y,Z).

The first clause is used to reduce the ps-goal r(t,u) when t is a ground term whatever u is. The second is used when t is a non-ground term and u is a ground term.

The same annotations are used in the clause body to create a coroutined execution between its subgoals. To be more precise, let ←$G_1, ..., G_m$ be a goal. Variables of any G_i can be annotated by one of the symbol ? or ^. The notation V? in G_i makes G_i a consumer of the variable V. It is the evaluation of $G_1, ..., G_{i-1}$ which binds V. The notation V^ makes G_i a producer of V. The bindings of V are then sent down to $G_1, ..., G_{i-1}$. As suggested, the evaluation of $G_1, ..., G_{i-1}$ is coroutined with that of G_i. Only one of the two processes are activated at one time but the two evaluations alternate. In particular, in case G_i is a consumer of V, each slice of the evaluation of $G_1, ..., G_{i-1}$ is employed for the generation of a new partial output binding of V whereas each slice of the evaluation of G_i consumes this partial output. This mechanism supports nested coroutining.

This weak form of parallelism is relaxed to a form that allows two or more processes to be executed in an unsynchronized fashion. This is specified by separating the goals by a || symbol, as in

$G_1 \| G_2 \| ... \| G_m$.

The effect is to fork the evaluation of $G_1, G_2, ..., G_m$ into m separate processes. This purely concurrent execution can be restricted to avoid inconsistent bindings for shared variables. To this end, an occurrence of a variable can be annotated by the ^ or the ? symbols, as in p(X,Z) || q(Z^,Y)   (or p(X,Z?) || q(Z,Y)).

In such cases, the s-goal p(X,Z) is suspended whenever it tries to bind Z. When suspended, it is reactivated each time the goal q binds Z.

IC-Prolog also offers another suspension mechanism. To make use of it, the programmer has to annotate some variable of a s-goal of the body of a clause with the ! symbol. If some goal reduction invokes that clause and if its evaluation reaches the annotated goal, then this process is suspended until the associated variable is bound by another goal evaluation. However, in case every other concurrent evaluation is suspended, the annotation is ignored. In contrast with the ? annotation, the ! symbol expresses no eager consumption.

Finally, IC-Prolog includes a guard-like mechanism. To our knowledge, it was the first logic language to propose it. Its effect in the clause

$H \leftarrow G_1, ..., G_m | B_1, ..., B_n$.

is to make the unification of H and the evaluation of $G_1, ..., G_m$ an indivisible unit. However, it is most commonly used to delay the communication of variable bindings resulting from the unification with the head H until after the successful evaluation of the guard $G_1, ..., G_m$. If the guard fails, the bindings are not transmitted to the other processes. This reminds Dijkstra's guarded commands ([Dijkstra, 1975]). The difference is that, in IC-Prolog, the successful evaluation of a guard does not exclude the possibility of using other clauses of the same procedure.

C. Comparison

For the same reasons as those explained above, we do not believe that augmenting a sequential language with parallel features is a good approach for parallel logic programming. A better approach is to deal with parallelism or parallel executions at the starting point and, when need be, to annotate parallel programs with sequential features. This provides a dynamic parallel behavior (defined implicitly) that should be contrasted with the static parallel behavior induced by explicit parallel declarations (as in parallel Prolog). To be more suggestive, consider the clause

p(X,Y) ← q(X), r(Y).

As q and r share no variables, it seems attractive to declare them as being parallel, thus writing in IC-Prolog terms

p(X,Y) ← q(X) || r(Y).

However, for queries of the form ←p(X,X), the two goals q(X) and r(X) are not independent and their parallel executions can lead to conflicting bindings. This is not true for instantiations of p(X,X) to ground atoms. To handle such cases, some additional clauses have to be written, including suitable run time tests. This leads to unnecessary complicated code. In contrast, this is not required in parallel schemes such as that of [Conery, 1983], in parallel languages or in Conclog. Conflicting bindings are indeed avoided by ordering the subgoals of conjunctions, by allowing only one binding per variable or by reconciling conflicting bindings, respectively.

It is furthermore reassuring to note that most parallel mechanisms of Prism and of IC-Prolog can also be coded in Conclog. Ouput constraints of IC-Prolog and clause ordering of Prism make exception. We have already explained in Section 6.2.3 why output constraints have not been incorporated in Conclog. As far as Prism clause orderings are concerned, we found them slightly tricky. We believe that their only use is to make some tests implicit. This is achieved in Conclog too (see Section 6.2.1.6).

8.1.2.2 Basic parallel strategy

Epilog ([Wise, 1984], [Porto, 1984a]) takes some departure from Prolog in adopting a parallel scheme at its basis. We however describe it in this section since Wise himself refers to reinterpreting and extending Prolog.

A. Description

Epilog is an or-parallel and and-parallel language where some sequencing or suspending constraints can be expressed. They are divided into two groups : fixed sequence contructs and data dependent constructs.

(i) Fixed sequence construct

Two fixed sequence constructs are provided.

1) First, a so-called CAND returns execution to a left-to-right pattern. Consider, for instance,

$$a \rightarrow [b,c] \rightarrow d.$$

The literal a is first evaluated. If it fails, then the whole conjunction fails. Otherwise, b and c are evaluated in parallel and if they, in turn, both succeed, then d is evaluated.

2) Second, a so-called COR has the semantics of a sequential or. For instance,

$$p \leftarrow q \parallel r.$$

states that q is evaluated first and, r is only reduced if and after q has failed. It is not evaluated in case q succeeds.

(ii) Data dependent constructs

The data dependent constructs include the thresholds criticized in Section 6.5 and variable-bindings annotations. They are

?X, !X, @X

to indicate that the variable X must be bound, unbound or bound to an atom at the time of the call, respectively.

B. Comparison

Though Epilog is in our research guidelines, its sequential features have to mature and to be completed. We refer the reader to Chapter 6 for a detailed discussion about these features. Furthermore, some problems are not discussed in [Wise, 1984] and [Porto, 1984a]. Among the crucial ones are the way in which conflicting bindings are treated and the way in which multiple solutions are managed.

8.2 Parallel execution models of Horn clause programs

Parallel execution models of Horn clause programs are discussed in this section. They are designed in order to work on Horn clauses free from annotations and this without making reference to Prolog. They issue from [Conery, 1983], [Conery, 1987b], [Li and Martin, 1986], [Kalé, 1987] and [Pollard, 1981]. They have already been discussed in Section 4.6. Here we further strengthen the fact that none of them deals with negation although this is practically required. Furthermore, just two of them, namely [Conery, 1983] and [Kalé, 1987], deal with annotations. They are used in the aim of easing the ordering of the s-goals of goals. This does not however remove the critics of Section 4.6. The undecidable problem of the automatic detection of the producer s-goal of a variable is, in fact, the only one that could be solved. This is indeed the case when the annotations provide sufficient information to determine it in a one-to-one fashion.

8.3 Guarded Horn clause languages

Most of the work in parallel logic programming refers to guarded Horn clauses. Among the well-known examples are Concurrent Prolog ([Shapiro, 1983]), Guarded Horn Clauses (subsequently abreviated by GHC to avoid confusion with guarded Horn clauses, [Ueda, 1986a]), Parlog ([Gregory, 1985]), P-Prolog ([Yang, 1986]) and the CP family of languages ([Saraswat, 1987]). The three first languages are certainly the most popular ones. They are called committed-choice languages.

All these languages make an intensive use of guarded Horn clauses. They are subsequently described according to the way they handle them. A comparison with Conclog then follows.

8.3.1 Committed-choice languages

Committed choice languages apply commitment at every reduction step. Only one unifiable clause whose guard evaluation succeeds is thus retained at each reduction step. A drastic decrease of the size of the computation results. However, at most one answer substitution can be computed and, in the bad cases, the computation fails whereas the and/or search tree indeed contains solutions. In other words, because of the commitment mechanism, these languages are not complete. This property is only obtained in the (restricted) cases where

- clauses, selected by the commitment mechanism, indeed lead to a solution, when any,
- all guards are mutually exclusive.

Concurrent Prolog, GHC and Parlog embody this approach. All of them are descendant of the Relational Language ([Clark and Gregory, 1981]), which itself is a descendant of IC-Prolog. We only describe the three first ones here since the Relational Language is somewhat obsolate with respect to its children.

Concurrent Prolog, GHC and Parlog essentially differ by the way and-parallelism is treated and particularly by the way suspension is declared. Some extra-logical features force the comparison to be slightly extended. In particular, Parlog relaxes the commitment mechanism by using all-solution relations. We will however exclude buit-in primitives dedicated to special applications from our discussion. They are only relevant to the programming of those applications and not for the general discussion we pursue.

A. Concurrent Prolog

Concurrent Prolog just uses read-only annotations (see Section 6.5, for their description) to suspend reduction steps. No other constraint can be stated in the calls or in the program clauses. As a result, variables may be bound by the reduction of any guard. This leads to some problems of efficiency. As we will explain in Subsection D, local environments need indeed to be managed and tests for consistency of such environments with the global one need to be performed in addition.

B. GHC

In constrast with other committed choice languages, GHC does not incorporate other annotations than the descriptor commit in guarded Horn clauses. Two suspension rules are rather used by the interpreter. They state as follows.

For any ps-goal G and for any guarded Horn clause $H \leftarrow C_g |_c C_b$,

(i) the unification of G and H and the reduction of the guard C_g cannot bind a variable appearing in G with a non-variable term or another variable of G until the clause is selected by commitment;

(ii) the reduction of the commit-body C_b cannot bind a variable appearing in the head H or the guard C_g with a non-variable term or another variable appearing in H or in C_g until the clause is selected by commitment.

Any reduction step that would break these suspension rules is suspended until it can further proceed without making the bindings prohibited by them. Under these rules, anything can be performed in any order. This has two important consequences.

- The unification of G and of H and the reduction of Cg can be done in parallel; even more, the latter can begin before the former is executed. However, the usual way of execution is to evaluate the guard Cg only after the unification of H and G has successfully terminated.
- The reduction of Cb may, but need not, start before the clause has been committed. The bindings made by it are unobservable from the reduction of Cb or the unification of G and H before the clause is selected by commitment, so the meaning of the program remains the same whether the reduction of Cb starts before or after commitment.

C. Parlog

A first version of Parlog appeared in [Clark and Gregory, 1983]. It has then been revised and modified in [Clark and Gregory, 1984] and finally in [Gregory, 1985]. We will refer to that last version in the sequel.

For efficiency and completeness reasons, two kinds of relations are defined in Parlog. They are called single-solution relations and all-solutions relations. The first ones embody the committed-choice side of the language. The second ones provide an additional dimension by excluding commitment and by making a search for all possible solutions. The two relations are interfaced by means of two set constructor primitives.

(i) Single-solution relations

Single solutions relations are used for the search of only one solution. They are defined by means of guarded Horn clauses where

- the only s-goals appearing in their body are calls (or their negation) to single-solution relations,
- the only annotations are the descriptor commit, the sequentialization operator and the sequential clause delimitor.

Each procedure defining a single solution relation must furthermore be declared with a mode declaration, stating the arguments as input or output, as seen in Section 6.5.

Commitment is applied at each step of the reduction of any call to a single-solution relation. This given, the reduction is performed according to the operational behavior we assigned to the annotations in Chapter 6. One important feature of Parlog is that the reduction of the guard of any clause cannot bind a variable of a call declared as an input by the mode declaration associated with the procedure to which the clause belongs. As a consequence, no local environment is needed to register bindings performed for these variables. Another attractive property of the single-solution relations of Parlog is that, thanks to the restricted form of the mode declarations, almost all of the unification involved by a call to a single-solution relation can be compiled. The only residue at run-time is a test that two terms are syntactically identical.

(ii) All-solution relations

All-solution relations are employed for the discovery of all solutions for a query. The associated procedures consist of a sequence of general Horn clauses with no associated mode declaration and no guards. Roughly speaking each call to an all-solution relation is reduced in a Prolog-like fashion. In fact, Parlog relaxes this stratgy

- by allowing s-goals of goals to be reduced in parallel but provided the two following conditions are fullfilled :
  - there is no communication of partial bindings between the subgoals of the goals,
  - the flow of binding is left-to-right, as in Prolog;
- by using clauses as or-parallel alternatives when calls to an all-solution relation is invoked as part of an eager set evaluation.

(iii) The set constructor

Finally, two set constructor primitives are provided to interface the all-solution relations with the single-solution relation : the eager set constructor and the lazy subset constructor.

The eager set constructor takes the form

set(List_sol,Term,Goal)

where List_sol is a list of terms, Term is a term and Goal is a goal formed of calls to all-solution relations separated by the sequentializing operator "&". It is defined with the implicit mode declaration (o,i,i). Its reduction involves an or-parallel search of all solutions of Goal. As a result, the list List_sol is incrementally bound to the various corresponding instantiations of Term. This list can be concurrently consumed by subgoals conjoined to the set subgoal.

The lazy subset constructor takes the form

subset(List_var,Term,Goal)

where List_var is a list of terms and Term and Goal are as above. It has the implicit mode declaration (i,i,i). The List_var argument must thus be given in the call or be generated by some other process. Its variables are bound to different instantiations of Term corresponding to various answer substitutions computed for Goal. The reduction of Goal is performed in a Prolog style. It is furthermore suspended when it produces an answer substitution and all variables of the List_var argument have already been instantiated thanks to previously computed answer substitution. As a consequence, the evaluation of any subset call cannot run ahead from the generation of the input list of variables List_var.

D. Safe and flat committed-choice languages

Or-parallelism resulting from the parallel reduction of guards is conceptually easy to handle : multiple environments have simply to be managed. To be more explicit, let us associate with each node of the and/or search tree, a process in charge of solving its associated s-goal or goal (as we did for the Conclog model). Let us furthermore call these processes, s-goal-processes or goal-processes, respectively. Given an s-goal, an s-goal-process is created for each unifiable guarded Horn clause. It unifies the s-goal and the clause head and launches the goal-process in charge of computing the guard of the clause. Since there are competing s-goal-processes, bindings made for variables in the s-goal must be hidden from processes that are not descendants of the associated s-goal-process. Therefore, from a conceptual standpoint, each s-goal-process has a local environment where these bindings are stored. The set of all other accessible bindings is referred to as its global environment. As the processes are organized according to the and/or search tree hierarchy, the local environments also form a tree. It dynamically expands and contracts as the computation proceeds.

Managing this tree evolution can be computationally expensive. In particular, two problems have to be solved : the value access control and the detection of inconsistencies between environments. As local environment evolves, bindings status evolves from private to public and, consequently, for most processes, from inaccessible to accessible. Hence, access to bindings has to be controlled during the computation. A more complicated problem is that of the detection of inconsistencies between environments. At the time of commitment, the local environment of an s-goal-process has to be merged with the environment of its grandfather s-goal-process. However, as competing brothers of its goal-process father can also change this environment, inconsistent bindings may occur.

There is no need to manage this dynamic tree if no local binding is made. Consequently, designers tried to develop so-called *safe languages*. The concept of safety was first introduced in [Clark and Gregory, 1985]. A language is defined to be safe if and only if, for any ps-goal and guarded Horn clause, the unification of the ps-goal and the head clause and the evaluation of the guard of the clause never construct a variable appearing in the ps-goal. Parlog and GHC are examples of safe languages. In Parlog, a program which may be unsafe is excluded as a dangerous program at compile time during mode analysis. GHC suspension rules can be paraphrased as follows : any attempt to make those bindings which should be stored in a local environment is suspended. Hence, the design philosophy of those languages excludes any program which requires multiple environments. In contrast, Concurrent Prolog is not safe. This is directly reflected in the complexity of commitment. In Parlog and GHC, committing the reduction to a clause only requires to confirm that no other competing clause has already been committed. In Concurrent Prolog, consistency checks of the environments have to be made in addition. An attempt has been made in [Codish, 1985] to limit the management of the local environments. It consists of augmenting Concurrent Prolog by output annotations and by programming in such a manner that for any ps-goal G and guarded Horn clause Cl, no binding for the variables of G is made during the unification of G and Cl and the computation of the guard of Cl, except those declared by output annotations. The management of local bindings becomes simpler since such bindings are syntactically predictable.

The interest of the commitment mechanism should be stressed again. By only selecting one guarded Horn clause to reduce a ps-goal, the number of bindings to be stored is considerably reduced. Some work have been done to further decrease this number. The flat committed choice languages Flat Parlog, Flat Concurrent Prolog, Flat GHC result from them. They are subsets of their respective language in which the guard parts are restricted to system predicates. Since no general computation is allowed in a guard, the computation structure is flat and no tree-structured environment is needed. This makes the implementation of committed-choice languages simpler. In particular, the implementation of Concurrent Prolog is greatly reduced although the problem of inconsistency checking is not eliminated. The implementation of GHC is also thereby simplified.

Strand ([Foster and Taylor, 1989a], [Foster and Taylor, 1989b]) is another flat committed-choice language that further simplifies the above mentioned ones. The simplifications essentially consist of reducing the predicates of the guards to simple tests, of forbidding self-referential and cyclic data structures and of instantiating variables of predicate calls by means of assignments. As a result, the language is characterized by static dataflow and allows very efficient implementations - according to [Foster and Taylor, 1989b], approximately three times faster than the implementation of Parlog of [Crammond, 1988] and the implementation of Flat Concurrent Prolog of [Houri and Shapiro, 1989].

8.3.2 Non committed-choice languages

We now turn to three attempts to introduce multi-solution and/or multi-directional procedures while using guarded Horn clauses : the CP family of languages, P-Prolog and Pandora.

A. The CP family of languages

The CP family of languages issues from [Saraswat, 1986] and [Saraswat, 1987]. It is composed of languages obtained by combining some extra-logical features according to the two following choices :
- any language can be declared as flat or not,
- any language can include the following annotations :
    - a wait annotation (see the ↓ annotations of Section 6.2.3),
    - a freeze construct, similar to that defined in Section 6.5,

- a don't care commit (see Section 6.5),
- a don't know commit (see Section 6.5),
- a sequential clause separator (see Section 6.5),
- a sequentialization operator (see Section 6.5),
- an otherwise predicate.

The following rules further restrict the combination of these annotations :
- at least one commit must be included in any combination,
- the freeze and the wait anotations cannot be combined,
- the otherwise predicate cannot be combined with the sequential clause separator.

The precise description of these annotations is out of purpose for our comparison. We refer the reader to [Saraswat, 1986] and [Saraswat, 1987]. It is here just sufficient to note that multi-solution and multi-directional procedures are supported in some CP languages thanks to the use of the don't known commit.

B. P-Prolog

P-Prolog is another alternative to get multi-solution and multi-directional procedures while using guarded Horn clauses. It is based on the concept of exclusively committable clauses, as defined in Section 6.5. Multi-solution and multi-directional procedures then arise from the fact that all clauses defined as non-exclusively committable are used in an or-parallel way.

C. Pandora

Pandora ([Baghat and Gregory, 1989]) is an extension of Parlog supporting a deadlock handling mechanism and a non-deterministic fork primitive. Based on these features, a new type of procedures, called the don't know relation procedures has been defined. They can be considered as a means to obtain multi-directional and multi-solution procedures. As before, we will restrict our description to what is needed for our comparison purposes and refer the interested reader to the above mentioned reference for more details.

According to our purposes, a Pandora program can be viewed as composed of two kinds of procedures: the single-solution relation procedures of Parlog and the newly introduced don't know relation procedures. The latter procedures have no declaration and are composed of clauses of the form

$H \leftarrow Cg : Cb.$

where Cg is a conjunction of calls to the primitives =, <, >, $\leq$, $\geq$ and where Cb is an unrestricted conjunction of s-goals. They influence the computations as follows. Any query may contain calls to the two kinds of procedures. The computation then first performs a deterministic phase where calls to single-solution relation procedures are reduced in a Parlog like manner and where calls to don't know relation procedures are also reduced provided they are deterministic, that is, using P-Prolog terminology with the obvious adaptation to the

Pandora context, are exclusively committable. Non-deterministic calls to don't know relation procedures are suspended. When the computation deadlocks with some s-goals being defined by don't know relation procedures, one such s-goal is selected and all the unifiable clauses of the corresponding procedure are used in parallel to reduce it. A new deterministic phase is then initiated for each resulting instances.

Multi-solution procedures are thus obtained by the parallel use of the clauses of don't know relation procedures. Multidirectionality is obtained by the fact that these procedures are not restricted by mode declarations, as the Parlog procedures are.

8.3.3 Comparison

A. Preliminary : logic programming is more than functional programming coupled with unification

To compare Conclog with guarded Horn clause languages, we first argue that logic programming is more than functional programming (understood in the sense of programming functions) coupled with unification. This claim is substantiated by recalling that logic programming is related to relational programming. Two important consequences follow. They distinguish the two programmings.

1) In contrast with functional programming, as many solutions as desired must be computable in any logic programming language. Note that, even if a predicate is used to compute a function, the same does not necessary hold for its defining subgoals. A convincing example is the naive sort defined as

sort(L,L_sorted) ← perm(L,L_sorted), ordered(L_sorted).

Generally, several solutions have to be computed by perm before the ordered permutation of L_sorted is generated.

2) The second consequence is related to multi-directionality. Even if using a procedure in a fully multi-directional manner is uncommon in practice, it often happens that procedures are called in several modes of use. For instance, the append procedure is rarely called with three variable arguments but often either
 - with the two first arguments instantiated and the third variable,
 - with the third argument instantiated and one or two of the two first arguments variable
 - or with all arguments instantiated.
A minimum to be ensured is certainly that a procedure built to construct some arguments could be used as a test procedure.

We believe that these properties are distinguishing characteristics of logic programming and that they should be embodied in any logic programming language. It is moreover worth noting that they are not utopian from a programming point of view. Indeed, as shown in

[Deville, 1990], programming a multi-directional many solutions procedure is not more difficult than building a directed single-solution procedure. Moreover, programming a procedure for each directionality leads to undesirable redundancy. The real challenge is to design an efficient computational model. This has been achieved in Prolog for the sequential context and is at the core of the current research in parallel programming.

B. Multi-solution and multi-directional procedures

The declarative properties developed above contrast with committed-choice languages. In their pure form, such languages only provide single-solution relations that are furthermore often directed. This is particularly clear for Parlog where the arguments of each relation have to be declared either as input or output. This implies such a strict pattern of use that procedures built to construct an argument cannot be used as testing devices. Rigid patterns of use also apply for GHC. Because of the suspension rules, an output argument must be represented as a variable at the head of a clause and unified after the clause has been committed. Concurrent Prolog read-only annotations also assume some patterns of use. Finally, because of the commitment mechanism, at most one solution to each call can be found (if any).

In fact, committed-choice languages can be viewed as parallel functional programming languages coupled with the unification mechanism. This has been clearly confessed in [Gregory, 1985] and in [Shapiro, 1986]. As we have just argued, parallel logic programming is more than that.

As a response to this criticism, two remedies have been proposed to improve the expressiveness of committed-choice languages. However, as we shall see, these are quite poor remedies.

1) On the one hand, Parlog has incorporated so-called all-solutions relations. But loss of uniformity and conciseness has resulted. For instance, the same procedure append to be employed in a functional sense (i.e. to determine in its third argument the concatenation of its two first list arguments) and in a relational one (for instance, with the last argument given and the others to be determined) has to be declared twice : as a single-solution relation and as an all-solution relation. Furthermore the search for all-solutions contrasts with that for single-solution relations. The former is done in a parallel Prolog-like fashion whereas the latter is done in a purely and-parallel fashion.

2) On the other hand, it has been shown how to transform an exhaustive search program into a deterministic program ([Ueda, 1986b], [Ueda, 1987], [Okumara and Matsumoto, 1987], [Tamaki, 1987]). Basically, the technique consists of constructing a new program that determines the set of all solutions (rather than the solutions) computed by the initial program. The counterpart is essentially that the resulting program has lost the declarative reading of the initial program. Furthermore, programs obtained in [Ueda, 1986b] and

[Ueda, 1987] embody little parallelism whereas those of [Okumara and Matsumoto, 1987] and [Tamaki, 1987] involve extra-computations.

The languages of the CP family including the don't know commit mitigates these drawbacks. However, it is regrettable that the don't know and don't care commits exclude one another. Hence, a same procedure can not be used in one mode with commitment and in another one without commitment, as we do with the merge procedure (see Section 6.2.1.5).

P-Prolog also claims to support multi-solution and multi-directional procedures. However, as we argued in Section 6.5, some patterns of use require the clauses to be declared as exclusively committable whereas others require them to be declared as non-exclusively committable. For example, using append with the two first arguments ground and the third argument to be determined requires the clauses to be declared as exclusively committable whereas using it with the two first arguments to be determined and the latter ground requires them to be non-exclusively committable. This should be related with our claim that more than one annotation is needed in a parallel logic programming language (see Section 6.2.3).

The don't know relation procedures of Pandora constitute another attempt to get multi-solution and multi-directional procedures. However, they suffer from several drawbacks. Firstly, they are used in a non-deterministic manner not in the initial mode of execution but in a deadlocking stage. It follows that the evaluation of calls to them is postponed at infinity if the first deterministic phase of the computation is infinite. This is particularly regrettable in the cases where the reduction of these calls do not interfere with the reduction of the calls solved in the deterministic phase. Secondly, and-parallelism is not employed when don't know relation procedures are used in a multi-solution purpose. A loss of parallel executions thus results. Finally, because no declaration can be associated with them, the don't know relation procedures cannot be employed in one pattern of use with commitment and in another pattern of use without commitment. As for Parlog, procedures have to be duplicated for that purpose.

It is worth noting that Conclog does not suffer from these drawbacks. Multi-solution and multi-directional procedures can indeed be coded in Conclog. Furthermore, commitment can be activated only for some calls or for some patterns of use. Hence, the same procedure can be used either by involving commitment or without involving it.

C. Ease of programming

Another criticism can be made to committed-choice languages. It is essentially due to the fact that only directed single-solution procedures can be computed. Annotations (in Parlog and in Concurrent Prolog) or carefull s-goal placing (in Guarded Horn Clause) must then be introduced to ensure a correct behavior of the programs, in particular, to avoid infinite suspensions and conflicting bindings. Hence, in committed-choice languages, the programmer must immediately reason in terms of parallel functional computations and handle annotations.

This is obviously far from the ideal of logic programming where one would ideally program in a declarative way.

The approach proposed in Conclog is quite different. Horn clauses can be computed without annotations in a quite sound and complete way (see Sections 4.5 and 5.5). Annotations are then introduced to optimize the executions and not to ensure their correctness. Part III will furthermore give correctness preserving transformations to this aim. Of course, these transformations could be applied to derive programs in Concurrent Prolog or in Parlog. However, the interest of the Conclog approach is that the annotations are in no point obligatory. For instance, the commit operator can be introduced only when need be. This avoids the problem of handling it when it is not desired.

The same criticism of ease of programming can also be applied to P-Prolog although with less strength. The concept of exclusiveness of guards is indeed quite declarative. The problems rather arise from the lack of kinds of annotations : the only concept of exclusively committable clauses and its complementary one of non-exclusively committable clauses are manifestly too weak to optimize all desired optimizable situations.

Languages of the CP family suffer from the obligation of incorporating one of the don't care and don't know commits and from their mutual exclusion. On the one hand, imposing the don't care commit leads to the problems of the committed-choice languages. On the other hand, although the don't know commit brings completion, it might be useful to use the don't care commit to optimize some computations. In contrast, Conclog allows to combine these two forms of commit and does not force to use them. A first advantage is that their presence is not required in any clause. A second one is that commitment may be activated in some patterns of use, only.

Pandora also suffers from the problem of forcing procedures to involve commitment or not whatever patterns of use are considered. Furthermore, because of the strategy used to reduce calls to don't know relation procedures, problems of fairness and deadlock have to be taken into account very rapidly by the programmer.

The treatment of negation should also be mentioned in this subsection. It was quite naturally introduced in Conclog. Furthermore, thanks to its similarity with the usual negation, it provides multi-directionality of procedures including ns-goals as well as a quite declarative coding of them (see for instance the efface procedure of Section 5.6.1). In contrast, none of the guarded Horn clause languages deal explicitly with negation. Classical negation is in fact employed in these languages, with the problems mentioned in Section 5.6.1.

D. Ease of implementation

The advantage of committed-choice languages seems to be their ease of implementation. Because only-one solution is provided and only one clause is retained at each reduction step, the exponential explosion of the and/or search tree is linearized and the memorization of bindings is considerably reduced. However, as suggested in Subsection 8.3.1.D, this is not so simple. In particular, commitment involves some necessary synchronizations. Multiple environments have to be managed in Concurrent Prolog, too. Furthermore, it has be pointed out in [Ratcliff and Syre, 1987] that the committed-choice language approach often leads to an explosion of processes which often brings very little parallelism for very much control and synchronization overhead.

Moreover, it is quite obvious to recognize that the more powerful a model is the more expensive its implementation is. Hence, the price to pay by Conclog to obtain the soundness and completeness properties, the ease of programming, inheritance of input contraints, of commit requirements is the efficiency of the computation. This is indeed true for the Conclog model without annotations. However, thanks to these annotations, the same computations as the Concurrent Prolog or Parlog ones and even their flat versions can be expressed in Conclog. This given, the efficiency of computations should be made similar. The only overhead in Conclog would be :

- at compile-time, a more elaborated compilation to detect the optimizations
- at run-time, some extra tests to perform.

The situation can thus be depicted as follows :

- in case they are correct, committed-choice programs should be computable in Conclog with similar performances or, at least, reasonably comparable performances,
- in other cases, programs can indeed be computed in Conclog whereas they cannot in committed-choice languages.

It is finally worth noting that the handling of multiple environments and the full use of or-parallelism are at the core of research at well-noted centers (see e.g. [Shen, 1986], [Hausmann et al., 1987], [Warren, 1987a], [Ali, 1988], [Carlson et al., 1988], [Buttler et al., 1988], [Gupta and Jayaraman, 1989], [Ramkumar and Kalé, 1989]). They should thus also be considered as viable.

8.4 Distributed logic languages

A distributed logic programming computation can be schematized as the simultaneous execution of several logic programs, each one being able to communicate with the others as well as to create and activate the execution of logic programs. Apart from the language Janus, exemplifying the distributed constraint programming framework and therefore studied in Section 8.5, the only language currently embodying distributed logic programming features is Delta-Prolog. It is still experimental and is expected to evolve. Two versions have been described in [Pereira and Nasr, 1984] and [Pereira et al., 1986]. We will essentially refer to the latter in this section though we will occasionally mention features from the former.

A. Description

Basically, the execution of a Delta-Prolog program consists of the simultaneous reductions of several ps-goals, each one by means of its own Prolog program. Each reduction is allowed to communicate with the others via message passing. Classical "rendez-vous" and CSP communication mechanisms are used for this purpose. They are embodied by so-called event s-goals. Each reduction can also split in the concurrent reductions of two subgoals thanks to split s-goals.

The major problem of Delta-Prolog is the handling of backtracking. Because each concurrent reduction is performed in a Prolog style, failure in one of them forces the Prolog bactracking to be applied. What happens should be quite clear as far as Prolog programs are concerned. It is less clear when message passing and rendez-vous strategy mechanisms are involved. This leads to a quite elaborated distributed backtracking strategy in [Pereira et al., 1986]. The precise description is out of purpose for our comparative purposes. The following rough one should be sufficient to suggest its complexity. When backtracking reaches one event s-goal, the message passing it embodies is undone. To this end, one of the two event s-goals that creates it is retried and the other is made failed to force backtracking to occur in the corresponding reduction. The problem is then which goal is retried and which one fails. There is an auxiliary problem related to the fact that, when one reduction jumps back to an event s-goal and undoes the computation therefrom, it may in particular jump over some other events with consequences to intervening processes.

B. Comparison

As Delta-Prolog computations basically consist of Prolog reductions, the discussion of Section 8.1 on Prolog applies to Delta-Prolog too. Some additional comments can furthermore be made from the distributed programming feature of Delta-Prolog. By involving message passing and rendez-vous, distributed logic programming is different from classical logic programming. As an argumentation, a new kind of logic, called distributed logic ([Monteiro, 1984]), has been used to provide the foundations of Delta-Prolog. It was a design choice of Conclog to use the classical framework of logic programming (see Chapter 1). Hence, from the basis, Conclog and Delta-Prolog already differ. Furthermore we believe that, because of the compexity of distributed backtracking, distributed programming in Delta-Prolog may be quite intricate. In contrast, because of its declarative appeal, Conclog is well suited for a quite natural programming. This will be substantiated in Part III. Hence, with regards to the ease of programming, programming in Conclog is easier than in Delta-Prolog.

8.5 Constraint concurrent logic programming languages

Constraint concurrent logic programming ([Saraswat, 1989]) has recently been proposed as a very powerful framework generalizing the concurrent logic programming one. We now briefly sketch this paradigm and explain why it is, to our opinion, orthogonal to our research.

A. Description

From a theoretical point of view, any computation of any kind can be described at any moment by a structure summing up the results of the computation sofar and, consequently, any computation can be viewed as the progressive updating of this structure. For instance, in the conventional imperative programming context, any computation can be described by means of a vector indicating the current values of the variables. The basic updating operations consist of reading the current value of a variable from the vector and of assigning (or writing) a new value for a variable in the vector. Constraint logic programming is another example of this general scheme. The structure, called the store, is here a constraint, that is a description of a set of valuations. It provides, in fact, partial information about the final possible values for the variables of the computation. The basic updating operations are the so-called Ask and Tell primitives. Their effect are respectively

- to check whether or not the current store entails a given constraint, that is whether every valuation permitted by the store is permitted by the constraint;
- to add a given constraint to the store provided that the resulting store is consistent that is permits at least one valuation.

Hence, a basic computation step does not change the value of a variable but may rule out certain values that were previously possible. The store is thus refined monotonically.

Though simple, this constraint scheme constitutes a very powerful paradigm for concurrent computations. It is easy to imagine that multiple agents can concurrently act and cooperate on a shared store. Furthermore, synchronization (of an asynchronous nature, in fact) may be achieved by means of a blocking version of the Ask primitive: an agent may be suspended if it attempts to ask a constraint that is not yet entailed by the current store as well as its negation is not. It remains suspended until other concurrently executing agents add enough constraints such that the resulting store entails the asked constraint or its negation.

This constraint paradigm has been investigated in details in [Saraswat, 1989]. A family of languages, named the cc family of languages, has been designed among other results. It has been argued to generalize many concurrent logic languages by taking the (usual) Herbrand universe as the domain of constraints. Moreover, many combinations of the Ask and Tell operators into complex behaviors such as interleaving executions, don't know and don't care choices, restriction and recursion, have been investigated. The extension of the framework to non-monotonic stores, local stores involving a reconciliation mechanism, extended clauses expressing synchronous communication, ... has also been taken into account. Finally, a distributed version of the constraint logic programming scheme has recently been tackled in [Saraswat et al., 1990]. One instantiation to the Herbrand universe has produced the language Janus. Its main features are the use of single-message, point-to-point, directional channels and the property of any clause that any variable occurs at most at two places, one of them having only the rights to tell constraints on the variable. Other interesting features are also the extension of the conventional logic programming idioms to the handling of arrays and the use of bags of unordered elements, which are particularly interesting to code many-to-one communication without using merge processes.

It is, of course, not the place here to expose in details the whole work contained in [Saraswat, 1989] and [Saraswat et al., 1990]. The interested reader is referred to these references for that purpose. Nevertheless, the above brief overview should be sufficient to understand the following comparison.

B. Comparison

While [Saraswat, 1989] has elaborated a very general framework and has highlighted the classical concurrent logic languages from a quite global perspective, our work has taken place in the classical logic programming framework (according to our objectives of Chapter 1). As a consequence, we could take profit of the specificity of the logic programming framework and develop notions tailored to this context. For instance, the role of idempotent substitutions in the reconciliation calculus, the extension of the notions of substitution, of term, of unification, of instantiation to tackle negative information, the reconciliation calculus and the algorithms supporting it cannot be developed in the more general setting of constraints. However, there is no doubt that some of these notions can be abstracted at a constraint level. This is partly achieved in [Saraswat, 1989]. In particular, a notion of reconciliation is proposed but has not received much attention. We believe that exploiting our ideas in the constraint framework could lead to enrich the cc family of languages with quite interesting languages.

Another originality of Conclog over the cc family of languages concerns the nature of the programming primitives. Although they are powerful, the Ask and Tell primitives of [Saraswat, 1989] are basic and elementary. In contrast, we have developed richer primitives (compare for instance the variety of primitives handling suspension with the only Ask primitive). As argued in Chapter 6, providing the programmer with a reasonably complete set of primitives is, to our opinion, fundamental in the design of a practical programming language.

Finally, our intention was not to design a distributed language and Conclog is certainly not one. From that perspective, it already differs from Janus. It should furthermore be recalled that Conclog programs are completely free from constraints on the occurrence of variables and on the way in which they should be annotated. Annotations are only introduced at will for optimization purposes. In that, Conclog also differs completely from Janus.

8.6 Parallel implementations of logic languages

For the sake of completeness, we finally mention that our work takes place at the language and programming levels and thus not at the implementation level. In that, it differs from work such as [Chassin and Robert, 1990], [Crammond, 1988], [Goto et al., 1988], [Gupta and Jayaraman, 1990], [Hermenegildo, 1986], [Hermenegildo and Rossi, 1990], [Nilsson and Tanaka, 1988], [Ramkumar and Kalé, 1989], [Taylor et al., 1986], [Warren, 1987b], ...

Conclusion

This second part has introduced a new concurrent logic programming language, called Conclog. It has been incrementally designed in three steps.

1) A parallel execution model of Horn clauses has first been pointed out. It uses or-parallelism and full and-parallelism. As a result, conjoined subgoals are solved independently even if they do share variables. A reconciliation procedure has then been developed to reconcile conflicting bindings. It is based on equation manipulations and makes use of idempotent substitutions.

This model has been described according to two views.

i) A tree view has characterized it in a global way in terms of and/or search trees. According to it, any computation appears as the construction of an and/or search tree slice by slice. This is achieved thanks to cycles, each one composed of an expanding generation phase followed by a re-organizing reconciliation phase. Two results of the latter phase are worth noting : newly computed anwer substitutions are delivered as a result of the computation and the generated part of the and/or search tree is pruned out of branches that are detected to participate to any solution.

ii) A process view has then refined the tree perception of the computation in a more dynamic way. According to it, any computation is described in terms of the behavior of processes of a process model. As a result, the above strict interleaving of the generation and reconciliation phases has been shown to be relaxed in several respects. Among others, some answer substitutions may be produced whereas others are still under computation.

The depth of the slices is a parameter of the model. A class of execution models is thus in fact defined. All of them have been proved to be sound and complete.

2) Negation has been integrated in a second step. It consists of a new form of the negation as failure rule. It has been designed in order to take profit of the main features of the basic model issued from the first design step while keeping them too. Hence, the equational framework used in the basic model has been extended to integrate inequations. The generalization of substitutions in n-substitutions has resulted. It has been motivated by the need to represent solutions of systems of equations and inequations in finite terms. Its justification thus results from theoretical results. Nevertheless, from a practical point of view, n-substitutions have turned out to be a very convenient and natural way of representing infinite number of solutions.

Goals have also been generalized to incorporate negative information. The instantiation concept, the unification concept and the reconciliation calculus have been generalized too, as a consequence.

This given, negative literals have been designed so as to behave as the "negators" of the set of answer n-substitutions computed by their associated positive literals. Some care has furthermore been taken for the way in which variables must be quantified at each reduction step. A form of negation very close to the real negation results. It has been proved to be sound with respect to the completion understanding of the programs. It has also been argued to be as complete as possible when the negation as failure rule and the classical resolution rule are used. Furthermore, as negative subgoals behave in an active way, the floundering problem has been shown to be of no concern.

3) Extra-logical features have been incorporated as a final design step. Their design has been guided by optimization and practicability purposes. On the one hand, annotations have been provided to optimize logic programs. In contrast with committed choice languages, their insertion is optional; in no way, they are required to ensure soundness and completeness. On the other hand, built-in primitives have been introduced to make Conclog practical. The whole set of extra-logical features has been argued to be minimal and "reasonably complete".

This design makes Conclog meet most of the requirements stated in Chapter 1.

i) It is manifestly general purpose and is built in the conventional logic programming framework.

ii) It is also concurrent at the basis and target machine independent.

iii) Furthermore, implementability results from the process model developed to express it.

iv) Finally, the ease of programming and the maximal expressiveness result from the following points. Thanks to the soundness and completeness properties of the model as it results from design steps 1 and 2, the execution of the program can be almost completely abstracted. In particular, multi-solution and multi-directional procedures are indeed supported. Efficient programs can also be coded thanks to the use of extra-logical features.

Ease of programming can then be argued as follows. Because of the soundness and completeness properties, one can essentially program in a declarative way. Annotations, of non-mandatory use, can then be introduced to optimize the programs. Transformations will be given to introduce them in a safe way in the next part. This claim of ease of programming will also be substantiated on practical examples there.

Similarly, expressiveness can be argued from a theoretical point of view : the whole power of general Horn clauses and of usual sequentializing, parallelizing and suspending features have indeed been embodied in Conclog. This claim will also be substantiated in a more concrete way through examples in the following part.

Part III

Programming in Conclog

Introduction

This third part is devoted to the programming in Conclog. It addresses two main issues.

On the one hand, a methodology of concurrent programming is proposed. It does not intend to be a "universal panacea" that ought to be employed in all cases. Rather it provides some guidelines that should ease the construction of a concurrent program. It is oriented to Conclog though most aspects can also be employed in other concurrent languages.

On the other hand, this third section intends to prove the expressiveness and ease of programming through the programming of examples. Two kinds of applications have been coded to this end : behavioral and non-behavioral applications. The former applications tackle the simulation of dynamic systems. They essentially require concurrent behavior constraints. The latter applications are free from such constraints. They can be regarded as the typical applications to which logic programming is dedicated. Those applications are furthermore used to illustrate and criticize the methodology of programming from a practical point of view.

This part is organized in three chapters. Chapter 9 presents the methodology. Non behavorial applications are then tackled in Chapter 10. Finally, behavorial ones are examined in Chapter 11.

Chapter 9

Towards a Methodology of Concurrent Logic Programming

9.1 Introduction

Programming is generally considered as a difficult task. It is even felt to be more difficult in a concurrent context because additional problems of interference, deadlock and starvation are furthermore to be feared. Concurrent logic programming is not an exception to the rule. Even if it could seem easier because of its declarative appeal, some care has to be taken to procedural aspects, as it was argued in Chapter 1. Hence, in spite of our concern of building Conclog as close as possible to the ideal of logic programming, some programming reasoning should also be applied when using Conclog. One of its features is that the above concern makes certainly the task easier. To further ease the programming, we develop hereafter a methodology for program construction. In no point, it intends to be a universal panacea that ought to be applied in all circumstances. It should rather be considered as a help to ease the construction of a program. It is furthermore worth noting that, although Conclog has been chosen as target language, parts of our methodology can also be applied when other concurrent logic languages are used.

This chapter presents an adaptation to the concurrent context of a methodology developed in [Deville, 1987] and refined in [Deville, 1990] for Prolog as target language. It rests on the same three phases. The first one deals with the specifications of the procedures. The second one describes the computed relations in logical terms. The last one derives Conclog programs from these logic descriptions. An interest of this approach is to separate the logical aspects of the construction of a program from its operational ones. Logic descriptions are only concerned by the declarative semantics. Conclog programs add the operational component.

The whole construction schema is drawn in Figure 9.1. It is however not so linear that it appears. The construction of a logic description may induce the modification of the specification. This arises for instance when some ambiguity is detected or when some precisions are required. Furthermore, logic descriptions and programs may be transformed to get more efficiency.

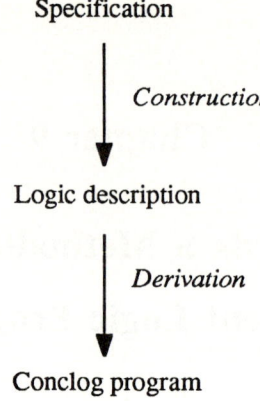

Figure 9.1

As our methodology is inspired of [Deville, 1987] and [Deville, 1990], part of the material is extracted from these references. This is duly signalled in most places. The comparative Section 9.5 will furthermore clarify our contribution. As a snapshot, the following rough description should suggest it. It is summed up in Figure 9.2.

As it is the more recent version, the latter of the above works, namely [Deville, 1990], is only referenced in the following.

i) The specification level

Basically, our specifications add information related to the concurrent framework to the specifications of [Deville, 1990]. Stated in our terminology, this has two main consequences.

1) On the one hand, environment properties of the procedures, composed only of preconditions in the sequential context, are augmented by invariant properties and event conditions. The first properties describe properties that must be satisfied all along the reduction of a call. The event conditions describe properties that are not required at the beginning of the reduction of a call but that should happen eventually.

2) On the other hand, operational properties, composed of preconditions and postconditions in the sequential context, are augmented by invariant properties and suspension conditions. The first ones describe properties that are ensured by the reduction of a call all along this reduction. The last conditions state conditions that force any call to suspend.

The type and relation specifications have been inherited from [Deville, 1990]. We however add another dimension to the type. They act here as preconditions and postconditions but also as invariants.

Phase	Sequential programming	Concurrent programming

Specification	• Type
	• Relation
	• Environment properties
	  - Preconditions
	
	• Operational properties
	
	  - Preconditions
	
	  - Postconditions
		• Type
		• Relation
		• Environment properties
		  - Preconditions
		  - Invariants
		  - Events
		• Operational properties
		  - Suspension conditions
		  - Preconditions
		  - Invariants
		  - Postconditions

Logic description	• Logic definition	• Logic definition • Logic properties
Logic program	• Prolog programs	• Conclog programs

Figure 9.2

ii) The logic description level

In the sequential context, the logic description consists of a wff characterizing the computed relation. This wff is called logic definition. We add to it so-called logic properties. They describe data dependency relations, test properties and exclusiveness properties of the relations used in the logic definition. They are essentially oriented to the concurrent context although some of them can be employed in a sequential context too.

iii) The program level

The program level handles Conclog programs here whereas Prolog ones are handled in [Deville, 1990]. However, the same two step derivations are still used. In the first one, the logic definition is translated in general Horn clauses thanks to syntactic transformations. A correct program is derived therefrom. In the second step, this first correct version is transformed in more efficient ones thanks to correctness preserving transformations.

Our contribution is at these two points. On the one hand, the notion of correctness has been adapted to our concurrent context. It calls the new notions of safety, weak termination and strong termination. On the other hand, some of the correctness preserving transformations are particular to our context too. Among them are transformations based on the logic properties.

9.2 Writing a specification

9.2.1 Introduction

As the term specification can be assigned different meanings, let us first make our understanding of it more precise.

Our specifications take place in the implementation phase of the software life cycle model proposed in [Sommerville, 1985]. At this stage, requirements that the software under construction must meet have been identified and specified. This software has furthermore been designed in a system of modules, each of which is the responsibility of an individual or a small group. The problem of designing executable code is then addressed. Restated in our context, the aim of the implementation phase is to implement the modules in Conclog.

As small programs represent the limit of what is reasonably possible to do rigorously, modules are generally composed of small pieces. Many small programs are thus generally to be managed. Several persons are furthermore generally concerned by a program :

- the implementer, who produces the code,
- the user, who uses the program
- the modifier, in charge of adapting the program.

Therefore, means of handling the programs efficiently are needed. To this end, programs are generally described by some concise and practical characterization. It is widely recognized that the code cannot play this role because many irrelevant coding details are involved. Rather a more abstract description, called specification, is usually used. The following characterization of a specification is to this end particularly illuminating :

"The specification must provide
> to the intended user
>> all the information that he will need to use the program correctly,
>> and nothing more.

The specification must provide
> to the implementer
>> all the information about the intended use that he needs to complete the program and
>> no additional information."   ([Parnas, 1972], [Deville, 1990])

Specifications can be approached in two ways. A first trend is to make formal specifications ([Liskov, 1975], [Parnas, 1977], [Balzer et al., 1983], ...). This trend has the merit of making things precise and unambiguous, of making automated analysis possible and of making use of formal proof techniques to verify the correctness of coded programs with respect to its formal specifications. Nevertheless, we use hereafter the second approach : following [Deville, 1990], specifications are made informal. We thus do not restrict ourselves to the use of one formalism but, rather, generally employ natural language. This approach has the merit of making the specification easier to express because no constraints to syntactic conventions is made. Note that using an informal language does not necessarily imply impreciseness and ambiguity. An important drawback seems however to lie in the proof of correctness of a program with respect to an informal specification. Some uncertainty is indeed introduced because to get complete certainty we should be able to add to the proof of correctness, a proof that this proof is correct and so on. In contrast, using a formal specification, it is possible to define a formal system such that the correctness proof of the program is reduced to a formal proof in the system. However, the problem is postponed of one step. Uncertainty is, of course, also introduced in this approach because the adaquation of the formal specification and what it really intends to mean has to be established. However, there is no formal way to do this.

A complete discussion about the virtues of formal and informal specifications can be found in [Le Charlier, 1985]. Such a discussion is out of the scope of the thesis. Roughly, we adopt informal specifications because we believe things are taken one step before. This does not mean that formal specifications are useless. On the contrary, it is often useful to transform informal specifications into formal ones to facilitate their analysis or the construction of a program. But we perceive this as a first programming step (where care to syntactic constructs has to be made, for instance). Moreover, needs for a high-level description remain. Hence, our use of informal specifications.

9.2.2 General form of a specification

Following [Deville, 1990], a specification is associated with each procedure. It contains information about the computed relation but also on operational properties. Some departure from [Deville, 1990] must thus be achieved in order to adapt the specifications to the concurrent context. A comparison between the two forms of specifications is presented in Section 9.5.

The specification of a procedure takes the following general form :

procedure proc_name(Par$_1$,...,Par$_m$)
- Type specification
- Relation specification
- Environment properties
  * Preconditions
  * Invariants
  * Events
- Operational properties
  * Suspension conditions
  * Preconditions
  * Invariants
  * Postconditions

All components are optional.

9.2.2.1 Type specification

The type specification component provides information on the type of the parameters. Basically, it is of the following form

Type :
   Par$_1$: Type$_1$,
   ...
   Par$_m$: Type$_m$.

The following example particularizes this form to the sort procedure.

Example 9.1

procedure sort(L,L_sorted).
- Type :
   L, L_sorted : lists of integers.

Types constitute a controversial issue in logic programming. Basically, logic programming languages are untyped languages. Nevertheless, we add type information in the specification because reasoning on the procedure is made easier when the forms of the parameters are known. Furthermore, this information appears quite naturally.

Types are assigned the classical meaning of subsets of the Herbrand base B_H. Integers, constants, atoms and lists are classical examples.

For ease of discussion, the following convention is adopted.

Convention 9.1 Given the types T_1, ..., T_m, we denote by $(T_1 \times ... \times T_m)^*$ the set of n-tuples of extended terms which have a ground instance that belongs to $T_1 \times ... \times T_m$ i.e.

$$(T_1 \times \ldots \times T_m)^* = \{ <(t_1,\Psi_1),\ldots,(t_m,\Psi_m)> : \exists \psi_1 \in \Psi_1, \ldots, \exists \psi_m \in \Psi_m$$
$$\exists \theta \in \text{ground}(<t_1,\ldots,t_m>,\psi_1) \cap \ldots \cap \text{ground}(<t_1,\ldots,t_m>,\psi_m) :$$
$$<t_1,\ldots,t_m> \theta \in T_1 \times \ldots \times T_m \}.$$

Type information act in three ways.

1° Precondition

First, it is a precondition on the parameters. Assume that the previous general form of type specification is stated. Then, when the procedure is invoked, the actual parameters $p_1, \ldots, p_m$ must be such that $<p_1,\ldots,p_m> \in (\text{Type}_1 \times \ldots \times \text{Type}_m)^*$. By convention, the effect of the procedure is undefined if the type preconditions are not satisfied.

2° Invariant

Second, type information acts as an invariant that any execution of the procedure must maintain. This covers two aspects. Assume the previous general type specification is stated. Then, for any call that verifies the preconditions of the procedure, the two following properties are required :

i) For any branch of the and/or/not search tree generated by the reduction of the call, the n-substitutions of this branch $v_1, \ldots, v_n$ and the actual parameter $p_1, \ldots, p_m$ of the call are such that, for any $i \in \{1,\ldots,m\}$, for any n-substitution v of $(v_1 \circ \ldots \circ v_n)$, the instantiation $p_i v$ is of type Type_i i.e.

$$<p_1 v,\ldots,p_m v> \in (\text{Type}_1 \times \ldots \times \text{Type}_m)^*.$$

ii) For any top part of a partial candidate solutions subtree (of the above and/or/not search tree), any n-reconciliation-substitution v is such that

$$<p_1 v,\ldots,p_m v> \in (\text{Type}_1 \times \ldots \times \text{Type}_m)^*.$$

Condition ii) is in general quite difficult to establish when some auxiliary procedures are called as subproblems. Fortunately, its verification is eased when some stronger condition can be proved. This latter condition is required by completing the specification declaration by a strong use declaration, as in

L : list; strong use

In such a case, types are required to be used in a strong sense. We will only limit in the following to strong use of lists whose elements are of arbitrary kind of terms. Nevertheless, the strong use idea may be extended to other kinds of types.

Stating strong use of types requires to verify the following condition ST.

(ST) Any actual parameter Par constrained by a strong use declaration verifies the two following properties. Let L be its positive part. Let Type be the type of the elements stated for L.

i)   L is bound in nmas to instances of the terms [], [H|T] where
    - T is itself constrained by a strong use and
    - H is required to be bound only to elements of the type Type;

ii) For any variable X of L, for any n-reconciliation-substitution v of any top part of a partial candidate solution subtree, the negative part v^- contains no binding Y/Z where Y is a variable of Xv^+ and Z is an instance of one of the following terms
    [H|T], [H1,H2|T], ..., [H1,...,Hm|T], ...
    where
    - T is an uninstantiated variable
    - the H's are either uninstantiated variables or are instantiated to all values of Type.

Manifestly, provided there is no conflict of instantiation of the elements H, condition ST implies the above conditions i) and ii).

Some procedures built to handle general lists are sometimes called with list parameters of a particular type. For such calls, it might be useful to qualify further the strong type use of the procedure. As a final extension to type specification, the strong use may then be required for lists whose elements are of some kinds of type. This is achieved by completing the strong use declaration as in one of the following two forms :

L : list, strong use for the type and all subtypes

L : list; strong use for the type and subtypes ST_1, ..., ST_p

where ST_1, ..., ST_p are subtypes for the elements of L. Here is an example.

    procedure append(L1,L2,L).
- Type
      L1, L2, L : strong use for the type and all subtypes.

In this case, condition ST is also required to hold when type Type is taken as any specified subtype.

3° Postcondition

Finally, type information acts as a postcondition. Assuming the above general type specification, for any call that verifies the preconditions, for any answer n-substitution v computed for it, the actual parameters of the call p_1, ..., p_m verify

$$<p_1v,...,p_mv> \in (Type_1 \times ... \times Type_m)^*.$$

Note that, this property results from property ii) of the above point 2°.

9.2.2.2 Relation specification

Logic programming belongs to a relational programming. One natural feature to be specified is thus the relation that the procedure intends to compute. Relations are also defined by means of the Herbrand base. In the following, an n-ary relation is considered as a set of ground n-tuples. Nevertheless, this set is not directly made explicit in the relation part of the specification. An informal description in natural language will rather be used. Example 9.2 gives our informal decription of the sort procedure.

Example 9.2

procedure sort(L,L_sorted).
- Relation
    L and L_sorted contain the same elements and L_sorted is ordered.

9.2.2.3 Environment conditions

Although, full and-parallelism is employed, reductions of subgoals interfere with one another. This results from two sources. On the one hand, after each reconciliation phase, bindings are published. Bindings generated in subtrees engendered by the reduction of some subgoal may thus be communicated to other subtrees generated by the reduction of other subgoals. On the other hand, annotations force bindings to be communicated from such subtrees to others. Hence, from an execution standpoint, the reduction of any call cannot be considered separately from concurrent reductions of other subgoals.

Modularity in the construction of a procedure is however still desired. The following environment properties are used for that purpose. They allow to abstract from reductions concurrent with the reduction of the call under consideration. The former reductions are subsequently referred to as the computing environment of the call. It thus consists of the part of the entire execution that is complementary to the reduction of the call. Restated in tree terms, it concerns the part of the computed and/or/not search tree which is complementary to the subtree engendered by the reduction of the call.

Besides such calls, shared resources may also be accessed by a call and influence its reduction. The association of these resources with the computing environment of the call is subsequently referred to as the environment of the call.

Environment properties state properties that the environment of any call ensures. It is thus not the responsability of any call to ensure them. Here we also take the convention that the effect of the procedure is undefined if they turn out to be violated.

Three kinds of environment properties can be stated : preconditions, invariants and events. The two first are quite familiar. Roughly speaking, they correspond to properties that hold at the time of the call and that hold during its computation. Postconditions of the environment are of no interest for the design of the procedure since the call is then completely computed. The event conditions are perhaps less expected. They state properties that ought to happen but that are not necessarily required at the time of the call.

A. Preconditions

Preconditions state properties that are assumed at the time of any call to the procedure that is when the associated ps-goal process is created. They may address several issues. Nevertheless, two of them are mostly stated. On the one hand, properties of the bindings of variables of the actual parameters of the considered call may be stated. For instance, the absence of bindings for them may be required. On the other hand, shared resources can be constrained. For instance, it may be assumed that some file has some status.

B. Invariants

Invariants state properties that are assumed during the entire reduction of any call to the procedure. They may also address several issues. Nevertheless, the two particular ones pointed out for the preconditions are also mostly stated.

C. Events

Events state properties that are assumed to hold eventually at some points of the execution of the environment. They may take many forms. The following will however just be used subsequently :

some term t is incrementally constructed to some other term u

It means that there exists, in the tree engendered by the execution of the environment, nmas's $\Theta_1, ..., \Theta_p$ that could be heard from any call to the procedure and such that their positive parts $\theta_1, ..., \theta_p$ verify

$t\theta_1...\theta_p = u.$

A classical example of use is that some list is incrementally constructed to a ground list of elements of some type.

9.2.2.4 Operational properties

Finally, operational properties characterize the computation of any call. They address properties on the calls that must be ensured by the actual parameters of the calls before their execution or that are ensured by them. These properties are composed of the expected preconditions, invariants and postconditions. Another kind of properties, called suspension conditions, have been added to them. They state conditions on which any call suspends. As suggested in Chapter 6, suspension is a major means of synchronization in concurrent logic programming. Suspension conditions have thus been stated in a section although some of them constitute invariants.

A. Suspension conditions

Although the format of suspension conditions is free, the following forms are generally employed. They can be grouped in two families. Using Par to denote some parameter and u, $v_1, ..., v_n$ to denote terms, they state as follows :

(i) "input family"

Par input .
Par input until u_1 or ... u_m .
Par element input

(ii) "form family"

Par non variable
Par ground
Par of the form v_1 or ... or v_m.

The forms of the "input family" can of course be combined with the forms of the other family. Nevertheless, as we will see, combining two forms of the same family is redundant and so should not be made.

Several suspensions may, in general, be stated altogether. They are called suspension patterns. Furthermore, several suspension patterns may be defined for a procedure. Any call is then suspended until the suspensions required by one pattern are fulfilled. In this case, everything occurs as if this pattern was only stated.

As an example, here is a fragment of the specification of the sort procedure.

Example 9.3

procedure sort(L,L_sorted).
- Operational properties
    * Suspension conditions : L input and non-variable.

The meaning of these specifications is as follows.

A.1 "THE INPUT FAMILY"

Specifications of the "input family" essentially declare the involved parameter as input or input until some point of instantiation. What this precisely means is defined as follows.

(i.1) *"Par input"* means that, for any call C to the procedure, the positive part t of the actual parameter Par cannot be constructed directly or indirectly by the reduction of

C. Stated in tree terms, for any branch of the subtree ST(C), the nmas's $\Theta_1, ..., \Theta_p$ of this branch verify the following property :

for any variable V of t^+, the functional restriction of any n-substitution of $\Theta_1 \circ ... \circ \Theta_p$ is ({},not{}).

(i.2) *"Par input until u_1 or ... u_m"* means that, for any call C to the procedure, the positive part t of the actual parameter Par cannot be constructed directly or indirectly by the reduction of C, except when the reduction has reached a point where t is known to be an instance of one u_i. Restated in tree terms, for any branch of the subtree ST(C) such that its nmas $\Theta_1, ..., \Theta_p$ do not verify the above property, there is a set of given general bindings, say $\{X_1/t_1\} \oplus \Psi_1, ..., \{X_q/t_q\} \oplus \Psi_q$ such that

$t \{X_1/t_1\} \circ ... \circ \{X_q/t_q\}$

is an instance of one u_i.

(i.3) *"Par element input"* may only be required for parameters Par of the list type. The intuitive meaning is that any call cannot construct the elements of the list but may instantiate these elements. The precise meaning results from the above point i.2. "Par element input" amounts to Par is input until [] or [H|T] where T is itself regarded as element input.

Example 9.4

1) Consider the procedure p(Par) and suppose that Par has been declared as

Par input.

Consider the call p(h(X)). Then, the reduction of p should suspend each time it would construct X directly or indirectly. Hence, the procedure

p(h(1)).
p(h(2)).

is not correct with respect to this specification whereas the following one is :

suspend p(Par?).
p(h(1)).
p(h(2)).

Note that this does not exclude that X can be instantiated during the reduction of p(h(X)) but such instantiations can only arise from bindings made for X in other subtrees.

2) Consider now the same procedure p but this time with the specification

Par input until h(Var).

Consider the call p(X). Its reduction should suspend each time it would construct X directly or indirectly. However, this restriction is overstepped when the reduction reaches a point where X is bound to some instance of h(Var). For instance, if X turns out to be instantiated to h(g(Y)) then, from this point, the reduction can instantiate Y.

3) Finally, consider the following specification

   Par element input.

Then the procedure p cannot construct the elements of Par but may instantiate them. The following procedure is thus correct with this respect.

   suspend p(!).
   p([]).
   p([H|T]) ← H=1, p(T).

A.2 THE "FORM FAMILY"

A specification of the "form family" requires that any call to the procedure is suspended until the specified parameter is of the form required by the specification. Precisely,

   Par ground (resp. Par non-variable)

requires that the parameter Par is ground (resp. non-variable) before the reduction can start. The form

   Par of the form v_1 or ... or v_n

requires that Par is an instance of one of the v_i's before the reduction of the call can occur.

Example 9.5 Consider again the procedure p(Par) and assume that Par is declared as

   Par of the form [] or [H|T].

Then, the reduction of the call p(L) suspends until L is intantiated to [] or some instance of [H|T].

B. Preconditions

Preconditions state properties that must be verified by the parameters of the procedure. For instance, assuming the specified procedure has two parameters, say Par_1 and Par_2, it might be required that, $Par_1 < Par_2$ holds. As for types, this means that at least one ground instance of the actual parameters must fulfill these conditions.

As before, we take the convention that the effect of the procedure is not defined if the preconditions are not satisfied.

C. Invariants

Properties may also be satisfied during the entire reduction of any call to the procedure. Although invariants are not, in principle, limited, we will only use the following two types of invariants.

1) The first ones state properties on parameters that hold for any branch of the and/or/not search tree engendered by the reduction of any call. Precisely, stating the relation

$R(Par_1,...,Par_m)$

between the parameters Par_1, ..., Par_m of the procedure means that, for any call C, for any branch B of the and/or/not search tree generated by the reduction of C, if (t_1,Ψ_1), ..., (t_m,Ψ_m) are the actual parameters, if Θ_1, ..., Θ_p are the nmas's and general bindings along B and if $Type_i$ is the type of Par_i then there is some μ of $ground(<t_1,...,t_m>;\psi_1) \cap ... \cap ground(<t_1,...,t_m>;\psi_m)$ for some $\psi_1 \in \Psi_1$, ..., $\psi_m \in \Psi_m$ such that

    (i) $t_i\mu \in Type_i$, for all $i \in \{1,...,m\}$
    (ii) $R(t_1\mu,...,t_m\mu)$.

2) Properties on the environment of the procedure can be required as invariants. In contrast with the environment properties, these properties are ensured by the reduction of any call to the procedure. Classical examples concern file status. For instance, it might be required that the reduction of any call does not alter the assignment of input and output files. As such file status invariants are satisfied by most procedures, we subsequently take the convention to state them implicitly.

D. Postconditions

Finally, some postconditions may be stated. Although the form of the postconditions is not limited, three kinds will usually be employed.

1) The first one generalizes the directionality specification of [Deville, 1990]. They are also called directionalities. They take the following form :

    inform : outform ; <Min-Max>

The inform and outform are of the form

    $<Set_1,...,Set_m>$

where m is the arity of the treated procedure and each Set_i is a subset of terms. The same abbreviations are also used :

    ground   for the set of ground terms
    var   for the set of variables
    ngv   for the set of non-ground and non-variable terms
    any   for the set of (non restricted) terms.

The Min and Max are integers, the special * symbol or the infinite ∞.

The meaning of such a specification is as follows. If the parameter of a call satisfies the inform then the instance of this call by any computed answer n-substitution verifies the outform. Furthermore, the Min and Max give lower and greater bounds on the number of computed answer n-substitutions, respectively. The * symbol is used to denote some unprecised finite number.

2) The second form of specification characterizes the form of the bindings made for some parameters in some suspension conditions and forms of the actual parameters. The format of such a specification is free. We will however just require the following general form :

Pattern_susp_cond and Set_param and Events : Bind_char$_1$ or ... or Bind_char$_r$

where

- Pattern_susp_cond is a conjunction of suspension conditions,
- Set_param is a conjunction of memberships of some actual parameters to the above Set$_i$ sets
- Events is a conjunction of events as specified in Subsection 9.2.2.3.C
- each Bind_char$_j$ is a characterization of bindings.

The format of such characterizations is free. We will however just use the following ones

Par is incrementally constructed,
Par is incrementally constructed to some term u,

where Par is the considered parameter.

The meaning is as follows. Assume the suspension patterns of Pattern_susp_cond are verified and the events of Events occur. Then, any call C verifies the following property (P) provided its actual parameters verify the preconditions of the procedure and the type membership of Set_param. Let ST(C) be the subtree engendered by the reduction of C. Let, furthermore, for any branch B of the subtree ST(N) attached to the node N,

Nmas(B)

be the serie $\Theta_1, ..., \Theta_p$ of nmas's situated on nodes of B that are not separated from N by an odd number of ns-goals and listed from N. Then, the property (P) is as follows :

- if Par is subject to the binding format
    Par is incrementally constructed
  then, for any answer n-substitution ν computed for the call C, there is a branch B of ST(C) such that the serie of the positive parts $\theta_1,...,\theta_p$ of Nmas(B) verifies
    Par($\theta_1 o ... o \theta_p$) = Par ν$^+$.

- if Par is subject to the binding format
    Par is incrementally constructed to u
  then, for any answer n-substitution ν computed for the call C such that Par ν$^+$ is an instance of u, there is a branch B of ST(C) such that the serie of the positive parts $\theta_1,...,\theta_p$ of Nmas(B) verifies
    Par($\theta_1 o ... o \theta_p$) = Par ν$^+$.

3) The last form of postconditions concerns the environment of the procedure. Particular examples are side effects of the procedure such as the modification of the status of some file.

9.2.3 Examples

Let us give some examples of specifications. The classical multi-directional procedure append is specified as follows.

procedure append(L1,L2,L).
- Type :
    L1, L2, L : lists; strong use for the type and all subtypes
- Relation :
    L is the list L2 appended to the list L1.

This example is quite simple and does not involve many parts. We now turn to the sort procedure.

procedure sort(L,L_sorted).
- Type :
    L, L_sorted : lists of integers
- Relation :
    L and L_sorted contain the same elements and L_sorted is ordered.
- Operational properties :
    1) Suspension condition :
        L input.
    2) Postconditions
        <ground,any> : <ground,ground>; <0-1>
        L input and L incrementally constructed to a ground list: L_sorted incrementally to a ground list.

As a third example, let us specify the more complicated efface example.

procedure efface(X,L,L_eff).
- Type :
    L, L_eff : lists whose elements are of the type of X
- Relation :
    X is an element of L and L_eff is L without the first occurrence of X.
- Operational properties :
    1) Suspension conditions :
        - Pattern1:
            X and L input,
            X ground
        - Pattern2 :
            L_eff input.
    2) Postconditions :
        <ground,ground,any> : <ground,ground,ground> ; <1-1>,

<any,any,ground> : <any,ngv,ground> ; <0-|L_eff|+1> [1]

Pattern1 & L incrementally contructed to a ground list : L_eff incrementally constructed

Pattern2 & L_eff incrementally constructed to a ground list : L incrementally constructed.

Finally, we specify an output procedure. It is assumed that the term Current Output Stream has been precisely defined.

procedure pretty_print_list(L).
- Type :
    L : list.
- Environment properties :
    1) Precondition :
        Assume the current output stream is the user terminal.
    2) Invariant :
        Assume the current output stream remains unchanged during the procedure execution.
- Operational properties :
    1) Suspension condition : L element input.
    2) Postcondition :
        The terms of L are successively printed on the user terminal.

9.3 Constructing a logic description

The next step in the methodology consists in constructing a logic description. It is composed of two parts : a definition part, called logic definition, and a set of properties, called logic properties. This section is organized with respect to them. A section is dedicated to each of these parts. Each one is furthermore organized according to the same structure :

- the general form of the definition or of the properties is first given,
- their correctness is then tackled,
- their construction is finally examined.

9.3.1 The definition part

The definition part of a logic description consists of the logic description of the relations proposed in [Deville, 1990]. It is thus not described in details here since all of them can be found in this book. This section rather aims at giving the background necessary to understand the methodology.

---

[1] As in Chapter 7, we denote by |L_eff| the length of L_eff.

9.3.1.1 General form

The logic definition of the relation is a closed wff taking the following form :

$$(\forall X_1 ... \forall X_n) \ (p(X_1,...,X_n) \Leftrightarrow F)$$

with $n \geq 0$ and F a first order formula. It is abbreviated as

$$p(X_1,...,X_n) \Leftrightarrow \text{Def}$$

when F has the form

$$\exists Y_1 ... \exists Y_n \ \text{Def}$$

with $X_i \neq Y_j$, for all i, j.

Example 9.4 Here is the definition of the relation associated with the sort(L,L_sorted) procedure :

    sort(L,L_sorted)   ⇔   L=[] ∧ L_sorted=[]
                                      ∨
                                      L=[H|T] ∧ partition(H,T,Smaller,Greater)
                                      ∧ sort(Smaller,Smaller_sorted) ∧ sort(Greater,Greater_sorted)
                                      ∧ append(Smaller_sorted,[H|Greater_sorted],L_sorted).

9.3.1.2 Correctness

Of course, all wff's are not suited for the development of procedures. Only a subclass has to be retained. Its wff's would intuitively be called correct. What this precisely means is defined as follows.

A. Intuition

Establishing the correctness of a logic definition consists in proving that there is an equivalence between the relation described in the specification and the logical consequences of the logic definition. Doing this directly is however not a simple task because subproblems are generally involved. Abstraction is then needed and correct logic definitions for the subproblems must be assumed. The correctness of a logic definition thus amounts to the correctness of a logic definition in a set of logic definitions. However, this is only fair when the logic definitions developed for the subproblems do not use the logic definition under study. Hence, the correctness of mutually recursive logic definitions must be stated simultaneously.

Logical consequences are generally understood by making reference to all models. However, the restriction to Herbrand models is made mainly because the domain under consideration when computing is the set of all ground terms. Furthermore, as agreed in Section 2.1 for all this work, we will refer to the whole language $\mathcal{L}$ (see Section 2.1) rather than to the constants, functors and predicates appearing in the programs under study.

B. Notations

The following notations will be used to express the correctness criteria.

Notation 9.2 Let S be a set of formulas and F be a formula. We note

$$S \models_H F$$

when F is true in all Herbrand models of S.

Notation 9.3 Let p be an m-ary procedure. Then,

i)   *p* denotes the relation associated with p
ii)   *LD(p)* denotes the logic definition of p under study
iii)   *domain(p)*, denotes the set of ground m-tuples $<t_1,...,t_m>$ that verify the types of p and the operational preconditions associated with p,
iv)   *prec(p)* denotes the set of tuples $<t_1,...,t_m>$ of extended terms for which one instance verifies the types of p and the operational preconditions associated with p,
v)   *susp(p)* denotes the set of tuples $<t_1,...,t_m>$ of extended terms of the form required by one suspension pattern. This means that each t_i^+ verifies the following constraints :
- if it is subject to a condition of the form
    Par non variable,
    Par ground,
    Par of the form v_1 or ... or v_m
then it must be non variable, ground or an instance of one v_i, respectively;
- if it is declared as input or element input then it is ground,
- if it is declared as input until u_1 or ... or u_m then it must be an instance of one u_i.

In case no suspension pattern is declared, susp(p) is defined as the set of extended terms of $\mathcal{L}$.

vi) $\bar{t}$ is used in $p(\bar{t})$ to denote some m-tuple $<t_1,...,t_m>$ of parameters

C. Correctness criteria

The correctness of a logic definition in a set of logic definitions is defined as follows.

Definition 9.4 Let p be an m-ary procedure and S be a finite set of logic definitions containing LD(p). Then, *LD(p) is correct in S wrt to the specification of p* iff any ground m-tuple $\bar{t}$ (of non-extended terms) verifies the following properties

1) $S \models_H p(\bar{t})$ iff $\bar{t} \in p$ and $\bar{t} \in$ domain(p),
2) $S \models_H \neg p(\bar{t})$ iff $\bar{t} \notin p$ or $\bar{t} \notin$ domain(p).

The correctness of m mutually recursive logic definitions is defined as follows.

Definition 9.5 Let $LD(p_1),...,LD(p_m)$ be logic definitions and $q_1, ..., q_n$ be all the predicate names appearing in them and distinct from $p_1, ..., p_m$. The logic definitions $LD(p_1),...,LD(p_m)$ *are correct with respect to the specification of the p_i's* iff, assuming the existence of a finite set S of logic definitions such that
   1) $LD(q_j)$ is correct with respect to the specification of q_j ($1 \leq j \leq n$),
   2) S contains no occurrences of $p_1, ..., p_m$
$LD(p_i)$ is correct in $S \cup \{LD(p_1),...,LD(p_m)\}$ with respect to the specification of p_i ($1 \leq i \leq m$).

Correct logic definitions have the interesting property that the existence of witnesses can be proved from them. When a logic algorithm is constructed, the literals used in it are not always ground but mostly existentially quantified. Their truth in all Herbrand models imply that, for any Herbrand model, a ground instance of the literal can be found such that it is true in the model. However, as we are interested in computations, the existence of ground instances is not sufficient. It is desired that the same ground instance can be used for all Herbrand models. Such ground instances of the parameters of these literals are called witnesses of the literals. The following property state the existence of such witnesses for correct logic definitions.

Proposition 9.6 Let p be an m-ary procedure, S be a set of logic definitions and $LD(p)$ be a correct logic definition in S. Then, any m-tuple $\bar{u}$ of non-extended terms verifies the following properties :

1) $S \models_H \exists(p(\bar{u}))$ iff
    there is some ground instance $\bar{t}$ of $\bar{u}$ such that $\bar{t} \in p$ and $\bar{t} \in domain(p)$,
2) $S \models_H \exists(\neg p(\bar{u}))$ iff
    there is some ground instance $\bar{t}$ of $\bar{u}$ such that $\bar{t} \notin p$ or $\bar{t} \notin domain(p)$,
3) $S \models_H \neg\exists(p(\bar{u}))$ iff
    there is no ground instance $\bar{t}$ of $\bar{u}$ such that $\bar{t} \in p$ and $\bar{t} \in domain(p)$,
4) $S \models_H \neg\exists(\neg p(\bar{u}))$ iff
    there is no ground instance $\bar{t}$ of $\bar{u}$ such that $\bar{t} \notin p$ or $\bar{t} \notin domain(p)$.

9.3.1.3 Construction

The construction of a correct logic definition is central to the construction of any logic program. It is extensively studied in [Deville, 1990]. We refer the reader to it for a detailed exposition. Nevertheless, the general scheme of construction is recalled hereafter in order to make the thesis as self-contained as possible. Its particularization to the concurrent framework is also tackled.

A. Structural induction techniques

The construction process proposed in [Deville, 1990] is based on structural induction (already used in [Knuth, 1968], [Burstall, 1974], [Manna and Waldinger, 1978], [Stoy, 1982] and [Turner, 1982]). It makes an intensive use of the notion of well-founded relation and minimal element. They are defined as follows.

Definition 9.7 A relation $<$ is *well-founded* over a set E iff there is no infinite decreasing sequence of elements of E i.e. there is no infinite sequence $x_1, \ldots, x_i, \ldots$ such that $x_1 > x_2 > \ldots > x_i > x_{i+1} > \ldots$.

Definition 9.8 An element e of a set E is *minimal* for the well-founded relation $<$ iff there is no element e' in E such that e'$<$e.

This given, the construction process produces a logic definition of the following form :

$$p(X_1,\ldots,X_m) \Leftrightarrow \begin{array}{c} C_1 \wedge F_1 \\ \vee \\ \ldots \\ \vee \\ C_n \wedge F_n \end{array}$$

where the X_i's are variable arguments for p and the C_i's and F_i's are formulas. Roughly speaking, each $C_i \wedge F_i$ deals with one of the various cases for some induction parameter on which a well-founded relation is defined. Each C_i determines a possible case of the induction parameter while the corresponding F_i verifies that p holds in this particular case. In practice, the C_i's are often literals and the F_i's are conjunctions of literals.

The construction process states as follows.

1°   Choose a parameter X_k; call it induction parameter,
2°   Define a well-founded relation, say $<$, over the type T_k of the induction parameter X_k
3°   Assume that X_k is of type T_k and construct a C_i for each structural form (including the minimal one) of the induction parameter X_k,
4°   Construct the corresponding F_i by the two following steps :
       4.1) Suppose that $<X_1,\ldots,X_m>$ is in the domain of p. Construct F_i such that, when C_i is true, $C_i \wedge F_i$ is true iff $<X_1,\ldots,X_m> \in p$. The formula F_i can be constructed by reducing the p to simpler subproblems (because of the particular structural form of X_k) and/or by using recursively p but in such calls $p(t_1,\ldots,t_m)$ that $t_k < X_k$.
       4.2) Verify that $C_i \wedge F_i$ is false when $<X_1,\ldots,X_m>$ is not in domain(p) and, if need be, modify it in consequence.

An important property of the resulting logic algorithms is that they are correct by construction.

Example 9.6 As an illustration, let us construct a logic definition for the sort procedure.

1° Choice of an induction parameter

There are two argument candidates : L and L_sorted. Let us arbitrarily choose the first one[1].

2° Choice of a well-founded relation

A classical relation on lists is the following :

$L_1 < L_2$ iff L_1 is a proper suffix of L_2.

This relation is furthermore well-founded because lists are always finite.

3° Construction of the C_i's

We now have to construct the C_i's for all different structural forms of L. A simple choice is

C_1 : L=[]
C_2 : L=[H|T] .

They indeed cover all the possible forms of L.

4° Construction of the F_i's

Each F_i must be constructed so that, given a ground n-tuple <L,L_sorted> of domain(sort) and assuming C_i holds, $C_i \wedge F_i$ is true iff <L,L_sorted>∈ sort.
1) if L=[] is true then, <L,L_sorted>∈ sort iff L=[]∧L_sorted=[];
2) if L=[H|T] is true then <L,L_sorted>∈ sort iff the following conjunction holds :
   L=[H|T] ∧ partition(H,T,Smaller,Greater)
   ∧ sort(Smaller,Smaller_sorted) ∧ sort(Greater,Greater_sorted)
   ∧ append(Smaller_sorted,[H|Greater_sorted],L_sorted).

(with the usual definitions of append and partition (see Sections 10.3 and 10.4 for a precise description)). Note that the recursive calls are allowed. Indeed, thanks to the definition of partition, Smaller≤T and Greater≤T so that Smaller<L and Greater<T.

It then remains to be verified that, for any i∈{1,2}, $C_i \wedge F_i$ is false when <L,L_sorted> is not in the domain of sort. This is indeed verified by the recursive calls and the usual specifications of append and partition.

Summing up, the following logic definition is pointed out for sort.

---

[1] Another logic definition is developed in the following Subsection B by taking L_sorted as induction parameter.

qsort(L,L_sorted) ⇔   L=[] ∧ L_sorted=[]
    ∨
    L=[H|T] ∧ partition(H,T,S,G) ∧
    qsort(S,S_sorted) ∧ qsort(G,G_sorted) ∧
    append(S_sorted,[H|G_sorted],L_sorted)

The creative aspect of the construction of a logic definition is thus reported in

- the choice of a parameter on which the induction is made,
- the choice of a well-founded relation,
- the choice of the C_i's and the F_i's.

According to these choices, several logic definitions result. The impact of the choices and a discussion about the merits of the resulting algorithms can be found in [Deville, 1990]. Additional techniques are furthermore given for transforming a logic definition into more efficient ones. Among them are generalization techniques, instantiation, unfolding, folding transformations, transformations by simplification and transformation with auxiliary definitions. Once more, we refer the interested reader to [Deville, 1990] for more details.

Remark Every language provides primitives. They are built-in procedures that must not be programmed. The existence of a correct logic definition may be assumed for them too. They are called primitive logic definitions and thus must not be constructed.

B. Particularization to the concurrent context

The logic definitions produced by the above general construction scheme are, of course, convenient for our context of concurrent programs. Nevertheless, some design choices may significantly change the inherent degree of parallelism and the efficiency of the resulting algorithms.

1° Choice of data representations

Among them, the choice of a data structure may be of importance. For instance, trees are generally of great interest since they generally contain a high potential for parallelism.

The choice of a data structure that leads to the maximum degree of parallelism or maximum efficiency is very difficult. There is, in fact, no universal panacea. Decisions may be heavily dependent on problem domain knowledge. The following general principle may however be stated:

choose a data structure that generates as many non interfering computations as possible or, at least, as many concurrent computations as possible.

Non interfering computations are particularly interesting because they allow parallel executions without need for reconciliation. Trees generally fit well in this framework. This is however not possible in all cases. When so, a good representation to look for is one that still allows concurrent executions such as stream parallelism. With this respect, lists are generally of great interest since they can be incrementally produced and consumed.

2° Choice of the subproblems

Decomposing a literal into a conjunction of other literals in the construction of the F_i's also greatly affects the inherent degree of parallelism and so the efficiency of the resulting algorithms. For instance, in order to sort a non-empty list, one could sort the list minus its first element and then place it in its good place. This is not a good decomposition because the insertion of the element can only be made after the remaining list is sorted or after at least a sufficient prefix is known. It is better to decompose the list to sort into two independent sublists and to sort them by recursive calls.

Here too, there is no universal panacea. The two above heuristics are also of application :

- choose a decomposition that produces as many non interfering computations as possible,
- choose a decomposition that produces literals that allow stream-parallelism .

Another heuristic can be added :

choose a decomposition that produces literals of same reduction complexity.

Finally, bad decompositions can be avoided by the application of the following heuristic :

avoid decompositions inducing dataflows that force the reduction of some literal to wait until other literals are completely reduced.

3° Choice of the induction parameter

Finally, the choice of an induction parameter also significantly determines the inherent degree of parallelism of the resulting procedures. In fact, it already determines the form of the resulting logic definitions significantly. As an example, let us take again the sort procedure and let us construct a logic definition by using L_sorted as induction parameter. We then get

$$\text{sort}(L,L\_sorted) \Leftrightarrow L\_sorted=[] \land L=[]$$
$$\lor$$
$$L\_sorted=[H|T] \land \text{element}(H,L,L\_rem) \land \text{list}(L\_rem)$$
$$\land \text{sort}(L\_rem,T) \land \text{ordered}(L\_sorted)$$

This logic definition significantly differs from the version constructed hereabove. What we do here is, in fact, generating permutations of the list L and looking for orderness.

Although all correct logic definitons can be transformed in Conclog programs, a good heuristic for the choice of the induction parameter is to take one declared as input in the suspension part of the specification and, when there are several patterns, one declared as input in as many suspension patterns as possible. Such an input parameter is indeed the starting point of a dataflow that we usually have in mind. The experience shows that this leads to the logic programs of best complexity when they are used with the corresponding parameter ground. Furthermore, choosing such a parameter for induction forces its structural form to be explained and will allow to apply some transformations to the logic programs to get more efficiency.

4° Combining the choices

It is finally worth noting that these choices are not independent from one another and usually interact. For instance, the choice of the data structure is crucial for determining the induction parameters. Indeed, their structure should be made easily explicit and well-founded relations should also be defined on them easily. Furthermore, some interesting decompositions are only possible when some clever choice of the induction parameters is made.

9.3.2 Logic properties

Logic properties constitute our contribution to the methodology at this second construction step. They capture, at the logic level, dependency relations of the C_i's and F_i's. They will be used for optimizations of logic programs in the next section. Although they are not limited, properties of three kinds will be used in the following. They are called data dependency properties, test dependency properties and exclusiveness properties. They are presented in the following according to the same scheme as logic definitions : general form, correctness and constuction.

9.3.2.1 General form

9.3.2.1.1 Data dependency property

A. Motivation

We motivate the introduction of the data dependency properties by considering again the sort procedure. Precisely, consider the case where L=[H|T]. As noted in Example 9.6, in this case, sort(L,L_sorted) reduces to

L=[H|T] ∧ partition(H,T,Smaller,Greater)
∧ sort(Smaller,Smaller_sorted) ∧ sort(Greater,Greater_sorted)
∧ append(Smaller_sorted,[H|Greater_sorted],L_sorted).

Intuitively, when L is input, it is the role of

partition(H,T,Smaller,Greater)

to generate bindings for Smaller and Greater. This has a counterpart at the declarative level :

$\forall H, T \in B_H$:
  $\{(\text{Smaller},\text{Greater}) \in B_H \times B_H :$
    $<H,T,\text{Smaller},\text{Greater}> \in \textit{partition} \cap \text{domain}(\textit{partition})\}$
  $=$
  $\{(\text{Smaller},\text{Greater}) \in B_H \times B_H : \exists \text{Smaller\_sorted},\text{Greater\_sorted},\text{L\_sorted} \in H_B :$
    $<H,T,\text{Smaller},\text{Greater}> \in \textit{partition} \cap \text{domain}(\textit{partition}),$
    $<\text{Smaller},\text{Smaller\_sorted}> \in \textit{sort} \cap \text{domain}(\textit{sort}),$
    $<\text{Greater},\text{Greater\_sorted}> \in \textit{sort} \cap \text{domain}(\textit{sort}),$
    $<\text{Smaller\_sorted},[H|\text{Greater\_sorted}],\text{L\_sorted}> \in \textit{append} \cap \text{domain}(\textit{append})\}.$

Such a property will be stated together with the logic definition. The following notation is provided as a shorthand :

For all H, T :
  partition(H,T,Smaller,Greater) $\rightarrow_{\{\text{Smaller},\text{Greater}\}}$
    (sort(Smaller,Smaller_sorted) $\wedge$ sort(Greater,Greater_sorted)
    $\wedge$ append(Smaller_sorted,[H|Greater_sorted],L_sorted)).

B. Description

In general, data dependency properties take the following form :

For all $X_1, ..., X_p : p_1(\bar{t_1}) \wedge ... \wedge p_r(\bar{t_r}) \rightarrow_{\{Y_1,...,Y_q\}} q_1(\bar{u_1}) \wedge ... \wedge q_s(\bar{u_s})$

where the $\bar{t_i}$'s and the $\bar{u_j}$'s are tuples of non-extended terms and where $\{X_1,...,X_p\}$ and $\{Y_1,...,Y_q\}$ partition the variables of the $\bar{t_i}$'s. The meaning is as follows. For any grounding values $<x_1,...,x_p>$ of $<X_1, ..., X_p>$, the two following sets S_1 and S_2 are identical

- S_1 is the set of the ground q-tuples $<y_1,...,y_q> \in H_B \times ... \times H_B$ such that, the ground tuple $<\bar{t_1},...,\bar{t_r}>\theta$, with
  $\theta = \{X_1/x_1,...,X_p/x_p,Y_1/y_1,...,Y_q/y_q\},$
  verifies, for any $i \in \{1,...,r\}$,
  $\bar{t_i}\theta \in p_i \cap \text{domain}(p_i).$

- S_2 is the set of the ground q-tuples $<y_1,...,y_q> \in H_B \times ... \times H_B$ such that, there exists a ground instance instance, say $<\bar{v_1},...,\bar{v_r},\bar{w_1},...,\bar{w_s}>$, of $<\bar{t_1},...,\bar{t_r},\bar{u_1},...,\bar{u_s}>\theta$, with
  $\theta = \{X_1/x_1,...,X_p/x_p,Y_1/y_1,...,Y_q/y_q\},$
  such that, for any $i \in \{1,...,r\}$ and $j \in \{1,...,s\}$,
  $\bar{v_i} \in p_i \cap \text{domain}(p_i),$
  $\bar{w_j} \in q_j \cap \text{domain}(q_j).$

9.3.2.1.2 Test dependency property

A. Motivation

Test data properties are motivated by the partition procedure. A logic definition for it is as follows :

$$\text{partition}(X,L,\text{Smaller},\text{Greater}) \Leftrightarrow$$
$$L=[] \land \text{Smaller}=[] \land \text{Greater}=[]$$
$$\lor$$
$$L=[H|T] \land$$
$$[\ (H \le X \land \text{Smaller}=[H|\text{Smaller\_rem}] \land \text{partition}(X,T,\text{Smaller\_rem},\text{Greater}))$$
$$\lor$$
$$(H>X \land \text{Greater}=[H|\text{Greater\_rem}] \land \text{partition}(X,T,\text{Smaller},\text{Greater\_rem}))\ ]\ .$$

Obviously, when L=[H|T], H≤X acts as a test to reduce partition(X,L,Smaller,Greater) to partition(X,L,Smaller,Greater_rem). At a logic level, we have

$$\forall X,L,H,T \in B_H : L=[H|T] \land H \le X \Rightarrow$$
$$\{\ \langle \text{Smaller},\text{Greater} \rangle \in B_H \times B_H :$$
$$\langle X,L,\text{Smaller},\text{Greater} \rangle \in \textit{partition} \cap \text{domain}(\textit{partition})\ \}$$
$$=$$
$$\{\ \langle \text{Smaller},\text{Greater} \rangle \in B_H \times B_H : \exists \text{Smaller\_rem} \in B_H :$$
$$S=[H|\text{Smaller\_rem}] \land$$
$$\langle X,L,\text{Smaller\_rem},\text{Greater} \rangle \in \textit{partition} \cap \text{domain}(\textit{partition})\ \}$$

This is abbreviated as

For all X, L, H, T :

$$L=[H|T] \land H \le X \xrightarrow{\text{partition}(X,L,\text{Smaller},\text{Greater})}$$
$$\text{Smaller}=[H|\text{Smaller\_rem}] \land \text{partition}(X,T,\text{Smaller\_rem},\text{Greater}).$$

B. Description

In general, test properties take the following form

$$\text{For all } X_1, ..., X_m : p_1(\overline{t_1}) \land ... \land p_r(\overline{t_r}) \xrightarrow{p(\overline{t})} q_1(\overline{u_1}) \land ... \land q_s(\overline{u_s})$$

where $\overline{t}$, the $\overline{t_i}$'s and the $\overline{u_j}$'s are tuples of non-extended terms and where $X_1, ..., X_m$ are all the variables of the $\overline{t_i}$'s. The meaning is as follows. Let $Y_1, ..., Y_n$ be the variables of $\overline{t}$ that are not in $\{X_1,...,X_m\}$. Then, for all ground m-tuples $\langle x_1,...,x_m \rangle$ of $\langle X_1,...,X_m \rangle$ such that, for all $i \in \{1,...,r\}$,

$$\overline{t_i}\theta \in p_i \cap \text{domain}(p_i)$$

with

$\theta = \{X_1/x_1,...,X_m/x_m\}$,

the following two sets S_1 and S_2 are identical

- S_1 is the set of ground n-tuples $<y_1,...,y_n> \in B_H \times ... \times B_H$ such that, if μ is the substitution
  $$\mu = \{X_1/x_1,...,X_m/x_m, Y_1/y_1,...,Y_n/y_n\},$$
  $\bar{t}\mu \in p \cap \text{domain}(p)$.

- S_2 is the set of ground n-tuples $<y_1,...,y_n> \in B_H \times ... \times B_H$ such that, using the above μ, there is a ground instance $<\bar{v}_1,...,\bar{v}_s>$ of $<\bar{u}_1,...,\bar{u}_s>\mu$ such that, for any $j \in \{1,...,s\}$, $\bar{v}_j \in q_j \cap \text{domain}(q_j)$.

9.3.2.1.3 Exclusiveness property

A. Motivation

The partition procedure can also be used to motivate the introduction of the exclusiveness properties. Intuitively, the conjunctions

L=[],
L=[H|T] ∧ H≤X
L=[H|T] ∧ H>X

exclude one another. That is, given a ground instance of the variables, only one of them is true. This is subsequently denoted as

For all L, X :
    L=[],
    L=[H|T] ∧ H≤X
    L=[H|T] ∧ H>X
are mutually exclusive.

B. Description

In general, exclusiveness properties take the following form :

For all $X_1, ..., X_m$:
    Conj_1,
    ...,
    Conj_n
are mutually exclusive,

where the X_i's are variables and the Conj_j's are conjunctions of literals. The meaning is as follows.

For any ground m-tuple $<x_1,...,x_m>$, at most one of the following properties P_i is verified ($1 \leq i \leq n$). Let $Conj_i$ be rewritten as
$$p_1(\overline{t_1}), ..., p_r(\overline{t_r})$$
and θ denotes the substitution $\{X_1/x_1,...,X_m/x_m\}$. Then, P_i states as follows : there is a ground instance $<\overline{u}_1, ..., \overline{u}_r>$ of $<\overline{t}_1, ..., \overline{t}_r>\theta$ such that, for any $j \in \{1,...,r\}$, one has
$$\overline{u}_j \in p_j \cap domain(p_j).$$

9.3.2.2 Correctness

The correctness of the logic properties is quite straightforward to define. Logic properties are correct iff the statements expressing their meaning hold.

9.3.2.3 Construction

The construction of the logic properties also requires creativity but, generally, results directly from the decomposition of the treated procedures into subprocedures.

A. Data dependency property

A good heuristic to discover data dependency properties is to take the parameters declared as input as a starting point and to examine the dataflow they induce. A first correct logic property generally results. The process can then be applied to the remaining subsequence by taking as input the variables produced in the first logic property. To be more specific, let us again consider the sort(L,L_sorted) procedure as an example. The specification provides L as given argument. Obviously, decomposing sort(L,L_sorted) in

partition(H,T,Smaller,Greater),
sort(Smaller,Smaller_sorted), sort(Greater,Greater_sorted),
append(Smaller_sorted,[H|Greater_sorted],L_sorted),

when L=[H|T], given L and so H and T, it is the role of partition(H,T,Smaller,Greater) to produce Smaller and Greater. Note that this does not hold in case the opposite directionality is stated. We thus obtain

For all H, T :
    partition(H,T,Smaller,Greater) $\rightarrow$ {Smaller,Greater}
        (sort(Smaller,Smaller_sorted), sort(Greater,Greater_sorted),
           append(Smaller_sorted,[H|Greater_sorted],L_sorted))

Assume now Smaller and Greater are fixed. Then, it is the role of sort(Smaller,Smaller_sorted) and sort(Greater,Greater_sorted) to produce Smaller_sorted and Greater_sorted, respectively. We thus have also

For all H, Smaller, Greater :
　sort(Smaller,Smaller_sorted),　sort(Greater,Greater_sorted)
　$\xrightarrow{\{\text{Smaller\_sorted},\text{Greater\_sorted}\}}$
　append(Smaller_sorted,[H|Greater_sorted],L_sorted) .

B. Test dependency property

As far as test dependency properties are concerned, a good heuristics is to look for procedures acting as tests i.e. literals such that, assuming their success, the whole procedure succeeds iff the remainder of the conjunction succeeds. For instance, referring to the partition procedure, assuming L=[H|T] and H≤X, partition(X,L,Smaller,Greater) succeeds iff

　Smaller=[H|Smaller_rem],　partition(X,T,Smaller_rem,Greater)

succeeds. Note that the same thing cannot be claimed if H≤X and partition(X,T,Smaller_rem,Greater) are interchanged. Indeed, assuming this partititon call succeeds, it is not because the test H≤X fails that partition(X,L,Smaller,Greater) should fail. Nevertheless, the following logic property is correct :

For all X,L,H,T,Smaller,Greater,Smaller_rem :
　L=[H|T] ∧ Smaller=[H|Smaller_rem] ∧ partition(X,T,Smaller_rem,Greater)
　$\xrightarrow{\text{partition}(X,L,\text{Smaller},\text{Greater})}$
　H≤X

It will be of no use later because the first conjunction contains a literal, namely Smaller=[H|Smaller_rem], that can not be considered as a test.

Note that L=[H|T] is one C_i and H≤X is some test used to decompose the partition procedure in elementary subprocedures. This can be generalized. A good strategy is indeed to examine the C_i's coupled with tests used in order to decompose the problem into subproblems.

C. Exclusiveness property

Finally, exclusiveness properties can be obtained by using the same heuristics. Taking the C_i's as starting points, it remains to look for additional literals that partition the treated procedure in disjoint cases. For instance, turning back to the partition procedure, the conjunctions

　L=[],
　L=[H|T] ∧ H≤X
　L=[H|T] ∧ H>X

manifestly points out all the cases to be treated.

D. Maximal properties

An additional heuristic can be applied in order to search for all kinds of logic properties. Logic properties should be searched so as to be maximally expressive. For instance, if the data dependency property

For all $X, Y : p(X,Y,T,U) \rightarrow_{\{T,U\}} [\ q(X,Y,T,U), r(X,Y,T,U), t(X,Y,T,U)\ ].$

holds, then the logic property

For all $X, Y : [\ p(X,Y,T,U), q(X,Y,T,U)\ ] \rightarrow_{\{T,U\}} [\ r(X,Y,T,U), t(X,Y,T,U)\ ]$

holds too. The latter is thus contained in the former and is thus less interesting to express. This can be transposed to logic properties of the other kinds. Hence, the following logic properties should be searched.

(i) Data dependency property

Search for data dependency properties

For all $X_1, ..., X_p : p_1(\bar{t_1}), ..., p_r(\bar{t_r}) \rightarrow_{\{Y_1,...,Y_q\}} q_1(\bar{u_1}), ..., q_s(\bar{u_s})$

such that the properties do not hold if $p_1(\bar{t_1}), ..., p_r(\bar{t_r})$ is replaced by a strict subset.

(ii) Test dependency property

Search for test dependency properties

For all $X_1, ..., X_m : p_1(\bar{t_1}), ..., p_r(\bar{t_r}) \xrightarrow{p(\bar{t})} q_1(\bar{u_1}), ..., q_s(\bar{u_s})$

such that the properties do not hold if $p_1(\bar{t_1}), ..., p_r(\bar{t_r})$ is replaced by a strict subset.

(iii) Exclusiveness property

Search for exclusiveness properties

For all $X_1, ..., X_m$:
    $Conj_1$,
    ...,
    $Conj_n$
are mutually exclusive,

such that

- they do not hold if one $Conj_i$ is replaced by a strict subconjuction
- their $Conj_i$'s conjunctions partition the set of cases to be treated in as many subcases as possible.

9.4 Deriving a concurrent logic program

We now turn to the last step of the proposed methodology. Given a specification and a correct logic description, a correct Conclog program is to be derived. In fact, more and more efficient Conclog programs are successively derived. This is achieved in two phases. A first correct Conclog program is derived from the logic definition. It is then transformed in more efficient versions thanks correctness-preserving transformations, some of them employing the logic properties and directionality hypotheses.

This section is organized as follows. The general form of the concurrent logic programs are first stated. Then, the correctness of concurrent logic programs is examined. Finally, correct concurrent logic programs are derived.

9.4.1 General form

The concurrent logic programs we manipulate are made of generalized Horn clauses where the Conclog annotations can be introduced. We will also use a more restricted form, called pure concurrent logic programs.

Definition 9.9 A *concurrent logic program (resp. procedure)* is a logic program (resp. procedure) where Conclog extra-logical features can be introduced. A *pure concurrent logic program (resp. procedure)* is a concurrent logic program (resp. procedure) where no such feature can be introduced.

9.4.2 Correctness

Obviously, our aim is to obtain correct Conclog programs. The exact meaning of correctness is precised hereafter. Although our target language is Conclog, most of the correctness definitions also apply, with slight modifications, to programs in other concurrent logic languages.

Obviously, the correctness of a concurrent logic program must be defined in terms of the correctness of its procedures.

Definition 9.10 A concurrent logic programs is *correct* iff all its concurrent logic procedures are correct.

As for logic definitions, the correctness of a concurrent logic procedure is desired independently of the concurrent logic procedures for its subproblems. Nevertheless, mutually recursive concurrent logic procedures must be treated together. We thus also define here the correctness of a concurrent logic procedure in a set of such logic procedures and the correctness of concurrent logic procedures. Some auxiliary concepts need first to be defined for that purpose.

9.4.2.1 Auxiliary concepts

Definition 9.11 Let

- p be an m-ary procedure,
- $\bar{t}$ be an m-tuple of (extended) terms
- ν be an n-substitution
- Ψ be a set of n-substitutions.

We denote by

$$\text{Sol}(p,\bar{t}),\ S_\nu(p,\bar{t}),\ S\Psi(p,\bar{t})$$

the following sets :

1) $\text{Sol}(p,\bar{t}) = \{\bar{u} \in p \cap \text{domain}(p) : \bar{u} \text{ is ground instance of } \bar{t}\,\}$

2) $S_\nu(p,\bar{t}) =$
   - $\emptyset$, if one of the component of $\bar{t}$ is not instantiable by ν,
   - $\{\bar{u} \in \text{domain}(p) : \bar{u} \text{ is ground instance of } \bar{t}\nu\}$, otherwise

3) $S\Psi(p,\bar{t}) = \bigcup_{\psi \in \Psi} S_\psi(p,\bar{t})$

They are also written as Sol, S_ν, $S\Psi$ when there is no doubt about the p and $\bar{t}$ arguments.

These notations given, the auxiliary concepts of g-soundness for a call, g-completeness for a call, redundancy for a call, safety for a call and termination for a call can be defined. The first two ones are adaptations of those proposed in [Deville, 1990]. The last ones are specific to our context.

A. G-soundness

The g-soundness property expresses that the n-substitutions of some set Ψ yields correct solutions.

Definition 9.12 Let Ψ be a set of n-substitutions, p be a procedure and $\bar{t}$ be an n-tuple of terms. We say that Ψ is *g-sound for* $p(\bar{t})$ iff

$$\text{Sol}(p,\bar{t}) \supseteq S\Psi(p,\bar{t})\ .$$

B. G-completeness

The completeness criteria expresses that every correct solution is covered by an n-substitution of Ψ.

Definition 9.13 Let Ψ be a set of n-substitutions, p be a procedure and $\bar{t}$ be an n-tuple of terms. We say that Ψ is *g-complete for* $p(\bar{t})$ iff

$$S\Psi(p,\bar{t}) \supseteq \mathrm{Sol}(p,\bar{t}).$$

C. Redundancy

The redundancy criteria expresses the fact that n-substitutions cover the same solutions.

Definition 9.14 Let Ψ be a set of n-substitutions, p be a procedure and $\bar{t}$ be an n-tuple of terms. We say that Ψ *is redundant for* $p(\bar{t})$ iff there are two n-substitutions ν and μ of Ψ such that

$$S_\nu(p,\bar{t}) \cap S_\mu(p,\bar{t}) \neq \emptyset$$

D. Safety

Another desired property is that no reduction of an s-goal remains idle forever. Basically, this amounts to requiring that the reduction of no subgoal issued from the reduction of the considered call, say $p(\bar{t})$, remains suspended forever. Two refinements are furthermore needed. On the one hand, the procedure cannot be blamed of infinite suspensions induced by its suspension patterns. The absence of suspension should thus only be required under the assumption that the environment of the procedure call eventually instantiates the call $p(\bar{t})$ to such an extent that the suspension patterns are verified (i.e. that $\bar{t}$ is instantiated to an element of susp(p)), and this in such a manner that all intermediate instantiations verify the preconditions of p (i.e. are in prec(p)). On the other hand, strong read-only annotated calls should also never suspend if the environment of the procedure call provide enough instantiations i.e. binds the read-only annotated variables to ground terms. Note that this property always results from the non suspending character of the non-annotated versions in the case where no extra-logical procedure, like those testing the read-only annotated restriction of variables, are used. Summing up, the precise definition of the safety property is as follows.

Definition 9.15 Let CP be a concurrent logic program, p be an n-ary procedure and $\bar{t}$ be an n-tuple of terms. The s-goal $p(\bar{t})$ *is safe under CP* iff, for any $\bar{t}^*$ obtained by read-only annotating some (possibly none) variables of $\bar{t}$, say $X_1, \ldots, X_n$, the reduction of no subgoal issued from the reduction of $p(\bar{t}^*)$ remains suspended forever, provided the following condition holds: $\bar{t}$ is progressively bound to an element $\bar{t}\theta$ of susp(p) such that for any read-only annotated variable X of $\bar{t}^*$, $X\theta$ is ground and this in such a manner that the (progressively) induced instances of $\bar{t}$ are in prec(p).

E. Termination

Termination will be used in two ways : in a weak one and in a strong one. In general, termination states that the computed and/or/not search tree engendered by the considered s-goal is finite. This is the sense we place in strong termination. However, this is not always possible. In this case, a weaker form, called weak termination, may hold. It requires the same property but under the assumption that reconciliation is provoked after a finite time. In other terms, it requires termination but only for the models whose R-depth parameters are finite.

Definition 9.16 Let CP be a concurrent logic program, p be an n-ary procedure and $\bar{t}$ be an n-tuple of terms.

1) The *s-goal* $p(\bar{t})$ *weakly terminates under CP* iff, for any model whose R-depth parameter is finite, the and/or/not search tree engendered by $p(\bar{t})$ is finite.
2) The *s-goal* $p(\bar{t})$ *strongly terminates under CP* iff, whatever value the R-depth parameter takes, the and/or/not search tree engendered by $p(\bar{t})$ is finite.

9.4.2.2 Correctness criteria

We are now in position to give correctness criterias. We begin by stating the correctness of a concurrent logic procedure in a set of concurrent logic procedures. In fact several forms of correctness are defined. They are called partial correctness, semi-correctness and total correctness. The first form does not care for termination and suspension. The second form further requires the safety and weak termination properties. Finally, the last one requires the strong termination property.

Before stating the definitions, the following remark is worth noting. Properties of the procedures should not be verified for all calls but only for those verifying the preconditions of the procedures. This justifies our interest for tuples of the prec(p) set in the following definitions.

Definition 9.17 Let CP be a concurrent logic program containing a concurrent logic procedure CLP(p) for the n-ary procedure p. Then, CLP(p) is *partially correct* in CP wrt to the specification of p iff the following conditions hold. For any n-tuple $\bar{t} \in$ prec(p), if Ψ denotes the set of answer n-substitutions computed for $p(\bar{t})$ by assuming that the environment properties, the safety property and termination property hold then

1) Ψ is g-sound and g-complete for $p(\bar{t})$,
2) Ψ is not redundant for $p(\bar{t})$,
3) the suspension conditions are verified,
4) the invariants are kept invariants during the reduction of $p(\bar{t})$,
5) the postconditions are fulfilled.

Definition 9.18 Let CP be a concurrent logic program containing a concurrent logic procedure CLP(p) for the n-ary procedure p. Then, CLP(p) is *semi-correct* in CP wrt to the specification of p iff the following conditions hold

1) CLP(p) is partially correct in CP with respect to the specification of p
2) for any $\bar{t} \in$ prec(p), $p(\bar{t})$ is safe under CP
3) for any $\bar{t} \in$ prec(p), if the set of answer n-substitutions Ψ computed for $p(\bar{t})$ is finite, then $p(\bar{t})$ weakly terminates under CP.

Definition 9.19 Let CP be a concurrent logic program containing a concurrent logic procedure CLP(p) for the n-ary procedure p. Then, CLP(p) is *totally correct in CP* or, more simply, *correct in CP*, wrt to the specification of p iff the following conditions hold

1) CLP(p) is semi-correct in CP with respect to the specification of p
2) for any $\bar{t} \in \text{prec}(p)$, if the set of answer n-substitutions Ψ computed for $p(\bar{t})$ is finite, then $p(\bar{t})$ strongly terminates under CP.

The correctness of mutually recursive concurrent logic procedures can now be stated.

Definition 9.20 Let $\text{CLP}(p_1), \ldots, \text{CLP}(p_m)$ be concurrent logic procedures and $q_1, \ldots, q_n$ be all the procedure names appearing in $\text{CLP}(p_1), \ldots, \text{CLP}(p_m)$ and distinct from $p_1, \ldots, p_m$. The concurrent logic procedures $\text{CLP}(p_1), \ldots, \text{CLP}(p_m)$ are correct (resp. semi-correct, partially correct) with respect to the specifications of $p_1, \ldots, p_m$ iff, assuming the existence of a concurrent logic program CP such that

- $\text{CLP}(q_j)$ is correct (resp. semi-correct, partially correct) in CP with respect to its specification, for all $j \in \{1,\ldots,n\}$,
- CP does not contain any occurrence of $p_1, \ldots, p_m$,

$\text{CLP}(p_i)$ is correct (resp. semi-correct, partially correct) in $\text{CP} \cup \{\text{CLP}(p_1),\ldots,\text{CLP}(p_m)\}$

An important property of correctness defined as before is that it is monotone.

Proposition 9.21 Let CP be a concurrent logic program containing no occurrence of a procedure q. Let CLP(q) be a concurrent logic procedure for q. Assume CLP(p) is correct (resp. semi-correct, partially correct) in CP with respect to its specification, then CLP(p) is correct (resp. semi-correct, partially correct) in $\text{CP} \cup \{\text{CLP}(q)\}$ with respect to its specification.
Proof Because CP contains no occurrence of q, the computed and/or/not subtree is the same whether it is computed with reference to CP or to $\text{CP} \cup \{\text{CLP}(q)\}$. ◊

9.4.3 Construction

The ultimate goal of the methodology is to construct correct concurrent logic programs. To this end, profit is, of course taken, from the logic descriptions developed in Section 9.3. We will proceed in two phases. Correct procedures are first derived from the logic definitions. They are then optimized by correctness-preserving transformations.

This section is organized according to this derivation process. It is composed of two parts.

1) In the first part, pure concurrent procedures are derived from the logic descriptions. They already meet some of the properties required to obtain correctness. It is one of the main characteristics of Conclog to obtain at this stage such a good approximation of correct programs. In particular, ideal logic procedures that do not refer to such operational conditions

are already semi-correct and can be executed. This contrasts with sequential languages or (concurrent) committed-choice languages where careful rearrangement of the literals and annotation insertions have generally to be operated. This property results from our concern for soundness and completeness.

Sequentialization constraints, suspension requirements and some operational invariants and postconditions are then achieved.

2) The second step of the derivation procedure consists in transforming the first versions into more efficient ones. This is achieved thanks to correctness-preserving transformations. Some of them are based on the logic properties.

9.4.3.1 Derivation of a first concurrent logic program

9.4.3.1.1 Primitive concurrent logic programs

As in any programming language, Conclog provides some built-in primitives. They are characterized by the fact that there is no need to write code to implement them. We can then assume the existence of concurrent logic programs that implement them. This is indeed operated in the mehodology.

9.4.3.1.2 From logic definitions to pure concurrent logic procedures

Let us now turn to non built-in procedures. The derivation of the first concurrent logic procedure is common to the derivation of a pure logic procedure in [Deville, 1990]. The same syntactic transformations are thus used.

A. The derivation process

Initial transformation

(0) Replace the logic definition $A \Leftrightarrow Def\_A$ by $A \Leftarrow Def\_A$

Intermediate transformations

The following transformations are extensions of the transformations presented in [Lloyd and Topor, 1984].

(1) Replace $A \Leftarrow W_1 \wedge ... \wedge W_{i-1} \wedge (V \vee W) \wedge W_{i+1} \wedge ... \wedge W_m$
by $A \Leftarrow W_1 \wedge ... \wedge W_{i-1} \wedge V \wedge W_{i+1} \wedge ... \wedge W_m$
$A \Leftarrow W_1 \wedge ... \wedge W_{i-1} \wedge W \wedge W_{i+1} \wedge ... \wedge W_m$.

(2) Replace $A \Leftarrow W_1 \wedge ... \wedge W_{i-1} \wedge \neg(V \vee W) \wedge W_{i+1} \wedge ... \wedge W_m$
by $A \Leftarrow W_1 \wedge ... \wedge W_{i-1} \wedge \neg V \wedge \neg W \wedge W_{i+1} \wedge ... \wedge W_m$.

(3) Replace $A \Leftarrow W_1 \wedge ... \wedge W_{i-1} \wedge \neg(V \wedge W) \wedge W_{i+1} \wedge ... \wedge W_m$
    by $A \Leftarrow W_1 \wedge ... \wedge W_{i-1} \wedge \neg V \wedge W_{i+1} \wedge ... \wedge W_m$
             $A \Leftarrow W_1 \wedge ... \wedge W_{i-1} \wedge \neg W \wedge W_{i+1} \wedge ... \wedge W_m$.

(4) Replace $A \Leftarrow W_1 \wedge ... \wedge W_{i-1} \wedge (V \Rightarrow W) \wedge W_{i+1} \wedge ... \wedge W_m$
    by $A \Leftarrow W_1 \wedge ... \wedge W_{i-1} \wedge \neg V \wedge W_{i+1} \wedge ... \wedge W_m$
             $A \Leftarrow W_1 \wedge ... \wedge W_{i-1} \wedge W \wedge W_{i+1} \wedge ... \wedge W_m$.

(5) Replace $A \Leftarrow W_1 \wedge ... \wedge W_{i-1} \wedge \neg(V \Rightarrow W) \wedge W_{i+1} \wedge ... \wedge W_m$
    by $A \Leftarrow W_1 \wedge ... \wedge W_{i-1} \wedge V \wedge \neg W \wedge W_{i+1} \wedge ... \wedge W_m$.

(6) Replace $A \Leftarrow W_1 \wedge ... \wedge W_{i-1} \wedge (V \Leftrightarrow W) \wedge W_{i+1} \wedge ... \wedge W_m$
    by $A \Leftarrow W_1 \wedge ... \wedge W_{i-1} \wedge V \wedge W \wedge W_{i+1} \wedge ... \wedge W_m$
             $A \Leftarrow W_1 \wedge ... \wedge W_{i-1} \wedge \neg V \wedge \neg W \wedge W_{i+1} \wedge ... \wedge W_m$.

(7) Replace $A \Leftarrow W_1 \wedge ... \wedge W_{i-1} \wedge \neg(V \Leftrightarrow W) \wedge W_{i+1} \wedge ... \wedge W_m$
    by $A \Leftarrow W_1 \wedge ... \wedge W_{i-1} \wedge \neg V \wedge W \wedge W_{i+1} \wedge ... \wedge W_m$
             $A \Leftarrow W_1 \wedge ... \wedge W_{i-1} \wedge V \wedge \neg W \wedge W_{i+1} \wedge ... \wedge W_m$.

(8) Replace $A \Leftarrow W_1 \wedge ... \wedge W_{i-1} \wedge \neg\neg W \wedge W_{i+1} \wedge ... \wedge W_m$
    by $A \Leftarrow W_1 \wedge ... \wedge W_{i-1} \wedge W \wedge W_{i+1} \wedge ... \wedge W_m$.

(9) Replace $A \Leftarrow W_1 \wedge ... \wedge W_{i-1} \wedge (\forall X_1 ... \forall X_n\, W) \wedge W_{i+1} \wedge ... \wedge W_m$
    by $A \Leftarrow W_1 \wedge ... \wedge W_{i-1} \wedge \neg(\exists X_1 ... \exists X_n\, \neg W) \wedge W_{i+1} \wedge ... \wedge W_m$.

(10) Replace $A \Leftarrow W_1 \wedge ... \wedge W_{i-1} \wedge \neg(\forall X_1 ... \forall X_n\, W) \wedge W_{i+1} \wedge ... \wedge W_m$
     by $A \Leftarrow W_1 \wedge ... \wedge W_{i-1} \wedge (\exists X_1 ... \exists X_n\, \neg W) \wedge W_{i+1} \wedge ... \wedge W_m$.

(11) Replace $A \Leftarrow W_1 \wedge ... \wedge W_{i-1} \wedge (\exists X_1 ... \exists X_n\, W) \wedge W_{i+1} \wedge ... \wedge W_m$
     by $A \Leftarrow W_1 \wedge ... \wedge W_{i-1} \wedge W \wedge W_{i+1} \wedge ... \wedge W_m$.

(12) Replace $A \Leftarrow W_1 \wedge ... \wedge W_{i-1} \wedge \neg(\exists X_1 ... \exists X_n\, W) \wedge W_{i+1} \wedge ... \wedge W_m$
     by $A \Leftarrow W_1 \wedge ... \wedge W_{i-1} \wedge \neg r(Y_1,...,Y_p) \wedge W_{i+1} \wedge ... \wedge W_m$
             $r(Y_1,...,Y_p) \Leftarrow (\exists X_1 ... \exists X_n\, W)$

where $Y_1,...,Y_p$ are all the free variables occurring in $(\exists X_1 ... \exists X_n\, W)$ and r is a new predicate.

Final transformation

(13) Replace $A \Leftarrow W_1 \wedge ... \wedge W_{i-1} \wedge W_i \wedge W_{i+1} \wedge ... \wedge W_m$
     by $A \leftarrow W'_1, ..., W'_{i-1}, W'_i, W'_{i+1}, ..., W'_m$
     where W'_j is W_j if W_j is a positive literal and $not(W''_j)$ if W_j is $\neg W''_j$.

B. Example

As an illustration, let us transform the following logic definition for the sort procedure

sort(L,L_sorted) ⇔ L=[] ∧ L_sorted=[]
         ∨
        L=[H|T]
         ∧ partition(H,T,Smaller,Greater)
         ∧ sort(Smaller,Smaller_sorted) ∧ sort(Greater,Greater_sorted)
         ∧ append(Smaller_sorted,[H|Greater_sorted], L_sorted).

The initial transformation gives rise to

sort(L,L_sorted) ⇐ L=[] ∧ L_sorted=[]
         ∨
        L=[H|T]
         ∧ partition(H,T,Smaller,Greater)
         ∧ sort(Smaller,Smaller_sorted) ∧ sort(Greater,Greater_sorted)
         ∧ append(Smaller_sorted,[H|Greater_sorted],L_sorted).

By (1) we get

sort(L,L_sorted) ⇐ L=[] ∧ L_sorted=[] .
sort(L,L_sorted) ⇐ L=[H|T]
         ∧ partition(H,T,Smaller,Greater)
         ∧ sort(Smaller,Smaller_sorted) ∧ sort(Greater,Greater_sorted)
         ∧ append(Smaller_sorted,[H|Greater_sorted],L_sorted).

By the final transformation, we finally get

sort(L,L_sorted) ← L=[], L_sorted=[] .
sort(L,L_sorted) ← L=[H|T],
        partition(H,T,Smaller,Greater),
        sort(Smaller,Smaller_sorted), sort(Greater,Greater_sorted),
        append(Smaller_sorted,[H|Greater_sorted],L_sorted).

C. Properties

The following properties can be established. We refer the reader to [Lloyd and Topor, 1984] and [Deville, 1987] for the demonstrations.

Property 9.22 The process of continually applying the transformation rules terminates within a finite number of steps on a set of pure logic procedures.

Property 9.23 Let
- S be a set of logic formulae of the form $p(X1,...,Xn) \Leftarrow W$
- S' be a set resulting from a single transformation (1) or (2) or ... or (13) applied to S

Then S and S' are logically equivalent. Furthermore comp(S) and comp(S') are logically equivalent.

Property 9.24 Let
- S be a set of logic definitions
- P be a concurrent logic program derived from S
- F be a closed formula containing only predicates which appear in S.

Then comp(P)|=F iff S |=F .

D. Correctness of the derived concurrent logic procedures

Concurrent logic programs derived from correct logic algorithms according to the above rules already verify some of the correctness criteria. We examine them hereafter and, for each of them verify whether the property holds or not. When it holds, a proof is given. Otherwise, when possible, transformations are given to make it hold. In the remaining cases, the proof of correctness is to be made on each specific case.

For simplicity of the presentation, mutual recursive algorithms are not considered. However, the following discussion can be easily extended to handle such algorithms.

D.1 NOTATION

The following notations will be used all along this subsection. Let
- p be an n-ary procedure
- LD(p) be a correct logic definition for p,
- $q_1, ..., q_m$ be all the predicate names appearing in LD(p) and distinct from p.

Assume the existence of a finite set S' of logic definitions such that

- LD(q_i) is correct in S' with respect to the specification of q_i, for any $i \in \{1,...,m\}$
- S' contains no occurrence of p.

Let furthermore S be S'∪{LD(p)}. We may assume that S is defined everywhere. Indeed, if this was not the case, we could add logic definitions of the form $s(\bar{x}) \Leftrightarrow s(\bar{x})$ for all predicates appearing in S but with no logic definition in S. This introduction does not change the logical consequences of S . The logic definition LD(p) thus remains correct.

The transformation rules presented in the above Subsection A produce a concurrent logic program from S. Let us denote by CP' the concurrent logic program derived from S' and by CLP(p), CLP(r_1), ..., CLP(r_k) the concurrent logic procedures derived from LD(p), with $r_1, ..., r_k$ the new procedure names introduced by application of the rule (12). We may also assume that CP' contains no occurrence of $r_1, ..., r_k$ (by restricting the new procedure names introduced by transformation rule (12)). Let us denote by CP the concurrent logic program CP'∪{CLP(p),CLP(r_1), ...,CLP(r_k)}.

Let $\bar{t}$ be an n-tuple of prec(p) and $\Psi(p,\bar{t})$ be the set of answer n-substitutions computed for p($\bar{t}$) under CP.

D.2 G-SOUNDNESS

The first property to verify is that the set of computed answer n-substitutions, $\Psi(p,\bar{t})$ is g-sound for $p(\bar{t})$.

Theorem 9.25 Assume that the two following properties hold for any s-goal, call and procedures involved in the reduction of $p(\bar{t})$:
1) procedures are called with their parameters verifying the preconditions,
2) environment properties of any procedure hold for any to call to them.

Then the set $\Psi(p,\bar{t})$ is g-sound for $p(\bar{t})$.

Proof Let v be an n-substitution of $\Psi(p,\bar{t})$. Let furthermore $\bar{u}$ be a ground instance of $Sol_v(p,\bar{t})$. We have to prove that $\bar{u} \in p$. Indeed, by g-soundness of the Conclog model (see Theorem 5.50), we have

$$Comp(CP) \models p(\bar{u}) ,$$

then, thanks to Proposition 9.24,

$$S \models p(\bar{u}) ,$$

and thus

$$S \models_H p(\bar{u}).$$

It follows, thanks to the correctness of LD(p) and to the hypotheses 1) and 2),

$$\bar{u} \in p. \ \lozenge$$

Two properties are thus required to obtain g-soundness. Let us examine them.

1° Preconditions

First, preconditions must be verified for any call involved in the reduction. This has to be done in each particular case because of the so many forms preconditions can take. We will just handle type preconditions here. Recall that logic definitions were designed so as to verify types. At the operational level, type acts as preconditions and must be fulfilled. Before explaining how this can be made, the following remark is worth noting. As auxiliary procedures may be considered as correct, type verification must in fact just be made for the s-goals of the clauses of the procedure p. This given, two cases must in fact be considered.

i) On the one hand, such a s-goal $q(\bar{u})$ results from the unification of a clause with a call to p. In this case, $\bar{u}$ generally verifies the type specification of q thanks to the type specification of p. It is here worth recalling that, as a variable may be instantiated to a term of any type, the more the call is instantiated the more difficult the verification of the type preconditions is. Hence, it is sufficient to verify the type precondition for any ground call to p.

ii) On the other hand, the call $q(\bar{u})$ participates in a conjunction instantiated by binding publication. Thus we also have to ensure that, for the body of any clause of p, the binding to be published for this body do not violate the type preconditions of the s-goals. Practically, this is generally ensured thanks to two properties :

- the strong typing of the parameters of s-goals of the clause body (recall that this may be assumed to hold since the auxiliary procedures q_i's may be assumed to be correctly implemented).
- the consistent use of the type of a same variable in the various q_i's. For instance, a parameter declared as a list should be used only in list parameters of q_i.

Nevertheless, if such type preconditions cannot be guaranteed, type check s-goals could be added in the clauses. This is achieved by replacing each call $q(\bar{u})$ by the following sequentialized goal

(type_test($Par_1,...,Par_n$) | $q(\bar{u})$)

where the Par_i's are the parameters whose types have to be tested.

2° Environment properties

Second, environment properties have to be ensured for any call involved in the reduction of $p(\bar{t})$. This is also to be ensured only for the s-goals composing the bodies of the clauses of p. This has to be verified in each particular case too, since such invariant properties can take so various forms. This is generally straightforwardly done since no environment properties are generally required. In the few cases where they occur, they are obtained thanks to the specifications of the procedures of conjoined calls.

D.3 G-COMPLETENESS

The second required property is that of g-completeness. However it can only be achieved in some conditions.

Theorem 9.26 Assume that the four following properties hold for any s-goal, call and procedures involved in the reduction of $p(\bar{t})$:

1) procedures are called with their parameters verifying the preconditions,
2) environment properties of any procedure hold for any call to them,
3) positive literals associated with ns-goals have a finite number of computed answer n-substitutions,
4) no reduction is infinitely suspended

Then, $\Psi(p,\bar{t})$ is g-complete for $p(\bar{t})$.

Proof Let $\bar{u} \in p \cap \mathrm{domain}(p)$ be a ground instance of $\bar{t}$. We have to prove that there is a computed answer n-substitution v of $\Psi(p,\bar{t})$ such that $\bar{u}$ is a ground instance of $\bar{t}v$. Indeed, as $\bar{u} \in p \cap \mathrm{domain}(p)$, we have, by correctness of LD(p) and assumptions 1) and 2),

$S \models_H p(\bar{u})$

and, thus by Proposition 9.24,

$\quad$ Comp(CP) $\models_H p(\overline{u})$

Then from Theorem 5.50 and assumptions 3) and 4), it is possible to find a computed answer n-substitution, say ν, such that $\overline{u} = \overline{t}\alpha$ for some $\alpha \in \text{ground}(\overline{t},\nu)$. Hence, as ν is idempotent and $\overline{t}$ is instantiable by any computed answer n-substitution, $\overline{u}$ is a ground instance of some $\overline{t}\nu$. ◊

Four hypotheses are thus required to obtain g-completeness. The two first one have been examined for the g-soundness property. Let us examine the two last ones.

1° Handling ns-goals

When ns-goals are involved in the reduction, their associated positive literals must compute a finite number of answer n-substitutions. This is generally straightforward to verify thanks to the <Min-Max> part of the directionalities stated in the specifications. Note that, because of the associated semantics, parameters declared as input and that are declared to be incrementally bound to some value, may be considered to have this value when directionalities are considered.

2° Safety

Non suspension of the calls is also to be ensured. It is however an assumption to get partial correctness. Then, when partial correctness is only tackled, the hypothesis is trivially verified. Nevertheless, it has to be verified to get semi-correctness and total correctness. How to achieve it is described in the following Subsection D.8.

D.4 REDUNDANCY

Non redundancy is also to be verified. This is generally straightforward since, by construction, the C_i's of the logic definitions have been chosen as mutually exclusive. It is thus sufficient to verify that, if they are disjunctions, the F_i's have been constructed so that all their components are mutually exclusive.

D.5 SUSPENSION CONDITIONS

Usual suspension conditions are quite easy to meet. A suspension declaration has simply to be formulated for each suspension pattern. It takes the following form :
- each parameter declared as input and constrained to be ground before reduction can occur is read-only annotated by the "?g" symbol,
- each parameter declared as input and constrained to be non-variable before reduction can occur is read-only annotated by the "?nv" symbol,
- other parameters declared as input are globally read-only annotated by the "?" symbol,
- suspension constraints of the form
    Par of the form v_1 or ... or v_n

are handled by means of a predicate in the Cond part of the suspension declarations. It takes the form
>   form(Par)

and is declared as
>   form(X) ← form_v_1(X).
>   ...
>   form(X) ← form_v_n(X).

where each form_v_i procedure is declared as
>   suspend form_v_i(X?).
>   form_v_i(v_i).

Other suspension conditions should be handled in each specific case. In particular, suspension conditions of the form

>   Par input until u

may require a careful analysis of the clause of p. However, they are usually achieved by unification predicates of the C_i's as well as suspension conditions of the q_j's.

Convention 9.27 We will subsequently take the convention of associating one and only one suspension declaration with each suspension pattern.

D.6 INVARIANT PROPERTIES

Invariant properties need also to be verified in each particular case since they can also take so many forms. Nevertheless, as for preconditions, we will also analyze the type conditions. Two conditions must in general be verified.

1° First, generated nmas's shoud verify the type conditions (see condition i in Subsection 9.2.2.1.2°). To check this, it is generally sufficient to verify that the literals of the C_i's and F_j's generate bindings of correct types. In particular, no variable occurs in parameters assigned to different types.

2° Second, any n-reconciliation-substitution of any top part of any partial solution subtree must verify the type condition too (see condition ii in Subsection 9.2.2.1.2°). This is generally difficult to prove. To suggest the difficulty, let us consider the following one clause procedure p

>   p(X) ← q(X), r(X).
>   q(X) ← X≠f(Y).
>   r(X) ← X≠g(Y).

Assume that p(T), q(T), r(T) require T to be of the following type.

>   {t∈ B_H : t is an instance of f(Z) or g(Z)}.

Then all generated nmas's (even those involved by the ns-goals X≠f(Y) and X≠g(Y)) verify the type. This is also the case for the n-substitutions computed by q(X) and r(X) i.e.

($\{\}$,not$\{$X/f(Y$_1$)$\}$) and ($\{\}$,not$\{$X/g(Y$_2$)$\}$), respectively. However, their reconciliation ($\{\}$,not$\{$X/f(Y$_1$),X/g(Y$_2$)$\}$) does not fulfill it.

In fact, in general, the following property should be enjoyed by all parameters :

Let $v_1, \ldots, v_r$ be the n-substitutions reconciled to form the computed answer n-substitution ρ for $p(\bar{t})$. Let P be a parameter of type T. Then, there is a common ground instance of $Pv_1, \ldots, Pv_r$ of type T.

In this case, it results directly from the definition of the reconciliation and from the idempotence of the n-substitutions that $P\rho$ is of type T.

The fact that each Pv_k is of type T can be ensured by the postconditions. It thus remains to be verified that a common ground instance of $Pv_1, \ldots, Pv_r$ is of type T. This might be achieved by looking at the directionality properties of the procedure involved in the C_i's and F_j's. In case type verification is not possible, one solution is to add a predicate call for type checking at the end of the considered $C_i \wedge F_i$, as

$C_i \wedge F_i \mid $ type$(\bar{u})$

where $\bar{u}$ is the vector of parameters for which types are not fulfilled and type is a predicate that performs the type check.

Fortunately, such a verification is not required when strong types are used. In this case, condition ST has simply to be checked. As for point 1°, it is generally sufficient to verify that the literals of the C_i's and F_j's use strong typing and that no variable occurs in parameters assigned to different types.

D.7 POSTCONDITIONS

Postconditions should also be verified. They can also take various forms and thus should be verified in each specific case. Nevertheless, it is worth noting that type postconditions result from the invariance of the types.

D.8 SAFETY

Given correct logic procedures for $q_1, \ldots, q_n$, safety can only be violated by inconsistent uses of suspension conditions of the q_i's. One must ensure that, for each call to p, every variable that may cause the suspension of some q_i because of the suspension conditions of q_i has another q_j as producer. This is to be analyzed in each situation but generally directly results from the decomposition of the problem into subproblems. To that effect, it is furthermore worth noting that an input parameter incrementally constructed ground can be regarded as ground. Finally, data-flow analysis and abstract interpretation techniques can be used for that purpose, too (see e.g. [Mellish, 1986], [Bruynooghe et al, 1987], …).

D.9 TERMINATION

Termination is to be verified in each case too. It generally results from the finiteness of the computed answer n-substitutions for the calls for the procedures $q_1, ..., q_n$.

D.10 SUMMARY

Summing up, the derived procedure CP(p) should be tested on the following points.

(i) Partial correctness

1. *Call verification.* For any clause C of CP(p), for any call $q(\bar{u})$ of C, check the following properties.
    1.1 for any ground $\bar{t} \in$ domain(p), the instantiation of $\bar{u}$ induced by the unification of $p(\bar{t})$ with C, verifies the type preconditions of q,
    1.2 when any, environment properties may be ensured for any call $q(\bar{u})$,
    1.3 for any ns-goal $q(\bar{u})$, the associated ps-goal engenders a finite number of answer n-substitutions.

2. *Types*

    For any parameter even those local to the clauses,
    2.1 Verify the strong type condition ST when strong types are used.
    2.2 Verify then the invariant conditions i) and ii) of Section 9.2.2.1 for parameters not covered by strong typing.

3. *Redundancy*

    Verify that each clause computes non redundant answer n-substitutions.

4. *Operational properties*
    4.1 Add suspension conditions to make suspension conditions hold.
    4.2 Verify the invariant properties.
    4.3 Verify the postconditions properties. For this purpose, note that, assuming safety, the above points ensure the g-soundness and g-completeness properties.

(ii) Semi-correctness

5. Verify the safety property
6. Verify the weak-termination property

(iii) Correctness

7. Verify the strong termination property.

9.4.3.2 Transformations of concurrent logic programs

At this stage of our construction, concurrent logic programs do not ressemble the procedures that a hacker programmer would have constructed. The following transformations aim at reaching a comparable level of performance. The point to stress is that such programs are far more difficult to understand than the logic definitions because logical aspects are hidden behind operational ones. Our construction process first focusses on the logical aspects and then turns to the operational ones thanks to systematic applications of the transformations.

The transformations proposed in this section will generally be regarded as correctness preserving. They are in fact more than that. Assuming the points 1 and 2 of the above Subsection D.10 hold, they conserve any property of the procedures. Hence, partially correct, semi-correct and correct procedures are transformed in partially correct, semi-correct and correct procedures, respectively. Some conditions of the application of the transformations issue from the necessity of preserving the safety property. They are thus not required when the safety property is not required to be conserved, for instance, when partial correctness is just to be conserved. They are signalled by the (*) mark.

The following notation is used all along this section : CP(p) is employed to denote a logic procedure for procedure p.

9.4.3.2.1 Transformations based on logic properties

9.4.3.2.1.1 Data dependency property

A. Motivation

Data dependency properties may be used to make explicit the data flow they express in the program. This is achieved by introducing read-only annotations in clause bodies. As a result, literals embodying type check may also be removed.

B. Description

B.1 IN-QUALIFIED VARIABLES

The transformations based on data dependency properties use a generalization of the property that arguments are input. Variables for which this generalizing property holds are called "in-qualified" for some conjunction. The meaning of in-qualified variables for a conjunction is that the bindings for these variables are made outside the conjunction. In other terms, for the conjunction, they can be considered as input. With regards to one clause, variables occurring in arguments declared as input in each suspension pattern are stated as in-qualified for the clause body. Other in-qualifications are done by applying the transformation.

From the intended meaning, it is obvious that in-qualified variables for a conjunction are in-qualified for any subconjunction.

B.2 FIRST TRANSFORMATION

Transformation 9.1 Introducing producer-consumer scheme Let

For all $X_1, ..., X_k : p_1(\overline{t_1}), ..., p_r(\overline{t_r}) \rightarrow_{\{Y_1,...,Y_\ell\}} q_1(\overline{u_1}), ..., q_s(\overline{u_s})$

be a logic property where the p_i's and q_j's are logical procedures and where $X_1, ..., X_k$ are the only variables that might be read-only annotated. Assume $X_1, ... X_k$ are in-qualified variables and $Y_1, ..., Y_\ell$ are incrementally constructed by the p_i's. Then

- replace the conjunction $p_1(\overline{t_1}), ..., p_r(\overline{t_r}), q_1(\overline{u_1}), ..., q_s(\overline{u_s})$ by the conjunction obtained from it
  1) by strong read-only annotating all occurrences of $Y_1,...,Y_k$ in $q_1(\overline{u_1}), ..., q_s(\overline{u_s})$;
  2) by removing in $q_1(\overline{u_1}), ..., q_s(\overline{u_s})$ type tests acting only on $Y_1,...,Y_\ell$ if they are fulfilled by postconditions of the p_i's.
- in-qualify the variables $Y_1,...,Y_\ell$ in $q_1(\overline{u_1}), ..., q_s(\overline{u_s})$.

Justification As the Y_i's are incrementally constructed by the p_i's, all solutions for the variables $Y_1,...,Y_\ell$ for the whole conjunction are produced by the subconjunction $p_1(\overline{t_1}), ..., p_r(\overline{t_r})$. As $X_1, ..., X_k$ are in-qualified for the conjunction $p_1(\overline{t_1}), ..., p_r(\overline{t_r})$, no infinite suspension can occur by strong read-only annotating the occurrences of $Y_1,...,Y_\ell$ in $q_1(\overline{u_1}), ..., q_s(\overline{u_s})$. Furthermore, in this case the type tests on $Y_1,...,Y_\ell$ in $q_1(\overline{u_1}), ..., q_s(\overline{u_s})$ are useless since they are already satisfied by the execution of $p_1(\overline{t_1}), ..., p_r(\overline{t_r})$. To conclude, note that $Y_1,...,Y_\ell$ satisfy the in-qualification meaning. ◊

Remark Note that the logic property is not necessary to ensure the correctness-preserving character of the transformation. Nevertheless, it is a good heuristic for discovering the suitable sets $\{X_1,...,X_k\}$, $\{Y_1,...,Y_\ell\}$. In view of this, we have introduced it in the hypotheses of the transformation.

Example 9.7 As an illustration, let us apply the transformation on the following version of the sort(L,L_sorted) procedure :

```
suspend sort(?,*).
sort(L,[]) ← L=[].
sort(L,L_sorted) ←   L=[H|T],
                     partition(H,T,Smaller,Greater),
                     sort(Smaller,Smaller_sorted), sort(Greater,Greater_sorted),
                     append(Smaller_sorted,[H|Greater_sorted],L_sorted).
```

We first have that

> For all L,
> L=[H|T] $\rightarrow_{\{H,T\}}$
> [partition(H,T,Smaller,Greater),
>   sort(Smaller,Smaller_sorted), sort(Greater,Greater_sorted),
>   append(Smaller_sorted,[H|Greater_sorted],L_sorted)]

As L is declared as input, Transformation 9.1 can be applied on the second clause. This yields

> sort(L,L_sorted) ← L=[H|T],
>   partition(H?,T?,Smaller,Greater),
>   sort(Smaller,Smaller_sorted), sort(Greater,Greater_sorted),
>   append(Smaller_sorted,[H?|Greater_sorted],L_sorted).

The following logic property holds too :

> For all H, T : partition(H,T,Smaller,Greater) $\rightarrow_{\{Smaller,Greater\}}$
>   [sort(Smaller,Smaller_sorted), sort(Greater,Greater_sorted),
>   append(Smaller_sorted,[H|Greater_sorted],L_sorted)] .

As, thanks to the previous application of Transformation 9.1, H and T are in-qualified for the conjunction

> partition(H?,T?,Smaller,Greater),
> sort(Smaller,Smaller_sorted), sort(Greater,Greater_sorted),
> append(Smaller_sorted,[H?|Greater_sorted],L_sorted).

Transformation 9.1 can be applied once again. This yields

> sort(L,L_sorted) ← L=[H|T],
>   partition(H?,T?,Smaller,Greater),
>   sort(Smaller?,Smaller_sorted), sort(Greater?,Greater_sorted),
>   append(Smaller_sorted,[H?|Greater_sorted],L_sorted).

Finally, Transformation 9.1 can be applied once again thanks to the logic property

> For all H, Smaller, Greater :
>   (sort(Smaller,Smaller_sorted), sort(Greater,Greater_sorted))
> $\rightarrow_{\{Smaller\_sorted,Greater\_sorted\}}$
>   (append(Smaller_sorted,[H|Greater_sorted],L_sorted)).

The following clause results

> sort(L,L_sorted) ← L=[H|T],
>   partition(H?,T?,Smaller,Greater),
>   sort(Smaller?,Smaller_sorted), sort(Greater?,Greater_sorted),
>   append(Smaller_sorted?,[H?|Greater_sorted?],L_sorted).

B.3 SECOND TRANSFORMATION

Logic properties of the first kind can thus be used to eliminate test type calls. Transformation 9.1 is however limited for this purpose. Indeed it only applies when the universally quantified variables of a logic property are in-qualified. This might however be too restrictive. Consider, for instance, the sort procedure with the two modes of use (i,*) and (*,i). Assume some type check calls list(Smaller) and list(Greater) have been added to the above procedure. No input argument is common to the two mode declarations so that no logic property can be applied. However, in this case, there is no need to make the tests list(Smaller) and list(Greater) since, in the two modes of use, the generator of Smaller and Greater ensure this. Transformation 9.1 can thus be extended. This gives rise to Transformation 9.2.

Transformation 9.2 Removing type checks Remove all calls of type testing procedures, type_test, such that, for every suspension condition SC, there is a logic property of the first kind such that type_test is removed by applying transformation 9.1 to CP(p) whose suspension conditions are restricted to SC.

Justification In this case, the type test call type_test is redundant with other calls of the procedure whatever suspension declaration is used. ◊

Note that read-only annotations cannot be inserted in the same way. Indeed, as illustrated by the sort procedure with two modes of use, this would lead to deadlock. For conflicting modes of use, a producer in one mode acts as a consumer in the other mode. Read-only annotating it when it is a consumer makes it a consumer in the other mode too. Hence, no producer remains and consumers can never be served.

C. Interest

The gain induced by Transformations 9.1 and 9.2 arises from two sources. On the one hand, an increase of performance results from the introduction of read-only annotations. As shown in Section 6.2.1.1, expliciting producer-consumer scheme may be quite substantial. On the other hand, some redundant type tests are removed. Besides the increase of performance, a further gain can result at the programming level. Type test predicates need not be programmed in case all calls to them are removed.

9.4.3.2.1.2 Test dependency property

A. Motivation

Test dependency properties may be used to sequentialize conjunctions. In fact, the sequentialization operator can be introduced in any place while g-soundness and g-completeness properties are preserved. However, introducing it in all cases is not interesting. Test dependency properties provide interesting situations where this can be done.

B. Description

The notion of deterministic calls is required to express the sequentialization transformation.

Definition 9.27 Let .
- $p_1, \ldots, p_m$ be logical procedures,
- $p_1(\bar{t_1}), \ldots, p_m(\bar{t_m})$ be calls to them,.
- $\{X_1,\ldots,X_n\}$ be the variables occuring in $\bar{t_1}, \ldots, \bar{t_m}$,
- $\{Y_1,\ldots,Y_p\}$ and $\{Z_1,\ldots,Z_q\}$ constitute a partition of $\{X_1,\ldots,X_n\}$.

Then, $\leftarrow p_1(\bar{t_1}), \ldots, p_m(\bar{t_m})$ is deterministic in $\{Y_1,\ldots,Y_p\}$ iff, for any ground p-tuple $<y_1,\ldots,y_p>$ there is at most one ground q-tuple $<z_1,\ldots,z_q>$ such that, for any $i \in \{1,\ldots,m\}$,

$\bar{t_i}$ is instantiable by θ,
$\bar{t}+\theta \in p \cap \text{domain}(p)$,

where θ denotes the substitution

$$\theta = \{Y_1/y_1,\ldots,Y_p/y_p,Z_1/z_1,\ldots,Z_q/z_q\}.$$

This given, the sequentialization transformation states as follows.

Transformation 9.3 Introducing sequentialization Let
- $p_1(\bar{t_1}), \ldots, p_r(\bar{t_r}), q_1(\bar{u_1}), \ldots, q_s(\bar{u_s})$ be a goal appearing in CP(p),
- For all $X_1, \ldots, X_m : p_1(\bar{t_1}), \ldots, p_r(\bar{t_r}) \xrightarrow{p(\bar{t})} q_1(\bar{u_1}), \ldots, q_s(\bar{u_s})$ be a correct logic property.
- $Y_1, \ldots, Y_k$ be the variables X_i's that are in-qualified.

Assume that the two following properties hold :

1) $\leftarrow p_1(\bar{t_1}), \ldots, p_r(\bar{t_r})$ is deterministic in $\{Y_1,\ldots,Y_k\}$,
2) the reduction of $\leftarrow p_1(\bar{t_1}), \ldots, p_r(\bar{t_r})$ does not suspend (*)

Then, replace the conjunction

$$p_1(\bar{t_1}), \ldots, p_r(\bar{t_r}), q_1(\bar{u_1}), \ldots, q_s(\bar{u_s})$$

by the conjunction

$$p_1(\bar{t_1}), \ldots, p_r(\bar{t_r}) \mid q_1(\bar{u_1}), \ldots, q_s(\bar{u_s}).$$

Justification By hypothesis, the introduction of the sequentialization operator does not violate the preconditions. Other operational properties are verified since they were verified for CP(p). Moreover, thanks to hypothesis 2), the introduction of the sequentialization operator does not introduce suspension. In these conditions, the introduction of the sequentialization operator does not perturbate the correctness properties. ◊

Remark Note that, as for Transformation 9.1, the logic property is not necessary to ensure the correctness-preserving character of the transformation. Nevertheless, we state it in the above transformation since it is a good heuristic to apply the transformation in a suitable manner. The same remark apply for the deterministic property.

Example 9.8 Let us illustrate this transformation of the following partition procedure

suspend partition(?,?,*,*).
partition(X,[],Smaller,Greater) ← L=[], Smaller=[], Greater=[].
partition(X,L,Smaller,Greater) ←
    L=[H|T], H≤X, Smaller=[H|Smaller_rem], partition(X,T,Smaller_rem,Greater).
partition(X,L,Smaller,Greater) ←
    L=[H|T], H>X, Greater=[H|Greater_rem], partition(X,T,Smaller,Greater_rem).

The following logic properties can be used :

For all X, L, H, T :

$$L=[H|T] \wedge H \leq X \xrightarrow{partition(X,L,Smaller,Greater)}$$
$$Smaller=[H|Smaller\_rem] \wedge partitition(X,T,Smaller\_rem,Greater).$$

For all X, L, H, T :

$$L=[H|T] \wedge H>X \xrightarrow{partition(X,L,Smaller,Greater)}$$
$$Greater=[H|Greater\_rem] \wedge partitition(X,T,Smaller,Greater\_rem).$$

Transformation 9.3 can be applied since

- X and L appear in an input parameter,
- ←L=[H|T] ∧ H≤X (resp. ←L=[H|T] ∧ H>X) is deterministic in {X,L},
- their reduction does not suspend,
- all the preconditions of
  Smaller=[H?|Smaller_rem] and partition(X,T,Smaller_rem,Greater)
  (resp. Greater=[H?|Greater_rem] and partitition(X,T,Smaller,Greater_rem))
  are fulfilled by any computed answer n-substitution for L=[H|T] ∧ H≤X (resp. L=[H|T] ∧ H>X).

This yields

suspend partition(?,?,*,*).
partition(X,L,Smaller,Greater) ← L=[], Smaller=[], Greater=[].
partition(X,L,Smaller,Greater) ←
    L=[H|T], H≤X | Smaller=[H|Smaller_rem], partition(X,T,Smaller_rem,Greater).
partition(X,L,Smaller,Greater) ←
    L=[H|T], H>X | Greater=[H|Greater_rem], partition(X,T,Smaller,Greater_rem).

C. Interest

The interest of Transformation 9.3 results from the gain engendered by the introduction of the sequentialization operator. The goal

$$\leftarrow p_1(\bar{t}_1), \ldots, p_r(\bar{t}_r)$$

can be regarded as a guard. Reducing

$$\leftarrow q_1(\bar{u}_1), \ldots, q_s(\bar{u}_s)$$

makes only sense when it can be reduced successfully. Introducing the sequentialization prevents the blind reduction of

$$\leftarrow q_1(\bar{u}_1), \ldots, q_s(\bar{u}_s).$$

It is only reduced when the guard successfully reduce and, in this case, for the answer n-substitutions computed for it. As illustrated in Section 6.2.1.3, some substantial gain can result.

Remark Note that goals

$$\leftarrow q_1(\bar{u}_1), \ldots, q_s(\bar{u}_s)$$

that would not act as guards but as the generator of small number of restrictive n-substitutions could be handled in a similar way. To this end, it is sufficient to replace in the above transformation the deterministic notion by a relaxed form characterizing such generators.

9.4.3.2.1.3 Exclusiveness property

A. Motivation

Exclusiveness properties are employed to reduce the computation effort drastically. They point out goals which exclude one another. The successful reduction of one of them allows thus to stop and reject the reduction of the others.

B. Description

Transformation 9.4 Introducing mutual exclusion Let

- CP(p) be composed of the following clauses
  $H_1 \leftarrow B_1.$
  ...
  $H_m \leftarrow B_m.$
- for any $i \in \{1,\ldots,m\}$, Conj_i be a goal formed from the logical s-goals of B_i and Comp_conj_i be the goal formed by the remaining s-goals.

Assume that

1) the following logic property holds
   For all $X_1, \ldots, X_n$,
   $Conj_1$,
   ...,
   $Conj_m$
   are mutually exclusif;
2) the variables $X_1, \ldots, X_n$ occur in parameters declared as input in one same suspension pattern SP,
3) SP has no activator commit operator and no activator commit operator has been declared for the whole procedure,
4) for each $i \in \{1,\ldots,m\}$, sequentialization operators and commit operators, if present, allow B_i to be rewritten in one of the following forms
   $Conj_i$, $Comp\_conj_i$
   $Conj_i$ | $Comp\_conj_i$,
   $Conj_i$ |$_c$ $Comp\_conj_i$,
5) for each $i \in \{1,\ldots,m\}$, the reduction of $Conj_i$ does not suspend. (*)

Then, for any $i \in \{1,\ldots,m\}$, replace each B_i by

$Conj_i$ |$_c$ $Comp\_conj_i$

and add a local commit-activator to the suspension declaration SP.

Justification Assuming that no activator commit is involved, thanks to the assumptions 4 and 5, for any $i \in \{1,\ldots,m\}$, the justification of Transformation 9.3 allows to rewrite B_i as

$Conj_i$ |$_c$ $Comp\_conj_i$.

Now, assume that activator commits are involved. The "|$_c$" symbol then does no more act as a sequentialization operator but handles commitment. Thanks to assumptions 3 and 4, the effect of activator commits that were present before the application of the transformation is not altered. The only perturbation could then result from the suspension declaration SP. With respect to it, assumptions 1 and 2 guarantee that commitment can indeed be applied. ◊

Example 9.9 Let us turn back to the partition procedure

suspend partition(?,?,*,*).
partition(X,L,Smaller,Greater) ← L=[], Smaller=[], Greater=[].
partition(X,L,Smaller,Greater) ←
    L=[H|T], H≤X, Smaller=[H|Smaller_rem], partition(X,T,Smaller_rem,Greater).
partition(X,L,Smaller,Greater) ←
    L=[H|T], H>X, Greater=[H|Greater_rem], partition(X,T,Smaller,Greater_rem).

The following logic property holds :

For all X, L :
   L=[],
   L=[H|T], H≤X,
   L=[H|T], H>X
are mutually exclusive.

It is easy to verify that the assumptions 2 to 5 of Transformation 9.4 indeed hold. Applying this transformation leads to

   suspend partition(?,?,*,*) with l_commit.
   partition(X,L,Smaller,Greater) ← L=[] |$_c$ Smaller=[], Greater=[].
   partition(X,L,Smaller,Greater) ←
       L=[H|T], H≤X |$_c$ Smaller=[H|Smaller_rem], partition(X,T,Smaller_rem,Greater).
   partition(X,L,Smaller,Greater) ←
       L=[H|T], H>X |$_c$ Greater=[H|Greater_rem], partition(X,T,Smaller,Greater_rem).

C. Interest

The interest of the transformation results from two mechanisms:

- from the commitment that allows, in view of the success of one guard, to stop the evaluation of other guards,
- from the sequentialization that postpones the evaluation of the commit body after the successful reduction of its associated guard.

As a drawback, however, the parallelism of the B_i's is reduced if they were not sequentialized before the application of the transformation. We then advise to use the transformation in the following cases :

- when only one suspension declaration is associated in the procedure p under consideration,
- when for each suspension declaration,
    - either, descriptor operators are placed or will be placed by further transformations in the place where the transformation places them and a commit activator is or will be associated with it,
    - or, a sequentialization operator is placed or will be placed by further transformations in the place where the transformation introduces the descriptor commit,
- when further transformations will embody the guard in the clause heads.

9.4.3.2.2 Transformations based on redundant subtree elimination

9.4.3.2.2.1 Selecting clauses

A. Motivation

The counterpart of Transformation 9.4 can be given for some kinds of calls. The following transformation introduces call-commits for such calls. A gain similar to that of Transformation 9.4 is then achieved for their reduction.

B. Description

Transformation 9.5 Introducing call-commits Let

- CP(p) be composed of the following clauses :
  $p(\bar{u}_1) \leftarrow B_1.$
  ...
  $p(\bar{u}_m) \leftarrow B_m.$
- $p(\bar{t})$ be a call for p, where $\bar{t}$ is a tuple of non-extended terms,
- for any $i \in \{1,...,m\}$, $Conj_i$ denote the equality $\bar{t}=\bar{u}_m$ conjoined with the guard of B_i if any.

Assume that

1) the following logic property hold :
   For all $X_1, ..., X_m$:
   $Conj_1,$
   ...,
   $Conj_m$
   are mutually exclusive,
2) $X_1, ..., X_m$ are strongly read-only annotated in $\bar{t}$ or occur in parameters declared as input in all suspension declarations.

Then replace the call $p(\bar{t})$ by the call $l\_commit(p(\bar{t}))$.

Justification Thanks to the hypothesis, whatever suspension declaration is used to reduce p, only one $Conj_i$ can be successfully reduced. Hence, commitment can indeed be applied to reduce $p(\bar{t})$. ◊

Example 9.10 Consider the following procedure

suspend p(?,?g).
p([],X) ← X<0 |c ... .
p([H|T],X) ← X≥0 |c ... .

Consider the call p(L,Nb). Obviously one has

For all L, Nb,
   L=[], Nb=X, X<0,
   L=[H|T], Nb=X, X≥0
are mutually exclusive.

Furthermore, L and Nb correspond to parameters declared as input. Transformation 9.5 can then be applied and the call can indeed be replaced by l_commit(p([H|T],X)).

C. Interest

The interest of Transformation 9.5 arises from the gain engendered by the commitment : in view of the successful reduction of one guard, the reduction of other guards can be stopped and eliminated.

9.4.3.2.2.2 Eliminating computed answer n-substitutions

A. Motivation

Some goals may involve calls for which only one n-substitution needs to be computed. The efficiency of the computation can then be increased by effectively computing only one of them. This is achieved by introducing the del and commit operators. The two following transformations are provided for that purpose.

B. Description

B.1 DEFINITIONS

Some definitions need first to be introduced.

Definition 9.28
1) The n-substitutions ν and μ are *equivalent* for the goal $\leftarrow$Cl iff the two following conditions hold :
   i) $\leftarrow$Cl is simultaneously instantiable by ν and μ;
   ii) if this is the case, the set of answer n-substitutions computed by $\leftarrow$Clν is equivalent to the set of answer n-substitutions computed by $\leftarrow$Clμ.
2) The set of n-substitutions $\Psi_1,\ldots, \Psi_n$ are equivalent for the goal $\leftarrow$Cl iff, for any i, j, for any $\psi \in \Psi_i$ there is a $\varphi \in \Psi_j$ such that ψ and φ are equivalent for $\leftarrow$Cl.

Definition 9.29 The s-goal G_k is *s-solvable* in $\leftarrow G_1,\ldots,G_m$ iff all the answer n-substitutions computed for G_k during the reduction of $\leftarrow G_1,\ldots,G_m$ are equivalent for the goal $\leftarrow G_1,\ldots,G_{k-1},G_{k+1},\ldots,G_m$.

Definition 9.30 The s-goal $G_k=p(\bar{t})$ ($1 \leq k \leq m$) is *s-reducable* in $\leftarrow G_1,\ldots,G_m$ with respect to CP(p) iff, whatever suspension declaration of CP(p) are chosen to reduce G_k, the sets of answer n-substitutions computed by the clauses are equivalent for $\leftarrow G_1,\ldots,G_{k-1},G_{k+1},G_m$.

B.2 ADDING del ANNOTATIONS

Transformation 9.6 Adding del annotations Let $\leftarrow G_1,\ldots,G_m$ be a goal whose reduction involves no side-effect. Replace any s-solvable s-goal G_k ($1 \leq k \leq m$) in $\leftarrow G_1,\ldots,G_m$ by the s-goal del(G_k).

Justification Introducing the del annotation may only influence the g-completeness of the computation. However, as all answer n-substitutions computed by G_k during the reduction of $\leftarrow G_1,\ldots,G_m$ are equivalent for $\leftarrow G_1,\ldots,G_{k-1},G_{k+1},\ldots,G_m$, the computation of one of them is sufficient. ◊

B.3 ADDING COMMIT OPERATORS

Transformation 9.7 Assume CP(p) involves no side-effect s-goals. Assume that the call $p(\bar{t})$ is s-reducable in $\leftarrow G_1,\ldots,G_{k-1},p(\bar{t}),G_k,\ldots,G_m$ with respect to CP(p). Then, replace $p(\bar{t})$ by l_commit($p(\bar{t})$).

Justification Thanks to the s-reducable hypothesis, the g-completeness property for

$\leftarrow G_1,\ldots,G_{k-1},p(\bar{t}),G_k,\ldots,G_m$

is indeed not altered. ◊

C. Interest

The interest of these two transformations arises from the increase of performance due to the non-computation of answer n-substitutions.

9.4.3.2.3 Transformations based on equivalent and/or/not search trees

A. Motivation

The repetition of the same reductions is manifestly not desired. The following transformations aim at avoiding them. They basically consist in rearranging the computed and/or/not search tree in equivalent ones.

B. Description

B.1 NOTATION

For ease of presentation, the transformations will be presented in the following form :

$H_1 \leftarrow B_1.$
...
$H_m \leftarrow B_m.$
___
$H'_1 \leftarrow B'_1.$
...
$H'_n \leftarrow B'_n.$

This means that the clauses above the line are transformed into the clauses below it. The two following points are furthermore stated implicitly :
- the $H_i \leftarrow B_i$ clauses represent all the clauses of the treated procedure,
- the suspension declarations, if any, are preserved by the transformation.

B.2 ELIMINATING IDENTICAL GOALS INSIDE CLAUSES

Our first transformation is based on the existence of identical conjunctions of literals inside different clauses. In this case, the computation of the conjunction is repeated every time one clause is used. This can be avoided by transforming the clauses as follows.

Transformation 9.7

$p(\overline{t}) \leftarrow T, S_1.$
...
$p(\overline{t}) \leftarrow T, S_n.$
___
$p(\overline{t}) \leftarrow T, q(\overline{u}).$
$q(\overline{u}) \leftarrow S_1.$
...
$q(\overline{u}) \leftarrow S_n.$

where
- $T, S_1, ..., S_n$ are some goals,
- q is a predicate name not used in the program under transformation,
- $\overline{u}$ is the vector of all the variables occurring in $T, S_1, ..., S_n$.

Justification Instead of being reduced n times by n concurrent processes of the S_i's, T is evaluated once in concurrence with a process, itself of charge of reducing the S_i's. Equivalent computed and/or/search trees are thus indeed computed.◊

The same transformation holds when the parallel "," goal separator is replaced by the "|" operator and/or when the "." clause delimiter is replaced by the "," one. The more general Transformations 9.8 and 9.9 hold thus too.

Transformation 9.8

$p(\bar{t}) \leftarrow T, S_1 \quad \text{end\_clause}_1$

...

$p(\bar{t}) \leftarrow T, S_n \quad \text{end\_clause}_n$

$p(\bar{t}) \leftarrow T, q(\bar{u}).$
$q(\bar{u}) \leftarrow S_1 \quad \text{end\_clause}_1$

...

$q(\bar{u}) \leftarrow S_n \quad \text{end\_clause}_n$

where

- $T, S_1, ..., S_n$ are some goals,
- q is a predicate name not used in the program under transformation,
- $\bar{u}$ is the vector of all the variables occurring in $T, S_1, ..., S_n$,
- each end_clause$_i$ is either "." or ";" ($1 \leq i \leq n$).

Justification Straightforward adaptation of the justification of Transformation 9.7. ◊

Transformation 9.9

$p(\bar{t}) \leftarrow T \mid S_1 \quad \text{end\_clause}_1$

...

$p(\bar{t}) \leftarrow T \mid S_n \quad \text{end\_clause}_n$

$p(\bar{t}) \leftarrow T \mid q(\bar{u}).$
$q(\bar{u}) \leftarrow S_1 \quad \text{end\_clause}_1$

...

$q(\bar{u}) \leftarrow S_n \quad \text{end\_clause}_n$

where

- $T, S_1, ..., S_n$ are goals,
- q is a predicate name not used in the program under transformation,
- $\bar{u}$ is the vector of all the variables occurring in $T, S_1, ..., S_n$.
- each end_clause$_i$ is either "." or ";" ($1 \leq i \leq n$).

Justification Straightforward adaptation of the justification of Transformation 9.7. ◊

B.3 ELIMINATING IDENTICAL GOALS APPEARING NEGATED AND UNEGATED

Ns-goals may also lead to the repeated evaluation of a goal. The following transformations adapt the two previous ones to this context.

Transformation 9.10

$p(\bar{t}) \leftarrow G, S_1.$
$p(\bar{t}) \leftarrow \text{not}(G), S_2.$

$p(\bar{t}) \leftarrow \text{call}(G,\text{Res}), q(\bar{u},\text{Res})$
$q(\bar{u},\text{succeeded}) \leftarrow S_1.$
$q(\bar{u},\text{failed}) \leftarrow S_2.$

where

- G is a ground goal,
- S_1 and S_2 are goals,
- q is a predicate name not used in the program under transformation,
- $\bar{u}$ is the vector of all the variables occurring in S_1 and S_2.

Justification Instead of being reduced twice, one time in concurrence with S_1 and another time through negation in concurrence with S_2, G is evaluated once in concurrence with a process in charge of S_1 and S_2. Thanks to the Res argument, the answer n-substitutions computed by S_1 or S_2 are discarded according as the reduction of G fails or succeeds. ◊

Transformation 9.11

$p(\bar{t}) \leftarrow G \mid S_1.$
$p(\bar{t}) \leftarrow \text{not}(G) \mid S_2.$

$p(\bar{t}) \leftarrow \text{call}(G,\text{Res}) \mid q(\bar{u},\text{Res})$
$q(\bar{u},\text{succeeded}) \leftarrow S_1.$
$q(\bar{u},\text{failed}) \leftarrow S_2.$

where

- G is a ground goal,
- S_1 and S_2 are goals,
- q is a predicate name not used in the program under transformation,
- $\bar{u}$ is the vector of all the variables occurring in S_1 and S_2.

Justification Instead of being reduced twice, one time before S_1 and another time, through negation, before the reduction of S_2, G is reduced once before S_1 or S_2 is reduced. Thanks to the Res argument, the correct reduction is indeed performed. ◊

These two transformations straightforwardly extend when G or not(G) is involved in more than one clause and/or when the "." clause delimiter is replaced by the ";" one. This yields the following transformations.

Transformation 9.12

$p(\bar{t}) \leftarrow G'_1, S_1 \quad \text{end\_clause}_1$

...

$p(\bar{t}) \leftarrow G'_n, S_n \quad \text{end\_clause}_n$

$p(\bar{t}) \leftarrow \text{call}(G,\text{Res}), q(\bar{u},\text{Res})$
$q(\bar{u},\text{res}_1) \leftarrow S_1 \quad \text{end\_clause}_1$

...

$q(\bar{u},\text{res}_n) \leftarrow S_n \quad \text{end\_clause}_n$

where

- for any $i \in \{1,...,n\}$, G'_i is either G or not(G) where G is a ground goal,
- $S_1, ..., S_n$ are goals,
- q is a predicate name not used in the program under transformation,
- $\bar{u}$ is the vector of all the variables occurring in $S_1, ..., S_n$,
- for any $i \in \{1,...,n\}$, res_i is succeeded or failed according as G'_i is G or not(G).

Justification Straightforward extension of the justification of Transformation 9.10. ◊

Transformation 9.13

$p(\bar{t}) \leftarrow G'_1 \mid S_1 \quad \text{end\_clause}_1$

...

$p(\bar{t}) \leftarrow G'_n \mid S_n \quad \text{end\_clause}_n$

$p(\bar{t}) \leftarrow \text{call}(G,\text{Res}) \mid q(\bar{u},\text{Res})$
$q(\bar{u},\text{res}_1) \leftarrow S_1 \quad \text{end\_clause}_1$

...

$q(\bar{u},\text{res}_n) \leftarrow S_n \quad \text{end\_clause}_n$

where

- for any $i \in \{1,...,n\}$, G'_i is either G or not(G) where G is a ground goal,
- $S_1, ..., S_n$ are goals,
- q is a predicate name not used in the program under transformation,
- $\bar{u}$ is the vector of all the variables occurring in $S_1, ..., S_n$,
- for any $i \in \{1,...,n\}$, res_i is succeeded or failed according as G'_i is G or not(G).

Justification Straightforward extension of the justification of Transformation 9.11. ◊

Transformation 9.14 Transformations 9.9 to 9.13 can be applied to procedures for which the G part is not ground but whose use is restricted so that it becomes ground after the clause is unified with any call.

Justification Indeed, in this case, everything occurs as if G were ground. ◊

Finally, when commitment is required by suspension declarations, the evaluation of the G goal can be performed once without requiring any meta-call. The transformation is subsequently stated in the more general case involving m clauses.

Transformation 9.15 Assume CP(p) verifies the following property : all suspension declarations specify an activator commit operator or are covered by a global declaration of commit operator. Assume the clauses of CP(p) are as follows :

$H_1 \leftarrow G_1 |_c B_1$.
...
$H_m \leftarrow G_m |_c B_m$;
$H \leftarrow not(G_1), ..., not(G_m) |_c B$.

with $G_1, ..., G_m$ ground goals. Then replace these clauses by the following ones :

$H_1 \leftarrow G_1 |_c B_1$.
...
$H_m \leftarrow G_m |_c B_m$;
$H \leftarrow B$.

Justification Indeed, because of the ";" clause separator and because commitment is involved by any call, the last clause is only used when the previous m ones have been rejected. In this case, the reductions of all the guards G_i have failed. Hence, when the last clause is selected, the reduction of its guard always succeeds. It is ground and so cannot communicate any bindings to B. It can thus be removed. ◊

Transformation 9.16 Transformation 9.15 can be applied to procedures for which the G_i's are not ground but whose use is restricted so that they become ground after the clause has been unified with any call.

Justification Indeed, in this case, everything occurs as if the G_i's were ground. ◊

C. Interest

The interest of these transformations arises from the elimination of the repetition of redundant reductions. This results in an obvious increase of the computation.

9.4.3.2.4 Transformation based on partial evaluation

A. Motivation

Some gain can also result by partially evaluating literals. Although this technique may cover quite complicated evaluations, we will just limit here to the opening of literals. The gain of the search for unifiable clauses results.

B. Description

Transformation 9.17

$p(\bar{t}) \leftarrow \ldots q(\bar{u}) \ldots$
$q(\bar{v}) \leftarrow T .$

$p(\bar{t}) \leftarrow \ldots (\bar{u} = \bar{v}_r \mid T) \ldots$
$q(\bar{v}) \leftarrow T .$

where
- q is a procedure defined by the only clause $q(\bar{v}) \leftarrow T$ and by at most one suspension declaration containing no Cond part,
- $\bar{v}_r$ is $\bar{v}$ where variables have been read-only annotated according to the suspension declaration.

Justification The correctness of the transformation is obvious because calling $q(\bar{u})$ amounts to unifying $\bar{u}$ and $\bar{v}$ with respect to the suspension declaration of q and, when successful, to evaluating T. ◊

C. Interest

The interest of this transformation is twofold. On the one hand, it arises from the gain of searching for a unifiable clause in the program. On the other hand, a further gain could be achieved by the application of transformations based on equality substitutions. In particular, Transformation 9.17 is particularly well-adapted when T is a short sequence of literals with equalities (this is often the case for most procedures implementing simple operations on abstract data types).

9.4.3.2.5 Transformations based on equality substitutions

A. Motivation

It is of usual practice to make unification equalities implicit in the parameter of calls as well as in the head of clauses. The interest of such a practice is twofold. On the one hand, the reduction of the equalities is avoided. On the other hand, the production of bindings inconsistent with the equalities is avoided during the reduction of conjoined calls. In particular, in our reconciliation based approach, some substantial reconciliation work can be avoided.

The following transformations are provided for this purpose.

B. Description

Transformation 9.18 Let $p(\overline{t}) \leftarrow B$ be a clause of CP(p) free from calls to extra-logical procedures. Let Y=u (or u=Y) be a literal of B. Let u^* be u without its read-only annotations. Then

- apply the substitution $\{Y/u^*\}$ to the other literals of B [1],
- instantiate $p(\overline{t})$ with $\{Y/u^*\}$ in the following cases :
  1) CP(p) has no suspension declaration,
  2) CP(p) has a suspension declaration but, for any suspension declaration, Y appears in a parameter globally read-only annotated.
  3) CP(p) has a suspension declaration, Y appears in a parameter not read-only annotated but all the parameters read-only annotated in one suspension declaration are ground.
- if there remains no other occurrence of Y than that Y=u (or u=Y) then remove this equality from B [2].

Justification As far as body literals are concerned, the transformation simply forward substitutes Y to its value and is thus quite correct. Furthermore, no suspension is to be feared because suspension only occurs when the arguments of the call are not sufficiently instantiated.

As far as the substitution in the head of the clause is concerned, the transformation is obviously correct when no suspension declaration is associated with p. Furthermore, when suspension declarations are involved, condition 2 guarantees that if suspension occurs it would have occured in B during the reduction of the equality Y=u. Finally, condition 3 guarantees that if it occurs after having applied the transformation, suspension would have occurred before applying it. ◊

Note that the substitution of Y by u in $p(\overline{t})$ cannot be done without restriction since suspension may be introduced for calls whose arguments share variables. For instance, if p is a two-ary procedure with the following suspension declaration

suspend p(!,*),

a call of the form p(X,X) does not suspend when it unifies with the clause

p(Y,Z) ← Z=a, ...

---

[1] In particular, this implies the inheritance of read-only annotations, as defined in Definition 6.2.
[2] In case Y=t appears in a conjunction of the form (Y=t|T), the | operator is removed as well so that the conjunction takes the form T.

whereas it suspends for the clause

   p(Y,a) ← ... .

Note furthermore that non-sharing of the variables is not sufficient. For instance, the call p(V,W!) does not suspend when the first clause is used whereas it suspends when the second one is used.

Nevertheless, the substitution can be achieved when a precondition of p requires that calls to p are such that their arguments do not share variables and no variables are locally read-only annotated. Such procedures are called call-free.

Definition 9.31 A procedure is *call-free* iff one precondition stipulates that arguments of the call never share variables and its variables are never locally read-only annotated.

Transformation 9.19 Let $p(\bar{t})$ ← B be a clause of CP(p) and Y=u (or u=Y) be a literal of B. Let u^* be u without its read-only annotations. Assume p is call-free. Then remove Y=u (resp. u=Y) from B, apply the substitution $\{Y/u^*\}$ to the remaining conjunction and to the head $p(\bar{t})$.

Justification The justification is similar to that of Transformation 9.18. No suspension is to be feared thanks to the call-free hypothesis. ◊

Example 9.11 Let us illustrate these transformations on the sort(L,L_sorted) procedure. Assume the following procedure has been derived.

   suspend sort(?,*).
   sort(L,L_sorted) ← L=[], L_sorted=[].
   sort(L,L_sorted) ←
       L=[H|T], partition(H?,T?,Smaller,Greater),
       sort(Smaller?,Smaller_sorted), sort(Greater?,Greater_sorted),
       append(Smaller_sorted?,[H?|Greater_sorted?],L_sorted).

The application of Transformation 9.18 gives rise to

   suspend sort(?,*).
   sort([],L_sorted) ← L_sorted=[].
   sort([H|T],L_sorted) ←
       partition(H?,T?,Smaller,Greater),
       sort(Smaller?,Smaller_sorted), sort(Greater?,Greater_sorted),
       append(Smaller_sorted?,[H?|Greater_sorted?],L_sorted).

Assuming that sort is call-free, Transformation 9.19 gives rise to

```
suspend sort(?,*).
sort([],[]).
sort([H|T],L_sorted) ←
    partition(H?,T?,Smaller,Greater),
    sort(Smaller?,Smaller_sorted), sort(Greater?,Greater_sorted),
    append(Smaller_sorted?,[H?|Greater_sorted?],L_sorted).
```

C. Interest

The interest of this transformation is twofold. On the one hand, it induces a double increase of the computation :

- the reduction of the equalities is avoided
- in reductions of other calls, the production of bindings inconsistent with the equalities is avoided; in particular, a substantial reconciliation work can be avoided.

On the other hand, combined with unfolding, it allows to simplify the suspension declarations (see the following transformations).

9.4.3.2.6 Transformations based on the simplification of annotations

A. Motivation

Finally, redundant annotations may be eliminated or simplified. This given, their handling is reduced and a more efficent code results. The following transformations are provided for that purpose.

B. Description

B.1 REMOVING READ-ONLY ANNOTATIONS

Transformation 9.20 Remove, in any call to p, global read-only annotations corresponding to parameters declared as input in all suspension patterns.
Justification The global read-only annotations are manifestly redundant with the input declarations in suspension patterns. ◊

A similar transformation rests on a syntactic anaysis of CP(p).

Transformation 9.21 Let Par be a parameter globally (resp. locally or globally) read-only annotated in all suspension declaration. Remove, in any call to p, global (resp. local) read-only annotations of variables occurring in place of Par.
Justification The read-only annotations are manifestly redundant with those stated in the suspension declarations. ◊

Global read-only annotations of suspension declarations are inherited in the clause bodies. This is performed explicitly by the following transformation.

Transformation 9.22 For any argument Arg_k declared as input in all suspension patterns,

- for any clause C of p, for any variable V occuring in place of Arg_k in the head of C, globally read-only annotate any occurrence of V in the body of C;
- replace the global read-only annotations of Arg_k by local ones in the suspension declarations of CP(p).

Justification The global read-only annotations in the clause bodies simply perform explicitly what would be done at run-time. Thanks to this explicit inheritance of the global annotations, the global read-only annotations can then be simplified in local ones. ◊

Suspension declarations can be simplified from redundant suspension tests.

Transformation 9.23 Let Par be a parameter. Assume all heads of clauses of CP(p) have a non-variable term (resp. ground term) in place of Par. Then replace, in all suspension declarations, the "?nv", "!nv" (resp. "?g", "!g") annotations of Par by the "?" (resp. "!") annotation.

Justification Such annotations are indeed performed during the unification thanks to the "?" (resp. "!") read-only constraint and the form of the corresponding head argument. ◊

Finally, local read-only annotations may be removed in some cases.

Transformation 9.24 For any suspension declaration, remove the local read-only annotation "!" if all the parameters are distinct variables in all the clause heads.

Justification Local read-only annotations "!" do not manifestly act when the corresponding clause head parameters are distinct variables. ◊

B.2 REMOVING GLOBAL ACTIVATOR COMMITS

Similar transformations can be stated for global activator commits.

Transformation 9.25 Assume CP(p) verifies one of the two following properties :

- a global (resp. local or global) commit activator is globally stated
- all its suspension declarations are associated with a global (resp. local or global) activator commit.

Then, replace, any annotated call $g\_commit(p(\overline{t}))$ (resp. $l\_commit(p(\overline{t}))$) by the unannotated call $p(\overline{t})$.

Justification The commit activators of the calls are indeed manifestly redundant with the commit activator stated with in CP(p). ◊

Transformation 9.26 Assume CP(p) verifies one of the following properties :

- a global activator commit is stated for the whole procedure;
- a global activator commit is associated with any suspension declaration.

Then,

- for any s-goal of any clause body of CP(p), perform the following :
    - if the s-goal is not annotated by an activator commit, then annotate it with a global one,
    - if the s-goal is annotated by a local activator commit, then replace it by a global one,
- replace the global activator commit declarations by local activator commit ones.

Justification This transformation performs explicitly the implicit propagation of global commit operators. The first part of the transformation is thus correct. As a result, this implicit propagation does not need to occur and global activator commit declarations can be replaced by local ones. ◊

B.3 REMOVING SUSPENSION CONDITIONS

Suspension declarations may be removed when they state no information.

Transformation 9.27 Remove any simple suspension declaration annotating no parameters with read-only annotations.

Justification Any suspension declaration stating no constraints can, of course, be removed. ◊

Finally, conditions of complex suspension declarations can be removed when they are already stated by the suspension declarations.

Transformation 9.28 Let

suspend $p(Par_1,...,Par_i,...,Par_n)$ with G_1, $q(Par_i)$, G_2.

be a complex suspension declaration of CP(p) where G_1 and G_2 are goals. Assume Par_i is read-only annotated. Assume q is defined as follows :

suspend q(Par!).   (resp. suspend q(Par?).)
$q(form_1)$.
...
$q(form_n)$.

Assume finally that each head clause of CP(p) has an instance of one $form_j$ as i^{th} parameter. Then, remove the $q(Par_i)$ test in the suspension declaration.

Justification Thanks to the read-only declaration of Par_i and the form of the ith paramater in each clause head, the test $q(Par_i)$ is already performed by the clause unification. ◊

Remark Note that this could be generalized in a straightforward way to variants of the Cond part of the suspension such that

$G_1, q(Par_i) | G_2$
$G_1 | q(Par_i), G_2$
$G_1 | q(Par_i) | G_2$.

C. Interest

The interest of these transformations arises from the fact that the useless handling of redundant annotations is avoided. This has a slight impact when the transformations are considered alone. However, combined, they may avoid the handling of inheritance of some annotations, even those made explicitly. Furthermore, the last transformation reduces the complexity of the handling of complex suspension declarations. In particular, the number of reductions required by them is decreased.

9.5 Comparison with related work

The methodology proposed in this chapter uses the transformational approach already developed in the imperative framework by work such as [Burstall and Darlington, 1977], [Balzer et al., 1983], ... Our contribution consists of transposing this approach in the concurrent logic framework. In particular, the transformations of Section 9.4.2 have no counterpart in this work.

A methodology for constructing imperative programs is developed in [Lengauer and Hehner, 1982]. Despite the target language, one significant difference with our methodology is that our transformations optimize the programs by restricting the parallel executions whereas, in [Lengauer and Hehner, 1982], the efficiency of the programs is improved by relaxing the (non-deterministic) sequential executions in concurrent ones. The reason for this difference results certainly from the following points.

i) On the one hand, programming in a logic programming language involves using the first order logic framework. It is inherently non-deterministic. This feature has convinced us to build Conclog so as to express at the basis all the sources of parallelism. Hence, programs are basically executed in a fully parallel way. They are thus optimized by eliminating the undesirable parallel executions.

ii) On the other hand, programming in an imperative language implies reasoning in terms of assignations, loops, ... that is in terms of actions. Those actions are most easily combined in sequences. It is thus natural to improve the programs by replacing sequential executions by concurrent ones.

A. Writing a specification

Our methodology is mostly connected with [Deville, 1990]. It is in fact an adaptation to the concurrent context. The same three phases of program construction have been conserved. We review them hereafter and point out our contribution for each of them.

A. Writing a specification

Roughly speaking, our contribution at the specification level consists of inserting information about the concurrent behavior of the reduction of a call in the specifications of [Deville, 1990]. We take this as an opportunity to re-organize the latter specifications. To be more specific, let us briefly describe them. They take the following form

procedure pred_name(Par$_1$,...,Par$_m$).
- Type
- Restriction on parameters
- Relation
- Application conditions
    * Directionalities
    * Environment preconditions
- Side effects

The type specification has been conserved in our specifications. However, types act in three ways in our methodology. Besides the preconditions and the postconditions already stated in the sequential framework, they act as invariants too. This has led us to introduce the notion of strong typing.

The relation specification has been conserved without any adaptation.

Restrictions on parameters, directionalities and side effect properties have been inserted in our operational properties. Four kinds of such properties may be stated : suspension conditions, preconditions, invariants and postconditions. The restrictions on parameters are examples of preconditions. Directionalities and side effect properties are stated as postconditions. Our format of preconditions and postconditions is free so that other forms can be stated in our methodology. For instance, some of our postconditions state properties about the effective way in which answer n-substitutions are constructed.

The two other kinds of operational properties are original to our specifications. They are particular to the concurrent framework. Invariants express properties that are kept invariant during the reduction of any call. Suspension conditions state conditions on which the reduction of any call suspends.

Finally, the environment preconditions are made part of our environment conditions. They act also as preconditions. Besides them, we allow to specify invariants and events. Those are also specific to the concurrent framework and thus original to our approach. Invariants state properties that should be guaranteed during the reduction of any call. Events state properties that are not required at the beginning of the reduction of a call but that should eventually occur during it.

B. Constructing a logic description

Our logic description part is composed of two parts : a definition part and a set of logic properties. The definition part issues from [Deville, 1990]. Our contribution with respect to that part is that several heuristics have been provided to construct logic definitions embodying as much parallel sources of parallelism as possible. The set of logic properties are original to our methodology. They describe, at the logic level, properties linking relations used in the definition part. They have been used in correctness-preserving transformations oriented to the concurrent framework. Nevertheless, they could also be used in the sequential one. For instance, the data dependency property could be used to order literals in clause bodies. The exclusiveness property could also be used to introduce Prolog cuts.

C. Deriving a logic program

At the program level, our methodology handles concurrent programs rather than sequential ones. This lead us to review the definition of correctness. The notion of safety, weak-termination, strong termination explained in our definition are peculiar to our work. The distinction between the partial correctness, semi-correctness and total correctness is also particular to our work.

Despite the difference of target languages, the two same derivation steps are used in our methodology. In the first step, the same syntactic transformations are first used to derive general Horn clause programs from the logic definitions. They are then made correct. As the programs are different and the correctness criterias are different, the points to verify and the way to do this are different too. The second step also consists in transforming the correct programs in more efficient versions. Several correctness preserving transformations have been provided for this purpose. Some of them, namely the transformations based on equivalent tree generation, partial evaluation and equality substitutions, are adaptations to the concurrent context of the transformations already presented in [Deville, 1990]. The other transformations are peculiar to our methodology. Among them are the transformations based on logic properties.

9.6 Conclusion

Chapter 1 has shown that any logic programming language must take some departure from the ideal of logic programming. Hence, despite our concern for obtaining soundness and completeness properties, some aspects have to be tackled when programming in Conclog. This does not however rule out the possibility of using logic as a basis for computing. Simply, two kinds of problems must be addressed : one the one hand, the construction of a solution for the problem to solve and, on the other hand, its translation in executable code.

This chapter has presented a methodology for programming in Conclog. One of its interests is precisely to separate the logical aspects from the procedural ones. It consists of an adaptation to the concurrent context of a methodology proposed in [Deville, 1990] for Prolog as target language. It rests on the same three phases.

The first one is the usual specification phase. Our specifications are formulated in natural language but are organized in four parts : type, relation, environment conditions and operational properties. They are assigned the following meaning. The type specification describes the type of the parameters. It acts in three ways :

- as a precondition that must be verified by the actual parameters,
- as an invariant that must be fulfilled by the reduction of calls,
- as a postcondition that must be verified by the computed answer n-substitutions.

The relation specification describes the computed relation. The environment conditions describe properties that must be ensured by the environment of the procedure call. They are classified in three parts : preconditions, invariants and events. The two first kinds are quite self-explanatory : they state properties that must hold at the beginning of the execution of a call and during the entire reduction, respectively. The last kind of properties specifies properties that are not required at the begining of the reduction but that must eventually occur. Finally, the operational properties state properties that must be ensured by the execution of the call. Four kinds of operational properties may be stated : preconditions, invariants, postconditions and suspension conditions. The three first ones are quite suggestive. They specify properties that should be verified by the actual parameters, properties verified during the entire execution of a call and properties to be verified by the computed answer n-substitutions or after the termination of the procedure calls. The suspension conditions express conditions that force the reduction of the calls to suspend.

The second phase of the methodology consists in constructing a logic description. It is composed of two parts : a definition part and a set of logic properties. The definition part consists of a well formed formula of first order logic. It defines the computed relation. It is called logic definition. The set of logic properties describes properties of the relations involved in the logic definition. Three kinds of such properties have been pointed out. We do not pretend the set to be complete. Discovering other such properties is left for future research.

The final step of the methodology consists in deriving a Conclog program from a logic description. This is achieved in three steps. In the first one, a set of general Horn clauses is derived by syntactic transformations from the logic definition. It is then transformed in a correct program. In a second step, this first correct version is optimized thanks to correctness preserving transformations. Some of them use the logic properties. Here too, we do not claim that the set of transformations is complete. The discovery of other transformations is left for future research.

The three following points are worth stressing.

1) We do not claim that the developed methodology is a universal panacea that ought to be applied for constructing any program. It rather gives guidelines that should help in constructing procedures.

2) A clear separation of the logical aspects from the operational ones was partly possible because of the nature of Conclog. For instance, if committed-choice languages were used, we would have to tackle functions at the logic level with the dataflows they induce. Also, we would have to construct the logic definitions so as to make appear guards acting only as tests.

3) Nevertheless, despite this point, parts of the methodology can also be applied to such languages. In particular, some of the proposed transformations can be straightforwardly adapted to them.

Chapter 10

Programming non-behavioral applications

10.1 Introduction

The aim of this chapter is twofold. On the one hand, it intends to be an illustration and a practicability test of the methodology developed in Chapter 9. On the other hand, it aims at presenting programming examples using Conclog while arguing two features of the language : its ease of programming and its expressiveness.

Non-behavioral applications are only programmed here. They are free from concurrency behavior constraints. They can thus be regarded as classical applications of the declarative logic programming paradigm. Therefore, they offer a good opportunity to illustrate and test both Conclog and the methodology on problems to which logic programming is widely acknowledged to be dedicated.

This chapter is organized as follows. Classical relational database programming is first addressed. Simple multi-directional and multi-solution procedures are then tackled. More elaborated single-solution directed procedures are developed thereafter. Some of them involve quite complex algorithmic. Tree related procedures are coded in a fourth section. Finally, procedures built on the classical generate and test programming paradigm are addressed.

10.2 Relational database programming

A classical introductory example to logic programming concerns the description and the reasoning on the relationships defined between members of a family. It illustrates the use of logic programming for database applications. Although Conclog is not devoted to database programming, it would be a considerable deficiency if so simple programs could not be programmed in it.

10.2.1 Programming samples

Consider a database of facts coupled with rules expressing family relationships. Traditionally, four basic predicates, namely

    father(Father,Child), mother(Mother,Child), male(Person), female(Person), [1]

are declared by means of facts. Other relations such as

    brother(Brother,Sibling), daughter(Daughter,Parent), parent(Parent,Child), grandparent(Grandparent,Grandchild),

are built from them by using rules. The following program gives one instance

    father(john,peter).   mother(isabelle,cathy).
    father(harry,cathy).   mother(mary,peter).

    male(harry).   female(isabelle).
    male(john).   female(cathy).
    male(peter).   female(mary).

    parent(Dad,Child) ← father(Dad,Child).
    parent(Mum,Child) ← mother(Mum,Child).

    brother(Brother,Sib) ←
          parent(Parent,Brother), parent(Parent,Sib), male(Brother), Brother≠Sib.

    grand_parent(Grandparent,Grandchild) ←
          parent(Grandparent,Parent), parent(Parent,Grandchild).

    daughter(Woman,Parent) ← parent(Parent,Woman), female(Woman).

Such clauses are quite intuitive. It is quite direct to establish that any logical consequence of them corresponds to the (non formalizable) perception of the relations we have in mind. Furthermore, thanks to the g-soundness and g-completeness theorems of Section 5.5, their computation in Conclog produces g-sound and g-complete results.

Thanks to these properties, the operational behavior of the computation may thus be completely discarded here. Nevertheless, for efficiency, it is worth looking at it. Consider, for instance, the procedure grand_parent. As it is stated, it is fully multi-directional. That is, it can be used whatever instantiation of the parameters is. In this context, any call to it is reduced by reducing independently the induced instance of the two subgoals parent(Grandparent,Parent) and parent(Parent,Grandchild). Consider now the following case. The grand_parent procedure is called with the Grandparent parameter ground. In this case, the reduction of the first s-goal parent(Grandparent,Parent) behaves in a quite efficient manner : it produces, for the Parent

---

[1] Recall that, in Conclog, variables are represented by strings beginning with a higher case letter and predicates are denoted by strings beginning with a lower case letter (see Section 2.1).

parameter, any child of Grandparent. In contrast, the s-goal parent(Parent,Grandchild) behaves in an inefficient and blind way : it produces all pairs (Parent,Grandchild) such that Parent is a parent of Grandchild. Most of these pairs are uninteresting for the reduction of the grand_parent(Grandparent,Grandchild) call since their first parameter Parent is not a child of the ground Grandparent parameter. In computational terms, most of them will thus not reconcile with the values for Parent generated by the reduction of parent(Grandparent,Parent). It would thus be better to reduce the s-goal parent(Grandparent,Parent) first and then, for any value generated for Parent, to reduce the induced instance of parent(Parent,Grandchild). This is obtained by sequentializing the two subgoals as follows :

>parent(Grandparent,Parent) | parent(Parent,Grandchild).

The same analysis applies by interverting the role of the subgoals in the case the second parameter Grandchild of the grand_parent(Grandparent,Grandchild) call is ground. In this case, it would thus be better to write

>parent(Parent,Grandchild) | parent(Grandparent,Parent).

The two sequentializations are conflictory so that two clauses should be provided to handle the grandparent procedure more efficiently. Tests should furthermore be added to use them in the right case. This is achieved by means of the ground built-in primitive that tests whether or not the given parameter is ground. The following clauses thus result :

>grand_parent(Grandparent,Grandchild) ←
>   ground(Grandparent) | parent(Grandparent,Parent) | parent(Parent,Grandchild).
>
>grand_parent(Grandparent,Grandchild) ←
>   ground(Grandchild) | parent(Parent,Grandchild) | parent(Grandparent,Parent).

Defining the grand_parent procedure just by them prevents us from using the procedure to produce all pairs (Grandparent,Grandchild) of the *grand_parent* relation. The initial clause

>grand_parent(Grandparent,Grandchild) ←
>   parent(Grandparent,Parent), parent(Parent,Grandchild).

should thus also be conserved. It is to be used only when the first two ones cannot. This is achieved by separating it from them by the ";" sequentialization delimitor. A final optimization should be made. As the procedure is stated all the clauses could be used to reduce any call whose parameters are ground. This would lead to reduce the two subgoals

>parent(Grandparent,Parent), parent(Parent,Grandchild)

three times. This may be avoided by selecting one of them arbitrarily. This is achieved by introducing commitment. To this end, the sequentialization operator "|" following the ground calls are replaced by the "|c" descriptor commit, the true |c guard is introduced in the last clause and commitment is activated by adding an activator commit. The following procedure results.

```
L_commit grand_parent.
grand_parent(Grandparent,Grandchild) ←
    ground(Grandparent) |c parent(Grandparent,Parent) | parent(Parent,Grandchild).
grand_parent(Grandparent,Grandchild) ←
    ground(Grandchild) |c parent(Parent,Grandchild) | parent(Grandparent,Parent) ;
grand_parent(Grandparent,Grandchild) ←
    true |c parent(Grandparent,Parent), parent(Parent,Grandchild).
```

Note that the expected behavior is indeed obtained. Whatever the actual parameters of a grand_parent call are, only one clause is selected. The two first ones are selected when the Grandparent and Grandchild parameters are ground, respectively. Finally, the last clause is only used in the more general cases where the first two ones cannot be used.

The brother and daughter relations can be improved in a similar way. Other database examples can also be programmed with similar ease and simplicity.

10.2.2 Evaluation

The following points are here worth stressing.

1° A first version of the procedures can be coded in Conclog quite directly and easily. It is directly issued from a declarative programming style. It has no extra-logical features although it is correct. Such features were then added to get more efficiency.

2° Compared with committed-choice languages, the database examples reveal three characteristics of Conclog. First, all solutions can be found in Conclog quite naturally whereas this is not possible in committed choice-languages[1]. Furthermore, multi-directionality is guaranteed naturally whereas this is not possible in committed-choice languages too (see Section 8.3.3). Finally, in contrast with them, commitment can be applied without preventing all the solutions to be discovered. This results from the weak commitment form required by local commit operators.

3° Compared with Prolog, all solutions can be found in parallel in the general case while the efficiency of directed dataflow computations may also be reached in the appropriate cases.

10.3 Simple multi-directional list processing

Database programming is mostly characterized by the manipulation of terms of weak complexity, with many facts and very simple rules. We now turn to more usual logic

---

[1] For completeness, let us recall that all solutions can also be programmed in Parlog. However, as signalled in Section 8.3.3, this requires to declare the clauses in a Prolog-like manner and to use special set built-in primitives.

programming, characterized by the manipulation of more elaborate terms, facts in minor number and rules of higher complexity.

As suggested in the previous chapters, relations on lists are very common in logic programming. Some multi-directional procedures handling them are programmed hereafter as first examples. They are quite elementary but will nevertheless be used to program more elaborate examples. The methodology developed in Chapter 9 is, of course, used to construct the programs. Hence, each procedure is handled in three steps :

- a specification is first given,
- a logic description is then constructed,
- a concurrent program is derived therefrom and then optimized.

10.3.1 Programming samples

10.3.1.1 The append procedure

A. Specification

The append procedure may be specified as follows :

procedure append(L1,L2,L).
- Type
    L1, L2, L : lists; strong use for the type and all subtypes
- Relation
    L is L1 concatenated with L2.

This specification is quite elementary and will be completed in Section 10.4. Nevertheless, it provides a good elementary example to program.

B. Logic description

The logic definition part will just be needed. It is obtained by taking L1 as induction parameter and by using the usual $<_{list}$ well-founded relation on lists :

$L_1 <_{list} L_2$ iff L_1 is a proper suffix of L_2.

It is as follows :

append(L1,L2,L) ⇔   L1=[] ∧ L2=L ∧ list(L)
                    ∨
                    L1=[H|T] ∧ L=[H|L_rem] ∧ append(T,L2,L_rem).

The list(L) type check call arises from the fact that the logic definition must ensure type checking. Type checking for the other paramaters L1 and L2 in

L1=[] ∧ L2=L ∧ list(L)

is ensured by the unifications L1=[] and L2=L. It is ensured in

L1=[H|T] ∧ L=[H|L_rem] ∧ append(T,L2,L_rem)

by the unifications and the recursive call.

C. Concurrent logic procedure

Applying the derivation process of Section 9.4.3.1.2 leads to the following clauses :

append(L1,L2,L) ← L1=[], L2=L,list(L).
append(L1,L2,L) ← L1=[H|T], L=[H|L_rem], append(T,L2,L_rem).

Let us verify that the resulting procedure is semi-correct. Referring to Subsection B.10 of Section 9.4.3.1.2, the following points need to be verified :

1. *Call verification.* The only subgoals in the procedure are unifications and a recursive call to append. No ns-goal is furthermore involved. As unification is constrained to no preconditions, the only property to verify is thus that append(T,L2,L_rem) verifies the type conditions of append. This is the case since
   - T and L_rem are local and are thus variables whatever call to append is treated,
   - L2 results from the treated call and thus verifies the list type.

2. *Types.*
   The only produced nmas's arise from the unifications L1=[], L2=L, L1=[H|T], L=[H|L_rem]. No negation is involved. Strong type condition SC is thus straightwardly verified. As a result, the parameter L is always guaranteed to be instantiated to a list. The list(L) s-goal is thus redundant and can be removed.

3. *Redundancy* The mutual exclusion of the unifications L1=[] and L1=[H|T] ensure non redundancy.

4. *Operational properties.* No operational properties are stated and thus need to be verified.

5. *Safety.* No annotations that might lead to suspension are involved so that no suspension can occur.

6. *Weak-termination.* The computed answer n-substitutions are finite only for the calls for which L1 or L are specified to be of finite length. Otherwise, the computed n-substitutions are instances of a infinite subserie of the serie :

   ({L1/[],L/L2},not{}),

   ({L1/[H],L/[H|L2]},not{}),

   ...

   ({L1/[H_1,...,H_m],L/[H_1,...,H_m|L2]},not{}),

   ...

   As the subtree engendered by any unification is finite, any tree engendered by a call is infinite iff the subtree engendered by the recursive subgoal append(T,L2,L_rem) is infinite. However, this subtree produces some instance of the above serie where L1 and L are replaced by T and L_rem, respectively. Because of the length constraint, only a finite number of n-substitutions of the serie are reconcilable with the n-substitutions issued from the concurrent unifications L1=[H|T] and L=[H|L_rem].

Note that the above procedure is not strong terminating since the recursive call is launched with two local variables (thus unconstrainted) as parameters T and L_rem. Let us apply Transformation 9.18. It results

append([],L,L).
append([H|T],L2,[H|L_rem]) ← append(T,L2,L_rem).

This time, as the finiteness constraint of the first and latter parameter are propagated by unification, the procedure is terminating even in the Conclog model with an infinite R-depth parameter.

10.3.1.2 The length procedure

A. Specification

The specification of the length procedure is as follows :

procedure length(L,Nb).
- Type
    L : list; strong use of the type and all subtypes
    Nb : integer
- Relation
    Nb is the number of elements of L.

Integers are here used in the $s^n(0)$ representation. Precisely, the integer type is defined as follows :

0 is an integer
if N is an integer, then s(N) is an integer.

B. Logic description

The logic definition part is also sufficient here. It could be obtained by taking the L parameter as induction parameter. As an exercise, let us use the Nb parameter. The well-founded relation chosen on integers is the usual one :

$0 < s(N)$ for any N,
if $N<M$ then $s(N) < s(M)$.

The following logic definition results :

length(L,Nb) ⇔ Nb=0 ∧ L=[]
∨
Nb=s(Nb_aux) ∧ L=[H|T] ∧ length(T,Nb_aux).

Type checking is ensured by the unifications and the recursive call. No type check call needs thus to be inserted.

Note that this is exactly the logic definition that would be obtained by using L as induction parameter with the $<_{list}$ relation. This results from the simplicity of the relation.

C. Concurrent logic procedure

The application of the derivation process of Section 9.4.3.1.2 leads to the following procedure :

length(L,Nb) ← Nb=0, L=[].
length(L,Nb) ← Nb=s(Nb_aux), L=[H|T], length(T,Nb_aux).

It can be proved semi-correct using similar arguments as for the append procedure. It is not correct since, whatever the actual parameters L and Nb are, the recursive call is reduced with two local variables, thus unrestricted in the Conclog model. Nevertheless, Transformation 9.18 circumvents this problem. The usual length procedure results :

length([],0).
length([H|T],s(Nb_aux)) ← length(T,Nb_aux).

10.3.1.3 The prefix procedure

A. Specification

The prefix procedure is specified as follows :

procedure prefix(P,L).
- Type
    P, L : list; strong use of the type and all subtypes
- Relation
    P is some prefix of L.

B. Logic description

Here too, the logic definition is sufficient. The two parameters can in principle be chosen as induction parameters. The choice of the former is better since the form of the prefix P determines the form of the list L. The following logic definition results from it. The used well-founded relation is the usual $<_{list}$ one.

prefix(P,L) ⇔ P=[] ∧ list(L)
∨
P=[H|P_rem] ∧ L=[H|L_rem] ∧ prefix(P_rem,L_rem).

As for the append procedure, the list(L) s-goal is introduced for type checking purposes. Because of the unifications and the recursive call, it is the only required one.

C. Concurrent logic procedure

The derivation process of Section 9.4.3.1.2 delivers the following clauses :

prefix(P,L) ← P=[], list(L).
prefix(P,L) ← P=[H|P_rem], L=[H|L_rem], prefix(P_rem,L_rem).

Using the same scheme of reasoning as for the append procedure, it can be proved semi-correct. The type check call list(L) can be removed similarly. The above procedure is however not correct because of the local variables P_rem and L_rem. Here too, Transformation 9.18 eliminates this problem. It delivers the usual prefix procedure

prefix([],L).
prefix([H|P_rem],[H|L_rem]) ← prefix(P_rem,L_rem).

10.3.1.4 The member procedure

A. Specification

Our final example consists of the member procedure. Its specification is as follows.

procedure member(X,L).
- Type
    L : list whose elements are of the type of X
- Relation
    X is a member of L.

B. Logic description

As for the previous example, the logic definition part is also sufficient here. Two parameters can be chosen as induction parameters. Chosing X is not well-suited since its structure cannot be represented easily by finite terms. Let us thus use the L parameter together with the usual $<_{list}$ well-founded relation. The following logic definition results. The list(L) predicate is used for the usual purposes of type checking.

member(X,L) ⇔ L=[] ∧ false
∨
L=[H|T] ∧ list(L) ∧ (X=H
∨ X≠H ∧ member(X,T)).

It can be simplified in the following definition

member(X,L) ⇔ L=[H|T] ∧ list(L) ∧ (X=H ∨ X≠H ∧ member(X,T)).

C. Concurrent logic procedure

The derivation process of Section 9.4.3.1.2 delivers the following concurrent logic procedure :

member(X,L) ← L=[H|T], X=H, list(L).
member(X,L) ← L=[H|T], X≠H, member(X,T), list(L).

Let us verify that it is semi-correct. Referring to Subsection B.10 of Section 9.4.3.1.2, the following points need to be verified.

1. *Call verification.* The only subgoals in the procedure are unifications, the negation of a unification and a recursive call to member. As the unification is constrained to no preconditions and engender a finite subtree, the only property to verify is thus that member(X,T) verifies the type conditions of member. This the case since
   - X is constrained to no type,
   - T is a local variable (it can thus be instantiated to some ground term of the list type).

2. *Types.*
   The only produced nmas's arise from the unifications L=[H|T], X=H. The strong condition property ST is thus verified. As a result, the L variable is always guaranteed to be of the list type. The list(L) s-goal is thus redundant and can be removed. Finally, type conditions of X are obviously verified by the unification X=H.

3. *Redundancy* The mutual exclusion of the conjunctions
   L=[H|T], X=H,
   L=[H|T], X≠H,
   for any ground values of X and L, ensures non redundancy.

4. *Operational properties.* No operational properties are stated and thus need to be verified.

5. *Safety.* No annotations that might lead to suspension are involved so that no suspension can occur.

6. *Weak-termination.* The computed answer n-substitutions are finite only for the calls for which the L parameter is specified to be of finite length. Otherwise, the computed n-substitutions are instances of an infinite subserie of the serie :
   ({L/[H]},not{}),
   ...

$(\{L/[H_1,\ldots,H_m]\},\text{not}\{\})$,
...

As the subtree engendered by any unification is always finite, any tree engendered by a call is infinite iff the subtree engendered by the recursive subgoal member(X,T) is infinite. This subtree produces some instance of the above serie where L is replaced by T. However, because of the length constraint, only a finite number of them are reconcilable with the n-substitutions issued from the concurrent unifications L=[H|T].

The above procedure is not strong terminating since the recursive call is launched with, a local variable (thus unconstrainted) for parameter T. Let us apply Transformation 9.18. It results

member(X,[X|T]).
member(X,[H|T]) ← X≠H, member(X,T).

This time, as the finiteness constraint of the second parameter L is propagated by unification, the procedure is terminating even in the Conclog model with an infinite R-depth parameter.

10.3.2 Evaluation

The simplicity and elegance of the above procedures should be underlined. They result from the fact that Conclog has been built as close as possible to the ideal of logic programming. In particular, our concern for g-soundness and g-completeness has allowed to state results (see Section 4.5 and 5.5) while abstracting most aspects of the computation. Although this might be surprising at first sight, it is thus quite natural that the above reasoning has paid little attention to the computation mechanisms.

Such an abstraction of the operational aspects contrasts with committed-choice languages. In Concurrent Prolog, for instance, one would have to introduce read-only annotations to ensure that one solution will indeed be computed. In Parlog, the corresponding mode declarations would have to be introduced whereas unifications would have to be carefully placed in GHC. Note furthermore, that commitment and guards will have to be placed whereas this is in fact not required by the computation.

Conclog should also be contrasted with these languages and with Prolog as far as the ease of obtaining multi-solution and multi-directional procedures is concerned. Among others, this results from our almost complete version of the negation as failure mechanism. Consider, for instance, the call

member(X,[1,Y,3]).

Figure 10.1 draws the Conclog computations. The following solutions are produced :

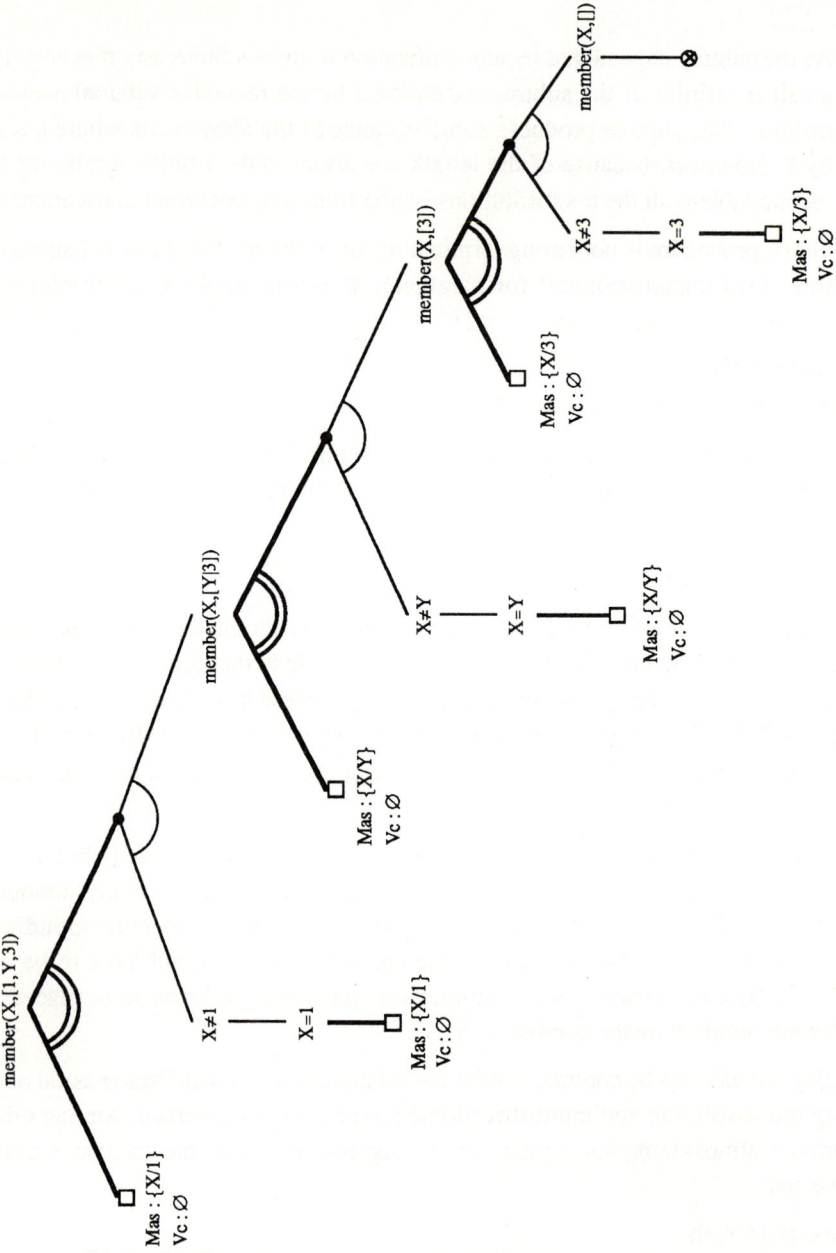

Figure 10.1 : the generation phase

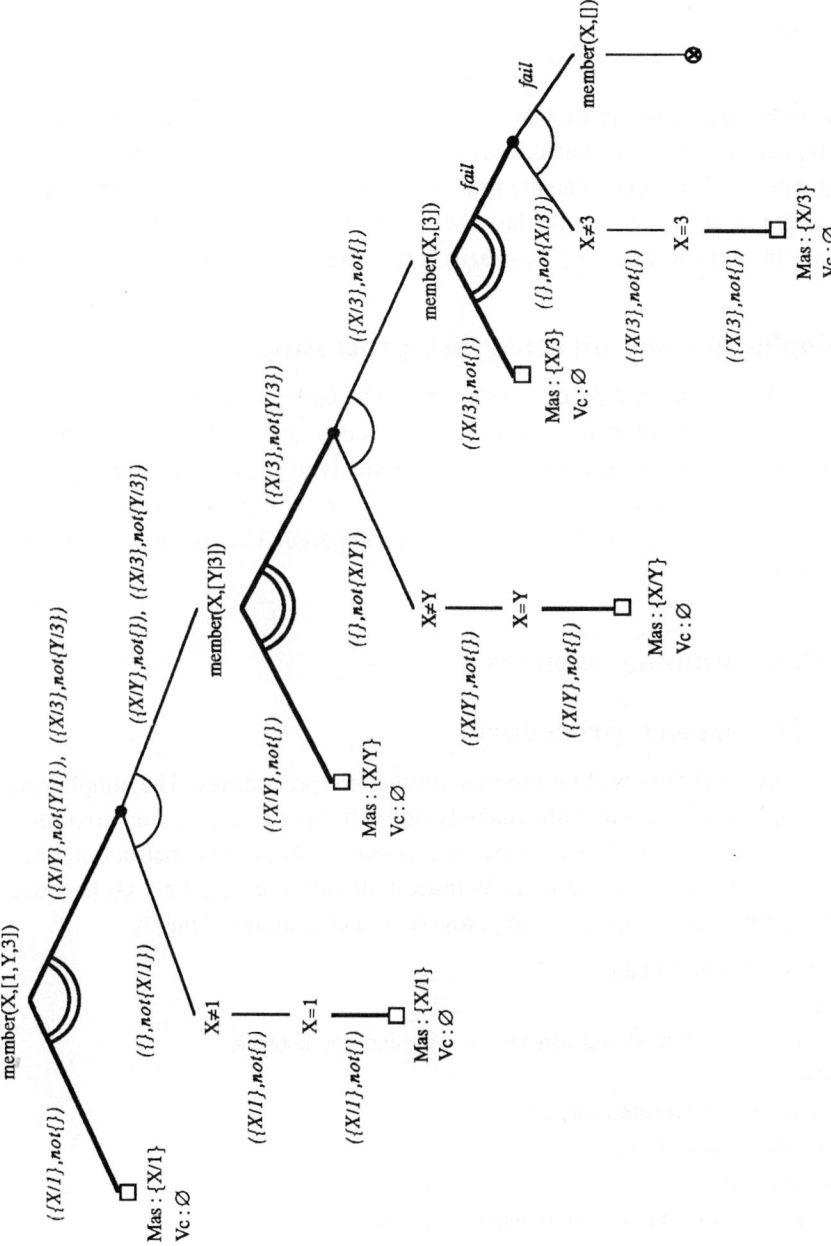

Figure 10.1 continued : the reconciliation phase

({X/1},not{}),
({X/Y},not{Y/1}),
({X/3},not{Y/3}).

In contrast, in Prolog, only the first solution might be produced because the s-goal X≠1 fails. Furthermore, because of commitment, only this solution might also be produced by committed-choice languages. This occurs when the first clause is selected for commitment. Note that, if the X≠H test is not placed in a guard, the last clause may be selected. In this case, failure would be returned since the negation in these languages acts as the Prolog one.

10.4 Single-solution directed list processing

Single-solution directed procedures may also be coded in Conclog. We illustrate this on several well-known examples : the reverse, compress and sort procedures. At the methodological level, an interest of these procedures is to provide the opportunity to handle operational properties. Furthermore, as they are more complex, several versions may be designed for them. Several are indeed coded and compared. This is particularly illustrated on the sort example.

10.4.1 Programming samples

10.4.1.1 The append procedure

The append procedure will be used by subsequent procedures. The simple specification given in Subsection 10.3.1.A is unfortunately not sufficient to prove the correctness of these programs. It is completed here. This does not however destroy the construction of Subsection 10.4.1.A : the program presented there is indeed already correct. This section thus aims at completing the information on an existing program rather than modifying it.

>   procedure   append(L1,L2,L).
>   - Type
>   L1, L2, L : lists; strong use for the type and any subtype
>   - Relation
>   L is L1 concatenated with L2.
>   - Operational properties :
>   Postconditions :
>   <ground,ground,any> : <ground,ground,ground>; <0-1>
>   L1 input and L1 incrementally constructed ground and L2 incrementally constructed ground : L incrementally constructed ground
>   L input ∧ L incrementally constructed ground : L1 and L2 incrementally constructed ground.

The added postconditions are quite intuitive. The first one simply states that if the actual parameters L1 and L2 are ground, then at most one answer n-substitution is computed. It furthermore binds L to a ground value. The two last ones state dataflow behaviors of the procedure. The former states that, for any call append(L1?,L2,L), if L1 and L2 are incrementally constructed ground then so is L. The latter charaterizes the reversed dataflow : if L is globally read-only annotated and incrementally constructed ground, then so are L1 and L2.

All these properties can be established by an inductive reasoning. We will for instance prove the second one. Let us reason inductively on the length of the value computed for L1. If L1 is bound to the empty list then the thesis is straightforward. Because, it is read-only annotated, only the first clause can be used. It binds L to L2 which is incrementally constructed. This is furthermore the restriction of the computed answer n-subsitution for the call. Otherwise, the second clause can only be used. It binds the head of L to the head of L1. Then its tail results from the recursive append call whose first parameter is of length strictly less than L1. The induction hypothesis can then be applied. The thesis follows from it.

10.4.1.2 The reverse procedure

A. Specification

The reverse procedure basically consists in reversing some given list. It is specified as follows.

    procedure reverse(L,L_reverse)
- Type
    L, L_reversed : lists; strong use
- Relation
    L_reversed is composed of the elements of L presented in the reversed order
- Operational properties
    1) Suspension condition
        L input
    2) Postconditions
        <ground,any> : <ground,ground>; <0-1>
        L_input ∧ L eventually constructed ground : L_reversed effectively constructed ground.

The type specification, relation specification and suspension condition are quite expected. The postconditions are perhaps less expected. They are introduced for illustrative purposes.

B. Logic description

Two logic definitions are presented in this section. The first one arises from the natural choice of L as induction parameter and $<_{list}$ as well-founded relation. A logic property is described for it. The second logic definition is derived from the first one thanks to a generalization transformation.

B.1 FIRST LOGIC DESCRIPTION

Taking L as the induction parameter and $<_{list}$ as the well founded relation leads to the following logic definition :

$$\begin{aligned}
\text{reverse(L,L\_reversed)} \Leftrightarrow\ & \text{L=[]} \wedge \text{L\_reversed=[]} \\
& \vee \\
& \text{L=[H|T]} \wedge \text{reverse(T,T\_reversed)} \\
& \wedge \text{append(T\_reversed,[H],L\_reversed).}
\end{aligned} \quad (LD_1)$$

The following logic properties may be associated with it :

For all L :
$\quad$ L=[H|T] $\rightarrow_{\{H,T\}}$
$\quad\quad$ reverse(T,T_reversed) $\wedge$ append(T_reversed,[H],L_reversed). $\quad (LP_1)$

For all H, T :
$\quad$ reverse(T,T_reversed) $\rightarrow_{\{T\_reversed\}}$
$\quad\quad$ append(T_reversed,[H],L_reversed). $\quad (LP_2)$

B.2 SECOND LOGIC DESCRIPTION

The logic definition LD_1 is quite correct. It may however be expected to lead to an inefficient algorithm. Indeed, whatever call is considered, an append call is involved. As the append procedure is implemented, this leads to re-analyze the T_reversed list. Fortunately, the append call can be removed thanks to the following generalization procedure ([Burstall and Darlington, 1977], [Deville, 1990]). It consists of generalizing the [H] parameter in a Acc parameter, of considering the common variable T_reversed as a local variable and of defining a new predicate for the other parameters on the basis of the conjunction

$\quad$ reverse(T,T_reversed) $\wedge$ append(T_reversed,[H],L_reversed).

Hence, a new predicate, called gen_reverse(L,Acc,L_reversed), is defined as follows :

$\quad$ gen_reverse(L,Acc,L_reversed) $\Leftrightarrow$ reverse(L,P), append(P,Acc,L_reversed).

Note that it is indeed a generalization of reverse since, taking [] as Acc list, one has

$\quad$ gen_reverse(L,[],L_reversed) $\Leftrightarrow$ reverse(L,P), append(P,[],L_reversed)

and, as [] is a neutral element of append,

$\quad$ gen_reverse(L,[],L_reversed) $\Leftrightarrow$ reverse(L,L_reversed).

Furthermore, a logic definition for gen_reverse can be derived from LD_1. Using unfolding in the definition of gen_reverse, one gets

gen_reverse(L,Acc,L_reversed) ⇔
    (L=[] ∧ P=[] ∧ append(P,Acc,L_reversed))
    ∨
    (L=[H|T] ∧ reverse(T,T_reversed) ∧ append(T_reverse,[H],P)
        ∧ append(P,Acc,L_reversed)).

Then, by associativity of append, one gets

append(T_reversed,[H|Acc],L_reversed)

from

append(T_reversed,[H],P) ∧ append(P,Acc,L_reversed).

The neutral property of append and the type definitions associated with it leads to

L=[] ∧ P=[] ∧ append(P,Acc,L_reversed)
⇔
L=[] ∧ L_reversed=Acc ∧ list(Acc).

In this condition, by folding, the above equivalence for gen_reverse may thus be simplified in

gen_reverse(L,Acc,L_reversed) ⇔
    (L=[] ∧ L_reversed=Acc ∧ list(L_reversed))
    ∨
    (L=[H|T] ∧ gen_reverse(T,[H|Acc],L_reversed)).

A second logic definition for reverse follows :

reverse(L,L_reversed) ⇔ gen_reverse(L,[],L_reversed).

gen_reverse(L,Acc,L_reversed) ⇔
    (L=[] ∧ L_reversed=Acc ∧ list(L_reversed))
    ∨
    (L=[H|T] ∧ gen_reverse(T,[H|Acc],L_reversed)). (Def$_2$)

The use of append has been replaced by the use of an extra-argument. As we will see in a moment, it collects in fact all the H's in good order. It thus acts as an accumlator. For this reason, it has been named Acc.

This version may be considered as more efficient since the same recursive scheme avoiding the append call results. The derived logic procedure will confirm this opinion.

C. Concurrent logic procedure

Two concurrent logic procedures are derived from the logic definitions.

C.1 First Concurrent Logic Procedure

Applying the derivation process of Section 9.4.3.1.2 on the logic definition LD_1 delivers the following concurrent logic procedure :

reverse(L,L_reversed) ←
    L=[], L_reversed=[].
reverse(L,L_reversed) ←
    L=[H|T], reverse(T,T_reversed), append(T_reversed,[H],L_reversed).

Let us prove that it is partially correct. Referring to Subsection B.10 of Section 9.4.3.1.2, the following points need to be verified :

1. *Call verification.* The subgoals in the procedure are
   - unifications, namely L=[], L_reversed=[], L=[H|T],
   - a call to the append procedure, namely append(T_reversed,[H],L_reversed),
   - a recursive call, namely reverse(T,T_reversed).

   No ns-goal is thus involved. As unification is constrained to no preconditions, the only property to verify is thus that, for any lists L, L_reversed, the calls
   append(T_reverse,[H],L_reversed),
   reverse(T,T_reversed)
   verify the type preconditions of the append and reverse procedures, respectively. This is straightforward since
   - T and T_reverse are local variables, thus unconstrained in the Conclog model
   - [H] is manifestly a list,
   - L_reversed is a list by hypothesis.

2. *Types.*
   The only produced nmas's arise from the unifications L=[], L_reversed=[], L=[H|T] and append(T_reversed,[H],L_reversed). Thanks to the strong use of type in append, the strong type condition ST is thus fulfilled.

3. *Redundancy* The mutually exclusive unifications L=[] and L=[H|T] ensure non redundancy.

4. *Operational properties.*
   4.1 The following suspension declaration is added to make the suspension condition holds :
       suspend reverse(?,*).
   4.2 No invariant property is stated and so needs to be verified.
   4.3 The postconditions are verified as follows :
       i) <ground,any> : <ground,ground>; <1-1>.
           For any ground L, the relation specification specifies that there is one and one L_reversed such that <L,L_reversed>∈ *reverse*. This

L_reversed is furthermore ground. Thanks to the above points, the procedure is g-sound and g-complete. There is thus at least one n-substitution returned to cover this solution. Moreover, it bounds L_reversed to a ground term. Thanks to the non redundancy criteria (point 3) above, there is only one.

ii) L input and L incrementally constructed ground : L_reversed incrementally constructed ground.

As it is stated, the procedure cannot ensure this precondition. Indeed, the specification of append guarentees that the subgoal

append(T_reversed,[H],L_reversed)

constructs L_reversed ground only if T_reversed is ground. In the parallel context, an equivalent condition is that T_reversed is restricted to be input and is constructed ground by concurrent reductions. This can however not be ensured. Some annotations must be introduced for this purpose. Although Transformation 9.1 cannot be applied to ensure correctness, the logic properties LP_1 and LP_2 can be used for inspiration. It suggests to annotate T_reversed by a global read-only annotation. Doing so ensures the postcondition. This is easily verified by an inductive reasoning. Assume L is constructed to an empty list. Then, using the first clause, L_reversed is incrementally constructed to an empty list. This is indeed part of a computed answer n-substitution. Assume now L is incrementally constructed to a non empty list. Then, thanks to the unification L=[H|T], T is constructed in this way. As it is an input parameter of the call

reverse(T,T_reversed)

and is such that T $<_{list}$ L, the specification of reverse can be recursively applied. This ensures that T_reversed is incrementally constructed. Now, applying the specification of append, L_reversed is incrementally constructed. Because of the dataflow induced by the computation, it is indeed a reversed list of L.

To ensure partial correctness, the procedure is thus modified as follows :

```
suspend reverse(?,*).
reverse(L,L_reversed) ←
     L=[], L_reversed=[].
reverse(L,L_reversed) ←
     L=[H|T], reverse(T,T_reversed), append(T_reversed?,[H],L_reversed).
```

To obtain correctness, let us transform it by applying Transformation 9.18. It results

```
suspend reverse(?,*).
reverse([],[]).
reverse([H|T],L_reversed) ←
        reverse(T,T_reversed), append(T_reversed?,[H],L_reversed).        (CP₁)
```

Correctness can now be established.

5. *Safety.* The first clause is free from annotations and thus cannot induce suspension. Nevertheless, annotations are involved in the second clause. They could in fact introduce suspensions. Fortunately, for any ground value for L, the dataflow in the procedure is as follows.
   - Head unification instantiates T, in a progressive way to a ground value;
   - Then, the recursive call reverse(T,T_reversed) suspends until T is of the form [] or [H|T]. A recursive reasoning then leads to the facts that T_reversed is incrementally constructed to a ground value and that reverse(T,T_reversed) involves no suspension.
   - The specification of append then ensures that the call
       append(T_reversed?,[H],L_reversed)
     involves no suspension.

6. *Strong termination.* Strong termination results from the following property : given any ground value for L, the engendered and/or/not search tree is finite. Indeed, thanks to the above dataflow, an inductive reasoning leads to the fact that the subtree engendered by the call reverse(T,T_reversed) is finite. Furthermore, T_reversed is instantiated progressively to a ground finite value. In these conditions, thanks to the
       <ground,any,any> : <ground,any,any>; <1-1>
   property and given the fact that T_reversed is input for append, the subtree engendered by
       append(T_reversed?,[H],L_reversed)
   is finite too.

The above procedure can be transformed while conserving its correctness. Applying Transformation 9.22 first leads to the following procedure

```
suspend reverse(!,*).
reverse([],[]).
reverse([H|T],L_reversed) ←
        reverse(T?,T_reversed), append(T_reversed?,[H?],L_reversed).
```

Applying Transformation 9.20 then leads to the following procedure

```
suspend reverse(!,*).
reverse([],[]).
reverse([H|T],L_reversed) ←
    reverse(T,T_reversed), append(T_reversed?,[H?],L_reversed).
```

C.2 SECOND CONCURRENT LOGIC PROCEDURE

Applying the derivation process of Section 9.4.3.1.2 on the logic definition LD_2 delivers the following concurrent logic procedure :

```
reverse(L,L_reversed) ← gen_reverse(L,[],L_reversed).

gen_reverse(L,Acc,L_reversed) ← L=[], L_reversed=Acc, list(L_reversed).
gen_reverse(L,Acc,L_reversed) ← L=[H|T], gen_reverse(T,[H|Acc],L_reversed).
```

Let us try to prove that it is partially correct. Referring to Subsection B.10 of Section 9.4.3.1.2, the following points need to be verified.

1. *Call verification.* The only subgoals in the procedure are unifications and calls to the procedure gen_reverse. No ns-goal are involved. The unifications and the gen_reverse procedure are constrained to no preconditions. Call verification is thus immediate.

2. *Types.*
   The only produced nmas's arise from the unifications L=[], L=[H|T]. Strong type condition ST is then fulfilled. As a result, the list(L_reversed) type check s-goal can be removed.

3. *Redundancy.* The mutually exclusive unifications L=[] and L=[H|T] ensure non redundancy.

4. *Operational properties.*
   4.1 The following suspension declaration is added to make the suspension condition holds :

           suspend reverse(?,*).

   4.2 No invariant properties are stated and so need to be verified.

   4.3 The postconditions are verified as follows :

   i) <ground,any> : <ground,ground>; <1-1>.

       For any ground L, the relation specification specifies that there is one and one L_reversed such that <L,L_reversed>∈ *reverse*. This L_reversed is furthermore ground. Thanks to the above points, the procedure is g-sound and g-complete. There is thus at least one n-substitution returned to cover this solution. Moreover, it binds L_reversed to a ground term. Thanks to the non redundancy criteria (point 3) above, there is only one.

ii) L input and L incrementally constructed ground : L_reversed incrementally constructed ground.

As it is stated, the procedure cannot ensure this postcondition. Indeed, as the call

gen_reverse(T,[H|Acc],L_reversed)

is reduced in a completely independent way from L=[H|T], the incremental construction of L cannot be communicated to the T parameter. This problem may be circumvented by applying Transformation 9.18 to the gen_reverse procedure. Then, thanks to head unification, the T parameter of the recursive gen_reverse call is now incrementally constructed. In these conditions, an inductive reasoning proves that L_reversed is indeed incrementally constructed to a ground list.

Summing up, to get partial correctness, the reverse procedure has been transformed into the following procedure.

suspend reverse(?,*).
reverse(L,L_reversed) ← gen_reverse(L,[],L_reversed).

gen_reverse([],L_reversed,L_reversed).
gen_reverse([H|T],Acc,L_reversed) ← gen_reverse(T,[H|Acc],L_reversed).   (CP$_2$)

It is correct. To prove this, two properties have to be established.

5. *Safety.* No annotations that might lead to suspension are involved so that no suspension can occur.
6. *Strong termination.* Strong termination is quite easy to establish since each clause body reduces to one call. It has to be proved for any ground value for the L parameter. In this condition, the thesis results from the fact that the and/or/not tree engendered by any call

gen_reverse(L,Acc,L_reversed)

whose L and Acc parameters are ground is finite. This may be easily proved by an inductive reasoning on L.

The procedure CP$_2$ may finally be optimized. Transformations 9.22 and 9.23 deliver the following procedure

reverse(L,L_reversed) ← gen_reverse(L?,[],L_reversed).

gen_reverse([],L_reversed,L_reversed).
gen_reverse([H|T],Acc,L_reversed) ← gen_reverse(T,[H|Acc],L_reversed).

The gen_reverse procedure is private to the reverse procedure. It may then be annotated according to the call in the reverse procedure. Hence, the following suspension declaration can be added :

suspend gen_reverse(?,*,*).

and the first parameter of the gen_reverse procedure can be declared as input. Then, Transformations 9.20 and 9.22 deliver

reverse(L,L_reversed) ← gen_reverse(L,[],L_reversed).

suspend gen_reverse(!,*,*).
gen_reverse([],L_reversed,L_reversed).
gen_reverse([H|T],Acc,L_reversed) ← gen_reverse(T,[H|Acc],L_reversed).

D. Comparison

As announced, the second logic procedure is more efficient than the first one. This is due to the fact that each time the clause

reverse([H|T],L_reversed) ←
    reverse(T,T_reversed), append(T_reversed?,[H],L_reversed).

is used, the T_reversed list is re-examined by the append call. The reason of the presence of this call is that it is not possible to insert H at the end of T_reversed by using such a simple construct as [H|...]. The second version avoids this examination by precisely providing some counterpart to the [H|...] operation. In fact, the H's are simply stocked in reversed order in the Acc parameter. Hence, the Acc name for accumulator. Assuming it is empty at the call, its contents then delivers the reversed list L_reversed when all elements of L have been examined.

As far as the construction of the procedure is concerned, proving the correctness of CP_2 has been made in a smaller way than for CP_1. This results from two facts.

1) First, information about procedures not in CP_1 have to be used. This necessitates to carry information in specifications. In contrast, as CP_2 uses no procedures exterior to it, inductive proofs could be employed to prove the correctness of CP_2.

2) Second, in contrast with CP_1, CP_2 could be transformed very simply so that the body of any clause contains at most one call. This simplifies greatly the handling of the dataflow.

10.4.1.3 The compress procedure

Our second single directed procedure concerns the compress procedure. Its has been defined in [Vasak, 1986] and has been intensively treated in [Deville, 1990]. Roughly speaking, it consists in condensing a list by replacing each sequence of same character by the character followed by the number of occurrences. For instance, the compression of the list [a,a,b,b,b,c,d,d,d,d] is [a,2,b,3,c,1,d,4].

The precise definition requires some auxiliary notions. The construction of the procedure also requires three auxiliary procedures. Such concepts and procedures are first defined. Two versions for the compress procedures will be coded next.

A. Auxiliary concepts

A *compact list of characters* is a list of the form $[c_1,n_1,...,c_k,n_k]$ where $k \geq 0$, the n_i's are positive integers and the c_i's are characters such that $c_i \neq c_{i+1}$. Given a list L of characters $[c_1,...,c_n]$, a *max subsequence* of L is a sublist $[c_p,...,c_q]$ of L such that

$1 \leq p \leq q \leq n$
$c_p = c_{p+1} = ... = c_{q-1} = c_q$
$c_{p-1} \neq c_p$ if $p > 1$
$c_q \neq c_{q+1}$ if $q < n$

Finally, the *compression of a list of characters* L is a compact list where each max subsequence of L is replaced by the character occurring in this subsequence and the length of this subsequence.

B. Auxiliary procedures

Three auxiliary procedures will be used : add, sequence and first. They are used for the following purposes.

1) The add(A,B,C) procedure is motivated by a future need of counting the number of occurrences of a same character. It is built to be multi-directional. It determines whether C is A+B.

2) The sequence(C,Lg,L_char) is motivated by a strategy of compacting a list : find the first sequence of maximal length formed by the same character and compress the tail of the list. The first task will thus require to identify a sequence of some length of the same character. This is the goal assigned to the sequence(C,Lg,L_char) procedure.

3) The first(C,L) procedure also results from this strategy. Maximality of a sequence requires that the head of the tail list differs from the character forming the sequence. Testing the head of a list is precisely the goal assigned to the first(C,L) procedure.

Precisely, the specifications of these procedures are as follows :

1)   procedure add(A,B,AplusB)
- Type
   A, B, AplusB : integers

- Relation

    AplusB is the sum of A and B.

2) procedure sequence(C,Lg,L_char)

- Type

    C : character

    Lg : positive integer

    L_char : list of characters; strong use

- Relation

    L_char is the list composed of Lg occurrences of C

- Operational properties

    Postcondition :

    L_char input ∧ L_char incrementally constructed ground : C constructed ground and Lg incrementally constructed ground.

3) procedure first(C,L).

- Type

    C : character

    L : list of characters; strong use

- Relation

    C is the first character of L.

- Operational properties

    Postconditions :

    <any,any> : <any,any>; <0-1>

    L input ∧ L incrementally constructed ground : C constructed ground.

C. The procedures

C.1 SPECIFICATION

The compress procedure is specified as follows.

procedure compress(L,CL)

- Type

    L : list of characters

    CL : compact list of characters

- Relation

    CL is the compression of L

- Operational properties

    1) Suspension condition

        L is input

2) Postconditions

<ground,any> : <ground,ground>; <0-1>

L input ∧ L incrementally constructed ground : CL incrementally constructed ground.

C.2 LOGIC DESCRIPTION

Two logic descriptions will be constructed subsequently. They result from two choices of input parameters.

C.2.1 First logic description

The first logic description results from the natural choice of the induction parameter : the parameter declared as input, namely L. The well-founded relation associated with it is the usual $<_{list}$ relation. The following logic definition results :

compress(L,CL) ⇔
    L=[] ∧ CL=[]
    ∨
    L=[C] ∧ CL=[C,1] ∧ char(C)
    ∨
    L=[C1,C2|T] ∧ compress([C2|T],CL_aux) ∧
      (C1≠C2 ∧ CL=[C1,1|CL_aux] ∧ char(C1)
        ∨
        C1=C2 ∧ CL_aux=[C2,Lg_aux|CL_aux_rem]
        ∧ add(Lg_aux,1,Lg) ∧ CL=[C1,Lg|LC_aux_rem]) .   (LD$_1$)

It will be useful to characterize the add predicate. The following logic properties are given for this purpose. The three first ones express, at the relational level, the dataflow intuitively induced by taking L as input parameter. The two last ones express that

    L=[C1,C2|T] ∧ C1≠C2   (resp. L=[C1,C2|T] ∧ C1=C2)

acts as a test to reduce compress(L,CL).

1) For all L :
    L=[C1,C2|T] → {C1,C2,T}
      compress([C2|T],CL_aux) ∧ C1=C2 ∧ CL_aux=[C2,Lg_aux|CL_aux_rem]
      ∧ add(Lg_aux,1,Lg) ∧ CL=[C1,Lg|LC_aux_rem]   (LP$_1$)

2) For all C1, C2, T :
    compress([C2|T],CL_aux) → {CL_aux}
      CL_aux=[C2,Lg_aux|CL_aux_rem] ∧ add(Lg_aux,1,Lg)
      ∧ CL=[C1,Lg|LC_aux_rem]   (LP$_2$)

3) For all CL_aux, C2 :
   CL_aux=[C2,Lg_aux|CL_aux_rem] → {Lg_aux, CL_aux_rem}
   add(Lg_aux,1,Lg) ∧ CL=[C1,Lg|LC_aux_rem].   (LP$_3$)

4) For all L, C1, C2, T
   L=[C1,C2|T] ∧ C1≠C2 $\xrightarrow{\text{compress(L,CL)}}$
   compress([C2|T],CL_aux) ∧ CL=[C1,1|CL_aux] ∧ char(C1)   (LP$_4$)

5) For all L, C1, C2, T
   L=[C1,C2|T] ∧ C1=C2 $\xrightarrow{\text{compress(L,CL)}}$
   CL_aux=[C2,Lg_aux|CL_aux_rem] ∧ add(Lg_aux,1,Lg)
   ∧ CL=[C1,Lg|LC_aux_rem]   (LP$_5$)

C.2.2 Second logic description

The second logic description is based on the other choice of the induction parameter : CL. The associated well-founded relation is as follows. Let $cl_1=[c_1,m_1,...,c_p,m_p]$ and $cl_2=[d_1,n_1,...,d_q,n_q]$ be two compact lists of characters. Then,

$$cl_1 < cl_2$$

holds iff cl_1 is a proper suffix of cl_2. The following logic definition results :

compress(L,CL) ⇔
   CL=[] ∧ L=[]
   ∨
   CL=[C,Lg|CL_rem] ∧ sequence(C,Lg,First_seq) ∧ compress(T,CL_rem)
   ∧ append(First_seq,T,L) ∧ not(first(C,CL_rem)).   (LD$_2$)

The following logic properties can be stated. They translate the best dataflow to use when L is given as ground.

1) For all L :
   append(First_seq,T,L) →{First_seq,T}
   CL=[C,Lg|CL_rem] ∧ sequence(C,Lg,First_seq) ∧ compress(T,CL_rem)
   ∧ not(first(C,CL_rem)).   (LP$_6$)

2) For all First_seq, T :
   sequence(C,Lg,First_seq) ∧ compress(T,CL_rem) →{C,CL_rem}
   CL=[C,Lg|CL_rem] ∧ not(first(C,CL_rem)).   (LP$_7$)

C.3. CONCURRENT LOGIC PROCEDURES

A concurrent logic procedure can be derived from each logic description. The resulting procedures are compared at the end of this section.

C.3.1 First concurrent logic procedure

Applying the derivation process of Section 9.4.3.1.2 on the logic definition LD_1 delivers the following concurrent logic procedure :

compress(L,CL) ← L=[], CL=[].
compress(L,CL) ← L=[C], CL=[C,1], char(C).
compress(L,CL) ←
    L=[C1,C2|T], compress([C2|T],CL_aux), C1≠C2, CL=[C1,1|CL_aux], char(C1).
compress(L,CL) ←
    L=[C1,C2|T], compress([C2|T],CL_aux), C1=C2,
    CL_aux=[C2,Lg_aux|CL_aux_rem], add(Lg_aux,1,Lg), CL=[C1,Lg|LC_aux_rem].

The type check predicates can be removed thanks to the following reasoning. Any call must satisfy the type constraints. Hence, the L and CL parameters must always be a list and a compact list of character. It follows that char(C) is redundant with L=[C]. Indeed, if the reduction of the s-goals L=[C] and CL=[C,1] let C variable, then C can obviously be instantiated to a character. Otherwise, C must be bound to a character and char(C) is trivially met. The same reasoning can be applied for char(C1). Hence, the type check tests char(C) and char(C1) can be removed.

Let us try to prove that the resulting procedure is semi-complete. To this end, the following points must be established.

1. *Call verification.*
    1.1 The only calls in the logic procedures are as follows :
    - unifications,
    - a ns-goal, namely C1≠C2,
    - a call to the add procedure, namely add(Lg,1,Lg_aux),
    - two identical recursive calls, namely compress([C2|T],CL_aux).

    The unifications are unconstrained. The type conditions for the add procedure are met since Lg and Lg_aux are local variables. Finally, the C2, T and CL_aux being local variables too, the type preconditions of compress are also trivially met.
    1.2 No environment property is stated so that the environment properties are trivially verified.
    1.3 The subtree engendered by the ns-goal C1≠C2 is manifestly finite.
2. *Types.*
    Nmas's produced during the reduction of a call to the compress procedure arise only from the unifications and from the add call. Calling the specification of add, the strong type ST is thus verified.

3. *Redundancy.* The mutual exclusion of the conjunctions
   L=[],
   L=[C],
   L=[C1,C2|T], C1≠C2,
   L=[C1,C2|T], C1=C2
   for any ground value of L, ensures the non-redundance of the computed answer n-substitutions.

4. *Operation properties.*

   4.1 The following suspension declaration is added to ensure the suspension condition :

   suspend compress(?,*).

   4.2 No invariant property is stated and so needs to be verified.

   4.3 The postconditions are verified as follows :

   i) <ground,any> : <ground,ground>; <0-1>

   The relation specification of compress ensures that, for any ground list L, there exists one and only one ground CL such that

   <L,CL>∈ *compress*

   Thanks to the above points, the compress procedure is g-sound and g-complete. At most one n-substitution is thus computed for any compress call whose L parameter is ground, when any. It is the only one thanks to the non-redundancy criteria. Finally, the g-soundness property ensures that the CL parameter is made ground by the n-substitution.

   ii) L input ∧ L incrementally constructed ground : CL incrementally constructed ground.

   This property is ensured as follows. Thanks to the suspension declaration, the compress([C2|T],CL_aux) calls cannot construct [C2|T]. This list can however be consumed incrementally thanks to the L=[C1,C2|T] unification. This given, by inductive reasoning, the list CL_aux is proved to be incrementally constructed to a ground list. In these conditions, the unifications

CL=[]	(first clause),
CL=[C,1]	(second clause),
CL=[C1,1,CL_aux]	(third clause),
CL=[C1,Lg_aux|CL_aux_rem]	(fourth clause)

   and the specification of add, ensure that CL is incrementally constructed ground.

5. *Safety*. Suspension may only occur because of the suspension declaration of compress. The above reasoning however ensures that any compress([C2|T],CL_aux) call cannot suspend indefinitely.
6. *Weak-termination*. To prove weak termination, let us first note that, thanks to the specification of add, non-termination can only arise from the use of the recursive calls compress([C2|T],CL_aux) in the third and fourth clauses. However, using them infinitely implies making L grow infinitely (because of the L=[C1,C2|T] unifications.

Let us now prove the weak-termination property. Let L be ground. Because of the above reasoning, only a finite number of subtrees engendered by the compress([C2|T],CL_aux) subgoals can reconcile with the bindings generated by the L=[C1,C2|T] unifications. The tree engendered by the treated compress call is thus indeed finite.

Summing up, to get semi-completion, the procedure compress has been modified as follows :

suspend compress(?,*).
compress(L,CL) ← L=[], CL=[].
compress(L,CL) ← L=[C], CL=[C,1].
compress(L,CL) ←
    L=[C1,C2|T], compress([C2|T],CL_aux), C1≠C2, CL=[C1,1|CL_aux].
compress(L,CL) ←
    L=[C1,C2|T], compress([C2|T],CL_aux), C1=C2,
    CL_aux=[C2,Lg_aux|CL_aux_rem], add(Lg_aux,1,Lg_aux), CL=[C1,Lg|LC_aux_rem].

It is not complete since, even when the L parameter is ground, the subgoal

compress([C2|T],CL_aux)

generates an infinite subtree if reconciliation is not provoked. This results from the fact that, even if the suspension declaration declares [C2|T] as input, the subgoal can use the third and fourth clause an infinite number of times. To circumvent this property, let us instantiate the head clause by applying Transformation 9.18. The following (still semi-correct) procedure results :

suspend compress(?,*).
compress([],[]).
compress([C],[C,1]).
compress([C1,C2|T],[C1,1|CL_aux]) ←
    compress([C2|T],CL_aux), C1≠C2.
compress([C1,C1|T],[C1,Lg|LC_aux_rem]) ←
    compress([C1|T],[C1,Lg_aux|CL_aux_rem]), add(Lg_aux,1,Lg).

This time as the head parameter [C1,C2|T] and [C1,C1|T] are more instantiated than the call parameter [C2|T], the subgoal

compress([C2|T],CL_aux)

cannot use the third and fourth clauses directly. It must suspend until the [C2|T] parameter is more instantiated. This can only occur by head unification of the first parameters. In these conditions, an inductive reasoning proves that the subtree engendered by the subgoal

    compress([C2|T],CL_aux)

is finite.

The procedure can finally be transformed. Intuitively, in the last clause, it is the role of the recursive compress call to instantiate Lg_aux. This is not explicitly stated by one of the logic properties LP_1 to LP_3. Nevertheless, combining them gives the following property :

    For all C1, T :
        compress([C1|T],[C1,Lg_aux|CL_aux_rem]) →{Lg_aux}
        add(Lg_aux,1,Lg)

Transformation 9.1 then transforms the last clause by annotating the add(Lg_aux,1,Lg) call :

    compress([C1,C1|T],[C1,Lg|LC_aux_rem]) ←
        compress([C1|T],[C1,Lg_aux|CL_aux_rem]), add(Lg_aux?,1,Lg).

Then, by successively applying Transformations 9.22 and 9.20, the procedure results in

    suspend compress(!,*).
    compress([],[]).
    compress([C],[C,1]).
    compress([C1,C2|T],[C1,1|CL_aux]) ←
        compress([C2|T],CL_aux), C1≠C2.
    compress([C1,C1|T],[C1,Lg|LC_aux_rem]) ←
        compress([C1|T],[C1,Lg_aux|CL_aux_rem]), add(Lg_aux?,1,Lg).

Transformation 9.3 can then be applied to force C1≠C2 to behave as a test before the recursive compress call is reduced. It rests on logic property LP_4. The following procedure results :

    suspend compress(!,*).
    compress([],[]).
    compress([C],[C,1]).
    compress([C1,C2|T],[C1,1|CL_aux]) ←
        C1≠C2 | compress([C2|T],CL_aux).
    compress([C1,C1|T],[C1,Lg|LC_aux_rem]) ←
        compress([C1|T],[C1,Lg_aux|CL_aux_rem]), add(Lg_aux?,1,Lg).

C.3.2 Second concurrent logic procedure

Let us now turn to the second logic description. Applying the derivation process of Section 9.4.3.1.2 on it delivers the following concurrent logic procedure :

```
compress(L,CL) ← CL=[], L=[].
compress(L,CL) ←
    CL=[C,Lg|CL_rem], sequence(C,Lg,First_seq), compress(T,CL_rem),
    append(First_seq,T,L), not(first(C,CL_rem)).
```

Let us try to prove that it is correct. The following points must be handled for this purpose.

1. *Call verification.* The procedure involves the following calls :
   - unifications,
   - a recursive call, namely compress(T,CL_rem),
   - a call to the sequence procedure, namely sequence(C,Lg,First_seq),
   - a call to the append procedure, namely append(First_seq,T,L),
   - a call to the first procedure, namely first(C,CL_rem).

   The only ns-goal is the ns-goal not(first(C,CL_rem)). No environment properties are required for the calls. Two properties must thus be verified.
   - The above calls verify the preconditions of the specifications. This is straightforward, since T, CL_rem, C, Lg, First_seq are local variables (thus uninstantiated at the time of the calls) and L is a list thanks to the parameter specification of the compress procedure.
   - The ps-goal first(C,CL_rem) engendered a finite number of n-substitutions. This is ensured by the specification of the first procedure.

2. *Types.* Types are ensured by the specifications of the sequence, append and first procedures

3. *Redundancy.* The mutual exclusion of the s-goals
   CL=[],
   CL=[C,Lg|CL_rem]
   for any ground value of CL ensures the non-redundancy of the computed answer subtitutions.

4. *Operational properties*
   4.1 The following suspension declaration is introduced to make the suspension condition holds :
       suspend compress(?,*).
   4.2 No invariant property is stated and thus needs to be verified.
   4.3 The postconditions are verified as follows.
       i) <ground,any> : <ground,ground>; <0-1>
          This is verified as for the first concurrent program.
       ii) L input ∧ L incrementally constructed ground : CL incrementally constructed ground.
          Proving this property directly on the procedure is not feasible. Specifications must be used for the calls to auxiliary procedures and

none of them provides enough information to handle the so general calls of the second clause. The second clause should thus be first modified to establish the postcondition. To this end, we take some inspiration of logic properties LP_6 and LP_7. They induce the following modifications,

    CL=[C?,Lg?|CL_rem?], sequence(C,Lg,First_seq?),
    compress(T?,CL_rem), append(First_seq,T,L),
    not(first(C?,CL_rem?)).

They translate, in fact, the dataflow for L input. This given, the postcondition is immediately verified thanks to the specifications of the auxiliary procedures.

5. *Safety.* Safety is also ensured by the incremental construction of the lists and by the specified dataflow.

6. *Weak termination.* Weak termination is ensured thanks to the dataflow and the incremental construction of the lists.

7. *Strong termination.* Strong termination is however not ensured since the compress(T,CL_rem) call can use the second clause an infinite number of time. In fact, even if equality substitution is operated, the input character of the list L and the knowledge of L is not sufficient to determine whether or not the clause should be used. It is unifiable an infinite number of times (even with the dataflow). To restrict its use, some auxiliary knowledge must be provided in it. In general, it is sufficient to split the clause into two clauses one for each elementary structure of L :

    L=[] and L=[H_L|T_L].

Here, the relation specification forces L and CL to be simultaneously empty. Hence, the information that L is of the form [H_L|T_L] need to be introduced. When so, strong termination is ensured since the compress(T,CL_rem) call must then wait until T is instantiated to an instance of [H_L|T_L] before it uses the second clause. As, for any ground value of L, T is constructed to a (finite) ground list by the append(First_seq,T,L) subgoal, the compress(T,CL_rem) call can thus use the second clause only a finite number of times. Strong termination of the other procedures then ensures the strong termination of any call to the compress procedure.

Summing up, the procedure is of the form

    suspend compress(?,*).
    compress([],[]).
    compress([H_L|T_L],[C,Lg|CL_rem]) ←
        sequence(C,Lg,First_seq?), compress(T?,CL_rem),
        append(First_seq,T,[H_L|T_L]), not(first(C?,CL_rem?)).

It can be further simplified by using Transformations 9.20 and 9.22 :

    suspend compress(!,*).
    compress([],[]).
    compress([H_L|T_L],[C,Lg|CL_rem]) ←
        sequence(C,Lg,First_seq?), compress(T,CL_rem),
        append(First_seq,T,[H_L?|T_L?]), not(first(C?,CL_rem?)).   (CP$_2$)

D. Comparison

The procedures CP$_1$ and CP$_2$ are worth comparing both from the efficiency and methodological points of view.

As far as efficiency is concerned, it is worth recalling that the procedures have been built with the first parameter L input. We can then compare them by considering this parameter as ground. For such calls, CP$_1$ behaves better than CP$_2$. This is easily confirmed by examining the reduction of such calls. On the one hand, using CP$_1$, the call is reduced by linearly inspecting L. On the other hand, using CP$_2$, the call is reduced by first partitioning L in all possible sublists First_seq and T, by recursively applying the process to T and by concurrently testing whether First_seq is a maximal subsequence. This is quite expensive !

From a methodological point of view, the construction of CP$_1$ is less tricky than that of CP$_2$. The form of the parameter in the clause head results naturally from the logic description. In contrast, some trick in CP$_2$ has to be employed to ensure strong termination.

To conclude, it is worth recalling that CP$_1$ has been obtained by reasoning on the input parameter whereas CP$_2$ has ben obtained by reasoning on the other one. The compress procedure thus suggests that, more efficient and easier procedures to construct are obtained by using the input argument as induction parameter. This conclusion may be generalized and taken as a good heuristic to find good concurrent logic procedures.

10.4.1.4 The sort procedure

Our final example deals with the sort procedure. It has already been partially treated in illustration of Chapter 9. It is now completely tackled. Four concurrent procedures are subsequently constructed and compared.

A. Auxiliary concepts

For ease of discussion, let us first introduce some auxiliary concepts.

1) Let L1=[a_1,...,a_m] and L2=[b_1,...,b_n] be two lists. Then, L1 is a permutation of L2 iff the multi-set {a_1,...,a_m} and {b_1,...,b_n} are identical. In particular, in this case, m and n are equal.

2) Let L=[e_1,...,en] be a list of integers. Then L is ordered iff, for any i, j∈ {1,...,m}, one has e_i≤e_j if i≤j.

B. Auxiliary procedures

Four auxiliary procedures will be used in the construction of the sort procedures. Two of them arise from a rough way of sorting a list : generate all permutations and take the ordered one. One procedure is associated with each task. They are specified as follows.

procedure perm(L,L_rem).
- Type
    L, L_perm : lists; strong use of the type and any subtype
- Relation
    L_perm is L where the elements are possibly permutated
- Operational properties
    1) Suspension condition
        L input
    2) Postconditions
        <ground,any> : <ground,ground>; <0-n!>
            where n is the length of L
        L input ∧ L incrementally constructed ground : L_perm incrementally constructed ground.

procedure ordered(L).
- Type
    L : list of integers
- Relation
    L is ordered
- Operational properties
    1) Suspension condition
        L input
    2) Postcondition
        L input : ordered(L) succeeds only when L has been constructed to a ground list.

Another procedure arises from a more clever sorting strategy : partition the list into two sublists, sort them and combine the sorted sublists. To ease the last step, the partitioning is chosen such that any element of one sublist is less than equal to any element of the other sublist. The following partition procedure results.

procedure partition(X,L,S,G).
- Type
    X : integer,
    L, S, G : list of integers; strong use

- Relation

    The lists S and G partition L in the elements that are less or equal to X and the elements that are strictly greater than X. Those elements are listed in S and G according to the order in which they appear in L.

- Operational properties

    1) Suspension conditions

        X ground and L input

    2) Postconditions :

        <ground,ground,any,any> : <ground,ground,ground,ground>; <0-1>
        X ground & L input & L incrementally constructed ground : S and G incrementally constructed ground.

The final auxiliary procedure issues from a third sorting strategy : extract one element from the list to sort, sort the remainder of the list and insert the element in the sorted list at its right place. The place procedure deals with the last task. It is defined by the following specification.

procedure place(X,L1,L2).

- Type

    X : integer

    L1, L2 : list of integers; strong use

- Relation

    L2 is ordered and contains X and the elements of L1.

- Operational properties

    1) Suspension condition

        X ground and L1 is input

    2) Precondition

        L1 is ordered

    3) Postconditions

        <ground,ground,any> : <ground,ground,ground>; <0-1>
        X ground & L1 input & L1 incrementally constructed ground : L2 incrementally constructed ground.

C. The sort procedures

C.1 Specification

Roughly speaking, the sort procedure consists in sorting one input list. This is made more precise by the following specification.

procedure sort(L,L_sorted).

- Type

    L, L_sorted : lists of integers; strong use

- Relation
    L_sorted is an ordered permutation of L
- Operational properties
    1) Suspension condition
        L is input
    2) Postconditions
        <ground,any> : <ground,ground>; <0-1>
        L input & L incrementally constructed ground : L_sorted incrementally constructed ground.

C.2 Logic description

In general, several logic definitions can be constructed according to the choice of the induction parameter, the well-founded relation and the decomposition of the problem into subproblems. Four versions are pointed out here. The compress procedure has illustrated the impact of the first choice. We here illustrate the influence of the decomposition of the problem into subproblems. The same input parameter L is taken as induction parameter.

C.2.1 LOGIC DESCRIPTION BASED ON DIRECT DECOMPOSITION

A first logic definition can be obtained directly from the relation specification : L_sorted is a permutation of L that is ordered. Hence, the following equivalence. It is manifestly correct.

sort(L,L_sorted) ⇔ perm(L,L_sorted), ordered(L_sorted).   (LD_1)

C.2.2 LOGIC DESCRIPTIONS BASED ON INDUCTIVE REASONING

Another strategy to discover a logic definition is to reason inductively on the structure of the input argument L. The most natural well-founded relation to take is the $<_{list}$ one. Two C_i's are thus pointed out :

C_1 : L=[]
C_2 : L=[H|T]

The formula F_1 to associate with C_1 is quite obvious : L_sorted=[]. In contrast, F_2 is not so immediate. There is at least two possible solutions to find it. The most apparent one is to sort T recursively and to insert H at its right place. F_2 is thus

sort(T,T_sorted) ∧ place(H,T_sorted,L_sorted).

Another possibility is to partition T into two sublists, say S and G, to sort them and to append the resulting sorted sublists while inserting H between them. The following F_2 results :

partition(H,T,S,G) ∧ sort(S,S_sorted) ∧ sort(G,G_sorted)
∧ append(S_sorted,[H|G_sorted],L_sorted).

Hence, the two following logic definitions :

sort(L,L_sorted) ⇔
 L=[] ∧ L_sorted=[]
 ∨
 L=[H|T] ∧ sort(T,T_sorted) ∧ place(H,T_sorted,L_sorted).   (LD$_2$)

sort(L,L_sorted) ⇔
 L=[] ∧ L_sorted=[]
 ∨
 L=[H|T] ∧ partition(H,T,S,G) ∧ sort(S,S_sorted) ∧ sort(G,G_sorted)
  ∧ append(S_sorted,[H|G_sorted],L_sorted).   (LD$_3$)

The following logic property can be stated for the former :

For all L, H, T :
 L=[H|T] ∧ sort(T,T_sorted) →$_{\{H,T\_sorted\}}$ place(H,T_sorted,L_sorted). (LP$_1$)

The following logic properties can be stated for the latter :

For all L, H, T :
 L=[H|T] ∧ partition(H,T,S,G) →$_{\{S,G\}}$
  sort(S,S_sorted) ∧ sort(G,G_sorted)
  ∧ append(S_sorted,[H|G_sorted],L_sorted).   (LP$_2$)

For all S, G :
 sort(S,S_sorted) ∧ sort(G,G_sorted) →$_{\{S\_sorted,G\_sorted\}}$
  append(S_sorted,[H|G_sorted],L_sorted).   (LP$_3$)

All of them result from the dataflow induced by taking L as input.

C.2.3 LOGIC DESCRIPTION BASED ON GENERALIZATION

The last definition contains an append call. It results that the local lists S_sorted and G_sorted are manipulated twice : in the sort call and in the append call. As for the reverse procedure, this append call can be removed by a generalization technique ([Burstall and Darlington, 1977], [Deville, 1990]). To this end, the [H|G_sorted] is generalized to an Arg parameter and a new literal is introduced for the s-goals sharing the local list S_sorted. It takes the other variables as parameters. It is called sort_gen. The following definition results :

 sort_gen(S,L_sorted,Arg) ⇔ sort(S,S_sorted) ∧ append(S_sorted,Arg,L_sorted).   (1)

It is also a generalization of the sort procedure. By taking [] as Arg parameter, one has

 sort_gen(S,L_sorted,[]) ⇔ sort(S,S_sorted) ∧ append(S_sorted,[],L_sorted)

and thus, thanks to the neutral property of [] for append,

 sort_gen(S,L_sorted,[]) ⇔ sort(S,L_sorted).

A logic definition for sort_gen can be derived from that of sort as follows. By unfolding the logic definition for sort with (1), one gets

sort_gen(S,L_sorted,Arg) ⇔
   [S=[] ∧ S_sorted=[]
      ∨
      S=[H|T] ∧ partition(H,T,Sa,Ga) ∧ sort(Sa,Sa_sorted) ∧ sort(Ga,Ga_sorted)
        ∧ append(Sa_sorted,[H|Ga_sorted],S_sorted)   ]
   ∧
   append(S_sorted,Arg,L_sorted)

i.e., by distributing ∧ over ∨,

sort_gen(S,L_sorted,Arg) ⇔
   S=[] ∧ S_sorted=[] ∧ append(S_sorted,Arg,L_sorted)
   ∨
   S=[H|T] ∧ partition(H,T,Sa,Ga) ∧ sort(Sa,Sa_sorted) ∧ sort(Ga,Ga_sorted)
      ∧ append(Sa_sorted,[H|Ga_sorted],S_sorted)
      ∧ append(S_sorted,Arg,L_sorted)

Then it results from the properties of = and of append :

sort_gen(S,L_sorted,Arg) ⇔
   S=[] ∧ Arg=L_sorted ∧ list(L_sorted)
   ∨
   S=[H|T] ∧ partition(H,T,Sa,Ga) ∧ sort(Sa,Sa_sorted) ∧ sort(Ga,Ga_sorted)
      ∧ append(Sa_sorted,[H|L_aux],L_sorted) ∧ append(Ga_sorted,Arg,L_aux)
      ∧ append(S_sorted,Arg,L_sorted)

Folding twice with (1), one then gets

sort_gen(S,L_sorted,Arg) ⇔
   S=[] ∧ Arg=L_sorted ∧ list(L_sorted)
   ∨
   S=[H|T] ∧ partition(H,T,Sa,Ga)
      ∧ sort_gen(Sa,L_sorted,[H|L_aux])
      ∧ sort_gen(Ga,L_aux,Arg).

i.e. by renaming the variables to more significant names,

sort_gen(L,L_sorted,Arg) ⇔
   L=[] ∧ Arg=L_sorted ∧ list(L_sorted)
   ∨
   L=[H|T] ∧ partition(H,T,S,G)
      ∧ sort_gen(S,L_sorted,[H|G_sorted]) ∧ sort_gen(G,G_sorted,Arg).

Summing up, the following logic definition has been pointed out for sort :

sort(S,L_sorted) ⇔ sort_gen(S,L_sorted,[]).

sort_gen(L,L_sorted,Arg) ⇔
    L=[] ∧ Arg=L_sorted ∧ list(L_sorted)
    ∨
    L=[H|T] ∧ partition(H,T,S,G)
        ∧ sort_gen(S,L_sorted,[H|G_sorted]) ∧ sort_gen(G,G_sorted,Arg).   (LD$_4$)

It corresponds to the well-known quicksort procedure using difference lists. The following logic property can be stated for it :

For all H, T : partition(H,T,S,G) →$_{\{S,G\}}$
    sort_gen(S,L_sorted,[H|G_sorted]) ∧ sort_gen(G,G_sorted,Arg).   (LP$_4$)

Intuitively speaking, it states that, for any H, T, the lists S, G such that

    partition(H,T,S,G) ∧ sort_gen(S,L_sorted,[H|G_sorted]) ∧ sort_gen(G,G_sorted,Arg)

are produced by the reduction of partition(H,T,S,G).

C.3 Concurrent logic procedure

Let us now derive the concurrent logic procedures from the logic procedures. To avoid ambiguity, each resulting sort procedure has been renamed to a typical name : nsort (for naive sort), psort (for place sort), qsort (for quicksort), qsort_dl (for quicksort with difference list).

C.3.1 THE nsort PROCEDURE

The nsort procedure is obtained by applying the derivation process of Section 9.4.3.1.2 to the logic definition LD$_1$.

    nsort(L,L_sorted) ← perm(L,L_sorted), ordered(L_sorted).

It is called naive sort because it consists in generating all permutations of L and of testing them for orderness. Let us try to prove that it is correct. The following points need to be verified for this purpose.

1. *Call verification*. Two calls are involved in the procedure : perm(L,L_sorted), ordered(L_sorted). Furthermore, no ns-goal and no environment property are involved. Thus, type precondition of the calls needs just to be verified. This is clearly achieved since, for any call to sort, the L and L_sorted parameters are lists of integers.

2. *Types*. Strong use of the type is obtained thanks to the strong use of types declared for the perm and ordered procedure.

3. *Redundancy*. Let L be ground. Let n be its length. Assume L_sorted can be instantiated to a permuted ordered version of L. The answer n-substitutions computed

for any call sort(L,L_sorted) arise by n-reconciling the n-substitutions computed by the subgoals perm(L,L_sorted) and ordered(L_sorted). To prove their non redundancy character, the following points are worth noting :
1) On the one hand, thanks to the correctness of the perm procedure, n! answer n-substitutions are computed by the perm(L,L_sorted) subgoal. Furthermore, they are not redundant. Only one of them thus contains the ordered L_sorted list.
2) On the other hand, the ordered procedure just acts as a test (see its specification). It consumes the lists constructed by perm(L,L_sorted) for L_sorted and returns, as computed answer n-substitutions, the ordered lists.

Summing up, only one of the n-substitutions computed by the perm(L,L_sorted) will pass the ordered test. Just one n-substitution is thus computed by any call.

Suppose now that L_sorted cannot be instantiated to a permuted ordered version of L. Then, no answer n-substitution is returned by perm(L,L_perm) or the evaluation of the call ordered(L_sorted) fails. In these situations, no n-substitution is computed and non-redundancy is proved.

4. *Operational properties*.
   4.1 The following suspension condition is added to make the suspension condition hold :

   suspend nsort(?,*).

   4.2 No invariant properties are stated and thus need to be verified.
   4.3 The postconditions are achieved as follows :

   i) <ground,any> : <ground,ground>; <0-1>

   The dataflow discussed in point 3 above proves that
   - one answer n-substitution is computed when L is ground and when L_sorted can be instantiated to a sorted version of L.
   - no answer n-substitution is computed when L is ground and when L_sorted cannot be instantiated to a sorted version of L.

   ii) L input ∧ L incrementally constructed ground : L_sorted incrementally constructed ground.

   This is directly ensured by the specification of the perm procedure.

5. *Safety*. Given L ground, the correctness of perm(L,L_sorted) with respect to its specification ensures that no infinite suspension occurs and that the list L_sorted is incrementally constructed ground. As a result, the ordered(L_sorted) call cannot suspend infinitely either.

6. *Strong termination*. Strong termination results from the same scheme of reasoning.

Summing up, the following nsort procedure has been proved correct :

suspend nsort(?,*).
nsort(L,L_sorted) ← perm(L,L_sorted), ordered(L_sorted).

It can be further transformed. Applying Transformation 9.22 first delivers

suspend nsort(!,*).
nsort(L,L_sorted) ← perm(L?,L_sorted), ordered(L_sorted).

The suspension declaration can be removed by Transformation 9.24. Then, thanks to the suspension condition of the perm and ordered procedures, Transformation 9.20 can be applied. The following procedure results.

nsort(L,L_sorted) ← perm(L,L_sorted), ordered(L_sorted).

C.3.2 THE psort PROCEDURE

The psort procedure is obtained by applying the derivation process of Section 9.4.3.1.2 to the logic definition LD_2.

psort(L,L_sorted) ← L=[], L_sorted=[].
psort(L,L_sorted) ← L=[H|T], psort(T,T_sorted), place(H,T_sorted,L_sorted).

Let us try to prove that it is correct. The following points need to be verified.

1. *Call verification.* The procedure contains no ns-goal and no environment condition is stated for the procedures called in it. Type preconditions need thus just to be verified. As the parameters T, T_sorted, H, T_sorted are local variables, <T,T_sorted> verifies the type preconditions of psort and <H,T_sorted,L_sorted> verifies the type preconditions of place.

2. *Types.* Bindings may only be produced by the unification L=[H|T] and the place call. Strong use of the types then results from the specification of the place procedure and from the fact that unification links types in a coherent way.

3. *Redundancy.* The non-redundancy of the computed answer n-substitutions is ensured by the exclusiveness of the unifications L=[] and L=[H|T].

4. *Operational properties.*
   4.1 The following suspension declaration is added to make the suspension condition hold :
      suspend psort(?,*).
   4.2 No invariant property is required and thus needs to be verified.
   4.3 The postconditions are proved as follows.
      i) <ground,any> : <ground,ground>; <0-1>
         For any ground L, the relation specification specifies that there is at least one L_sorted such that <L,L_sorted>∈ *sort* . This L_sorted is furthermore ground. Thanks to the above points, the procedure is g-

sound and g-complete. When there is such a L_sorted, at least one n-substitution is thus returned to cover this solution. Thanks to the non redundancy criteria (point 3 above), there is only one. Moreover, it bounds L_sorted to a ground term.

ii) L input and L incrementally constructed ground : L_sorted incrementally constructed ground.

The fact that L is eventually bound to a ground list allows us to reason inductively. If L is bound to the empty list then the thesis is obvious. Otherwise, assume the thesis holds for any L list of length strictly less than n. Let us show that it holds for a list L of length n. Indeed, thanks to the L=[H|T] unification, T is then bound incrementally to a list of integers of length strictly less than n. By the recursive hypothesis and since T is input by the sort specification, T_sorted is then incrementally constructed ground. Then, thanks to the specification of the place procedure and since H is constructed ground by the unification L=[H|T], the list L_sorted is incrementally constructed ground.

5. *Safety.* Safety results from the same dataflow reasoning.

6. *Weak termination.* Assume L is incrementally constructed to a ground list. There are two possible sources of non-termination : psort(T,T_sorted) and place(H,T,L_sorted).
   - The first call can engender an infinite subtree only by using the second clause an infinite number of times. However, at each use, the list L is required to have an additional element (thanks to the L=[H|T] unification). Infinitely using the clause thus requires that T is of infinite length which is not possible since L is instantiated to a ground list by hypothesis and T is linked with L by the L=[H|T] call.
   - The place(H,T,L_sorted) can also only engender a finite subtree provided reconciliation is provoked. Thanks to the first postcondition property of sort, all solutions for T_sorted are ground. Furthermore L=[H|T] instantiates H to a ground value. Hence, thanks to the specification of place, the place(H,T,L_sorted) call can engender a finite subtree when reconciliation is provoked.

7. *Strong termination.* Even if the suspension conditions impose the dataflow described in point 4.3.ii, strong termination does not occur. Indeed, if reconciliation is not provoked, the psort(T,T_sorted) call can use the second clause an infinite number of times. The form of the head parameter is indeed not sufficient to make qsort(T,T_sorted) suspend until T is constructed. This is achieved by applying Transformation 9.18. As a result, the L head parameter is replaced by [H|T].

Summing up, the following procedure results.

```
suspend psort(?,*).
psort([],[]).
psort([H|T],L_sorted) ← psort(T,T_sorted), place(H,T_sorted,L_sorted).
```

It may be simplified by applying Transformations 9.22 and 9.21 successively. The following procedure results :

```
suspend psort(!,*).
psort([],[]).
psort([H|T],L_sorted) ← psort(T,T_sorted), place(H,T_sorted,L_sorted).
```

Note that logic property LP_1 may be applied too. The induced annotation is however redundant with the suspension conditions stated for the procedures.

C.3.3 THE qsort PROCEDURE

The qsort procedure is obtained by applying the derivation process of Section 9.4.3.1.2 to the logic definition LD_3.

```
qsort(L,L_sorted) ← L=[], L_sorted=[].
qsort(L,L_sorted) ←
    L=[H|T], partition(H,T,S,G), qsort(S,S_sorted), qsort(G,G_sorted)
    append(S_sorted,[H|G_sorted],L_sorted).
```

Let us try to prove its correctness. The following points need to be verified for this purpose.

1. *Call verification.* The procedure contains no ns-goal. No environment condition is stated for the procedures called in it. Thus type preconditions need just to be verified. Let L and L_sorted be ground lists of integers. Then, as the parameters H, T, S, G, S_sorted, G_sorted are local variables, the following properties hold :
   - <H,T,S,G> verifies the type precondition of partition,
   - <S,S_sorted> and <G,G_sorted> verifies the type precondition of qsort,
   - <S_sorted,[H|G_sorted],L_sorted> verifies the type precondition of append.

2. *Types.* Bindings may only be produced by the unifications and the append call. Strong use of the types then results from the specification of the append procedure and from the fact that the unifications link types in a coherent way.

3. *Redundancy.* The non-redundancy of the computed answer n-substitutions is ensured by the exclusiveness of the unifications L=[] and L=[H|T].

4. *Operational properties.*
   4.1 The following suspension declaration is added to make the suspension condition hold :

suspend qsort(?,*).

4.2 No invariant property is required and thus needs to be verified.

4.3 The postconditions are proved as follows.

i) <ground,any> : <ground,ground>; <0-1>

The justification is similar to that given for the psort procedure.

ii) L input and L incrementally constructed ground : L_sorted incrementally constructed ground.

The fact that L is eventually bound to a ground list allows us to reason inductively. If L is bound to the empty list then the thesis is obvious. Otherwise, assume the thesis holds for any list L of length strictly less than n. Let us show that it holds for a list L of length n. Indeed, thanks to the L=[H|T] unification, H is instantiated to a ground integer and T is bound incrementally to a list of integers of length strictly less than n. Then, thanks to the specification of the partition procedure, S and G are incrementally constructed to a ground list of integers. Their length is less than that of T. They are thus strictly less than n. By the induction hypothesis, S_sorted and G_sorted are then incrementally constructed to a ground list of integers. The specification of the append procedure then allows to conclude that L_sorted is incrementally constructed to a ground list of integers.

5. *Safety*. Safety results from the same dataflow reasoning.

6. *Weak termination*. Weak termination is established using this dataflow too. Let qsort(L,L_sorted) be some call with L being incrementally constructed to a ground list of integers. There are four possible sources of non-termination : partition(H,T,S,G), qsort(S,S_sorted), qsort(G,G_sorted) and append(S_sorted,[H|G_sorted],L_sorted). Let us reason inductively on the length of L. If L is empty then the thesis is obviously proved. Otherwise, the specification of partition ensures that the subtree engendered by partition(H,T,S,G) is finite even if reconciliation is not provoked. The lists S and G are furthermore incrementally constructed to ground lists of integers. Then, by the inductive hypothesis, the subtrees engendered by qsort(S,S_sorted) and qsort(G,G_sorted) are finite. There is thus a limited number of S_sorted lists and [H|G_sorted] lists in the subtree engendered by the qsort(L,L_sorted) call. It follows, thanks to the specification of append that, when reconciliation is provoked, the and/or/not search tree is finite.

7. *Stong termination*. Strong termination is not ensured by the procedure as it results from the above points. There are two reasons for this.

- First, the head parameter of the second clause and the suspension declaration are not sufficient to prevent the qsort(S,S_sorted) and qsort(G,G_sorted) from using the second clause of the qsort procedure an infinite number of times.

- Second, as it is stated, the append(S_sorted,[H|G_sorted],L_sorted) call engenders an infinite subtree too.

To obtain strong correctness, the procedure must thus be transformed. Let us first use the logic properties. Applying Transformation 9.1 to logic properties LP_2 and LP_3 leads to

```
suspend qsort(?,*).
qsort(L,L_sorted) ← L=[], L_sorted=[].
qsort(L,L_sorted) ←
       L=[H|T], partition(H,T,S,G), qsort(S?,S_sorted), qsort(G?,G_sorted)
       append(S_sorted?,[H|G_sorted?],L_sorted).
```

Then, by applying Transformation 9.18, one gets

```
suspend qsort(?,*).
qsort([],[]).
qsort([H|T],L_sorted) ←
       partition(H,T,S,G), qsort(S?,S_sorted), qsort(G?,G_sorted)
       append(S_sorted?,[H|G_sorted?],L_sorted).
```

This procedure does not suffer from the two above problems.
- On the one hand, the form of the first parameter forces some call to qsort to employ the second clause only when its first parameter is instantiated to some instance of [] or [H|T]. Given a first parameter L ground and the dataflow described above, the second clause can thus be employed a finite number of times by qsort(S?,S_sorted) and qsort(G?,G_sorted).
- On the other hand, as S_sorted is declared as input for the append call and since it is incrementally constructed by the qsort(S?, S_sorted), the specification of append ensures that the subtree engendered by append(S_sorted,[H|G_sorted],L_sorted) is finite.

Finally, the procedure can be simplified. Transformation 9.22 produces the following code

```
suspend qsort(!,*).
qsort([],[]).
qsort([H|T],L_sorted) ←
       partition(H?,T?,S,G), qsort(S?,S_sorted), qsort(G?,G_sorted)
       append(S_sorted?,[H?|G_sorted?],L_sorted).
```

Then thanks to the suspension required in the specification, most read-only annotations can be removed. Transformation 9.20 is applied for this purpose. It delivers the final qsort procedure :

```
suspend qsort(!,*).
qsort([],[]).
qsort([H|T],L_sorted) ←
    partition(H,T,S,G), qsort(S,S_sorted), qsort(G,G_sorted)
    append(S_sorted?,[H?|G_sorted?],L_sorted).
```

C.3.4 THE qsort_dl PROCEDURE

The qsort_dl procedure results from the logic definition LD_4. Applying the derivation process of Section 9.4.3.1.2 delivers the following procedure.

```
qsort_dl(L,L_sorted) ← sort_gen(L,L_sorted,[]).

sort_gen(L,L_sorted,Arg) ← L=[], Arg=L_sorted, list(L_sorted).
sort_gen(L,L_sorted,Arg) ←
    L=[H|T], partition(H,T,S,G),
    sort_gen(S,L_sorted,[H|G_sorted]), sort_gen(G,G_sorted,Arg).
```

Let us try to prove that it is correct.

1. *Call verification.* Call verification is immediate. No ns-goals are involved in the procedure and no environment properties are required for the calls of the procedure. Furthermore, the only call constrained by type preconditions is the partition(H,T,S,G) one. The fulfillment of these preconditions is obvious since H, T, S and G are local variables.

2. *Types.* Strong property of the type is also immediate. In particular, the list L_sorted is always bound to a list. The list(L_sorted) s-goal can thus be removed.

3. *Redundancy.* The mutual exclusion of the L=[] and L=[H|T] unifications ensures the non redundancy of the computed answer n-substitutions.

4. *Operational properties.*
    4.1 The following suspension declaration is added to make the suspension condition hold:
        suspend qsort_dl(?,*).
    4.2 No invariant property is stated and thus needs to be verified.
    4.3 The postconditions properties are verified as follows.
        i) <ground,any> : <ground,ground>; <0-1>
            If L is ground then sort_gen is called with its first and third argument ground. To prove the thesis, let us prove that whenever gen_sort is called with these parameters ground it returns, when any, a ground value for its second parameter L_sorted. To this end, let us reason in an inductive way.
            1° The thesis is obvious if L is [].

2° Assume then the thesis holds when L is of length strictly less than n. Let us prove that it holds when it is of length n. In this case, the partition(H,T,S,G) s-goal engenders a ground value for the S and G lists. By definition of the relation *partition*, the S and G lists are of length less than T i.e., thanks to the L=[H|T] unification, of length strictly less than n. The recursive hypothesis can then be applied. It follows that the sort_gen(G,G_sorted,Arg) call engenders a ground value for G_sorted. As a result, the induction hypothesis can be applied once again and the sort_gen(S,L_sorted,[H|G_sorted]) call returns, when any, a ground value for L_sorted. Summing up a ground value is thus returned for L_sorted.

This establishes the <ground,any> : <ground,ground> part of the specification. The min and max numbers result from the g-soundness, the g-completeness (obtained by the above points) and non redundancy character of the computed answer n-substitutions (obtained in point 3).

ii) L input and L incrementally constructed ground : L_sorted incrementally constructed ground.

This property is proved by proving that for any lists L and Arg input and incrementally constructed, the list L_sorted is incrementally constructed. This is achieved by an inductive reasoning on the length of L. If it is nul i.e. if L is constructed to [], then the thesis is obvious. Otherwise, assume it holds for any L of length strictly less than n and let us prove that it holds for any list L of length n. To this end, let us first note that, thanks to the partition specification, the s-goal partition(H,T,S,G) incrementally constructs the lists S and G. These lists are furthermore of length strictly less than L. To use the inductive hypothesis, let us annotate the recursive calls. Using logic property LP_4, their S and G parameters are globally read-only annotated. Then, a read-only annotation is placed to the Arg parameter of the last recursive calls. The hypothesis can then be used and it results that G_sorted is incrementally constructed to a ground list. Then, annotating the G_sorted and H term by a read-only annotation, the hypothesis can be used once more for the sort_gen(S,L_sorted,[H|G_sorted]) call. It results that the list L_sorted is indeed incrementally constructed to a ground list.

5. *Safety*. Safety results from the same inductive reasoning.
6. *Weak termination*. Weak termination is established by the same inductive reasoning.

7. *Strong termination.* Strong termination is not ensured because of the lack of instantiation of the head parameter of the clauses. This is circumvented by applying Transformation 9.18.

Summing up, to be correct, the qsort_dl procedure is presented in the following form :

suspend qsort_dl(L?,*).
qsort_dl(L,L_sorted) ← sort_gen(L,L_sorted,[]).

sort_gen([],L_sorted,L_sorted).
sort_gen([H|T],L_sorted,Arg) ←
    partition(H,T,S,G),
    sort_gen(S?,L_sorted,[H?|G_sorted?]), sort_gen(G?,G_sorted,Arg?).

Using Transformation 9.22, the qsort_dl definition may be modified as follows :

suspend qsort_dl(L!,*).
qsort_dl(L,L_sorted) ← sort_gen(L?,L_sorted,[]).

The first parameter of any sort_gen call is thus globally read-only annotated. The last one can be also considered as globally annotated. As sort_gen is private to the qsort_dl procedure, the first and third argument may be required to be input. A suspension declaration may thus be added. The following procedure follows.

suspend sort_gen(?,*,?).
sort_gen([],L_sorted,L_sorted).
sort_gen([H|T],L_sorted,Arg) ←
    partition(H,T,S,G),
    sort_gen(S?,L_sorted,[H?|G_sorted?]), sort_gen(G?,G_sorted,Arg?).

Transformation 9.21 allows to remove the global read-only annotation of the call

sort_gen(L?,L_sorted,[]).

Then successive applications of Transformations 9.22 and 9.21 deliver the following procedure:

suspend qsort_dl(L!,*).
qsort_dl(L,L_sorted) ← sort_gen(L,L_sorted,[]).

suspend sort_gen(!,*,!).
sort_gen([],L_sorted,L_sorted).
sort_gen([H|T],L_sorted,Arg) ←
    partition(H,T,S,G),
    sort_gen(S,L_sorted,[H|G_sorted]), sort_gen(G,G_sorted,Arg).

Finally, the first suspension declaration may be removed thanks to Transformation 9.24. The final version of the quick sort coded with difference list results. It is more generally presented by denoting the L_sorted and Arg parameters of the sort_gen procedure as a unique parameter presented in the difference list notation L_sorted-Arg. This motivates our appellation "quick sort with difference list".

D. Comparison

This section has illustrated the impact of the decomposition strategy. Four procedures have been pointed out. Let us analyze them from the efficiency standpoint. The first parameter L is input. The discussion may thus be limited to the case where L is ground.

The qsort_dl procedure has the best behavior. Using it, the list L is analyzed first linearly by the partition s-goal. Each produced sublist is then re-analyzed by the recursive qsort_dl s-goals. Assuming a fair distribution of the elements in the list to sort, an algorithm of complexity $n \log_2 n$ thus results. The "n" symbol there denotes the length of the list. Furthermore, one interest of the algorithm is that it embodies a great source of parallelism : the sublists resulting from the partition call can be treated in a completely independent way and therefore concurrently.

The behavior of the qsort procedure is similar but the sorted sublists are combined in a less efficient way. An append call is used for this purpose. It involves a re-analysis of one sorted sublist, namely S_sorted. An algorithm of complexity $(3n/2) \log_2 n$ results.

The psort procedure is still less efficient. It involves less potential for parallelism. The only potential one arises from an incremental consumption of the list T_sorted by the place call. Furthermore, this place call implies a re-analysis of the sorted list. Assuming the same fair distribution of the elements, an algorithm of complexity n^2 results.

Finally, the nsort procedure is the less efficient one. It behaves as follows. All permutations of the list to sort are generated and then tested for orderness. An algorithm of complexity $n!$ results. A suitable choice of the R-depth parameter may however decrease this computation effort. In fact, a better performance is obtained by pruning as early as possible the permutations in view of their prefix. The best computation is then obtained by coroutining the reduction of the perm(L,L_sorted) s-goal, generating the permutations, and the reduction of the ordered(L_sorted) s-goal, testing for ordereness. This is achieved by fixing the R-depth parameter to 1.

It is worth noting that, from a methodological point of view, the nsort procedure was the easiest one to construct. In fact, all implementation problems have been reported in the construction of the auxiliary procedures perm and ordered. At the opposite, the qsort_dl procedure has required the most elaborated construction. In this case, the gain of performance is thus compensated by a loss of ease of construction.

10.4.2 Evaluation

As a conclusion of this section, four points result from the construction of the procedures.

1° Comparing the construction process of the multi-directional procedures of Section 10.3 with that of the single directed procedures of this section, an obvious conclusion is that the latter is more complex than the former. This results from two factors. First, the relations manipulated in this section are intrisically more complex that those of Section 10.3. This has allowed to construct several procedures for a same specification. Second, operational properties have been managed here. An interest of Conclog is that the operational behavior can be almost abstracted when logical aspects are just tackled. This is, of course, no more true when operational properties describing the operational behavior are treated. Furthermore, handling such a behavior requires to handle the same properties for the auxiliary procedures used in a procedure. As an example, the multi-directional procedure append constructed in Section 10.3 had to be further characterized.

2° Logic properties have revealed to have two possible uses. On the one hand, they have been used as hints to obtain correctness properties even the partial one (see for instance, Point 1.4.3.ii of Subsection 10.4.1.2.C). On the other hand, they have been used to apply transformations while preserving correctness (see for instance, the same Subsection 10.4.1.2.C).

3° The three step construction of the procedures may appear to be quite tiresome. Nevertheless, it has the merits of separating the three aspects of the construction of any procedure : the specification, the conceptual characterization of the algorithm underlying the procedure (achieved by the logic description) and the real coding of the algorithm (achieved by the concurrent logic procedures). The two following points are moreover worth noting.

At the logic description level, several design decisions have been analyzed. Some logic description have furthermore been derived from other ones. Several procedures have resulted from all these logic descriptions. Some of them are generally considered to embody advanced programming. It is not clear at all that such procedures could be obtained by directly manipulating the procedure codes.

At the logic procedure level, proving correctness has forced us to identify several problems of the derived procedures in a systematic way. At this level too, we do not believe that, by directly coding the procedures, all problems to solve would have effectively been handled.

4° As a final conclusion, the examples of this section have established that Conclog is also well suited for handling directed list procedures. Procedures resulting either from a declarative description of the computed relation (as the nsort procedure) or from an elaborated scheme of reasoning (such as the gen_reverse and qsort_dl procedure) have been programmed using Conclog. Some of them involve the same dataflow and the same suspension mechanisms as the corresponding procedures of the committed-choice languages. For these procedures, the same efficient procedures can then be coded. Moreover, in contrast with those languages, procedures requiring s-goals to produce several solutions, could also be coded (see for instance the second compress procedure and the nsort procedure).

10.5 Handling trees

So far, we only handled lists as data structure. Conclog also supports the manipulation of more complex structures. As an illustration, this section deals with binary tree structures.

Binary trees are recursively defined as follows. The empty tree is denoted by the constant void. Non-empty trees are represented by the ternary structure tree(Element,Left,Right) where Element is the element at the root, Left and Right are the left and right subtrees, respectively. Element can itself be of a complex structure. For instance, it is usual to give it the structure element(Key,Information) - or el(Key,Info) for short - in order to manipulate the tree as a dictionary.

An interest of binary trees is that they embody a lot of potential parallelism. The examples of this section should be quite convincing for this purpose. They are presented with the aim of proving that this parallelism can indeed be coded in Conclog. We will thus subsequently focus on operational aspects and pass under silence the three step construction of the procedures. Nevertheless, in view of the previous sections, those are quite straightforward so that the comprehension of the procedures is not deteriorated.

10.5.1 Programming samples

A. Tree membership

Our first example concerns the relation *tree_member*. It determines whether some term is in some tree. The associated procedure is specified as follows.

procedure tree_member(El,Tree).
- Type
    El : element,
    Tree : binary trees
- Relation
    El is an element of Tree.

It is implemented by reasoning inductively on the structure of the tree Tree.

tree_member(X,tree(X,Left,Right)).
tree_member(X,tree(Y,Left,Right)) ← X≠Y | tree_member(X,Left).
tree_member(X,tree(Y,Left,Right)) ← X≠Y | tree_member(X,Right).

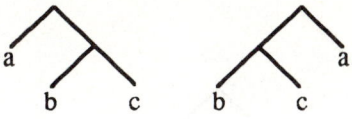

Figure 10.2

Clearly, the search for an element in a tree generally involves the search in the left and right subtrees. Both searches are independent and should be done in parallel. This is embodied as or-parallelism in our code. For any call tree_member(El,Tree), the second and third clauses can be used in paralllel. They examine the left and right subtrees, respectively.

B. Isomorphic trees

The second example provides still more parallelism. It consists of testing two binary trees for isomorphism. Two binary trees are called *isomorphic* if one of them can be obtained from the other by reordering some branches. For instance, the trees of Figure 10.2 are isomorphic.

Precisely, the isomorphism relation can be recursively defined as follows

1) two empty trees are isomorphic;
2) two non-empty trees are isomorphic if they have identical elements at their root and one of the following conditions hold :
   2.1) the left subtrees are isomorphic and the right subtrees are isomorphic
   2.2) the left subtree of one is isomorphic to the right subtree of the other and the two other subtrees are isomorphic.

The following isotree procedure verifies whether two subtrees are isomorphic. It is specified as follows :

procedure isotree(Tree1,Tree2)
- Type
    Tree1, Tree2 : binary trees
- Relation
    Tree1 and Tree2 are isomorphic.

Its implementation results from the above definition and by reasoning on the structure of the trees. It is as follows

```
isotree(void,void).
isotree(tree(X,Left1,Right1),tree(X,Left2,Right2)) ←
    isotree(Left1,Left2),  isotree(Right1,Right2).
isotree(tree(X,Left1,Right1),tree(X,Left2,Right2)) ←
    isotree(Left1,Right2),  isotree(Right1,Left2).
```

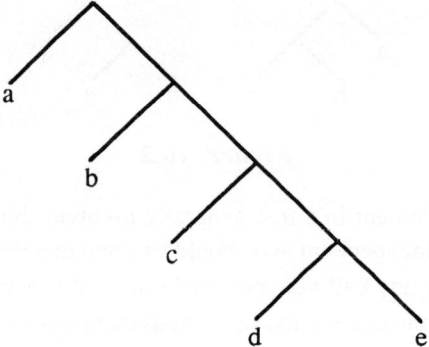

Figure 10.3

Various sources of parallelism can be pointed out from the above definition. They are the parallel verifications of 2.1 and 2.2 and, for each of them, the parallel verifications for isomorphism of the two pairs of subtrees. They are embodied by the isotree procedure. On the one hand, the parallel verifications of 2.1 and 2.2 is implemented as or-parallelism : for any call, the second and third clauses can be used in parallel. On the other hand, the parallel verifications of the isomorphism of the pairs of subtrees is coded by and-parallelism : in each clause the isotree recursive calls can indeed be reduced in parallel.

C. Balanced trees

Trees are usually used for efficient information retrieval. Algorithms of complexity O(n) for list structures are generally improved in algorithms of complexity $O(\log_2 n)$ for tree structures, where n is the number of the involved elements. Compare for instance the efficiency of member(X,List) with tree_member(X,Tree). Nevertheless, to obtain such efficiency, the binary trees must be well-balanced. This avoids bad situations of the form of Figure 10.3 where trees behave as lists.

The well-balanced character is defined as follows. It calls the auxiliary concept of height of a tree.

1) The *height* of a tree is
   - 0 if the tree is empty,
   - 1+max{HL,HR}, otherwise, where HL and HR are the heights of the left and right subtrees of the tree, respectively.
2) A tree is called *well-balanced* if it is empty or if the height of its subtrees at most differ from one unit.

The following height procedure determines the height of a tree. It is specified as follows.

procedure height(Tree,Height)
- Type
    Height : integer,
    Tree : binary tree
- Relation
    Height is the height of the tree Tree
- Suspension condition
    Tree input.

It is implemented by reasoning inductively on the structure of Tree. The following piece of code results :

suspend height(!,*).
height(void,0).
height(tree(E,Left,Right),N) ← height(Left,N1), height(Right,N2), max(N1,N2,N3), N is 1+N3.

The max procedure is used to determine the maximum of two positive numbers. It is specified as follows :

procedure max(N1,N2,Max)
- Type
    N1, N2, Max : positive integers
- Relation
    Max is the maximum of N1 and N2
- Suspension condition
    N1 and N2 ground.

It is implemented as follows.

suspend max(!g,!g,*).
max(N1,N2,N1) ← N1>N2.
max(N1,N2,N2) ← N1≤N2.

The definition of the height of two procedures points out one source of parallelism : the height of a non empty tree may be determined by concurrently determining the length of the left and right subtrees. This is embodied in the height procedure by the concurrent reductions of the two subgoals height(Left,N1) and height(Right,N2).

The well-balanced tree relation is computed by the following well-balanced_tree(T) procedure. This is specified as follows.

procedure well_balanced_tree(Tree).
- Type
    Tree : binary tree

- Relation

    Tree is a well_balanced tree
- Suspension condition

    Tree input.

It is implemented by reasoning inductively on the structure of Tree.

> suspend well_balanced_tree(!).
> well_balanced_tree(void).
> well_balanced_tree(t(X,Left,Right)) ← height(Left,N1), height(Right,N2), one_unit(N1,N2).

The procedure one_unit is used there to determine whether two input numbers differ by one unit. It is specified as follows.

> procedure one_unit(N1,N2).
> - Type
>
>   N1, N2 : integers
> - Relation
>
>   N1 and N2 differ by one unit
> - Suspension condition
>
>   N1 and N2 ground.

It is implemented as follows.

> suspend one_unit(!g,!g).
> one_unit(N1,N2) ← N is abs(N1-N2), N≤1.

Here too, it is worth noting that the well_balanced_tree procedure embodies the concurrent determination of the height of subtrees by means of the concurrent reduction of the height(Left,N1) and height(Right,N2) subgoals.

D. Handling balanced trees

Generally, the efficiency of the search in a binary tree is still improved by incorporating some key information in the element part of the tree and by arranging the tree so that the following property holds : for every non-empty tree, any key in the left subtree is less than the key at the root, itself less than any key in the right subtree. The retrieval of an element thus only requires the examination of one subtree. The counterpart is some extra computation to maintain the tree well-balanced when adding or deleting an element in it. It is easy to see that insertion or deletion can at most disrupt the tree by increasing or decreasing one subtree height by one unit, respectively. Hence four unbalanced tree situations may result. For each of them, we give a transformation to balance the tree and associate a clause translating it. Furthermore, in order to avoid the computation of the height of the trees, we incorporate this information in the tree structure. As a consequence, binary trees are now defined as void or structures of the form tree(El,Height,Left,Right).

In the two first situations, the tree is unbalanced because of its left subtree SL. In the first case, this is due to the left subtree of SL. The whole tree is balanced by switching the two roots and moving the subtree B2 from the right sub-subtree place to the left subtree of the right subtree place. In the second case, unbalancing is due to the right subtree of SL. It contains two subtrees one of which is only of height h-1. This is because the whole tree is assumed to be balanced before each operation. The transformation does not care which one is of height h-1. It consists in splitting the right subtree, conserving its left part in the left subtree and moving its right part to the right subtree. The two last situations deal with the symmetric situations.

The four situations and transformations are depicted in Figure 10.4. The corresponding clauses are as follows.

1st situation

```
balance_tree(  tree( A,  H_3,  tree(B,H_2,B1,B2), A2),
               tree( B,  H_2,  B1, tree(A,H_1,B2,A2) ) ←
                   height(B1,H_1), height(B2,H), height(A2,H),
                   H_1 is H+1, H_2 is H+2, H_3 is H+3.
```

2nd situation

```
balance_tree(  tree( A,  H_3,  tree(B,H_2,B1,tree(C,H_1,C1,C2)), A2),
               tree( C,  H_2,  tree(B,H_1,B1,C1), tree(A,H_1,C2,A2) ) ←
                   height(B1,H), height(A2,H)
                   H_1 is H+1, H_2 is H+2, H_3 is H+3.
```

3rd situation

```
balance_tree(  tree( A,  H_3,  A1, tree(B,H_2,tree(C,H_1,C1,C2),B2)),
               tree( C,  H_2,  tree(A,H_1,A1,C1), tree(B,H_1,C2,B2) ) ←
                   height(A1,H), height(B2,H)
                   H_1 is H+1, H_2 is H+2, H_3 is H+3.
```

4th situation

```
balance_tree(  tree( A,  H_3,  A1, tree(B,H_2,B1,B2)),
               tree( B,  H_2,  tree(A,H_1,A1,B1), B2) ) ←
                   height(A1,H), height(B1,H), height(B2,H_1),
                   H_1 is H+1, H_2 is H+2, H_3 is H+3.
```

These clauses can be used to define a predicate balance_tree(Tree,Newtree) determining whether Newtree is a balanced version of the tree Tree. In fact, the only case to be added concerns already balanced binary trees which are their balanced versions. This is expressed in the two following clauses

612 PROGRAMMING NON-BEHAVIORAL APPLICATIONS

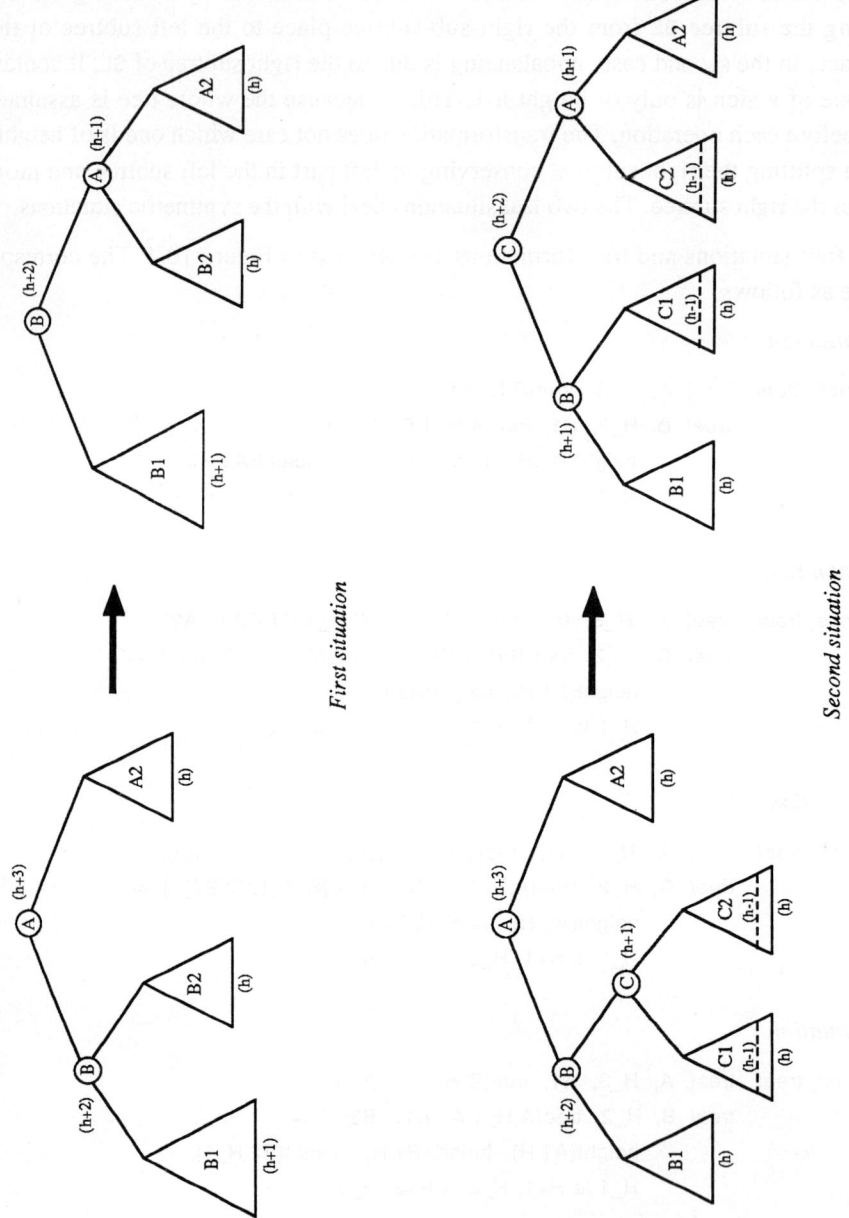

Figure 10.4

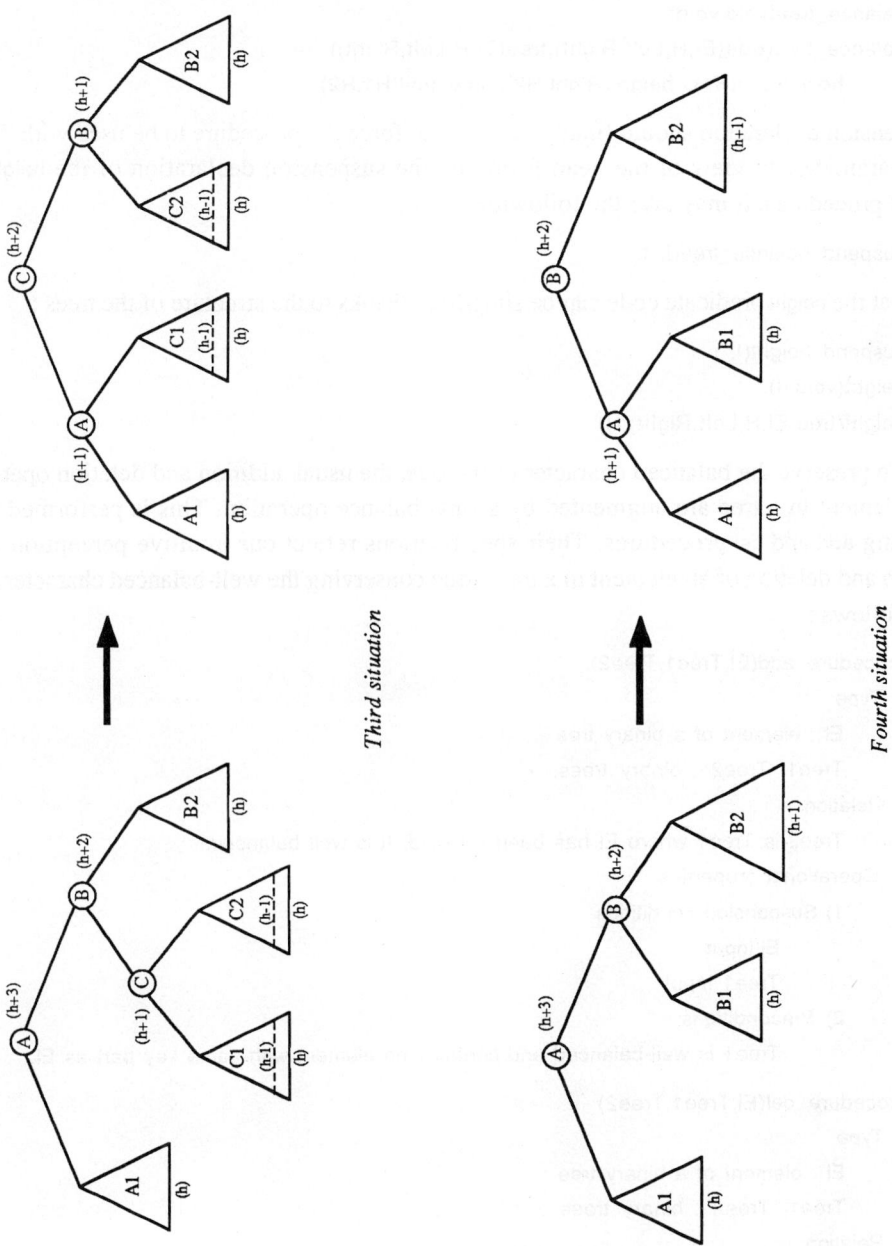

Figure 10.4 continued

balance_tree(void,void).
balance_tree(tree(El,H,Left,Right),tree(El,H,Left,Right)) ←
    height(Left,H1), height(Right,H2), one_unit(H1,H2).

A suspension declaration should finally be added to force the procedure to be used with Tree as input parameter. In view of the head form and the suspension declaration of the height and one_unit procedures, it may take the following form

suspend balance_tree(!,*).

Note that the height predicate code can be simplified thanks to the structure of the trees :

suspend height(!,*).
height(void,0).
height(tree(El,H,Left,Right),H).

To preserve the balanced character of the tree, the usual addition and deletion operations of an element in a tree are augmented by a final balance operation. This is performed in the following add and del procedures. Their specifications reflect our intuitive perception of the addition and deletion of an element in a tree while conserving the well-balanced character. They are as follows :

procedure add(El,Tree1,Tree2).
- Type
    El : element of a binary tree
    Tree1, Tree2 : binary trees
- Relation
    Tree2 is Tree1 where El has been inserted. It is well balanced.
- Operational properties
    1) Suspension conditions
        El input
        Tree1 input
    2) Preconditions
        Tree1 is well-balanced and contains no element with same key part as El.

procedure del(El,Tree1,Tree2).
- Type
    El : element of a binary tree
    Tree1, Tree2 : binary trees
- Relation
    Tree2 is Tree1 where El has been removed. It is well balanced.

- Operational properties
    1) Suspension conditions
        El input
        Tree1 input
    2) Precondition
        Tree1 is well-balanced.

In view of the above well-balanced operations, they can be implemented as follows. Note that the balanced operation is performed once the tree is effectively updated thanks to the suspension declarations of the balance_tree and height procedures.

```
suspend add(?,?,*).
add( el(Key,Info), void, tree(el(Key,Info),1,void,void)).
add( el(Key,Info), tree(el(Key_r,Info_r),H,Left,Right), New_tree) ←
    Key < Key_r |
    add(el(Key,Info),Left,New_Left),
    balance_tree(tree(el(Key_r,Info_r),_,New_left,Right),New_tree).
add( el(Key,Info), tree(el(Key_r,Info_r),H,Left,Right), New_tree) ←
    Key_r < Key |
    add(el(Key,Info),Right,New_Right),
    balance_tree(tree(el(Key_r,Info_r),_,Left,New_Right),New_tree).

suspend del(?,?,*).
del( el(Key,Info), tree(el(Key,Info), 1, void, void), void).
del( el(Key,Info), tree(el(Key,Info),Height,tree(El,H,SL,SR),Right), New_tree) ←
    del(El,tree(El,H,SL,SR),New_Left),
    balance_tree(tree(El,_,New_Left,Right),New_tree).
del( el(Key,Info), tree(el(Key,Info),Height,Left,tree(El,H,SL,SR)), New_tree) ←
    del(El,tree(El,H,SL,SR),New_Right),
    balance_tree(tree(El,_,Left,New_Right),New_tree).
del( el(Key,Info), tree(el(Key_r,Info_r),Height,Left,Right), New_tree) ←
    Key < Key_r |
    del(el(Key,Info),Left,New_Left),
    balance_tree(tree(el(Key_r,Info_r),_,New_Left,Right),New_tree).
del( el(Key,Info), tree(el(Key_r,Info_r),Height,Left,Right), New_tree) ←
    Key_r < Key |
    del(el(Key,Info),Right,New_Right),
    balance_tree(tree(el(Key_r,Info_r),_,Left,New_Right),New_tree).
```

It is worth noting that a similar performance can be obtained at a lower programming price when the existence of arbitrarily many processes can be assumed and when deletion is not concerned. In this case, there is no need to manipulate key information and to maintain the key property. Keeping the tree balanced can be achieved just by inserting the element in the subtree of lower height. The counterpart is that the whole tree must be searched when retrieving the element, not just one subtree. However, as the availability of arbitrarily many processors is assumed, a performance in $O(log_2 n)$ is still maintained.

10.4.2 Evaluation

It is widely recognized that trees embody a great potential of parallelism. This has been illustrated in this section by some typical examples. Conclog has also been proved able to support the coding of this parallelism in a quite natural way. Furthermore, assuming infinite resources, balancing of trees have been argued to be achievable in a simpler way than the usual one thanks to the fully parallel search ability of the language.

Compared with sequential languages such as Prolog, Conclog thus differs by its ability to use the parallelism offered by the tree representation. As far as committed-choice languages are concerned, the commitment to one clause forces to use the guard in a quite strange way : the entire body of the clause must be placed in the guard. Nevertheless, despite this placement, procedures cannot be used in a fully multi-directional way in such languages. For instance, the isotree procedure cannot be used to produce all trees isomorphic to an input tree.

10.6 Generate and test programming

We finally address one very popular style in logic programming : the generate and test style. It consists of generating candidate solutions and testing them for adequacy. Generally, resulting programs are easier to construct than the programs that compute the solution(s) directly. However, they are also less efficient. As a consequence, they are usually transformed to obtain better performances. The classical technique is to insert the tester inside the generator as deeply as possible, thus creating some interleaving between the generator and the tester. This is however not always so easy. Furthermore, transformed programs are generally so complex that they completely lose their declarative reading. An interest of Conclog is to achieve this interleaving between the generator and the tester in a fully transparent manner to the programmer by means of reconciliation. A gain of generated s-goals results too. It is however counterbalanced by an overhead due to reconciliation. This is illustrated in this section on the following classical 4 queens problem.

10.6.1 Programming sample

A. The problem

The 4 queens problem consists of placing 4 queens on a chessboard so that no queen can attack the others i.e. two queens are never on the same horizontal, vertical or diagonal line. In view of the two first restrictions, solutions can be represented by lists of the form [Q1,Q2,Q3,Q4] indicating that the queen number i occupies the position (Qi,i). For instance, the solution depicted in following Figure 10.5 is represented as [2,4,1,3]. The solution to the problem is then easy. It consists of generating the permutations of [1,2,3,4] and of testing, for each of them, that no queen attacks another one.

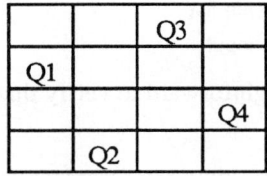

Figure 10.5

B. The program

This solution may be implemented in a quite easy way :

4_queens(Queens) ← perm([1,2,3,4],Queens), safe(Queens). (1)

The perm procedure has been described above. To specify and construct the safe procedure, let us introduce some auxiliary concepts.

1) A list $[e_1,...,e_n]$ is said to be queen-safe iff, for any $i \in \{1,...,n\}$, for any $j \in \{i+1,...,n\}$, one has $e_i - e_j \neq \pm(i-j)$.
2) An integer Q is attackable by the list $[e_1,...,e_n]$ at distance D iff there is some $i \in \{1,...,n\}$ such that $Q - e_i = \pm(D-i+1)$.

The $(e_i - e_j) \neq \pm(i-j)$ disequality expresses that the queens are not on a same diagonal line. The safety qualification thus states that no queen attacks another one. Similarly, the attackable character of a queen Q in a list at some distance D expresses that Q is attacked by one queen of the list when Q is placed at first place and the queens of the list are placed at places D+1, ..., D+n, respectively.

The two following properties are worth noting :

1) A list L is queen-safe iff one of the following conditions holds :
   i) L is empty
   ii) L is not empty, say it is $[e_1,...,e_n]$ (n≠0), and the two following conditions hold:
      ii.1) e_1 is not attackable by $[e_2,...,e_n]$ at distance 1,
      ii.2) $[e_2,...,e_n]$ is queen-safe
2) An integer Q is attackable by $[e_1,...,e_n]$ at distance D iff one of the following conditions holds :

- $Q-e_1=\pm D$
- Q is attackable by $[e_2,...,e_n]$ at distance $D+1$.

Let us now turn back to the safe procedure. It is specified as follows.

procedure safe(Queens).
- Type : Queens : list of integers
- Relation : Queens is a queen-safe list
- Suspension condition : Queens input.

With such a specification, it is straightforward to verify that the clause (1) indeed delivers one solution to the 4 queens problem.

The implementation of the procedure safe(Queens) rests on property 1 above. The test for condition ii.1 needs in fact just to be coded. This is achieved by implementing a procedure testing for attackability by a list at some distance D. The following procedure is provided for this purpose.

procedure attack(Q,L,D).
- Type

    Q, D : integers,

    L : list of integers.
- Relation

    Q is attackable by L at distance D
- Suspension conditions

    Q and D ground, L input.

Given this procedure, the safe procedure can be coded as follows : [1]

suspend safe(!).
safe([]).
safe([Q|Qs]) ← not(attack(Q,Qs,1)), safe(Qs).

The implementation of the attack procedure rests on property 2 above. It is as follows :

suspend attack(Q!g,L!,D!g).
attack(Q1,[Q2|Qs],D) ← Q1 is Q2-D.
attack(Q1,[Q2|Qs],D) ← Q1 is Q2+D.
attack(Q1,[Q2|Qs],D) ← D_aux is D+1, attack(Q1,Qs,D_aux).

---

[1] The logic description phase and the derivation process are straightforward. They have been skipped for purposes of conciseness.

C. Operational behavior

In general, the permutations of the list [1,2,3,4] do not need to be completely constructed to determine that they are unsafe. The unsafeness of one prefix implies the unsafeness of the entire list. The permutations are generated by appending to some prefix, say of length Lg, (4-Lg)! suffixes. Hence, removing such an unsafe prefix prevents from generating (4-Lg)! useless suffixes. A substantial gain may thus result. This is exactly what is obtained by interleaving the generator and testor. One of the interests of Conclog is that such an interleaving is achieved naturally thanks to the interleaving of the generation and reconciliation phases. Table 10.1 compares the number of reductions obtained by fixing the R-depth parameter to 1, 2, 3, 4.[1] The best computation is obtained by fixing the R-depth parameter to 1. This is quite expected since the generator and testor are then coroutined.

R-depth value	Number of involved reduction steps
1	291
2	386
3	472
4	752

Table 10.1

The gain obtained by restricting the generation is however counterbalanced by the overhead induced by the reconciliation. Table 2 compares the number of reconciliations involved when the R-depth parameter is chosen as 1, 2, 3 and 4, respectively. All the reconciliations have been counted there even those reducing to simple compositions. As illustrated, the situation is then reversed. Fixing the R-depth to 1 requires the maximal number of reconciliation. Fixing it to 4 requires the minimum number of reconciliation.

R-depth value	Number of involved reduction steps
1	106.520
2	21.081
3	17.870
4	14.106

Table 10.2

---

[1] The perm procedure used for this purpose is that of Appendix 1.

To conclude, it is worth recalling that, assuming infinite resources, the computation of answer n-substitutions is not delayed by the computation of useless reductions, as this is the case in Prolog for instance. This property results from the fact that or-parallelism and and-parallelism are employed. Hence, discarding the size of the computation, the best computations are obtained by fixing the R-depth parameter to the infinite value. Nevertheless, computing resources are generally finite. In this case, useless computations influence the speed of the computation of answer n-substitutions. Fixing the R-depth parameter to 1 has the interest of decreasing to its minimal value the size of the computation i.e. the number of involved s-goals. It has however the drawback of maximizing the overhead due to the reconciliation. This causes however just a cost in execution time. At the opposite, fixing the R-depth parameter to 4 has the advantage of minimizing the reconciliation overhead but has the drawback of requiring the larger computation size. There is unfortunately no universal best choice for the R-depth parameter : it depends on the available resources.

D. Pruning in an "a priori way"

Discarding the reconciliation overhead, some inefficiency still remains. It results from the fact that candidate solutions are eliminated in a "a posteriori way". Prefixes are indeed extended by the perm procedure in all possible ways without taking care for safety. It is however better to generate only safe values for the suffixes. Useless suffixes are then discarded in a "a priori" way. A technique for performing such a priori pruning has been proposed in [Van Hentenrijck, 1987]. Its essential advantage is to obtain such pruning while perturbing programs just by domain declarations. At an operational level, the only required adaptation is to extend unification in order to incorporate the constraints performed by these domains. This technique has not been incorporated in Conclog. It could however be extended in an easy way thanks to the equational paradigm.

10.6.2 Evaluation

This section has shown that generate and test programming is supported in Conclog in a very natural way. Interleaving the generator and the testor is achieved in a fully transparent manner to the programmer. It results from the provoked reconciliation.

The ease and efficiency of handling such programming in Conclog should be constrasted with those of Prolog and committed-choice languages. Prolog supports similar programs. However, the safety test is made after the permutations have been completely generated ! As far as committed-choice languages are concerned, because of the commitment, only one clause is retained at each step. This implies that only one permutation over the 4! ones is computed. Hence there is N/4! chances to find a solution (with N the number of solutions, generally 1) !

10.7 Conclusion

This chapter has addressed the coding of non behavioral applications in Conclog. Such applications are free from behavior constraints. They can be regarded as the applications to which logic programming is widely acknowledged to be dedicated. One of our goals was to build Conclog as close as possible to what we called the "ideal of logic programming". It should thus be well suited to tackle these applications. This has been illustrated in this chapter through their coding. Ease of programming and expressiveness of the language have moreover been argued.

Five points have been developed as an argumentation.

1) Database programming has first been shown to be supported in a quite declarative way. This property results from our care for g-soundness and g-completeness properties. Thanks to them, the operational behavior could be abstracted.

2) Multi-directional mutli-solution list procedures were then coded in a second step. Ease and simplicity of the construction has particularly been pointed out.

3) Single-solution directed list procedures have been programmed in a third step. For one specification, several procedures have furthermore been constructed. Some of them result from the declarative characterization of the computed relations. Others embody what is generally agreed to be elaborated programming techniques.

4) A fourth section has handled trees. It has been shown that the sources of parallelism they embody can indeed be programmed very naturally. This results from the use of full and-parallelism and or-parallelism adopted at the basis of the design of Conclog.

5) Finally, procedures built using the generate and test paradigm have been proved to be supported by Conclog too. It has furthermore been shown that the interleaving of the generator and the testor, generally achieved by program transformation, is obtained in Conclog very naturally by means of the provoked reconciliation.

The methodology developed in Chapter 9 has also been illustrated in this chapter. It does not aim at being a universal panacea. Nevertheless, one of its interests is to provide systematic guidelines in the construction process. This has particularly been taken into profit to construct procedures acknowledged to be of advanced programming. Logic descriptions resulting from natural choices have first been defined. They were then transformed to give other logic descriptions. Concurrent logic procedures were finally derived therefrom. Obtaining such procedures directly is generally considered to be difficult, especially in a concurrent framework.

Chapter 11

Programming behavorial applications

11.1 Introduction

Chapter 10 has presented typical applications of logic programming. We now abandon the first order logic framework and turn to behavioral applications. Our goal in doing so is to test the ability of Conclog to handle such applications. To this end, this chapter tackles classical programming of systems of infinite processes as well as the programming of classical concurrent programming problems. Among others, the coding of the following systems is achieved : airline reservation systems, unix shell, and lift systems. Furthermore, semaphores are simulated and the seminal dining philosopher problem is solved.

11.2 Programming infinite processes

All the applications handled in this chapter are based on the manipulation of potentially infinite streams by several processes. Typically, lists of potentially infinite length are shared by subgoals of goals, one of them being the answer list. A classical illustration is the computation of the infinite list of prime numbers from 2 using the Sieve of Eratosthenes. It is pictured in Figure 11.1. The algorithm consists of generating the sequence of integers from 2 in increasing order (in the picture the list Int) and of cleaning it from elements that are multiples of preceding ones. This delivers the answer list Prime_list.

The Conclog program is developed as follows. It is built around the primes procedure. This intends to compute the list of primes. Its specification is as follows :

procedure primes(Prime_list).
- Type : Prime_list : list of integers
- Postcondition : Prime_list is incrementally constructed to the list of primes from 2 listed in increasing order.

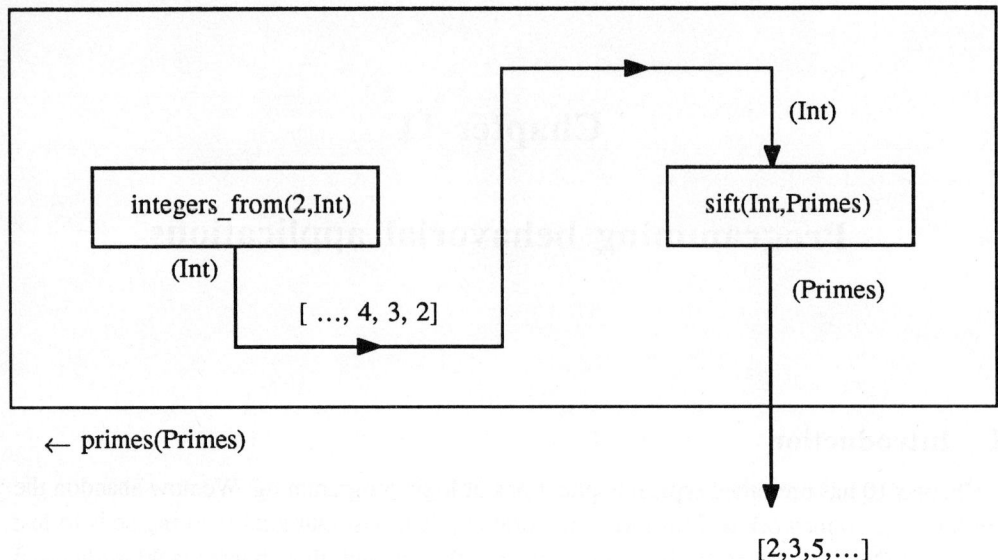

Figure 11.1

It is implemented by means of two procedures in charge of the two subtasks pointed out above : integer_from(Int,List) and sift(List,Sifted_list). The integer_from(Int,List) generates the sequence of integers greater than Int in increasing order. The sift(List,Sifted_list) cleans the list from elements that are multiples of the preceding ones. This is made precise in the following specifications.

    procedure integer_from(Int,List).
- Type :
    - Int : integer
    - List : list of integers
- Operational properties
    1) Suspension condition : Int ground
    2) Postcondition : List is incrementally constructed to the list of integers listed in increasing order.

    procedure sift(List,Sifted_list).
- Type :
    - List, Sifted_list : list of integers,

- Operational properties
    1) Suspension condition : List input
    2) Precondition : the elements of List are listed in increasing order
    3) Postcondition : Sifted_list is incrementally constructed to the list obtained from List by removing any element that is a multiple of a preceding one.

These procedures may be implemented as follows.

1) The list List of the Integer_from(Int,List) procedure is composed of the following elements:

- its head is Int
- its tail is the list L_rem that verifies integer(Succ_Int,L_rem) where Succ_Int is the successor of Int.

The integer_from procedure may thus be implemented by means of a recursive call.

2) The Sifted_list of the sift(List,Sifted_list) is composed of the following elements :

- its head is the head element H of List
- its tail is the list obtained by first removing all multiples of H in the tail of List and then by sifting the resulting list.

The second task may be achieved by calling recursively the sift procedure. The first task is achieved by the filter(Int,List,Filtered_list) procedure. It is specified as follows :

procedure filtered(Int,List,Filtered_list).
- Type :
    Int : integer
    List, Sifted_list : list of integers,
- Operational properties
    1) Suspension conditions : Int ground and List input
    2) Precondition : the elements of List are listed in increasing order
    3) Postcondition : Filtered_list is incrementally constructed to the list obtained from List by removing any element that is a multiple of Int.

It may manifestly be coded without calling any auxiliary procedure. Elements of List need simply to be tested for multiplicity with Int. The non multiple ones form the Filtered_list list.

The following piece of code results :

primes(Prime_list) ← integers_from(2,Int), sift(Int,Prime_list).

suspend integers_from(!g,*).
integers_from(Int,[Int|Ints_rem]) ← Succ_Int is Int + 1, integers_from(Succ_int,Int_rem).

```
suspend sift(!,*).
sift([Int|Ints],[Int|Sift_list_rem]) ←
    filter(Int,Ints,Filtered_list),  sift(Filtered_list,Sift_list_rem).

suspend filter(!g,!,*).
filter(Int,[Num|Nums],[Num|Filtered_Nums]) ←
    not(0 is Num mod Int) | filter(Int,Nums,Filtered_Nums).
filter(Int,[Num|Nums],Filtered_Nums) ←
    0 is Num mod Int | filter(Int,Nums,Filtered_Nums).
```

A similar algorithm is presented in [Clark and Gregory, 1986] using Parlog.

The operational behavior of the computation is worth noting. The computation starts by reducing the s-goal primes(Primes_list). This launches the reduction of the integers_from(2,Int) and sift(Int,Prime_list) s-goals. The first reduction incrementally generates the list of integers Int. The last one consumes it. The two reductions proceed concurrently but, the former is unconstrained whereas the latter is constrained by the availability of integers in Int. This contraint results from the following points :

- the suspension declaration,
- the fact that the actual parameter Int is a variable
- the form of the first parameter of the head of the clause defining sift : [Int|Ints_rem].

They ensure the suspension of the reduction until the integers are effectively produced in Int. Furthermore, the induced hearing of bindings forces the Int list to be effectively communicated from the reduction of the integers_from(2,Int) s-goal to the reduction of the sift(Int,Prime_list) s-goal.

The same situation happens for the two subgoals engendered by the sift(Int,Prime_list) s-goal. The filter(Int,Ints,Filtered_list) subgoal consumes the list Ints and produces the Filtered_list which is consumed by the recursive sift(Filtered_list,Sift_list) subgoal.

Clearly, such s-goals manipulating infinite lists do not terminate. This is however of no concern. What really matters is that any finite prefix of each list is computed after a finite time. This unterminating feature can furthermore be exploited to program perpetual processes. Such processes repeatdly change from one state to another, the set of reachable states being finite. They sometimes suspend, waiting for some event to happen. They can be simulated in Conclog by means of a recursive call and the handling of an infinite list. Suspension is achieved by means of read-only annotations and suspension declarations. It occurs because the head of the list is not sufficiently constructed. The associated event thus corresponds to the construction of the head of the list, allowing the reduction to resume.

The above integers_from, sift and filter s-goals constitute examples of perpetual processes. The filter one is particularly worth illustrating. The reduction of filter(Int,Ints,Filtered_list)

produces an infinite number of filter(Int,Num,Filtered_nums) s-goals thanks to the recursive calls in the filter procedure. The incremental consumption of the Ints list and the suspension for the availability of the elements is provided by means of the second read-only annotation of the suspension declaration and by the form of the second parameter of the head of the clauses :

[H|T]

More practical examples are given in the following sections where this paradigm is fully taken into account.

By definition, at any time, any process moves from one state to another one, determined deterministically or not. Procedures will be subsequently constructed so as to reflect this feature. In particular, for any parameter to be constructed by the reduction of any expected call, bindings for these parameters are made at places such that they will never be removed by further computation and reconciliation. For instance, the following procedure p

suspend p(!,*).
p([H|T],1) ← test_1, ...
p([H|T],2) ← test_2, ...

constructed for calls of the form p(X,Y) where Y is an uninstantiated variable, is rewritten as

suspend p(!,*).
p([H|T],Z) ← test_1 | Z=1, ...
p([H|T],Z) ← test_2 | Z=2, ...

when, for some instance x^* of [H|T], the unification of $p(x^*,Y)$ with p([H|T],1) (resp. p([H|T],2)) does not ensure that the reduction of the induced instance of test_1 (resp. test_2) will succeed. It follows that the provoked reconciliation is useless here. The R-depth parameter will then be instantiated to ∞ for all progams of this section. Note however that the programs could also be run with another choice of the R-depth parameter. Intermittent reconciliations are simply useless.

11.3 Programming abstract data types

A very popular technique in software engineering is to reason in terms of abstract data types. It consists of describing a data structure by defining its properties and some associated operations. Those are the only means to access the data type from outside. A major interest of this approach is the capacity to hide non-relevant information to external world. For instance, the implementation of the structure is completely hidden. This is furthermore strengthened by the abstract algebraic techniques usually applied to specify the operations.

11.3.1 General framework

Conclog turns out to be a very useful tool to simulate abstract data types. The general scheme employed to this end is described hereafter. It will be exemplified in the following Subsections B and C.

Any instance, say Iadt, of an abstract data type is associated with a perpetual process Padt. It is accessed by means of a (possibly infinite) list of operations. Classically, this list is incrementally generated by some perpetual process conjoined to Padt. It is constructed by terms possibly containing free variables. These terms represent operations to be performed by Iadt. Their treatment generally results in modifying the internal structure of Iadt and of instantiating the free variables. This instantiation is considered as the answer of Iadt to the operation.

In more precise programming terms, any abstract data type is represented by a unary predicate, say adt(L_op). The parameter L_op is the list of operations by which the abstract data type can be accessed. It is the only means of accessing it. As a result, the restriction to access the abstract data type by the only use of operations is ensured.

One instance of the abstract data type is represented by a call to the adt(L_op) procedure. As described above, the reduction of the call may be interpreted as the behavior of a perpetual process.

The implementation details are hidden in the definition of the predicate adt(L_op) where an auxiliary predicate of the form imp_adt(L_op,Int_state) is called. This really constitutes the data structure. The local variable Int_state represents its internal structure and is inaccessible from outside. Many imp_adt predicates can generally be defined, each corresponding to a different representation of the data structure or, equivalently, to a different structure of Int_state. Finally, suspension declarations are used to ensure that the process only acts in response to the arrival of the operations. Back communication is used to deliver the results.

11.3.2 The stack abstract data type

A. Simple stack

As a first illustration, we program the classical stack abstract data type. Assume it is accessed by the two following operations :

1) push(X) : puts X on top of the stack;
2) pop(X) : assuming the stack is non-empty, instantiates X to its top and remove it from the stack.

Following the above guidelines, we define a stack predicate with one parameter : stack(L_op). The list L_op is the only means of communication with sibling subgoals. At this point, no implementation feature is apparent. Such features only appear in the definition of the stack predicate. We naturally choose a list to represent the internal state of the stack and write

$$\text{stack(L\_op)} \leftarrow \text{imp\_stack(L\_op,[]).} \qquad (1)$$

The imp_stack really implements the abstract data type stack. It is defined according to the definition of the push and pop operations.

suspend imp_stack(!,!).
imp_stack([push(X)|L_op_rem],Actual_stack) ←
    imp_stack(L_op_rem,[X|Actual_stack]).   (2)
imp_stack([pop(X)|L_op_rem],[Top_stack|Rem_stack]) ←
    X=Top_stack, imp_stack(L_op_rem,Rem_stack).   (3)

The following programming details are worth noting.

1) The suspension declaration is used to force any call to the imp_stack procedure to behave as a consumer of its parameter. A local read-only anotation is however used for the first parameter to allow the reduction of the call to instantiate inner variables of terms (as the X variable is in the second clause).

2) The assignment of X to the top element Top_stack cannot be made directly by head unification. Since, if we wrote the head as
    stack([pop(X)|L_op_rem],[X|Rem_stack]) ← ...
deadlock would result since unification forces X to be bound to the top of the stack whereas the suspension declaration forbids it.

Except for these implementation details, the rules defining imp_stack resemble their non-formal definition.

B. Towards a more complex stack

An attractive property of the abstract data type approach is the possibility to increase the operations easily. This is also true in the Conclog implementation. In a first step, we introduce two new operations

contents(X) : instantiates X to the actual contents of the stack;

height(X) : instantiates X to the height of the actual stack.

They are implemented by adding two new clauses to imp_stack.

imp_stack([contents(X)|L_op_rem],Actual_stack) ←
    X=Actual_stack, imp_stack(L_op_rem,Actual_stack).   (4)
imp_stack([height(X)|L_op_rem],Actual_stack) ←
    length(Actual_stack?,X), imp_stack(L_op_rem,Actual_stack). (5)

The length procedure is that described in Section 10.2. It is multi-directional. However, thanks to the read-only annotation, the Actual_stack parameter of the length(Actual_stack,X) call is implicitly decorated with a read-only annotation. In other terms, this call is prevented from constructing the Actual_stack structure.

In a second step, we extend the pop(X) operation to the case where the stack is empty. If so, X is instantiated to undefined. The following clause is added to this end.

imp_stack([pop(X)|L_op_rem],[]) ←
    X=undefined, imp_stack(L_op_rem,[]). (6)

Finally, we add a clause to allow the termination of the imp_stack process.

imp_stack([],_). (7)

C. Operational behavior

Programming abstract data types in this way results from the possibility to perform concurrent reductions. To make things more specific, let us consider the following query

← produce_op(L_op), stack(L_op)

Assume that the produce_op procedure is conceived so that any call to it consists of incrementally constructing the L_op list with terms of the form push(X), pop(X), contents(X), height(X), ... The reduction of the query results in the concurrent reductions of the two subgoals produce_op(L_op) and stack(L_op). The former thus produces incrementally L_op. The reduction of the stack(L_op) s-goal uses the clause

stack(L_op) ← imp_stack(L_op,[]).

and launches the reduction of the body imp_stack(L_op,[]). Because of the suspension declaration, the imp_stack(L_op,[]) first waits until some operation has been produced by the reduction of produce_op(L_op). Then, according to the operation placed in L_op, one of the clauses (2) to (6) is selected. The instance of its body induced by unification is then reduced. Whatever clause is selected, this always involve the reduction of a recursive call to the imp_stack procedure, say imp_stack(L_op_rem,New_stack). It operates in a similar way. Thus, it first waits until some operation has been placed in L_op_rem i.e. until a second operation has been placed by the reduction of produce_op(L_op) in L_op. Then, it selects one of the clauses (2) to (6) and the process repeats. This given, the second parameter Stack of any subgoal imp_stack(L,Stack) can be regarded as the actual contents of the treated instance of the actual instance of the stack abstract data type. The changing of this contents is represented by the various values of the parameter in the imp_stack(L,Stack) subgoals successively generated. Note that it is internal to the stack since it cannot be directly accessed by the reduction of the produce_op(L_op) s-goal.

Concurrently to the reduction of the imp_stack(L_op_rem,New_stack) subgoal, the reductions of some conjoined s-goals may be performed. They aim at instantiating some free variables of the treated operation terms. Examples of such s-goals are the X=Top_stack, X=Actual_stack, X=undefined unifications of clauses (3), (4), (6), respectively, and the length(Actual_stack?,X) s-goal of clause (5).

Such a scheme may, of course, be programmed in other concurrent logic programming languages, such as the committed-choice ones (as this has been illustrated in [Shapiro, 1987b], for instance). In contrast, this is not possible in sequential languages such as Prolog. Nevertheless, the corroutined execution of the reduction of the produce_op(L_op) and stack(L_op) s-goals can be simulated but, as shown hereafter, by involving some undesired features. First, perpetuality of the processes must be simulated by using recursivity. For instance, for the above query, a procedure, say p, must be declared as follows :

p(...) ← seq_produce_op(Op), stack(Op,...), p(...).

The seq_produce_op(Op) s-goal is the counterpart of the produce_op(L_op) s-goal of the Conclog program. To allow operations to be generated according to the answer given to previous operations, it must generate each operation after having received the answer to the previous one. As an incremental communication cannot occur in Prolog, any call to the seq_produce_op must thus instantiate the Op variable to one operation only. Some parameters of the adt and p procedures have been unspecified. Making them precise depends on the way the internal state of the abstract data type is recorded. In Prolog, this can only be achieved in two ways : by using assert and retract procedures or by using parameters. The first solution has the advantage of hiding the internal value of the stack in the stack procedure. Using it, one would, for instance, write

stack(push(X)) ←
    retract(stack_contents(Actual_contents)),
    assert(stack_contents([X|Actual_contents])).

The stack_contents predicate is some predicate declared in the program by a single clause. This clause is modified by the assert and retract built-in primitives. It has one parameter which records the last updated value for the stack. The drawback of the method is that, as the name is unique, only one instance can be employed for the stack. This is manifestly too drastic. The procedure needs thus to be adapted. To conserve the assert and retract approach, a second argument to the stack procedure is needed. It aims at referring to the instance of the data type under consideration. As a result, one of the nice features of the Conclog program is lost : the possiblity to create a new instance by a simple call to the procedure embodying the abstract data type without referencing the instance by an identifier. Note furthermore that some auxiliary problems then arise from the fact that it is not possible in Prolog to write constructs of the form Instance_stack_contents(Actual_stack) where Instance_stack_contents is a variable. The above stack_contents predicate cannot thus be particularized so easily to the instance under consideration. Nevertheless this is possible by using structure handling built-in primitives. This solution looks thus a little bit "tricky".

Let us now turn to the second approach. It consists of adding two extra parameters to the stack procedure. One represents the Old value of the stack and the other the updated one. The stack procedure is then modified in consequence :

```
stack(push(X),Initial_stack,[X|Initial_stack]).
stack(pop(X),[X|Rem_stack],Rem_stack).
stack(pop(undefined),[],[]).
stack(contents(Actual_stack),Actual_stack,Actual_stack).
stack(length(X),Actual_stack,Actual_stack) ← length(Actual_stack,X).
```

The procedure p is then modified as follows :

p(Initial_state) ← seq_produce_op(Op), stack(Op,Initial_state,Final_state), p(Final_state).

The advantage of this solution is that the program is not poluted with some tricky built-in primitives. The drawback is that the internal state of the abstract data type is made apparent and therefore can be accessed.

Summing up, in contrast with Conclog, implementation details are made apparent. Two solutions may be employed. One of them requires to identify the instances explicitly. Furthermore, it involves some built-in primitives destroying the declarative aspects of the programs. The second solution is more declarative but requires the explicit and apparent handling of the internal state of the data type. It is thus no more inaccessible.

11.3.3 The dictionary abstract data type

We further illustrate the implementation information hidding of Conclog by implementing a dictionary abstract data type in two different manners. The dictionary structure is defined at an abstract level as a set of elements composed of two items :

- a key field, which acts as an identifier;
- an information field, which contains information of any form.

The associated operations are the usual add, delete and retrieve primitives. We increase them by a test for membership of an element. Clearly, the abstract data type generalizes many "database applications".

Following the general scheme of Subsection A., we define this abstract data type as

dictionary(L_op) ← imp_dictionary(L_op,...).

Some representation choice of the internal state has to be made in order to make the imp_dictionary predicate precise. We give here two different representations. The resulting predicates are prefixed by the chosen structure in order to distinguish them.

In a first version, we choose a list representation. The dictionary abstract data type is then defined as

    dictionary(L_op) ← list_imp_dictionary(L_op,[]).

with list_imp_dictionary defined as

    suspend list_imp_dictionary(!,!).
    list_imp_dictionary([add(El)|L_op_rem],Actual_dict) ←
        list_imp_dictionary(L_op_rem,[El|Actual_dict]).
    list_imp_dictionary([delete(El)|L_op_rem],Actual_dict) ←
        delete(El,Actual_dict,Dict_rem),
        list_imp_dictionary(L_op_rem,Dict_rem).
    list_imp_dictionary([retrieve(El)|L_op_rem],Actual_dict) ←
        member(El,Actual_dict?), list_imp_dictionary(L_op_rem,Actual_dict).
    list_imp_dictionary([exist(El)|L_op_rem],Actual_dict) ←
        member(El,Actual_dict?) |
        El=true, list_imp_dictionary(L_op_rem,Actual_dict).
    list_imp_dictionary([exist(El)|L_op_rem],Actual_dict) ←
        not(member(El,Actual_dict?) |
        El=false, list_imp_dictionary(L_op_rem,Actual_dict).

The member procedure is described in Section 10.2. It is multi-directional. Read-only annotations have then been inserted to use the annotated parameters in an input way only. The delete procedure consists of removing an element of a list, this resulting in a new list. It is the specified as follows :

    procedure delete(El,L1,L2).
- Type
      L1, L2 : lists
- Relation
      L2 is L1 where the occurrences of El have been removed
- Operational properties
      1) Suspension conditions
          El input and L1 element input
      2) Postconditions
          El and L1 input and L1 incrementally constructed to a ground list : L2 incrementally constructed to a ground list

In a second version, we use balanced binary trees. The dictionary is then defined as

    dictionary(L_op) ← btree_imp_dictionary(L_op,void).

with btree_imp_dictionary defined as

```
suspend btree_imp_dictionary(!,!).
btree_imp_dictionary([add(El)|L_op_rem],Actual_dict) ←
    add(El,Actual_dict,New_dict),
    btree_imp_dictionary(L_op_rem,New_dict).
btree_imp_dictionary([delete(El)|L_op_rem],Actual_dict) ←
    del(El,Actual_dict,New_dict),
    btree_imp_dictionary(L_op_rem,New_dict).
btree_imp_dictionary([retrieve(El)|L_op_rem],Actual_dict) ←
    tree_member(El,Actual_dict?),
    btree_imp_dictionary(L_op_rem,Actual_dict).
btree_imp_dictionary([exist(El)|L_op_rem],Actual_dict) ←
    tree_member(El,Actual_dict?) |
    El = true, btree_imp_dictionary(L_op_rem,Actual_dict).
btree_imp_dictionary([exist(El)|L_op_rem],Actual_dict) ←
    not(tree_member(El,Actual_dict?)) |
    El = false, btree_imp_dictionary(L_op_rem,Actual_dict).
```

The add and del predicates refer to those manipulating well-balanced binary trees in section 10.4. The tree_member predicate is an obvious extension of that of the same section for binary trees.

As already said, the implementation of the data structure is completely transparent to the user of the abstract data type dictionary. Whether the dictionary is represented as a list or a binary tree only concerns the implementer of the data type.

11.4 Programming systems of processes

The previous section has foccussed on the description of a single process. We now turn to systems of processes and show how to implement them in Conclog.

Roughly speaking, the processes are embodied in conjoined s-goals sharing lists. Each s-goal behaves as a perpetual process. It divides its life into sending messages to sibling goals, executing some appropriate actions in response to received messages and waiting for the arrival of messages. Messages are transmitted by means of the shared lists. Waiting is ensured by means of read-only annotations, suspension declarations and suitable values for the clause head parameters. Merge processes are used as arbitrors. They ensure the mutual exclusive access to the shared ressources.

It is worth noting that the Conclog processes thus act in an object-oriented spirit. It should be clear from the above description that all object-oriented applications that do not require inheritance can immediately be translated in Conclog. Inheritance can also be programmed by using Shapiro and Takeuchi's technique of inheritance by delegation ([Shapiro and

Takeuchi, 1983]). Roughly speaking, subclasses processes are extended to call their superclass process when an unrecognized message is sent to them. To overcome the resulting verbosity, a new language, called Vulcan, has recently been proposed ([Kahn et al., 1987]). It is of a higher level than the concurrent logic programming ones. It describes objects and their methods in a purely object-oriented approach. The programs are then translated into Concurrent Prolog. They can be transformed in Conclog as well, since Conclog provides features as powerful as the Concurrent Prolog ones.

This section will only deal with applications that do not require such elaborated mechanisms. We refer the reader to the above references for further information and suggest him to transpose the Concurrent Prolog programs into Conclog ones.

11.4.1   An airline reservation system

11.4.1.1   Problem   description

Our first application deals with an airline reservation system. Bryant and Dennis (1982) used it as a benchmark problem for comparing different approaches to concurrent programming. Later, Shapiro gave a Concurrent Prolog version ([Shapiro, 1983]). We give hereafter the Conclog version.

The description of the problem reads as follows :

"The process for the airline reservation system contains information about flights of a single airline. Initially, each flight has 100 seats available. The system can accept two kinds of commands. To reserve seats on a flight an agent gives the command ('reserve',f,n). If at least n seats are available on flight f, the seats will be reserved and the system will respond with the message true. If that many seats are not available, the system will respond with the message false. To find out how many seats are available on flight f, a system user gives the command ('info',f). The system will respond with the number of seats which are available on the flight at the time the command is processed" (from [Briant and Dennis, 1982], p. 430)

We will furthermore postulate the existence of two system users, acting concurrently. Generalization to more users is straightforward.

11.4.1.2   The Conclog program

A.   Overview of the solution

The whole system thus includes three actors : the two users and the airline database. Communication occurs from the users to the database and inversely from the database to the users. No communication is to be achieved between the two users. We use a merge process at the front of the database to group the queries from the users and to make the number of users transparent to the database process. It furthermore ensures exclusive access to the database. The situation can thus be depicted by Figure 11.2.

The Conclog description reflects this structure. It is

airline_reservation_system ← user(1,L1), user(2,L2),
merge(L1,L2,L_request),
database(L_requests).

The lists L1, L2 and L_request represent the communication channels. Their contents is described in the next subsection. Similarly, the user, merge and database procedures are constructed there.

B. The program

B.1 SPECIFICATIONS

The user, merge and database procedures are specified as follows.

1) Procedure user(Id,L).

The user(Id,L) procedure is constructed so that the reduction of any call user(Id,L), with Id a ground term and L an uninstantiated variable, simulates some arbitrary user. The Id parameter is an identifier of the described user. It is of no significance for the program. The L parameter is a list, acting as a channel by which the user can communicate with the database. It is incrementally produced by the user. It is constructed with instances of the following terms :

reserve(Flight*,Seats*,Response),
info(Flight*,Seats),
create(Flight*),
delete(Flight*).

The two first terms correspond to the operations required by the description of Subsection A. The last ones are used to create and delete a flight, respectively. The instances of these terms are constrained by the two following rules :

- variables ended by a "*" symbol must be instantiated by a ground term,
- the other variables must be kept free.

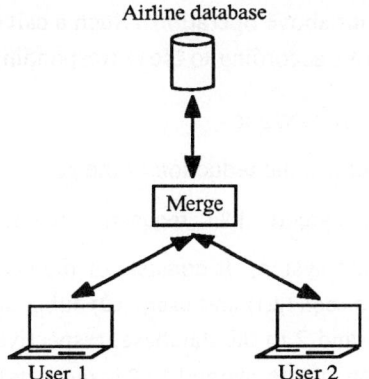

Figure 11.2

2) The merge(L1,L2,L) procedure

The merge(L1,L2,L) procedure aims at merging the lists L1 and L2 into the list L. The lists L1 and L2 are incrementally consumed and, thus, are declared as input. The list L is incrementally produced therefrom. Only one arbitrary merged version of the lists L1 and L2 is constructed for L. It is required to be fair in the sense that any element of any list is eventually placed in L. Precisely, the merge procedure obeys the following specification.

    procedure merge(L1,L2,L)
- Type

    L1, L2, L : lists; strong use
- Relation

    L is a merged version of L1 and L2
- Operational properties

    1) Suspension condition

        L1 and L2 element input

    2) Precondition

        L variable

    3) Postcondition

        L1 and L2 input and incrementally constructed :

            L incrementally constructed,

            only one version is constructed for L

3) The database(L) procedure

The database(L) procedure is constructed so that any call whose L parameter is variable simulates the database component as described in Subsection A. The L parameter is a list of

B.2 THE AIRLINE RESERVATION SYSTEM

Thanks to these specifications, the reduction of the goal

← user(1,L1), user(2,L2), merge(L1,L2,L_request), database(L_requests).

simulates the airline reservation system. It consists of the concurrent reductions of the four subgoals. The reduction of the user(1,L1) and user(2,L2) subgoals constructs incrementally the lists of requests of the users 1 and 2 to the database, respectively. These requests are merged incrementally by the reduction of the merge(L1,L2,L_requests) subgoal, this resulting in the incremental construction of the list L_request. Finally, the reduction of the database(L_requests) subgoal treats the requests as the real database would do. As a result, the Response and Seats variables of the reserve(Flight*,Seats*,Response) and info(Flight*,Seats) terms are instantiated. Their values may then be consumed by the user calls.

Let us now implement the auxiliary user, merge and database procedures.

B.3 THE user PROCEDURE

The specification of the user procedure does not much restrict the behavior of the user. Very complex ones can thus be programmed. The program presented hereafter describes a very simple one. It reflects cyclic screen sessions, each consisting of the impression of the prompt 'Command?', the reading of the desired command and the writing of the answer :

user(Id,[Request|L_mess_rem]) ←
    nl | write('Command ?') | read(Request) | nl | write_answer(Request) |
    user(Id,L_mess_rem).

The "|" is used to sequentialize the operations of the screen session. The write_answer procedure writes, when any, the answer returned by the database in a user-friendly way.

suspend write_answer(!g).
write_answer(info(Flight,Seats)) ← write('Seats = ',Seats).
write_answer(reserve(Flight,Seats,true)) ← write(Seats,' seats reserved').
write_answer(reserve(Flight,Seats,false)) ← write('not enough seats').
write_answer(create(Flight)).
write_answer(delete(Flight)).

B.4 THE merge PROCEDURE

The merge(L1,L2,L) procedure is implemented by an inductive reasoning on both L1 and L2. One has

```
merge(L1,L2,L) ⇔
    L1=[] ∧ L2=L
    ∨
    L1=[H1|T1] ∧ L=[H1|L_rem] ∧ merge(T1,L2,L_rem).
```

and

```
merge(L1,L2,L) ⇔
    L2=[] ∧ L1=L
    ∨
    L2=[H2|T2] ∧ L=[H2|L_rem] ∧ merge(L1,T2,L_rem).
```

The first logic definition gives rise to the following clauses :

```
merge([],L2,L2).
merge([H1|T1],L2,H1|L_rem]) ← merge(T1,L2,L_rem).
```

The second logic definition gives rise to the following clauses :

```
merge(L1,[],L1).
merge(L1,[H2|T2] ,[H2|L_rem]) ← merge(L1,T2,L_rem).
```

Using only the two first clauses or the two last ones would not ensure fairness. For instance, if the two first clauses are retained, elements of L2 would then be placed in L only after all elements of L1 have been placed in it. This never occurs in case L1 is infinite. The solution is to use the four clauses. Commitment must also be applied in order to guarantee that only one merged version of L1 and L2 will be constructed in L. Finally, a suspension declaration is added to force the reduction of merge(L1,L2,L) to consume the lists L1 and L2 really.

Summing up, the merge procedure is as follows :

```
suspend merge(!,!,*) with l_commitment.
merge([],L2,L2).
merge(L1,[],L1).
merge([H1|T1],L2,[H1|L_rem]) ← merge(T1,L2,L_rem).
merge(L1,[H2|T2],[H2|L_rem]) ← merge(L1,T2,L_rem).
```

B.5 THE database PROCEDURE

The database procedure is an obvious instance of the dictionary abstract datatype. Its internal structure is implemented by using a list representation. Its elements are of the form el(Flight,Seats) where Flight is the identifier of some flight and Seats is the number of available seats in the flight. At any moment, at most one such structure is registered for each flight.

The database procedure is as follows :

```
database(L_request) ← imp_db(L_request,[]).

suspend imp_db(!,!).
imp_db([info(Flight,Seats)|L_requests_rem],DB) ←
    member(el(Flight,Seats),DB?),
    imp_db(L_request_rem,DB).
imp_db([reserve(Flight,Required_seats,Response)|L_requests_rem],DB) ←
    member(el(Flight,Free_seats),DB?),
    Required_seats ≤ Free_seats |
    Response = true,
    New_free_seats is Free_seats - Required_seats,
    modify(el(Flight,New_free_seats),DB,New_DB),
    imp_db(L_requests_rem,New_DB).
imp_db([reserve(Flight,Required_seats,Response)|L_requests_rem],DB) ←
    member(el(Flight,Free_seats),DB?),
    Required_seats > Free_seats |
    Response = false,
    imp_db(L_requests_rem,DB).
imp_db([create(Flight)|L_request_rem],DB) ←
    imp_db(L_requests_rem,[el(Flight,100)|DB]).
imp_db([delete(Flight)|L_requests_rem],DB) ←
    delete(el(Flight,_),DB,New_DB),
    imp_db(L_requests_rem,New_DB).
```

In principle, calls updating the database, calls delivering answers to the request and recursive calls to the imp_db procedure can be performed concurrently. Wrong answers are indeed removed by the failure of the whole goal in which they participate (see Point 3 of Subsection 6.2.1.1.B.2.2). Nevertheless, the sequentialization operator has been introduced in the second and third clauses to ensure a better simulation : the response true or false is then constructed only after the corresponding situation has been detected.

The member procedure is that of Section 10.2. The modify and delete procedures are called for modifying the number of seats available in some flight and for suppressing the flight, respectively. They are specified as follows.

procedure modify(El,L1,L2).
- Type
    El : of the form el(Id,Inf)
    L1, L2 : lists of elements of the form of El; strong use
- Relation
    L2 is L1 where the element whose Id subcomponent is that of El is replaced by El.

- Operational properties
    1) Suspension conditions
        El ground, L1 input
    2) Precondition
        L1 contains an element whose Id subcomponent is that of El
    3) Postcondition
        El ground and L1 input and L1 incrementally constructed to a ground list : L2 incrementally constructed to a ground list.

procedure delete(El,L1,L2).
- Type
    El : of the form el(Id,Inf)
    L1, L2 : lists of elements of the form of El; strong use
- Relation
    L2 is L1 where the element whose Id subcomponent is that of El is removed.
- Operational properties
    1) Suspension conditions
        El ground, L1 input
    2) Precondition
        L1 contains an element whose Id subcomponent is that of El
    3) Postcondition
        El ground and L1 input and L1 incrementally constructed to a ground list : L2 incrementally constructed to a ground list.

Their implementation directly results from a scheme of reasoning similar to that employed in Section 10.3. They state as follows :

suspend modify(!g,?,*).
modify(el(Id,New_Inf),[el(Id,Old_Inf)|DB_rem],[el(Id,New_Inf)|DB_rem]).
modify(el(Id,New_Inf),[el(Id_e,Inf_e)|DB_rem],[el(Id_e,Inf_e)|New_DB_rem]) ←
    Id ≠ Id_e |
    modify(el(Id,New_Inf),DB_rem,New_DB_rem).

suspend delete(!g,?,*).
delete(el(Id,_),[el(Id,Inf)|DB_rem],DB_rem).
delete(el(Id,_),[el(Id_e,Inf_e)|DB_rem],[el(Id_e,Inf_e)|New_DB_rem]) ←
    Id ≠ Id_e |
    delete(el(Id,_),DB_rem,New_DB_rem).

B.6 Ending the computation

Stated as above the processes are perpetual. To program more realistic sessions, terminating clauses are added. This is quite simple as far as the database procedure is concerned. The clause

imp_db([],_).

needs simply to be added. In contrast, the user procedure cannot be extended so simply. A halt command ending the session is first added to the user commands. The user behavior is then adapted according to the typed command. It is split in two parts : a fixed screen session one and a response to command one. The latter varies according as the command is halt or not. If it is halt the user procedure is halted. This is achieved by a clause with empty body. Otherwise, the user procedure is called recursively (as before) after the answer for the previous request has been output. The resulting user procedure is as follows.

user(Id,L_mess) ← screen_session(Command) | response_to_cmd(Id,Command,L_mess).

screen_session(Command) ← nl | write('Command ?') | read(Command).

suspend response_to_cmd(!,!,*).
response_to_cmd(Id,halt,[]).
response_to_cmd(Id,Request,[Request|Lm_rem]) ←
    Request≠halt | write_answer(Request) | user(Id,Lm_rem).

The final Conclog program is listed in Appendix 2.

C Programming remarks

As a conclusion, the two following facts are worth noting.

First, there is no need to use two half-duplex channels between the user and merge processes or between the merge process and the database process to achieve two-way communication. Back communication allows to send partially instantiated messages (e.g. info(Flight,Seats) or reserve(Flight,Seats,Response)) whose variables are instantiated in response. As a consequence, messages do not need to be tagged by an identifier to make explicit the process to which the answer must be returned. This should be contrasted with parallel functional languages !

Second, mutually exclusive access to the database and fairness of this access are ensured by the commit operator of the merge procedure. Indeed, as a result, at each reduction step of a call to this procedure, only one unifiable clause is taken into account. It follows that only one request from L1 or L2 is selected at any time. Furthermore, as commitment is assumed to be fair, a fair merging of the requests results. Fairness of the access to the database is then ensured.

11.4.2 A simple operating system

Our second application consists of programming a simple operating system. It shows how a UNIX-like operating system can be implemented in Conclog. It is inspired from [Clark and Gregory, 1983] and [Clark and Gregory, 1984] where a similar operating system has been programmed using Parlog. A more elaborate discussion of logic operating systems can be found in [Foster, 1987].

11.4.2.1 Problem description

We will just program here a layer subset of the real UNIX operating system. We consider the following components :
- a file system connected to a filestore and a spooler;
- two terminals, each with its keyboard and screen.

The system may be understood from a logical point of view as follows. A process is associated with the file system, a second with the filestore and a third with the spooler. Each terminal is associated with three processes : a keyboard process, a screen process and a term process. A merge process is finally used to interface the two term processes with the file system.

Precisely, the specification of the processes is as follows.
- the file system process is in charge of the file management;
- the filestore process is in charge of the file storing;
- the spooler process is in charge of the file printing;
- the keyboard processes collect the strings of characters introduced at the associated keyboards;
- the screen processes display the strings of characters on the associated screens;
- the term processes process the requests formulated through strings sent by its keyboard process and merge these keyboard inputs with the request responses to form the screen outputs;
- the merge process merges its two input streams into a third one.

These processes are organized as illustrated in Figure 11.3. The annotations along the arrows are used as labels for the communication channels. Their direction indicates in which sense the communication occurs.

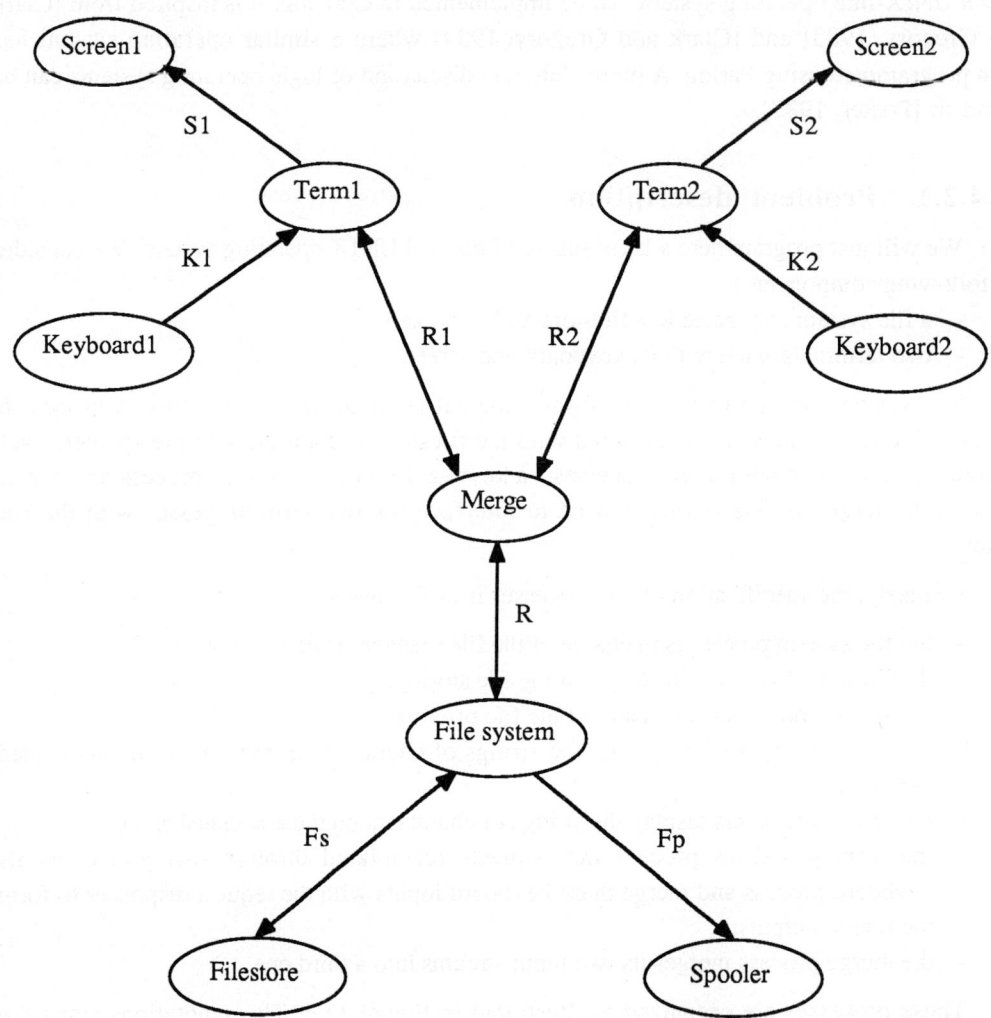

Figure 11.3

11.4.2.2 The Conclog program

The Conclog implementation reflects this description. A process is associated with a call to a procedure. Its reduction intends to simulate the behavior of the process. In view of this correspondence, the name of the associated predicate is chosen as the name of the process.

All the processes behave concurrently. The whole operating system can thus be simulated by the reduction of the following goal

    ←   screen(1,S1), keyboard(1,K1), term(K1,S1,R1),
         screen(2,S2), keyboard(2,K2), term(K2,S2,R2),
         merge(R1,R2,R),
         file_system(R,Fs,Fp), file_store(Fs), spooler(Fp).

The adequacy of the reduction of the subgoals with respect to the process they intend to simulate is ensured by the construction of the procedures. Each one is examined subsequently.

The remainder of this section is organized with respect to this examination. It is divided as follows :

1. The keyboard, screen and merge procedures
2. The file_system procedure
3. The file_store procedure
4. The spooler procedure
5. The term procedure

The term procedure constitutes the core of the program. It is constructed in three steps. The command language is first defined. Its parsing is examined in a second step. Finally, the real handling of the commands is constructed progressively. To this end, a simple shell is first given. It is then extended to handle failure, to abord foreground commands, to kill background processes and to handle priorities.

11.4.2.2.1 The keyboard, screen and merge procedures

The keyboard and screen procedures are assumed to be built-in. The merge procedure is the one defined in Section 11.4.1 for the construction of the airline reservation system.

11.4.2.2.2 The file_system procedure

A. The file system process

To program the file system procedure, let us first describe the file system process in more details. It receives a list of queries of the form

```
get(File_name,File_contents),
replace(File_name,File_contents),
print(File_name).
```

It uses two other channels to communicate with the file store process and the spooler process. It acts as follows. Each get(File_name,File_contents) query is transmitted to the file store process in order to get the contents of the file named File_name. Each replace(File_name,File_contents) query is also transmitted to it to order the replacing of the contents of the file named File_name by File_contents. Finally, each reception of a print(File_name) order first generates a get query in order to search for the contents of the file named File_name and then a priniting order for this contents.

B. Specification

The call file_system(R,Fs,Fp) intends to simulate this behavior. The parameters R, Fs, Fp aim at representing the list of queries, the channel with the file store system and the channel with the spooler, respectively. The specification of the procedure results.

```
procedure file_system(R,Fs,Fp).
```
- Type
    R : list of terms of the form
        get(File_name,File_contents),
        replace(File_name,File_contents),
        print(File_name);
    Fs : list of terms of the form
        get(File_name,File_contents),
        replace(File_name,File_contents),
    Fp : list of terms of the File_contents type.
- Operational properties
    1) Suspension condition
        R element input
    2) Precondition
        Fs, Fp variables
    3) Postcondition
        Provided R is incrementally constructed, the lists Fs and Fp are incrementally constructed as follows :
          - any get(...) term of R is placed in Fs
          - any print(File_name) of R gives rise to a get(File_name,File_contents) in Fs and the insertion of File_contents in Fp.

C. Conclog code

The program is easily derived from this specification

```
suspend file_system(!,*,*).
file_system([get(File_name,File_contents)|L_queries_rem],
                [get(File_name,File_contents)|L_filestore_rem],L_spooler) ←
    file_system(L_queries_rem,L_filestore_rem,L_spooler).
file_system([replace(File_name,File_contents)|L_queries_rem],
                [replace(File_name,File_contents)|L_filestore_rem],L_spooler) ←
    file_system(L_queries_rem,L_filestore_rem,L_spooler).
file_system([print(File_name)|L_queries_rem],
                [get(File_name,File_contents)|L_filestore_rem],
                [File_contents|L_spooler]) ←
    file_system(L_queries_rem,L_filestore_rem,L_spooler).
```

Note that, thanks to the back communication mechanism, there is no need to order the printing of File_contents only after the treatment of get(File_name,File_contents) has returned its value. It is thus correct to construct the L_filestore and L_spooler parameters simultaneously.

11.4.2.2.3 The file_store procedure

A. The file store process

The file store process receives queries of the form get(File_name,File_contents) and replace(File_name,File_contents). In the first case, it answers the File_contents. In the second case, it just replaces the actual contents of the file File_name by File_contents.

B. The procedure

Clearly, the file_store process is an instance of the dictionary abstract data type. The corresponding procedure is coded by using a list representation of the internal state.

```
file_store(L_queries) ← imp_file_store(L_queries,Init_FS).

suspend imp_file_store(!,!).
imp_file_store([get(File_name,File_contents)|L_rem],FS) ←
    member(el(File_name,File_contents),FS?),
    imp_file_store(L_rem,FS).
imp_file_store([replace(File_name,File_contents)|L_rem],FS) ←
    modify(el(File_name,File_contents),FS,New_FS) |
    imp_file(L_rem,New_FS).
```

The member and modify procedures have been described in Sections 10.2 and 11.4.1.C.4, respectively.

11.4.2.2.4 The spooler procedure

A. The spooler process

The spooler process receives a list of file contents to be printed. Here we define a spooler with two printers. Extension to more printers can be easily made. A fair distribution between the printers is requested.

B. Specification

The spooler(L) procedure thus uses the list L in an input way. It is in charge of printing its elements.

C. Conclog code

Its implementation is achieved by means of two procedures : printer(L) and rev_merge(L,L1,L2). The first procedure is assumed to be built-in. It simulates the printing of the elements of L. It declares L as input. The second procedure acts in the reverse way of the merge procedure: it splits a list into two sublists with a fair repartition between the sublists. Precisely, its specification is as follows.

    procedure rev_merge(L,L1,L2).
- Type

    L, L1, L2 : lists, strong use of type and all subtypes,
- Relation

    L is a merged version of L1 and L2
- Operational properties
    1) Suspension condition

        L element input
    2) Precondition

        L1 and L2 variables
    3) Postcondition

        Assume L is incrementally constructed. Then, L1 and L2 are incrementally constructed. Only one value is generated for L1 and L2. Furthermore, the elements of L are fairly distributed between L1 and L2.

The rev_merge procedure is coded by reasoning inductively on L. One has

    rev_merge(L,L1,L2) $\Leftrightarrow$
        L=[] $\wedge$ L1=[] $\wedge$ L2=[]
        $\vee$
        L=[H|T] $\wedge$ (L1=[H|L1_rem] $\wedge$ rev_merge(T,L1_rem,L2)
            $\vee$
            L2=[H|L2_rem] $\wedge$ rev_merge(T,L1,L2_rem)).

The following procedure results. The commit operator is used to ensure that one and only one couple (L1,L2) is produced.

 suspend rev_merge(!,*,*) with l_commit.
 rev_merge([],[],[]).
 rev_merge([H|T],[H|L1_rem],L2) ← rev_merge(T,L1_rem,L2).
 rev_merge([H|T],L1,[H|L2_rem]) ← rev_merge(T,L1,L2_rem).

The spooler procedure can then be implemented as follows :

 spooler(Files) ← rev_merge(Files,P1,P2), printer(P1), printer(P2).

11.4.2.2.5 The term procedure

A. The term process

The term process is the core of our operating system. It does really the job. It receives a string of characters representing commands, executes them and sends the input strings together with the computation results as output. It has three streams : one for the input stream of characters, another for the output streams of characters and a third one to converse with the file system process.

B. The Conclog procedure

The term(L_in,L_out,File_request) procedure simulates this behavior. It takes three parameters L_in, L_out and File_request for the input stream, the output stream and the conversation with the file system process, respectively. The first one is input. It is implemented by means of three auxiliary procedures :

 parser_cmds(L_in,L_cmds),
 shell(L_cmds,File_request,L_out),
 merge(L1,L2,L).

The first one aims at transforming the input stream of characters into a list of UNIX-like commands. It uses the L_in list as input and constructs the L_cmds list of commands. The second procedure aims at processing the commands of the L_cmds list. It uses this list as input. It dialogues with the file system by means of the File_request list and produces some display in L_out. Finally, the last procedure is the merge procedure already detailed. It is used for merging the input stream of characters with that delivered from the execution of the commands in order to form the stream to be output.

Thanks to these procedures, the term procedure can be coded as

```
term(L_in,L_out,File_requests) ←
    parser_cmds(L_in,L_cmds),
    shell(L_cmds,File_requests,L_out_aux),
    merge(L_in,L_out_aux,L_out).
```

Let us now refine the parser_cmds and shell procedures.

B.1 The parser_cmds procedure

The parser_cmds procedure is constructed in two steps. The syntax of the user command language is defined first. Its parsing in UNIX like commands is then addressed.

B.1.1 The command language

We subsequently use a UNIX like language command, inspired of that of [Clark and Gregory, 1983].

A user command consists of a sequence of characters divided up into four command fields :

- a non-empty list of program names,
- an input specifier,
- an output specifier,
- an optional "&" specifier to indicate that the command is to run in background.

The command terminates by a CR. Blanks are used at will to separate the fields or the program names but the first typed character must be non-blank.

If more than one is given, the program names are separated by the "||" symbol, as in

P1 || P2 || ... || Pn .

This indicates that the programs P1, P2, ..., Pn are to be run concurrently with the output of each program Pi being fed to program Pi+1.

The input specifier indicates the source of the input to the first program in the list. There are three possibilities.

(1) If absent then there is no input.
(2) If the input specifier is of the form "<Fn", the file with name Fn is taken as input.
(3) If the input specifier reduces to the "<" symbol on its own, then the standard input is taken as input. This means that the string of characters following the command and terminated by the next CR character is taken as input. For simplification, we force each such sequence to begin by the % symbol and assume that no file name and no command name start with it

The output specifier can be of two kinds.

(1) If it is ">Fn", the file with name Fn is taken as output.
(2) If it is not specified, the output is standard, that is, it is sent to the same stream as the responses to the commands.

The internal representation of the commands is as follows

cmd(L_prgms,File_name,File_name,Tag).

The first argument, L_prgms, is a list of program names to be executed in a pipelined way. The second and third ones basically represent the name of a file. The former can take three forms :

- file(File_name) to refer to a specified file,
- std to refer to the standard input,
- none when no input file is specified.

The latter can only take the two first forms. Finally the Tag argument takes the values fg or bg to indicate that the programs are to run in foreground or background, respectively.

For instance, the commands

"print <Fn CR",
"P || Q < CR"
"R >Gn & CR"

are represented as

cmd([print],Fn,std,fg),
cmd([P,Q],std,std,fg),
cmd([R],none,G,bg),

respectively.

The internal representation of the input introduced on the keyboard takes the following form :

txt(L_chars)

where L_chars is the list of characters introduced after the % symbol and till the CR end delimitor. For instance, the input

"%A simple operating system CR"

is represented as

txt([A, ,s,i,m,p,l,e, ,o,p,e,r,a,t,i,ng, ,s,y,s,t,e,m,])

B.1.2 The parsing

The parsing of the strings of the list L_in is made in a classical manner. We assume that L_in is a list of ASCII code representing characters. Nevertheless, in order to be as suggestive as possible, we do not include the ASCII code in our programs but instead represent them by their logical name written in bold characters. For instance, **BL**, **CR**, **||**, **&** represent the ASCII codes for the blank character, the control return character, the "||" symbol and the & character, respectively. Note that other arguments, except those lists of characters included in txt(...) representations, refer to logical Conclog terms.

The parser_cmds(L_in,L_cmds) procedure is built thanks to the auxiliary procedure read_cmd_txt(L_in,Cmd_txt,L_in_rem). It consists of reading the first command or the first input text of L_in. This delivers the value of the Cmd_txt parameter. The L_in_rem parameter delivers the remainder of the list L_in.

The read_cmd_txt procedure is specified as follows.

procedure read_cmd_txt(L_in,Cmd_txt,L_in_rem).
- Type
    L_in, L_in_rem : lists of ASCII code
    Cmd_txt : command or text
- Relation
    Cmd_txt is the first command or text of L_in and L_in_rem is L_in cut off the strings representing Cmd_txt.
- Operational conditions
    1) Suspension condition
        L_in input
    2) Precondition
        L_in represents a list of commands and/or texts
    3) Postcondition
        <ground,var,var> : <ground,ground,ground>; <1-1>
        L_in input and L_in incrementally constructed to a ground list : L_in_rem incrementally constructed to a ground list.

Assuming its existence, the parser_cmd(L_in,Cmd_txt) procedure can be coded by an inductive reasoning on L_in :

suspend parser_cmds(?,*)
parser_cmds([],[]).
parser_cmds([H|T],[Cmd_txt|L_cmd_txt_rem]) ←
    read_cmd_txt([H|T],Cmd_txt,L_in_rem),
    parser_cmds(L_in_rem,L_cmd_txt_rem).

The implementation of the parser_cmd procedure rests on two procedures. One is in charge of reading an input text and the other is in charge of reading a command. They are called after the first character of the parsed list L_in has determined whether a command or a text is in front of L_in. This can be determined by testing whether or not this character is % or not. They are specified as follows :

procedure read_txt(L_in,Txt,L_in_rem)
- Type
    L_in, L_in_rem : lists of ASCII code
    Txt : text
- Relation
    Txt is txt(String) where String is the list of characters of L_in up to the first CR character, this character being excluded. L_in_rem is the remainder of L_in, the CR character being also excluded.
- Operational conditions
    1) Suspension condition
        L_in input
    2) Postconditions
        <ground,var,var> : <ground,ground,ground>; <1-1>
        L_in input and L_in incrementally constructed to a ground list : L_in_rem incrementally constructed to a ground list.

procedure read_cmd(L_in,Cmd,L_in_rem)
- Type
    L_in, L_in_rem : lists of ASCII code
    Cmd : command
- Relation
    Cmd is the first command of L_in and L_in_rem is L_in cut off the strings representing Cmd_txt.
- Operational conditions
    1) Suspension condition
        L_in input
    2) Precondition
        A command is in front of L_in
    3) Postconditions
        <ground,var,var> : <ground,ground,ground>; <1-1>
        L_in input and L_in incrementally constructed to a ground list : L_in_rem incrementally constructed to a ground list.

Thanks to these procedures, the read_cmd_txt procedure can be coded as follows :

suspend read_cmd_txt(!,*,*).
read_cmd_txt([%|L_in],Txt,L_in_rem) ←
    read_txt(L_in,Txt,L_in_rem).
read_cmd_txt([Char|L_in],Cmd,L_in_rem) ←
    Char ≠ % | read_cmd([Char|L_in],Cmd,L_in_rem).

The read_txt procedure is quite straightforward to implement. For generality, we will use an auxiliary procedure that reads some list until some character is determined. It is specified as follows.

procedure read_until(X,L,Prefix,Suffix)
- Type
    L, Prefix, Suffix: lists, strong use
- Relation
    Prefix is the list of elements of L up to the first occurrence of X, this occurrence excluded. Suffix is the remainder of L, the occurrence excluded too.
- Operational conditions
    1) Suspension condition
        X ground and L input
    2) Postconditions
        <ground,ground,any,any> : <ground,ground,ground>; <0-1>
        X ground and L input and incrementally constructed to a ground list : Prefix and Suffix incrementally constructed to a ground list.

Its implementation results from an inductive reasoning on L. It is as follows :

suspend read_until(!g,!,*,*).
read_until(_,[],[],[]).
read_until(X,[X|T],[],T).
read_until(X,[Y|T],[Y|L1_rem],L2) ← X≠Y | read_until(X,T,L1_rem,L2).

The implementation of read_txt is then

suspend read_txt(!,*,*).
read_txt(L_in,txt(L_char),L_in_rem) ←
    read_until(CR,L_in,L_char,L_in_rem).

Implementing the read_cmd procedure is a little bit more complicated since undesirable blanks must occur between the fields or the program names. To eliminate them, we will adopt the convention that each field reading begins at a non-blank character.

Four auxiliary procedures are subsequently used. Each one aims at determining one field of the command. They are specified as follows :

procedure read_prgms(L_in,L_prgms,L_in_rem)
- Type
    L_in, L_in_rem : lists of ASCII code
    L_prgms : list of atoms
- Relation
    L_prgm is the list of the program names contained in front of L_in; L_in_rem is the remainder list cut off blanks placed in front.

- Operational conditions
    1) Suspension condition
        L_in input
    2) Precondition
        A command is in front of L_in
    3) Postconditions
        <ground,var,var> : <ground,ground,ground>; <1-1>
        L_in input and L_in incrementally constructed to a ground list : L_in_rem incrementally constructed to a ground list.

procedure read_input(L_in,Input_file,L_in_rem)
- Type
    L_in, L_in_rem : lists of ASCII code
    Input file : of one of the three following forms
        file(File_name) where File_name is the name of a file,
        std,
        none
- Relation
    Input file is the input file designator in front of L_in;
    L_in_rem is the remainder list cut off the blanks placed in front.
- Operational conditions
    1) Suspension condition
        L_in input
    2) Precondition
        L_in is not empty and its head is a non-blank character
    3) Postcondition
        <ground,var,var> : <ground,ground,ground>; <1-1>
        L_in input and L_in incrementally constructed to a ground list : L_in_rem incrementally constructed to a ground list.

procedure read_output(L_in,Output_file,L_in_rem)
- Type
    L_in, L_in_rem : lists of ASCII code
    Output_file : of one of the two following forms
        file(File_name) where File_name is the name of a file
        std,
- Relation
    Output file is the output file designator in front of L_in;
    L_in_rem is the remainder list cut off blanks placed in front.

- Operational conditions
    1) Suspension condition
        L_in input
    2) Precondition
        L_in is not empty and its head is a non blank character
    3) Postcondition
        <ground,var,var> : <ground,ground,ground>; <1-1>
        L_in input and L_in incrementally constructed to a ground list : L_in_rem incrementally constructed to a ground list.

procedure read_tag(L_in,Tag,L_in_rem)
- Type
    L_in, L_in_rem : lists of ASCII code
    Tag : either "bg" or "fg"
- Relation
    Let P be the list of characters of L_in up to the first occurrence of the CR character, this character included. Then,
    if the head of L_in is **&** then Tag is "bg" and L_in_rem is L_in cut off P
    if the head of L_in is **CR** then Tag is "fg" and L_in_rem is the tail of L_in cut off P
- Operational conditions
    1) Suspension condition
        L_in input
    2) Precondition
        L_in non empty and its head is either **&** or **CR**.
    3) Postconditions
        <ground,var,var> : <ground,ground,ground>; <1-1>
        L_in input and incrementally constructed to a ground list : L_in_rem incrementally constructed to a ground list.

Thanks to these procedures, the read_cmd procedure may be implemented as follows :

read_cmd(L_in,cmd(L_prgms,Input_file,Output_file,Tag),L_in_rem) ←
    read_prgms(L_in,L_prgms,L_in_1),
    read_input(L_in_1,Input_file,L_in_2),
    read_output(L_in_2,Output_file,L_in_3),
    read_tag(L_in_3,Tag,L_in_rem).

Implementing these auxiliary procedures requires the four following procedures. They are used

- for removing blanks placed in front of a list,
- for reading some name and removing blanks following it

- for testing whether a character is a limitator or not
- for connecting an atom with the list of ASCII code representing it,

respectively. They are specified as follows.

1) procedure read_blank(L_in,L_out).
   - Type

     L_in, L_out : lists of ASCII code
   - Relation

     L_out is L_in cut off the blank characters placed in front of it
   - Operational properties
     1) Suspension condition

        L_in input
     2) Postconditions

        <ground,any> : <ground,ground>; <0-1>

        L_in input and L_in incrementally constructed ground : L_out incrementally constructed ground.

2) procedure read_name(L_in,Name,L_in_rem).
   - Type

     L_in, L_in_rem : lists of ASCII code

     Name : atom
   - Relation

     Let P be the list of characters of L_in upto the first occurrence of a **CR**, **BL**, **&**, **||**, **<** or **>** character. Then
     - Name is the atom corresponding to P,
     - L_in_rem is L_in cut off P.
   - Operational properties
     1) Suspension condition

        L_in input
     2) Precondition

        L_in is not empty and its head is not a **CR** or blank character
     3) Postconditions

        <ground,any,any> : <ground,ground,ground>; <0-1>

        L_in input and L_in incrementally constructed ground : L_in_rem incrementally constructed ground

3) procedure limitator(C).
   - Type

     C : character
   - Relation

     C is either **BL**, **CR**, **&**, **||**, **<**, **>**

- Operational properties
    1) Suspension condition
        C ground
    2) Postcondition
        <any> : <ground>, <0-1>
4) procedure name(Atom,L)
    - Type
        Atom : atom,
        L : list of ASCII code
    - Relation
        L is the list of ASCII characters corresponding to the atom Atom
    - Operational properties
        1) Suspension conditions
            Pattern1 : Atom ground
            Pattern2 : L input
        2) Postconditions
            Pattern1 : L incrementally constructed
            <ground,any> : <ground,ground>; <0-1>
            <any,ground> : <ground,ground>; <0-1>

The read_prgms(L_in,L_prgms,L_in_rem) procedure can then be coded thanks to the following algorithm :

read the string of the first program name in L_in, thanks to the read_name procedure,
transform it into an atom thanks to the name procedure,
read the blank characters following the name
if the next character is ||
    then read blanks and repeat the process
    else stop, all program names have been read.

This is embodied in the following piece of code :

read_prgms(L_in,[Prgm|L_prgms_rem],L_in_rem) ←
    read_name(L_in,Prgm_string,L_rem1),
    name(Prgm,Prgm_string),
    read_blanks(L_rem1,L_rem2),
    end_read_prgm(L_rem2,L_prgms_rem,L_in_rem).

```
suspend end_read_prgm(!,*,*,*).
end_read_prgm([Char|Lin_rem],L_prgms,L_rem) ←
    Char = || |
    read_blanks(Lin_rem,L1),
    read_prgms(Lin_rem,L_prgms,L_rem).
end_read_prgm([Char|Lin_rem],L_prgms,L_rem) ←
    Char ≠ || |
    L_prgms = [],
    L_rem = [Char|Lin_rem].
```

No suspension declaration is needed to reflect the suspension condition of the read_prgms procedure thanks to the suspension conditions of the read_name, name and read_blank procedures and thanks to the suspension declaration of the end_read_prgm procedure. For the same reasons, no sequentialization operator is needed in the body of its clause to express the sequentiality of the above algorithm.

The end_read_prgm procedure is used to express the last if statement. It takes as paramaters

- the part of the L_in list which has not been examined yet, say L_in_rem,
- the list of program names to be read in L_in_rem,
- the list L_rem as it results after the reading of all program names.

The code of the procedure reflects the if instruction. One point is worth noting. In the second clause, the list L_prgms is instantiated to [] only after the test to detect whether all program names have been read is made. This is to prevent erroneous instantiations of the L_prgms list.

The precondition of the read_input procedure ensures that the first character to be read is always non blank. It can thus be of the following form :

CR
&
>
<

The three first cases correspond to the case where no input specifier is specified. In these cases, the Input file name should be instantiated to none. The list L_in is then the list L_in_rem. In the last case, the input file name is std or file(File_name) according as a file name follows the "<" symbol or not. This amounts to test that the character following the "<" symbol is a limitator or not. In both cases, blanks following the "<" symbol or the file name should be read to determine the list L_in_rem delivered by the procedure. The following piece of code follows :

```
suspend read_input(?,*,*).
read_input([CR|Chars],none,[CR|Chars]).
read_input([&|Chars],none,[&|Chars]).
read_input([>|Chars],none,[>|Chars]).
read_input([<,Char|Chars],Input_file,L) ←
    limitator(Char) |
    File_input = std,
    read_blanks([Char|Chars],L).
read_input([<,Char|Chars],Input_file,L) ←
    not(limitator(Char)) |
    Input_file = file(File_name),
    read_name([Char|Chars],File_name_string,L_aux) ,
    name(File_name,File_name_string) ,
    read_blanks(L_aux,L).
```

The read_output procedure is constructed in a similar way. The following piece of code results.

```
suspend read_output(?,*,*).
read_output([CR|Chars],std,[CR|Chars]).
read_output([&|Chars],std,[&|Chars]).
read_output([>,Char|Chars],File_name,L_rem) ←
    read_name([Char|Chars],File_name_string,L_aux) ,
    name(File_name,File_name_string) ,
    read_blanks(L_aux,L_rem).
```

The read_tag procedure directly follows from its specification :

```
suspend read_tag(?,*,*).
read_tag([&|Chars],bg,L) ← read_until(CR,Chars,_,L).
read_tag([CR|Chars],fg,Chars).
```

To complete the parser program, the auxiliary read_blanks, read_name, limitator and name procedure remains to be specified. We assume the latter to be a built-in procedure. The two first ones are coded by inductively reasoning its L_in parameter :

```
suspend read_blanks(!,*).
read_blanks([BL|Lin_rem],Lout) ← read_blanks(Lin_rem,Lout).
read_blanks([Char|Lin_rem],Lout) ← Char ≠ BL.| Lout = [Char|Lin_rem].
```

```
suspend read_name(?,*,*).
read_name([Char|Chars],Name,L_rem) ←
    limitator(Char) |
    Name = [], L_rem = [Char|Chars]
read_name([Char|Chars],Name,L_rem) ←
    not(limitator(Char)) |
    Name = [Char|Name_rem] ,read_name(Chars,Name_rem,L_rem).
```

Finally, the limitator procedure directly results from its specification :

```
suspend limitator(!).
limitator(CR).
limitator(BL).
limitator(&).
limitator(||).
limitator(<).
limitator(>).
```

B.2 The shell procedure

We now program the shell process. It receives a stream of commands and is in charge of executing them. To this end, it can make some file requests to the file system. Some output may furthermore results from the execution of the commands.

Many shell processes can in fact be pointed out. They vary from the strategies they embody. We program several ones hereafter. We begin with a simple one and complicate it by introducing failure handling, abortion of commands and process priorities.

The shell procedure will be designed in such a way that the reduction of any call of the form

    shell(L_cmds,File_request,Output),   (*)

where L_cmds is a list of commands and File_request and Output are variables, reflects the behavior of the shell process. As the shell process consumes the commands and do not generate them, the L_cmds parameter is declared as element input whatever shell is considered.

B.2.1 THE SIMPLE SHELL

As the behavior of the shell process simply consists of executing commands, coding the shell procedure by the following clause might seem satisfactory :

```
shell([Cmd|Cmds],File_request,Output) ←
    execute(Cmd,File_request_1,Output_1),
    shell(Cmds,File_request_2,Output_2),
    merge(File_request_1,File_request_2,File_request),
    merge(Output_1,Output_2,Output).
```

The execute procedure is assumed to execute some command possibly with some file requests and some output.

Using this procedure, the reduction of a call of the form (*) above results in the concurrent execution of four processes. One is in charge of executing the first command. The second one is in charge of executing the commands following it. The third one merges the requests to the file system made by the two first ones. Finally, the last one merges the output generated by them.

This solution is not fully satisfactory for two reasons :

1) Text input may occur between some commands. It is not handled by the above clause.
2) Commands should not always be executed concurrently. They can be executed either in foreground or in background. However, in the above clause, all of them are executed concurrently.

The first problem is solved by adding two parameters to the execute procedure. The former, Cmd_txt receives the flow from the input stream. This may be necessary to execute commands requiring an input text. The second parameter is used to output this flow, possibly cut off some employed input text. This avoids the shell to handle text explicitly : input texts are consumed and removed from the flow of command/text before they are passed to the shell. In terms of the program, the shell procedure may then only embody clauses for the commands.

The second problem is solved by duplicating the clause in order to have a clause for foreground commands and a clause for background ones. They are the same except that, in the first one, the execute and shell calls are sequentialized. They thus form a sequentialized goal. This translates the fact that any foreground command should be executed before any subsequent command. As they are suspended on their two first list parameters, the merge calls may still be executed concurrently with this sequentialized goal.

The simple shell is then defined as follows :

suspend shell(!,*,*).
shell([cmd(L_prgms,Infile,Outfile,fg)|Cmd_txt],File_request,Output) ←
    merge(File_request_1,File_request_2,File_request),
    merge(Output_1,Output_2,Output),
    [execute(cmd(L_prgms,Infile,Outfile,fg),Cmd_txt,Cmd_txt_rem,
                                    File_request_1,Output_1) |
        shell(Cmd_txt_rem,File_request_2,Output_2)   ] .
shell([cmd(L_prgms,Infile,Outfile,bg)|Cmd_txt],File_request,Output) ←
    merge(File_request_1,File_request_2,File_request),
    merge(Output_1,Output_2,Output),
    execute(cmd(L_prgms,Infile,Outfile,fg),Cmd_txt,Cmd_txt_rem,
                                    File_request_1,Output_1)
    shell(Cmd_txt_rem,File_request_2,Output_2).

It remains to implement the execute procedure. It aims at making the reduction of the call

execute(Cmd,Cmd_txt,Cmd_txt_rem,File_request,Output)

behave as the execution of a command. This execution is as follows. Let

cmd(L_prgms,Infile,Outfile,Tag)

be the command Cmd to be executed. Program codes for the programs of L_prgms are first searched thanks to file requests. When need be, input information are also searched. This might require inspecting the flow of commands and input text or searching for files. Thereafter, the command is really executed. Output in the Output file may result.

The following specification follows.

procdure execute(Cmd,Cmd_txt,Cmds_txt_rem,File_request,Output).
- Type
    Cmd : command
    Cmd_txt, Cmd_txt_rem : lists of commands and texts
    File_request : list whose elements are of the form
        get(File_name,File_contents)
        replace(File_name,
    Output : list of ASCII codes
- Relation
    Cmd_txt_rem is
        - Cmd_txt where the first input text has been removed, if the input field of Cmd is std,
        - Cmd_txt, otherwise

Output is
- [] if the output file of the command is some file,
- the text generated by the execution of the command otherwise

File_request is composed of
- a get(Prgm_name,Prog_code) term for each program involved by the procedure
- a replace(Outfile,Txt) term if an output file is specified in the output specifier of the command. In this case, Outfile is this file and Txt is the text resulting from the execution of the procedure.

- Operational properties

    1) Suspension condition

    Cmd input, Cmd_txt element input

    2) Precondition

    Cmd_txt_rem, File_request, Output : variables

    3) Postconditions

    <ground,ground,var,var,var> : <ground,ground,ground,ground,ground>; <1-1>
    Cmd_txt input and incrementally constructed : Cmd_txt_rem incrementally constructed

To implement the procedure, assume that the reduction of the four following s-goals behave as follows :

1° The s-goal

progs(L_progms,Prgms_code,File_request),

incrementally consumes the list of programs L_progms and searches for the code of these programs by means of the file requests to the file system.

2° The s-goal

input(Infile,Cmd_txt,Cmd_txt_rem,In_txt,File_request)

waits for the Infile parameter to be ground and consumes the list of commands and texts Cmd_txt. It acts as follows according to the value of the Infile parameter

- If the input specifier Infile is std then the first text of Cmd_txt is taken as input data. This means that the variable In_txt is bound to this text. Furthermore, Cmd_txt_rem is bound to the list Cmd_txt cut off this text.
- If the input specifier Infile designates some file, then the contents of this file is obtained by means of a request message to the file store system. In this case, In_txt is bound to the contents of this file and Cmd_txt_rem is bound to Cmd_txt.
- If the input specifier Infile is none, then no input text is searched and the variables In_txt and Cmd_txt_rem are bound to [] and Cmd_txt, respectively.

3° The s-goal

output(Outfile,Out_txt,Output,File_request),

waits for the Outfile parameter to be ground and uses the Out_txt parameter as element input. It regards them as an output specifier and a list of ASCII code, respectively. Then, according to the value of Outfile, the following operations are performed. If this value is std then the Output variable is bound to Out_txt and the File_request variable is bound to the empty list. Otherwise, Outfile is of the form file(File_name). In this case, the Output variable is bound to the empty list and the File_request variable is bound to the list [replace(File_name,Out_txt)].

4° The s-goal

run(Prgm_code,In_txt,Out_txt,File_request).

incrementally consumes the list of program codes Progm_code and execute them. To this end, it also consumes the input text of the In_txt parameter and constructs the variable File_request by some messages for the file system. As a result of the execution, some text may be constructed. The Out_txt variable is bound to it.

The implementation of the execute procedure then basically consists of launching, in parallel, the reduction of these s-goals together. A process in charge of merging the messages for the file system must furthermore be launched concurrently. These five concurrent executions may be simulated by the reduction of the following goal

    ←   progs(L_prgms,Prgms_code,File_request_1),
          input(Infile,Cmd_txt,Cmd_txt_rem,In_txt,File_request_2),
          output(Outfile,Out_txt,Output,File_request_3),
          run(Prgms_code,In_txt,Out_txt,File_request_4),
          merge(File_request_1,File_request_2,File_request_12),
          merge(File_request_3,File_request_4,File_request_34),
          merge(File_request_12,File_request_34,File_request).

Three merge calls are used to merge the successively merge the file system messages to the file system. Note that the concurrent reduction of the subgoals is allowed thanks to their assumed suspension behavior.

Summing up, the execute procedure is as follows

```
suspend execute(?,?,*,*,*).
execute(cmd(L_prgms,Infile,Outfile,_),Cmd_txt,Cmd_txt_rem,File_request,Output) ←
    progs(L_prgms,Prgms_code,File_request_1),
    input(Infile,Cmd_txt,Cmd_txt_rem,In_txt,File_request_2),
    output(Outfile,Out_txt,Output,File_request_3),
    run(Prgms_code,In_txt,Out_txt,File_request_4),
    merge(File_request_1,File_request_2,File_request_12),
    merge(File_request_3,File_request_4,File_request_34),
    merge(File_request_12,File_request_34,File_request).
```

The progs, input, output and run procedures are constructed in order to reflect the above behavior of the reduction of the associated calls.

1° The progs procedure results directly from this description. It is as follows :

```
suspend progs(!,*,*).
progs([],[],[]).
progs([Prog_name|Prog_names_rem],[Prog_code|Prgms_code_rem],
                    [get(Prog_name,Prog_code)|File_requests_rem]) ←
    progs(Prog_names_rem,Prgms_code_rem,File_requests_rem).
```

As usual, the incremental consumption is achieved by the "!" read-only annotation and the explicit form of the list in the clause head.

2° The input procedure also follows from the above description. We use an auxiliary procedure to search for the first input text in the stream of commands/texts Cmd_txt. It is constructed in the more general aim of searching an element in a list. Its specification is as follows

procedure search(X,L,L_rem).
- Type
    L, L_rem : lists whose elements are of the type of X; strong use
- Relation
    L_rem is L where the first element that unifies with X has been removed
- Operational properties
    1) Suspension condition
        L element input
    2) Postcondition
        L incrementally constructed : L_rem incrementally constructed.

It is implemented by an inductive analysis of the input list L. The following piece of code results:

```
suspend input(!g,?,*,*,*).
input(none,Cmds_txts,[],Cmds_txts,[]).
input(std,Cmds_txts,L_char,Cmds_txts_rem,[]) ←
      search(txt(L_char),Cmds_txts,Cmds_txts_rem).
input(file(Fn),Cmds_txts,File_txt,Cmds_txts,[get(Fn,File_txt)]).

suspend search(*,!,*) with l-commit.
search(X,[X|L_rem],L_rem);
search(X,[Y|T],[Y|L_rem]) ← search(X,T,L_rem).
```

3° The output procedure results also from the above description. It is as follows:

```
suspend output(!g,!,*,*).
output(std,Out_txt,Out_txt,[]).
output(file(File_name),Out_txt,[],[replace(File_name,Out_txt)]).
```

4° Finally, the run procedure is constructed by means of an auxiliary built-in procedure:

```
exec(Prog_code,In_txt,Out_txt,File_request)
```

It declares its two first parameters as input. Assuming the two last ones are variables, the reduction of the above call then results in adding the Prog_code to the run time system and executing it. This involves the consumption of the In_txt text, the sending of messages to the file system by constructing the File_request list and the output of some text by instantiating the Out_txt variable.

The run procedure is then coded to reflect the pipeline execution of the list of program codes: the input of the $i+1^{th}$ program is the output of the ith one. The following piece of code results.

```
suspend run(?,?,*,*).
run([Prg_code],In_txt,Out_txt,File_request) ←
      exec(Prg_code,In_txt,Out_txt,File_request).
run([Prg_code_1,Prg_code_2|Prgms_rem],In_txt,Out_txt,File_request) ←
      exec(Prg_code_1,In_txt,Out_txt_aux,File_request_1),
      run([Prg_code_2|Prgms_rem],Out_txt_aux,Out_txt,File_request_2),
      merge(File_request_1,File_request_2,File_request).
```

Pipeline is achieved in the second clause by passing as input text of the recursive call the output text generated by the exec call. A merge call is used to merge the message to the file system arising from the exec and run calls. Note that all subgoals can be reduced concurrently thanks to the suspension declarations.

B.2.2 HANDLING FAILURE

The simple shell suffers from one drawback : it fails whenever a command execution fails. This is not what one would expect from a practical operating system. If a user program fails, the operating system should not crash. Moreover, output from a user program should be incrementally available whether or not it ultimately fails.

To circumvent this problem, we make use of the simplified form of our meta-call primitive, namely call(Goal,Status). It has only two parameters : the goal to be launched and a variable to memorize the result of the computation : failed or succeeded.

The code is then modified as follows. The

  execute(...)

calls are replaced by the

  call(execute(...),Status)

calls. Such a call always succeeds even when the command execution fails. However, in this case, the File_request and Ouput channels contain a variable as tail sublist. To terminate properly, we furthermore close these channels. This is achieved by a generalized form of the merge procedure, called g_merge, that takes the result of the computation into account. It is specified as follows.

  procedure g_merge(Status,L1,L2,L).
- Type
    Status : failed or succeeded
    L1, L2, L : lists; strong use
- Operational properties
    1) Suspension conditions
        Status : input
        L1, L2 : element input
    2) Precondition
        L is a variable
    3) Postcondition
        Assume that L1 and L2 are incrementally constructed. Assume that Status is eventually bound to succeeded or failed. Let L1_pref be
        - the prefix constructed for L1 when Status is bound to failed, if this is the case,
        - L1, otherwise.
        Assume that L1 is no more constructed when Status becomes bound to failed. Then, L is incrementally constructed to one merged version of L1_pref and L2.

Such a procedure may be coded from the merge procedure. It must just be extended in two ways. First, the merge predicate must be extended from one parameter : Status. It is kept unprecised in the head of the four clauses defining the merge procedure since until Status is not bound to failed the g_merge procedure acts as the classical merge. The second extension deals with this event. When Status is bound to failed then the elements of L1 are discarded and only those of L2 are inserted in L. This is achieved by the following clause.

    g_merge(failed,L1,L2,L2).

Commitment is conserved. It ensures that only one merged version is constructed for L. The following procedure results :

    suspend g_merge(!,!,!,*) with l_commit.
    g_merge(Status,[H|T],L2,[H|L_rem]) ← g_merge(Status,T,L2,L_rem).
    g_merge(Status,L1,[H|T],[H|L_rem]) ← g_merge(Status,L1,T,L_rem).
    g_merge(Status,[],L2,L2)
    g_merge(Status,L1,[],L1)
    g_merge(failed,L1,L2,L2).

The list L is required to be bound by the elements of L2 as soon as Status becomes bound to failed. One might thus expect that only the last clause should be used as soon as Status becomes bound to failed. This is not guaranteed by the procedure. Indeed, in this case, the first four clauses may remain unifiable. The specification is however still met since it is assumed that the list L1 is no more constructed as soon as Status become bound to failed. Only, the second clause and the fourth one can then be used. Both of them construct L with elements of L2.

The shell procedure then rewrites as

    suspend shell(!,*,*).
    shell([cmd(L_prgms,Infile,Outfile,fg)|Cmd_txt],File_request,Output) ←
        g_merge(Status,File_request_1,File_request_2,File_request),
        g_merge(Status,Output_1,Output_2,Output),
        [call(execute(cmd(L_prgms,Infile,Outfile,fg),Cmd_txt,Cmd_txt_rem,
                                      File_request_1,Output_1),
            Status)
        | shell(Cmd_txt_rem,File_request_2,Output_2)] .
    shell([cmd(L_prgms,Infile,Outfile,bg)|Cmd_txt],File_request,Output) ←
        g_merge(Status,File_request_1,File_request_2,File_request),
        g_merge(Status,Output_1,Output_2,Output),
        call(execute(cmd(L_prgms,Infile,Outfile,fg),Cmd_txt,Cmd_txt_rem,
                                    File_request_1,Output_1),
        Status),
    shell(Cmd_txt_rem,File_request_2,Output_2).

B.2.3 ABORTING FOREGROUND COMMAND EXECUTION

We further complicate the shell by allowing the execution of foreground commands to be aborted. To this end, a new command is introduced : abort. Its effect is to abort the execution of the foreground process under execution.

This extension is achieved by replacing the process in charge of executing a foreground command by three concurrent conjoined processes : the execution of the foreground command, a search process for an abort command and an arbitrator process. They act as follows :

1° The process executing the command basically acts as in the basic shell. It still consumes the flow of commands/texts Cmd_txt, dialogues with the file system by means of the File_request_1 list and outputs the unused commands/texts of Cmd_txt in Cmd_txt_rem as well as some results in Output_1. The novelty is that it hears for a stop order resulting from the discovery of an abort command. It stops its processing when such a stop message is heard.

This may be coded in Conclog by calling the execute procedure as before but now through the three-argument meta call primitive :

```
call( execute(cmd(L_prgms,Infile,Outfile,fg),Cmd_txt,Cmd_txt_rem,
                                        File_request_1,Output_1),
      Status, Control).
```

While the Control variable remains uninstantiated, the reduction of this call amounts to the reduction of the execute(...) call. Instantiating the Control variable to [stop] has the effect of stopping the latter reduction.

2° The search process is in charge of searching in the flow of commands Cmd_txt for an abort command. As a result, it produces the list Cmd_txt cut off the first occurrence of the abort command. To be useful, such a search must succeed before the foreground command is completely executed. In case this execution terminates, the search then becomes useless and is stopped. Therefore, the search process should also hear for stop messages and stop when one occurs.

The search may be implemented thanks to the search procedure of Subsection B.2.1 above. Stopping the search is made possible by using the three arguments meta-call primitive. The following s-goal then embodies the search process :

```
call( search(cmd(abort,_,_,_),Cmd_txt,Cmd_txt_rem),
      Status,Control).
```

3° Finally, the role of the arbitrator process is to monitor the results of the computation of the two previous processes. On the one hand, it stops the process executing the command if the search for an abort command is successful. On the other hand, it stops the search process if the command process terminates. In both cases, it furthermore selects the appropriate continuation points.

This is achieved by the following arbitrator procedure. Its parameters include the Status and Control variables of the two processes, the remainder of the flow of commands/texts computed by the process executing the foreground command, the remainder of this flow computed by the search process and the flow of commands to consider after the execution of these three concurrent processes. The arbitrator predicate is thus of the following form.

arbitrator(Status_exec,Control_exec,Status_search,Control_search,
 Cmd_txt_exec,Cmd_txt_search,Cmd_txt_rem)

Its reduction is as follows.Two cases must be considered.

1) In the first one, the execution of the command terminates first. This is signalled by the binding of Status_exec to [failed] in case the execution fails or [succeeded] in case the execution succeeds (see Section 6.2.2). The search process is then required to stop. This is achieved by instantiating the Control_search variable to [stop]. In this case, the commands/texts to be considered are those of Cmd_txt_exec.

2) In the second case, the search process terminates first. This is signalled similarly by the binding of Status_search to [failed] in case of failure or to [succeeded] in case of success. In case of failure, no abort has been found and the execution of the foreground command should be pursued. The flow of commands/texts to be considered after its execution is that computed by it. Consequently, the Cmd_txt_rem variable is bound to Cmd_txt_exec in this case. In case of success, an abord command has been found. The execution of the foreground command is then stopped. This is achieved by instantiating the Control_exec variable to [stop]. The commands/texts to be considered after execution of the foreground command are then those of Cmd_txt_search.

This behavior of the arbitrator process can be coded in the following procedure :

```
suspend arbitrator(!,*,!,*,!,!,*) with l_commit.
arbitrator([succeeded],_,_,[stop],Cmd_txt_exec,_,Cmd_txt_exec).
arbitrator([failed],_,_,[stop],Cmd_txt_exec,_,Cmd_txt_exec).
arbitrator(_,[stop],[succeeded],_,_,Cmd_txt_search,Cmd_txt_search).
arbitrator(_,_,[failed],_,Cmd_txt_exec,_,Cmd_txt_exec).
```

The form of the clause heads and the read-only annotations of the suspension declaration ensure that the reduction of an arbitrator call whose parameters are variables only occurs in one of the two above situations. The commit operator ensures that if they occur simultaneously, one of them is chosen arbitrarily.

Replacing the two-arguments meta-call by the three-arguments one forces the g_merge procedure to be adapted. Two modifications are required. First, the procedure should be adapted to the new forms of the Status variable. Second, it should be extended in order to handle the new [stopped] issue. In this case, the channel should also be closed as for the failed case. The following g_merge_2 procedure results :

```
suspend g_merge_2(!,!,!,*).
g_merge_2(Status,[H|T],L2,[H|L_rem]) ← g_merge_2(Status,T,L2,L_rem).
g_merge_2(Status,L1,[H|T],[H|L_rem]) ← g_merge_2(Status,L1,T,L_rem).
g_merge_2(Status,[],L2,L2)
g_merge_2(Status,L1,[],L1)
g_merge_2([failed],L1,L2,L2).
g_merge_2([stopped],L1,L2,L2).
```

The shell clause for the foreground command is obtained by noting the following fact. Foreground commands require that the commands stated after them are executed only after they are completely executed. This end of execution may be understood either as a natural termination or as a provoked one due to the discovery of an abort command. In terms of the Conclog program, this termination coincides with the termination of the reduction of the arbitrator call. Furthermore the flow of commands and texts to take into account is the one delivered by this call.

Summing up, the following clause results.

```
shell([cmd(L_prgms,Infile,Outfile,fg)|Cmd_txt],File_request,Output) ←
    g_merge_2(Status_exec,File_request_1,File_request_2,File_request),
    g_merge_2(Status_exec,Output_1,Output_2,Output),
    call( execute(cmd(L_prgms,Infile,Outfile,fg),Cmd_txt,Cmd_txt_rem_exec,
                                    File_request_1,Output_1),
          Status_exec,Control_exec).
    call( search(cmd(abort,_,_,_),Cmd_txt,Cmds_rem_search),
          Status_search,Control_search),
    [  arbitrator( Status_exec,Control_exec,Status_search,Control_search,
                   Cmd_txt_rem_exec,Cmd_txt_rem_search,Cmd_rem)
    |  shell(Cmd_rem,File_request_2,Output_2) ] .
```

B.2.4 KILLING BACKGROUND COMMAND EXECUTION

An additional refinement to the shell consists of allowing the execution of background commands to be killed. This requires the following extensions.

Firstly, a list of commands under execution must be kept by the shell. It consists of a list of command identifiers, referred to in the following by Cmd_id. Every command is then augmented by an identifier. This can be implemented as a prompt number incremented and inserted by the term process.

A second extension concerns the commands. In addition to the already known ones, a kill command is provided. It takes the form

   kill(Cmd_id).

Its action is to kill the process identified by Cmd_id.

We seize this opportunity to refine the internal structure of the keyboard strings. There are now of three forms

   - the interrupt form : interrupt(abort) or interrupt(kill(Proc_id))
   - the text form : txt(L_chars) ,
   - the command form : cmd(Cmd_id,L_prgms,Infile,Outfile,Tag).

The first form is a new one. The others refer to the already known forms. It is not difficult to extend the parser in order to handle the interrupt form.

The shell procedure is then modified as follows. First, it is extended so as to handle a list of active processes in charge of the execution of the background commands. It is subsequently referred to as Lap. As this list is internal to the shell, we will keep it also private in the Conclog procedure. This is achieved, as for abstract data types, by calling an auxiliary procedure. It is named kernel_shell and reflects in fact the real behavior of the shell. The list of active processes is empty when the shell process is launched. Consequently, the shell procedure is implemented as follows :

   shell(Cmd_txt,File_request,Output) ← kernel_shell(Cmd_txt,File_request,Output,[]).

A suspension declaration follows from that of the shell procedure. Basically, the added parameter is just consulted. The internal structure of its terms will however be accessed and modified later. It is thus declared as element input. The following suspension declaration results:

   suspend kernel_shell(!,*,*,!).

The core of the kernel_shell is constructed with respect to the two old foreground and background commands and the newly introduced kill command. A clause is associated with each of them.

1° The treatment of foreground commands is not modified by the introduction of interrupt commands. The clause of the kernel_shell procedure corresponding to foreground commands is thus directly derived from that of the above Subsection B.2.3. It is as follows :

```
kernel_shell([cmd(Cmd_id,L_prgms,Infile,Outfile,fg)|Cmd_txt],File_request,Output,Lap) ←
    g_merge_2(Status_exec,File_request_1,File_request_2,File_request),
    g_merge_2(Status_exec,Output_1,Output_2,Output),
    call(  execute(cmd(Cmd_id,L_prgms,Infile,Outfile,fg),Cmd_txt,Cmds_rem_exec,
                                              File_request_1,Output_1),
           Status_exec,Control_exec).
    call(  search(interrupt(abort),Cmd_txt,Cmds_rem_search),
           Status_search,Control_search),
    [ arbitrator( Status_exec,Control_exec,Status_search,Control_search,
                  Cmd_txt_rem_exec,Cmd_txt_rem_search,Cmd_rem)
    | kernel_shell(Cmd_rem,File_request_2,Output_2,Lap) ] .
```

2° Background commands are basically handled as before. The only extension is that the shell process should now be able to kill their execution when it receives a kill command. To this end, the execution of the commands need first to be extended in order to be stopped on demand. In Conclog terms, this is achieved by replacing the execute call by a three arguments meta-call of it. Binding its Control component to stop has exactly the expected effect of stopping the execution of the command. To complete the mechanism, some means must be provided to bound this Control variable easily. This is achieved by inserting the identifier of the command together with the Status and Control variables in the list of active processes.

The clause of the kernel_shell procedure corresponding to background commands is thus as follows :

```
kernel_shell([cmd(Proc_id,L_prgms,Infile,Outfile,bg)|Cmd_txt],File_request,Output,Lap) ←
    g_merge_2(Proc_status,File_request_1,File_request_2,File_request)),
    g_merge_2(Proc_status,Output_1,Output_2,Output)),
    call(  execute(cmd(Cmd_id,L_prgms,Infile,Outfile,bg),Cmd_txt,Cmd_txt_rem,
                                              File_request_1,Output_1),
           Proc_status,Proc_control),
    kernel_shell(Cmd_txt_rem,File_request_2,Output_2,
                                 [proc(Cmd_id,Proc_status,Proc_control)|Lap]).
```

3° Handling of kill commands remains to be explained. When a killed command is received by the shell, the specified process is simply searched in the list of active processes and its Control variable is set to [stop]. Subsequent commands are then handled.

Such an instantiation of the Control variable is achieved by means of the following kill procedure. It is specified as follows.

procedure kill(Proc_id,Lap,New_lap)
- Type
    Proc_id : identifier of a process
    Lap, New_lap : lists of terms of the form proc(X,Y,Z)
- Relation
    Lap contains a term proc(Proc_id,Proc_status,Proc_control) - where Proc_id is the first parameter - and New_lap is Lap where the first occurrence of the term has been removed.
- Operational properties
    1) Suspension conditions
        Proc_id ground
        Lap element input
    2) Postconditions
        Lap element input and incrementally constructed : New_lap incrementally constructed
        As a side effect, the Proc_control component of the first occurrence referred to in the relation specification is bound to [stop].

Its implementation directly results from an inductive reasoning on Lap. It is

suspend kill(!g,!,*).
kill(Proc_id,[],[]).
kill(Proc_id,[proc(Proc_id,Proc_status,Proc_control)|Procs_rem],Procs_rem) ←
    Proc_control = [stop].
kill(Proc_id,[proc(Proc_id_aux,Proc_status,Proc_control)|Procs_rem],L) ←
    Proc_id ≠ Proc_id_aux |
    L = [proc(Proc_id_aux,Proc_status,Proc_control)|L_rem],
    kill(Proc_id,Procs_rem,L_rem) .

Note that the side effect property is achieved through head unification and the back communication mechanism.

The clause for kill commands is then as follows :

kernel_shell([interrupt(kill(Proc_id))|Cmd_txt],File_request,Output,Lap) ←
    kill(Proc_id,Lap,New_Lap),
    kernel_shell(Cmd_txt,File_request,Output,New_Lap).

B.2.5 HANDLING PRIORITIES

As a final refinement, we introduce priority in the shell. In our previous shell programs, the execution of background commands continue to run even when a foreground command is executed. We might wish to give a higher priority to the foreground commands so that background commands are effectively executed only when there is no active foreground command to be executed.

This extension is subsequently performed in two ways. In a first solution, the execution of background commands is suspended as soon as a foreground command is detected. In the second one, the execution of background commands is suspended when the execution of the foreground command is effectively ready to be executed.

i) First solution

The first solution is implemented by calling background executions with a common control parameter, say Fg_control. It is incrementally constructed with a suspend order when a foreground command is invoked and with a continue order when the foreground command is executed. As a result, the execution of background commands is suspended and resumed each time the execution of a foreground command is started and ended, respectively. To be propagated in the reduction of the kernell_shell call, this control parameter is inserted as a parameter of the kernel_shell procedure. It is submitted to no suspension declaration since the reduction of the kernel_shell calls may instantiate it.

Let us examine, in more details, the impact of this extension on the three clauses of the kernel_shell procedure.

1° The clause handling foreground command is augmented by two incremental constructions of the Fg_control parameter. The first one occurs at the begining of the execution of the foreground commands. The Fg_control parameter can thus be constructed by head unification. The head parameter [suspend|Fg_control_rem_1] results. The second incremental construction occurs when the execution of the foreground command is ended i.e. after the call

  arbitrator(Status_exec,Control_exec,Status_search,Control_search,
    Cmd_txt_rem_exec,Cmd_txt_rem_search,Cmd_rem)

is reduced. It consists of adding the continue order in the Fg_control list. This is achieved by instantiating Fg_control_rem_1 as follows

  Fg_control_rem_1 = [suspend|Fg_control_rem_2]

The kernel_shell procedure is then recursively called with Fg_control_rem_2 as Fg_control parameter in order to pursue the incremental construction of the Fg_control list of the initial call to the kernel_shell procedure. The following clause results.

```
kernel_shell([cmd(Cmd_id,L_prgms,Infile,Outfile,fg)|Cmd_txt],File_request,Output,
                                            Lap,[suspend|Fg_control_rem_1]) ←
    g_merge_2(Status_exec,File_request_1,File_request_2,File_request),
    g_merge_2(Status_exec,Output_1,Output_2,Output),
    call(  execute(cmd(Cmd_id,L_prgms,Infile,Outfile,fg),Cmd_txt,Cmd_rem_exec,
                                            File_request_1,Output_1),
           Status_exec,Control_exec),
    call(  search(interrupt(abort),Cmd_txt,Cmd_rem_search),
           Status_search,Control_search),
    [   arbitrator( Status_exec,Control_exec,Status_search,Control_search,
                    Cmd_txt_rem_exec,Cmd_txt_rem_search,Cmd_rem)
     |  Fg_control_rem_2=[continue|Fg_control_rem_2],
        kernel_shell(Cmd_rem,File_request_2,Output_2,Lap,Fg_control_rem_2) ] .
```

2° The clause handling background commands is modified in order to suspend and resume their execution. They are, in fact, already submitted to stop orders that may arise from the kill commands. The extension is then easy. It is sufficient to merge these stop orders with the orders published by means of the Fg_control parameter. This is achieved by the following s-goal

    merge(Fg_control,Proc_control,Real_control)

The following clause results.

```
kernel_shell([cmd(Cmd_id,L_prgms,Infile,Outfile,bg)|Cmd_txt],File_request,Output,
                                            Lap,Fg_control) ←
    g_merge_2(Proc_status,File_request_1,File_request_2,File_request)),
    g_merge_2(Proc_status,Output_1,Output_2,Output)),
    merge(Fg_control,Proc_control,Real_control),
    call(  execute(cmd(Cmd_id,L_prgms,Infile,Outfile,fg),Cmd_txt,Cmd_txt_rem,
                                            File_request_1,Output_1),
           Proc_status,Real_control),
    kernel_shell(Cmd_txt_rem,File_request_2,Output_2,
                                            [proc(Cmd_id,Proc_status,Proc_control)|Lap).
```

This merging has some consequences on the value that can now be generated for the Proc_status variable. This may now be constructed to more elaborate values than the [stopped] one. The g_merge_2 procedure needs thus to be revised. The modification is however minor since the (incrementally generated) suspended and continued values may be simply omitted. The two following clauses need thus simply to be added :

    g_merge_2([continued|Status_rem],L1,L2,L) ← g_merge(Status_rem,L1,L2,L).
    g_merge_2([suspended|Status_rem],L1,L2,L) ← g_merge(Status_rem,L1,L2,L).

3° Priority of foreground commands over background ones has no effect on the kill commands. The clause of kernel_shell procedure for kill clauses is then just extended by the addition of the new parameter Fg_control in the clause head and in the recursive call. It is as follows.

kernel_shell([interrupt(kill(Proc_id))|Cmd_txt],File_request,Output,Lap,Fg_control) ←
    kill(Proc_Id,Lap,New_Lap),
    kernel_shell(Cmd_txt,File_request,Output,New_Lap,Fg_control).

ii) Second solution

The first solution has the drawback that the execution of background commands is suspended even when the execution of foreground commands is waiting for input text on the screen. To remedy this situation, we let the background processes run until input text is available. The execution of foreground commands requiring such input text (i.e. those whose input specifier is std) does not consequently order suspension at the beginning of their execution but when an input text has been detected in the flow of commands/texts.

This is implemented by duplicating the clause handling foreground commands.

One clause handles commands whose input specifier is not std. It is a reformulation of the original clause. The only difference is that the construction of the Fg_control parameter is not made by head unification but after the test on the input specifier is performed. This prevents the reduction from generating an undesirable suspend order when the input specifier is std.

The other clause handles foreground commands whose input specifier is std. It differs from the original clause by the way in which suspension is ordered. This is no more achieved by head unification with a Fg_control parameter of the form [suspend|Fg_control_rem_1] but by means of a wait_txt call. Its reduction searches in the commands/texts flow Cmd_txt for an input text. When it has encountered it, it instantiates the Fg_control parameter with the [suspend|Fg_control_rem_1] list. Precisely, the wait_txt procedure is specified as follows.

    procedure wait_txt(Cmd_txt,Fg_control,Fg_control_rem).
- Type
    Cmd_txt : list of commands/texts
    Fg_control, Fg_control_rem : lists whose elements are either suspend, continue, stop
- Operational properties
    1) Suspension condition
        Cmd_txt input
    2) Precondition
        Fg_control and Fg_control_rem are variables
    3) Postcondition
        Assume Cmd_txt is incrementally constructed. Then Fg_control is bound to [suspend|Fg_control_rem] when an input text constructs Cmd_txt.

Its implementation results directly from an inductive reasoning on Cmd_txt :

    suspend wait_txt(!,*,*).
    wait_txt([cmd(_,_,_,_,_)|Cmd_txt_rem],Fg_control,Fg_control_rem) ←
        wait_txt(Cmd_txt_rem,Fg_control,Fg_control_rem).
    wait_txt([interrupt(_)|Cmd_txt_rem],Fg_control,Fg_control_rem) ←
        wait_txt(Cmd_txt_rem,Fg_control,Fg_control_rem).
    wait_txt([txt(_)|Cmd_txt_rem],[suspend|Fg_control_rem],Fg_control_rem)).

Given this procedure, the two clauses for handling foreground commands are as follows :

kernel_shell([cmd(Cmd_id,L_prgms,Infile,Outfile,fg)|Cmd_txt],File_request,Output,
                                                                                                 Lap,Fg_control) ←
    Infile≠std |
        Fg_control=[suspend|Fg_control_rem_1]) ←
        g_merge_2(Status_exec,File_request_1,File_request_2,File_request),
        g_merge_2(Status_exec,Output_1,Output_2,Output),
        call(execute(cmd(Cmd_id,L_prgms,Infile,Outfile,fg),Cmd_txt,Cmd_txt_rem_exec,
                                                          File_request_1,Output_1),
                Status_exec,Control_exec),
        call(search(interrupt(abort),Cmd_txt,Cmd_txt_rem_search),
                Status_search,Control_search),
        [arbitrator(Status_exec,Control_exec,Status_search,Control_search,
                          Cmd_txt_rem_exec,Cmd_txt_rem_search,Cmd_txt_rem)
          | Fg_control_rem_2=[continue|Fg_control_rem_2],
            kernel_shell(Cmd_txt_rem,File_request_2,Output_2,Lap,Fg_control_rem_2)] .

kernel_shell([cmd(Cmd_id,L_prgms,std,Outfile,fg)|Cmd_txt],File_request,Output,
                                                                              Lap,Fg_control) ←
        g_merge_2(Status_exec,File_request_1,File_request_2,File_request),
        g_merge_2(Status_exec,Output_1,Output_2,Output),
        wait_txt(Cmd_txt,Fg_control,Fg_control_rem_1),
        call(execute(cmd(Cmd_id,L_prgms,Infile,Outfile,fg),Cmd_txt,Cmd_txt_rem_exec,
                                                          File_request_1,Output_1),
                Status_exec,Control_exec),
        call(search(interrupt(abort),Cmd_txt,Cmd_txt_rem_search),
                Status_search,Control_search),
        [arbitrator(Status_exec,Control_exec,Status_search,Control_search,
                          Cmd_txt_rem_exec,Cmd_txt_rem_search,Cmd_txt_rem)
          | Fg_control_rem_1=[continue|Fg_control_rem_2],
            kernel_shell(Cmd_rem,File_request_2,Output_2,Lap,Fg_control_rem_2)] .

11.4.2.2.6 The final program

The whole program is listed in Appendix 3. Compared with the previous procedure, the two following modifications have been made.

1) First, the g_merge_2 procedure has been renamed as g_merge.

2) Second, the term procedure has been extended so as to handle command identifiers. The essential extension concerns the parser_cmds procedure which really performs the identification of commands. This has required two major alterations.

- On the one hand, because commands identifiers are now inserted in the screen display before each command, the stream of characters forming commands and texts is now output explicitly by the parser_cmds procedure. As a result, the read_cmd_txt, read_txt, read_cmd, read_prgms, read_input, read_output, read_tag and read_blanks procedures are also extended to handle the part of the stream they compute.

- On the other hand, the commands formatted by the old parser procedure are now reformatted for the new format of commands. This includes the handling of commands of the interrupt form. This re-formatting is achieved by means of the procedure transform_cmd_txt.

Comparing the procedures of Appendix 3 with those presented in this section, the ease of modification of the latter procedures should be noted.

11.4.3 A lift system

Our last programming example of systems of processes consists of making a prototype from an informal specification. Specification prototyping is generally considered as a necessary step of program development. It is a powerful tool for making the real needs precise and for clarifying the specifications. In particular, inconsistencies and underdefinitions are easily highlighted by using it. It is now widely recognized that such problems have to be detected as early as possible to minimize the development costs. Hence, the interest taken in specification prototyping.

Prolog has often been claimed to be a powerful language for rapid prototyping (see e.g. [Venken and Bruynooghe, 1984], [Habra and van Lamsweerde, 1988]). We show here that Conclog is as interesting for rapid proptotyping of reactive systems. Such systems move in the physical world, react to a set of external stimuli and are subject to a set of dynamic, temporal and control constraints. The example developed in this section is a lift system. The informal description given hereafter is inspired from that published in the call for papers of the 4th International Workshop of Software Specifications and Design ([FWSS, 1987]).

11.4.3.1 Problem description

The lift system is composed of a set of n lifts moving between m floors. Each lift has a set of buttons, one for each floor. When pressed, these cause the lift to visit the corresponding floor. Each floor has a button. When pressed, this causes some lift to be called in the floor. A lift with no request to service remains at its final destination and awaits further requests. Finally, the system must ensure the following requirements :
- all requests for lifts from floors must be served eventually, with all floors given equal priority;
- all requests for floors within lifts must be served eventually, with floors being serviced sequentially in the direction of travel.

The system can be further complicated by placing, for instance, two buttons at each lift, one for requesting an up-lift and one for requesting a down-lift. For ease of discussion, we will limit to the above simple system. Nevertheless, the solution we will give can be easily augmented to incorporate this extension. For the same reason of simplicity, we ignore the existence of such components as doors, cables and engines which do not affect the design of the system but are used for physical implementation.

11.4.3.2 The Conclog program

A. Global description of the system

As for the previous examples, we build the Conclog program to reflect the basic concepts. Here, the lift system is obviously formed from two main components : the lifts and the floors. The Conclog description of the system is thus something of the form

```
← lift_1(...), lift_2(...), ..., lift_m(...), floor_1(...), ..., floor_n(...).
```

In order to avoid repetition in the description of the lifts and the floors, this basic scheme is first modified by including the identifying number as parameter. We thus write lift(i,...) and floor(i,...) instead of lift_i(...) and floor_i(...), respectively. The other parameters are used for the necessary communication between the floors and the lifts. As requests can occur in the two directions, we give two communication lists to each component : an "in" one and and "out" one. The precise description is finally obtained by adding a message manager to manage the communications. The Conclog description of the lift system is therefore

```
←    lift(1,Lin_1,Lout_1), lift(2,Lin_2,Lout_2), ..., lift(n,Lin_n,Lout_n),
     floor(1,Fin_1,Fout_1), floor(2,Fin_2,Fout_2), ..., floor(m,Fin_m,Fout_m),
     mess_manager( lifts_in(Lin_1, Lin_2, ...,Lin_n),
                   lifts_out(Lout_1, Lout_2, ...,Lout_n),
                   floors_in(Fin_1, Fin_2, ..., Fin_m),
                   floors_out(Fout_1, Fout_2, ..., Fout_m) ).
```

We now have to describe the lift, floor and mess_manager procedures. Of course, the two first intend to simulate the behavior of the lift and floor components of the system. To go further, the interaction between lifts and floors must be further specified. It is as follows. Each time a non-activated button is pressed, a request for service (of the form request(Id) with Id being the floor identifier) is sent to some lift. Lifts thus share their time between waiting for such requests and treating them. This treatment includes the sending of a message of visit (of the form served(Floor_Id) with Floor_id being a floor identifier) each time a floor has been served. It is the role of the message manager to manage the request(Id) and served(Floor_Id) messages and to ensure a fair repartition of the floor requests.

B. The floor procedure

The Conclog floor(Id,L_in,L_out) procedure is constructed so as the execution of any call floor(Id,L_in,L_out), where id is the (ground) identifier of a floor, reflects the behavior of the floor components. This may be modelized as follows.

- From an outside point of view, any floor receives a sequence of served messages as input and outputs a sequence of request messages.
- From an internal point of view, it embodies a generator of button stimulations and a state that tells whether its button is stimulated or not.

The type of the Id, L_in and L_out parameters should thus be specified as follows :

- Id is a floor identifier,
- L_in is a list whose elements are of the form served(Id),
- L_out is a list whose elements are of the form request(Id).

They should be submitted to the following suspension conditions :

Id ground and L_in input.

The core of the procedure should then be constructed in such a way that the reduction of any call floor(Id,L_in,L_out) behaves as a perpetual process. It should conserve the state of the floor button as internal state. This state should change according to the arrival of the served(Id) messages and to the activation of the button associated with the floor. As a side effect of this change, some request messages should furthermore be sent. Precisely, the state change and sending of the request message should be governed by the following rules.

1. If the button is activated then
    1.1 if the state of the button indicates that it is stimulated then
     - this state is not changed
     - no request message is sent.

1.2 if the state of the button indicates that it is not stimulated then
- the state is changed to indicate that the button is stimulated
- a request(Id) message is sent; its Id parameter is the identifier of the floor under consideration.
2. If a served message is received then
- the state is changed to indicate that the button is no more stimulated
- no request message is sent.

To implement this behavior, we will use two auxiliary procedures : stimulator(L_stimuli) and button(Id,L_in,L_out,State).

1) The stimulator(L_stimuli) procedure is used to simulate the stimulation of the button. It is assumed to be built-in and to be constructed so as any call to it, whose parameter is a variable, constructs L_stimuli incrementally to an infinite list of put_on terms. The rate of the production of the put_on terms is assumed to be random.

2) The button(Id,L_in,L_out,State) procedure is used to simulate the above perpetual button process. The Id, L_in and L_out parameters have the form indicated above. The State parameter is of the type {off,on}. The off value is used to indicate that the button is not stimulated. The on one is used to indicate that the button is stimulated. The Id, L_in and State parameters are ruled by the following suspension declaration :

Id and State ground, L_in element input.

The Conclog code results directly from the above description. It is as follows :

```
suspend button(!g,!,*,!).
button(Id,[put_on|L_in_rem],[request(Id)|L_out_rem],off) ←
    button(Id,L_in_rem,L_out_rem,on).
button(Id,[put_on|L_in_rem],L_out,on) ← button(Id,L_in_rem,L_out,on).
button(Id,[served(Id)|L_in_rem],L_out,on) ← button(Id,L_in_rem,L_out,off).
```

Given these procedures, the floor procedure can be coded as follows :

```
floor(Id,L_in,L_out) ←
    stimulator(L_stimuli),
    button(Id,L_in_button,L_out,off),
    merge(L_in,L_stimuli,L_in_button).
```

It is easy to verify that the reduction of any call floor(id,L_in,L_out) with id the identifier of some floor simulates the intuitive behavior of a floor. Indeed, the reduction of such a call results in the concurrent reduction of the three subgoals

```
stimulator(L_stimuli),
button(id,L_in_button,L_out,off),
merge(L_in,L_stimuli,L_in_button).
```

The reduction of the first one simulates the activation of the button at the floor. Stated in computational terms, it incrementally constructs L_stimuli with put_on terms (see the specification of the stimulator procedure). Those are merged with the served messages sent to the floor by means of the L_in list to form the list L_in_button (see specification of the merge procedure in Section 11.4.1). The reduction of the

>   button(Id,L_in_button,L_out,off)

subgoal consumes this list and generates, when need, be the request message in the L_out list (see the above specification of the button procedure).

C. The lift procedure

The lift(Id,F_in,F_out) procedure is also constructed in such a way that the reduction of any call floor(id,F_in,F_out), where id is the identifier of a lift and F_in and F_out are variables, simulates the behavior of a lift. To construct it, let us first modelize this behavior too.

C.1 THE LIFT BEHAVIOR

From an external point of view, any lift receives a stream of request messages and outputs a stream of served messages. From an internal point of view, it embodies a generator of requests for visiting floors and moves between floors. The exact moving and sending of served messages is ruled by the received request messages and by the visiting requests. To explain it, we first characterize the lift by a set of attributes. We then distinguish two basic operations of the lift behavior. It is finally described in term of them.

C.1.1 The lift attributes

The behavior of the lift is charaterized by means of the four following items :

- a State attribute of value "waiting", "up" and "down".
    It aims at describing the deplacement of the lift, when any, or the absence of deplacement. The lift is always in one of these states. It is in the waiting state when it is not moving. It is in the up (down) state when it is executing an ascending (descending) deplacement.

- a Lcsf attribute and a Lwf attribute.
    These attributes should be read as the list of the currently satisfied floors and the list of waiting floors, respectively. The first one describes the floors that are going to be visited in the current deplacement of the lift and the floors that will be satisfied when the lift will change its deplacement direction and will come bak.

- a Floor attribute.
    We assume that the lift is always at one floor and we neglect the transition times between adjacent floors. The floor attribute indicates the floor where the lift is currently.

These four attributes will be sufficient to describe the lift. The lift will thus be subsequently regarded as a 4-tuple

<State,Lcsf,Lwf,Floor>.

The behavior of the lift then consists of moving from such 4-tuples to other 4-tuples and of sending messages. The initial 4-tuple is as follows :

- the initial value of the State attribute is set to the waiting value,
- the initial value of the Lcsf and Lwf attributes are set to the empty list,
- the value of the Floor attribute is some arbitrary floor.

The following properties are kept invariant all along the behavior of the lift :

I_1. if the lift is in the waiting state then the Lcsf and Lwf lists are empty,
I_2. if the lift is in the up state then
- the Lcsf list is in increasing order, is not empty and all its element are greater than the value of its floor attribute,
- the Lwf list is in decreasing order
I_3. if the lift is in the the down state then
- the Lcsf list is in decreasing order, is not empty and all its elements are less than the value of the floor attribute
- the Lwf list is in increasing order.

C.1.2 *The lift atomic actions*

The lift behavior (and consequently the transition between 4-tuples) may be explained in terms of two basic atomic actions : registering of a requested floor and serving a registered floor.

i) *Registering a requesting floor*

Registering a requested floor is operated in two circumstances : by the arrival of a request(Id) message simulating the stimulation of a button or directly by the introduction of users in a lift serving a floor. Basically, the registration consists of recording the floor identifier in one of the lists Lcsf or Lwf. The lift is furthermore woken up if it is in the waiting state. The precise meaning is described by the following algorithm.

Algorithm Register_floor(Id) Let

- Id the identifier of the floor to register
- <State_init,Lcsf_init,Lwf_init,Floor_init> be the value of the <State,Lcsf,Lwf,Floor> 4-tuple before the registration,
- <State_post,Lcsf_post,Lwf_post,Floor_post> be the value of the <State,Lcsf,Lwf,Floor> 4-tuple after the registration.

Then, the <State_post,Lcsf_post,Lwf_post,Floor_post> 4-tuple is determined as follows.

    Floor_post = Floor_init = F

    if State_init = waiting then
      if Id ≤ F then
        Lcsf_post = [Id], Lwf_post = [], State_post = down
      if Id > F then
        Lcsf_post = [Id], Lwf_post = [], State_post = up

    if State_init = up then
      if Id ≤ F then
        insert F in Lwf_init according to its decreasing order, this delivers Lwf_post
        Lcsf_post = Lcsf_init,
        State_post = up
      if Id > F then
        insert F in Lcsf_init according to its increasing order, this delivers Lcsf_post
        Lwf_post = Lwf_init ,
        State_aux = up

    if State_init = down then
      if Id ≤ F then
        insert F in Lcsf_init according to its decreasing order, this delivers Lcsf_post
        Lwf_post = Lwf_init,
        State_post = down
      if Id > F then
        insert F in Lwf_init according to its increasing order, this delivers Lwf_post
        Lcsf_post = Lcsf_init ,
        State_aux = down.

The following property is worth noting.

Property 11.1 Algorithm Register_floor keeps properties I_1, I_2 and I_3 invariant. Furthermore, after execution the value of the State attribute is either up or down and the value of the Lcsf attribute is non-empty.

Proof Simple verification ◊

ii) *Serving a registered floor*

Intuitively speaking, serving a registered floor involves the deplacement of the lift to the floor, the sending of a served message to the floor (to indicate that it is served), the memorization of the requests from possible users at the floor and the change of state when no floor remains to be satisfied in this direction or at all.

The precise meaning is described also in terms of the lift attributes and the sending of served messages. It is stated by the following algorithm.

Algorithm Serve_floor Let

- <State_init,Lcsf_init,Lwf_init,Flour_init> be the value of the <State,Lcsf,Lwf,Flour> 4-tuple before the operation,
- <State_post,Lcsf_post,Lwf_post,Flour_post> be the value of the <State,Lcsf,Lwf,Flour> 4-tuple after the operation.

Assume that Lcsf_init is not empty and that State_init is either up or down. Let Id be the first floor identifier of Lcsf_init and Lcsf_rem be its remainder. Serving the floor identified by Id determines the 4-tuple <State_post,Lcsf_post,Lwf_post,Floor_post> and provokes the sending of served messages as follows.

1) A served(Id) message is sent to the floor identified by Id,

2) The requests of the user entering in the lift at floor Id are then registered by applying the Register_floor algorithm with <State_init,Lcsf_rem,Lwf_post,Id> as initial 4-tuple; let <State_aux,Lcsf_aux,Lwf_aux,Floor_aux> be the resulting 4-tuple.

3) Finally, the 4-tuple <State_post,Lcsf_post,Lwf_post,Floor_post> is determined as follows :

    if Lcsf_aux = [] and Lwf_aux = [] then
      Lcsf_post = [],
      Lwf_post =[],
      State_post = waiting

    if Lcsf_aux = [] and Lwf_aux ≠ [] then
      Lcsf_post = Lwf_aux,
      Lwf_post =[],
      if State_aux = up
        then State_post = down
        else State_post = up

    if Lcsf_aux ≠ [] then
      Lcsf_post = Lcsf_aux,
      Lwf_post =Lwf_aux,
      State_post = State_aux.

4) Set Floor_post to Id.

Property 11.2 Assuming Lcsf_init is not empty and State_init is either up or down, the algorithm Serve_floor keeps properties I_1, I_2 and I_3 invariant.
Proof Simple verification. ◊

C.1.3 The lift algorithm

We are now in position to describe the lift behavior algorithm. Two behaviors are in fact described. They are called elementary and realistic.

i) The elementary behavior

The elementary behavior consists of the infinite repetition of the following cycle.

Wait until one of the two following actions is executable
Non-deterministically and fairly choose one of them
Execute it.
The two actions are :
    1) register some request(Id) message, if any
    2) serve some registered requesting floor, if any.

Note that because of Property 11.1, the floors are always served correctly i.e. when the assumptions of Algorithm Serve_floor are fulfilled.

Note also that, as the two actions may be chosen non-deterministically, some requesting floor may thus be registered before previously registered ones are served.

ii) The realistic behavior

The above behavior is called elementary since, using it, the lift can go over some floor without stopping although a requesting message floor has been sent. The second behavior remedies this situation. It makes the choice between the two actions deterministic : the second action is executed only when the first one cannot be executed.

C.2 THE CONCLOG PROCEDURE

C.2.1 The lift and lift_body procedures

Let us now turn to the Conclog procedures. As for the floor procedure, the lift(Id,L_in,L_out) procedure is constructed so that the reduction of any call of the form lift(id,L_in,L_out), where id is some (ground) identifier of a lift, reflects the behavior of the lift (just descibed above).

It is worth noting that the parameters of the lift procedure reflects the lifts external behavior. They constitue the information visible from the outside of the lift. The core of the procedure further requires to take the internal component of the lift into account. This is the reason why the lift procedure is implemented by means of an auxiliary procedure, called body_lift. It adds the four attributes of the lift to the parameters of the lift procedure. The associated predicate is thus of the following form

lift_body(Id,L_in,L_out,State,Lcsf,Lwf,Floor).

It is constructed so that the reduction of any call, whose attribute parameters verify the invariants I_1, I_2 and I_3, behaves as a perpetual process reflecting the lift behavior, both from the internal and external point of views. This given, the implementation of the lift procedure is easy. It is sufficient to call the lift_body procedure with the initial value of the attributes. The initial position of the lift is arbitrarily taken as the first floor. The following clause results :

lift(Id,L_in,L_out) ← lift_body(Id,L_in,L_out,waiting,[],[],1).

The lift_imp procedure is implemented thanks to two auxiliary procedures : gen_service and memorize_request. They are specified as follows.

1° The gen_request procedure.

The gen_request(Floor,L_floor) procedure is used to simulate the requests made by the users entering the lift when it visits the floor identified by Floor. The Floor parameter is submitted to a suspension declaration stating it as input. The procedure is designed for calls whose L_floors parameter is a variable. The reduction of any such call consists of instantiating L_floors to a (possibly empty) list of floor identifiers distinct from Floor.

Note that this indeed corresponds to the reality. On the one hand, several users may enter the lift at the same floor and require several destinations. On the other hand, no user can enter the lift or the lift can be requested to visit the floor where the users expect to go. In this case, no request is made. Finally, in all cases, requested floors should be different from the floor just visited.

2° The memorize_request procedure

The memorize_request procedure is used to register requests. It essentially consists of the register_floor algorithm. We extend it in order to handle a (possibly empty) list of floor identifiers rather than just one. The way in which a non empty list should be treated is quite clear : it is sufficient to apply successively the algorithm Register_request. The way in which an empty list should be treated is less intuitive. It is guided by the case where the floor stops at a floor without embarking any user. This case is precisely treated at step 3) of the algorithm Serve_floor. We thus specify the memorize_request procedure as follows :

procedure memorize_request(L_req_floors,F,Lcsf_init,Lwf_init,State_init,
                          Lcsf_post,Lwf_post,State_post)
- Type
    L_req_floor : list whose elements are of the form request(Id) where Id is the
        identifier of a floor,
    F : identifier of a floor
    Lcsf_init, Lcsf_post, Lwf_init, Lwf_post : lists of floor identifiers
    State_init, State_post : either up, down or waiting.
- Suspension conditions :
    F, State_init : ground,
    L_req_floors, Lcsf_init, Lwf_init : input
- Preconditions
    L_req_floors, Lcsf_init and Lwf_init are eventually constructed to one ground list.
- Postconditions
    - If the ground value for L_req_floors is not empty, then, using the same notations,
      Lcsf_post, Lwf_post and State_post have the values determined by applying
      successively the algorithm Register_floor with the successive elements of L_floors.
    - Otherwise, Lcsf_post, Lwf_post and State_post are determined by applying step 3)
      of the algorithm Serve_floor.
    - In all cases, L_csf_post and Lwf_post are incrementally constructed.

The lift_body is then implemented with respect to its lift process interpretation stated above. Two versions are given for the two behaviors of the lift.

1° Elementary lift

The procedure for the elementary lift is coded by associating a clause with each elementary action. The first one corresponds to the registration of a request message. The second one to the serving of a floor. A commit operator is used to simulate the non-deterministic choice between the two actions. A suspension declaration is used to declare the input arguments. Thanks to the form of the clause heads, it further ensures that the lift acts only when a request message has been sent to it or when the lift has floors to serve.

The following procedure results.

suspend lift_body(!g,!,*,o,!g,!,!,!g) with l_commit.
lift_body(Id,[request(Floor_req)|L_reqs_rem],L_out,Floor,Lcsf,Lwf,State) ←
    memorize_requests([Floor_req],Floor,Lcsf,Lwf,State,New_Lcsf,New_Lwf,New_state),
    lift_body(Id,Floor,L_reqs_rem,L_out,New_Lcsf,New_Lwf,New_state).
lift_body(Id,L_in,[served(Calling_floor)|L_out_rem],Floor,
                                    [Calling_floor|Lcsf_rem],Lwf,State) ←
        gen_service(Calling_floor,L_floors_gen),
        memorize_requests(L_floors_gen,Calling_floor,Lcsf_rem,Lwf,State,
                                    New_Lcsf,New_Lwf,New_state),
        lift_body(Id,Calling_floor,L_in,L_out_rem,New_Lcsf,New_Lwf,New_state).

2° The realistic lift

In the above program, commitment selects arbitrarily one clause when both of them are unifiable. The realistic behavior requires that a floor is served only when no request has been addressed to the lift. In programming terms, this means that the second clause should only be selected when the second parameter list L_in is not constructed with a request(Id) term. This condition may be tested by means of the var_syst predicate. The list L_in is not constructed iff the call var_syst(L_in) succeeds. The lift_body is then coded as an if-then-else instruction. The call var_syst(L_in) is first reduced through the two-arguments meta-call primitive

    call(var_syst(L_in),Result).

The lift_body_end procedure is used thereafter to select the body of one of the right clause. It takes the Result variable as parameter as well as all the parameters of the lift_body procedure. The Result parameter is submitted to the following suspension declaration

    Result ground.

The others inherit their suspension declaration from the Lift_body procedure. It acts as follows. If Result is succeeded (i.e. if var_syst(L_in) is successfully reduced), then the second clause is used. Otherwise, L_in is of the form [request(Id)|L_in_rem] and the first clause is used. As the choice between the two clauses is now deterministic, the l_commit operator is finally removed.

The following program results.

    suspend lift_body(!g,!,*,o,!g,!,!,!g).
    lift_body(Id,L_in,L_out,Floor,Lcsf,Lwf,State) ←
        call(var_syst(L_in),Result) |
        lift_body_end(Result,Id,L_in,L_out,Floor,Lcsf,Lwf,State).

```
suspend  lift_body_end(!g,!g,!,*,o,!g,!,!,!g).
lift_body_end(succeeded,Id,L_in,[served(Calling_floor)|L_out_rem],Floor,
                                            [Calling_floor|Lcsf_rem],Lwf,State) ←
        gen_service(Calling_floor,L_floors_gen),
        memorize_requests(L_floors_gen,Calling_floor,Lcsf_rem,Lwf,State,
                                                    New_Lcsf,New_Lwf,New_state),
        lift_body(Id,Calling_floor,L_in,L_out_rem,New_Lcsf,New_Lwf,New_state).
lift_body_end(failed,Id,[request(Floor_req)|L_reqs_rem],L_out,Floor,Lcsf,Lwf,State) ←
        memorize_requests([Floor_req],Floor,Lcsf,Lwf,State,New_Lcsf,New_Lwf,New_state),
        lift_body(Id,Floor,L_reqs_rem,L_out,New_Lcsf,New_Lwf,New_state).
```

Remark Note that because of its temporal character, the call var_syst(L_in) cannot be simply inserted in the two clauses of the elementary lift, negated in the first one and unegated in the second one.

C.2.2 The gen_request and memorize_request auxiliary procedures

i) The gen_request procedure

The gen_request procedure is not constructed here. It is assumed to be built-in. Nevertheless, it can be implemented in various ways, for instance by using a perpetual screen process.

ii) The memorize_request procedure

The memorize_request procedure is implemented by an inductive reasoning on the list L_req_floors and from the case analysis performed in Algorithms Register_floor and Serve_floor. Three auxiliary procedures will be useful : inc_insert(X,L,_res), dec_insert(X,L,L_res) and reverse(State1,State2). The two first ones aim at inserting X in L with respect to an increasing and decreasing listing of elements, respectively. The last one is used to reverse the direction of the displacement of the lift. These procedures are specified as follows.

1)   procedure inc_insert(X,L,L_res)
   - Type
        X : integer
        L, L_res : lists of integers; strong use
   - Relation
        L_res is L where X has been inserted so that all elements of L_res appears in increasing order.
   - Operational properties
        1) Precondition
            The elements of L appear in increasing order

2) Suspension conditions
X ground and L input
3) Postcondition
<ground,ground,var> : <ground,ground,ground>; <1-1>
X ground and L input and L incrementally constructed ground : L_res incrementally constructed ground.

2) procedure dec_insert(X,L,L_res).
Similar specification where the increasing order is replaced by a decreasing one.

3) procedure reverse(State1,State2).
- Type
State1, State2 : either up or down
- Relation
(State1=up ∧ State2=down) ∨ (State1=down ∧ State2=up).
- Operational properties
1) Suspension condition
State1 ground
2) Postcondition
<ground,var> : <ground,ground>, <1-1>

Thanks to these procedures, the memorize_request procedure can be coded as follows. For more suggestivity, names of the parameters have been inserted in the suspension declaration.

```
suspend memorize_request(L_req_floors!,Floor!g ,Lcsf_init!,Lwf_init!,State_init!g,
                         Lcsf_post ,Lwf_post,State_post)
memorize_requests([],Floor,[],[],State,[],[],waiting).
memorize_requests([],Floor,[],[H|T],State,[H|T],[],New_state) ←
    reverse_dir(State,New_state).
memorize_requests([],Floor,[H|T],Lwf,State,[H|T],Lwf,State).
memorize_requests([Floor_req|L_floors_rem],Floor,[],[],waiting,
                         New_Lcsf,New_Lwf,New_state) ←
    Floor ≤ Floor_req |
    memorize_requests(L_floors_rem,Floor,[Floor_req],[],up,
                New_Lcsf,New_Lwf,New_state).
memorize_requests([Floor_req|L_floors_rem],Floor,[],[],waiting,
                         New_Lcsf,New_Lwf,New_state) ←
    Floor > Floor_req |
    memorize_requests(L_floors_rem,Floor,[Floor_req],[],down,
                New_Lcsf,New_Lwf,New_state).
```

```
memorize_requests([Floor_req|L_floors_rem],Floor,Lcsf,Lwf,up,
                         New_Lcsf,New_Lwf,New_state) ←
    Floor ≤ Floor_req |
    inc_insert(Floor_req,Lcsf,Lcsf_aux),
    memorize_requests(L_floors_rem,Floor,Lcsf_aux,Lwf,up,
                         New_Lcsf,New_Lwf,New_state).
memorize_requests([Floor_req|L_floors_rem],Floor,Lcsf,Lwf,up,
                         New_Lcsf,New_Lwf,New_state) ←
    Floor > Floor_req |
    dec_insert(Floor_req,Lwf,Lwf_aux),
    memorize_requests(L_floors_rem,Floor,Lcsf,Lwf_aux,up,
                         New_Lcsf,New_Lwf,New_state).
memorize_requests([Floor_req|L_floors_rem],Floor,Lcsf,Lwf,down,
                         New_Lcsf,New_Lwf,New_state) ←
    Floor ≥ Floor_req |
    dec_insert(Floor,Lcsf,Lcsf_aux),
    memorize_requests(Floor,L_floors_rem,Lcsf_aux,Lwf,down,
                         New_Lcsf,New_Lwf,New_state).
memorize_requests([Floor_req|L_floors_rem],Floor,Lcsf,Lwf,down,
                         New_Lcsf,New_Lwf,New_state) ←
    Floor < Floor_req |
    inc_insert(Floor,Lwf,Lwf_aux),
    memorize_requests(L_floors_rem,Floor,Lcsf,Lwf_aux,down,
                         New_Lcsf,New_Lwf,New_state).
```

The auxiliary procedures inc_insert and dec_insert can be implemented thanks to a inductive reasoning on the list L. The following piece of code results.

```
suspend inc_insert(!g,!,*).
inc_insert(Num,[],[Num]).
inc_insert(Num,[Num|T],[Num|T]).
inc_insert(Num,[H|T],L) ← Num < H | L = [Num,H|T].
inc_insert(Num,[H|T],L) ← Num > H | L= [H|New_T], inc_insert(Num,T,New_T).

suspend dec_insert(!g,!,*).
dec_insert(Num,[],[Num]).
dec_insert(Num,[Num|T],[Num|T]).
dec_insert(Num,[H|T],L) ← Num > H | L = [Num,H|T].
dec_insert(Num,[H|T],L) ← Num < H | L= [H|New_T], dec_insert(Num,T,New_T).
```

The code of the reverse_dir procedure directly results from its specification. It is as follows :

suspend reverse_dir(!g,*).
reverse_dir(up,down).
reverse_dir(down,up).

D. The `mess_manager` procedure

We finally program the message manager component. Recall that it takes the following form

mess_manager(lifts_in(Lin_1, Lin_2, ...,Lin_n),
              lifts_out(Lout_1, Lout_2, ...,Lout_n),
              floors_in(Fin_1, Fin_2, ..., Fin_m),
              floors_out(Fout_1, Fout_2, ..., Fout_m))

Its effect is to connect the Fin_j's with the Lout_k's and the Lin_p's with the Fout_q's. The first connection is deterministic whereas the second is indeterministic. For the latter, a fair distribution of the requests from the floors to the lifts must be ensured.

D.1 FIRST CONNECTION

The first connection is achieved by first merging the Lout_k and by distributing the served(Floor_id) messages according to the floor identifier Floor_id. This is performed by means of two auxiliary procedures : gen_merge and service_lift. They are defined as follows.

i) The gen_merge procedure

The gen_merge procedure is a generalization of the merge procedure. It takes m input lists and merges them to form one output list. It could be defined directly but this requires the definition of the merge of (m-1) lists, of (m-2) lists, ... and of 2 lists. Rather we define all these merge by using list of lists as input parameter. The precise specification is as follows.

procedure gen_merge(L_list,L).
- Type
    L_list : list of lists; strong use of type and of all subtypes
    L : list; strong use of type and of all subtypes
- Relation
    Let L_list be [L1,...,Lm]. Then L is one fair merged version of the lists L1, ...,Lm.
- Operation properties
    1) Suspension conditions
        L_list element input and each list of L_list element input
    2) Preconditions
        L_list contains at least one element
        L variable

3) Postconditions

    <ground,var> : <ground,ground>; <1-1>

    L_list incrementally constructed and each list of L_list incrementally constructed: L incrementally constructed.

Note that this is indeed a generalization of the merge procedure of Section 11.4.1 since one has

merge(L1,L2,L) = gen_merge([L1,L2],L).

Conversely, the gen_merge is implemented subsequently by using the merge procedure. One auxiliary procedure will furthermore be needed. It is used to partition the list of L_list into two lists of lists. Its specification is as follows.

partition_lists(L,L1,L2).

- Type

    L, L1, L2 : lists, strong use

- Relation

    Let L be $[e_1,...,e_m]$. Then $L1=[e_1,e_3,...,e_r]$ and $L2=[e_2,e_4,...,e_s]$ where r and s are defined as follows :

        if m is even then r=m-1 and s=m,

        if m is odd then r=m and s=m-1.

- Operational properties

    1) Suspension condition

        L element input

    2) Precondition

        L contains at least one element

    3) Postconditions

        <ground,any,any> : <ground,ground,ground> :<0-1>

        L element input and L incrementally constructed : L1 and L2 incrementally constructed.

Given this procedure, the gen_merge(L_list,L) can be easily constructed by induction on L_list. If L_list is empty then L is empty. If L_list reduces to an element then L is simply this element. Otherwise, it is sufficient to partition L_list, to apply gen_merge recursively on the two produced sublists and to merge the resulting lists. This is implemented in the following procedure.

```
suspend gen_merge(!,*).
gen_merge([],[])
gen_merge([L],L).
gen_merge([L1,L2],L) ← merge(L1,L2,L).
gen_merge([L1,L2,L3|Ll_rem],L) ←
    partition_lists([L1,L2,L3|Ll_rem],P1,P2),
    gen_merge(P1,Lm1), gen_merge(P2,Lm2),
    merge(Lm1,Lm2,L).
```

The partition(L,L1,L2) procedure results from an inductive reasoning on the L parameter. The following piece of code follows :

```
suspend partition_lists(!,*,*).
partition_lists([],[],[]).
partition_lists([L],[L],[]).
partition_lists([L1,L2|Ll_rem],[L1|P1_rem],[L2|P2_rem]) ←
    partition_lists(Ll_rem,P1_rem,P2_rem).
```

ii) The service_lift procedure

The service_lift(L,Lift_1,...,Lift_m) procedure aims at distributing the served(l) messages of the list L in the list Lift_l according to the lift identifier I. Its first parameter is declared as input. It is specified as follows.

procedure service_lift(L,Lift_1,...,Lift_m).
- Type
    L, Lift_1, ..., Lift_m : lists whose elements are of the form served(Id)
- Relation
    For any i, the ith list Lift_i contains, in the same order, the elements served(i) of L
- Operational properties
    1) Suspension condition
        L input
    2) Postcondition
        L input and incrementally constructed ground : Lift_1, ..., Lift_m incrementally constructed ground.

The procedure is implemented by an inductive reasoning on L as well as a case analysis of its elements.

```
suspend service_lift(!,*,*,...,*).
service_lift([],[],...,[]).
service_lift([served(1)|Lout_rem],[served(1)|F1rem],F2,...,Fm) ←
    service_lift(Lout_rem,F1rem,F2,...,Fm).
service_lift([served(2)|Lout_rem],F1,[served(2)|F2rem],...,Fm) ←
    service_lift(Lout_rem,F1,F2rem,...,Fm).
...
service_lift([served(m)|Lout_rem],F1,F2,...,[served(m)|Fmrem]) ←
    service_lift(Lout_rem,F1,F2,...,Fmrem).
```

iii) First connection

Given these gen_merge and service_lift procedures, the first conjunction may be achieved by the following goal

← gen_merge(Lout_1,Lout_2,...,Lout_n,Lout), service_lift(Lout,Fin_1,...,Fin_m).

D.2 SECOND CONNECTION

The second connection is achieved by first merging the Fout_n lists and then by distributing the requests on the Lin_m lists. The merge may be performed thanks to the above gen_merge procedure. The distribution of the requests is achieved by the reversed version of the merge process. This is performed by the

rev_merge(L,L1,...,Lm)

procedure. Its first parameter is input. The others are constructed in such a way that one merged version of them constitutes L. Only one version is constructed for them. Precisely, the rev_merge is specified as follows.

procedure rev_merge(L,L1,...,Lm).
- Type
    L, L1, ..., Lm : lists, strong use of the type and all subtypes
- Relation
    L is a merged version of L1, ..., Lm
- Operational properties
    1) Suspension condition
        L element input
    2) Precondition
        L1, ..., Lm variables
    3) Postcondition
        L element input and incrementally constructed :
            - L1, ..., Lm incrementally constructed
            - only one list is constructed for each of them.

The implementation of the procedure results directly from an inductive reasoning on L. It is as follows.

```
suspend rev_merge(!,*,*,...,*) with l_commit.
rev_merge([],[],[],...,[]).
rev_merge([X|Lin_rem],[X|L1_rem],L2,...,Ln) ←
      rev_merge(Lin_rem,L1_rem,L2,...,Ln).
rev_merge([X|Lin_rem],L1,[X|L2_rem],...,Ln) ←
      rev_merge(Lin_rem,L1,L2_rem,...,Ln).
...
rev_merge([X|Lin_rem],L1,L2,...,[X|Ln_rem]) ←
      rev_merge(Lin_rem,L1,L2,...,Ln_rem).
```

D.3 THE mess_manager PROCEDURE

Summing up, the message manager is defined as follows.

```
mess_manager( lifts_in(Lin_1, Lin_2, ...,Lin_n),
              lifts_out(Lout_1, Lout_2, ...,Lout_n),
              floors_in(Fin_1, Fin_2, ..., Fin_m),
              floors_out(Fout_1, Fout_2, ..., Fout_m) ) ←
                      gen_merge([Lout_1,Lout_2,...,Lout_n],Lout),
                      service_lift(Lout,Fin_1,...,Fin_m),
                      gen_merge([Fout_1,Fout_2,...,Fout_m],Fout),
                      rev_merge(Fout,Lin_1,Lin_2,...,Lin_n).
```

E. Final program

The whole is program is listed in Appendix 4.

11.5 Classical concurrent programming

Classical concurrent programming is generally illustrated by some well-known problems. Among them are the dining philosophers problem, the sleeping barber problem, the readers and writers problem, ... These problems are part of the concurrent programming folklore and benchmarks for the expressiveness of concurrent programming languages. It would be a considerable default for one concurrent language if one of these classical problems would reveal to be unprogrammable using it. Although Conclog has been designed for another aim (i.e. to execute general Horn clause programs in a concurrent fashion), it turns out that classical concurrent problems can be solved using it. As an argumentation, we show how to simulate semaphores and solve the dining philosophers problem.

11.5.1 Semaphores in Conclog

A. Description

The semaphore is a central notion in imperative concurrent programming. Any problem that refers to concurrency can be programmed using it. As a consequence, its single simulation in a concurrent language gives it the full power of expressiveness in concurrent programming.

A semaphore is a global integer variable, incremented and decremented during the computation. It is initialized by an assignment at the beginning of the program and is accessed in any procedure of the program by using two primitives : P and V. Basically, the former is used to decrement the semaphore from one unit, the latter to increment it from one unit. To provide its full power to the semaphore, these operations have been somewhat complicated. The execution of the P operation only succeeds when the semaphore is strictly positive. Otherwise, it is suspended. On the other hand, the execution of the V operation only increments the semaphore when no execution of a P operation is suspended. Otherwise, one suspended execution is woken up and the semaphore is kept to its value.

A semaphore can thus be viewed to some extend as an abstract data type. It has two internal components : its value, hereafter denoted by Value, and a list of waiting processes, hereafter denoted by Wait_proc. It can be accessed by two primitives P and V, renamed to the more expressive primitives : wait and signal. Their effect is as follows

- wait : If Value>0 then Value := Value - 1, else the execution of the process executing the wait operation is suspended and queued in Wait_proc.
- signal : If there are suspended processes in Wait_proc then one of them is woken up and removed from Wait_proc, otherwise Value := Value +1.

It is however not entirely an abstract data type since one internal component, namely Value, is accessed directly by instantiation.

B. Simulation

The above description suggests that semaphores may be programmed in Conclog following the guidelenes stated in Section 11.2 for the simulation of abstract data types. As initialization makes their Value structure apparent, they will however be directly coded by the instance of the imp_adt procedure rather than by the instance of the adt procedure. Two such programs are given subsequently. The first one directly results from the imp_adt procedure rather than from that of the adt procedure. The latter generalizes it in order to allow semaphores to handle signal and wait calls not relevant for them. All of them use a list structure to represent the Wait_proc list. It is organized as a queue in order to ensure a fair waking up of the suspended processes.

B.1 SIMPLE SEMAPHORE

Instantiating the imp_adt procedure of Section 11.2 to the semaphore context leads to the following semaphore(L_op,Wait_proc,Value) procedure. The Wait_proc and Value parameters have just been described. The L_op parameter is the list through which the semaphore is accessed. It is constructed by means of the wait and signal operations. The first one is presented in a slightly different form : wait(Resp). The Resp parameter is used to inform the calling process of the success of the execution of the wait call. It is bound to ok in two situations : at the call if Value is strictly positive or, otherwise, when the calling process is woken up.

```
suspend semaphore(!,!,!g).
semaphore([wait(Resp)|L_mess_rem],Wait_proc,0) ←
    append(Wait_proc?,[m(wait,Resp)],New_Wait_proc),
    semaphore(L_mess_rem,New_Wait_proc,0).
semaphore([wait(Resp)|L_mess_rem],[],Value) ←
    Value > 0 |
    New_value is Value - 1, Resp = ok,
    semaphore(L_mess_rem,[],New_value).
semaphore([signal|L_mess_rem],[m(wait,Resp)|Wait_proc_rem],0) ←
    Resp = ok,
    semaphore(L_mess_rem,Wait_proc_rem,0).
semaphore([signal|L_mess_rem],[],Value) ←
    New_value is Value + 1,
    semaphore(L_mess_rem,[],New_value).
```

B.2 MORE COMPLEX SEMAPHORE

Many semaphores will generally be employed in the program. To allow an easy referencing, we first extend the above semaphore procedure with a Name parameter. Furthermore, in order to avoid the explicit dispatching of the wait and signal calls to their addressed semaphore, we generalize the semaphore procedure to enable it to treat wait and signal calls not addressed to them. It follows that the above semaphore procedure is modified in three points.

1° Firstly, a new parameter is added to it : the name of the semaphore. It is subsequently denoted by Name.
2° Secondly, wait and signal calls are tagged by the name of the semaphore to which they are addressed. The terms of the L_op list are thus of the form wait(Name,Resp) and signal(Name).
3° Finally, two clauses are added to handle wait and signal calls addressed to other semaphores. They are simply discarded.

The following semaphore procedure results :

```
suspend semaphore(!g,!,!,!g).
semaphore(Name,[wait(Name,Resp)|L_mess_rem],Wait_proc,0) ←
    append(Wait_proc?,[wait(Name,Resp)],New_Wait_proc),
    semaphore(Name,L_mess_rem,New_Wait_proc,0).
semaphore(Name,[wait(Name,Resp)|L_mess_rem],[],Value) ←
    Value > 0 |
    New_value is Value - 1, Resp = ok,
    semaphore(Name,L_mess_rem,[],New_value).
semaphore(Name,[signal(Name)|L_mess_rem],[wait(Name,Resp)|Wait_proc_rem],0) ←
    Resp = ok,
    semaphore(Name,L_mess_rem,Wait_proc_rem,0).
semaphore(Name,[signal(Name)|L_mess_rem],[],Value) ←
    New_value is Value + 1,
    semaphore(Name,L_mess_rem,[],New_value).
semaphore(Name,[wait(Other_name,Resp)|L_mess_rem],Wait_proc,Value) ←
    Name ≠ Other_name,
    semaphore(Name,L_mess_rem,Wait_proc,Value).
semaphore(Name,[signal(Other_name)|L_mess_rem],Wait_proc,Value) ←
    Name ≠ Other_name,
    semaphore(Name,L_mess_rem,Wait_proc,Value).
```

C. Application

The classical use of the semaphore is schematized by the following procedure :

```
procedure p
  begin
    repeat
      wait(S);
      critical region;
      signal(S);
      remainder
    forever
  end.
```

This procedure repeats forever the following cycle. It first waits to obtain exclusive access to some resource, enters its critical region, liberates the resource by a signal operation at the end of the critical region and performs some remainder operations.

The procedure can be transformed in a Conclog procedure as follows. To avoid confusion let us call conclog_p the resulting Conclog procedure.

1) A parameter L_op is added to the procedure conclog_p. It consists of a list of wait(S,Resp) and signal(S) calls to the semaphore S. It is incrementally constructed by the execution of p.
2) The cycle is simulated by using tail recursivity.
3) Sequentialization of the algorithm is achieved by using the sequentialization operator.
4) Let us now turn to the core of the cycle. The wait(S) call in p should first be simulated. This is is achieved by sending a wait(S,Resp) term to the semaphore S. Practically, this means instantiating the head of the list L_op as follows :

    L_op = [wait(S,Resp)|L_op_rem1].

The critical section can then be entered when the execution of the wait(S) instruction has succeeded. This success is represented by the fact that the Resp variable is instantiated to ok. Suspension until success of the execution of wait(S) may thus be simulated by the suspension induced by the unification

    Resp? = ok.

Then, the critical section can be executed. When it terminates, the signal(S) instruction has to be executed. This is simulated, as for the wait(S) instruction, by the sending of a signal(S) term to the semaphore. Practically, this means that the L_op list is further instantiated by the term signal(S). This is achieved by the following operation

    L_op_rem1 = [signal(S)|L_op_rem2].

The remainder section can then be executed. When it terminates, a new cycle must be undertaken. This is simulated by a recursive call where the L_op_rem2 is passed to pursue the communication with the S semaphore.

The following conclog_p procedure results :

conclog_p(L_op) ←
    L_op = [wait(S,Resp)|L_op_rem1] |
    Resp? = ok |
    code of critical region |
    L_op_rem1=[signal(S)|L_op_rem2] |
    code of remainder |
    conclog_p(L_op_rem2).

This transformation can be easily generalized to handle more general programs of the form

```
procedure p
  begin
    repeat
      Sequence_init;
      wait(S1); ...; wait(Sn);
      critical region;
      signal(Sn); ...; signal(S1);
      Sequence_rem
    forever
  end.
```

where S1, ..., Sn are semaphores and Sequence_init and Sequence_rem are sequences of instructions not referring to the semaphores. In this case, the procedure derived in Conclog is

```
conclog_p(L_op) ←
    code of Sequence_int |
    L_op = [wait(S1,Resp1),...,wait(Sn,Respn)|L_op_rem1] |
    Resp1? = ok, ..., Respn? = ok |
    code of critical region |
    L_op_rem1=[signal(Sn),...,signal(S1)|L_op_rem2] |
    code of Sequence_rem |
    conclog_p(L_op_rem2).
```

11.5.2 The dining philosophers

A. Problem description

The problem of the dining philosophers has been proposed in [Dijkstra, 1971]. It is set here in a monastory of five monks. There, each monk shares its time between thinking and eating. When a philosopher wishes to eat, he enters the dining room, takes a seat, eats and then returns to his cell. The refectory is shown in Figure 11.4. Five bowls and five chopsticks are arranged alternately around a circular table. Each philosopher has his own place at the table. In the center of the table is a large bowl of rice that is assumed to be continually replenished. Eating rice requires two chopsticks. A philosopher may only use the ones that are on either side of his bowl. A choptsick can be used by one philosopher at a time.

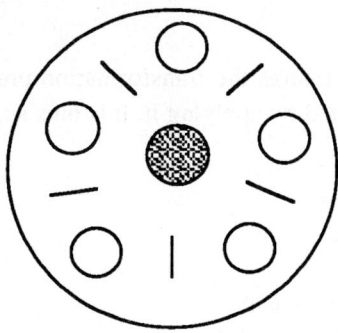

Figure 11.4

The challenge is to write a program that refects the philosophers' life and that avoids the problems of deadlock and starvation.

B. Classical imperative solution

The classical solution consists of allowing at most four philosophers to enter the room. Then, a philosopher behavior consists of waiting for his two forks, eating when they are available and liberating the forks at the end of the meal. The restriction to four philosophers prevents deadlock and starvation.

In imperative programming, this is translated into the following piece of code.

```
program dining_philosophers.
   var room : semaphore; fork : array[0...4] of semaphore;
   procedure philosopher(i)
      repeat
         think;
         wait(room);
         wait(fork[i]);
         wait(fork[(i+1)mod5]);
         eat;
         signal(fork((i+1)mod5]);
         signal(fork[i]);
         signal(room)
      forever;
   begin
      room := 4;
      for i:=0 to 4 do fork[i] := 1;
      philosopher(0) || ... || philosopher(4).
   end.
```

C. The Conclog solution

We translate this solution thanks the transformation presented in Section 11.5.1. The philosopher procedure is transformed by applying it. It is thus augmented by the L_op parameter and now rewrites as

```
conclog_philosopher(Id,L_op) ←
        Succ_id is (Id+1)mod5,
        think |
        L_op = [ wait(room,Resp_room),
                 wait(fork(Id),Resp_fork_id),
                 wait(fork(Succ_id),Resp_fork_succ_id) | L_op_rem1]  |
        Res_room?=ok, Resp_fork_id?=ok, Resp_fork_succ_id?=ok |
        eat |
        L_op_rem1 = [ signal(fork(Succ_id)), signal(fork(Id)), signal(room) | L_op_rem2]  |
        conclog_philosopher(Succ_id,L_op_rem2).
```

The Succ_id is (Id+1)mod5 s-goal does not arise from the transformation. It is due to the technical problem that, in logic programming, (Id+1)mod5 is interpreted as a structure and not as the corresponding value. The eat and think procedures are never programmed. We do not program them here either. They can be simulated by waiting for a random time.

The core of the program is then translated as follows. Calls to the conclog_philosopher procedure are launched concurrently to simulate the

philosopher(0) || ... || philosopher(4).

instruction. This may be achieved by reducing the goal

← conclog_philosopher(0,L_op_0), ..., conclog_philosopher(4,L_op_4).

Signal and wait operations for the semaphores in the philosopher procedure have been simulated by the insertion of the corresponding terms in the L_op lists of the conclog_philosopher procedure. To complete the scheme, it thus remains to link these L_op lists with the calls in charge of the simulation of the semaphores. This is achieved by means of a subgoal concurrent with the above conclog_philosopher subgoals. It is called arbitrator. It takes all the L_op lists as parameter. Intuitively, its reduction activates the semaphores and communicates them the signal and wait of the executions of the philosopher procedures. The first task is easy to achieve : it is sufficient to call the semaphore procedure for each semaphore. The Value parameter is instantiated as indicated in the philosopher program. The second task may be achieved quite simply thanks to our general form of the semaphore : it is sufficient to merge all the L_op lists and to communicate the resulting merged list to all semaphore calls. Note that, without this general form, we should have to handle six lists for the semaphores and explicitly determine to which semaphore the wait and signal calls refer. This would have quite complicated the merge procedure.

In conclusion, the execution of the imperative program dining philosospher is thus simulated by the reduction of the goal

    ← conclog_philosopher(0,L_op_0),
       conclog_philosopher(1,L_op_1),
       conclog_philosopher(2,L_op_2),
       conclog_philosopher(3,L_op_3),
       conclog_philosopher(4,L_op_4),
       arbitrator(L_op_0,L_op_1,L_op_2,L_op_3,L_op_4).

with the arbitrator procedure stated as

    arbitrator(L_op_0,L_op_1,L_op_2,L_op_3,L_op4) ←
       gen_merge([L_op_0,L_op_1,L_op_2,L_op_3,L_op_4],L_op),
       semaphore(room,L_op,[],4),
       semaphore(fork(0),L_op,[],1),
       semaphore(fork(1),L_op,[],1),
       semaphore(fork(2),L_op,[],1),
       semaphore(fork(3),L_op,[],1),
       semaphore(fork(4),L_op,[],1).

The gen_merge procedure has been defined in Section 11.4.3.

11.6 The producer-consumer paradigm

Most of the procedures we have studied in this chapter can be schematized by the producer-consumer scheme. This scheme is basically as follows. Two conjoined s-goals share a common list, say L. They are reduced concurrently, as usual in Conclog. The particularity is that the reduction of one of them incrementally constructs L whereas the reduction of the other declares L as element input and incrementally consumes it. The former s-goal is called the producer of L and the latter s-goal is called its consumer. This situation may be schematized in the following goal :

    ← producer(L), consumer(L).

Clearly, in this producer-consumer scheme, the consumer cannot run ahead the producer : it can just consume the elements of L at the rate they are produced. In contrast, the producer can produce L without any care for the rate in which it is consumed. We examine hereafter three schemes constraining the production rate of the producer. A first one makes the producer produce only on demand by the consumer. It has the drawback that the consumer can request without care for the producer. The second scheme remedies this problem : the consumer and producer behave at the same rate. The last scheme relaxes a little bit this synchronization by allowing the producer to run ahead the consumer to some extend.

11.6.1 Lazy producer

Suspension declarations and constructions based on structural induction on the input parameter ensure that the consumer process cannot run ahead the producer process. However, the producer is not restricted and so can exceed the rate at which the values are used by the consumer. The producer is thus eager in the sense that it produces values at will. Clark and Gregory ([Gregory, 1985], [Clark and Gregory, 1986]) have shown how to transform the program in order to make the producer lazy. Roughly speaking, their transformation consists of inverting the communication. The consumer is made the producer of variables that are instantiated by the producer. Some auxiliary adaptations of the code are furthermore needed for the following purposes:

- to ensure that the consumer process does not deadlock,
- to make sure that the producer - that now behaves as a tester - can yet construct values for the given variables
- to eliminate some undesirable non determinism.

In particular, this always involves reversing the suspension declarations.

We prove that this transformation is feasible in Conclog and illustrate it on the following simple producer and consumer.

```
← producer(L), consumer(L,0).

producer(L) ← producer_a(L1), producer_b(L2), merge(L1,L2,L).
producer_a([a|Lrem]) ← producer_a(Lrem).
producer_b([b|Lrem]) ← producer_b(Lrem).

suspend consumer(!,*).
consumer([a|L_rem],Count) ← New_count is Count + 1, consumer(L_rem,New_count).
consumer([b|L_rem],Count) ← consumer(L_rem,Count).

suspend merge(!,!,*) with l_commit.
merge([H|T],L2,[H|Lrem]) ← merge(T,L2,Lrem).
merge(L1,[H|T],[H|Lrem]) ← merge(L1,T,Lrem).
merge([],L2,L2).
merge(L1,[],L1).
```

The merge(L1,L2,L) procedure is that defined in Section 11.2. It is easy to verify that the reduction of any call producer_a(L) (resp. producer_b(L)) incrementally constructs L with a's (resp. b's). The reduction of the s-goal producer(L) thus produces a list of a's and b's, arbitrarily interleaved. Moreover, it is easy to see that the reduction of the consumer(L,0) s-goal simply counts the number of a's and discards all b's. Because of the suspension declaration of consumer, it can only consume the list L. The reduction of the goal

← producer(L), consumer(L,0).

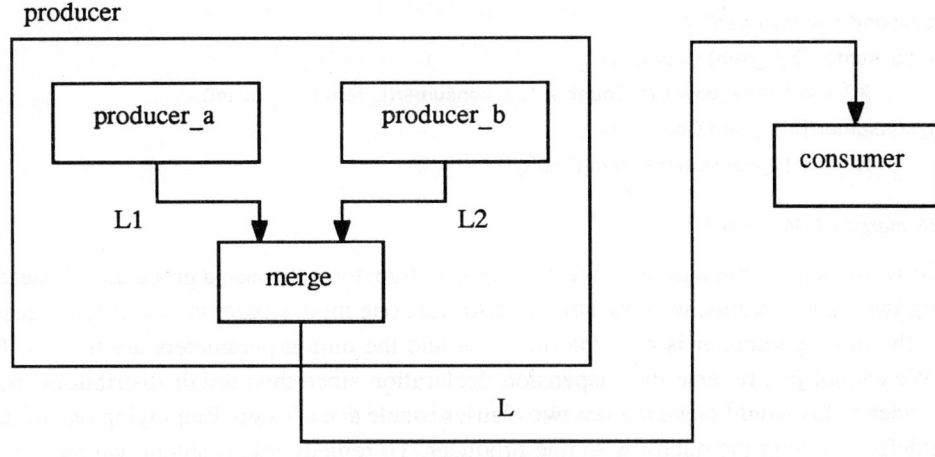

Figure 11.5

thus consists of an instance of the producer-consumer scheme. The dataflow is represented in Figure 11.5.

The producer is made lazy by transforming the consumer, merge and producer procedures as follows.

A. THE consumer PROCEDURE

The consumer is made a producer of a list but now of variables to preserve the original consumer character. These variables will be instantiated later by the producer. The transformed version of the consumer process, denoted by t_consumer, thus looks like

    t_consumer([X|L_rem],Count).

The values a and b for X cannot be embodied in the head since it is the role of the producer to give X a value. We thus include them in the body of the clauses. As they act as tests to select the clause to be used, we place them in the front and separate them by a sequentialization operator from the rest of the clauses. Furthermore, as X=a (resp. X=b) immediately succeeds by instantiating X to a (resp. b), we add a global read-only annotation in order to make X=a (resp. X=b) a real test that suspends until X is instantiated to some ground value. Finally, the suspension declaration must be changed. The first argument cannot be declared as input since the consumer is now a producer of the first parameter. It is changed to "*". The consumer procedure thus rewrites as

```
suspend t_consumer(*,?).
t_consumer([X|L_rem],Count) ←
    X? = a | New_count is Count + 1, t_consumer(L_rem,New_count).
t_consumer([X|L_rem],Count) ←
    X? = b | t_consumer(L_rem,Count).
```

B. THE merge PROCEDURE

Moving back on the dataflow, we now have to transform the merge procedure. Instead of merging two input streams, we now have to distribute one input stream in two output streams. Hence, the input parameter is now the third one and the output parameters are the two first ones. We cannot just reverse the suspension declaration since then unfair distribution could result. Indeed, this would make the last two clauses usable at each step. Employing one of them would definitely bind the dataflow to one producer. To remedy this problem, we modify the merge code to reflect the structure of the input parameter in the clause heads. The two first clauses treat the case where it is of the form [H|T]. We thus dedicate the two last clauses for the case where it is empty. In this case, the two first parameters are empty. A single clause is thus sufficient.

The transformed version of merge is thus

```
suspend t_merge(*,*,!).
t_merge([H|T_rem],L2,[H|T]) ← t_merge(T_rem,L2,T).
t_merge(L1,[H|T_rem],[H|T]) ← t_merge(L1,T_rem,T).
t_merge([],[],[]).
```

Note that this is is the reversed merge we programmed in Section 11.4.3.

C. THE producer_a AND producer_b PROCEDURES

The producer_a and producer_b procedures must finally be transformed. Both are now consumers of a list of variables, that they must instantiate to a and b, respectively. A naive solution could be to just add a

   suspend producer_a(!) (resp. suspend producer_b(!))

suspension declaration. However, deadlock would result since the clause unification would instantiate the head list to a and b, respectively. The variable assignments have thus to be made in the body of the clauses. The correct transformed clauses are thus

```
suspend t_producer_a(!).
t_producer_a([X|L_rem]) ← X=a, t_producer_a(L_rem).
suspend t_producer_b(!).
t_producer_b([X|L_rem]) ← X=b, t_producer_b(L_rem).
```

11.6.2 Synchronous producer and consumer

One problem remains. The producer now cannot run ahead the consumer but the consumer can generate variables at a rate superior to their instantiation by the producer. We now show how to make the producer and consumer processes behave at a same rate. To this end, we transform the initial producer-consumer program so that the producer can only produce a new binding when the previous one has been consumed.

Our transformation takes profit of the recursive calls in the producer and consumer definitions. It consists of polluting the list of values by inserting a Resp variable between two values. This variable is instantiated to ok by the consumer after consumption of the preceding value. It furthermore constitutes an extra parameter of the producer_a and producer_b procedures. It is declared as input. Hence, the producer can only proceed when the variable is bound to ok i.e. when the consumer has consumed the value. Moreover, the consumer cannot run ahead the producer since it needs some value to proceed. It should be noted that the modifications are minor and only concern the producer and the consumer processes. For instance, the merge process is not affected.

The transformed code is as follows.

```
← producer(L), consumer(L).

producer(L) ← producer_a(L1,ok), producer_b(L2,ok), merge(L1,L2,L).

suspend producer_a(*,!).
producer_a([a,Resp|L_rem],ok) ← producer_a(L_rem,Resp).

suspend producer_b(*,i).
producer_b([b,Resp|L_rem],ok) ← producer_b(L_rem,Resp).

suspend consumer(!,!).
consumer([a,Resp|L_rem],Count) ←
      New_count is Count + 1 |
      Res=ok, consumer(L_rem,New_count).
consumer([b,Resp|L_rem],Count) ← Res=ok, consumer(L_rem,Count).

suspend merge(!,!,*) with l_commit.
merge([H|T],L2,[H|Lrem]) ← merge(T,L2,Lrem).
merge(L1,[H|T],[H|Lrem]) ← merge(L1,T,Lrem).
merge([],L2,L2).
merge(L1,[],L1).
```

11.6.3 Asynchronous consumer and producer

We finally slightly relax the constraint on the producer by allowing some a's and b's to be bufferred. We do this essentially by interposing a buffer between the producer and the consumer. Slight modifications on the producer and consumer procedures will furthermore result.

A. The buffer procedure

The buffer is assigned three tasks :

1) it receives the a's and b's produced by the producer and record them in case they cannot be consumed by the consumer,
2) it constraints the rate of production of the producer
3) it provides the consumer with a's and b's at the rate it can consume them. That is, it sends such a value when it is available (that is has been communicated by the producer) and when the consumer has consumed the last sent value.

Two natural features of a buffer are its size and its contents. The first one specifies the number of elements the buffer can record. The last one registers elements. Moreover, two streams appear naturally in the above scheme: the stream of a's and b's produced by the producer and the stream of same values sent to the consumer. All these features and streams are embodied in the buffer procedure. They are used by it as parameters. Four other parameters are added to them, namely :

- a Status parameter,
- a Num_el parameter,
- a Ack_cons parameter,
- a Ack_prod parameter.

Their presence is justified as follows.

1) The Num_el parameter is added for ease of the implementation. It aims at counting the number of elements registered in the buffer.
2) The Status parameter aims at indicating whether the two following properties hold :
   - the buffer can still record one element,
   - the buffer should record one sent element.

   The reason for which the first condition might be violated is quite clear : the buffer has registered all the elements it can. At the opposite, the buffer can be empty when the consumer signals to it that it has consumed the last received value. In this case, some value communicated by the producer should not be registered but should be directly transmitted to the consumer.

   The Status parameter is allowed to take three values :
   - indebted, to indicate that a value is expected by the consumer,

- full, to indicate that there is no room for further value in the buffer,
- free, to indicate that at least one value can be buffered

3) The Ack_cons parameter is used to receive acknowledgement messages from the consumer.
4) The Ack_prod parameter is used to send acknowledgment messages to the producer.

Summing up, the buffer predicate is as follows :

buffer(Status,Size,Num_el,Contents,Ack_prod,Ack_cons,Prod_list,Cons_list).

The five first arguments are explicit by their name. The In_list and Out_list correspond to the stream sent by the producer to the buffer and to the stream sent by the buffer to the consumer, respectively. The Status, Size, Num_el are declared as input. The Contents, Ack_cons, In_list lists are declared as element input.

The buffer procedure is implemented as a perpetual process. Thus it calls itself recursively. Change of states are represented by modification of the parameters in the recursive calls. Its implementation rests on the two following principles.

- Each time it has consumed an a or b, the consumer sends an acknwoldgement message to the buffer. It is represented by the ok atom.
- Each time, it produces an a or b, the producer produces simultaneously a Resp variable in the Ack_prod list. It is acknowledged by the buffer by instantiating it to ok. This is performed each time the buffer is not full.

The two following properties follow :

- once its status is full, the buffer cannot receive an a or b from the producer;
- once its status is undebted, the buffer cannot receive an acknowledgment message from the consumer.

In these conditions, the buffer procedure is governed by the following algorithm :

1. If an a or b value is received from the producer then
    1.1 if Status is free then
    - register the value in the buffer,
    - update the buffer components,
    - if it remains free then instantiate the first Resp variable of the Ack_prod list by ok,
    1.2 if Status is undebted then send the value to the consumer and acknowledge the producer by instantiating the first Resp variable of the Ack_prod list by ok.

2. If an acknowledgment message is received from the consumer then
    2.1 if Num_el is 0 then move the Status parameter to the undebted value,
    2.2 if Num_el is not null then
        2.2.1 If Status is free then
        - take the oldest element of the buffer and send it to the consumer,

- update the buffer components,
2.2.2 If Status is full then
- take the oldest element of the buffer and send it to the consumer,
- update the buffer components,
- acknowledge the producer by instantiating the first Resp variable of the Ack_prod list to ok.

The buffer procedure is implemented according to this algorithm. A clause is associated with each case. A suspension declaration is added to declare the input arguments. It incorporates a commit operator that simulates the indeterministic arrival of a and b values produced by the producers and the acknowledgment messages sent by the consumer. Fair choice is ensured as usual by instantiating the clause heads as much as possible.

The procedure new_status(Size,Num_el,Status) is finally used to update the status component. It is specified as follows.

procedure status(Size,Num_el,Status).
- Type
    Size, Num_el : integers
    Status : of the three forms stated in the above point 2)
- Relation
    Status is free if Num_el<Size
    Status is full if Num_el=Size
- Operational properties
    1) Suspension condition
        Size and Num_el ground
    2) Precondition
        Num_el≤Size
    3) Postcondition
        <ground,ground,any> : <ground,ground,ground>; <0-1>

Its implementation is straightforward. It is as follows :

suspend new_status(!g,!g,*).
new_status(Size,Size,full).
new_status(Size,Nb,Status) ← Nb<Size | Status=free.

This given, the code of the buffer procedure is as follows.

suspend buffer(!g,!g,!g,?,!,!,!,*).

buffer(free,Size,Num_el,Contents,[Res|Ack_prod_rem],Ack_cons,[X|Prod_list_rem],
                                                            Cons_list) ←
    New_num_el is Num_el+1,
    new_status(Size,New_num_el,free) |$_c$
    Res=ok,
    append(Contents,[X],New_contents),
    buffer(free,Size,New_num_el,New_contents,Ack_prod_rem,Ack_cons,
                                                    Prod_list_rem,Cons_list).

buffer(free,Size,Num_el,Contents,[Res|Ack_prod_rem],Ack_cons,[X|Prod_list_rem],
                                                            Cons_list) ←
    New_num_el is Num_el+1,
    new_status(Size,New_num_el,full) |$_c$
    append(Contents,[X],New_contents),
    buffer(full,Size,New_num_el,New_contents,[Res|Ack_prod_rem],Ack_cons,
                                                    Prod_list_rem,Cons_list).

buffer(undebted,Size,Num_el,Contents,[Res|Ack_prod_rem],Ack_cons,[X|Prod_list_rem],
                                                    [X|Cons_list_rem]) ←
    Res=ok,
    buffer(undebted,Size,Num_el,Contents,Ack_prod_rem,Ack_cons,Prod_list_rem],
                                                            Cons_list_rem).

buffer(Status,Size,0,Contents,Ack_prod,[ok|Ack_cons_rem],Prod_list,Cons_list) ←
    buffer(undebted,Size,0,Contents,Ack_prod,Ack_cons_rem,Prod_list,Cons_list).

buffer(free,Size,Num_el,[X|Contents_rem],Ack_prod,[ok|Ack_cons_rem],Prod_list,
                                                    [X|Cons_list_rem]) ←
    Num_el>0 |$_c$
    New_num_el is Num_el-1,
    buffer(free,Size,New_num_el,Contents_rem,Ack_prod,Ack_cons_rem,Prod_list,
                                                            Cons_list).

buffer(full,Size,Size,[X|Contents_rem],[Res|Ack_prod_rem|,[ok|Ack_cons_rem],Prod_list,
                                                    [X|Cons_list_rem]) ←
    New_num_el is Num_el-1, Res = ok,
    buffer(free,Size,New_num_el,Contents_rem,Ack_prod_rem,Ack_cons_rem,Prod_list,
                                                            Cons_list).

B. The producer and consumer procedures

The producer_a and producer_b procedures are those of Section 11.6.2 but where the a and b values are grouped with their Resp variable by means of pair constructors. The two lists generated by the producers are then merged as before. An auxiliary dispatcher is finally used to separate the a's and b's from the Resp variables and to put them in their corresponding Prod_list and Ack_prod lists. Furthermore, it ensures that the order of the values in Prod_list corresponds to the order of their corresponding Resp variables in Ack_prod.

```
producer(Prod_list,Ack_prod) ←
    producer_a(La), producer_b(Lb), merge(La,Lb,Laux), split(Laux,Prod_list,Ack_prod).

producer_a([(a,Res)|Lrem]) ← producer_a(Lrem).
producer_b([(b,Res)|Lrem]) ← producer_b(Lrem).

suspend split(!,*,*).
split([],[],[]).
split([(X,Resp)|T],[X|L_rem],[Resp|Resps_rem]) ← split(T,L_rem,Resps_rem).

suspend consumer(*,!,!).
consumer(Ack_cons,[a|L_rem],Count) ←
    New_count is Count + 1 |
    Ack_cons = [ok|Ack_cons_rem],
    consumer(Ack_cons_rem,L_rem,New_count).
consumer(Ack_cons,[b|L_rem],Count) ←
    Ack_cons = [ok|Ack_cons_rem],
    consumer(Ack_cons_rem,L_rem,Count).
```

C. The producer-consumer goal

As a conclusion, the original

```
← producer(L), consumer(L)
```

query is now modified as

```
←   producer(Prod_list,Ack_prod),
    buffer(free,N,0,[],Ack_prod,Ack_cons,Prod_list,Cons_list),
    consumer(Ack_cons,Cons_list,0).
```

11.7 Conclusion

This chapter has tackled behavioral applications. Several representative examples have been programmed using Conclog. They include an airline reservation system, a unix shell and a lift system. Other classical concurrent programming problems have also been addressed. It has been shown how to simulate semaphores and how to code the seminal dining philosophers problem.

One conclusion of this chapter is that programming such applications is indeed feasible in Conclog. This results from the interpretation of the reduction of subgoals as perpetual processes. On a programming standpoint, this has been made possible thanks to the extra-logical features. Suspension of the perpetual processes could not have been simulated without read-only annotations and suspension declarations. Non deterministic choice of these processes could not have been simulated without the commit operators either.

It is here worth stressing that these extra-logical features were originally introduced in Conclog to optimize programs constructed from a logical perspective and not to code behavioral applications. Hence, optimizing programs in a minimal and "reasonably complete" manner has provided a framework to tackle those applications. Nevertheless, we believe that programming them could be made easier by using extra-logical features devoted to them. The definition of such features is however out of the scope of this book and is left for future research.

Some of the Conclog extra-logical features have also been introduced in other forms in other concurrent logic languages such as the committed choice ones. Conclog thus shares its ability to support behavioral applications with such concurrent programming languages. In contrast, as these applications require concurrency, sequential languages such as Prolog are not suited to tackle them.

The first order logic framework has not been much used in this chapter. This is not really surprising since the programs presented in this chapter have been dedicated to simulate behaviors. As a result, the methodology proposed in Chapter 9 has not been much used either. Nevertheless, the specifications proposed in it have revealed to be quite suited to describe the procedures. Some of them have furthermore been constructed by using structural induction.

Conclusion

This part has addressed the programming in Conclog. Two major issues have been addressed.

Methodological guidelines have first been given. Chapter 1 has shown that whatever logic programming language is used, procedural aspects of the computations must be taken into account. Although it has been built to be as close as possible to the ideal of logic programming, Conclog is not an exception to the rule. This does not mean that logic cannot be used as a basis for computing. Simply, two aspects must be handled : the declarative construction of a solution to the problem to solve and its translation in executable code. It is thus important to associate a methodology of programming with the design of the language. The proposed methodology rests on three phases. The first one consists in writing a specification of the problem to solve. The second one consists in constructing a logic description from the specification. The third one consists in deriving a Conclog program therefrom. One of its features is thus to separate the logical aspects from the procedural ones. As argued in Chapter 9, this has been possible in such a clear way thanks to our concern of building Conclog as close as possible to the ideal of logic programming. Using committed-choice languages for instance would have imply to reason in terms of functions and the induced dataflows in order to build the logic description. Nevertheless, parts of the methodology could be used when such languages are used as target languages.

Practical examples of programming have then been given. They have been classified in two kinds of applications : the behavioral and the non-behavioral ones.

1) The behavioral applications consist of the simulation of dynamic systems. Their specification thus essentially state behavioral requirements. We succeeded in programming several behavioral applications : an airline reservation system, a unix-like shell and a lift system. Classical concurrent programs have also been tackled. For instance, the seminal dining philosopher problems has been solved using Conclog.

2) The non-behavioral applications are free from behavioral requirements. They can be regarded as the typical applications to which logic programming is widely acknowledged to be dedicated. Several applications have been handled. We succeeded in programming relational database, multi-directional and multi-solution procedures, single-solution directed procedures. Parallelism of trees has also been shown to be expressible in Conclog. Futhermore, the generation and test paradigm has been shown to be supported quite elegantly.

These two kinds of applications have established the ease of programming and the expressiveness of Conclog. This has been contrasted in some cases with other languages such as Prolog and the committed-choice languages.

Although it does not intend to be a universal panacea, the methodology has been used as a support to program the applications. It has intensively been taken into profit in order to handle non-behavioral applications. In particular, it has revealed useful to guide the construction of procedures widely acknowledged to be of advanced programming. To our opinion, constructing them directly is more difficult, especially in the concurrent framework. The methodology has been used in a lesser extend to program behavioral applications. This results from the fact that, by nature, such applications do not fit the first order logic framework. Nevertheless, the specifications proposed in the methodology have been used to describe the procedures. Some of them have furthermore been constructed using the construction guidelines of the methodology.

Part IV

Conclusion

Chapter 12

Conclusion

A concurrent logic programming language and a methodology for programming with it have been introduced in this book. As a conclusion, we recall their main features and suggest future research.

12.1 The Conclog language

Our main concern for designing Conclog was to build it as close as possible to the ideal of logic programming. Desired properties of ease of programming, simplicity of the semantics, expressiveness, completeness and soundness have resulted. Multi-directional and multi-solution procedures have also followed quite naturally.

An original approach has been taken to achieve these features. Instead of directly dealing with operational tricks to ensure efficiency, the ideal of logic programming has been taken as a reference. A parallel execution model of Horn clauses was first constructed. It has been explained according to two views. In the more global tree view, the computations are seen as the progressive construction slice by slice of an and/or search tree by means of two interleaving phases. They are called generation and reconciliation phases. Any generation phase aims at extending the constructed top part of the and/or search tree from one slice. To this end, or-parallelism and and-parallelism are employed in an unrestricted way. It follows that conflicting bindings may be produced. They are intermittently reconciled by the reconciliation phases. Precisely, any reconciliation phase takes the part of the and/or search tree resulting from the preceding generation and acts in three ways. Branches that are detected to contribute to no solution are removed from the tree. Bindings pointed out to be common to any solution by the reconciliation are communicated between the subtrees. Finally, solutions contained in the newly constructed slice are delivered as the results of the computation.

The tree view has been refined in a more dynamic and more real perception of the computations. This rests on the behavior of processes of a process model. Many parallel computations have then been pointed out. They relax the apparent strict interleaving of the generation and reconciliation phases.

The depth of the slices has been incorporated as a parameter of the model. Hence, a class of models has in fact been defined. All of them are proved to be sound and complete.

Negation has been introduced in a second design step. It has been proved necessary to incorporate negative information. This has led us to generalize substitutions and mgus to n-substitutions and n-mgus, respectively. The Conclog negation then consists of an improved form of the classical negation as failure rule. It is based on our equational framework. Referring to the usual completion understanding of the programs, the extended models are proved to be sound and as complete as possible when the resolution and negation as failure rules are used. Classical problems with the usual negation as failure rule are ruled out. For instance, the floundering problem is of no concern. Furthermore, negative information turn out to be an elegant way of representing an infinite number of solutions and to obtain more multi-directional procedures.

Extra-logical features have finally been incorporated in a third design step. They have been introduced both for purposes of efficiency and practicability. On the one hand, annotations have been provided to increase the performance of the procedures. Their use is not mandatory. They express various forms of suspension, synchronization, clause selections, ... On the other hand, built-in primitives have been provided for practicability. They include the necessary input/output facilities, arithmetic ones, meta-call ones, ... The whole set of extra-logical primitives has been argued to be minimal and reasonably complete in the sense that

- for any extra-logical feature, it is practically not convenient to simulate it by a combination of other ones (minimality);
- most desirable forms of synchronization, communication or, more generally, computations can indeed be programmed by using the Conclog extra-logical features (reasonable completion).

The language has been tested on various examples ranging from the behavioral applications to the non-behavioral ones.

Because of our intial concern of making Conclog as close as possible to the ideal of logic programming, programs could be obtained by using a declarative style of programming. In particular, multi-directional multi-solution procedures are supported quite naturally. No annotation is, furthermore, required to make them sound and complete. Annotations may then be introduced to improve the efficiency. Correctness preserving transformations have furthermore been provided to this end in the methodological part. Procedures of efficiency similar to those of other concurrent languages, such as the commited-choice, can then be obtained.

Programs simulating dynamic systems have also been developed. Such behavioral applications are not related to the first order logic foundation of logic programming. Nevertheless, they could effectively be programmed thanks to the power of the extra-logical features. For example, an airline reservation system, a unix shell and a lift system have been programmed. Classical concurrent applications have also been coded. For instance, the seminal dining philosopher problem has been solved in Conclog. Finally, programming in an object-oriented manner has been proved to be feasible too.

Conclog contrasts with other concurrent programming languages by its ability to support multi-directional multi-solution procedures. Chapter 8 has argued that committed-choice languages (Concurrent Prolog [Shapiro, 1983], Parlog [Gregory, 1985], Guarded Horn Clauses [Ueda, 1986a]) essentially embody functional parallel programming coupled with unification. Because the commitment mechanism is applied at each reduction step, at most one solution can be computed for any procedure call. Furthermore, strict use of annotations and/or careful placing of literals make the procedures usable in some modes only. Some remedies have been proposed to solve this problem (such as the use of bagof built-in primitives, all-solution relations, program transformations) but they have been shown to deviate too much from the parallel logic programming paradigm. P-Prolog ([Yang and Aiso, 1986]) and the CP family of languages are other attempts to get multi-directionality while conserving the power of the commitment mechanism. The set of the annotations they provide has been argued to be less powerful than ours. It follows that procedures are made more easily multi-directional in Conclog.

It is worth noting that the ease of obtaining this multi-directionality property also results from our careful treatment of negation. In fact, in the above languages, negation is treated in the usual manner. No real treatment is operated. In contrast, in Conclog, we take advantadge of the basic model (particularly of the search for all solutions induced by or-parallelism and of the mutli-equational framework) to build a negation very close to the real one.

Handling of annotations should also be contrasted with that required by the above languages. Correctness of the procedure requires a careful design of the guards of the clauses. Furthermore, in addition to the guard annotation, auxiliary annotations are required to handle the dataflow correctly or even are required by the definition of the language (as in Parlog). In contrast, in Conclog, there is no need of introducing annotations to ensure soundness and completeness. They may then be optionally introduced in order to get more efficiency. Of course, they are also required to code behavioral constraints.

Compared with parallel Prolog dialects ([Clark and Mac Cabe, 1979], [Kasif et al., 1983], [Butler et al., 1986], [Shen, 1986], [Hausman et al., 1987], [Whesphal et al., 1987], [Butler et al., 1988], [Calderwood and Szeredi, 1989], [Szeredi, 1989]), we argued that parallelizing Prolog is not a good approach to design concurrent logic programming languages. It is, in fact, at the basis, a contradictory approach since the logic programming framework, naturally parallel, is first sequentialized to give Prolog and then parallelized to give the parallel Prolog versions. This has the consequence of keeping Prolog drawbacks of non termination and incomplete computations. The necessary introduction of parallel features or of parallel versions of sequential ones (such as the cut) may furthermore lead to complicated programming. Finally, the advantages of literal ordering can be conserved by appropriate annotations.

Compared with other parallel execution models ([Pollard, 1981], [Conery, 1983], [Li and Martin, 1986], [Kalé, 1987]), Conclog first differs by dealing explicitly with negation. Other differences are as follows.

The parallel execution model of [Pollard, 1981] rests on a reconciliation-based approach too. However it differs in the way in which substitutions are reconciled and in the way the and/or search tree is pruned. Reconciliation of substitutions made there was proved to be not completely satisfactory. In contrast, our equational framework fits well this purpose. Our and/or search tree pruning is achieved by conserving the equational framework and involves less concepts while conserving the same performance. Finally, communication of bindings is achieved in Conclog and not in [Pollard, 1981].

The three other models share the feature of determining, in a conjunction of s-goals, a producer s-goal for each shared variable. They paradoxally suffer from the impossibility of automatically designating the right producer s-goal (i.e. that leading to the most efficient and complete computation). As a result, they use heuristics which, in bad cases, lead to quite unappropriate dataflows. We have preferred to address the designation of producers at the programming level by making the programmer responsible for the insertion of annotations. Moreover schemes of [Conery, 1983] and [Li and Martin, 1986] are proved incomplete, in contrast with Conclog.

In contrast with [Saraswat, 1989], which has highlighted the concurrent logic languages from the general perspective of constraint programming, Conclog has taken place in the classical logic programming framework (according to our objectives of Chapter 1). As a consequence, we could take profit of the specificity of the logic programming framework and develop notions tailored to this context. For intance, the role of idempotent substitutions in the reconciliation calculus, the extension of the notions of substitution, of term, of unification, of instantiation to tackle negative information, the reconciliation calculus and the algorithms supporting it cannot be developed in the more general setting of constraints. However, there is no doubt that some of these notions can be abstracted at a constraint level (which is partly achieved in [Saraswat, 1989]) and we believe that exploiting our ideas in the constraint framework could lead to enrich the cc family of constraint languages with quite interesting languages.

12.2 The methodology

Although it is desired, a complete abstraction of the operational features of the computation is not possible. The semi-decidability character of first order logic creates a first gap between the declarative and the operational semantics of any logic programming language. Moreover, extra-logical features must also be taken into account for practicability. They definitively break the hoped equivalence between the two semantics. Conclog is not an exception to the rule. A methodology of programming in it has thus been associated with its design. It adapts, to the concurrent context, a methodology proposed in [Deville, 1990] for Prolog as target language. It also covers the entire construction process. It rests on the same three phases.

The first phase deals with specification. They are described in natural language and are structured in type specification, relation specification, environment conditions and operational properties. Here our contribution was to introduce information specific to concurrent executions. Briefly, types are used as invariants, invariants are introduced as environment conditions and operational properties, event conditions are introduced in the environment conditions and suspension conditions are introduced in the operational properties.

The second phase consists in constructing logic descriptions. They are composed of two parts : a definition part and a set of properties. The first part, called logic definition, is taken from [Deville, 1990]. It consists in defining the computed relation by a well formed formula of first order logic. We adopted Deville's correctness criterias and construction process. Our contribution was to point out some heuristics that may lead to procedures involving as much parallelism as possible. The second part constitutes our main contribution at this level. It states properties between the relations involved in the logic definition. They include data dependency properties, test dependency properties and exclusiveness properties. They are particularly interesting in a parallel context but can be used in a sequential one as well.

The third phase of the methodology consists in deriving correct concurrent procedures from the logic definition. One of our contributions was to review the concept of correctness. Auxiliary concepts of partial correctness, semi-correctness, safety, weak termination and strong termination were introduced. The derivation of the procedure is achieved in two steps, similar to those used in the sequential context. At a first step, the same syntactic transformations are applied on the logic definition to derive a set of general Horn clauses. It is then made correct. At the second step, this first correct version is improved thanks to correctness preserving transformations. Some of them make use of the logic properties. Here one contribution was to design such a set of transformations. Some of them, namely the transformations based on equality substitutions, partial evaluation and generation of equivalent search trees, have counterparts in the sequential framework. The other ones are specific to our work.

The methodology highlights Conclog features from another point of view. Conclog ease of use has been claimed. This is reflected in the methodology. The logical aspects could be clearly separated from the operational ones during the construction of a program. This is highly desired in a logic programming context, but as argued in Chapter 9, cannot be achieved in a so-clear way when committed-choice languages are used as target languages. Because of their relationship to a functional paradigm, a functional reasoning involving dataflow handling has already to be employed in the construction of a logic description. Nevertheless, despite this point, parts of the methodology can also be applied in order to design concurrent programs in these languages.

Moreover, it should be stressed that, because of our concern for completeness and soundness, the set of general Horn clauses derived from the logic definition already meets all the logical correctness criterias. There is thus no need of ordering s-goals of clause bodies judiciously or of determining a producer s-goal for each shared variable. Compatibility of types, absence of infinite suspension, termination, behavioral properties, if any, remain to be fulfilled to obtain correctness.

12.3 Future work

Any language gives rise to at least three levels of works : its definition, its implementation and programming with it. At these three points, work remain to be performed. We suggest some part hereafter.

A. Definition

A great part of the thesis has discussed the design of Conclog. No formal semantics has been given. Some research should be done in this direction. It could draw its inspiration from some pieces of work already performed for other concurrent logic programming languages (see e.g. [Levi and Palamidessi, 1985], [Levi and Palamidessi, 1987], [de Bakker and Kok, 1988], [Gerth et al., 1988], [Saraswat, 1989], [de Boer et al., 1989a], [de Boer et al., 1989b], ...).

B. Implementation

The process model designed in Part II proves the implementability character of Conclog. A Prolog interpreter has furthermore been constructed to test the language and to employ it on practical benchmarks. Nevertheless, a lot of work remain to be done in this domain. Research should first be made for efficient memory management. Because and-parallelism and or-parallelism are combined, multiple environments have to be managed. This is central in some current work ([Yang, 1986], [Warren, 1987a], [Butler et al., 1988], [Ramkumar and Kalé, 1989], ...). Conclog gives an additional dimension to them: bindings should be connected so as to facilitate the manipulation of the corresponding equations when reconciliation is performed. Some research should also be made to detect optimization situations, for instance, where reconciliation reduces to simple composition. Finally, another connected subject of research is to design an abstract machine for Conclog. A good approach could be to modify Warren's WAM to the Conclog context.

Note that as the process model has been conceived in such a way that processes need to share a minimum of information, Conclog could be implemented on shared memory systems or on distributed ones.

C. Programming

A lot of work should also be performed at the programming level. Our methodology could be completed in three points :

- additional heuristics to find logic definitions well suited for concurrent executions could be searched;
- additional logic properties could be pointed out;
- additional correctness preserving transformations could be conceived.

Some guidelines should also be searched to discover infinite suspensions or non-terminating computations. Abstract interpretations techniques (see e.g. [Cousot and Cousot, 1977], [Mellish, 1986], [Bruynooghe et al., 1987], [Marriot and Sondergaard, 1988], [Winsborough, 1989], ...) seem well suited for this purpose. Also of interest are work based on semantic research (see e.g. [Baudinet, 1988]).

The construction of an integrated system supporting the methodology constitutes another direction of research.

Finally, the methodology has been developed essentially for applications fitting the first order logic framework, namely the non-behavioral applications. Some research should also be made to provide guidelines to construct programs for behavioral applications. In this direction, two points should particularly be investigated :

- to provide a counterpart of the logic description that suits system simulation;
- to provide a derivation process to transform such descriptions into correct Conclog programs.

Appendices

Appendices

Appendix 1

The perm and element procedures

1. Specifications

A. The perm procedure

procedure perm(L,L_rem).
- Type
    L, L_perm : lists; strong use of the type and any subtype,
- Relation
    L_perm is L where the elements are possibly permutated
- Operational properties
    1) Suspension condition
        L input
    2) Postconditions
        <ground,any> : <ground,ground>; <0-n!>
            where n is the length of L
        L input $\wedge$ L incrementally constructed ground : L_perm incrementally constructed ground.

B. The element procedure

procedure element(X,L,L_rem).
- Type
    L, L_perm : lists whose elements are of the type of X; strong use of the type and any subtype,
- Relation
    X is one element of L and L_rem is L where X has been removed
- Operational properties
    1) Suspension condition
        L element input

2) Postconditions

<any,ground,any> : <ground,ground,ground>; <0-1>

L element input ∧ L incrementally constructed ground : L_rem incrementally constructed ground.

2. Codes

A. The perm procedure

    suspend perm(!,*).
    perm([],[]).
    perm([H|T],[H_perm|T_perm]) ←
        element(H_perm,[H|T],L_aux),
        perm(L_aux,T_perm).

B. The element procedure

    suspend element(*,!,*).
    element(X,[X|T],T).
    element(X,[H|T],[H|T_rem]) ← X≠H, element(X,T,T_rem).

Appendix 2

An airline reservation system

% *The airline reservation system*

    airline_reservation_system   ←   user(1,L1), user(2,L2),
                                      merge(L1,L2,L_request),
                                        database(L_requests).

% *The user component*

    user(Id,L_mess) ← screen_session(Command) | response_to_cmd(Id,Command,L_mess).

    screen_session(Command) ← nl | write('Command ?') | read(Command).

    suspend response_to_cmd(!,!,*).
    response_to_cmd(Id,halt,[]).
    response_to_cmd(Id,Request,[Request|Lm_rem]) ←
        Request≠halt | write_answer(Request) | user(Id,Lm_rem).

    suspend write_answer(!g).
    write_answer(info(Flight,Seats)) ← write('Seats = ',Seats).
    write_answer(reserve(Flight,Seats,true)) ← write(Seats,' seats reserved').
    write_answer(reserve(Flight,Seats,false)) ← write('not enough seats').
    write_answer(create(Flight)).
    write_answer(delete(Flight)).

% *The merge component*

    suspend merge(!,!,*) with l_commitment.
    merge([],L2,L2).
    merge(L1,[],L1).
    merge([H1|T1],L2,[H1|L_rem]) ← merge(T1,L2,L_rem).
    merge(L1,[H2|T2],[H2|L_rem]) ← merge(L1,T2,L_rem).

% *The airline database*

```
database(L_request) ← imp_db(L_request,[]).

suspend imp_db(!,!).
imp_db([],_).
imp_db([info(Flight,Seats)|L_requests_rem],DB) ←
    member(el(Flight,Seats),DB?),
    imp_db(L_request_rem,DB).
imp_db([reserve(Flight,Required_seats,Response)|L_requests_rem],DB) ←
    member(el(Flight,Free_seats),DB?),
    Required_seats ≤ Free_seats |
    Response = true,
    New_free_seats is Free_seats - Required_seats,
    modify(el(Flight,New_free_seats),DB,New_DB),
    imp_db(L_requests_rem,New_DB).
imp_db([reserve(Flight,Required_seats,Response)|L_requests_rem],DB) ←
    member(el(Flight,Free_seats),DB?),
    Required_seats > Free_seats |
    Response = false,
    imp_db(L_requests_rem,DB).
imp_db([create(Flight)|L_request_rem],DB) ←
    imp_db(L_requests_rem,[el(Flight,100)|DB]).
imp_db([delete(Flight)|L_requests_rem],DB) ←
    delete(el(Flight,_),DB,New_DB),
    imp_db(L_requests_rem,New_DB).

suspend  modify(!g,?,*).
modify(el(Flight,New_seats),[el(Flight,Old_seats)|DB_rem],[el(Flight,New_seats)|DB_rem]).
modify(el(Flight,New_seats),[el(Flight_e,Seats_e)|DB_rem],
                                [el(Flight_e,Seats_e)|New_DB_rem]) ←
    Flight ≠ Flight_e |
    modify(el(Flight,New_seats),DB_rem,New_DB_rem).

suspend  delete(!g,?,*).
delete(el(Flight,_),[el(Flight,Seats)|DB_rem],DB_rem).
delete(el(Flight,_),[el(Flight_e,Seats_e)|DB_rem],[el(Flight_e,Seats_e)|New_DB_rem]) ←
    Flight ≠ Flight_e |
    delete(el(Flight,_),DB_rem,New_DB_rem).
```

Appendix 3

An operating system

% *The operating system*

    operating_system ←
        screen(1,S1), keyboard(1,K1), term(K1,S1,R1),
        screen(2,S2), keyboard(2,K2), term(K2,S2,R2),
        merge(R1,R2,R),
        file_system(R,Fs,Fp), file_store(Fs), spooler(Fp).

% *The keyboard and screen procedures*

    keyboard(I,KI) ← *primitive*.

    screen(I,SI) ← *primitive*.

% *The file_system procedure*

    suspend file_system(!,*,*).
    file_system([get(File_name,File_contents)|L_queries_rem],
                    [get(File_name,File_contents)|L_filestore_rem],L_spooler) ←
        file_system(L_queries_rem,L_filestore_rem,L_spooler).
    file_system([replace(File_name,File_contents)|L_queries_rem],
                    [replace(File_name,File_contents)|L_filestore_rem],L_spooler) ←
        file_system(L_queries_rem,L_filestore_rem,L_spooler).
    file_system([print(File_name)|L_queries_rem],
                    [get(File_name,File_contents)|L_filestore_rem],
                    [File_contents|L_spooler]) ←
        file_system(L_queries_rem,L_filestore_rem,L_spooler).

% The *File_store* procedure

    file_store(L_queries) ← imp_file_store(L_queries,Init_FS).

    suspend imp_file_store(!,!).
    imp_file_store([get(File_name,File_contents)|L_rem],FS) ←
        member(el(File_name,File_contents),FS?),
        imp_file_store(L_rem,FS).
    imp_file_store([replace(File_name,File_contents)|L_rem],FS) ←
        modify(el(File_name,File_contents),FS,New_FS) |
        imp_file(L_rem,New_FS).

% The *spooler* procedure

    spooler(Files) ← rev_merge(Files,P1,P2), printer(P1), printer(P2).

% The *term* procedure

    term(L_in,L_out,File_requests) ←
        parser_cmds(L_in,Cmd_txt,Out_cmd_txt),
        shell(Cmd_txt,File_requests,Output_shell),
        merge(Out_cmd_txt,Output_shell,L_out).

% The *parser_cmds* procedure

    parser_cmds(L_in,Cmd_txt,Out_cmd_txt) ←
        imp_parser_cmds(L_in,Cmd_txt,Out_cmd_txt,0).

    suspend imp_parser_cmds(!,*,*,!g).
    imp_parser_cmds([],Cmd_txt,[],_).
    imp_parser_cmds([H|T],[Formatted_cmd_txt|Cmd_txt_rem],Out_cmd_txt,Num) ←
        Succ_Num is Num+1 |
        read_cmd_txt([H|T],Cmd_txt,Char_cmd_txt,L_in_rem),
        transform_cmd_txt(Cmd_txt,Num,Formatted_cmd_txt),
        append(Char_cmd_txt?,[**CR**,Succ_num,@|Out_cmd_txt_rem],Out_cmd_txt),
        imp_parser_cmds(L_in_rem,Cmd_txt_rem,Out_cmd_txt_rem,Succ_Num).

    suspend read_cmd_txt(?,*,*,*).
    read_cmd_txt([%|L_in],Txt,[%|Char_txt],L_in_rem) ←
        read_txt(L_in,Txt,Char_txt,L_in_rem).
    read_cmd_txt([Char|L_in],Cmd,Char_cmd,L_in_rem) ←
        Char ≠ % | read_cmd([Char|L_in],Cmd,Char_cmd,L_in_rem).

read_txt(L_in,txt(L_char),L_char,L_in_rem) ←
    read_until(**CR**,L_in,L_char,L_in_rem).

read_cmd(L_in,cmd(L_prgms,Input_file,Output_file,Tag),Char_cmd,L_in_rem) ←
    read_prgms(L_in,L_prgms,Char_prgms,L_in_1),
    read_input(L_in_1,Input_file,Char_input_file,L_in_2),
    read_output(L_in_2,Output_file,Char_output_file,L_in_3),
    read_tag(L_in_3,Tag,Char_tag,L_in_rem),
    append(Char_prgms?,Char_input_file,Char_aux_1),
    append(Char_aux_1?,Char_output_file,Char_aux_2),
    append(Char_aux_2?,Char_tag,Char_cmd).

suspension read_prgms(?,*,*,*).

read_prgrms(L_in,[Prgm|L_prgms_rem],Char_l_prgm,L_in_rem) ←
    read_name(L_in,Prgm_string,L_rem1),
    name(Prgm,Prgm_string),
    read_blanks(L_rem1,Blanks,L_rem2),
    end_read_prgm(L_rem2,L_prgms_rem,Char_l_prgm_rem,L_in_rem),
    append(Prgm_string?,Blanks,Char_prgm),
    append(Char_prgm?,Char_l_prgm_rem,Char_l_prgm).

end_read_prgm([Char|Lin_rem],L_prgms,Char_prgms,L_rem) ←
    Char = || |
    read_blanks(Lin_rem,Blanks,L1),
    read_prgms(Lin_rem,L_prgms,Char_l_prgm,L_rem),
    append([|||Blanks?],Char_l_prgm,Char_prgms).

end_read_prgm([Char|Lin_rem],L_prgms,Chars_prgm,L_rem) ←
    Char ≠ || |
    L_prgms = [],
    Char_prgm = [],
    L_rem = [Char|Lin_rem].

suspend read_input(?,*,*,*).
read_input([**CR**|Chars],none,[],[**CR**|Chars]).
read_input([&|Chars],none,[],[&|Chars]).
read_input([>|Chars],none,[],[>|Chars]).
read_input([<,Char|Chars],Input_file,Chars_input_file,L) ←
    limitator(Char) |
    File_input = std,
    read_blanks([Char|Chars],Blanks,L),
    Chars_input_file = [<|Blanks].

```
read_input([<,Char|Chars],Input_file,Chars_input_file,L) ←
    not(limitator(Char)) |
    Input_file = file(File_name),
    read_name([Char|Chars],File_name_string,L_aux) ,
    name(File_name,File_name_string) ,
    read_blanks(L_aux,Blanks,L),
    append([<|File_name_string?],Blanks,Chars_input_file).
suspend  read_output(?,*,*,*).
read_output([CR|Chars],std,[],[CR|Chars]).
read_output([&|Chars],std,[],[&|Chars]).
read_output([>,Char|Chars],file(File_name),Char_output_file,L_rem) ←
    read_name([Char|Chars],File_name_string,L_aux) ,
    name(File_name,File_name_string) ,
    read_blanks(L_aux,Blanks,L_rem) ,
    apend([>|File_name_string?],Blanks,Char_output_file).
suspend  read_tag(?,*,*,*).
read_tag([&|Chars],bg,[&|Chars_tag],L) ←  read_until(CR,Chars,Chars_tag,L).
read_tag([CR|Chars],fg,[],Chars).
suspend  read_until(!g,!,*,*).
read_until(_,[],[],[]).
read_until(X,[X|T],[],T).
read_until(X,[Y|T],[Y|L1_rem],L2) ←  X≠Y | read_until(X,T,L1_rem,L2).
suspend  read_blanks(!,*,*).
read_blanks([BL|Lin_rem],[BL|Blanks_rem],Lout) ←
    read_blanks(Lin_rem,Blanks_rem,Lout).
read_blanks([Char|Lin_rem],Blanks,Lout) ←
    Char ≠ BL| Lout = [Char|Lin_rem], Blanks = [].
suspend  read_name(?,*,*).
read_name([Char|Chars],Name,L_rem) ←
    limitator(Char) |
    Name = [], L_rem = [Char|Chars]
read_name([Char|Chars],Name,L_rem) ←
    not(limitator(Char)) |
    Name = [Char|Name_rem], read_name(Chars,Name_rem,L_rem).
```

```
suspend limitator(!).
limitator(CR).
limitator(BL).
limitator(&).
limitator(<).
limitator(>).
limitator(||).

suspend  transform_cmd_txt(!,!g,*).
transform_cmd_txt(txt(L),_,txt(L)).
transform_cmd_txt(cmd(Lprgms,Input_file,Output_file,Tag),Num,Transf_cmd) ←
        not(interrupt(Lprgms)) |
        Transf_cmd = cmd(Num,Lprgms,Input_file,Output_file,Tag).
transform_cmd_txt(cmd(Lprgms,Input_file,Output_file,Tag),Num,Transf_cmd) ←
        interrupt(Lprgms) |
        Transf_cmd = interrupt(Lprgms).
```

% *The shell procedure*

```
shell(Cmd_txt,File_request,Output) ←
        kernel_shell(Cmd_txt,File_request,Output,[],Fg_control).
suspend  kernel_shell(!,*,*,!,*).
kernel_shell([cmd(Cmd_id,L_prgms,Infile,Outfile,fg)|Cmd_txt],File_request,Output,
                                                     Lap,Fg_control) ←
    Infile≠std |
        Fg_control=[suspend|Fg_control_rem_1]) ←
        g_merge(Status_exec,File_request_1,File_request_2,File_request),
        g_merge(Status_exec,Output_1,Output_2,Output),
        call(  execute(cmd(Cmd_id,L_prgms,Infile,Outfile,fg),Cmd_txt,Cmd_txt_rem_exec,
                                                     File_request_1,Output_1),
               Status_exec,Control_exec).
        call(  search(interrupt(abort),Cmd_txt,Cmd_txt_rem_search),
               Status_search,Control_search),
        [  arbitrator( Status_exec,Control_exec,Status_search,Control_search,
                       Cmd_txt_rem_exec,Cmd_txt_rem_search,Cmd_txt_rem)
            |  Fg_control_rem_2=[continue|Fg_control_rem_2],
               kernel_shell(Cmd_txt_rem,File_request_2,Output_2,Lap,Fg_control_rem_2) ] .
```

```
kernel_shell([cmd(Cmd_id,L_prgms,std,Outfile,fg)|Cmd_txt],File_request,Output,
                                                       Lap,Fg_control) ←
    g_merge(Status_exec,File_request_1,File_request_2,File_request),
    g_merge(Status_exec,Output_1,Output_2,Output),
    wait_txt(Cmd_txt,Fg_control,Fg_control_rem_1),
    call( execute(cmd(Cmd_id,L_prgms,Infile,Outfile,fg),Cmd_txt,Cmd_txt_rem_exec,
                                         File_request_1,Output_1),
        Status_exec,Control_exec),
    call( search(interrupt(abort),Cmd_txt,Cmd_txt_rem_search),
        Status_search,Control_search),
    [ arbitrator( Status_exec,Control_exec,Status_search,Control_search,
                Cmd_txt_rem_exec,Cmd_txt_rem_search,Cmd_txt_rem)
      | Fg_control_rem_1=[continue|Fg_control_rem_2],
        kernel_shell(Cmd_rem,File_request_2,Output_2,Lap,Fg_control_rem_2) ] .

kernel_shell([cmd(Cmd_id,L_prgms,Infile,Outfile,bg)|Cmd_txt],File_request,Output,
                                                       Lap,Fg_control) ←
    g_merge(Proc_status,File_request_1,File_request_2,File_request)),
    g_merge(Proc_status,Output_1,Output_2,Output)),
    merge(Fg_control,Proc_control,Real_control),
    call( execute(cmd(Cmd_id,L_prgms,Infile,Outfile,fg),Cmd_txt,Cmd_txt_rem,
                                         File_request_1,Output_1),
        Proc_status,Real_control),
    kernel_shell(Cmd_txt_rem,File_request_2,Output_2,
                                  [proc(Cmd_id,Proc_status,Proc_control)|Lap]).

kernel_shell([interrupt(kill(Proc_id))|Cmd_txt],File_request,Output,Lap,Fg_control) ←
    kill(Proc_id,Lap,New_Lap),
    kernel_shell(Cmd_txt,File_request,Output,New_Lap,Fg_control).

suspend  wait_txt(!,*,*).
wait_txt([cmd(_,_,_,_,_)|Cmd_txt_rem],Fg_control,Fg_control_rem) ←
    wait_txt(Cmd_txt_rem,Fg_control,Fg_control_rem).
wait_txt([interrupt(_)|Cmd_txt_rem],Fg_control,Fg_control_rem) ←
    wait_txt(Cmd_txt_rem,Fg_control,Fg_control_rem).
wait_txt([txt(_)|Cmd_txt_rem],[suspend|Fg_control_rem],Fg_control_rem)).
```

suspend kill(!g,!,*).
kill(Proc_id,[],[]).
kill(Proc_id,[proc(Proc_id,Proc_status,Proc_control)|Procs_rem],Procs_rem) ←
    Proc_control = [stop].
kill(Proc_id,[proc(Proc_id_aux,Proc_status,Proc_control)|Procs_rem],L) ←
    Proc_id ≠ Proc_id_aux |
    L = [proc(Proc_id_aux,Proc_status,Proc_control)|L_rem],
    kill(Proc_id,Procs_rem,L_rem)

suspend arbitrator(!,*,!,*,!,!,!,*) with l_commit.
arbitrator([succeeded],_,_,[stop],Cmd_txt_exec,_,Cmd_txt_exec).
arbitrator([failed],_,_,[stop],Cmd_txt_exec,_,Cmd_txt_exec).
arbitrator(_,[stop],[succeeded],_,_,Cmd_txt_search,Cmd_txt_search).
arbitrator(_,_,[failed],_,Cmd_txt_exec,_,Cmd_txt_exec).

suspend execute(?,?,*,*,*).
execute(cmd(L_prgms,Infile,Outfile,_),Cmd_txt,Cmd_txt_rem,File_request,Output) ←
    progs(L_prgms,Prgms_code,File_request_1),
    input(Infile,Cmd_txt,Cmd_txt_rem,In_txt,File_request_2),
    output(Outfile,Out_txt,Output,File_request_3),
    run(Prgms_code,In_txt,Out_txt,File_request_4),
    merge(File_request_1,File_request_2,File_request_12),
    merge(File_request_3,File_request_4,File_request_34),
    merge(File_request_12,File_request_34,File_request).

suspend progs(!,*,*).
progs([],[],[]).
progs([Prog_name|Prog_names_rem],[Prog_code|Prgms_code_rem],
                    [get(Prog_name,Prog_code)|File_requests_rem]) ←
    progs(Prog_names_rem,Prgms_code_rem,File_requests_rem).

suspend input(!g,?,*,*,*).
input(none,Cmds_txts,[],Cmds_txts,[]).
input(std,Cmds_txts,L_char,Cmds_txts_rem,[]) ←
    search(txt(L_char),Cmds_txts,Cmds_txts_rem).
input(file(Fn),Cmds_txts,File_txt,Cmds_txts,[get(Fn,File_txt)]).

suspend output(!g,!,*,*).
output(std,Out_txt,Out_txt,[]).
output(file(File_name),Out_txt,[],[replace(File_name,Out_txt)]).

```
suspend run(?,?,*,*).
run([Prg_code],In_txt,Out_txt,File_request) ←
    exec(Prg_code,In_txt,Out_txt,File_request).
run([Prg_code_1,Prg_code_2|Prgms_rem],In_txt,Out_txt,File_request) ←
    exec(Prg_code_1,In_txt,Out_txt_aux,File_request_1),
    run([Prg_code_2|Prgms_rem],Out_txt_aux,Out_txt,File_request_2),
    merge(File_request_1,File_request_2,File_request).

exec(Prg_code,In_txt,Out_txt,File_request) ← primitive.
```

% *Auxiliary procedures*

```
append([],L,L).
append([H|T],L2,[H|L_rem]) ← append(T,L2,L_rem).

member(X,[X|T]).
member(X,[H|T]) ← X≠H | member(X,T).

suspend modify(!g,?,*).
modify(el(Id,New_Inf),[el(Id,Old_Inf)|DB_rem],[el(Id,New_Inf)|DB_rem]).
modify(el(Id,New_Inf),[el(Id_e,Inf_e)|DB_rem],[el(Id_e,Inf_e)|New_DB_rem]) ←
    Id ≠ Id_e |
    modify(el(Id,New_Inf),DB_rem,New_DB_rem)

suspend merge(!,!,*) with l_commit.
merge([],L,L).
merge(L,[],L).
merge([H|T],L2,[H|L_rem]) ← merge(T,L2,L_rem).
merge(L1,[H|T],[H|L_rem]) ← merge(L1,T,L_rem).

suspend rev_merge(!,*,*).
rev_merge([],[],[]).
rev_merge([H|T],[H|L1_rem],L2) ← rev_merge(T,L1_rem,L2).
rev_merge([H|T],L1,[H|L2_rem]) ← rev_merge(T,L1,L2_rem).

suspend g_merge(!,!,!,*).
g_merge(Status,[H|T],L2,[H|L_rem]) ← g_merge(Status,T,L2,L_rem).
g_merge(Status,L1,[H|T],[H|L_rem]) ← g_merge(Status,L1,T,L_rem).
g_merge(Status,[],L2,L2)
g_merge(Status,L1,[],L1)
g_merge([failed],L1,L2,L2).
g_merge([stopped],L1,L2,L2).
g_merge([continued|Status_rem],L1,L2,L) ← g_merge(Status_rem,L1,L2,L).
g_merge([suspended|Status_rem],L1,L2,L) ← g_merge(Status_rem,L1,L2,L).
```

suspend search(*,!,*) with l_commit.
search(X,[X|L_rem],L_rem);
search(X,[Y|T],[Y|L_rem]) ← search(X,T,L_rem).

Appendix 4

A lift system

% *The lift system*

    lift_system ←
        lift(1,Lin_1,Lout_1), lift(2,Lin_2,Lout_2), ..., lift(n,Lin_n,Lout_n),
        floor(1,Fin_1,Fout_1), floor(2,Fin_2,Fout_2), ..., floor(m,Fin_m,Fout_m),
        mess_manager(lifts_in(Lin_1, Lin_2, ...,Lin_n),
                          lifts_out(Lout_1, Lout_2, ...,Lout_n),
                          floors_in(Fin_1, Fin_2, ..., Fin_m),
                          floors_out(Fout_1, Fout_2, ..., Fout_m)).

% *The lift procedure*

    floor(Id,L_in,L_out) ←
        stimulator(L_stimuli),
        button(Id,L_in_button,L_out,off),
        merge(L_in,L_stimuli,L_in_button).

    suspend button(!g,!,*,!).
    button(Id,[put_on|L_in_rem],[request(Id)|L_out_rem],off) ←
        button(Id,L_in_rem,L_out_rem,on).
    button(Id,[put_on|L_in_rem],L_out,on) ← button(Id,L_in_rem,L_out,on).
    button(Id,[served(Id)|L_in_rem],L_out,on) ← button(Id,L_in_rem,L_out,off).

% *The floor procedure*

    lift(Id,L_in,L_out) ← lift_body(Id,L_in,L_out,waiting,[],[],1).

% Elementary lift

suspend lift_body(!g,!,*,o,!g,!,!,!g) with l_commit.
lift_body(Id,[request(Floor_req)|L_reqs_rem],L_out,Floor,Lcsf,Lwf,Status) ←
    memorize_requests([Floor_req],Floor,Lcsf,Lwf,Status,New_Lcsf,New_Lwf,New_status),
    lift_body(Id,Floor,L_reqs_rem,L_out,New_Lcsf,New_Lwf,New_status).
lift_body(Id,L_in,[served(Calling_floor)|L_out_rem],Floor,
                                                        [Calling_floor|Lcsf_rem],Lwf,Status) ←
    gen_service(Calling_floor,L_floors_gen),
    memorize_requests(L_floors_gen,Calling_floor,Lcsf_rem,Lwf,Status,
                                          New_Lcsf,New_Lwf,New_status),
    lift_body(Id,Calling_floor,L_in,L_out_rem,New_Lcsf,New_Lwf,New_status).

% Realistic lift

suspend lift_body(!g,!,*,o,!g,!,!,!g).
lift_body(Id,L_in,L_out,Floor,Lcsf,Lwf,Status) ←
    call(var_syst(L_in),Result) |
    lift_body_end(Result,Id,L_in,L_out,Floor,Lcsf,Lwf,Status)

suspend lift_body_end(!g,!g,!,*,o,!g,!,!,!g).
lift_body_end(succeeded,Id,L_in,[served(Calling_floor)|L_out_rem],Floor,
                                                        [Calling_floor|Lcsf_rem],Lwf,Status) ←
    gen_service(Calling_floor,L_floors_gen),
    memorize_requests(L_floors_gen,Calling_floor,Lcsf_rem,Lwf,Status,
                                          New_Lcsf,New_Lwf,New_status),
    lift_body(Id,Calling_floor,L_in,L_out_rem,New_Lcsf,New_Lwf,New_status).
lift_body_end(failed,Id,[request(Floor_req)|L_reqs_rem],L_out,Floor,Lcsf,Lwf,Status) ←
    memorize_requests([Floor_req],Floor,Lcsf,Lwf,Status,New_Lcsf,New_Lwf,New_status),
    lift_body(Id,Floor,L_reqs_rem,L_out,New_Lcsf,New_Lwf,New_status).

% The memorize_request procedure

suspend memorize_request(L_req_floors!,Floor!g ,Lcsf_init!,Lwf_init!,Status_init!g,
                                Lcsf_post ,Lwf_post,Status_post)
memorize_requests([],Floor,[],[],Status,[],[],waiting).
memorize_requests([],Floor,[],[H|T],Status,[H|T],[],New_status) ←
    reverse_dir(Status,New_status).
memorize_requests([],Floor,[H|T],Lwf,Status,[H|T],Lwf,Status).

memorize_requests([Floor_req|L_floors_rem],Floor,[],[],waiting,
                          New_Lcsf,New_Lwf,New_status) ←
        Floor ≤ Floor_req |
        memorize_requests(L_floors_rem,Floor,[Floor_req],[],up,
                          New_Lcsf,New_Lwf,New_status).
memorize_requests([Floor_req|L_floors_rem],Floor,[],[],waiting,
                          New_Lcsf,New_Lwf,New_status) ←
        Floor > Floor_req |
        memorize_requests(L_floors_rem,Floor,[Floor_req],[],down,
                          New_Lcsf,New_Lwf,New_status).
memorize_requests([Floor_req|L_floors_rem],Floor,Lcsf,Lwf,up,
                          New_Lcsf,New_Lwf,New_status) ←
        Floor ≤ Floor_req |
        inc_insert(Floor_req,Lcsf,Lcsf_aux),
        memorize_requests(L_floors_rem,Floor,Lcsf_aux,Lwf,up,
                          New_Lcsf,New_Lwf,New_status).
memorize_requests([Floor_req|L_floors_rem],Floor,Lcsf,Lwf,up,
                          New_Lcsf,New_Lwf,New_status) ←
        Floor > Floor_req |
        dec_insert(Floor_req,Lwf,Lwf_aux),
        memorize_requests(L_floors_rem,Floor,Lcsf,Lwf_aux,up,
                          New_Lcsf,New_Lwf,New_status).
memorize_requests([Floor_req|L_floors_rem],Floor,Lcsf,Lwf,down,
                          New_Lcsf,New_Lwf,New_status) ←
        Floor ≥ Floor_req |
        dec_insert(Floor,Lcsf,Lcsf_aux),
        memorize_requests(Floor,L_floors_rem,Lcsf_aux,Lwf,down,
                          New_Lcsf,New_Lwf,New_status).
memorize_requests([Floor_req|L_floors_rem],Floor,Lcsf,Lwf,down,
                          New_Lcsf,New_Lwf,New_status) ←
        Floor < Floor_req |
        inc_insert(Floor,Lwf,Lwf_aux),
        memorize_requests(L_floors_rem,Floor,Lcsf,Lwf_aux,down,
                          New_Lcsf,New_Lwf,New_status).

% *The mess_manager procedure*

```
mess_manager(  lifts_in(Lin_1, Lin_2, ...,Lin_n),
               lifts_out(Lout_1, Lout_2, ...,Lout_n),
               floors_in(Fin_1, Fin_2, ..., Fin_m),
               floors_out(Fout_1, Fout_2, ..., Fout_m) )  ←
                          gen_merge([Lout_1,Lout_2,...,Lout_n],Lout),
                          service_lift(Lout,Fin_1,...,Fin_m),
                          gen_merge([Fout_1,Fout_2,...,Fout_m],Fout),
                          rev_merge(Fout,Lin_1,Lin_2,...,Lin_n).

    smode  service_lift(!,*,*,...,*).
    service_lift([],[],...,[]).
    service_lift([served(1)|Lout_rem],[served(1)|F1rem],F2,...,Fm)  ←
        service_lift(Lout_rem,F1rem,F2,...,Fm).
    service_lift([served(2)|Lout_rem],F1,[served(2)|F2rem],...,Fm)  ←
        service_lift(Lout_rem,F1,F2rem,...,Fm).
    ...
    service_lift([served(m)|Lout_rem],F1,F2,...,[served(m)|Fmrem])  ←
        service_lift(Lout_rem,F1,F2,...,Fmrem).
```

% *Auxiliary procedures*

```
    suspend  inc_insert(!g,!,*).
    inc_insert(Num,[],[Num]).
    inc_insert(Num,[Num|T],[Num|T]).
    inc_insert(Num,[H|T],L)  ← Num < H | L = [Num,H|T].
    inc_insert(Num,[H|T],L)  ← Num > H | L= [H|New_T], inc_insert(Num,T,New_T).

    suspend  dec_insert(!g,!,*).
    dec_insert(Num,[],[Num]).
    dec_insert(Num,[Num|T],[Num|T]).
    dec_insert(Num,[H|T],L)  ← Num > H | L = [Num,H|T].
    dec_insert(Num,[H|T],L)  ← Num < H | L= [H|New_T], dec_insert(Num,T,New_T).

    suspend  reverse_dir(!g,*).
    reverse_dir(up,down).
    reverse_dir(down,up).
```

suspend gen_merge(!,*).
gen_merge([],[]).
gen_merge([L],L).
gen_merge([L1,L2],L) ← merge(L1,L2,L).
gen_merge([L1,L2,L3|Ll_rem],L) ←
    partition_lists([L1,L2,L3|Ll_rem],P1,P2),
    gen_merge(P1,Lm1), gen_merge(P2,Lm2),
    merge(Lm1,Lm2,L).

suspend partition_lists(!,*,*).
partition_lists([],[],[]).
partition_lists([L],[L],[]).
partition_lists([L1,L2|Ll_rem],[L1|P1_rem],[L2|P2_rem]) ←
    partition_lists(Ll_rem,P1_rem,P2_rem).

suspend rev_merge(!,*,*,...,*) with l_commit
rev_merge([],[],...,[]).
rev_merge([X|Lin_rem],[X|L1_rem],L2,...,Ln) ←
    rev_merge(Lin_rem,L1_rem,L2,...,Ln).
rev_merge([X|Lin_rem],L1,[X|L2_rem],...,Ln) ←
    rev_merge(Lin_rem,L1,L2_rem,...,Ln).
...
rev_merge([X|Lin_rem],L1,L2,...,[X|Ln_rem]) ←
    rev_merge(Lin_rem,L1,L2,...,Ln_rem).

suspend merge(!,!,*) with l_commitment.
merge([],L2,L2).
merge(L1,[],L1).
merge([H1|T1],L2,[H1|L_rem]) ← merge(T1,L2,L_rem).
merge(L1,[H2|T2],[H2|L_rem]) ← merge(L1,T2,L_rem).

References

References

References

[Abadi and Manna, 1987]
ABADI M., MANNA Z., *Temporal Logic Programming*, Proc. 4th Int. Symp. on Logic Programming, San Francisco, USA, IEEE Computer Society Press, 1987, pp. 4-16.

[Ali, 1988]
ALI K.A.M., *Or-Parallel Execution of Prolog on BC-Machine*, Proc. 5th Int. Conf. and Symp. on Logic Programming, Seattle, USA, The MIT Press, 1988, pp. 1531-1545.

[Apt and van Emden, 1982]
APT K.R., VAN EMDEN M.H., *Contributions to the Theory of Logic Programming*, Journ. ACM 29(3), July 1982, pp. 841-863.

[Apt et al., 1988]
APT K., BLAIR H., WALKER A., *Towards a Theory of Declarative Knowledge*, In [Minker, 1988], pp. 89-148.

[Bahgat and Gregory, 1989]
BAHGAT R., GREGORY S., *Pandora: Non-deterministic Parallel Logic Programming*, Proc. 6th Int. Conf. on Logic Programming, Lisbon, Portugal, The MIT Press, 1989, pp. 471-486.

[Balzer et al., 1983]
BALZER R., CHEATHAM N., WILE D., *Software Technology in the 1990's*, IEEE Trans. on Computer, vol. C-16(11), November 1983, pp. 39-45.

[Barbuti and Martelli, 1986]
BARBUTI R., MARTELLI M., *Completeness of the SLDNF-Resolution for a Class of Logic Programs*, Proc. 3rd Int. Conf. on Logic Programming, London, Great-Britain, Lecture Notes in Computer Science n° 225, Springer-Verlag, 1986, pp. 394-410.

[Barbuti et al., 1987]
BARBUTI R., MANCARELLA P., PEDRESCHI D., TURINI F., *Intensional Negation of Logic Program: Examples and Implementation Techniques*, Proc. International Joint Conference on Theory and Practice of Software Development, Lecture Notes in Computer Science n° 250, Springer-Verlag, 1987, pp. 96-110.

[Barbuti et al., 1990]
BARBUTI R., MANCARELLA P., PEDRESCHI D., TURINI F., *A Transformational Approach to Negation in Logic Programming*, Journ. of Logic Programming, vol. 8, 1990, pp.201-228.

[Baudinet, 1988]
BAUDINET M., *Proving Termination Properties of Prolog Programs: A Semantic Approach*, Proc. 3rd Symp. on Logic in Computer Science, Edinburgh, Great-Britain, IEEE Computer Society Press, 1988, pp. 336-347.

[Bowen et al., 1982]
BOWEN D.L., BYRD L., PEREIRA F.C.N., PEREIRA L.M., WARREN D.M.D., *DECsystem-10 Prolog user's manual*, Department of Artificial Intelligence, University of Edinburgh, November 1982.

[Bruynooghe, 1982]
BRUYNOOGHE M., *Adding Redundancy to obtain more reliable and readable Prolog Programs*, Proc. 1st Int. Conf. on Logic Programming, Marseille, France, 1982, pp. 129-133.

[Bruynooghe and Pereira, 1984]
BRUYNOOGHE M., PEREIRA L.M., *Deduction Revision by Intelligent Backtracking*, In [Campbell, 1984], pp. 194-215.

[Bruynooghe et al., 1987]
BRUYNOOGHE M., JANSSENS G., CALLEBAUT A., DEMOEN B., *Abstract Interpretation: towards the global optimization of Prolog Programs*, Proc. 4th Int. Symp. on Logic Programming, San Francisco, USA, IEEE Computer Society Press, 1987, pp. 192-204.

[Bryant and Dennis, 1982]
BRYANT R., DENNIS J.B., *Concurrent Programming*, Operating Systems Engineering, Springer-Verlag, 1982, pp. 426-452.

[Burstall, 1974],
BURSTALL R.M., *Program Proving as Hand Simulation with a Little Induction*, Proc. IFIP, North-Holland, 1974, pp. 308-312.

[Burstall and Darlington, 1977]
BURSTALL R.M., DARLINGTON J., *A Transformation System for Developing Recursive Programs*, Journ. ACM, vol 24(1), January 1977, pp. 44-67.

[Butler et al., 1986]
BUTLER R., LUSK E.L., OLSON R., OVERBEEK R.A., *ANLWAM: A Parallel Implementation of the Warren Abstract Machine*, Internal Report, Argonne National Laboratory, U.S.A., 1986.

[Butler et al., 1988]
BUTLER R., DISK T., LUSK E.L., OLSON R., OVERBEEK R.A., STEVENS R., *Scheduling Or-Parallelism: An Argonne Perspective*, Proc. 5th Int. Conf. and Symp. on Logic Programming, Seattle, USA, The MIT Press, 1988, pp. 1590-1605.

[Calderwood and Szeredi, 1989]
CALDERWOOD A., SZEREDI P., *Scheduling Or-parallelism in Aurora - the Manchester Scheduler*, Proc. 6th Int. Conf. on Logic Programming, Lisboa, Portugal, The MIT Press, 1989, pp. 419-435.

[Campbell, 1984]
CAMPBELL J., ed., *Implementations of Prolog*, Ellis Horwood, 1984.

[Carlson et al, 1988]
CARLSON M., DANHOF K., OVERBEEK R., *A simplified Approach to the Implementation of AND-Parallelism in an OR-Parallel Environment*, Proc. 5th Int. Conf. and Symp. on Logic Programming, Seattle, USA, The MIT Press, 1988, pp. 1565-1577.

[Cavedon and Lloyd, 1990]
CAVEDON L., LLOYD J.W., *A Completeness Theorem for SLDNF-Resolution*, to appear in Journ. of Logic Programming.

[Chan, 1988]
CHAN D., *Constructive Negation Based on the Completed Database*, Proc. 5th Conf. and Symp. on Logic Programming, Seattle, USA, The MIT Press, 1988, pp. 111-125.

[Chan, 1989]
CHAN D., *An Extension of Constructive Negation and its Application in Coroutining*, Proc. of the North American Conference on Logic Programming, Cleveland, USA, The MIT Press, 1989, pp. 477-496.

[Chang and Despain, 1985]
CHANG J.M., DESPAIN A.M., *Semi-intelligent Backtracking of Prolog based on Static Data Dependency Analysis*, Proc. 2nd Symp. on Logic Programming, Boston, USA, IEEE Computer Society Press, 1985, pp. 10-21.

[Chassin and Robert, 1990]
CHASSIN DE KERGOMMEAUX J., ROBERT P., *An Abstract Machine to Implement Efficiently Or-And Parallel Prolog*, Journ. of Logic Programming, vol. 7, 1990, pp. 249-264.

[Church, 1936]
   CHURCH A., *An unsolvable problem of elementary number theory*, American Journ. of Math., vol. 58, 1936, pp. 345-363.

[Clark, 1978]
   CLARK K.L., *Negation as Failure*, In [Gallaire and Minker, 1978], pp. 293-324.

[Clark, 1979]
   CLARK K.L., *Predicate Logic as a Computational Formalism*, Research Report Doc 79/59, Department of Computing, Imperial College, London, Great-Britain, 1979.

[Clark and Gregory, 1981]
   CLARK K.L., GREGORY S., *A Relational Language for Parallel Programming*, Proc. Conf. on Functional Programming Languages and Computer Architecture, Portsmouth, USA, ACM, 1981, pp. 171-178.

[Clark and Gregory, 1983]
   CLARK K.L., GREGORY S., *Parlog : a Parallel Programming Language*, Research Report Doc 83/5, Department of Computing, Imperial College, London, Great-Britain, 1983.

[Clark and Gregory, 1984]
   CLARK K.L., GREGORY S., *Parlog: Parallel Programming in Logic*, Research Report Doc 84/4, Department of Computing, Imperial College, London, Great-Britain, 1984.

[Clark and Gregory, 1985]
   CLARK K.L., GREGORY S., *Notes on the implementation of Parlog*, Journ. of Logic Programming, vol. 2, 1985, pp. 17-42.

[Clark and Gregory, 1986]
   CLARK K.L., GREGORY S., *Parlog: Parallel Programming in Logic*, ACM Trans. on Programming Languages and Systems, vol. 8, n°1, January 1986, pp. 1-49.

[Clark and Mac Cabe, 1979]
   CLARK K.L., MAC CABE F.G., *The Control Facilities of IC-prolog*, In [Michie, 1979], pp. 122-149.

[Clark and Tärnlund, 1982]
   CLARK K.L., TÄRNLUND S.A., *Logic Programming*, Academic Press, 1982.

[Clark et al., 1982]
   CLARK K.L., MAC CABE F.G., GREGORY S., *IC-PROLOG language features*, In [Clark and Tärnlund, 1982], pp. 253-266

[Clocksin and Mellish, 1981]
   CLOCKSIN W.F., MELLISH C.S., *Programming in Prolog*, Springer-Verlag, 1981.

[Codish, 1985]
CODISH M., *Compiling OR-parallelism into AND-parallelism*, Master Thesis, The Weizmann Institute of Science, Israel, 1985.

[Colmerauer, 1982]
COLMERAUER A., *PROLOG II Manuel de Référence et Modèle Théorique*, Groupe de Recherche en I.A., Université d'Aix-Marseille, Marseille, France, 1982.

[Colmerauer, 1987]
COLMERAUER A., *Opening the Prolog III Universe*, Rapport de Recherche, Groupe de Recherche en I.A., Université d'Aix-Marseille, Marseille, France, 1987.

[Colmerauer et al., 1973]
COLMERAUER A., KANOUI H., ROUSSEL P., PASERO R., *Un Système de Communication Homme-Machine en Français*, Rapport de Recherche, Groupe de Recherche en I.A., Université d'Aix-Marseille, Marseille, France, 1973.

[Colmerauer et al., 1983]
COLMERAUER A., KANOUI H., VAN CANEGHEM M., *Prolog, Theoretical Principles and Current Trends*, Technology and Science of Informatics 2, 4, 1983, pp. 255-292.

[Common and Lescanne, 1988]
COMMON H., LESCANNE P., *Equational Problems and Disunification*, Journ. of Symbolic Computation, vol. 7, 1989, pp. 371-426.

[Conery, 1983]
CONERY J.S., *The And/Or Process Model for Parallel Interpretation of Logic Programs*, Ph.D. thesis, University of California, USA, 1983, revised version published as [Conery, 1987a].

[Conery, 1987a]
CONERY J.S., *Parallel Execution of Logic Programs*, Kluwer Academic Press, 1987.

[Conery, 1987b]
CONERY J.S., *Implementing Backward Execution in Nondeterministic AND-Parallel Systems*, Proc. of 4th Int. Conf. on Logic Programming, Melbourne, Australia, The MIT Press, 1987, pp. 635-653.

[Conery and Kibler, 1981]
CONERY J.S., KIBLER D.F., *Parallel Interpretation of Logic Programs*, Proc. Conf. on Functional Programming Languages and Computer Architecture, Portsmouth, USA, ACM, 1981, pp. 163-170.

[Cousot and Cousot, 1977]
> COUSOT P., COUSOT R., *Abstract Interpretation : a Unified Framework for Static Analysis of programs by Construction or Approximation of Fixpoints*, Proc. 4th Symp. on Principles of Programming Languages, Los Angeles, USA, ACM, 1977, pp. 238-252.

[Cox, 1981]
> COX P.T., *On Determining the Causes of Non-Unifiability*, Technical Report 23, Department of Computer Science, University of Auckland, New Zealand, 1981.

[Cox, 1984]
> COX P.T., *Finding Backtrack Points for Intelligent Backtracking*, In [Campbell, 1984], pp. 216-233.

[Cox and Pietrzykowski, 1981]
> COX P.T., PIETRZYKOWSKI T., *Deduction Plans : a Basis for Intelligent Backtracking*, IEEE Trans. on Pattern Analysis and Machine Intelligence 3 (1), 1981, pp. 52-65.

[Crammond, 1988]
> CRAMMOND J., *Implementation of Committed-Choice Languages on Shared Memory Multiprocessors*, Ph. D. thesis, Heriot-Watt University, Edinburgh, Great-Britain, 1988.

[Dahl, 1980]
> DAHL V., *Two solutions for the Negation Problem*, Proc. Logic Programming Workshop, Dreceben, Hungary, 1980, pp. 61-72.

[Dantzig, 1963]
> DANTZIG, G.B., *Linear Programming and Extensions,* Princeton University Press, 1963.

[Darlington, 1982]
> DARLINGTON J., ed., *Functional Programming and its Applications*, Cambridge University Press, 1982.

[de Bakker and Kok, 1988],
> DE BAKKER J.W., KOK J.N., *Uniform Abstraction, Atomicity and Contractions in the Comparative Semantics of Concurrent Prolog*, Proc. Conf. on Fifth Generation Computer Systems, Tokyo, Japan, OHM, Springer-Verlag, Ltd., 1988, pp. 347-355.

[de Boer et al., 1989a]
> DE BOER F.S, KOK J.N., PALAMIDESSI C., RUTTEN J.J.M.M., *Control Flow versus Logic: a Denotational and a Declarative Model for Guarded Horn Clauses*, Proc. MFCS89, Lecture Notes in Computer Science n° 379, Springer-Verlag, 1989, pp. 165-177.

[de Boer et al., 1989b]
DE BOER F.S, KOK J.N., PALAMIDESSI C., RUTTEN J.J.M.M., *Semantics Models for a version of Parlog*, Proc 6th Int. Conf. on Logic Programming, Lisbon, Portugal, The MIT Press, 1989, pp. 621-636.

[De Groot and Lindström, 1986]
DE GROOT D., LINDSTRÖM G., eds., *Logic Programming: Relations, Functions and Equations*, Prentice Hall, 1986.

[Deville, 1987]
DEVILLE Y., *A Methodology for Logic Program Construction*, Ph.D. Thesis, University of Namur, Namur, Belgium, 1987, revised version published as [Deville, 1990].

[Deville, 1990]
DEVILLE Y., *Logic Programming: Systematic Program Development*, Addison-Wesley, 1990.

[Dijkstra, 1971]
DIJKSTRA E.W., *Hierarchical Ordering of Sequential Processes*, Acta Informatica, vol 1 (2), 1971, pp. 115-138.

[Dijkstra, 1975]
DIJKSTRA E.W., *Guarded Commands, Nondeterminacy and Formal Derivation of Programs*, Comm. ACM, vol 18(8), August 1975, pp. 453-457.

[Dincbas, 1980]
DINCBAS M., *Metacontrol of Logic Programming in METALOG*, Proc. Conf. on Fifth Generation Computer Systems, Tokyo, Elsevier/North-Holland, 1984, pp. 361-370.

[Eder, 1985]
EDER E., *Properties of Substitutions and Unifications*, Journ. of Symbolic Computation, 1, 1985, pp. 31-46.

[Foster, 1987]
FOSTER I.T., *Logic Operating Systems: Design Issues*, Proc. 4th Int. Conf. on Logic Programming, Melbourne, Australia, The MIT Press, 1987, pp. 910-926.

[Foster and Taylor, 1989a]
FOSTER I., TAYLOR S., *Strand: A Practical Parallel Programming Tool*, Proc. North American Conference on Logic Programming, Cleveland, USA, The MIT Press, 1989, pp. 497-512.

[Foster and Taylor, 1989b]
FOSTER I., TAYLOR S., *Strand: New Concepts in Parallel Programming*, Prentice-Hall, Englewood Cliffs, 1989.

[FWSS, 1987]
   Proceedings of the Fourth International Workshop on Software Specification and Design, Monterey, California, USA, April 3-4, IEEE Computer Society Press, 1987.

[Gallaire and Minker, 1978]
   GALLAIRE H., MINKER J., eds., *Logic and Databases*, Plenum Press, 1978,

[Gerth et al., 1988]
   GERTH R., CODISH M., LICHTENSTEIN, SHAPIRO E., *Fully Abstract Denotational Semantics for Concurrent Prolog*, Proc. 3rd Symp. on Logic in Computer Science, Edinburgh, Great-Britain, IEEE Computer Society Press, 1988, pp. 320-335.

[Giannesini et al., 1986]
   GIANNESINI F., KANOUI H., PASSERO R., VAN CANEGHEM M., *Prolog*, Intereditions, 1986.

[Goto et al., 1988]
   GOTO A., SATO M., NAKAJIMA K., TAKI K., MATSUMOTO A., *Overview of the Parallel Inference Machine Architecture (PIM)*, Proc. Conf. on Fifth Generation Computer Systems, Tokyo, Japan, OHM, Springer-Verlag, Ltd., 1988, pp. 208-229.

[Green, 1969]
   GREEN C.C., *Theorem-proving by Resolution as a Basis for Question-answering Systems,* Machine Intelligence 4, 1969, pp. 183-205.

[Gregory, 1985]
   GREGORY S., *Design, Application and Implementation of a Parallel Programming Language*, Ph. D. thesis, Department of Computing, Imperial College, London, Great-Britain, 1985, revised version published as [Gregory, 1987].

[Gregory, 1987]
   GREGORY S., *Parallel Logic Programming in Parlog: The Language and its Implementation*, Addison-Wesley, 1987.

[Gupta and Jayarama, 1989]
   GUPTA G, JAYARAMA B., *Combined And-Or Parallelism on Shared Memory Multiprocessors*, Proc. of the North American Conference on Logic Programming, Cleveland, USA, The MIT Press, 1989, pp. 332-349.

[Gupta and Jayarama, 1990]
   GUPTA G, JAYARAMA B., *Optimizing And-Or Parallel Implementations*, Proc. of the North American Conference on Logic Programming, Austin, USA, The MIT Press, 1990, pp. 605-623.

[Habra and van Lamsweerde, 1988]
   HABRA N., VAN LANSWEERDE A., *Generation de prototypes Prolog à partir de spécifications formelles de besoins*, Proc. 4th Conference-Exposition, Software Engineering, Paris, France, 1988, pp. 129-140.

[Hausman et al., 1987]
   HAUSMAN B., CIEPIELEWSKI A., HARIDI S., *Or-parallel prolog made efficient on shared memory multiprocessors*, Proc. 4th Symp. on Logic Programming, San Francisco, USA, IEEE Computer Society Press, 1987, pp. 69-79.

[Hayes, 1973]
   HAYES P.J., *Computation and deduction*, Proc. 2nd MFCS Symp., Czechoslovak Academy of Sciences, 1973, pp. 105-118.

[Herbrand, 1930]
   HERBRAND J., *Researches in the Theory of Demonstration*, In [Van Heijenoort, 1967], pp. 525-581.

[Hermenegildo, 1986]
   HERMENEGILDO M.V., *An Abstract Machine for Restricted AND-Parallel Execution of Logic Programs*, Proc. 3rd Int. Conf. on Logic Programming, London, Great-Britain, Lecture Notes in Computer Science n° 225, Springer-Verlag, 1986, pp. 25-39.

[Hermenegildo and Nasr, 1986]
   HERMENEGILDO M.V., NASR R.I., *Efficient Management of Backtracking in AND-Parallelism*, Proc. 3rd Int. Conf. on Logic Programming, London, Great-Britain, Lecture Notes in Computer Science n° 225, Springer-Verlag, 1986, pp. 40-54.

[Hermenegildo and Rossi, 1990]
   HERMENEGILDO M.V., ROSSI F., *Non-strict Independent And-Parallelism*, Proc. 7th Int. Conf. on Logic Programming, Jerusalem, Israël, The MIT Press, 1990, pp. 237-252.

[Houri and Shapiro, 1989]
   HOURI A., SHAPIRO E., *A sequential abstract machine for Flat Concurrent Prolog*, Journ. of Logic Programming, vol. 7, 1989, pp. 85-123.

[Huet, 1976]
   HUET G., *Résolution d'Equations dans des Languages d'Ordres 1, 2, ..., ω*, Thèse d'Etat, Université de Paris VII, 1976.

[Jacquet, 1987]
   JACQUET J.-M., *A Guided Tour Through Parallelism in Logic Programming*, Research Report, University of Namur, Namur, Belgium, 1987.

[Jacquet, 1989]
   JACQUET J.-M., *Conclog: a Methodological Approach to Concurrent Logic Programming*, Ph. D. thesis, University of Namur, Namur, Belgium, 1989.

[Jaffar and Lassez, 1987]
   JAFFAR J, LASSEZ J.L., *Constraint Logic Programming*, Proc. 14th Symp. on Principle of Programming Languages, Munich, Germany, ACM, 1987, pp. 111-119.

[Jaffar and Michaylov, 1987]
   JAFFAR J., MICHAYLOV S., *Methodology and Implementation of a CLP System*, Proc. 4th Int. Conf. on Logic Programming, Melbourne, Australia, The MIT Press, 1987, pp. 196-218.

[Jaffar et al., 1983]
   JAFFAR J., LASSEZ J.L., LLOYD J.W., *Completeness of the Negation as Failure Rule*, Proc. 8th International Joint Conference on Artificial Intelligence, Karlsruhe, Germany, 1983, pp. 500-506.

[Jaffar et al., 1986]
   JAFFAR J., LASSEZ J.L., MAHER M.J., *A Logic Programming Language Scheme*, In [De Groot and Lindström, 1986], pp. 441-468.

[Kahn et al., 1987]
   KAHN K., TRIBBLE E.D., MILLER M.S., BOBROW D.G., *Vulcan: Logic Concurrent Objects*, Research Directions in Object-oriented Programming, Cambridge, USA, 1987, pp. 75-112.

[Kalé, 1987]
   KALE L.V., *Parallel Execution of Logic Programs : the REDUCE-OR Process Model*, Proc. 4th Int. Conf. on Logic Programming, Melbourne, Australia, The MIT Press, 1987, pp. 616-632.

[Kalé et al., 1988]
   KALE L.V., RAMKUMAR B., SHU W., *A Memory Organization Independent Binding Environment for AND and OR Parallel Execution of Logic Programs*, Proc. 5th Int. Conf. and Symp. on Logic Programming, Seattle, USA, The MIT Press, 1988, pp. 1223-1240.

[Kasif et al., 1983]
   KASIF S., KOHLI M., MINKER J., *PRISM : A Parallel System for Problem Solving*, Proc. Logic Programming Workshop, Albufeira, Portugal, 1983, pp.544-546.

[Khabaza, 1984]
   KHABAZA T., *Negation as Failure and Parallelism*, Proc. 2nd Int. Conf. on Logic Programming, Uppsala, Sweden, Uppsala University Press, 1984, pp. 70-75.

[Kimura and Chikayama, 1987]
KIMURA Y., CHIKAYAMA T. *An Abstract KL1 Machine and its instruction set*, Proc. 4th Int. Symp. on Logic Programming, San Francisco, USA, IEEE Computer Society Press, 1987, 468-479.

[Knuth, 1968]
KNUTH D.A., *The Art of Computer Programming*, Volume 1: Fundamental Algorithms, Addison-Wesley, 1968

[Kowalski, 1974]
KOWALSKI R.A., *Predicate Logic as a Programming Language*, Proc. IFIP, North-Holland, 1974, pp. 569-574.

[Kowalski, 1979]
KOWALSKI R.A., *Logic for Problem Solving*, North-Holland, Amsterdam, 1979.

[Kowalski and van Emden, 1976]
KOWALSKI R.A., VAN EMDEN M.H., *The Semantics of Predicate Logic as a Programming Language*, Journ. ACM, vol. 23, n° 4, pp. 733-742, 1976.

[Lassez et al., 1988]
LASSEZ J.L., MAHER M.J., MARRIOT K., *Unification revisited*, In [Minker, 1988], 1988, pp. 587-626

[Le Charlier, 1985]
LE CHARLIER B., *Réflexions sur le Problème de la Correction des Programmes*, Ph. D. Thesis, University of Namur, Namur, Belgium, 1985.

[Lengauer and Hehner, 1982]
LENGAUER C., HEHNER E.C.R., *A Methodology for Programming with Concurrency*, Science of Computer Programming 2, 1982, pp. 1-52.

[Levi and Palamidessi, 1985]
LEVI G., PALAMIDESSI C., *The Declarative Semantics of Read-only Annotations*, Proc. 2nd Symp. on Logic Programming, Boston, USA, IEEE Computer Society Press, 1985, pp. 128-137.

[Levi and Palamidessi, 1987],
LEVI G., PALAMIDESSI C., *An Approach to the Declarative Semantics of Synchronization in Logic Languages*, Proc 4th Int. Conf. on Logic Programming, Melbourne, Australia, The MIT Press, 1987, pp. 877-893.

[Levy, 1987]
LEVY J., *A GHC Abstract Machine and Instruction Set*, Proc. 3rd Int. Conf. on Logic Programming, London, Great-Britain, Lecture Notes in Computer Science n° 225, Springer-Verlag, 1986, pp. 157-171.

[Li and Martin, 1986]
LI P.P., MARTIN A.J., *The Sync Model: A Parallel Execution Method for Logic Programming*, Proc. 3rd Symp. on Logic Programming, Salt Lake City, USA, IEEE Computer Society Press, 1986, pp. 223-235.

[Lin et al., 1986]
LIN Y., KUMAR V., LEUNG C., *An Intelligent Backtracking Algorithm for Parallel Execution of Logic Programs*, Proc. 3rd Int. Conf. on Logic Programming, London, Great-Britain, Lecture Notes in Computer Science n° 225, Springer-Verlag, 1986, pp. 55-68.

[Liskov, 1975]
LISKOV B.H., *Specification Techniques for Data Abstractions*, IEEE Trans. on Soft. Engineering, vol SE-1(1), March 1975, pp. 7-19.

[Lloyd, 1987]
LLOYD J.W., *Foundations of Logic Programming*, Springer-Verlag, 1987.

[Lloyd and Topor, 1984]
LLYOD J.W., TOPOR R.W., *Making Prolog more Expressive*, Journ. of Logic Programming, vol. 3, 1984, pp. 225-240.

[Lloyd and Topor, 1985]
LLYOD J.W., TOPOR R.W., *A Basis for Deductive Data Base Systems*, Journ. of Logic Programming, vol. 2, 1985, pp. 93-103.

[Lloyd and Topor, 1986]
LLYOD J.W., TOPOR R.W., *A Basis for Deductive Data Base Systems II*, Journ. of Logic Programming, vol. 3, 1986, pp. 55-67.

[Lugiez, 1989]
LUGIEZ D., *A Deduction Procedure for First Order Programs*, Proc. 6th Int. Conf. on Logic Programming, Lisbon, Portugal, The MIT Press, 1989, pp. 585-599.

[Maluszynski and Näslund, 1989]
MALUSZYNSKI J., NASLUND T., *Fail Substitutions for Negation as Failure*, Proc. of the North American Conference on Logic Programming, Cleveland, USA, The MIT Press, 1989, pp.461-476.

[Manna and Waldinger, 1977]
MANNA Z., WALDINGER R., *The Automatic Synthesis of Recursive Programs*, Proc. Symp. on Artificial Intelligence and Programming Languages, Rochester, USA, ACM, 1977, pp. 29-36.

[Manna and Waldinger, 1978]
MANNA Z., WALDINGER R., *Is "Sometimes" Sometimes Better than Always?, Intermittent Assertions in Proving the Correctness of Programs*, Comm. ACM, vol. 21(2), February 1978, pp. 159-172.

[Marriot and Sondergaard, 1988]
MARRIOT K., SONDERGAARD H., *Bottom-up Abstract Interpretation of Logic Programs*, Proc. 5th Int. Conf. on Logic Programming, Seattle, USA, The MIT Press, 1988, pp. 733-748.

[Martelli and Montanari, 1982]
MARTELLI A., MONTANARI U., *An Efficient Unification Algorithm*, TOPLAS, vol. 4, No. 2, April 1982, pp. 258-282.

[Mellish, 1986]
MELLISH C.S., *Abstract Interpretation of Prolog Programs*, Proc. 3rd Int. Conf. on Logic Programming, London, Great-Britain, Lecture Notes in Computer Science n° 225, Springer-Verlag, 1986, pp. 463-474.

[Michie, 1979]
MICHIE D., ed., *The Expert System in the Micro-electronic Age*, Edinburgh University Press, 1979.

[Minker, 1988]
MINKER J., *Foundations of deductive databases and logic programming*, Morgan Kaufmann, Los Altos, 1988.

[Monteiro, 1984]
MONTEIRO L., *A Proposal for Distributed Programming in Logic*, In [Campbell, 1984], pp. 329-340.

[Naish, 1985a]
NAISH L., *Negation and Control in Prolog*, Ph.D. Thesis, University of Melbourne, Melbourne, Australia, 1985, revised version published as Lecture Notes in Computer Science n° 238, Springer-Verlag, 1986.

[Naish, 1985b]
NAISH L., *Automating Control for Logic Programs*, Journal of Logic Programming, vol. 3 1985, pp. 167-183.

[Naish, 1986]
NAISH L., *Negation and Quantifiers in NU-Prolog*, Proc. 3rd Int. Conf. on Logic Programming, London, Great-Britain, Lecture Notes in Computer Science n° 225, Springer-Verlag, 1986, pp. 600-614.

[Neel, 1982]
: NEEL D., ed., *Tools and Notions for Program Construction*, Cambridge University Press, 1982.

[Nilsson and Tanaka, 1988]
: NILSSON M., TANAKA H., *Massively Parallel Implementation of Flat GHC on the Connective Machine*, Proc. Conf. on Fifth Generation Computer Systems, Tokyo, Japan, OHM, Springer-Verlag, Ltd., 1988, pp. 1031-1040.

[Okumura and Matsumoto, 1987]
: OKUMURA A., MATSUMOTO Y., *Parallel Programming with Layered Streams*, Proc. 4th Symp. on Logic Programming, San Francisco, USA, IEEE Computer Society Press, 1987, pp. 224-232.

[Overbeek et al., 1985]
: OVERBEEK R.A., GABRIEL J., LINDHOLM T., LUSK E.L., *Prolog on Multiprocessors*, Internal Report, Argonne National Laboratory, USA., 1985.

[Palamidessi, 1988]
: PALAMIDESSI C., *A Fixpoint Semantics for Guarded Horn Clauses*, Report CS-R8833, Centre for Mathematics and Computer Science, CWI, Amsterdam, The Netherlands, 1988.

[Palamidessi, 1990]
: PALAMIDESSI C., *Algebraic Properties of Idempotent Substitutions*, Proc. Int. Colloqium on Automata, Languages and Programming, Warwick, Great-Britain, Lecture Notes in Computer Science n° 443, Springer-Verlag, 1990, pp. 386-399.

[Parnas, 1972]
: PARNAS D.L., *A Technique for Software Module Specification with Examples*, Comm. ACM, vol. 15(5), 1972, pp. 330-336.

[Parnas, 1977]
: PARNAS D.L., *The Use of precise Specification in the Development of Software*, Proc. IFIP-77, North-Holland, 1977, pp. 861-867.

[Paterson and Wegman, 1978]
: PATERSON M.S., WEGMAN M.N., *Linear unification*, Journ. Comput. Syst. Sci. 16, 2, April 1978, pp. 158-167.

[Pereira and Nasr, 1984]
: PEREIRA L.M., NASR R., *Delta-Prolog: a Distributed Logic Programming Language*, Proc. Conf. on Fifth Generation Computer Systems, Tokyo, Japan, Elsevier/North-Holland, 1984, pp. 283-291.

[Pereira et al., 1986]
PEREIRA L.M., MONTEIRO L., CUNHA J., APARICIO N.J., *Delta-Prolog: a Distributed Backtracking Extension with Events*, Proc. 3rd Int. Conf. on Logic Programming, London, Great-Britain, Lecture Notes in Computer Science n° 225, Springer-Verlag, 1986, pp. 225-260.

[Plotkin, 1970]
PLOTKIN G., *A Note on inductive Generalization*, Machine Intelligence 5, 1970, pp. 101-124.

[Pollard, 1981]
POLLARD G.H., *Parallel execution of Horn clause programs*, Ph.D. thesis, Department of Computing, Imperial College, London, 1981.

[Porto, 1982]
PORTO A., *EPILOG : a Language for Extended Programming in Logic*, Proc. 1st Int. Conf. on Logic Programming, Marseille, France, 1982, pp. 31-37.

[Porto, 1984a]
PORTO A., *EPILOG : a Language for Extended Programming in Logic*, In [Campbell, 1984], pp. 268-278.

[Porto, 1984b]
PORTO A., *Two-Level PROLOG*, Proc. Int. Conf. on Fifth Generation Computer Systems, Tokyo, Japan, Elsevier/North-Holland, 1984, pp. 356-360.

[Ramkumar and Kalé, 1989]
RAMKUMAR B., KALE L.V., *Compiled Execution of the Reduce-Or process Model on Multiprocessors*, Proc. of the North American Conference on Logic Programming, Cleveland, USA, The MIT Press, 1989, pp. 313-331.

[Ratcliff and Syre, 1987]
RATCLIFF M., SYRE J.C., *A Parallel Logic Programming Language for PEPSys*, Technical Report, ECRC, Munich, Germany, 1987

[Reynolds, 1970]
REYNOLDS J., *Transformational Systems and the Algebraic Structure of Atomic Formulas*, Machine Intelligence 5, 1970, pp. 135-152.

[Robinson, 1965]
ROBINSON J.A., *A Machine-oriented Logic based on the Resolution Principle*, Journ. ACM 12, January 1965, pp. 23-41.

[Saraswat, 1986]
SARASWAT V.A., *Problems with Concurrent Prolog*, Research Report, Carnegie Mellon University, Pittsburgh, USA, 1986.

[Saraswat, 1987]
SARASWAT V.A., *CP as a logic programming language*, Research Report, Carnegie Mellon University, Pittsburgh, USA, 1987.

[Saraswat, 1989]
SARASWAT V.A., *Concurrent Constraint Programming Languages*, Ph.D. Thesis, Carnegie Mellon University, Pittsburg, USA, 1989.

[Saraswat et al., 1990]
SARASWAT V.A., KAHN K., LEVY J., *Janus: A Step towards Distributed Constraint Programming*, Proc. North American Conference on Logic Programming, Austin, USA, The MIT Press, 1990, pp. 431-446.

[Sato, 1982]
SATO T., *An Algorithm for Intelligent Backtracking*, Proc. of the R.I.M.S. Symposia on Software Science and Engineering, Lecture Notes in Computer Science n° 147, Springer-Verlag, 1982, pp. 88-98.

[Sato and Tamaki, 1984]
SATO T., TAMAKI H., *Transformational Logic Program Synthesis*, Proc. Conf. on Fifth Generation Computer Systems, Tokyo, Japan, Elsevier/North-Holland, 1984, pp. 195-201.

[Shapiro, 1983]
SHAPIRO E.Y., *A Subset of Concurrent Prolog and its interpreter*, Technical report TR-003, ICOT, Tokyo, Japan, 1983.

[Shapiro, 1986]
SHAPIRO E.Y., *Concurrent Prolog: a progress report*, IEEE Computer, August 1986, pp. 44-58.

[Shapiro, 1987a],
SHAPIRO E.Y., *An OR-Parallel Execution Algorithm for Prolog and Its FCP Implementation*, Proc. 4th Int. Conf. on Logic Programming, Melbourne, Australia, The MIT Press, 1987, pp. 311-337.

[Shapiro, 1987b]
SHAPIRO E.Y., ed., *Concurrent Prolog: Collected Papers*, volumes I and II, The MIT Press, 1987.

[Shapiro and Takeuchi, 1983]
SHAPIRO E.Y., TAKEUCHI A., *Object-oriented Programming in Concurrent Prolog*, New Generation Computing 1:1, 1983, pp. 25-48.

[Shen, 1986]
   SHEN K., *An Investigation of the Argonne Model of Or-Parallel Prolog*, Master's thesis, University of Manchester, Manchester, Great-Britain, 1986.

[Shepherdson, 1984]
   SHEPHERDSON J.C., *Negation as Failure: a Comparison of Clark's Completed Database and Reiter's Closed World Assumption*, Journ. of Logic Programming vol. 1, 1984, pp. 51-79.

[Siegel, 1987]
   SIEGEL P., *Représentation et utilisation de la connaissance en calcul propositionnel*, Thèse de doctorat, Université d'Aix-Marseille, Marseille, France, 1987.

[Sommerville, 1985]
   SOMMERVILLE I., *Software Engineering*, Addison-Wesley, 1985.

[Stoy, 1982]
   STOY J., *Some Mathematical Aspects of Functional Programming*, In [Darlington, 1982], pp. 217-252.

[Szeredi, 1989]
   SZEREDI P., *Performance Analysis of the Aurora Or-parallel Prolog System*, Proc. of the North American Conference on Logic Programming, Cleveland, USA, The MIT Press, 1989, pp. 713-734.

[Takeuchi and Furukawa, 1986]
   TAKEUCHI A., FURUKAWA K., *Parallel Logic Programming Languages*, Proc. 3rd Int. Conf. on Logic Programming, London, Great-Britain, Lecture Notes in Computer Science n° 225, Springer-Verlag, 1986, pp. 242-254.

[Tamaki, 1987]
   TAMAKI H., *Stream-based Computation of ground I/O Prolog into committed-choice languages*, Proc. 4th Int. Conf. on Logic Programming, Melbourne, Australia, The MIT Press, 1987, pp. 376-393.

[Tärnlund, 1977]
   TÄRNLUND S.A., *Horn clause computability*, BIT 17, pp. 215-226, 1977.

[Taylor et al., 1986]
   TAYLOR S., SAFRA S., SHAPIRO E., *A Parallel Implementation of Flat Concurrent Prolog*, Technical Report, Department of Computer Science, The Weizmann Institute of Science, Rehovot, Israël, 1986.

[Tuner, 1982]
   TUNER D.A., *Functional Programming and Proofs of Program Correctness*, In [Neel, 1982], pp. 187-209.

[Ueda, 1985]
UEDA K., *Guarded Horn Clauses*, Technical Report TR-103, ICOT, Tokyo, 1985.

[Ueda, 1986a]
Ueda K., *Guarded Horn Clauses*, Ph.D. Thesis, Faculty of Engineering, University of Tokyo, Tokyo, Japan, 1986.

[Ueda, 1986b]
UEDA K., *Making Exhaustive Search Programs Deterministic, Part 1*, Proc. 3rd Int. Conf. on Logic Programming, London, Great-Britain, Lecture Notes in Computer Science n° 225, Springer-Verlag, 1986, pp. 270-282.

[Ueda, 1987]
UEDA K., *Making Exhaustive Search Programs Deterministic, Part 2*, Proc. 4th Int. Conf. on Logic Programming, Melbourne, Australia, The MIT Press, 1987, pp. 356-375.

[Van Heijenoort, 1967]
VAN HEIJENOORT J., ed., *From Frege to Gödel: A Source Book in Mathematical Logic, 1879-1931*, Harvard University Press, 1967.

[Van Hentenryck, 1987]
VAN HENTENRYCK P., *Consistency Techniques in Logic Programming*, Ph.D. Thesis, University of Namur, Namur, Belgium, 1987, revised version published as [Van Hentenryck, 1989].

[Van Hentenryck, 1989]
VAN HENTENRYCK P., *Constraint Satisfaction in Logic Programming*, The MIT Press, Cambridge, USA, 1989.

[Vasak, 1986]
Vasak T., *Towards a Methodology for Logic Programming*, Ph.D. Thesis, University of New South Wales, Kensington, Australia, 1986.

[Venken and Bruynooghe, 1984]
VENKEN R., BRUYNOOGHE M., *Prolog as a Language for Prototyping of Information Systems*, In Approaches to prototyping, ed. R. Budd et al., Springer-Verlag, 1984, pp. 447-458.

[Wallace, 1987]
WALLACE M., *Negation By Constraints : a Sound and Efficient Implementation of Negation in Deductive Databases*, Proc. 4th Int. Symp. on Logic Programming, San Francisco, USA, IEEE Computer Society Press, 1987, pp. 253-263.

[Warren, 1979]
WARREN D.H.D., *Coroutining Facilities for Prolog Implemented in Prolog*, D.A.I. Research Paper, University of Edinburgh, Scotland, 1979.

[Warren, 1987a]
WARREN D.H.D., *Or-parallel Execution Models of Prolog*, Proc. Int. Joint Conf. on Theory and Practice of Software Development, vol. 2, Lecture Notes in Computer Science n° 250, Springer-Verlag, 1987, pp. 243-259.

[Warren, 1987b]
WARREN D.H.D., *The SRI Model for Or-Parallel Execution of Prolog: Abstract Design and Implementation*, Proc. 4th Int. Symp. on Logic Programming, San Francisco, USA, IEEE Computer Society Press, 1987, pp. 92-102.

[Whesphal et al., 1987]
WHESPHAL H., ROBERT P., CHASSIN J., SYRE J.C., *The PEPSys Model : Combining Backtracking, AND- and OR-parallelism*, Proc. 4th Int. Symp. on Logic Programming, San Francisco, USA, IEEE Computer Society Press, 1987, pp. 436-448.

[Winsborough, 1989]
WINSBOROUGH W.H., *Path-Dependent Reachability Analysis for Multiple Specialization*, Proc. of the North American Conference on Logic Programming, Cleveland, USA, The MIT Press, 1989, pp. 133-153.

[Wise, 1982]
WISE M.J., *A Parallel Prolog: the construction of a data driven model*, Proc. Symp. on Lisp and Functional Programming, Pittsburgh, USA, ACM, 1982, pp. 56-66.

[Wise, 1984]
WISE M.J., *EPILOG : reinterpreting and extending Prolog for a multiprocessor environment*, In [Campbell, 1984], pp. 341-351.

[Woo and Choe, 1986]
WOO N.S., CHOE K., *Selecting the backtrack literal in the AND process of the AND/OR Process Model*, Proc. 3rd Int. Symp. on Logic Programming, Salt Lake City, USA, IEEE Computer Society Press, 1986, pp. 200-210.

[Yang, 1986]
YANG R., *A Parallel Logic programming Language and its Implementation*, Ph.D. thesis, Dept. of electrical Engineering, Keio University, Yokohama, Japan, 1986, see also [Yang, 1987].

[Yang, 1987]
YANG R., *P-Prolog: A Parallel Logic Programming Language*, Series in Computer Science, vol. 9, World Scientific, 1987.

[Yang and Aiso, 1986]
    YANG R., AISO H., *P-Prolog : a Parallel Logic Language based on Exclusive Relation*, Proc. 3rd Int. Conf. on Logic Programming, London, Great-Britain, Lecture Notes in Computer Science n° 225, Springer-Verlag, 1986, pp. 255-260.

Index

Index

Index

!, !nv, !g 380
?, ?g, ?nv 380
<Srtriplets,Label> 168
⊥ 26
⊤ 26
$Ax_=$ 262
B_H 25
$Cform(v_1,...,v_m)$ 265
Cform(Snsubst) 265
$Cform^*(v_1,...,v_m)$ 265
$Cform^*$(Snsubst) 265
cod(v) 89
$cod(v^-)$ 89
$cod(\theta)$ 28
comp(P) 262
cp(T) 76
det(G) 405
$Dform(v_1,...,v_m)$ 264
Dform(Snsubst) 264
$Dform^*(v_1,...,v_m)$ 264
$Dform^*$(Snsubst) 264
$dom(\theta)$ 28
domain(p) 499
E_s_d 168
$E\theta$ 28; 383
eq(T) 70
$E \leq F, F \geq E$ 29
$E \equiv F$ 29
f_restriction(v) 276
Form(v) 263
$Form^*$(v) 263
front(T) 76
Funcs 21

g_commit(...) 408
g_commit pred_name 408
glb 26
ground(E) 266
ground(E;v) 266
ground(t) 265
ground(t;v) 265
hsyst(v) 89
$hsyst(v_1,...,v_m)$ 89
hsyst(Snsubsts) 89
id_child(I,Id) 147
id_father(Id) 147
inf(c,d) 30
$\mathcal{L}$ 22
l_commit(...) 408
l_commit pred_name 408
LD(p) 499
lub 26
mas 30
mgu 30; 62
v^+ 88
v^- 88
n-mgu 91; 104
neg(v) 274
nmas 245; 277
$Nreconc(v_1,...,v_m)$ 95
Nreconc(Snsubsts) 95
v|Svars 275
p 499
P |- $(A_1, ..., A_m)$ with θ 43
P |- $(L_1, ..., L_m)$ with v 334
P |- Int $(A_1, ..., A_m)$ with θ 43
P |- Int $(L_1, ..., L_m)$ with v 334

prec(p) 499
Preds 21
Proc_sol 168
$\theta_{|Svars}$ 27
$\rho_N(v_1,...,v_m)$ 96
$\rho_N(Snsubsts)$ 96
$S \models F$ 24
$S \models_H F$ 499
$\sigma \circ \tau$ 28
S^+ 86
S^- 86
S_d 168
Set_binds 168
Set_procs 168
$sneg(\{v_1,...,v_m\}$ 275
sol(n,G) 405
Sol(S) 54; 86
$\sigma\tau$ 28
ST(N,T) 146
susp(p) 499
suspend pred_name($m_1,...,m_n$) with
   g_commit 408
suspend pred_name($m_1,...,m_n$) with
   l_commit 408
suspend proc_name($Arg_1,...,Arg_n$) until
   Cond 391
$syst(\theta)$ 53
$syst(\theta_1,...,\theta_m)$ 53
$\sigma \leq \tau, \tau \geq \sigma$ 29
$\sigma \equiv \tau$ 29
$S \approx T$ 69; 90
T_P 26
$T \downarrow \alpha$ 26
$T \uparrow \alpha$ 26
$T \supseteq_{sol} S$ 87
$(T_1 \times ... \times T_m)^*$ 486
U_H 25
var(v) 89
Var(N,T) 146
var(v^-) 89

var(S) 28
varcod(v) 89
varcod(v^-) 89
varcod(θ) 28
Vars 21
Vc(N,T) 146
$\{v_1,...,v_m\}_{atom}$ 277
$\{v_1,...,v_m\}_{clause}$ 277
$\{\}$ 27
| 399
$|_c$ 407

activator commits 407
adequate instantiation 217
and-parallelism 40
and/or/not process model 242
and/or/not search tree 242
approximation 125
atom 22
atomic formula 22
atom subset 30
auxiliary unifier 226

binding 27
binding publication 125
body 23
bound 22; 28

c-goal 355
c-unsatisfiability 355
c-validity 355
cs-goal 355
call-commit 408
candidate-solution subtree 38; 145
clause 23
clause subset 30
closed wff 22
codomain 28; 89
commit-body 407
common part 76

compact system 70
completeness 44
completed definition 262
completed subtree 145; 289
completion 262
complex goal 399
complex solution 119
complex suspension declaration 392
composition of substitutions 28
compound term 22
computed and/or search tree 144
computed answer n-substitution 291; 322
computed answer substitution 152; 192
concurrent logic procedure 512
concurrent logic program 512
consistency 78; 267; 272
constant 22
constructed term 28
controlled and-parallelism 42
correctness 499; 509; 515

decreasing R-depth reduction operator 414
definite Horn clause 23
descriptor commit 407
direct binding 379
domain 24; 28; 89

e-equation 52
e-inequation 86
e-system 52
eager producer 42
eh-system 86
elementary equation 52
elementary hybrid system 86
elementary inequation 86
elementary set of n-substitutions 91
elementary system 62
en-reconciliation 95
en-substitution 88
entering generation 127
entering reconciliation 127

equation 52
equational restriction 276
equivalence 69; 87; 537
er-model 204
es-nsubst 91
event-driven reconciliation 437
exclusively commitable for a non-extended
    ps-goal 433
expression 22
extended (general) goal-node 245
extended expression 243
extended goal 244
extended s-goal 244
extended unification 244

filter 226
free variable occurrence 22
frontier 76
full and-parallelism 41
functional restriction 276
functor 22

g-completeness 335; 513
g-soundness 334; 513
general binding 277
general goal 241
general goal-node 241
general goal-process 242
general interpreter 334
general program 241
general query 241
general query-process 242
general s-goal 241
general s-goal-node 242
generation procedure 127
global call-commit 408
global procedure-commit 408
global read-only annotations 380
goal 33
goal-node 35
ground atom 25

ground instance   25
ground term   25
grounding substitution   27
guard   407
guarded clause   407

h-system   86, 89
head   23
Herbrand interpretation   25
Herbrand model   25
Herbrand universe   25
Horn clause   23
Horn clause program   23
hybrid system   86

idempotence of sets of n-substitutions   95
idempotent substitution   31
identity substitution   27
incompleted subtree   145; 289
increasing R-depth reduction operator   414
indirect binding   379
inequation   86
instance   28; 246; 266
instance subtree   216
instantiability   245
instantiation   27
instantiation es-nsubst   245
instantiation of a node   280
instantiation of a process   150
instantiation subtree   281
interpretation   24
interpreter   43

lazy producer   42
least Herbrand model   26
less general   29
literal   22
local call-commit   408
local procedure-commits   408
local read-only annotations   380
logical consequence   24

minimal element   501
model   24
more general than   29; 90; 91
most general common instance   244
most general unifier (mgu)   30; 53; 62; 69
multi-equation   69
multi-inequation   103
multi-set   68
multi-term   79

n-reconciliation   95
n-substitution   88, 90
n-unifier   91; 104
natural reconciliation   200
negation as failure   240
negation of an n-substitution   274
negation wrt to a set of variables   274; 275
negative literal   22
negative part of an n-substitution   88
negative simple goal   241
negative unifier   119
non-exclusive committability   433
normalized answer   355
ns-goal   241
ns-goal-node   241
ns-goal-process   242

optimal instantiation   314
or-parallelism   40

P-substitution   117
parallel goals   399
part   39
partial candidate solution subtree   145
partial correctness   515
partial solution subtree   145
partial solution subtree n-substitution   288
positive literal   22
positive part of an n-substitution   88
positive simple goal   241
positive unifier   119

primary unifier 226
procedure 23
procedure-commit 408
processes responsible of a variable for a suspended process 424
provoked reconciliation 200
ps-goal 241
ps-goal-node 241
ps-goal-process 242
pss-n-substitution 288
pure concurrent logic procedure 512
pure concurrent logic program 512

qn-reconciliation 273
query 33
query-node 35

R-depth 39
R-depth operator 414
R-triplet 128
reconciler operator 415
reconciliation 57
reconciliation procedure 127
reconciliation-substitution 146
reduction 228; 378
reduction step 33; 378
reduction strategy 33
redundancy 514
relaunch operator 415
removal message 190
renaming substitution 29
restricted and-parallelism 41

s-goal 33
s-goal-node 35
safe language 460
safety 514
scope 22; 226
semi-correctness 515; 516
sequentialized goal 399
simple cs-goal 355
simple goal 33

simple suspension declaration 392
solution 34; 86; 104
solution subtree 38; 145
solution-weaker system 56; 87
solvable system 54; 86
soundness 44
stream-parallelism 41
strong termination 515
subgoal 33
substitution 27
subsumption 226
success set 215
suspended process 383
suspended ps-goal-clause-process 383
suspension declarations 391
system of equations 52

term 22
term assignment 24
termination 515
term restriction 246
tree cut off its last slice of some R-depth 146
triplet-reconciliation messages 171
truth value 24

unification 30; 62
unifier 53; 69
unrestricted solution 208

variable assignment 24
variant (n-)substitution 29, 90
variant term 29
weak termination 515
well-formed formula 22
well-formed part 39
well-founded relation 501
wff 22

"∥-reduction step" 378

□-nodes 35
⊗-nodes 36

Lecture Notes in Computer Science

For information about Vols. 1–466
please contact your bookseller or Springer-Verlag

Vol. 467: F. Long (Ed.), Software Engineering Environments. Proceedings, 1989. VI, 313 pages. 1990.

Vol. 468: S.G. Akl, F. Fiala, W.W. Koczkodaj (Eds.), Advances in Computing and Information – ICCI '90. Proceedings, 1990. VII, 529 pages. 1990.

Vol. 469: I. Guessarian (Ed.), Semantics of Systems of Concurrent Processes. Proceedings, 1990. V, 456 pages. 1990.

Vol. 470: S. Abiteboul, P.C. Kanellakis (Eds.), ICDT '90. Proceedings, 1990. VII, 528 pages. 1990.

Vol. 471: B.C. Ooi, Efficient Query Processing in Geographic Information Systems. VIII, 208 pages. 1990.

Vol. 472: K.V. Nori, C.E. Veni Madhavan (Eds.), Foundations of Software Technology and Theoretical Computer Science. Proceedings, 1990. X, 420 pages. 1990.

Vol. 473: I.B. Damgård (Ed.), Advances in Cryptology – EUROCRYPT '90. Proceedings, 1990. VIII, 500 pages. 1991.

Vol. 474: D. Karagiannis (Ed.), Information Systems and Artificial Intelligence: Integration Aspects. Proceedings, 1990. X, 293 pages. 1991. (Subseries LNAI).

Vol. 475: P. Schroeder-Heister (Ed.), Extensions of Logic Programming. Proceedings, 1989. VIII, 364 pages. 1991. (Subseries LNAI).

Vol. 476: M. Filgueiras, L. Damas, N. Moreira, A.P. Tomás (Eds.), Natural Language Processing. Proceedings, 1990. VII, 253 pages. 1991. (Subseries LNAI).

Vol. 477: D. Hammer (Ed.), Compiler Compilers. Proceedings, 1990. VI, 227 pages. 1991.

Vol. 478: J. van Eijck (Ed.), Logics in AI. Proceedings, 1990. IX, 562 pages. 1991. (Subseries in LNAI).

Vol. 479: H. Schmidt, Meta-Level Control for Deductive Database Systems. VI, 155 pages. 1991.

Vol. 480: C. Choffrut, M. Jantzen (Eds.), STACS 91. Proceedings, 1991. X, 549 pages. 1991.

Vol. 481: E. Lang, K.-U. Carstensen, G. Simmons, Modelling Spatial Knowledge on a Linguistic Basis. IX, 138 pages. 1991. (Subseries LNAI).

Vol. 482: Y. Kodratoff (Ed.), Machine Learning – EWSL-91. Proceedings, 1991. XI, 537 pages. 1991. (Subseries LNAI).

Vol. 483: G. Rozenberg (Ed.), Advances in Petri Nets 1990. VI, 515 pages. 1991.

Vol. 484: R. H. Möhring (Ed.), Graph-Theoretic Concepts in Computer Science. Proceedings, 1990. IX, 360 pages. 1991.

Vol. 485: K. Furukawa, H. Tanaka, T. Fuijsaki (Eds.), Logic Programming '89. Proceedings, 1989. IX, 183 pages. 1991. (Subseries LNAI).

Vol. 486: J. van Leeuwen, N. Santoro (Eds.), Distributed Algorithms. Proceedings, 1990. VI, 433 pages. 1991.

Vol. 487: A. Bode (Ed.), Distributed Memory Computing. Proceedings, 1991. XI, 506 pages. 1991.

Vol. 488: R. V. Book (Ed.), Rewriting Techniques and Applications. Proceedings, 1991. VII, 458 pages. 1991.

Vol. 489: J. W. de Bakker, W. P. de Roever, G. Rozenberg (Eds.), Foundations of Object-Oriented Languages. Proceedings, 1990. VIII, 442 pages. 1991.

Vol. 490: J. A. Bergstra, L. M. G. Feijs (Eds.), Algebraic Methods II: Theory, Tools and Applicatlons. VI, 434 pages. 1991.

Vol. 491: A. Yonezawa, T. Ito (Eds.), Concurrency: Theory, Language, and Architecture. Proceedings, l989. VIII, 339 pages. 1991.

Vol. 492: D. Sriram, R. Logcher, S. Fukuda (Eds.), Computer-Aided Cooperative Product Development. Proceedings, 1989 VII, 630 pages. 1991.

Vol. 493: S. Abramsky, T. S. E. Maibaum (Eds.), TAPSOFT '91. Volume 1. Proceedings, 1991. VIII, 455 pages. 1991.

Vol. 494: S. Abramsky, T. S. E. Maibaum (Eds.), TAPSOFT '91. Volume 2. Proceedings, 1991. VIII, 482 pages. 1991.

Vol. 495: 9. Thalheim, J. Demetrovics, H.-D. Gerhardt (Eds.), MFDBS '91. Proceedings, 1991. VI, 395 pages. 1991.

Vol. 496: H.-P. Schwefel, R. Männer (Eds.), Parallel Problem Solving from Nature. Proceedings, 1990. XI, 485 pages. 1991.

Vol. 497: F. Dehne, F. Fiala. W.W. Koczkodaj (Eds.), Advances in Computing and Information - ICCI '91. Proceedings, 1991. VIII, 745 pages. 1991.

Vol. 498: R. Andersen, J. A. Bubenko jr., A. Sølvberg (Eds.), Advanced Information Systems Engineering. Proceedings, 1991. VI, 579 pages. 1991.

Vol. 499: D. Christodoulakis (Ed.), Ada: The Choice for '92. Proceedings, 1991. VI, 411 pages. 1991.

Vol. 500: M. Held, On the Computational Geometry of Pocket Machining. XII, 179 pages. 1991.

Vol. 501: M. Bidoit, H.-J. Kreowski, P. Lescanne, F. Orejas, D. Sannella (Eds.), Algebraic System Specification and Development. VIII, 98 pages. 1991.

Vol. 502: J. Bārzdiņž, D. Bjørner (Eds.), Baltic Computer Science. X, 619 pages. 1991.

Vol. 503: P. America (Ed.), Parallel Database Systems. Proceedings, 1990. VIII, 433 pages. 1991.

Vol. 504: J. W. Schmidt, A. A. Stogny (Eds.), Next Generation Information System Technology. Proceedings, 1990. IX, 450 pages. 1991.

Vol. 505: E. H. L. Aarts, J. van Leeuwen, M. Rem (Eds.), PARLE '91. Parallel Architectures and Languages Europe, Volume I. Proceedings, 1991. XV, 423 pages. 1991.

Vol. 506: E. H. L. Aarts, J. van Leeuwen, M. Rem (Eds.), PARLE '91. Parallel Architectures and Languages Europe, Volume II. Proceedings, 1991. XV, 489 pages. 1991.

Vol. 507: N. A. Sherwani, E. de Doncker, J. A. Kapenga (Eds.), Computing in the 90's. Proceedings, 1989. XIII, 441 pages. 1991.

Vol. 508: S. Sakata (Ed.), Applied Algebra, Algebraic Algorithms and Error-Correcting Codes. Proceedings, 1990. IX, 390 pages. 1991.

Vol. 509: A. Endres, H. Weber (Eds.), Software Development Environments and CASE Technology. Proceedings, 1991. VIII, 286 pages. 1991.

Vol. 510: J. Leach Albert, B. Monien, M. Rodríguez (Eds.), Automata, Languages and Programming. Proceedings, 1991. XII, 763 pages. 1991.

Vol. 511: A. C. F. Colchester, D.J. Hawkes (Eds.), Information Processing in Medical Imaging. Proceedings, 1991. XI, 512 pages. 1991.

Vol. 512: P. America (Ed.), ECOOP '91. European Conference on Object-Oriented Programming. Proceedings, 1991. X, 396 pages. 1991.

Vol. 513: N. M. Mattos, An Approach to Knowledge Base Management. IX, 247 pages. 1991. (Subseries LNAI).

Vol. 514: G. Cohen, P. Charpin (Eds.), EUROCODE '90. Proceedings, 1990. XI, 392 pages. 1991.

Vol. 515: J. P. Martins, M. Reinfrank (Eds.), Truth Maintenance Systems. Proceedings, 1990. VII, 177 pages. 1991. (Subseries LNAI).

Vol. 516: S. Kaplan, M. Okada (Eds.), Conditional and Typed Rewriting Systems. Proceedings, 1990. IX, 461 pages. 1991.

Vol. 517: K. Nökel, Temporally Distributed Symptoms in Technical Diagnosis. IX, 164 pages. 1991. (Subseries LNAI).

Vol. 518: J. G. Williams, Instantiation Theory. VIII, 133 pages. 1991. (Subseries LNAI).

Vol. 519: F. Dehne, J.-R. Sack, N. Santoro (Eds.), Algorithms and Data Structures. Proceedings, 1991. X, 496 pages. 1991.

Vol. 520: A. Tarlecki (Ed.), Mathematical Foundations of Computer Science 1991. Proceedings, 1991. XI, 435 pages. 1991.

Vol. 521: B. Bouchon-Meunier, R. R. Yager, L. A. Zadek (Eds.), Uncertainty in Knowledge-Bases. Proceedings, 1990. X, 609 pages. 1991.

Vol. 522: J. Hertzberg (Ed.), European Workshop on Planning. Proceedings, 1991. VII, 121 pages. 1991. (Subseries LNAI).

Vol. 523: J. Hughes (Ed.), Functional Programming Languages and Computer Architecture. Proceedings, 1991. VIII, 666 pages. 1991.

Vol. 524: G. Rozenberg (Ed.), Advances in Petri Nets 1991. VIII, 572 pages. 1991.

Vol. 525: O. Günther, H.-J. Schek (Eds.), Advances in Spatial Databases. Proceedings, 1991. XI, 471 pages. 1991.

Vol. 526: T. Ito, A. R. Meyer (Eds.), Theoretical Aspects of Computer Software. Proceedings, 1991. X, 772 pages. 1991.

Vol. 527: J.C.M. Baeten, J. F. Groote (Eds.), CONCUR '91. Proceedings, 1991. VIII, 541 pages. 1991.

Vol. 528: J. Maluszynski, M. Wirsing (Eds.), Programming Language Implementation and Logic Programming. Proceedings, 1991. XI, 433 pages. 1991.

Vol. 529: L. Budach (Ed.), Fundamentals of Computation Theory. Proceedings, 1991. XII, 426 pages. 1991.

Vol. 530: D. H. Pitt, P.-L. Curien, S. Abramsky, A. M. Pitts, A. Poigné, D. E. Rydeheard (Eds.), Category Theory and Computer Science. Proceedings, 1991. VII, 301 pages. 1991.

Vol. 531: E. M. Clarke, R. P. Kurshan (Eds.), Computer-Aided Verification. Proceedings, 1990. XIII, 372 pages. 1991.

Vol. 532: H. Ehrig, H.-J. Kreowski, G. Rozenberg (Eds.), Graph Grammars and Their Application to Computer Science. Proceedings, 1990. X, 703 pages. 1991.

Vol. 533: E. Börger, H. Kleine Büning, M. M. Richter, W. Schönfeld (Eds.), Computer Science Logic. Proceedings, 1990. VIII, 399 pages. 1991.

Vol. 534: H. Ehrig, K. P. Jantke, F. Orejas, H. Reichel (Eds.), Recent Trends in Data Type Specification. Proceedings, 1990. VIII, 379 pages. 1991.

Vol. 535: P. Jorrand, J. Kelemen (Eds.), Fundamentals of Artificial Intelligence Research. Proceedings, 1991. VIII, 255 pages. 1991. (Subseries LNAI).

Vol. 536: J. E. Tomayko, Software Engineering Education. Proceedings, 1991. VIII, 296 pages. 1991.

Vol. 537: A. J. Menezes, S. A. Vanstone (Eds.), Advances in Cryptology – CRYPTO '90. Proceedings. XIII, 644 pages. 1991.

Vol. 538: M. Kojima, N. Megiddo, T. Noma, A. Yoshise, A Unified Approach to Interior Point Algorithms for Linear Complementarity Problems. VIII, 108 pages. 1991.

Vol. 539: H. F. Mattson, T. Mora, T. R. N. Rao (Eds.), Applied Algebra, Algebraic Algorithms and Error-Correcting Codes. Proceedings, 1991. XI, 489 pages. 1991.

Vol. 540: A. Prieto (Ed.), Artificial Neural Networks. Proceedings, 1991. XIII, 476 pages. 1991.

Vol. 541: P. Barahona, L. Moniz Pereira, A. Porto (Eds.), EPIA '91. Proceedings, 1991. VIII, 292 pages. 1991. (Subseries LNAI).

Vol. 543: J. Dix, K. P. Jantke, P. H. Schmitt (Eds.), Nonmonotonic and Inductive Logic. Proceedings, 1990. X, 243 pages. 1991. (Subseries LNAI).

Vol. 544: M. Broy, M. Wirsing (Eds.), Methods of Programming. XII, 268 pages. 1991.

Vol. 545: H. Alblas, B. Melichar (Eds.), Attribute Grammars, Applications and Systems. Proceedings, 1991. IX, 513 pages. 1991.

Vol. 547: D. W. Davies (Ed.), Advances in Cryptology – EUROCRYPT '91. Proceedings, 1991. XII, 556 pages. 1991.

Vol. 548: R. Kruse, P. Siegel (Eds.), Symbolic and Quantitative Approaches to Uncertainty. Proceedings, 1991. XI, 362 pages. 1991.

Vol. 550: A. van Lamsweerde, A. Fugetta (Eds.), ESEC '91. Proceedings, 1991. XII, 515 pages. 1991.

Vol. 551:S. Prehn, W. J. Toetenel (Eds.), VDM '91. Formal Software Development Methods. Volume 1. Proceedings, 1991. XIII, 699 pages. 1991.

Vol. 552: S. Prehn, W. J. Toetenel (Eds.), VDM '91. Formal Software Development Methods. Volume 2. Proceedings, 1991. XIV, 430 pages. 1991.

Vol. 553: H. Bieri, H. Noltemeier (Eds.), Computational Geometry - Methods, Algorithms and Applications '91. Proceedings, 1991. VIII, 320 pages. 1991.

Vol. 554: G. Grahne, The Problem of Incomplete Information in Relational Databases. VIII, 156 pages. 1991.

Vol. 555: H. Maurer (Ed.), New Results and New Trends in Computer Science. Proceedings, 1991. VIII, 403 pages. 1991.

Vol. 556: J.-M. Jacquet, Conclog: A Methodological Approach to Concurrent Logic Programming. XII, 781 pages. 1991.